Myanmar (Burma)

a Lonely Planet travel survival kit

Joe Cummings
Tony Wheeler

Myanmar (Burma)

6th edition

Published by
Lonely Planet Publications
Head Office: PO Box 617, Hawthorn, Vic 3122, Australia
Branches: 155 Filbert St, Suite 251, Oakland, CA 94607, USA
10 Barley Mow Passage, Chiswick, London W4 4PH, UK
71 bis rue du Cardinal Lemoine, 75005 Paris, France

Printed by
SNP Printing Pte Ltd, Singapore

Script Typeset by
David Bradley

Photographs by
Joe Cummings, Bernard Napthine

Front cover: Shwedagon Paya (Bernard Napthine)

First Published
December 1979

This Edition
January 1996

National Library of Australia Cataloguing in Publication Data

Cummings, Joe
Myanmar.

6th ed.
Includes index.
ISBN 0 86442 324 1

1. Burma - Guidebooks.
I. Title. (Series: Lonely Planet travel survival kit).

915.91045

Joe Cummings

Joe has been involved in South-East Asian studies for many years and was a Peace Corps volunteer in Thailand during the 1970s. Since then he has been a translator/interpreter of Thai in San Francisco, a graduate student in Thai language and Asian art history (MA 1981) at the University of California at Berkeley, an East-West Center Scholar in Hawaii, a university lecturer in Malaysia and a bilingual consultant in the USA and Taiwan. He is also author of Lonely Planet's *Laos*, *Thailand* and *Bangkok* guidebooks and the *Thai phrasebook*, and a contributor to several other LP guides to East and South-East Asian countries.

Tony Wheeler

Tony was born in England but spent most of his younger years overseas due to his father's occupation with British Airways. Those years included a lengthy spell in Pakistan, a shorter period in the West Indies and all his high school years in the USA. He returned to England to do a university degree in engineering, worked for a short time as an automotive design engineer, returned to university again and did an MBA then dropped out on the Asian overland trail with his wife Maureen. They've been travelling, writing and publishing guidebooks ever since, having set up Lonely Planet Publications in the mid-1970s. Travelling for Tony and Maureen is considerably enlivened by their daughter Tashi and son Kieran.

From Joe

Thanks to Percy Win Swe, Nyan Min Din, Aung Win, White Horse Travels & Tours, the poet A M, Kin Zaw Nichols, Myat Wunna, Tour Mandalay, Ledo Road veteran Gerd Remus, Wolf & Jutta Koslowski, Vicky Bowman, Doug Glenn, Wun Zaw, Ko Ko Gyi, Daniel Gerbault, the Moustache Brothers, Zin Myo Laing, Rocky, Ko Kyaw, Sue Reitz, Sai Myint Aung, Thein Win, Martin Tatuch, Aung Kyaing, Kelvin Khin Zaw Win, Robertson Bwa, John DeModena, Khin Maung Than, L Thein Aung and Fred Neumann. Certain Burmese friends who were helpful with political information shall remain unnamed, as their association with a foreign writer might be misconstrued by the current regime.

Dedication This, the sixth edition of *Myanmar*, is dedicated to Daw Aung San Suu Kyi, under house arrest from July 1989 to July 1995.

This Book

The first three editions were researched and written by Tony while Joe took over the duties for the fourth, fifth and sixth editions.

From the Publisher

Producing this greatly expanded sixth edition was the collective task of a number of people at LP's Melbourne office. Megan Fraser was responsible for editing, Adam McCrow for design and layout and Glenn Beanland for mapping. Valerie Tellini took on the job of design coordination and creation of the temple sections and Greg Alford the task of proofreading, caption-writing and general advice.

Thanks to Helen Castle for assisting with editing, to Christine Niven and Jo Horsburgh for their help with proofing and to Adam McCrow, Chris Love and Trudi Canavan for their work on the maps. Thanks also to Simon Bracken for the front cover design and Adam McCrow for the back cover design, to Margie Jung, Ann Jeffree and Trudi Canavan for their illustrations, to Sally Woodward for map checking, to Kerrie Williams for indexing and to Samantha Carew for her editorial support during layout.

Sally Steward's input in the Burmese language sections was greatly appreciated; thanks also to David Bradley for compiling the Burmese script.

We would also like to acknowledge the sources of the temple illustrations appearing in the temple sections and on the title page. They were taken from the publications *Architectural Drawings of Temples in Pagan* (Department of Higher Education, Ministry of Education, Yangon, 1989) and *A Guide to Mrauk-U* (Sittway Degree College, Sittwe, 1992) by Tun Shwe Khine.

Thanks

Thanks to the following people and other travellers who took the time and trouble to write to us about their experiences in Myanmar:

Lin Ang (Bur), Martha Barkunsky (Sp), Ann & Tom Besson (USA), Michael & Christel Bohm (D), Elma de Bok (Nl), E Carter (UK), David Cox, Paul Curran, Rachel Fearnside (UK), Riep Florian (D), C J Fraser (Tai), Maria Giancola (I), Luke Golobitsh (D), Michael Hatamiya (J), Marc Heritier (CH), Robert Hickey (Aus), B Holtkemeyer (D), D R Hood (UK), R Rhodes James (UK), Sean Lawson (C), Rob Lober (UK), R Patrick MacDaniel (USA), John Margarson (UK), Narharidas Patel (UK), Paul Patrick (UK), Chen Rozen (Isr), H von Schaper (D), G Sobel (Isr), Lorenzo Sonelli (I), Ferd Steegh (Nl), Heather Storey (Aus), Mark Swaim (USA), Ulana Switucha (C), Steve & Joanne Tibbetts (USA), Jean Timberlake (UK), E YomTov (Isr) and Hans Verhoef (Nl).

Aus – Australia, B – Belgium, Bur – Myanmar (Burma), C – Canada, CH – Switzerland, D – Germany, I – Italy, Isr – Israel, J – Japan, N – Norway, Nl – The Netherlands, S – Sweden, Sp – Spain, Tai – Taiwan, UK – United Kingdom, USA – United States of America

Warning & Request

Things change – prices go up, schedules change, good places go bad and bad places go bankrupt – nothing stays the same. So if you find things better or worse, recently opened or long since closed, please write and tell us and help make the next edition better.

Your letters will be used to help update future editions and, where possible, important changes will also be included in a Stop Press section in reprints.

We greatly appreciate all information that is sent to us by travellers. Back at Lonely Planet we employ a hard-working readers' letters team to sort through the many letters we receive. The best ones will be rewarded with a free copy of the next edition or another Lonely Planet guide if you prefer. We give away lots of books, but, unfortunately, not every letter or postcard receives one.

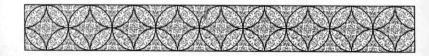

Contents

Map Legend

BOUNDARIES

.... International Boundary
.... Regional Boundary

ROUTES

.... Freeway
.... Highway
.... Major Road
.... Unsealed Road or Track
.... City Road
.... City Street
.... Railway
.... Underground Railway
.... Tram
.... Walking Track
.... Walking Tour
.... Ferry Route
.... Cable Car or Chairlift

AREA FEATURES

.... Parks
.... Built-Up Area
.... Pedestrian Mall
.... Market
.... Cemetery
.... Reef
.... Beach or Desert
.... Rocks

HYDROGRAPHIC FEATURES

.... Coastline
.... River, Creek
.... Intermittent River or Creek
.... Rapids, Waterfalls
.... Lake, Intermittent Lake
.... Canal
.... Swamp

SYMBOLS

✪ CAPITAL		National Capital
◉ Capital		Regional Capital
● CITY		Major City
● City		City
● Town		Town
● Village		Village
■	▼	Place to Stay, Place to Eat
☕	🍷	Cafe, Pub or Bar
✉	☎	Post Office, Telephone
❶	⑤	Tourist Information, Bank
●	Ⓟ	Transport, Parking
🏛	☗	Museum, Youth Hostel
✝	➕	Church, Cathedral
⚲	⊞	Paya, Meditation Centre
☪	✡	Mosque, Synagogue
⚑	ॐ	Chinese Temple, Hindu Temple
✚	★	Hospital, Police Station

◔	�ⓟ	Embassy, Petrol Station
✈	✝	Airport, Airfield
🛏	✿	Swimming Pool, Gardens
❖	🐘	Shopping Centre, Zoo
⚑	⛺	Golf Course, Picnic Site
←	A25	One Way Street, Route Number
🏛	⚱	City Hall, Monument
⛩	▣	Fortress, Tomb
⌂	⌂	Cave, Hut or Chalet
▲	❄	Mountain or Hill, Lookout
⛩	⚓	Lighthouse, Shipwreck
)(	◎	Pass, Spring
⚑	🏄	Beach, Surf Beach
	⁂	Archaeological Site or Ruins
		Ancient or City Wall
		Cliff or Escarpment, Tunnel
		Railway Station

Note: not all symbols displayed above appear in this book

Introduction

Then, a golden mystery upheaved itself on the horizon – a beautiful, winking wonder that blazed in the sun, of a shape that was neither Muslim dome nor Hindu temple spire. 'There's the old Shwedagon,' said my companion. The golden dome said 'This is Burma, and it will be quite unlike any land you know about'.

Rudyard Kipling, *Letters from the East* (1898)

To most of the West, Myanmar – until 1989 known as Burma – is still a geographic question mark, a slightly bizarre Eastern country that has been on some sort of total seclusion plus mad socialism binge since WW II. It has also been torn by continual internal strife involving a smorgasbord of dictators, anti-government rebels, guerrillas, insurgents and assorted malcontents.

True, true, true and yet somehow all false. There are places in Myanmar, like the great ruined city of Bagan (Pagan) or the glittering Shwedagon Paya in Yangon (Rangoon), with more 'magic' than almost anywhere on earth. Myanmar has been secluded and xenophobic – for many years no tourists were allowed

and until recently two weeks was all you got – yet the Burmese people are incredibly friendly and considerate. Myanmar's strict military rule is rightly regarded as an abomination by some members of the international community. And, yes, there is a whole assortment of rebel groups dedicated to the overthrow of the government, but even the mightiest kings of Bagan at its height never brought Myanmar's hill tribes to heel, so little has changed in that respect. Within the regions you're allowed to visit you are most unlikely to face any problems.

What has changed is the ruling party's determination to tighten its iron grip on all internal affairs, while at the same time lengthening the validity of tourist visas to 28 days. Contradictory? At times little about this country seems to make sense to outsiders, yet it continues to hold many of us in its spell.

Myanmar is far from the easiest or most comfortable country in Asia to visit. If you abide by the letter of law it can even be rather

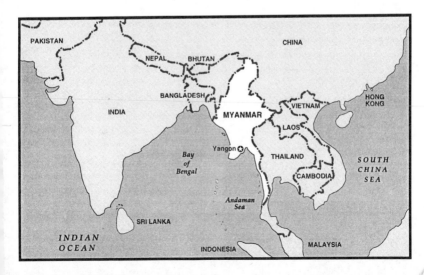

expensive. But the rewards are worth the effort – it's a most unusual, culturally rich and highly enjoyable country for the visitor. At the same time it offers a glimpse of an incredibly Orwellian society usually ignored by the world press.

Should You Visit Myanmar?

The State Law and Order Restoration Council (SLORC), the latest junta to run Myanmar, is abominable. As a ruling group it's continuing a tradition that has existed in Myanmar for centuries. Most Burmese monarchs, up to and including the last, King Thibaw Min, came to power by killing off all persons with claims to the throne. In many regards, Myanmar is still a hundred years behind the rest of South-East Asia. Corvée – involuntary civilian service to the state – was practiced in Thailand until early this century. It is still practiced in Myanmar.

We've read most of the non-governmental reports published in English on human rights in Myanmar. Though they surely provide an important balance against equally biased reports by international government agencies, it's obvious that every group has its own agenda. No group – governmental or non-governmental – can claim objectivity as long as their funds depend on the emotional manipulation of their financial supporters, either by inflaming their passions or calming their fears.

Our bias is that if people decide to visit Myanmar to see for themselves, that they'll go with as much advance information as possible. Many good-hearted Burmese citizens eke out a living from tourism, however small-scale. Since the package-tour requirement has been waived, the potential for ordinary people to benefit from tourist visitation has only increased. We believe – now more than ever – that the positives of travel to Myanmar outweigh the negatives.

Still, anyone contemplating a visit to Myanmar should bear in mind that any contribution they make to the nation's economy (no matter how small) may allow Myanmar's repressive, inept government to stay in power that little bit longer. On the other hand, keeping the Burmese isolated from international witnesses to the internal oppression may also help cement SLORC's fear-driven control over the people and seal Myanmar off from the outside world. This is why the government restricts tourism in the first place. It's your choice! ■

Facts about the Country

HISTORY
Early Pyu & Mon Kingdoms
Virtually nothing is known of Myanmar's prehistoric inhabitants though archaeological evidence suggests the area has been inhabited since at least 2500 BC. The country's history really begins with the struggle for supremacy between the various peoples who inhabited different regions of the country around a thousand years ago.

A group known as the Pyus created city-states in central Myanmar at Beikthano, Hanlin and Thayekhittaya (Sri Ksetra) during this millennium. Little is known about these people; the art and architecture they left behind indicates they practiced Theravada and Mahayana Buddhism mixed with Hinduism, and that they had their own alphabet. The Pyus were dispersed or enslaved by Yunnanese invaders during the 10th century, leaving central Myanmar without any clear political succession.

Around the 6th century the Mon – who may have originated in eastern India or who may have been indigenous to mainland South-East Asia – settled the fertile lowlands stretching from the Ayeyarwady (Irrawaddy) River delta across Thailand (then Siam) to western Cambodia. Inscriptions left behind by the civilization they developed referred to this area as Suvannabhumi or 'Golden Land'. According to official Burmese history, the Mon capital occupied the area around Thaton in present-day Myanmar, though outside scholars argue more convincingly that Suvannabhumi was centred in Thailand's Nakhon Pathom.

Enter the Burmans, who came south into Myanmar from somewhere in the eastern Himalayas around the 8th or 9th century AD. Once the Pyus were vanquished by the Yunnanese, the Burmans supplanted the Pyus in central Myanmar, a region which ever since has been the true cultural heartland of Myanmar. Shortly after they took over the central region, the Burmans came into conflict with the Mon in a long and complicated struggle for control of the whole country. By the time the Burmans had irrevocably ended up on top, the Mon had largely merged with Burman culture or, bearing in mind how much Mon culture the Burmans had absorbed, vice versa.

Great Kings of Bagan (Pagan)
It is thought that Bagan was actually founded on the banks of the Ayeyarwady in 849 AD but it entered its golden period 200 years later when Anawrahta ascended the throne in 1044. Anawrahta consolidated the kingdom, drawing several regions around it into satellite or vassal status – creating the first centralised government the country now called Myanmar had ever known. Virtually all written history pertaining to Myanmar begins with this era; legendary Bagan kings dating to the 2nd century of the Christian era are probably no more than invented personages.

Initially animists, the Burmans had picked up a hybrid form of Buddhism – part Tantric, part Mahayana – in their migration to Myanmar. When the Mon King Manuha of Thaton to the south would not co-operate willingly with Anawrahta's request for their *Tripitaka*, the holy canon of Theravada Buddhism, Anawrahta marched south and conquered Thaton in 1057. He took back not just the Buddhist scriptures, but also the king and most of his court. This injection of Mon culture inspired a phenomenal burst of energy from the Burmans. Bagan quickly became a city of glorious temples and the capital of the first Burmese kingdom to encompass virtually all of present-day Myanmar. What we today identify as 'Burmese' is really a fusion of Mon and Burman cultures that came about at the height of the Bagan era.

Anawrahta was accidentally killed by a wild buffalo in 1077. None of his successors had his vision or energy, and Bagan's power declined slowly but steadily. Kyanzittha (1084-1113) attempted to unify Myanmar's disparate peoples, and later kings like Alaungsithu or Htilominlo built beautiful shrines, but essentially Bagan reached its peak with Anawrahta.

Bagan's decline coincided with the rise to power of Kublai Khan and his Tartars in the north, and from Yunnan in China they invaded Myanmar in 1287. Bagan's rule immediately proved to be tenuous – it collapsed before the Tartar onslaught. Shan tribes – closely related to the Siamese – from the hills to the east took the opportunity to attack and grab a piece of the low country, while in the south the Mon broke free of Burman control to once again establish their own kingdom.

New States Arise
For the next 250 years Myanmar remained in chaos. In the south the Mon kingdom remained relatively stable, but in the north there was continuous strife. Between the two a weaker Burman kingdom was established at Taungoo, east of Pyay (Prome), and it retained its independence by playing off one major power against the other.

At first the Mon established their new capital close to the present Thai border at Mottama (Martaban) near Mawlamyine (Moulmein), but after a series of skirmishes with the Siamese it was shifted to Bago (Pegu), near Yangon (Rangoon), and the Mon country became known as the Kingdom of Hanthawady. In 1472 Dhammazedi, considered the greatest of the Bago kings, came to the throne. A major Buddhist revival took place and the first contact with Europeans was made. During this time the great Shwedagon Paya in Yangon began to assume its present form.

Meanwhile the Shan took over Upper Myanmar once again and founded the Kingdom of Ava near present-day Mandalay in 1364. Along the western coast the Rakhine (a people living near the Indian border) established Mrauk U (Myohaung), a Buddhist kingdom complete with fields of temples to rival Bagan. Surprisingly, it was

not the establishment of Bago, Ava or Mrauk U that was to provide the catalyst for the reunification of Myanmar, but tiny Taungoo, which had been founded by Burman refugees from the new Shan kingdoms.

In the 1500s a series of Taungoo kings

Myanmar's Capitals & Ruling Chronology

It's difficult to create a precise summary of the different historical periods in Myanmar because of the general lack of accurate historical records. The only clearly documented eras are those which have been considered 'Burmese' by Burmese historians: that is, the Rakhine, Pyu, Mon and Burman kingdoms. Periods of Shan or Siamese rule – even when power extended well into central Myanmar – aren't counted.

Rakhine

Dhanyawady	? to 6th C
Wethail	4th to 8th or 9th C
Mrauk U	13th to 18th C

Pyu

Beikthano	? to 5th C
Hanlin	3rd to 9th C
Thayekhittaya	3rd to 10th C

Mon

Thaton (Dvaravati)	? to 10th C
Hanthawady	10th to 16th C

Burman

Bagan	11th to 14th C
Sagaing	1315 to 1364
Ava	1364 to 1555
	1629 to 1752
	1765 to 1783
	1823 to 1837
Taungoo	1486 to 1573
Shwebo	1758 to 1765
Konbaung	1783 to 1823
	1837 to 1857
Mandalay (Yadanapon)	1857 to 1885

British

Sittwe & Mawlamyine	1826 to 1852
Mandalay	1852 to 1886
Yangon	1886 to 1947

extended their power north nearly to Ava, then south, taking the Mon kingdom and shifting their own capital to Bago. Their hold was initially fragile but in 1550 Bayinnaung came to the throne, reunified all of Myanmar and managed to defeat the neighbouring Siamese so convincingly that it was many years before the long-running friction between the Burmese and Siamese re-emerged. Burmese historians sometimes refer to this era as 'the Second Burmese Empire'.

With Bayinnaung's death in 1581 this new Burmese kingdom immediately went into decline; and when in 1636 the capital was shifted north from Bago to Ava, the idea of a kingdom taking in all of Myanmar was effectively renounced. Ava was the capital of Myanmar, but it was a long way from the sea and from communication with the outside world. This isolation eventually contributed to the conflict with the British.

Final Kings of Mandalay

In the 1700s the decline became serious as hill tribes once more started to raid central Myanmar and the Mon again broke away and established their own kingdom in Bago. In 1752 the Mon actually took Ava, but in the same year Alaungpaya came to power in Shwebo, 80 km north of Ava, and spent the next eight years rushing back and forth across Myanmar – conquering, defeating and destroying all who opposed him. He was the founder of the last Burmese dynasty and it was his near invincibility that later deluded the Burmese into thinking they could take on the British.

Alaungpaya's son Hsinbyushin charged into Thailand for good measure, and so thoroughly levelled the capital of Ayuthaya that the Siamese were forced to move south to their present capital of Bangkok. Bodawpaya, who came to power in 1782, was also a son of Alaungpaya and managed to bring Rakhine (Arakan) back under Burmese control. This was to be the direct cause of the first Anglo-Burmese conflict.

Rakhine, the eastern coast region of the Bay of Bengal, had long been a border region

between Myanmar and India; its people, although basically Burmese, were also to some extent Indian. Refugees from Rakhine fled into British India and from there planned to recapture their country. This so irritated the Burmese that they, in return, mounted raids across the border into British territory. This did not make the officials of the British Raj very happy.

At this time the British, Dutch and French were all vying for power in the East, and all had established at least some sort of contact with the Burmese. However, the Burmese showed little interest in dealing with European foreigners commercially. The British, increasingly worried about the threat posed by French interests in the region, sought to shore up their possessions in India by gaining some sort of control or influence of the eastern side of the Bay of Bengal. Border incidents in Rakhine and Assam gave the British the excuse they needed.

In 1819 Bagyidaw came to the throne in Myanmar. A hot pursuit across the Assam border by Burmese troops led to the declaration of war by the British. The increasing isolation of the Burmese court at Ava contributed to this disastrous (for the Burmese) war; but there is little doubt that the British were more motivated by geopolitical considerations than by concern for Assamese refugees. After an inept and mismanaged campaign lasting two years, the British finally forced the Burmese to surrender, and imposed the Treaty of Yandabo upon them. Under its terms, Britain gained control of Rakhine and Taninthayi (Tenasserim), and Myanmar had to pay a large reparation in silver to the British and accept a British 'resident' at Ava. Within a few years, however, various British residents managed to form reasonable relations with Bagyidaw.

Unfortunately, Bagyidaw was followed by the much less reasonable Tharawaddy Min, and he in turn by his even crazier son Bagan Min. It had long been the custom for a new king to massacre all possible pretenders to the throne, but Bagan Min took this policy to new extremes. In the first two years of his reign 6000 people were executed. The

British resident had been forced to withdraw during Tharawaddy's brief reign, and frontier incidents again began to flare up. The British seized upon an extortion incident in 1852 in Yangon whereby two British ship captains allegedly had been kidnapped by Burmese government officials in order to open hostilities in the Second Anglo-Burmese War.

In fact, it's possible that this incident never actually happened, and the British again were more motivated by the necessity of protecting their Indian possessions. In any case, most historians agree that this war was started on the basis of a grossly exaggerated pretext by the British. It's more likely that they had realised what a bad deal they had made in taking over Rakhine and Taninthayi, which were of little practical or commercial use. Rather, they sought the use of a suitable port, such as Yangon.

The British quickly took over Yangon, Mottama and Pathein (Bassein), and marched north to Pyay. Unlike the first war, the British conducted this campaign with stern efficiency, and met little opposition from the ill-equipped and disorganised Burmese forces. After a series of skirmishes and one-sided battles, the war was over – this time, the British annexed all of Lower Myanmar, which became a province of India.

Bagan Min, now extremely unpopular, was deposed and Mindon Min became king of Myanmar, or at least what remained of it, in 1853. Mindon proved to be a wise realist who eventually came to amicable terms with the British yet cleverly balanced their influence with that of other European (and American) powers. During this period the industrial revolution came to full flower in Europe, and Lower Myanmar became an important and profitable part of the British Empire due to its enormous teak resources and vast potential for growing rice.

Unhappily for the Burmese, Mindon made one important mistake – he did not adequately provide for a successor. When he died in 1878 the new king, Thibaw Min, was propelled into power by his ruthless wife and

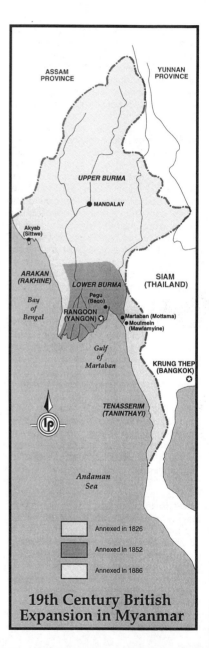

19th Century British Expansion in Myanmar

scheming mother-in-law. Thibaw was so far down the list of possible successors that the 'massacre of kinsmen' reached unheard-of heights, and in this new age of the telegraph and steamship the news soon reached Europe in lurid detail. Thus European and British attitudes towards the new king were tarnished from the start.

Thibaw proved to be a totally ineffective ruler. Upper Myanmar soon became a sorry scene as armed gangs and ruthless officials vied with each other to extort more money from the hapless peasants. Enormous numbers of Burmese fled to the stability of British Lower Myanmar, where there also happened to be a great demand for labour for the new rice trade.

Finally, in 1885, another Anglo-Burmese conflict flared up – the British resident had again withdrawn from Mandalay and a petty dispute over the exploits of the Bombay Burmah Trading Company was the excuse the British needed to send the gunboats north to Mandalay. In two weeks it was all over: the money Thibaw had thought was going into defence had actually gone into corrupt officials' pockets and the British took Mandalay after only the most token resistance.

In order to stamp their authority upon Upper Myanmar, the British undertook a brutal two-year military campaign throughout the region. Similar in motivation to the Highland Clearances of Scotland approximately a century earlier, British forces ruthlessly crushed any signs of opposition, killing many innocent civilians and destroying numerous villages.

British Period

So once again Myanmar was united, but this time with the British as masters. To the British, Myanmar was just another chunk of Asia that now had the good fortune to be part of the Raj. To the Burmese the situation was not nearly so pleasant: Upper Myanmar may have been only part of the whole country, but it was the heartland of Myanmar; Thibaw might have been a bad king, but he was a Burmese king.

Now Myanmar was just a part of British India – and what was worse, Indians, whom the Burmese had traditionally looked down on, came flooding in with the British. As the swampy delta-land of the south was turned into rice paddies, it was the Indians who supplied the money to improve the land, and those same Indians who came to own it when the less commercially experienced Burmese proved unable to make it pay or to pay for it. By 1930 half of Yangon's population was Indian. As Myanmar's national income grew, the country became increasingly dependent upon imports, and the profits from rice cultivation were whisked out of the country to pay for more and more imported goods.

The British applied direct rule only to the areas in which Burmans were the majority – central Myanmar, Rakhine and Taninthayi. The 'hill states' belonging to the Chin, Kachin, Shan, Karen and Kayah were permitted to remain largely autonomous though officially part of the Raj. This difference between direct and indirect rule has haunted Myanmar's political history ever since.

Burmese nationalism grew as a shadow of the movement in India, but grow it did, and in the 1920s and '30s the British were forced to make an increasing number of moves towards Myanmar's self-government. In 1937 Myanmar was separated from India, but internally the country was torn by a struggle between the opposing Burmese political parties. There had also been a peasants' uprising earlier in the 1930s and sporadic outbursts of anti-Indian and anti-Chinese violence.

WW II

Japanese-Burmese contacts had been made well before Japan entered WW II. Indeed Bogyoke Aung San, who had first made his name through university-level political action and was later to become the 'father figure' for independent Burma, had fled to the Japanese in 1940 following his arrest for participation in the Communist Party of Burma. Aided by the Burmese Independence Army (BIA), the Japanese army marched

Bogyoke Aung San, the father of Myanmar's independence movement and its most famous martyr

Soon an internal resistance movement sprang up and towards the end of the war the BNA hastily switched sides to the British. The Allies prevailed at a cost of some 27,000 casualties; nearly 200,000 Japanese perished in the fierce, protracted battles.

Independence

That Myanmar was heading rapidly towards independence after the war was all too clear, but who should manage this process was a different question. The British wanted a gradual transition allowing time to rebuild the shattered economy and political system before the handover. Bogyoke Aung San wanted independence immediately, because if given time, other political parties could gain ground on his strong position at the close of the war. He also wanted to establish a democratic, civilian government:

We must make democracy the popular creed. We must try to build up a free Burma in accordance with such a creed. If we should fail to do this, our people are bound to suffer. If democracy should fail the world cannot stand back and just look on, and therefore Burma would one day, like Japan and Germany, be despised. Democracy is the only ideology which is consistent with freedom. It is also an ideology that promotes and strengthens peace. It is therefore the only ideology we should aim for.

Aung San's incredibly prophetic views didn't win over the military nor the political right, however, and in late 1945 he made another prediction:

How long do national heroes last? Not long in this country, I do not give myself more than another eighteen months of life.

into Myanmar within weeks of Pearl Harbor and by mid-1942 had driven the retreating British-Indian forces, along with the Chinese Kuomintang (KMT) forces which had come to their aid, out of most of Myanmar. Japan declared Myanmar an independent country and allowed Aung San and his '30 comrades' to create the Burma National Army (BNA). One of the 30 was a Sino-Burmese native of Pyay named Shu Maung, who took the *nom de guerre* 'Ne Win', meaning 'brilliant like the sun'. Aung San took the position of defence minister; Ne Win became chief of staff of the BNA.

The Japanese were able to maintain Burmese political support for only a short while before their harsh and arrogant conduct managed to alienate the Burmese. The imaginative 'Chindit' anti-Japanese operation, mounted by the Allies with air-supplied troops behind enemy lines, also encouraged further anti-Japanese feeling.

Eighteen months and six days later, in July 1947, 32-year-old Aung San and six of his assistants were assassinated in a plot ascribed to U Saw, a pre-war political leader who had been imprisoned by the British during WW II after attempting to make a secret agreement with the Japanese. Many scholars today theorise General Ne Win may have ordered the assassination because Aung San had plans to demilitarise the government.

JOE CUMMINGS

JOE CUMMINGS

BERNARD NAPTHINE

JOE CUMMINGS

Top Left: Dressed for novitation, Mandalay
Top Right: Floating market vendor, Inle Lake
Bottom Left: Traditional face markings, Nyaungshwe
Bottom Right: Novice monk from Shwenandaw Kyaung, Mandalay

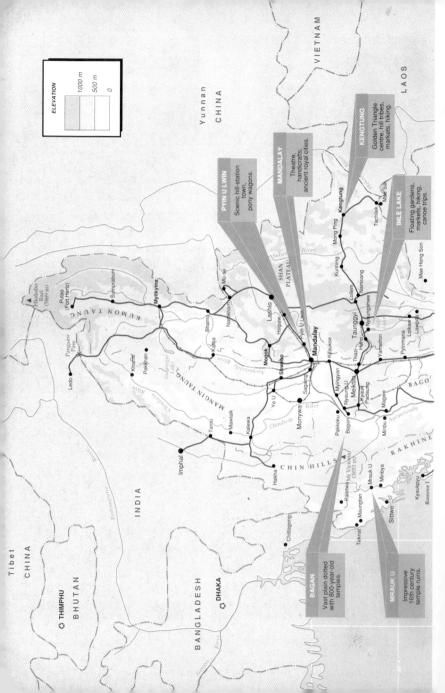

ELEVATION

1000 m
500 m
0

Tibet
CHINA

BHUTAN
✛ THIMPHU

INDIA

BANGLADESH
✛ DHAKA

Chittagong

PYIN U LWIN
Scenic hill-station town, pony wagons.

MANDALAY
Theatre, handicrafts, ancient royal cities.

KENGTUNG
Golden Triangle centre, hill tribes, markets, hiking.

INLE LAKE
Floating gardens, markets, hiking, canoe trips.

BAGAN
Vast plain dotted with 800-year-old temples.

MRAUK U
Impressive 16th century temple ruins.

VIETNAM

LAOS

Yunnan
CHINA

Mae Sai

Tachilek

Mae Hong Son

Mong Ping

Kengtung

Kunhing

Loilem

Namsang

Lawpita

Lokaw

Pyinmana

Yamethin

BAGO

Kyaukse

Meiktila

Nyaung-U

Kyauk Padaung

Magwe

Minbu

Bagan

Pakokku

Myingyan

Sagaing

Monywa

Ye U

Mandalay

Shwebo

Mogok

Thazi

Heho

Nyaungshwe

Taunggyi

SHAN PLATEAU

Salween River

Pyin U Lwin

Lashio

Hsipaw

Kutkai

Muse

Namkham

Bhamo

Kaba

Katha

Pakhan

Khamti

Mawlaik

Kalewa

Tamu

Imphal

Hakha

CHIN HILLS

Mt Victoria (3053 m)

Palewa

Maungtan

Teknat

Mrauk U

Minbya

Sittwe

Kyaukpyu

Ramree I.

RAKHINE

Irrawaddy River

Chindwin River

Indawgyi Lake

Putao (Fort Hertz)

Hkakabo Razi (5889 m)

KUMON TAUNG

MANGIN TAUNG

Sumprabum

Myitkyina

Pangsaw Pass

Ledo

Brahmaputra River

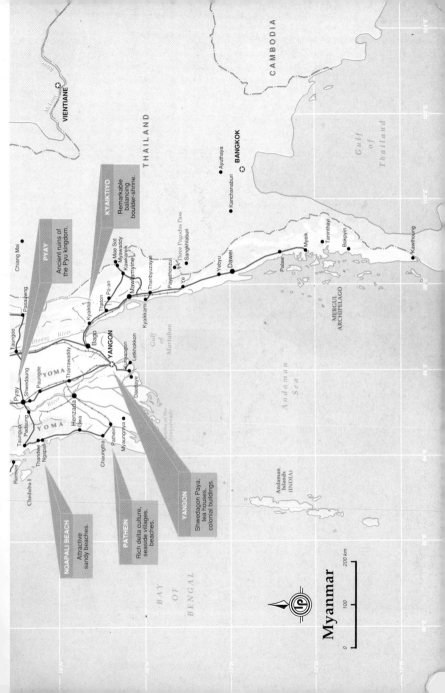

Myanmar

PYAY
Ancient ruins of the Pyu kingdom.

KYAIKTIYO
Remarkable balancing boulder-shrine.

NGAPALI BEACH
Attractive sandy beaches.

PATHEIN
Rich delta culture, seaside villages, beaches.

YANGON
Shwedagon Paya, tea houses, colonial buildings.

CAMBODIA

THAILAND

Gulf of Thailand

BANGKOK

Kanchanaburi

Ayutthaya

Chiang Mai

Pasawng

Taungoo

Mae Sot

Myawaddy

Kawkareik

Pa-an

Thaton

Kyaikto

Mawlamyine

Three Pagodas Pass

Sangklaburi

Thanbyuzayat

Ye

Payathonzu

Yebyu

Dawei

Palaw

Myeik

Taninthayi

Bokpyin

Kawthoung

MERGUI ARCHIPELAGO

Andaman Sea

Gulf of Martaban

Bago

YANGON

Kyaikkami

Kunyangon

Lehkokkon

Daedaye

YOMA

Thanwaddy

Tharrawaddy

Henzada

Shwedaung

Paungde

Pyay

Taungup

Padaung

YOMA

Gwa

Myaungmya

Chaungtha

Pathein

Thandwe

Ngapali

Taungup

Remmee

Cheduba I

Mouths of the Ayeyarwady

Andaman Islands (INDIA)

BAY OF BENGAL

VIENTIANE

Mekong River

Sittoung River

0   100   200 km

Top Left: The verdant rice fields of Nanthe, Inle Lake
Top Right: The magnificient Thanboddhay Paya, near Monywa
Bottom Left: An ancient deva image at Nanthe's Kyaukpyugyi Paya, Inle Lake
Bottom Right: Bullock cart heading home, Hmawza village

On 4 January 1948, at an auspicious middle-of-the-night hour, Myanmar became independent and left the British Commonwealth. Almost immediately the new government of U Nu was faced with the complete disintegration of Myanmar. The hill tribe people, who had supported the British and fought against the Japanese throughout the war, were distrustful of the Burmese and went into armed opposition. The communists withdrew from the government and attacked it. Muslims from the Rakhine area also opposed the new government. The Mon, long thought to be totally integrated with the Burmese, revolted. Assorted factions, private armies, WW II resistance groups and plain mutineers further confused the picture.

In early 1949 almost the entire country was in the hands of one rebel group or another, and even Yangon suffered fighting right in its suburbs. At its worst stage the government was almost on the point of surrendering to the communist forces, but gradually, and with particularly valuable assistance from loyal hill tribe contingents, the government fought back and through 1950 and 1951 regained much of the country.

Although much of Myanmar was now at least tenuously under government control, a new problem sprang up for the battered Burmese. With the collapse of Chiang Kai-Shek's KMT forces before Mao Zedong, the tattered remnants of his army withdrew into Myanmar and mounted raids from northern Myanmar into Yunnan, the bordering Chinese province. Unable to counter the Chinese communists, the KMT decided to carve their own little fiefdom out of Burmese territory. The Burmese government now found itself fighting not only a mixed bag of rebels, communists and out-and-out gangs of brigands and *dacoits* (highwaymen), but also a US-supported, anti-communist, Chinese army. Amazing as it may seem, while operating an embassy in Yangon and espousing friendly relations with the new Burmese government, the USA was also flying in supplies to the Chinese forces encamped within Myanmar's borders; forces whose

main source of income was the cultivation of opium poppies for the production of heroin!

Burmese Road to Socialism

In the mid-1950s, although the central government strengthened its hold on the country, the economic situation went from bad to worse. A number of grandiose development projects succeeded only in making foreign 'advisors' rather wealthy, and in 1953 the Burmese bravely announced that aid or assistance from the USA was no longer welcome as long as US-supplied Chinese nationalist forces were at large within Myanmar. Despite the sickly economy, U Nu managed to remain in power until 1958 when, with political turmoil about to become armed chaos yet again and the KMT problem still unresolved, he voluntarily handed the reins over to a military government under General Ne Win.

Freed from the 'democratic' responsibilities inherent in a civilian government, Ne Win was able to make some excellent progress during the 15 months his military government operated. A degree of law and order was regained, rebel activity was reduced and Yangon was given a massive and much-needed cleanup.

In early 1960, elections were held and U Nu came back to power with a much improved majority, but once again political turmoil developed. His party threatened to break up into opposing groups and in early 1962 Ne Win assumed power again, abolished the parliament and established his own 17-member Revolutionary Council, announcing that the country would 'march toward socialism in our own Burmese way'. This time U Nu did not hand over power voluntarily, and along with his main ministers was bundled into prison, where he remained until forced into exile in 1966. He later ineffectively opposed the Ne Win government from abroad. In 1980, U Nu returned from exile under an amnesty programme for political offenders and devoted himself to translating Buddhist scriptures except for a brief period of political involvement in 1988. U Nu died of a heart attack at age 88 in Yangon in February 1995.

Soon after coming to power in 1962, Ne Win announced the new path which Myanmar would henceforward follow: 'The Burmese Road to Socialism'. It was a steadily downhill path. Nationalisation policies were extended right down to the retail shop level in 1966 when it was announced that a long list of items would only be available from 'Peoples' Shops'. The net result was frightening: many everyday commodities immediately became available only on the black market, and vast numbers of people were thrown out of work by the closure of retail outlets.

A disingenuous 'sock the rich' measure demonetised the largest banknotes (K50 and K100); anybody so unfortunate as to have those notes found them to be worthless. Many of the retail traders who became unemployed following the nationalisation of retail trade were Indians and Chinese, and they were hustled out of the country with draconian thoroughness. No compensation was paid for their expropriated businesses, and each adult was allowed to depart with only K75 to his or her name plus K250 in gold – even a woman's jewellery in excess of that amount was to be confiscated. As many as a quarter of a million people of Indian and Chinese descent left Myanmar during the 1960s. Anti-Chinese riots in Yangon in 1967 – spurred by fears that the Chinese were about to 'import' China's Cultural Revolution – killed hundreds of Chinese.

In late 1974 there were serious student disturbances over the burial of former UN secretary-general and long-time Ne Win political foe, U Thant, yet overall the government appeared firmly in control and determined to continue its strange progress towards a Burmese Utopia. In late 1981 Ne Win retired as president of the republic (retaining his position as chair of the Burmese Socialist Programme Party, the country's only legal political party at the time), but his successor was more or less a hand-picked man and the government was still very much guided by Ne Win's political will.

1988 Anti-Government Uprising

As Myanmar's economy stagnated, the country's standard of living slid downhill year after year. Finally, in 1987 and 1988, the long-suffering Burmese people decided they had had enough of their incompetent and arrogant government and packed the streets in huge demonstrations, insisting that Ne Win had to go.

Ne Win voluntarily retired in July 1988, but it was too late to halt the agitation of the people. Spurred by the further demonetisation of large notes and a prophecy that on the auspicious date of 8-8-88 Burma would become a 'free country', massive pro-democracy demonstrations were brutally crushed, with at least 3000 deaths over a six-week period.

Ne Win's National Unity Party (formerly the Burmese Socialist Programme Party) was far from ready to give up control and the

Nobel laureate Aung San Suu Kyi, whose release from house arrest brings new hope for democracy in Myanmar

public protests continued as two wholly unacceptable Ne Win stooges succeeded him. The third Ne Win successor came to power after a military coup in September 1988 which, it is generally believed, was organised by Ne Win.

A newly formed State Law and Order Restoration Council (SLORC) established martial law under the leadership of General Saw Maung, commander in chief of the armed forces, and promised to hold democratic National Assembly elections in May 1989. The SLORC also changed the country's official name from the Union of Burma to the Union of Myanmar, claiming that 'Burma' was a vestige of European colonialism.

The opposition quickly formed a coalition party called the National League for Democracy (NLD) and campaigned for all they were worth. U Nu tried to declare a parallel government based on the 1945 constitution, but the long-suppressed Burmese population rallied around charismatic NLD spokesperson Aung San Suu Kyi, daughter of national hero Bogyoke Aung San. Suu Kyi, conversant in Burmese, Japanese, French and English and married to an Oxford University professor, brought a hitherto unseen sophistication to Burmese politics.

Nervous, the SLORC tried to appease the masses with new roads and paint jobs in Yangon, and then attempted to interfere in the electoral process by shifting villages from one part of the country to another and by postponing the election. Perhaps the biggest surprise came with the announcement that the government was abandoning socialism in favour of a capitalist economy in all but a few industries.

In July 1989 Aung San Suu Kyi was placed under house arrest; she was to be finally released six years later in July 1995.

1990 Free Election

Once the government was confident it had effectively reduced the opposition, in May 1990 it allowed the country's first free election in 30 years. In spite of all preventive measures, the National Unity Party lost the election to the NLD, which took 392 of the 485 contested seats. The SLORC barred the elected members of parliament from assuming power, however, decreeing that a state-approved constitution had to be passed by national referendum first.

In October 1990 the military raided NLD offices and arrested key leaders. Since then 111 elected parliamentarians have been disqualified, imprisoned, exiled or killed. Although many political prisoners have since been released, most signs indicate that the current government will never hand over the reigns of power peacefully.

After the events of 1988-89, the world press at first gave amazingly little coverage to politics in Myanmar. In January 1991 Suu Kyi was awarded the Sakharov Prize for freedom of thought by the European Parliament, and in October of the same year she was honoured with the Nobel Peace Prize; both awards were issued as tributes to her selfless leadership in Myanmar's prodemocracy movement. Yet another international honour came her way in June 1992 when UNESCO awarded Suu Kyi with the Simon Bolivar Prize for action contributing to 'freedom, independence and dignity of peoples and to the strengthening of a new international economic, social and cultural order'.

Although Western pressure on the government to release Aung San Suu Kyi and to instate the elected government steadily increased during the early 1990s, leaders of the ASEAN countries (Thailand, Malaysia, Singapore, Brunei, Indonesia and the Philippines) rejected a US bid to participate in economic sanctions against Myanmar, saying they preferred a policy of 'constructive engagement'. As Singapore Prime Minister Goh put it, 'The policy of isolating Myanmar in our view has not worked because it has chosen to be isolated for many years. To further isolate it will not bring results.'

Thailand has halted its timber and mineral deals with the Burmese, however, following border skirmishes between the Thai and Burmese forces. The Burmese have repeat-

Name Changes

One of the cursory changes instituted by the government since the 1988 uprising has been a long list of Roman spelling changes for geographic names in a further effort to purge the country of its colonial past. In most of the name changes, the new Romanised versions bring the names phonetically closer to the everyday Burmese pronunciation.

Myanmar versus Burma In 1989 the official English name of the country was changed from the Union of Burma to the Union of Myanmar to conform to Burmese usage. There has been no change in the Burmese name for the country. 'Myanmar' has in fact been the official name since at least the time of Marco Polo's 13th-century writings; the first Burmese-language newspaper, published in 1868, was called *Myanmar Thandawzin*, translated by the British as 'Burma Herald'. In the country's 1947 Constitution, the Burmese version reads 'Myanmar,' the English version 'Burma'.

In Burmese literary contexts, 'Myanmar' is used to refer to the whole country, 'Bamar' (from whence the English got 'Burma') to refer to Burman ethnicity or to the Burman language. In everyday parlance, 'Bamar-pyi' (or 'Land of the Burmans') may also be used to refer to the country. The new government position finds 'Myanmar' more equitable since it doesn't identify the nation with any one ethnic group. If the current military regime releases control of the government to the National League for Democracy, however, there's always the possibility all the names could revert back to their colonial versions.

Linguistically speaking the change is quite reasonable, but it has become something of a political football between the opposition and the government. The official United Nations designation is now 'Myanmar' and Amnesty International uses this name as well; some English-language periodicals – such as *Asiaweek* – recognise the change, while others (eg *Time*) don't.

The 'r' at the end of 'Myanmar' is merely a British English device used to lengthen the preceding 'a' vowel; it is not pronounced. State enterprises that use 'Myanmar' in their titles typically spell the word without an 'r', eg Myanma Airways, Myanma Five Star Line, Myanma Timber Enterprise and so on.

Old Name	New Name	Old Name	New Name
Burma	Myanmar	Pagan	Bagan
Rangoon	Yangon	Pegu	Bago
Akyab	Sittwe	Prome	Pyay (or Pyi)
Amherst	Kyaikkami	Sandoway	Thandwe
Arakan	Rakhine	Syriam	Thanlyin
Bassein	Pathein	Taunggyi	*no change*
Mandalay	*no change*	Tavoy	Dawei
Martaban	Mottama	Yaunghwe	Nyaungshwe
Maymyo	Pyin U Lwin	Chindwin River	*no change*
Mergui	Myeik (or Beik)	Irrawaddy River	Ayeyarwady River
Moulmein	Mawlamyine	Salween River	Thanlwin River
Myohaung	Mrauk U	Sittang River	Sittoung River

edly shelled Thai territory since 1992 while attacking pro-democracy and Karen insurgent armies in eastern Myanmar. In April 1995 Burmese and Christian Karen troops marched across the Thai border, raided five refugee camps, torched several hundred homes and repatriated Karen refugees to Myanmar at gunpoint. This did not set well with the Thai government, who are beginning to re-think their Myanmar policy.

Due to Yangon's continued persecution of Rohingya Muslims in Myanmar's Rakhine State, Indonesia and Malaysia have begun withdrawing their limited support of the Myanmar government. An estimated 200,000 Muslim refugees fled to Bangladesh in 1992 to avoid military repression in a situation that alienated the Muslim community around the world. Under the auspices of the UN High Commissioner for Refugees, over 115,000 had returned to Myanmar by the end of 1994.

Political & Economic Expansion

However reprehensible SLORC's coming to power has been, Burmese politics have stabilised considerably since the events of 1988 to 1991. Truces with 15 different insurgent groups, along with major military victories against the Karen and Mon rebels along the Thai border, have only consolidated Yangon rule.

A growing number of foreign investors – most of them Asian – have grown confident enough to risk huge amounts of foreign currency in private development projects, especially in the central Yangon to Mandalay corridor. Singaporean, Thai and Japanese companies continue to hold significant investments in the country, while China remains the junta's biggest military supporter.

The land border between Myanmar and China stands wide open to legal and illegal trade, and provides the main supply line for a contracted billion dollars worth of Chinese weaponry destined for Myanmar's military, along with another estimated billion in consumer goods annually. Beijing considers Yangon a seaport for western China, conveniently linked to Yunnan Province by the WW II-era Burma Road. A 1994 visit to Yangon by Chinese Premier Li Peng – the man who ordered the Tiananmen Square massacre one year after Myanmar's bloody 1988 putdown – reaffirmed China's 100% approval of SLORC rule. The recent US renewal of 'Most Favoured Nation' trade status for China was received with delight in Yangon. In fact, as long as China remains a major foreign trade hub in Asia, Myanmar need not fear potential trade sanctions from other nations.

Meanwhile the repression of free speech and other human rights continues under SLORC leadership. A report commissioned by the International Commission of Jurists (ICJ) in Geneva describes systematic human rights violations, including: arbitrary arrests of anyone opposed to SLORC, torture of detainees, severe media restrictions, forced relocation of a half million urban dwellers, and forced conscription of civilians to serve as porters and human mine sweepers for the military. The government also often requests 'volunteer beautification' labour from city, town and village residents, requiring them to paint their houses, dig drainage ditches, build walls and weed the roadside.

Still it must be said that those Burmese who don't openly express dissent, and who have the wherewithal to participate in Myanmar's current economic growth, seem more satisfied with the government now than at any time since the 1970s. A genuine middle class, however small, has appeared and is growing. The government, on its part, seems to believe the general citizenry won't risk relative political stability and prosperity by open revolt and so it is a little more likely to further loosen restrictions enacted during the standoff of 1988-90. This social truce of sorts has gained, if not unqualified support from neighbouring countries, at least encouragement from those who perceive an overall improvement in the country's political condition.

Pressure from Western countries ebbs and flows. The German government, formerly one of Myanmar's most vocal critics, has lately been holding high-level trade talks – Germany is now Myanmar's second-largest trading partner in the West. Australia restored military relations in 1994 after a three-year moratorium over Myanmar's human rights record. And the USA has stationed drug enforcement agents in the country after withholding all anti-narcotics aid for a similar length of time. In 1995 the British parliament's House of Lords discussed and then ruled out possible sanctions against Myanmar. Individual Western companies, however, have taken direct action to discontinue doing business in Myanmar; in the USA, kingpin retailers Levi Strauss, Macy's and Liz Clairborne each halted imports of textiles from Myanmar.

Aung San Suu Kyi was honoured with a fourth international award in May 1995 when India presented the leader in absentia with the Jawaharlal Nehru Award for International Understanding, citing her as 'brave, non-violent and unyielding'. Much to the joy of the Burmese people and her supporters abroad, the government finally released Suu Kyi from house arrest in July 1995 after nearly six years. Suu Kyi's detention was the most potent symbol of government repression and the biggest magnet for international attention, but many other high-level dissidents, including the NLD's Tin U and Kyi Maung, have also been recently released. These opposition leaders are talking amongst themselves and with the ruling regime for the first time since 1988. The content of such dialogues has been encouraging enough to stave off the most virulent official criticism from other countries yet vague enough that it promises little in terms of substantial change in the near future. Still there is more hope and a greater potential for positive change than at any time since the NLD won the election in 1990.

Meanwhile the NLD membership at large has lost much strength. The original NLD symbol – a conical farmer's hat with red star on top – has been banned. Government propaganda leaflets label Suu Kyi an 'opportunist' and 'genocidal prostitute'. Like South Africa's Nelson Mandela or South Korea's Kim Young Sam, however, she's becoming a figure who seems destined to move from arrest to political office.

Many Burmese say they expect major political changes to occur only after Ne Win (85 years old in 1996) dies. A revolt among progressive officers in the military is seen as one possible – but unlikely – alternative to the current political situation. Another is that the generals will actually hand over the reigns to a civilian government, as promised, when the new constitution is ratified (see the Government section later in this chapter). More likely the best-case scenario will imitate the Indonesian model, where the military is guaranteed a certain number of seats in the national legislature. An old Burmese proverb seems to sum up the current prevailing attitude: 'Water flows, fish follow'.

GEOGRAPHY
Size & Shape
Myanmar has an area of 671,000 sq km, sandwiched between Thailand and Laos to the east and Bangladesh to the west with India and China bordering on the north. The country extends from approximately 28°N latitude to 10°N latitude; the Tropic of Cancer crosses the country just above

Mogok in the Mandalay Division and also intersects the Chin, Kachin and Shan states.

The shape has been likened to a parrot facing west, with the beak touching Sittwe (Akyab), the claws gripping Yangon, the tail extending down the Taninthayi peninsula, and outstretched wings forming the three northernmost states. Its greatest length north to south extends approximately 2000 km, while the widest east to west distance is around 1000 km.

The Bay of Bengal and the Andaman Sea form the southern boundaries of the country. The central part of the country is marked by expansive plains and wide rivers emptying into the Bay of Bengal and the Gulf of Martaban (the upper Andaman Sea). Mountains rise to the east along the Thai border and to the north where you find the easternmost end of the Himalayas (highest elevations around 6000 metres).

Rivers
Most of the country's agriculture is centred along the floodplains of the 2000-km Ayeyarwady River (spelt Irrawaddy in fomer times), which flows south from its source 27 km north of Myitkyina to a vast delta region along the Gulf of Martaban south-west of Yangon. Navigable year-round for at least 1500 km, the Ayeyarwady has played a major role in domestic transport and communications for centuries. At the height of British rule as many as nine million passengers a year were carried along this huge river by the colonial Irrawaddy Flotilla Company. The company even operated a class of luxury paddle wheelers fitted with polished brass and wood trim.

Other major rivers are the Chindwin (navigable for 792 km), which joins the Ayeyarwady between Mandalay and Bagan; the Kaladan (navigable for 177 km), which flows from Paletwa in the southern Chin State to the Bay of Bengal at Sittwe; the Sittoung (formerly Sittang; non-navigable due to strong currents), which flows through Taungoo and meets the sea between Bago and Mawlamyine; and the Thanlwin (formerly Salween; navigable for just 89 km), which has its headwaters in China and for some distance forms the border between Myanmar and Thailand before eventually reaching the sea at Mawlamyine. The Mekong River forms the border between Myanmar and Laos.

Mountains

The Himalayas rise in the north of Myanmar, and Hkakabo Razi, right on the border between Myanmar and Tibet, is the highest mountain in South-East Asia at 5889 metres. Gamlang Razi is only slightly lower at 5835 metres. West of Bagan towards Rakhine, Mt Victoria rises to 3053 metres. A wide expanse of comparatively dry plain stretches north of Yangon, but hill ranges running north-south separate the central plain from Myanmar's neighbours.

Coastline

Myanmar's coastline extends 2832 km from the mouth of the Naaf River near Bangladesh to the southern tip of Taninthayi Division near Ranong, Thailand. Coastal barrier and delta islands are common in the estuarial areas stretching from the Rakhine State to Mawlamyine. Off peninsular Myanmar farther south, over a thousand continental islands dot the littoral sea, forming a mostly uninhabited island group sometimes called the Mergui Archipelago.

Resources

Myanmar is fortunate in possessing huge stands of teak and other hardwoods. According to the most recent World Development Report put out by the UN, Myanmar has an estimated natural forest area of 43%, down 12% from 10 years ago, and is ranked 33rd among the world's top 100 countries (ahead of the USA, Australia and most European countries). The Bago Yoma (*yoma* means 'mountain range' in Burmese), extending between the Ayeyarwady and Sittoung river valleys, is the most heavily forested area and the source of most of the country's teak.

If timber concessions (and smuggling) to India, Hong Kong, Japan, Thailand and other Asian countries continue at current rates (0.3% per annum), however, widespread deforestation is inevitable. Even where the Yangon rulers have the wherewithal to curb the timber trade (in many parts of the country they don't, since most forests lie in ethnic rebel territory), they seem content to sell it off as quickly as they can to increase or maintain the strength of the Tatmadaw ('armed forces').

The country's lengthy coastline provides a wealth of saltwater fisheries. Until recently all fisheries were state-owned, but since 1991 several private domestic and foreign companies have begun large-scale processing of marine products along the coast. The harvesting of shrimp in particular – estimated at a potential 13,000 metric tonnes per year – promises to be a major source of national revenue in the future.

The country is also rich in gems, oil, natural gas and mineral deposits, which, like timber, serve as direct sources of foreign currency for the Tatmadaw.

CLIMATE

Myanmar undergoes an annual three-season cycle that follows the classic 'dry and wet monsoon climate' pattern common to other parts of mainland South-East Asia. The south-west monsoon starts between mid-May and mid-June, bringing frequent rains that continue into late October. The rain tends to fall mainly in the afternoons and evenings. Although it takes the edge off the intense heat, it does tend to make things unpleasantly humid. Generally speaking, travelling in the rainy season is not particularly difficult, though unpaved roads may occasionally be impassable. In central Myanmar it rains most during August and September, when occasional floods may occur.

The November to May dry period that follows begins with lower relative temperatures because of the influences of Asia's north-east monsoon. This second monsoon bypasses all but the south-easternmost reaches of Myanmar below Myeik (fomerly Mergui; off limits to visitors) but results in cool breezes throughout the country. As a

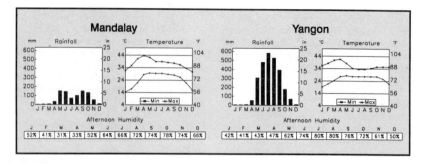

result, during December and January the temperature can drop to near freezing at night in the highlands of the Kalaw-Taunggyi area.

In February the temperatures start to rise, and during March, April and May it can be unpleasantly hot. In Yangon the temperature often tops 40°C and in Mandalay and Bagan – part of the 'dry zone' lying in the rain shadow of the Rakhine Yoma (Arakan Range) – it gets even hotter. The annual water festival, when people douse each other with cold water, takes place in April at the height of the hot season.

Dry season rains known as 'mango showers' occasionally bring welcome but temporary relief. In May the rains start as the south-west monsoon again sweeps northward from the Indian Ocean. In October the rain tapers off and you're back to the cool, dry winter season.

The geography of Myanmar considerably affects the monsoon rains. The delta region around Yangon gets about 250 cm a year, but the rainfall rapidly diminishes as the monsoon continues north; the central area of Myanmar (which includes Bagan) is a large, comparatively dry zone with 60 cm to 110 cm of rain a year. Then north of Mandalay the hill ranges force the winds higher and the rain again gets heavier, reaching a drenching annual total of around 350 cm. The Rakhine coastal area near Bangladesh and the Taninthayi coastal strip beside southern Thailand are exposed to the full force of the south-west monsoon rains, which are often held over the region by the mountain ranges

inland. Thus these coastal areas get very heavy rainfall; Sittwe reaches over 500 cm a year, Mawlamyine around 440, most of which falls during the south-west monsoon.

ECOLOGY & ENVIRONMENT

From the snow-capped Himalayas in the north to the coral-fringed Mergui Archipelago in the south, Myanmar's 2000-km length crosses three distinct ecological regions within the vast Indo-Malay biogeographic realm: the Indian subregion along the Bangladesh and India borders; the Indochinese subregion in the north bordering Laos and China; and the Sundaic subregion bordering peninsular Thailand. Together these regions produce what is quite likely the richest biodiversity in South-East Asia.

Very little natural history research has been carried out in Myanmar due to the country's self-imposed isolation from the rest of the world since independence. Most of the studies available date to the British colonial era and are not reliable by today's standards. Tertiary education in the country, which has never approached an international level, has further declined in quality since the 1970s, hence native research is even more scant. So far Myanmar's new openness to tourism and foreign investment has not extended to the reception of trained wildlife researchers, but indications are this may soon change.

Flora

As in the rest of tropical Asia, most indigenous vegetation in Myanmar is associated with two basic types of tropical forest: monsoon forest (with a distinctive dry season of three months or more) and rainforest (where rain falls more than nine months per year).

Monsoon forests are marked by deciduous tree varieties which shed their leaves during the dry season to conserve water; rainforests are typically evergreen. The area stretching from Yangon to Myitkyina mainly contains monsoon forests while peninsular Myanmar south of Mawlamyine is predominantly a rainforest zone. There is much overlap of the two – some forest zones support a mix of monsoon forest and rainforest vegetation.

In the mountainous Himalayan region above the Tropic of Cancer, Myanmar's flora is characterised by subtropical broadleaf evergreen forest up to 2000 metres; temperate semi-deciduous broadleaf rainforest from 2000 to 3000 metres; and evergreen coniferous and subalpine snow forest passing into alpine scrub above 3000 metres.

Along the Rakhine and Taninthayi coasts, tidal forests occur in river estuaries, lagoons, tidal creeks and along low islands. Such woodlands are characterised by mangrove and other coastal trees which grow in mud and are resistant to sea water. Beach and dune forests, which grow along these same coasts above the high tide line, consist of palms, hibiscus, casuarinas and other tree varieties which can withstand high winds and occasional storm-sent waves.

The country's most famous flora includes an incredible array of fruit trees (see the Food section in the Facts for the Visitor chapter), over 25,000 flowering species, a variety of tropical hardwoods and bamboo. Of the latter, considered one of Asia's more renewable plant resources, Myanmar may possibly contain more species than any country outside China. One pure stand of bamboo in Rakhine State extends over 7770 sq km. Cane and rattan are also plentiful.

As mentioned earlier, Myanmar currently boasts natural forest cover of 43%, ranking it 33rd among the top 100 countries. Another 31% of the land surface features secondary forest, most of which is subject to shifting 'slash-and-burn' cultivation.

Myanmar holds 75% of the world's reserves of *Tectona grandis*; better known as teak to English speakers, *kyun* to the Burmese. This dense, long-wearing, highly prized hardwood is one of Myanmar's most important exports, for which the biggest consumers are (in descending order) Hong Kong, Singapore, Thailand and India.

Fauna

When Marco Polo visited Myanmar in the 13th century, he described 'vast jungles teeming with elephants, unicorns and other wild beasts'. Though Myanmar's natural biodiversity has no doubt altered considerably since that time, it's difficult to say just how much.

The most comprehensive wildlife survey available today was undertaken by the Bombay Natural History Society between 1912 and 1921 and published as the *Mammal Survey of India, Burma and Ceylon*. In Myanmar *The Wild Animals of Burma*, published in 1967, is the most recent work available and even this volume simply contains extracts from various surveys carried out by the British between 1912 and 1941, with a few observations dating to 1961.

As with flora, Myanmar's wildlife variation is closely affiliated with geographic and climatic differences. Hence the indigenous fauna of the country's northern half is mostly of Indo-Chinese origin while that of the south is generally Sundaic (ie typical of Malaysia, Sumatra, Borneo and Java). In the Himalayan region north of the Tropic of Cancer, fauna shares the Indian realm with areas of north-eastern India. The large overlap area between zoogeographical and vegetative zones – extending from around Myitkyina in the north to the Bago Yoma in the central region – means that much of Myanmar is a potential habitat for plants and animals from all three zones.

Myanmar is rich in bird life, with an estimated one thousand resident and migrating species. Coastal and inland waterways of the delta and the southern peninsula are especially important habitats for South-East Asian waterfowl.

Distinctive mammals of renown – found in dwindling numbers within the more heavily forested areas of Myanmar – include leopards, jungle cats, fishing cats, civets, Indian mongoose, crab-eating mongoose, Himalayan bear, Asiatic black bears, Malayan sun bears, gaur (Indian bison), banteng (wild cattle), serow (an Asiatic mountain goat), wild boar, sambar, barking deer, mouse deer, tapirs, pangolin, gibbons, macaques, dolphins and dugongs.

An estimated 2000 tigers are thought to inhabit the primary forests, about four times as many as in neighbouring Thailand. Around 10,000 Asiatic elephants – roughly a third of all those trodding the planet – are widely distributed in Myanmar. Among these are 6000 pachyderms that make up the world's largest herd of working elephants, most of which are used in logging and agriculture. It's encouraging that this number exceeds by a thousand that tallied by English scholar F T Morehead in his 1944 treatise *The Forests of Burma*.

Burmese Tuskers
The *Elephas maximus* plays such an important role in montane Myanmar that the Burmese use different names for male elephants according to tusk characteristics:

With two tusks	swai-son
With one tusk	tai
Without tusks	hine
Widely spread, curving tusks	swai-gar
Straight, downward-curving tusks	swai-saik
Short, stumpy tusks	swai-tok
Stumpy tusks shaped like banana buds	hnget-pyaw-bu

According to a 1955 edition of the *Journal of the Bombay Natural History Society*, the old rule of thumb that an Asian elephant's shoulder height is about twice the circumference of one of its forefeet is accurate more than 95% of the time. ■

Both the one-horned ('Javan') rhinoceros and the Asiatic two-horned ('Sumatran') rhinoceros are believed to survive in very small numbers near the Thai border in the Kayin State. The rare red panda (or cat bear) was last sighted in northern Myanmar in the early 1960s but is still thought to live in Kachin State forests above 2000 metres.

Herpetofauna include four sea-turtle species along with numerous snake varieties, of which an astounding 52 are venomous. These include the common cobra, king cobra (hamadryad), banded krait, Malayan viper, green viper and Russell's pit viper.

Environmental Policy
Myanmar claims to have three national parks and 17 wildlife sanctuaries (including two marine and three wetland environments) which together protect about 1% of the nation's total land surface. Compared to international averages, this is a very low coverage (Thailand, by comparison, has 12% coverage); the government reports plans to raise protection to 5% by the end of the century.

At the moment deforestation by the timber industry poses the greatest threat to wildlife habitats. The state-owned Myanma Timber Enterprise (MTE) accounts for most of the logging undertaken throughout the country. The most valued woods are teak and cherrywood *(padauk)*. Reportedly the company follows a sustainable 'selective tender' system devised by the British in 1856 to maintain forest cover. The latest government plan calls for the complete elimination of all log exports, figuring that the greatest potential revenue comes from processed wood products rather than raw timber. If this plan is carried out, cutting should slow even further. Unfortunately illegal logging in areas of the country controlled by insurgent armies – particularly in the Shan and Kayin states – is not controlled. These areas – rather than the MTE – are the greatest source of timber smuggled to neighbouring countries.

In areas where habitat loss isn't a problem, hunting threatens to wipe out the more rare animal species. Even in the nation's nominally protected lands, wildlife laws are seldom enforced due to corruption and a general lack of manpower. While many animals are hunted for food, tigers and rhinos are killed for the lucrative overseas Chinese pharmaceutical market. Among the Chinese, the ingestion of tiger penis and bone are thought to have curative effects. Taipei, where at least two-thirds of the pharmacies deal in tiger parts (in spite of the fact that such trade is contrary to Taiwanese law), is the world centre for Burmese tiger consumption.

Marine resources are threatened by a lack of long-range conservation goals. For the moment, Myanmar's lack of industrialisation means the release of pollutants into the seas is relatively low. But overfishing, especially in the delta regions, is a growing problem. The country must also deal with illegal encroachment on national fisheries by Thai and Malaysian fishing boats.

GOVERNMENT
The System
The Tatmadaw ('armed forces') and their political junta, the State Law and Order Restoration Council (SLORC), rule Myanmar with an iron fist these days. The only political party with any actual power is Ne Win's National Unity Party (originally the Burmese Socialist Programme Party). General Saw Maung headed the party from 1988 until his nervous breakdown in late 1991, during which he made rambling speeches on such mystical topics as Jesus' supposed sojourn in Tibet. The government is now led by another Ne Win appointee, General Than Shwe, who seems moderate compared to his predecessor; 2000 political prisoners and 'prisoners of conscience' were released in April 1992 when Than Shwe took over. According to Aung San Suu Kyi, however, around 40 political dissidents remain imprisoned.

Environmental Consciousness
At the moment Myanmar lacks the legal structure for a viable national park system and there are virtually no organised environmental movements as yet. Most Burmese recycle non-biodegradable materials as a matter of course; unlike in wealthier countries, disposability is still considered a luxury reserved for the rich. Rubbish isn't yet a serious problem in Myanmar due to this thrifty recycling ethic. As the country develops economically, however, its natural resources and environmental purity will come under increasing pressure.

What can the average visitor to Myanmar do to minimise the impact of tourism on the environment?

In outdoor areas where rubbish has accumulated, consider organising an impromptu cleanup crew to collect plastic, styrofoam and other non-biodegradables for delivery to a regular rubbish pickup point. If there isn't a pickup somewhere nearby, enquire about the location of the nearest collection point and deliver the refuse yourself.

By expressing your desire to use environmentally friendly materials – and by taking direct action to avoid the use and indiscriminate disposal of non-biodegradables – you can provide an example of environmental consciousness not only for the Burmese but for other international visitors.

Visitors might also avoid all restaurants serving 'exotic' wildlife species (eg barking deer, pangolin, bear). The main patrons of this type of cuisine are wealthy Burmese, along with visiting Chinese from Singapore, Hong Kong and Taiwan.

When using hired boats in the vicinity of coral reefs, insist that boat operators avoid lowering their anchors onto coral formations. Likewise, volunteer to collect (and later dispose of) rubbish if it's obvious that the usual mode is to throw everything overboard.

Naturally, you should refrain from purchasing coral or items made from coral while in Myanmar. In Chaungtha many souvenir stalls offer coral clusters; although talking to the vendors won't get you anywhere, try expressing your concern to the village officials who may take action if they receive enough complaints. Burmese sensitive to Western paternalism are quick to point out that on a global scale the so-called 'developed' countries contribute far more environmental damage than do the poorer countries of South-East Asia; for example, per capita greenhouse emissions for Australia, Canada or the USA average over five tons each while the South-East Asian countries contribute less than 0.5 tonnes per capita.

Hence in making complaints or suggestions to the Burmese employed in the tourist industry it's important to emphasise that you want to work *with* them rather than against them in improving environmental standards. ∎

Behind the scenes, real control remains in the hands of postal clerk-turned-dictator Ne Win (commonly spoken of as 'the Old Man'), as it has since 1962. Ne Win is said to be obsessed with astrology and numerology to the extent that virtually every major tactical decision at the national level is based on consultations with horoscopes and obscure number charts. One result was the introduction of K45 and K90 banknotes in the late 1980s. Ne Win reveres the number nine; both 45 and 90 are factors of nine, and the digits of both numbers add up to nine. He has been married seven times, his wealth is said to rival that of the late Ferdinand Marcos and he owns property in England, Germany and Japan.

While Burmese citizens have relative economic freedom in all but state-owned trade spheres (naturally these are the big ones, like timber and oil), their political freedom is strictly curtailed. Peaceful political assembly is banned and citizens are forbidden to talk to foreigners about politics. All government workers in Myanmar, from mail carriers to university professors, must sign a pledge not to discuss the government among themselves or risk losing their jobs. In everyday practice, plenty of Burmese talk to foreigners about political issues as long as they know no Burmese are listening, voicing such common laments as 'Our government is run by a bunch of idiots'.

The opposition movement that began in 1988 appears to be quelled now, with many leaders and spokespersons under arrest and the SLORC firmly in control. Although its impossible to know what goes on out of public eye, the government has only carried out four official executions in the last 25 years.

George Orwell (who wrote *Animal Farm* and *1984* and who once served with the British colonial police in Burma) could hardly envision a more Orwellian regime than that currently held in place by the Tatmadaw. It has turned friend against friend and family member against family member in a web of mutual suspicion. The military employs a large network of informers who circulate in cinemas, teashops, offices and private homes to ferret out 'minions of colonialism' – anyone who voices opposition to the government. A national dress code requires all citizens to dress in proper Burmese attire; trousers (for men or women), for example, are frowned upon unless necessary in one's occupation. Foreign music (ie any music with foreign lyrics) is banned from the radio waves.

Among the most visible signs of the government's current strategy are the prominent red-and-white signboards posted in public areas of all Myanmar's major cities. They carry slogans, in Burmese (and occasionally in English), such as these:

- Only when there is discipline will there be progress.
- The strength of the nation lies only within.
- Crush all destructive elements.
- Beware of aboveground and underground destructive elements.
- Observance of discipline leads to safety.
- Anyone who is riotous, destructive and unruly is our enemy.
- The Tatmadaw shall never betray the national cause.

Cynics say that the opposition never stood a chance and that the 1990 election was either a small tactical error on the part of the military or a simple way of identifying the opposition (anybody who ran for election against the SLORC was immediately put on the arrest list). Some even contend that had the opposition taken over, Myanmar would now be in a state of anarchy. Many younger Burmese, however, still harbour hopes that they will be able to some day wrest control of the country from the feared and hated Tatmadaw.

Movement toward a somewhat more tolerant atmosphere came in 1992 with the release of large numbers of political prisoners and the repeal of a national 11 pm to 4 am curfew imposed since 1988. Cynics contend that many of the freed 'political prisoners' were in fact just common criminals and that very few real opponents to the SLORC were released.

Each year since 1992, however, has seen the release of more prisoners; on March 27 (Armed Forces Day), 1995, the government released 31 high-profile political prisoners, including Tin U, co-founder of the original NLD and former army chief of staff. Another sign that the government is at least recognizing the opposition was the state-sponsored public funeral of U Nu in 1995 – the only democratically elected prime minister Myanmar has ever known. In the same year, the government also reduced by a third the prison terms of 23,000 convicts who had participated in construction projects around the country.

The Constitution

Myanmar has had three constitutions since gaining independence from the British in 1948, the most recent of which was suspended by the SLORC in 1989. In 1995, after five years of snail-like progress, the government finally organised the National Convention, which consists of 702 delegates given the task of drafting a new national charter. Most delegates were selected by the junta; less than 15% hail from the NLD, which has largely been co-opted by the NUP.

In no uncertain terms the delegates have been instructed to draft a charter giving the military leadership special 'emergency powers' that include the right to suspend ordinary government procedures. The parameters also dictate that the charter disqualifies anyone married to a foreigner. Government estimates as to how long it will take to finish the new constitution range from six months to two years. The SLORC has repeatedly promised that once the constitution is ratified – whether by public referendum or by other means has yet to be decided – civilian rule will come. As trade minister Lieutenant General Tun Kyi told international reporters in 1994: 'When the constitution is completed, democracy will be restored.'

Administrative Divisions

For administrative purposes, Myanmar is divided into seven divisions *(tain)* where Burmans are in the majority (Yangon, Ayeyarwady, Bago, Magwe, Mandalay, Sagaing, Taninthayi); and into seven states *(pyi)* where non-Burmans are in the majority (Shan, Kachin, Chin, Rakhine, Kayah, Kayin, Mon).

Each state and division is subdivided into villages *(kyay)*, village tracts *(kyay ywa oksu)*, township *(myonei)* and district *(khayain)*. At the moment, every one of these subdivisions has a SLORC office.

The Military

Myanmar's Tatmadaw totals approximately 300,000 regulars, about the same size as standing armies in Indonesia and Thailand, and is ranked 21st on a global scale. Military expenditures account for an estimated 14% of the national budget; in this category Myanmar ranks 36th worldwide, well behind Saudi Arabia (61%), Singapore (25%), the USA (20%), Switzerland (20%) and Vietnam (20%).

The military's main weapons supplier is China, which has a government contract to supply a billion dollars' worth of arms to the Tatmadaw. Singapore acts as an arms broker to Myanmar for weaponry manufactured elsewhere.

ECONOMY
Pre & Post-WW II Economics

Myanmar's value to the British during the colonial era can be summed up in one word – rice. The 19th century was a time of major upheaval in world economies. With industrialisation, a world market for agricultural products suddenly emerged as some countries found it more profitable to produce industrial goods and import food with the proceeds rather than grow their own food. Myanmar proved ideally suited for supplying a large proportion of the world's rice.

Prior to WW II, Myanmar exported as much as 3.5 million tonnes of rice a year, but much of the profit from this enterprise went to British or other foreign parties. As in a number of other colonial countries, it was a frequent complaint that foreign rule had turned Myanmar into a one-product country

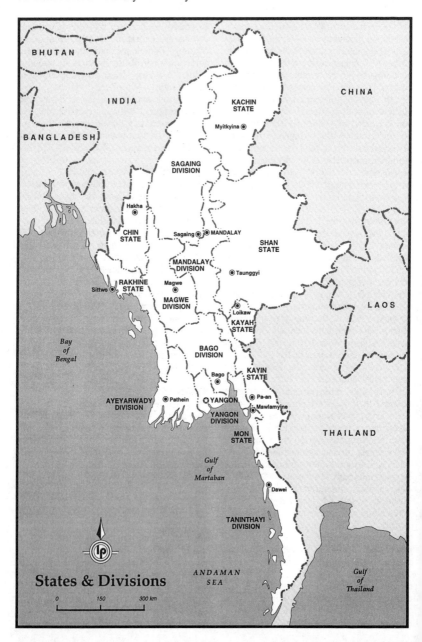

States & Divisions

0   150   300 km

with all the dangers this entailed. Myanmar's rice-growing potential was devastated along with many other of the country's assets during WW II, and the path of development since the war has not been a happy one.

Myanmar suffered major damage from WW II, far more than most of its neighbours: Malaysia and Indonesia were quickly overrun and thus suffered little damage; Thailand collaborated and thus also escaped damage; and the war never physically reached most of India. Yet in Myanmar, air and ground battles raged right to the end and caused enormous loss. Furthermore, Myanmar quickly threw off the colonial yoke after the war and never enjoyed the benefits of overseas aid for reconstruction and replacement of ruined assets. Internal conflicts following independence and a shift toward a command economy in the 1960s and '70s further complicated the situation and prevented efficient restoration.

For a time, Myanmar remained dependent upon rice as a major source of foreign earnings while at the same time its efficiency as a rice producer steadily declined. Despite all the worldwide advances in agriculture – miracle rice, fertilisers, etc – the Burmese were managing to produce less per hectare even two decades after independence. By the mid-1960s, the area under rice production was slightly above pre-war levels but the actual output was slightly lower. Yet the population had increased by over 50% compared to the pre-war figures and by now is probably 100% higher. The upshot is that after WW II there was little rice to export and barely enough to feed the country. By 1987, Myanmar was one of the 10 poorest countries in the world.

Since the government abandoned socialism in 1989 the economy has changed rapidly. As of 1995 the economy was growing at a rate of 6.4% per year, the highest since before Ne Win took power in the early 1960s. Myanmar now ranks sixth in world rice exports, behind Thailand, the USA, Pakistan, China and Australia. Processing and manufacturing have tripled over the last eight years and now provide more of the country's GDP than agriculture. Nominal per capita income is US$890, but when adjusted for purchasing power parity this amounts to US$676, still the lowest in Asia.

Inflation runs an estimated 30% per annum when adjusted for dollar usage and purchasing power parity – more like 50% if judged by a *kyat* (Burmese currency) index alone. The country carries a modest foreign debt of US$6.4 billion, equal to Sri Lanka's and one tenth that of Thailand's; hard-currency reserves have increased to between US$40 million and US$60 million – roughly one month's revenue from exports.

Certain key commodities and services remain in government control or are fully state-owned. One of the most profitable state corporations is Myanma Petrochemical Enterprise, which posted a profit of K3 billion in the 1992-93 financial year, followed by Myanma Railways (K2 billion), Myanma Gems Enterprise (K1.8 billion) and Myanma Timber Enterprise (K1.6 billion).

Despite solid growth, all is not rosy with the economy. Merchants and entrepreneurs prosper while farmers and workers are barely able to scrape by. The retail price of rice multiplied nine times between 1984 and 1993; the wholesale price increased 21 times. The maximum government salary is US$15 per month, and Burmese citizens must typically spend around 65% of their monthly income on food. This leaves little to spend on consumer goods, so most Burmese, for example, rely on discarded, second-hand clothes imported by ship from Singapore, Malaysia and Japan in huge bales. Most of the clothes you see hanging in upcountry markets are 'bale' clothing, which fetch around K40 to K50 per piece for shirt or blouse, just K100 for a used denim jacket.

International Trade

Since 1990 the government has moved towards more economic involvement with the outside world and has a number of major foreign-aided projects underway, along with many joint ventures with foreign-owned companies. Under new investment laws, even wholly owned foreign enterprises are now permitted in certain sectors. Over 25 foreign banks have opened branches in Yangon.

Between 1989 and 1993, the number of exporters and importers registered in Myanmar increased from 986 to 4813. Myanmar's main export revenues come from timber (US$95 million per year), pulses (US$66 million), rice (US$25 million), and gems and pearls (US$10 million), followed by much lesser incomes from maize, rubber, cotton, jute, minerals and marine products.

Hong Kong is currently the biggest buyer of Burmese timber, purchasing US$10 million worth from April to September of 1994 alone; it was followed by Singapore (US$4.75 million), Thailand (US$2.86 million), India (US$1.5 million) and Japan (US$1.2 million). By far the largest importers of Burmese commodities are India and Singapore (about US$60 million each in 1993), followed by Thailand, China, Japan, Hong Kong and Pakistan, each of which imported over US$15 million worth in 1993.

In the reverse direction, most imports to Myanmar originate in Japan, China, Thailand, Singapore and Malaysia. When it comes to foreign investment in Myanmar, the single largest player is Singapore; the latter's presence in Yangon is becoming so great that many Burmese complain that Myanmar is becoming an Singaporean economic colony. Some distance behind Singapore march the USA, South Korea, Thailand, Britain and Japan.

Legal civilian trade with China totals over US$1 billion annually, and Myanmar has a contract with the Chinese government to import another US$1 billion in arms. Although not specifically included in the official state agreements, there is also a brisk trade in Burmese jade, gems and teak in exchange for advanced Chinese weaponry to be used against anti-Yangon forces in Upper Myanmar.

Among Western countries the largest trade partners are the USA (US$74 million in 1992-93), Germany (US$65 million), the Netherlands (US$19 million) and the UK (US$10 million). Oil companies are among the largest private investors in Myanmar's economy: eg the USA's Texaco, France's Total and the Anglo-Dutch Shell.

Sectors of the economy hitherto entirely controlled by the government are now dominated by private enterprise. Foreign investment in fishery projects, for example, went from zero to US$7.9 million between 1990 and 1993, while the value of hotel and tourism projects rose from zero to US$6.4 million during the same period. Foreign-owned hotels worth another US$17 million were either under construction or on the drawing board in 1995-96.

The government continues to control all legal foreign trade in timber, minerals, gems, oil and gas – although foreign companies have been contracted for the exploration and extraction of some minerals and petroleum. These and other large private ventures – such as international hotels – must be underwritten or sponsored by someone in the government. Ministers typically take a piece of every project that requires their approval, often as much as 5% of the project's estimated value. Tatmadaw officers thus enriched live in colonial-style villas in Yangon's best suburbs and are chauffeured about in the latest-model Japanese cars. Most conduct multiple business affairs that assure a comfortable retirement.

Many Chinese who fled Myanmar following nationalisation in the 1960s are now returning to participate in the liberalised economy. Those who can speak Burmese are able to get national ID cards even though they aren't Burmese citizens; this permits overseas Chinese to use kyats to purchase goods and services that usually require US dollars, enabling them to enjoy lifestyles that are extremely extravagant by ordinary Burmese standards.

Many South-East Asia speculators are moving investments from Vietnam – the previous darling of 'emerging market' entrepreneurs – to Myanmar. Political risks for both countries are considered equal, but businesspeople are finding that Myanmar's government doesn't place as many obstacles in the way of foreign investors. British commercial law still dominates Myanmar's legal system and contracts are said to be much more easily enforced than under Vietnam's patchwork of French, Soviet and Roman law. London's *Financial Times* reports there is much less red tape in Myanmar than in Vietnam; corruption, surprisingly, is also reckoned to be substantially lower.

Underground Economy

Although the black market is no longer the only game in town, it still plays a major role in Myanmar's economy. Many Burmese with civil service jobs hang up their coats at the office, then leave to do business elsewhere for the rest of the day, buying and selling a variety of home-grown commodities and smuggled consumer goods. Without income earned (and goods purchased) on the black market, virtually no civil servant in present-day Myanmar could survive.

Beyond simple subsistence, the objective of most black-market traders is to stockpile as many US dollars as they can as hedges against inflation and the vagaries of Burmese currency. The difference between the official exchange rate for kyat and the free-market rate is enormous: in 1995 it was around 5.5 per US$1 at the official rate versus 100 per US$1 on the free market.

In northern Myanmar, rural cash economies revolve around opium. In 1994 over 3000 metric tonnes of raw opium were produced; more than half the heroin sold in North America is reportedly refined from opium grown in Myanmar.

Tourism

Tourism, an obvious source for hard currency, came to a temporary halt following the 1988 uprising, but is quickly building up again with the liberalised visa regulations and expanding tourist infrastructure.

Pre-1988 tourism peaked in 1986-87 at 41,000 arrivals per year. During the restrictive 1990-92 period the incoming stream slowed to around 4000 per annum. By 1992-93 it was back up to 22,000 and in 1994-95 around 60,000 reportedly visited. German, Italian, Japanese and American tourists topped the list, though no one nationality sent more than 1200 in any one year. Even by 1993 the yearly receipts earned via tourism amounted to only US$600,000, most of which is thought to have been spent by business travellers.

During 'Visit Myanmar Year 1996' – which officially runs from October 1996 to October 1997 – the national tourist industry hopes to see a half million visitors. This figure is absurdly unrealistic given the current deficiency of hotel, restaurant and transportation infrastructure in the country and the lack of promotion outside the country. Other significant factors that make the projected number untenable include the lack of repeat visitation due to the offensive two-tiered pricing system for hotels, the high admission fees for historic and religious sites and the excessive paperwork for visiting areas outside the Yangon-Mandalay-Bagan-Inle Lake quadrangle. The country's poor human rights image also acts as a deterrent to tourism. Independent observers estimate arrivals won't exceed 160,000 to 200,000 per annum by the end of 1997.

POPULATION

Since the government does not control the entire country, a complete census has not been possible since the British days. A census taken in 1983 counted 34 million; as of 1993 the population is estimated to be about 46 million with an annual growth rate of around 2.1%. Approximately 74% live in rural areas.

The largest cities, in declining order, are Yangon, Mandalay, Pathein, Mawlamyine, Taunggyi and Sittwe. Population statistics for each of these cities have not been made public since 1973, and local estimates vary wildly depending on whom you ask; Yangon appears to have 3 or 4 million, Mandalay around 800,000, the remainder 300,000 or fewer.

Vital Statistics

The Burmese have an overall national literacy rate of 81.5%, an infant mortality rate of 79 per 1000 and an average life expectancy

INSURGENCY

Independent Myanmar has been plagued by rebellion since its inception in 1948. By 1992, outside observers estimated there were as many as 35 insurgent factions operating inside the country, including national or ethnic liberation parties, 'warlord organisations' and Kuomintang (KMT) remnants. The estimated numbers in these individual groups range from as few as 50 (Tai National Army, Palaung State Liberation Organisation, Kayah New Land Revolution Council) to the tens of thousands (Mong Tai Army/Shan United Army). Most have formed loose affiliations amongst themselves, while some are splinter groups or factions vying for local supremacy (Ma Ha San faction of the Wa National Army; Karenni People's United Liberation Front versus the Karenni Liberation Army). Others are tactical wings for political parties, such as the Karen National Liberation Army (KNLA) for the Karen National Union (KNU).

The naming can be quite confusing. One group may have more than one title, such as the United Pa-O Organisation and the Pa-O Shan State Independence Party, while different, unaffiliated groups may have similar names, such as the Shan State Army (ethnic Shans; member of the National Democratic Front or NDF), the Shan United Revolutionary Army (ethnic Shans; ally of the Third Chinese Irregular Forces – a remnant of the 93rd Nationalist Chinese Army) and the Shan United Army or SUA (a 'warlord' group made up of ethnic Shans, Chinese and other minorities, under the leadership of the infamous Khun Sa, who is also known as Chang Chi-fu and Sao Mong Khawn). In 1985 Khun Sa and the SUA merged with the Mong Tai Army under the Tai-land Revolutionary Council ('Tai' is what the Shan call themselves).

These groups operate primarily in the various states of outer Myanmar, where Burmans are in the minority, as opposed to 'Myanmar proper', where the Yangon government has control. They do occasionally cause mischief outside their own territory; the Karen have attacked Burman strongholds in Bago, Dawei and Kyaikto, and were responsible for bombings in the delta area near Yangon and in the primarily Karen suburb of Insein on the outskirts of the capital in 1984. In early 1992 a band of Karen rebels were routed by the Myanmar army just south of Yangon.

The situation is complicated by the fact that insurgency in the 'Golden Triangle' area is in many cases linked to the thriving opium trade there. Some Western opponents of the trade, which is largely controlled by the Shan, Wa and Kokang, have expressed qualified support of Burmese efforts to eradicate insurgency in the north-east. Thus the opium trade has helped to splinter foreign attitudes toward Yangon; governments that might otherwise support anti-Yangon movements have been forced to tolerate the ruling regime in the name of the 'war on drugs'. Yangon, in turn, exploits foreign ambivalence to the full, identifying all insurgency with the opium trade.

Among these insurgent groups, the most significant government opponent has been the NDF, an alliance of nine non-communist insurgent groups formed in 1976. The avowed purpose of the NDF was to provide military assistance to members under government attack and to work towards common political ends on a national level while retaining local independence. The nine or 10 member groups may share a combined force of over 25,000 soldiers, though it's doubtful they could ever rally together for a truly unified offensive.

During the mid-1980s, the NDF sought to enter into negotiations with the Burmese government in order to come to a peaceful resolution of the age-old majority-minority conflict. Meetings arranged and conducted by the Burmese proved unsuccessful and since the 1988 Yangon uprising the NDF has refused to talk again until representatives of both parties can meet outside Myanmar under a neutral chairmanship. Following the truces of 1989-94 and the 1995 Burmese military victories against the KNU – the backbone of the NDF – a bilateral settlement is highly unlikely to occur in the near future.

Until recently the most conspicuous non-participant in the NDF was the Burmese Communist Party (BCP), a seasoned group that reached peak numbers (12,000 to 15,000 troops) in the late 1970s and early '80s. The BCP became increasingly isolated due to changes in attitude in China dating to 1979, when Beijing began distancing itself from the heavily Maoist BCP. In contrast, Chinese relations with the Burmese government have improved greatly since the end of the Chinese Cultural Revolution – Ne Win finally paid a visit to Beijing in 1985, just one month after China stopped broadcasting the Voice of the People of Burma from across the border.

Other non-ethnic opposition groups include the Democratic Alliance of Burma, the National League for Democracy in Liberated Areas, the National Coalition Government of the Union of Burma and the All Burma Students' Democratic Front. Most of the latter groups operate from refugee camps along the Thai-Burmese border or in KNU-protected villages in eastern Myanmar. None field their own armies and although they meet endlessly and produce stacks of bold declarations and mission statements, they yield very little real power.

Karen National Union

The 47-year-old KNU has offered armed resistance against the Burmese government ever since independence, claiming that the autonomy promised them in the Panglong Agreement of 1947 was never honoured by the Burmese. Until recently the KNU and its tactical arm, the KNLA, controlled most of the Kayin State, home to perhaps a million Karen. Their independent territory, called Kawthoolei by the Karen, was long headquartered in Manerplaw, across the Thanlwin River from Tha Song Yang, Thailand, near the Thai-Burmese border.

Manerplaw also served as headquarters for the Democratic Alliance of Burma (DAB), an alliance of a dozen rebel groups fighting for regional autonomy. It was also the seat of the National Coalition Government of the Union of Burma (NCGUB), a 'parallel government' established by a group of disaffected National League for Democracy members who won parliamentary seats in the ill-fated May 1990 national elections. The prime minister of the parallel government is Dr Sein Win, cousin to Aung San Suu Kyi and son of U Ba Win (who along with his brother Aung San was assassinated in 1947). Along with the exiled MPs, the coalition included an alliance of ethnic insurgent groups led by Karen general Bo Mya and Kachin leader Brang Seng. The NCGUB was severely weakened by the departure of many of its ethnic partner groups to take advantage of government truces.

In January 1992, the Burmese army's 22nd and 44th divisions along with part of the 66th Light Infantry Battalion – a combined strength of 20,000 troops – advanced on Manerplaw from the west but suffered heavy casualties. Outmaneuvered by the KNLA, the government declared unilateral ceasefire.

After a rift between Christian and Buddhist Karen caused the KNU to split into two hostile factions, the Burmese army violated the ceasefire in January 1995 to offer support to the Buddhist faction, the Democratic Karen Buddhist Organisation (DKBO); this time around they were able to take Manerplaw. The KNU leadership headed south but lost their second capital, Kawmoora (opposite Sai Yok, Thailand), at the end of February 1995.

Up until now the Yangon policy has been one of containment, but this now seems to have changed to 'exterminate them once and for all'. Fighting with the KNLA is now concentrated close to a proposed underground gas pipeline from the Gulf of Martaban to Thailand. After eight Burmese petroleum engineers were killed by the KNLA near Dawei in 1995, the government immediately pulled all engineers out of the field and began heavy military operations in the area.

Shan Rebels

If the Burmese government is able to vanquish the KNU – an outcome not by any means assured at this point – its final and perhaps most powerful remaining adversaries are the Shan. Opium warlord Khun Sa remains very powerful in southern Shan State. From his fortress at Ho Mong, opposite Thailand's Mae Hong Son, the 60-year-old insurgent veteran has declared himself president of an independent Shan state called 'Tai-land' and reportedly commands 25,000 troops. These are said to make up the largest, most well-trained and most well-equipped ethnic army in Myanmar nowadays, with an arsenal that includes Russian SAM-7 anti-aircraft missiles. Khun Sa's Shan United Army, in conjunction with the allied Shan State Army and Mong Tai Army, operate their own military academy where cadets begin training as young as age 12.

Khun Sa's downfall may be the increased centralisation around Ho Mong, which has a population of well over 20,000 and boasts gem-refining workshops, sawmills and other industries. As in the case of KNU development in Manerplaw, the concentration of so much of the economy and the military in Ho Mong seems the very antithesis of classic guerrilla strategy, creating an ever larger target for the Yangon government.

Some observers speculate that the Burmese military won't make too much of an effort to defeat the Shan because of mutual benefits obtained via the opium trade. But they may go after Khun Sa's headquarters to create the appearance of waging a war on drugs – American courts indicted Khun Sa on drug charges in 1989 and he is also wanted in Thailand – and to show other insurgent groups that their leaders can be captured. The infamous Lo Hsing-han, a Shan warlord rival of Khun Sa's, has been seen playing golf with Burmese army officers near Bago; one current theory says Khun Sa will gradually be isolated in such a way that the Shan rebel movement – and Shan opium production – remain intact.

Truces

Over the last five or six years the anti-Yangon insurgency has weakened considerably. In 1989 the ethnic rank and file of the BCP – many of them Wa troops – revolted against their Burman leadership and eliminated the 41-year-old BCP in one fell stroke during the so-called 'Pangsang Mutiny'. Burman communist leaders fled to China and BCP territory passed on to the Wa National Army, who quickly negotiated a truce with Yangon.

Next came a similar truce with the Kachin Independence Organisation (KIO), one of the best armed and most organised of the insurgent armies. The KIO truce was followed by similar agreements with Kayah and Pa-O, also major players in the insurgency game. In June 1995 the New Mon State Party and its Mon National Liberation Front, who had been fighting the government since 1949, signed a ceasefire with the Burmese military. This raised the total of signed truces with ethnic insurgent groups to 15. In some cases, especially among the Wa, Pa-O and Kokang, such agreements mean turning a blind eye toward opium and heroin trafficking. In many such instances the Burmese army is thought to be actively cooperating in the narcotics trade – like rival Mafia dons who've agreed to end hostilities in order to share criminal profits.

The only armies of significance still fighting belong to the Karen (KNU/KNLA) and Shan (MTA/Shan State Progress Party, allied with Shan State Army – the SSA). The Karen rebels were hit hard during a succession of Burmese offensives in 1994 and 1995. The much feared SSA lost its foremost military and political leader, the widely admired Sao Sai Lek, who died in early 1995.

On the political front, Yangon has taken a lesson from the Thai battle against insurgency during the 1970s and early '80s by declaring amnesty for all groups except the Shan and by building hospitals, schools and roads in frontier areas to win villagers away from rebel leadership.

None of these political and military successes mean that insurgency in Myanmar has been defeated. But a steady movement toward peace if not total reconciliation seems obvious. Meanwhile the military leadership in Yangon uses the widespread insurgency as an excuse for continuing human rights abuses and as an explanation for draining public funds into military confrontations with rebel forces. ∎

of 59 years. The average citizen consumes 2448 calories per day; in Asia only Afghanistan, Nepal and Cambodia have lower calorie intakes. In the percentage of daily calories taken from rice consumption, Myanmar ranks first worldwide. According to the 1994 World Development Report, 74% of Burmese citizens have access to safe drinking water, a 252% increase since 1980.

PEOPLE

Myanmar's population can be divided into four main ethnological groups – Tibeto-Burman, Mon-Khmer, Austro-Thai and Karennic. The Tibeto-Burman group includes the majority Burmans and over 30 smaller tribal groups including the Rakhine, Chin, Kachin, Lisu, Lahu and Akha. Most of the Mon-Khmer are Mon living in the Gulf

Kachin couple in traditional dress, from northern Myanmar

Karen couple; the Karen mainly live in eastern Myanmar and in the Ayeyarwady delta area

Chin couple, who inhabit western Myanmar, bordering India and Bangladesh

of Martaban area, along with smaller groups in the north such as the Intha, Wa and Palaung. Most of the Austro-Thais are Shan living in the north; 'Shan' in fact comes from the same Austro-Thai root as 'Siam,' both meaning 'free'. The Karennic groups include the numerous Karen and Kayah (known to the British as the Karenni) tribes living along or near the central Thai-Burmese border.

Altogether 67 tribal groups are recognised by the government, officially clustered by language origin into just seven 'national races': Shan, Mon, Karen (Kayin), Kayah, Chin, Kachin and Rakhine. The fact that the government doesn't include the Burmans (Bamar) when speaking of 'tribes' – while including the non-tribal Rakhine, Mon and Shan – shows how its classification system is designed to marginalise all non-Burman peoples.

The exact percentage belonging to each group is a hotly debated topic both inside and outside Myanmar. In the absence of any scientifically conducted census, no one can claim to know the true ethnic breakdown. Best estimates run as follows: Burman 65%, Shan 10%, Karen 7%, Rakhine 4%, and Chin, Kachin and Mon around 2.3% each. Chinese, Indian, Assamese and other minorities comprise less than 1% each.

Obviously the Burmese are not a homogeneous people, a fact which has caused the country many problems over the years. For centuries Myanmar was torn by the struggle for supremacy between the Burmans and the Mon, a conflict which eventually ended with the Burmans in control, only to be overwhelmed by the British and the long arm of the Raj. The British gave a certain amount of autonomy to the Shan and Kayin states, later guaranteed in the Burmese constitution but disregarded by Ne Win and subsequent regimes.

Since independence the internal instabilities have shown themselves again, and today sizeable tracts of the country are only nominally under government control, if at all. The main opposition comes from ethnic minorities living along the Thai and Chinese borders. These groups were long distrustful

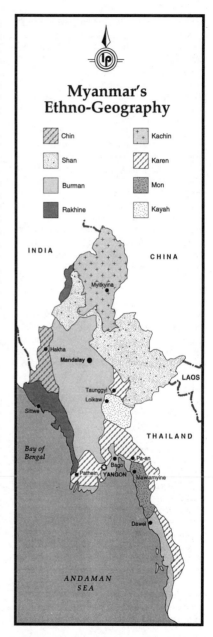

Myanmar's Ethno-Geography

of the lowland Burmese, and with British 'protection' gone their distrust grew into armed resistance, which the central government has taken many years to mollify or overcome.

Under the British many other nationalities also came into Myanmar – particularly Indians and Chinese. Prior to independence, Yangon was much more an Indian city than a Burmese one, for the Indians were generally preferred by British employers. A large proportion of the Indian population has been expelled since independence, although there are still many people of Indian descent in Myanmar. The Chinese have got equally short shrift from time to time – particularly during the Cultural Revolution in China, when many Chinese found themselves very unpopular in Myanmar. During the wholesale nationalisation of the economy in the 1960s and '70s, many Indian and Chinese business-owners fled overseas; some are returning now that socialism has become sufficiently diluted.

ARTS

Burmese culture, at the court level, has not had an easy time since the collapse of the last kingdom – architecture and art were both royal activities which without royal support have floundered and faded. On the other hand, at the street level, Burmese culture is vibrant and thriving, as you'll see at the first *pwe* ('show') you visit.

Drama

Drama, the key to modern Burmese culture, is accessible and enjoyable for visitors. The pwe is the everyday Burmese theatre: a religious festival, wedding, funeral, celebration, monastic ordination, fair, sporting event – almost anything can be a good reason for a pwe. Once under way a pwe traditionally goes on all night, which is no strain – if the audience gets bored at some point during the performance they simply fall asleep and wake up when something more to their taste is on.

There are various forms of pwe. In *anyein pwe* the emphasis is on comedy, slapstick and dancing but the borderline to the more serious theatre is often crossed, and indeed

in an all-night performance there is plenty of time for both.

Pwes are great fun; you immediately sense that the audience is really enjoying itself and the surprising thing is that you can enjoy it too. Particularly during the comedy segments it is very easy to understand what is happening – slapstick comedy hardly needs to be translated. In one pwe we saw in Yangon a prolonged skit involved an obviously hen-pecked and accident-prone husband who, at every opportunity, showed his nervousness by untying, hitching up and then retying his *longyi*. An equivalent gesture in our culture might be compulsively straightening a necktie or fiddling with a ballpoint pen. It soon had the audience, and us, falling around with laughter. That's a comic pwe, but you'll also see more serious dance, drama and music.

Pwe comedians in rural areas often work subtle political commentary into their routines. A famous Mandalay pwe comedian was once arrested for comparing farmer's hats with his cohort on stage. The cohort said 'My hat is so large it protects my head from sun and rain all day long', to which the comedian replied 'My hat is so large it protects all Myanmar', a reference to the star-topped hat that served as a symbol for the NLD before Aung San Suu Kyi was arrested in 1989.

Dance

Myanmar's truly indigenous dance forms are those that pay homage to the *nats* or members of the spirit world. In special *nat pwes*, one or more nat is invited to possess the body and mind of a medium; sometimes members of the audience are possessed instead, an event greatly feared by most Burmese. Nat dancing styles are very fluid and adaptable, and are handed down from older pwe dancers to their offspring or apprentices.

In contrast, few of Myanmar's classical dance-drama styles are entirely indigenous. Most arrived from Thailand during periods of Burmese conquest of Thai kingdoms. Today the dances most obviously taken from Thailand are known as *yodaya zat* or

'Ayuthaya theatre', as taught to the Burmese by Thai theatrical artists taken as war captives from Ayuthaya by King Hsinbyushin in the late 1700s. Around this same period *zinmai pannatha* or 'Chiang Mai plays' were translated into Burmese, providing the text for another entire dance-drama genre.

The most Burmese of the dances feature solo performances by female dancers who wear dresses with long white trains which they kick into the air with their heels during the foot movements – some outside observers see a Chinese influence in these movements (they do seem to resemble certain aspects of Chinese opera). A *zat pwe* involves a recreation of an ancient legend or Buddhist *jataka* (life story of the Buddha) while the *yamazat* picks a tale from the Indian epic *Ramayana*. The arm and head movements often seek to mimic those of Burmese marionette theatre. Around 2000 dance movements are catalogued by Burmese dance scholars, including 13 kinds of head movements, 28 eye movements, nine neck movements, 24 ways of moving only one hand plus 23 using both hands, 38 leg movements, eight body postures and 10 walking movements.

Classical dance-drama is currently enjoying a revival in Myanmar and is occasionally performed at the National Theatre in Yangon. Shorter, excerpted performances may be seen at large banquet-style restaurants in Yangon and Mandalay. Since Burmese classical dancing emphasises pose rather than movement, and solo rather than ensemble performances, it can soon become a little boring for TV-hyped Western tastes. By contrast the less common but more lively *yein pwe* features singing and dancing performed by a chorus or ensemble.

Marionette Theatre

Yok-thei pwe or Burmese marionette theatre presents colourful puppets up to a metre high in a spectacle that many aesthetes consider the most expressive of all the Burmese arts. Developed during the reign of King Bagyidaw in the Konbaung period, it was so influential that it became the forerunner to

zat pwe as later performed by actors rather than marionettes. As with dance-drama, the genre's 'golden age' began with the Mandalay kingdoms of the late 18th century and ran through to the advent of cinema in the 1930s.

The Burmese have great respect for an expert puppeteer; indeed a yok-thei pwe is thought to demand a more skilled and artistic performance than a live zat pwe. Some marionettes may be manipulated by a dozen or more strings; certain nats may sport up to 60 strings, including one for each eyebrow. The marionette master's standard repertoire requires a troupe of 28 puppets including Thagyamin ('king of the gods'); a Burmese king, queen, prince and princess; a regent; two court pages; an old man and an old woman; a villain; a hermit; four ministers; two clowns; one good and one evil nat; a Brahmin astrologer; two ogres; a *zawgyi* (an alchemist); a horse; a monkey; a *makara* or mythical sea serpent; and an elephant. These figures bring together the talents of singers, puppeteers, musicians, woodcarvers, embroiderers and set designers.

Marionette theatre declined following WW II and is now mostly confined to tourist venues in Mandalay and Bagan. Rather less frequently it appears at pwes sponsored by wealthy patrons.

Music

Burmese music, which features strongly in any pwe, can be rather hard for unaccustomed Western ears to enjoy. As with other Asian music it is very short on the harmony so important in Western music and tends to sound 'harsh, tinkly and repetitive'. The perceived harshness is probably due to the fact that Burmese scales are not 'tempered' as Western scales have been since the Bach era. As in Western music, the Burmese diatonic scale has seven tones, but they are arranged equidistantly within the octave, and there is no tempering or re-tuning of the 4th and 7th intervals as with Western scales.

Traditional Burmese music is primarily two-dimensional in the sense that rhythm and melody provide much of the musical structure, while repetition is a key element in developing this structure; subtle shifts in rhythm and tonality provide the modulation usually supplied by the harmonic dimension in Western music. These techniques have been 'rediscovered' in Western musical trends like the minimalism of Steve Reich, Philip Glass and Brian Eno. There is also a significant amount of improvisation in live performance, an element traditional Burmese music shares with jazz.

Classical Music The original inspiration for much of Myanmar's current musical tradition came from Thailand (then Siam) during the reign of King Hsinbyushin, particularly after the second conquest of Thailand in 1767. During this period, Siamese court musicians, dancers and entertainers from Ayuthaya were brought to Myanmar by the hundreds in order to effect 'cultural augmentation'. Myanmar's kings were very good at 'capturing' culture (the same was done with Mon culture from Thaton). Burmese classical music as played today was codified by Po Sein, a colonial-era musician, composer and drummer who also designed the *saing waing* (also known as *pat waing)* and formalised classical dancing styles. Such music is meant to be played as an accompaniment to classical dance-dramas which enact scenes from the jatakas or from the Indian epic *Ramayana*.

Musical instruments are predominantly percussive, but even the circle of tuned drums, the saing waing, may carry the melody. These drums are tuned by placing a wad of *pat-sa* ('drum food') – made from a kneaded paste of rice and wood-ash – onto the centre of the drum head, then adding or subtracting a pinch at a time till the desired drum tone is attained. By the use of multiple hand and stick strokes, Burmese percussionists can create melodic and chordal patterns on the large banks of drums employed in a typical performance.

In addition to the saing waing, the traditional Burmese ensemble *(saing)* of seven to 10 musicians will usually play: the *kyaynaung*, a circle of tuned brass gongs; the *saung kauk*, a boat-shaped harp with 13 strings; the *pattala*, a sort of xylophone; the *hne*, an oboe-type instrument related to the Indian *shanai*; the *palwe*, a bamboo flute; the *michaung* or crocodile lute; the *patma*, a bass drum; and the *yagwin* (small cymbals) and *wa-let-khoke* (bamboo clappers), which are purely rhythmic in nature and are often played by Burmese vocalists. It is also not uncommon to see a violin or two in a saing, and even the Dobro (an American acoustic slide guitar played on the lap) is occasionally used. At the National Museum in Yangon you can view an exhibit of Burmese musical instruments, including old Mon violins, the use of which may predate that of violins in Europe.

An older performance mode features duets of two female musicians playing Burmese harp and crocodile lute. This style of playing originated during the reign of King Badomintara in the late 18th century, when court maidens were trained on these instruments.

Folk & Pop Older still is an enchanting vocal folk music tradition still heard in rural areas where the Burmese may sing without instrumental accompaniment while working. Such folk songs set the work cadence and provide a distraction from the physical strain and monotony of pounding rice, clearing fields, weaving and so on.

Via radio and cassette tapes, Myanmar's urban ears are fed by a huge pop music industry based in Yangon. The older generation prefer a pop sound created in the 1950s and '60s by combining traditional Burmese melodies and rhythms with Western instrumental settings. Younger Burmese listen to heavily Western-influenced sounds –

The traditional shape of the Burmese oboe

the pervasive power of rock music has even penetrated the SLORC prohibition on Western music (except for lyrics, which must always be sung in Burmese).

Modern Burmese pop borrows from many sources – Burmese folk melodies and old Scottish reels, as well as modern tunes taken directly from international pop hits. Burmese heavy metal groups with names like Iron Cross, Wild Ones and Emperor have become very successful in recent years. Other than bans on non-Burmese lyrics, headbangers are restricted by the regulation (not very well enforced) that hair not fall below the shoulders.

Art & Literature

Early Burmese art was always a part of religious architecture – paintings were something you did on the walls of temples, sculpture something to be placed inside them. Since the decline of temple-building, the old painting skills have considerably deteriorated. Modern Burmese paintings in the Western style reflect only a pale shadow of the former skill, and the one painter of any renown, U Ba Kyi, paints murals and canvases commissioned for the larger hotels and government offices.

Religious texts inscribed onto Myanmar's famous *kammawas* (lacquered scriptures) and *parabaiks* (folding manuscripts) were the first literature as such, and began appearing in the 12th century. Until the 1800s, the only other literature available were royal geneaologies, poetry and law texts. A Burmese version of the Indian epic *Ramayana* – called *Yama Thagyin* or *Yama Yagan* in Burmese – was first written in 1775 by poet U Aung Pyo. The first printed books in the country were produced by missionaries; the American Baptist Mission was responsible for virtually all publishing until the late 19th century, when the first Burmese-owned press began printing a Burmese-language newspaper.

Today the Burmese are great readers, as you'll realise from the piles of books in the street at every night market. Because of the heavy restrictions placed on verbal expression by the military government, topics are greatly circumscribed. Of the 3660 books published in Myanmar in 1993, 1171 had to do with arts and culture, 713 pertained to religion and only 129 to language and literature. A paltry 22 titles came out in the fields of political and social sciences.

Wall painting from Tilawkaguru cave temple, Sagaing Hill, outside Mandalay

Buddhist Sculpture Remarkably little research has been carried out on the topic of Burmese religious sculpture other than that from the Bagan and Mandalay eras. A rich Buddhist sculptural tradition in wood, bronze, stone and marble existed among the Shan, Mon and Rakhine peoples but these have received short shrift from both Burman and foreign scholars. Even Burman sculpture is hard to come by in the country.

Compared to the inhabitants of neighbouring countries, the Burmese have had a difficult time preserving historical, nonarchitectural art. Seldom does one come across any Buddha images older than a

Shapes of the Buddha

Despite stylistic variations, Buddha images in Myanmar are remarkably similar in overall shape and form. This is because sculptors are traditionally bound by certain iconographical parameters that specify the hand and body positions the Buddha may assume, as well as the physical characteristics which the sculptor is required to depict. The way the monastic robes drape over the body, the direction in which the hair curls, the proportions for each body part – all are to some degree canonised by these texts. The tradition does leave room for innovation, however, allowing the various 'schools' of Buddhist art to distinguish themselves over the centuries.

One aspect of the tradition that almost never varies is the posture of the Buddha image. Four basic postures (Pali: *asana*) are portrayed: standing, sitting, walking and reclining. The first three postures are associated with the daily activities of the Buddha: namely, teaching, meditating and offering refuge to his disciples, which can be accomplished in any of these three asanas. The reclining position represents the Buddha's dying moments when he attained *parinibbana* or ultimate nirvana. Another key iconographical element is the figure's *mudra* or hand position.

Bhumisparsa ('touching the earth') – In this classic sitting posture the right hand touches the ground while the left rests in the lap. This hand position symbolises the point in the Buddha's legendary life story when he sat in meditation beneath the legendary banyan tree in Bodh Gaya, India, and vowed not to budge from the spot until he gained enlightenment. Mara, the Buddhist equivalent of Satan, tried to interrupt the Buddha's meditation by invoking a series of distractions (including tempests, floods, feasts and nubile young maidens); the Buddha's response was to touch the earth, thus calling on nature to witness his resolve. The bhumisparsa mudra is one of the most common mudras seen in Buddhist sculpture; it's also known as the *maravijaya* ('victory over Mara') mudra.

Dhyana ('meditation') – Both hands rest palms up on the Buddha's lap, with the right hand on top, signifying meditation. This mudra is always accompanied by a sitting posture.

Vitarka or Dhammachakka ('exposition' or 'turning of the wheel of dharma') – When the thumb and forefinger of one hand (vitarka) or both hands (dhammachakka) form a circle with the other fingers curving outward (similar to the western 'OK' gesture), the mudra evokes the first public discourse on Buddhist doctrine. A sitting posture is most common with these mudras, though it's occasionally seen in standing images.

Abhaya ('no fear') – In this posture, one or both hands extend forward, with palms out and fingers pointing upward, to symbolise the Buddha's offer of protection or freedom from fear to his followers. This mudra is most commonly seen in conjunction with standing or walking Buddhas, and occasionally with sitting images.

Dana ('giving' or 'offering') – Either one or both hands extend forward in this posture, with palms up and parallel to the ground, to signify the offering of *dhamma* (Buddhist teachings) to the world. Rarely seen in seated images, this is almost always accompanied by a standing posture.

Bhumisparsa

Dhyana

Vitarka

Physical Characteristics According to the Mahapadana Sutta of the Pali canon, there are 32 bodily marks whereby one can recognise a Buddha. Most of these can easily be seen on any Burmese Buddha image:

1. Well-planted feet
2. Wheel marks on the base of the feet
3. Projecting heels
4. Long fingers
5. Soft, delicate hands and feet
6. Hands and feet covered with a network of lines
7. Arched feet
8. Antelope limbs
9. Hands that can reach to the knees without bending
10. Private member in a sheath
11. Golden complexion
12. Delicate skin
13. One hair for every pore
14. Body hairs standing straight up
15. Upright limbs
16. Protuberances on the hands, feet and shoulders
17. Lion chest
18. Full shoulders
19. Rotundity of a banyan tree
20. Well-rounded branching of the trunk
21. Superior delicacy of taste
22. Lion jaw
23. Forty teeth
24. Even teeth
25. Teeth without gaps
26. Very white teeth
27. Large and thin tongue
28. Brahman voice
29. Dark eyes
30. Ox-like lashes
31. White tuft between the eyebrows
32. Protuberance on the crown of the head

easily find more Burmese religious sculpture on display in Hong Kong, San Francisco and London than in Myanmar.

Buddhist Woodcarving Burmese woodcarving was mainly reserved for royal palaces, which were always made of timber and were showpieces for the skilful woodcarver. When royal palaces ceased to be built, woodcarving skills rapidly declined although the new construction boom has brought about a small but growing woodcarving renaissance – again mostly seen in hotels.

hundred years in Burmese *payas* (pagodas) or *kyaungs* (monasteries) – after a few weeks of looking one gets the definite impression that most such sculptures have been sold or stolen. This may be partially due to the Burmese belief that images from old kyaungs or payas may be unlucky, so why collect them? Mandalay's Mahamuni Buddha image, a Rakhine sculpture, is just about the only famous image with any age – probably because it's too heavy to steal! Unfortunately the years of war and poverty have taken their toll on the arts and you'll

A bronze crowned Buddha in royal robes from the 18th century, Myothit, near Magwe

Architecture

Traditional temple architecture brings together all the *pan seh myo* or 'ten types of flower', the traditional Burmese arts schemata:

- Gold and silversmithing *(ba-dein)*
- Blacksmithing *(ba-be)*
- Bronze, copper and brass casting *(ba-dine)*
- Woodcarving *(ba-bu)*
- Lathe-work *(pan-buq)*
- Painting *(ba-gyi)*
- Lacquerware *(pan-yun)*
- Stucco work *(pan-daw)*
- Stone carving *(pan-ta-maw)*
- Masonry (pa-yan) and stone-cutting *(pan-ywe)*

It is in architecture that one sees the strongest evidence of Burmese artistic skill and accomplishment. Myanmar is a country of stupas or Buddhist reliquaries, often called 'pagodas' in English. The Burmese seem unable to see a hilltop without wanting to put a religious monument on top of it. Wherever you are – boating down the river, driving through the hills, even flying above the plains – there always seems to be a stupa in view. It is in Bagan that you see the most dramatic results of this national enthusiasm for religious monuments; for over two centuries a massive construction programme here resulted in thousands of shrines, stupas, monasteries and other sacred buildings.

Pagoda = Paya Paya (pa-YAH), the most common Burmese equivalent to the often misleading English term 'pagoda', literally means 'holy one' and can refer to people, deities and places associated with religion. For the most part it's a generic term for what students of Hindu-Buddhist architecture call a 'stupa'. There are basically two kinds of payas: the solid, bell-shaped *zedi* and the hollow square or rectangular *pahto*. A zedi or stupa is usually thought to contain 'relics' – either objects taken from the Buddha himself (especially pieces of bone, teeth or hair) or certain holy materials such as Buddha images and other religious objects blessed by a famous *sayadaw* (Burmese Buddhist master). Both zedis and pahtos are often associated with Buddhist monasteries or kyaung.

The term pahto is sometimes translated as 'temple' though 'shrine' would perhaps be more accurate since priests or monks are not necessarily in attendance. The so-called 'Mon-style' pahto is a large cube with small windows and ground-level passageways; this type is also known as a *ku* or *gu* (from the Pali-Sanskrit *guha* or cave). In later Bagan structures, indoor passages led to outside terraces on several levels, a style usually ascribed to the Burmans rather than the Mon. The overall Burman concept is similar to that of the Mayan and Aztec pyramids of Mesoamerica; both architectural styles are designed so that worshippers climb a symbolic mountain while viewing religious reliefs and frescoes along the way.

If all this seems too confusing, just remember that the generic Burmese term for all these structures is 'paya'. The famous Mon zedi in Yangon is called Shwedagon Paya, and Bagan's greatest pahto is known as Ananda Paya.

Payas function basically as a focus for meditation or contemplation. In the case of solid payas (zedis), if there is a need for some sheltered gathering place or a place to house images or other paraphernalia, then this will usually be an ancillary to the paya. There may be small shrines, pavilions, covered walkways or other such places all around a major paya. These are often more heavily ornamented than the zedis themselves. *Hman-si-shwe-cha*, which describes the combination of giltwork with coloured glass mosaic, is one of the most popular types of ornamentation in Mon and Burman temples.

Zedi Styles Zedis go under different names in other Buddhist countries; they may be called *dagobas* in Sri Lanka, *chedis* or *jedis* in Thailand, *stupas* or *chaityas* in India, but basically they all refer to the same idea. Although at first glance all zedis may look alike, you'll soon realise there have been many, often subtle, design changes over the years. Early zedis were often hemispherical (see the Kaunghmudaw at Sagaing near Mandalay) or bulbous (the Bupaya in Bagan), while the more modern style is much more graceful – a curvaceous lower bell merging into a soaring spire as in the Shwedagon Paya in Yangon. Style is not always a good indicator of a zedi's original age since Myanmar is earthquake-prone and many have been rebuilt over and over again, gradually changing their design through the centuries.

One thing many zedis seem to have in quantity is an air of tranquillity. Even when it's noisy around a zedi, when some sort of festival or ceremony is going on, the atmosphere is still charged with that tranquil magic that seems to pervade everything around it. High above you can hear the wind bells tinkling from the *hti*, the decorative metal 'umbrella' that tops the structure. Around the base people are meditating, or strolling around, or simply chatting. Zedis have a warmth, an easygoing feeling of friendliness, that is quite unmatched by any other religious building.

Other Buildings Traditionally, only the zedi, gu and pahto have been made of permanent materials; until quite recently all secular buildings – and most monasteries – were constructed of wood and thus there are few wooden buildings of any age to be seen. Even the great palaces were all made of wood, and with the destruction of Mandalay Palace during WW II there is no remaining Burmese wooden palace. There are only a few reminders of these beautifully carved buildings left in Myanmar, and even these are deteriorating today due to lack of protection.

Although so little remains of the old wooden architectural skills, there are still many excellent wooden buildings to be seen. The Burmese continue to use teak with great skill, and a fine country home can be a very pleasing structure indeed. Unhappily the Burmese have proved far less adept with more modern materials, and Myanmar boasts some appalling corrugated-iron-roofed buildings and concrete monstrosities. Even with the finer, older buildings the emphasis has

---

Burmese Iconography

Buddhist architecture in Myanmar – whether old or new – tends to employ a set of common decorative motifs taken from Hindu-Buddhist mythology. These may appear as free-standing sculptures, often placed near gates and doorways; as bas relief on the exterior walls of *theins* or *pahtos*; or as goldleaf paintings or woodcarvings on doors. Each motif symbolises a particular positive quality associated with the religion and is meant to confer that quality upon the place as well as the people who enter the place.

Motif	Burmese	Pali/Sanskrit	Meaning
lion	chinthe	singa	courage, royalty
goose ('Brahminy duck')	hintha	hamsa	unity
human from the waist up,	keinnayi (male)	kinnari	love
ostrich-like bird waist down	keinnaya (female)	kinnara	
sphinx-like, half lion,	Manoutthiha	Manussingha	security
half human			
eagle-like bird	kalon	garuda	strength
legless dragon	naga	naga	peace, prosperity
ogre	bilu	yaksha	protection
sea serpent	makan	makara	blessing
earth goddess	wathondayei	vasundhara	maternal protection
peacock	daun	–	sun or patriotism
rabbit	youn	–	moon or peace
crowned Buddha-like figure	Lokanat	Lokanatha or	world peace,
holding a lotus flower		Avalokitesvara	future Buddhahood

always been more on quantity than quality – Myanmar boasts no great buildings of meticulous artistry like India's Taj Mahal. But when it comes to location – balancing a delicate stupa on a towering hilltop or perching one on the side of a sheer precipice – the Burmese have no match.

Although historical monuments in the Burman-majority areas are fairly well preserved, elsewhere in Myanmar this is sadly not the case. An extraordinarily beautiful, 100-year-old Shan-style palace in Kengtung was razed to build a 14-storey hotel on the new Thailand-China route. Other palaces in this area are also in line to be demolished.

CULTURE & SOCIETY
Bamahsan Chin
The social ideal for most Burmese citizens – no matter what their ethnic background may be – is a standard of behaviour commonly termed *bamahsan chin* or 'Burmese-ness'.

The hallmarks of bamahsan chin include: an acquaintance with Buddhist scriptures (and the ability to recite at least a few classic verses); showing respect for elders; being able to speak idiomatic Burmese; dressing modestly; showing discretion in behaviour toward members of the opposite sex; and most importantly, exhibiting modes of expression and comportment that value the quiet, subtle and indirect rather than the loud, obvious and direct.

The degree to which a Burmese can conform to these ideals matches the degree of respect he or she will receive from associates. Although high rank – civil, military or clerical – will exempt certain individuals from chastisement by inferiors, it doesn't exempt them from the way they are perceived by other Burmese. This goes for foreigners as well, even though most first-time visitors can hardly be expected to speak idiomatic Burmese or recite Buddhist scripture.

Avoiding Offence
The usual Asian rules of conduct apply in Myanmar, plus there's a few specially

Burmese ones. As elsewhere in Asia it is unseemly to show too much emotion – losing your temper over problems and delays gets you nowhere, it just amazes people. Stay calm and collected at all times. The Burmese frown on such displays of anger just as much as they frown on too open a display of affection.

As in other Buddhist countries the head is the highest part of the body – spiritually as well as literally. You should never deliberately touch somebody else on the head or pat a child on the head. Equally, the feet are the lowest part of the body – don't point your feet at somebody.

Buddha images are sacred objects, so don't pose in front of them for pictures and definitely do not clamber upon them.

A couple of rules apply specifically to women. Women should never ride on the roof of vehicles or boats, which would be a cultural insult to any male passengers below. Those males who weren't gravely offended might take the roof-sitting as licence to harrass such 'loose women'.

Monks are not supposed to touch or be touched by women. If a woman wants to hand something to a monk, the object should be placed within reach of the monk, not handed directly to him.

Dress
One should dress neatly (no shorts or sleeveless shirts) when visiting religious sites. Most important of all in Myanmar, remember to take off your shoes and socks before entering the grounds of any Theravada Buddhist shrine, zedi, temple, paya or monastery. Even at the most dilapidated, run-down, ruined paya in Bagan the 'no footwearing' rule still applies. You must go barefoot in every part of a Buddhist compound, not just in the shrine buildings as in neighbouring Buddhist countries. In the middle of the day barefooting it can get a little painful as the paved area around a paya often becomes very hot. At major payas there will often be a mat walkway around the platform.

At one time this restriction caused quite a

stir between the Burmese and the British. As part of the growing surge of nationalism between the wars, and a neat way to put the British in their place, the Burmese decided to rigidly enforce the no-footwear rules, from which the Europeans had previously been exempted. Signs also suddenly appeared announcing that there was to be 'no umbrellaring' – in case you've never seen anyone do this, it means using an umbrella to point things out!

Shoes – but not necessarily socks – are also taken off before entering private homes. Actually the Burmese very rarely wear socks. You'll find it easier to deal with temples and private homes if you follow their example and go sockless. Or take it a step further and wear slip-on sandals – the most convenient footwear for travelling in Myanmar – like the locals do.

Beach attire or sloppy lounge clothes are not considered appropriate for walking around town. The attitude of 'this is how I dress at home and no one is going to stop me' gains nothing but disrespect or disgust from the Burmese. Men as well as women should keep their shoulders covered except at the beach or when bathing. Likewise long trousers, longyis or skirts are considered more appropriate than shorts in all situations except at the beach.

SPORT
Burmese Martial Arts
Myanmar has a tradition of kickboxing that's said to date back to the Bagan era, although the oldest written references are found in chronicles of warfare between Burma and Thailand during the 15th and 16th centuries. Burmese kickboxing *(myanma let-hwei)* is very similar in style to Siamese kickboxing or *muay thai* although not nearly as well developed as a national sport. In fact Burmese boxing matches are never seen or heard on television or radio, and only occasionally reported in the newspaper.

The most common and traditional kickboxing venues are temporary rings set up at *paya pwe* ('pagoda festivals') rather than sports arenas. Within the last five years,

the martial art's status has raised perceptibly and nowadays occasional championship matches are also occasionally held at Aung San Stadium in Yangon. Finding out in advance about such public events can be difficult. If you're interested it's best to drop in on one of the kickboxing classes at Yangon's YMCA and ask whether there are any upcoming matches in the area.

As in Thai boxing, almost anything goes in the ring. All surfaces of the body are considered fair targets and any part of the body except the head may be used to strike an opponent. Common blows include high kicks to the neck, elbow thrusts to the face and head, knee hooks to the ribs and low crescent kicks to the calf. A contestant may even grasp an opponent's head between his hands and pull it down to meet an upward knee thrust. Punching is considered the weakest of all blows and kicking merely a way to 'soften up' one's opponent; knee and elbow strikes are decisive in most matches.

Competition isn't nearly as formalised in Myanmar as in Thailand; in fact you probably won't find two people anywhere in the country who agree on the rules! What's obvious is that the structure and limitations of each match varies with its context and with the calibre of the participants. Unlike Thai boxing, which has borrowed a great deal from the Queensbury rules in international or Western boxing, Burmese boxing represents a more traditional form once shared by the two countries. Rules tend to follow situational norms; fighters, managers and judges get together before each match and work out time limits and scoring criteria.

In the simplest rural matches, fought in a dirt circle, there's no time limit and a fighter loses once he has wiped blood from his face or body three times. In more organised amateur matches, boxers fight in square rings (5.8 by 5.5 metres), for three to five rounds of three minutes each, usually with two minutes rest between. Professional matches in larger towns and cities begin with five rounds but may increase round by round to 12 rounds when the scoring is tight – even longer if no clear winner emerges earlier in the match. When such extensions occur, boxers can request a five-minute rest period for every seven rounds fought. Such marathons – gruelling in the extreme by most international standards – are somewhat rare. At both amateur and pro matches, two referees officiate in the ring – this contrasts with Thailand, where there's only one. At ringside are three judges who score the match by pooling their impressions of stamina, skill and bravery.

Fighters bandage their hands but do not wear gloves; they fight barefoot except for nylon anklets worn to absorb perspiration. Simple, dark-coloured shorts rather than baggy boxing trunks are usually worn; if the shorts worn by the contestants appear too similar in colour, the fighters may sew coloured bandanas over the front to make it easier for spectators to differentiate the opponents. In championship matches Burmese fighters are beginning to imitate the Thai boxers they see on TV by wearing big, gaudy trunks.

Before the match begins each boxer performs a dance-like ritual in the ring to pay homage to Buddha and to Khun Cho and Khun Tha, the nats whose domain includes Burmese kickboxing. The winner repeats the ritual at the end of the match. A small musical ensemble consisting of drums, hne, cymbals and bamboo clappers performs during the rituals and throughout the match; the volume and tempo of the music rise and fall along with events in the ring.

There are no weight divisions in Burmese boxing – perhaps because the pool of professional fighters is relatively small. Instead boxers are ranked by skill into first, second, and third class. The best boxers are said to hail from the Ayeyarwady Division, Mandalay Division, Kayin State and Mon State, and these regions are where you'll see the best matches. At present Myanmar's most celebrated boxer is 22-year-old national champion Shwe Du Won from Pa-an, Kayin State. A pro boxer earns around K10,000 for winning in a big match. Many of the more accomplished Burmese professionals end up migrating to the better-paying boxing stadiums of provincial Thailand; some go back and forth.

Myanmar's most famous myanma lethwei teacher is 38-year-old Saya Pan Thu, founder of the Institute of Myanmar Traditional Advanced Boxing and one of three trainers at Yangon University. Pan Thu comes from a teaching lineage that emphasises Myanmar's most traditional style of kickboxing, but also incorporates a few grappling and wrestling techniques from the judo-like Burmese art of *bando*. Due largely to Pan Thu's steady promotion of Burmese martial arts, the country is on the verge of establishing the Myanma Traditional Boxing Federation, an organisation that will regulate boxing rules, introduce new safety measures to the ring and develop overall professionalism.

Another thread follows the YMCA school developed by Nilar Win, who now teaches in Paris. The YMCA/Nilar Win tradition appeals to both the amateur and the aspiring professional with its relative emphasis on physical fitness and on precision of movement. It also borrows more from modern martial techniques outside Myanmar, particularly from Thailand.

Chinlon

The Burmese term *chinlon* refers to games in which a woven rattan ball about 12 cm in diameter is kicked around. It also refers to the ball itself, which resembles the *takraw* of Thailand and Malaysia. Informally any number of players can form a circle and keep the chinlon airborne by kicking it soccer-style from player to player; a lack of scoring makes it a favourite pastime with Burmese of all ages.

In formal play six players stand in a circle of 22-foot circumference. Each player must keep the ball aloft using a succession of 30 techniques and six surfaces on the foot and leg, allotting five minutes for each part. Each successful kick scores a point, while points are subtracted for using the wrong body part or dropping the ball.

A popular variation – and the one used in intramural or international competitions – is played with a volleyball net, using all the same rules as in volleyball except that only the feet and head are permitted to touch the ball. It's amazing to see the players perform aerial pirouettes, spiking the ball over the net with their feet.

RELIGION

Around 87% of the Burmese are Buddhist. During the U Nu period Buddhism functioned as a state religion of sorts – as embodied in such catch-phrases as 'the Socialist Way to Nibbana'. Nowadays there is complete freedom of religion, though within the government Buddhists tend to attain higher rank more easily than non-Buddhists, simply because Buddhism is considered a key element in bamahsan chin or 'Burmese-ness'.

An appreciation of Buddhism and its history in Myanmar is an absolute prerequisite for outsiders wishing to understand the Burmese mind.

Burmese Buddhism

Early Buddhism & Theravada Reform The Mon were the first people in Myanmar to practice Theravada Buddhism, called the 'Southern School' since it took the southern route from India, its place of origin. King Asoka, the great Indian emperor and devout Buddhist convert, is known to have sent missions during the 3rd century BC to Suvannabhumi or the 'Golden Land' – an area taken to be the fertile river deltas of what are today Myanmar, Thailand and Cambodia. A second wave is thought to have arrived in South-East Asia via Sinhalese missionaries from present-day Sri Lanka sometime between the 6th and 10th centuries.

By the 9th century the Pyus of Upper Myanmar were combining Theravada with elements of Mahayana and Tantric Buddhism brought with them from their homelands on or near the Tibetan Plateau. When the Burmans of Bagan supplanted the Pyus they inherited this amalgamated form.

During the early Bagan era (11th century), Burman King Anawrahta decided that the Buddhism practiced in his realm should be 'purified' of all non-Theravada elements, a task he set for Mon monks captured by his armies in Thaton, Lower Myanmar. Although Burmese Buddhism was never totally rid of Mahayana, Tantric, Hindu and animist elements, his efforts were remarkably successful in bringing the Burmese around to a predominantly Theravada world-view.

History & Tenets Strictly speaking, Theravada Buddhism is not a theism like Hinduism, Judaism, Islam or Christianity since it is not centred around a god or gods, but rather is based on a psycho-philosophical system. Today it covers a wide range of interpretations of the basic beliefs which all start from the enlightenment of Siddhartha Gautama, a prince-turned-ascetic, in northern India around 2500 years ago. Gautama was not the first Buddha, nor is he expected to be the last.

Neither Buddha ('The Enlightened') nor his immediate pupils ever wrote the *dhamma* or Buddhist teachings down, so a schism developed a thousand years after Gautama's death and today there are two major schools of Buddhism. The Theravada or 'doctrine of the elders' school holds that to achieve *nibbana* (nirvana), the eventual aim of every Buddhist, you must 'work out your own salvation with diligence'. In other words it is up to each individual to work out his or her own fate.

The Mahayana, or 'large vehicle', school holds that individuals should forego the experience of nibbana until all humankind is ready for salvation. The goal is to become a bodhisattva or 'Buddha-to-be' rather than a fully enlightened Buddha. From this perspective, no one can enter nibbana without the intervention of a bodhisattva.

The Mahayana school have not rejected the other school, but claim they have extended it. Hence the Mahayanists often refer to Theravada as 'Hinayana' or 'small vehicle' Buddhism. The Theravadins, on the other hand, see Mahayana as a misapprehension of the Buddha's original teachings. To those who would choose, Mahayana offers the 'soft option' ('have faith and all will be well'), while the Theravada is more austere and ascetic, and, some might say, harder to practise.

In the Buddhist world today, Theravada Buddhism is followed in Sri Lanka, Laos, Cambodia, Thailand and Myanmar. Mahayana Buddhism is practised in Vietnam, Japan and China, and amongst Chinese Buddhists in Taiwan, Singapore and Hong Kong. There are other more esoteric divisions of Buddhism such as the Hindu-influenced Tantric Buddhism of Tibet and Nepal, and the Zen Buddhism of Japan, all of which are forms of Mahayana in general principle since they adhere to the bodhisattva ideal.

Today the majority of Buddhists in Myanmar belong to the Theravada sect; those who profess Mahayana Buddhism total fewer than 1%, virtually all of whom are of Chinese descent.

Buddha taught that the world is primarily characterised by *dukkha* (unsatisfactoriness), *anicca* (impermanence) and *anatta* (insubstantiality), and that even our happiest moments are only temporary, empty and unsatisfactory. The ultrapragmatic Buddhist perception of cause and effect – *kamma* in Pali, *karma* in Sanskrit, *kan* in Burmese – holds that birth inevitably leads to sickness, old age and death, hence every life is insecure and subject to dukkha. Through rebirth, the cycle of *thanthaya* (Pali: *samsara)* repeats itself endlessly as long as ignorance and craving – the remote and proximate causes of birth – remain. Only by reaching a state of complete wisdom and non-desire can one attain true happiness. To achieve wisdom and eliminate craving one must turn inward and master one's own mind through meditation, most commonly known to the Burmese as *bhavana* or *kammathan*.

Buddha preached four noble truths:

1. Life is dukkha (unsatisfactoriness).
2. Dukkha comes from *tanha* (selfish desire).
3. When one forsakes selfish desire suffering will be extinguished.
4. The 'eightfold path' is the way to eliminate selfish desire.

The 'eightfold path' is divided into three stages: *sila* – morality; *samadhi* – concentration; and *pañña* – wisdom and insight. The eightfold path consists of:

1. Right speech
2. Right action
3. Right livelihood
4. Right exertion
5. Right attentiveness
6. Right concentration
7. Right thought
8. Right understanding

This is an evolutionary process through many states of spiritual development until the ultimate goal is reached – death, no further rebirths, entry to nibbana. To the Western mind this often seems a little strange – for most Westerners death is the end, not something to be looked forward to but something to be feared.

In addition to the four noble truths and the eightfold path, devout Burmese Buddhists adhere to five lay precepts or moral rules *(sila)* which require abstinence from: 1) killing; 2) stealing; 3) unchastity (usually interpreted among laypeople as adultery); 4) lying; and 5) intoxicating substances.

Along with the moral and philosophical tenets outlined above, Buddhism emphasises love, compassion, non-violence and tolerance of other belief systems. This tolerance has often resulted in its assimilation into other religions, as eventually happened in India with Hinduism, or in its absorption of already extant beliefs, as happened with the Burmese nats. The personal experience one has of Buddhism remains similar from country to country despite local adaptations, changes, amalgamations and inclusions: an overriding impression of warmth and gentleness, and a religion practised by sympathetic people who are always eager to explain their beliefs.

Rebirth vs Reincarnation In Myanmar the Buddhist concept of rebirth has been corrupted over the years into a common belief in reincarnation. If you're good, some say, 'women can be reborn as men, poor men as rich men, non-Burmese as Burmese – it's all very logical'. Actually Buddha taught that there is no part of a person which is called the soul, and that rebirth is the continuation of a mental or physical process rather than the transfer of a spiritual entity from one life rank to another.

Nibbana – liberation from the mundane world of mental and physical bondage – is the only goal worth pursuing, since all lives, rich or poor, beautiful or ugly, are forever subject to suffering, impermanence and lack of meaning. Effectively, nibbana is an end to the cycle of rebirths (both moment to moment and life to life) that define existence.

Kamma is central to the doctrine of rebirth, but it's not 'fate' as sometimes described, but rather the ultimate law of causation. Not only does rebirth result from actions we have committed in a previous life, but each moment in our lives is the result of previous moments – during each of which we made conscious or unconscious choices that determined our current lot. At each and every moment one has the opportunity to improve one's kamma; thus, in Theravada Buddhism each person alone is responsible for his or her destiny, not only from life to life but from moment to moment. Buddha did not claim that his way was the only way, simply that no one can escape the natural laws of causation.

In spite of these obviously profound truths, the most common Burmese approach is to try for a better future life by feeding monks, giving donations to temples and performing regular worship at the local paya. For the average Burmese everything revolves around the 'merit' *(kutho*, from the Pali *kusala* or 'wholesome') one is able to accumulate through such deeds. One of the more typical rituals performed by individuals visiting a stupa is to pour water over the Buddha image at their astrological post (determined by the day of the week they were born) – one glassful for every year of their current age plus one extra to ensure a long life. Asked what they want in their next life, most Burmese will put forth such seemingly mundane and materialistic values as beauty and wealth – or rebirth somewhere beyond the reach of SLORC.

Monks & Nuns Socially, every Burmese male is expected to take up temporary monastic residence twice in his life: once as a *samanera* or novice monk between the ages of 5 and 15 and again as a fully ordained monk or *pongyi* sometime after age 20. Almost all men or boys under 20 years of age participate in the *shinpyu* or novitiation ceremony – quite a common event since a family earns great merit when one of its sons takes robe and bowl. A samanera adheres to 10 precepts or vows, which include the usual prohibitions against stealing, lying, killing, intoxication and sexual involvement, along with ones forbidding: eating after noon; listening to music or dancing; wearing jewellery, garlands or perfume; sleeping on high beds; and accepting money for personal use. A novice usually lasts a week or two – nine days is an auspicious number.

Later in life a male should spend three months as a pongyi at a monastery during the Buddhist Lent (Waso) which begins in July and coincides with the rainy season. For many men the post-rice harvest, hot-season hiatus between January and April is a more convenient time. Some men spend as little as three to nine days to accrue merit as monks. Others may enter the monkhood yet a third time, since three is considered an especially lucky number.

There are currently an estimated 250,000 monks in Myanmar; this number includes the many monks who have ordained for life as well as those undergoing temporary ordination. Of these a significant percentage become scholars and teachers, while some specialise in healing, folk magic or nat exorcism.

All things possessed by a monk must be offered by the lay community. Upon ordination a new monk is typically offered a set of three robes (lower, inner and outer), costing around K1280 for a standard grade cloth of cotton or dacron, a bit more for the thick acrylic robes worn during the cool season. Bright red robes are usually reserved for novices under 15, darker colours for older, fully ordained monks. Other possessions he is permitted include a razor, cup, filter (for keeping insects out of drinking water), umbrella and alms bowl. The latter are usually plain black lacquer bowls made in Ava or Sagaing; monks carry them to gather their daily food from householders in their monastery precincts.

At one time the Theravada Buddhist world had a separate Buddhist monastic lineage for females, who called themselves *bhikkhuni* and observed more vows than monks did – 311 precepts as opposed to the 227 followed by monks. Started in Sri Lanka around two centuries after the Buddha's lifetime by the daughter of King Asoka, the bhikkhuni tradition in Sri Lanka eventually died out and was unfortunately never restored.

In Myanmar, the modern equivalent are women who live the monastic life as *dasasila* or 'Ten-Precept' nuns. Burmese nuns shave their heads, wear pink robes, and take vows in an ordination procedure similar to that undergone by monks. Burmese nuns don't go out on daily alms-food rounds but they do collect dry food provisions every 15 days in most locales, or as often as once a week in some places.

Generally speaking, nunhood isn't considered as 'prestigious' as monkhood. The average Burmese Buddhist makes a great show of offering new robes and household items to the monks at their local kyaung but pay much less attention to the nuns. This is mainly due to the fact that nuns generally don't perform ceremonies on behalf of laypeople, so there is often less incentive for self-interested laypeople to make offerings to them. Furthermore, many Burmese equate the number of precepts observed with the total Buddhist merit achieved, hence nunhood is seen as less 'meritorious' than monkhood since nuns keep only ten precepts – the same number observed by male novices.

This difference in prestige represents social Buddhism, however, and is not how those with a serious interest in Buddhist practice regard the nuns. Nuns engage in the same fundamental eremitic activities – meditation and dhamma study – as monks do, activities which are the core of monastic life. When more than a few nuns reside at one temple, it's usually a sign that the teachings there are particularly strong.

Monasteries Monastic communities are called *kyaungtaik, pongyi-kyaung* or simply *kyaung* for short. The most important structure on the monastery grounds is the *thein* (Pali: *sema*), a consecrated hall where monastic ordinations are held. Kyaungs may also be associated with one or more zedis (stupas) or pahtos (square, enclosed shrine halls containing Buddha images). An open-sided rest house or pavilion *(zayap)* may be available for gatherings of laypeople during festivals or pilgrimmages.

Non-Theravada Elements in Burmese Buddhism The Theravada Buddhism practiced by the Burmese is no more a 'pure' form of the belief system than Mexican Catholicism is 'pure' Roman Catholicism. In everyday life it is blended with bits of spirit worship, Hinduism and Mahayana Buddhism. The nat cult in particular plays an important role in the religious life of most Burmese, who, it is said, 'love the Buddha, but fear the nats'. See the aside on Nat Worship for more detail on this fascinating aspect of Burmese metaphysical life.

Mahayana elements survive in the worship of at least two *arahats* (enlightened disciples) of the Buddha whose images are often encountered at Burmese payas. In Mahayana Buddhism these would be considered bodhisattvas. The monk Sivali (Shin Thiwali in Burmese) is shown holding a walking staff and fan; he is believed to bring prosperity and good fortune to those who make offerings or pay homage to him, especially in preparation for travel. Upagupta (Shin Upagot) sits crosslegged on a lotus raft in the middle of the ocean with a begging bowl and appears to anyone who faces physical danger. Offerings to Shin Upagot insure that the monk will save the devotee's life in instances of mortal danger; others pray to Upagot for good weather. Burmese Buddhists also worship Lokanatha, otherwise known as Avalokitesvara, a Mahayana deity who is thought to be protecting the world between the passing of the last Buddha and the coming of the next. The crowned Lokanatha sits on a lotus pedestal, with his left thigh parallel to the pedestal and his right knee upright, while holding a lotus flower in his right hand. Almost all major payas in central Myanmar feature separate shrines to these three figures somewhere in the grounds.

Hinduism survives mainly in the form of Burmese astrology, which is based on the Indian system of naming the zodiacal planets for Hindu deities and is very important for deciding the proper dates for weddings, funerals, ordinations and other life-cycle ceremonies. A cabalistic ritual called Paya-kozu ('Nine Gods'), held on behalf of those who have fallen ill or have experienced serious misfortune, similarly invokes Hindu deities. A *ponna* or Brahman priest – usually but not always of Indian descent – often officiates at rituals such as these and may also divine the most auspicious moment for significant occasions.

Ne Win's infamous fascination with numerology is shared by many Burmese Buddhists. Nearly everyone in Myanmar reveres the number 'nine', thought to have an inherent mystic significance. In Burmese the word *ko* or 'nine' also means 'to seek protection from the gods'; *nat-ko* signifies propitiation of the nats, and offerings are often made in nines, eg nine candles, nine kinds of food, nine cups of tea and so on.

Recommended Reading If you're interested in learning more about Buddhism, the following books are recommended:

The Wisdom of the Buddha by Jean Boisselier (Thames & Hudson, London, 1994; French version, Gallimard, 1993)
Buddhism by Christmas Humphreys (Pelican, London, 1949)
Living Buddhist Masters by Jack Kornfield (Buddhist Publication Society, Kandy, Sri Lanka, 1989)
What Buddhism Is (Department of Religious Affairs, Yangon)

What the Buddha Taught by Walpola Rahula (Haw Trai Foundation, Bangkok)
Buddhism in the Modern World edited by Heinrich Dumoulin (MacMillan Publishing, New York, 1976)
The Central Conception of Buddhism by Th Stcherbatsky (Motilal Banarsidass, Delhi, 1974)
Buddhist Dictionary by Mahathera Nyanatiloka (Island Hermitage Publications, Kandy, Sri Lanka, 1950)
The Initiation of Novicehood and the Ordination of Monkhood in the Burmese Buddhist Culture by Sao Htun Hmat Win (Department of Religious Affairs, Yangon, 1986)
Essential Themes of Buddhist Lectures Given by Ashin Thittila (Department of Religious Affairs, Yangon, 1987)

Meditation Centres In Yangon there are several centres for the study and practice of *satipatthana vipassana,* or insight-awareness meditation, based on instructions in the Maha Satipatthana Sutta (Sutra) of the Theravada Buddhist canon. This type of meditation is also commonly practised in Sri Lanka and Thailand, though the tradition of lay practice is probably stronger in Myanmar. Many Westerners have come to Myanmar to practise at the various centres for periods of time ranging from 10 days to more than a year. Visitors typically attach themselves to a respected *sayadaw* (master) in the Buddhist tradition for the duration.

The most famous centre in Yangon is the Mahasi Meditation Centre *(Mahasi Thathana Yeiktha* in Burmese), founded in 1947 by the late Mahasi Sayadaw, perhaps Myanmar's greatest meditation teacher. The Mahasi Sayadaw technique strives for intensive, moment-to-moment awareness of every physical movement, every mental and physical sensation, and ultimately, every thought. The centre is on Thathana Yeiktha Rd (formerly Hermitage Rd) off Kaba Aye Pagoda Rd, north of Kandawgyi (Royal) Lake, about 10 minutes from the city centre or 20 minutes from the airport.

Two of the Mahasi centre's chief meditation teachers, Sayadaw U Pandita and Sayadaw U Janaka, have established their own centres – Panditarama and Chanmyay Yeiktha – which are also highly regarded.

NAT WORSHIP

The widespread adoption of Buddhism in Myanmar suppressed but never replaced the pre-Buddhist practice of *nat* worship. Originally animistic – associated with hills, trees, lakes and other natural features – the Burmese nat has evolved into a spirit that may hold dominion over a place (natural or human-made), person, or field of experience. Orthographically the written Burmese word 'nat' is derived from the Pali-Sanskrit *natha*, which means 'lord' or 'guardian' though this spelling may have overlaid an existing indigenous term. Despite the continued efforts of some Buddhist leaders to downgrade the nat cult, it remains an important dimension of everyday Burmese life.

Before King Anawrahta came to power in Bagan in the 11th century, it was common for the Burmese to build small shrines or 'spirit houses' dedicated to land nats who were displaced by the construction of houses, monasteries or other buildings, or by the planting of rice and other crops. The owners or tenants of the buildings made daily offerings of food, incense and flowers at the shrines to placate these 'guardian' nats. Unpropitiated, such nats might cause misfortune to befall the land's human tenants.

Separate larger shrines were built for a higher class of nats descended from actual historic personages (including previous Thai and Burman kings) who had died violent, unjust deaths. These supra-human nats, when correctly propitiated, could aid worshippers in accomplishing important tasks, vanquishing enemies and so on. A few Hindu *devas* and Mahayana Buddhist *bodhisattvas* – each with its own magico-religious function – also participated in the nat pantheon.

In his push to make Theravada Buddhism the national faith, King Anawrahta tried to ban nat worship in Bagan, which was (and still is) the strongest bastion of spirit worship in Myanmar. As part of his anti-nat campaign, he ordered the destruction of all nat shrines in the kingdom and banished all Hindu images to a desecrated Vishnu temple renamed Nathlaung Kyaung or 'Monastery of the Prisoner Nats'. He also forbade the practice of animal sacrifice at nearby Mt Popa, a volcanic outcropping considered the abode of the 36 most powerful human nats in the Burman spirit pantheon. Instead of abandoning their belief in nats, however, the Burmans merely took their practices underground, rebuilding the guardian nat shrines in their homes.

Realizing he was turning the people away from Buddhism rather than destroying their faith in the nats, the king rescinded his total ban and decided to allow nat images and shrines on *paya* grounds. He himself led the way by placing images of the 36 nats from Mt Popa at the base of the sacred *zedi* of Shwezigon. To these universally recognised 36, Anawrahta added a 37th, Thagyamin, a Hindu deity based on Indra who he crowned 'king of the nats'. Thagyamin thus outranked the previous nat king, Mahagiri-nat ('Lord of the Great Hill', a reference to Mt Popa). Since in traditional Buddhist mythology Indra paid homage to Buddha on behalf of the Hindu pantheon, this theistic insertion effectively made all nats subordinate to Buddhism.

Anawrahta's scheme worked, and today the commonly believed cosmology places Buddha and his teachings at the top, with the Hindu and Burman nats at second and third ranks. In spite of the nats' lower position in the hierarchy, the Burmese nat cult is nearly as strong as ever. The Burmese merely divide their devotions and offerings according to the sphere of influence: Buddha for future lives, and the nats – both Hindu and Burman – for problems in this life. A misdeed, for example, might be redressed by offerings made to Thagyamin, who once a year records the names of those who perform good deeds in a book made of gold leaves, those who do evil in a book made of dogskin. Offerings to Thurathati (Sanskrit: Saraswati), a nat in charge of education, may help a student pass a tough exam.

Since the Bagan era the house guardian nat has stayed indoors and merged with Mahagiri to form Eindwin-Min Mahagiri or 'Lord of the Great Mountain (who is) in the House'. In most homes this dual nat is represented by a large, unhusked coconut which is dressed with a red *gaung-baung* or turban, perfumed, and hung from a pillar or post somewhere in the house. This nat must receive daily offerings from the house's inhabitants; for many Burmese this is the only nat worshipped on a regular basis. Other nats, particularly in Burman-dominated central Myanmar, have shrines in paya or monastery grounds which receive occasional offerings only during pilgrimages or bimonthly full/new moon visits.

Some of the more animistic guardian nats remain outside home and paya. A tree spirit shrine, for example, may be erected beneath a particularly venerated old tree thought to wield power over the immediate vicinity. These are especially common beneath larger banyan trees *(Ficus religiosa)* since this tree is revered as a symbol of Buddha's enlightenment; an offering made to a banyan nat conveniently doubles as a Buddhist offering. A village may well have a nat shrine off in a wooded corner somewhere for the propitiation of the village guardian spirit. Such tree and village shrines are simple dollhouse-like structures of wood or bamboo; their proper placement is divined by a local *saya*, a 'teacher' or shaman trained in spirit lore.

Knowledge of the complex nat world is fading fast among the younger Burmese generation, many of whom pay respect only to the coconut-head house guardian. Red and white are widely known to be nat colours; drivers young and old tie red and white strips of cloth onto the side-view mirrors and hood ornaments of their vehicles for protection from the nats. Those with a general fear of nats will avoid eating pork, which is thought to be offensive to the spirit world. The main fear is not simply that spirits will wreak havoc on your daily affairs but rather that one may enter your mind and body, then force you to perform unconscionable acts in public – acts that would cause other Burmese to shun you. Spirit possession – whether psychologically induced or metaphysical – is a real phenomenon in Myanmar.

Staunch Burmese Buddhists claim to pay no attention to the nats, as if for them the nats didn't exist. On close questioning, however, they will usually admit this is only because they 'outrank' nats due to their adherence to Buddhism, and thus they have no reason to fear them. It is commonly believed that Buddhists can stay out of the nats' reach as long as they keep the five lay precepts against lying, stealing, killing, harmful sexual behaviour and intoxication. Drunkenness in particular is considered an invitation to spirit possession.

Nat Festivals

On certain occasions the nat cult goes behind simple propitiation of the spirits (via offerings) and steps into the realm of spirit invocation. Most commonly this is accomplished through *nat pwes*, special musical performances designed to attract nats to the performance venue. Virtually all indigenous Burmese music is designed for this purpose; the 'classical' forms seen in tourist restaurants came relatively late in the country's music history. When enough money is available, a nat pwe may be hosted the night before a *shinpyu* or Buddhist novitiation ceremony as a way of receiving the nats' blessings – perhaps on some level even asking the nats' permission for the novice ordination. Often the nat pwe is part of a variety of musical, dramatic and comedic performances that last from dusk till dawn; those spectators who object to nat pwes (or are fearful of the nat world) can then leave during the nat pwe and return later for the rest of the show.

The nats like loud and colourful music, so nat pwe musicians bang away at full volume on their gongs, drums and xylophones, producing what sounds like some ancient form of rock and roll. Such music lures the nats to the vicinity of the pwe but it still takes a spirit medium or *nat-gadaw* (literally, 'nat wife') to make one materialise. Most nat-gadaws are either women or male transvestites who sing and perform special dances that invite specific nats to possess them. Once possessed they continue to sing and dance while in trance, often performing various feats that 'prove' a spirit has taken them over – such as dancing with a large bowl of water balanced on their heads or bending over backwards to snatch an offered K50 bill with their mouths. The highly entertaining androgyny displayed by some nat-gadaws brings the spectacle even closer to rock and roll à la Mick Jagger or David Bowie at their most outrageous.

Every nat pwe is accompanied by a risk that the invited spirit may choose to enter, not the body of the medium, but one of the spectators. One of the most commonly summoned spirits at nat pwes is Ko Gyi Kyaw, a drunkard nat who responds to offerings of liquor imbibed by the nat-gadaw. When he enters someone's body he's given to lascivious dancing, so a chance possession by Ko Gyi Kyaw (Big Brother Kyaw) is especially embarrassing. During his last visit to Bagan, Joe attended a nat pwe near Lawkananda Paya in which Ko Gyi Kyaw possessed a 14-year-old girl in the audience. Her family was mortified when she began dancing drunkenly around the tent, her longyi flapping away immodestly to show her legs.

Once possessed by a nat, the only way one can be sure the spirit won't return again and again is to employ the services of an older Buddhist monk skilled at exorcism – a process that can take days if not weeks. Without undergoing such a procedure, anyone who has been spirit-possessed may carry the nat stigma the rest of their lives. Girls who have been so entered are considered unmarriageable unless satisfactorily exorcised. *Nat-gadaws,* who choose to devote their minds and bodies to nat possession and thus live on the fringe of 'normal' Burmese society, usually have a history of involuntary nat trance. By the time they become spirit mediums they're considered strong enough to handle such trance states.

Though nat pwes are commonly held as an adjunct to festivals throughout Burman Myanmar, the grandest of all occur during the annual nat festival in Taungbyon, about 20 km north of Mandalay. Held each August (more specifically for six days up to and including the full moon of Wagaung) since Anawrahta's reign, the Taungbyon festival honors the so-called 'Muslim Brothers', Byat-wi and Byat-ta, two of the most famous nats from the Bagan era. Nat-gadaws and nat devotees from all over Myanmar convene in a Woodstock-like collection of tents for a week of drinking, wild music and nat possession. Another nat festival, rather smaller than the one at Taungbyon, follows immediately afterwards at Yedana-gu, a town between Amarapura and Sagaing. This one revolves around the ritual bathing of nat images on the banks of the Ayeyarwady River; many festival-goers arrive by sampan from Amarapura. ■

Although each presents its own slight twist on the Mahasi Sayadaw technique, the basic meditation instructions are similar.

Another famous centre is the International Meditation Centre, founded by the late U Ba Khin, a well-known lay teacher. The U Ba Khin technique focuses on a deep appreciation of impermanence and on consciously moving or 'sweeping' one's mental awareness throughout the body. Instruction at all of the above centres is given to foreigners in English. The late Mogok Sayadaw's Mogok Meditation Centre is also highly respected but instruction is available only in Burmese – primarily from taped lectures recorded by the late Sayadaw.

To obtain the necessary 'special-entry visa' for a long-term stay, applicants must receive a letter of invitation from the centre where they would like to study, which may in turn require a letter of introduction from an affiliated meditation centre abroad. This invitation is then presented to a Burmese consulate or embassy that will issue a visa for an initial stay of six to 12 weeks, as recommended by the centre. This may be extended in Yangon at the discretion of the centre and Burmese immigration.

Important points to remember: the special-entry visa takes eight to 10 weeks to be issued and cannot be applied for while a person is in Myanmar on a tourist visa. Food and lodging are provided at no charge at the centres but meditators must follow eight precepts, which include abstaining from food after noon and foregoing music, dancing, jewellery, perfume and high or luxurious beds. Daily schedules are rigorous and may involve nearly continuous practice from 3 am till 11 pm. Students may be given permission to travel in Myanmar at the end of a long period of study but this is not automatic. Finally, Westerners who have undergone the training say it is not recommended for people with no previous meditation experience.

For further information, write to:

Chanmyay Yeiktha Meditation Centre
655-A Kaba Aye Pagoda Rd, Yangon
(☎ 01-61479)

International Meditation Centre
31-A Inya Myaing Rd, Yangon (☎ 01-31549)
Mahasi Meditation Centre
16 Thathana Yeiktha Rd, Yangon
Mogok Meditation Centre
82 Natmauk Rd, Yangon
Panditarama
80/A Shwetaunggyaw Rd, Yangon (☎ 01-31448)

For further information on the teachings of Mahasi Sayadaw, U Ba Khin and Mogok Sayadaw, read *Living Buddhist Masters* by Jack Kornfield (see the Recommended Reading section earlier).

Other Religions

Among non-Buddhist Burmese citizens, 5% are animist, 4.5% Christian, 4% Muslim and 1.5% are Hindu. Most of the Muslims and Hindus, as well as many of the Christians, are of Indian descent.

Most of the country's other Christians are found among the tribal minorities, though the majority of the latter remain animist. Christian missionaries have been active in Myanmar for over 150 years. The American Baptists were first on the scene, but apart from certain hill tribes they have had little success with the Burmese. The Church of Myanmar – formerly the Church of England – has about 30,000 members and a large cathedral in Yangon.

LANGUAGE

Burmese is the predominant language although substantial tribal minorities speak their own dialects. English is also quite widely spoken although, as in other Asian countries, it's easy to be deceived in the cities into believing that English is more widespread than it actually is. Many English words – eg car, bus, telephone, doctor, film, TV – are part of everyday Burmese vocabulary. But it doesn't take a long bus ride into the country to raise a few communication problems. If you do experience difficulty in making yourself understood, a simple rule of thumb is to look for somebody older. There are more likely to be English speakers amongst the older generation.

Peculiar English pronunciations to watch

out for include the 'oy/oi' diphthong, which almost always comes out 'wai' so that 'boy' becomes 'bwai', 'oil' is 'wile' and 'boil' is 'bwile'. Final consonants are often dropped, so that 'sidecar' becomes 'sai-kah' (which means 'trishaw' in Burmese English).

The Burmese have their own alphabet and script – it looks rather like a lot of mating bubbles and circles. You're hardly going to have time in Myanmar to pick up the alphabet, but it is worth making the effort to learn the numerals, if only so you can read bus numbers. The fervent de-anglicisation of Myanmar resulted in many English signs being taken down and nothing being substituted. It can be very difficult to determine how far you've come while on a Burmese train, as railway station signs are very rare.

Since Burmese has its own alphabet there can be a variety of interpretations of Burmese words into our script. Words descended from Pali are sometimes transcribed following their original Pali pronunciation rather than the more common Burmese pronunciation; the formal term for 'gem', *yadana*, may appear in its Pali spelling *ratana* even though this isn't the way it's pronounced in everyday Burmese language. Further confusion is added by the practice of sometimes running words together, sometimes separating. For example, the Shwe San Daw and the Shwesandaw are exactly the same paya in Thandwe; both mean 'Golden Hair Relic'.

Language Study

Finding good Burmese-language study materials can be difficult. Lonely Planet publishes a *Burmese phrasebook* that deals with the language in more detail than we have space for here.

The serious Burmese-language student will want to seek out John O'Kell's four-volume textbook and tape series, published by Northern Illinois University. *Burmese: An Introduction to the Spoken Language, Books 1 & 2* covers the spoken aspects of the language, while *Burmese: An Introduction to the Script* and *Burmese: An Introduction to the Literary Style* cover the written aspects.

Audio tapes for each of these volumes can be purchased separately.

Forms of Address

The Burmese have a greater variety of forms of address than our basic Mr, Mrs, Miss and Ms, and it is not possible to tell a person's marital status from the prefix to their name. Some examples include:

U (or Oo as it is pronounced) literally means 'uncle' and is a respectful form of address for any adult male.

Ko literally means 'elder brother' – it's a familiar term usually used among males of similar age.

Maung is used to address a younger male or a small boy, but it is also used by some men as a sign of modesty.

Bo is a 'leader', usually a military officer.

Ma means 'sister' and can be used for any woman from a little girl to an older lady, but should always be used for young girls.

Daw means 'aunt' and is a respectful form of address for an adult woman of any age, married or single.

Saya literally means 'teacher' or 'master' and is used for teachers and employers.

Each of the ethnic minorites have their own titles of course, some of which are used by the Burmese when referring to members of these groups. The male/female equivalents for *U/Daw* for the Shan is *Sai/Nang*, for the Karen *Saw/Nan*, for the Mon *Mahn/Nai* and for the Chin *Sai/Sai*.

The Burmese have no 'family names'. A person's name consists solely of his or her given name, whether one, two or three syllables, normally preceded by one of the customary forms of address mentioned above. In other words, you cannot discern the blood relationship between people by their names; even the terms 'brother' or 'sister' are of no help since these can be used among friends.

Likewise, Burmese women do not sacrifice their own names when they marry. Thus, when U Hla Tun and Daw Than Mya are married, the wife does not become Mrs Hla Tun or Than Mya Tun; her name remains exactly the same as before marriage.

A final thing to remember about Burmese names is that two or three-syllable given names cannot be shortened by omitting one or more of the syllables. Thein Lwin is always called Thein Lwin, never Thein or Lwin. While travelling in Europe, he might call himself 'Mr Thein Lwin' instead of 'U Thein Lwin' to avoid confusion, but not Mr Lwin. It helps to remember that a Burmese name is a complete semantic unit; for example, Ne Win means 'bright sun', while Aung Sein is 'victorious diamond'. Would you call Mr Hopkins 'Mr Hop' or 'Mr Kins'?

Pronunciation

In this section and the Food section of this book, Burmese pronunciation is shown in the system of Cornyn, which is used in most places where the language is taught outside Myanmar. This will help give you an idea of how words are spoken.

Tones There are three tones, plus two other possibilities, for any syllable. Every syllable has one of these five alternatives.

Creaky Tone

This is made with the voice tense, producing a high-pitched and relatively long creaky sound. It is indicated here by an acute accent above the vowel, for example *ká* 'dance'.

Even Tone

This is made with the voice relaxed, staying at a low pitch for a fairly long time, and not rising or falling in pitch. It is indicated by no accent above the vowel, for example *ka* 'shield'.

Heavy (Falling) Tone

This is made with more effort, but not creakiness. The pitch of the voice starts quite high, then falls for a reasonably long time. It is indicated by a grave accent above the vowel, for example *kà* 'car'.

Stopped (Short) Syllable

This is a very short syllable, on a high pitch, cut off at the end by a sharp catch in the voice (a glottal stop); abit like the Cockney pronunciation of 't' in a word like 'bottle'. It is indicated here by a single quotation mark afterthe vowel, for example *ka'* 'join'.

Reduced (Minor) Syllable

This is a shortened syllable, usually the first

syllable of a two-syllable word, and it sounds like the first syllable of 'again' in English. It is indicated here by a ˘ above the vowel. For example *ălou'* 'work'.

Vowels There are seven vowels, and two combinations of vowels, *ai* and *au*. Five of the vowels and the two combinations occur nasalised; six plus the two combinations occur in stopped syllables; and all seven, but not the two combinations, occur in non-nasalised, non-stopped syllables.

Nasalisation of vowels is like that found in French; speakers of English or other languages can approximate this by putting a weak 'n' at the end of such a syllable.

i	*i (in)*	like English 'e' as in 'be'
ei	*e (ein)*	like the 'a' as in 'bay'
e	*e*	like the short vowel in 'bet'
a	*a (an)*	like the vowel in the first syllable of 'father'
o		as in 'law'
ou	*ou (oun)*	as in 'go'
u	*u (un)*	as in 'loop'
ain	*ai*	as in 'I'; nasalised or stopped
aun	*au*	like the combination in 'out'; nasalised or stopped

Consonants There are 30 consonants, which only occur at the beginning of a syllable. Many of these are similar to consonants in English or other European languages; the following are different.

th	like English 'th' in 'thin'
ny	similar to the beginning of 'new'

hm, hn, hny, hng, hl	all made with a puff of air just before the nasal or 'l' sound
hp, ht, hs, hc, hk	aspirated
p, t, c, k	unaspirated

The aspirated sounds are made with a puff of air after the sound; this is the way English 'p', 't', 'k' are pronounced at the beginning of a word. The unaspirated sounds are without this puff of air, as in English 'p', 't', 'k' after an 's', as in 'spin' 'stir' 'skin'.

Greetings & Civilities

Hello. (lit. It's a blessing)
mingălă ba မင်္ဂလာပါ။

Are you well?
(hkămyà/shin) nei ခင်ဗျား:/ရှင်
kàunbadhălà? နေကောင်းပါသလား။

(I) am well.
nei kàunbade နေကောင်းပါတယ်။

Have you eaten?
(hkămyà/shin) ခင်ဗျား:/ရှင်
htămìn sàpyìbabyìlà? ထမင်း:စား:ပြီ:ပါပြီလား။

(I) have eaten.
sàpyìbabyi စား:ပြီ:ပါပြီ

Where are you going?
(hkămyà/shin) ခင်ဗျား:/ရှင်
begou thwàmălè? ဘယ်ကိုသွား:မလဲ။

(I) am going to the
market.
zèigou thwàme ဈေး:ကိုသွား:မယ်။

Thank you. (not
commonly said)
cèizù ba ကျေး:ဇူး:ပါ။

It's nothing.
(you're welcome)
kei'sá măshíbabù ကိစ္စမရှိပါဘူး:။

I'm leaving now.
(Goodbye)
thwàbaòunme သွား:ပါအုံး:မယ်။

Useful Words & Phrases

(I) don't understand.
nàmălebabù နာ:မလည်ပါဘူး:။

Please say it again.
hkămyà/shin ခင်ဗျား:/ရှင်
pyanpyòba ပြန်ပြောပါ။

Can you speak English?
hkămyà/shin ...lou ခင်ဗျား:/ရှင်
pyòda'thălà လိုပြောတတ်ပါသလား။
ìngălei' အင်္ဂလိပ်

What is your name?
hkămyà/shin name belou hkobadhălè?
ခင်ဗျား:/ရှင် နာမည် ဘယ်လိုခေါ်ပါသလဲ။

My name is...
căno/cămá nanme...lóu hkobade
ကျွန်တော်/ကျွန်မနာမည်...လို့ ခေါ်ပါတယ်။

I'm glad to meet you.
hkămyà/shinne twéida wùn thabade
ခင်ဗျား:/ရှင်နဲ့ တွေ့ တာဝမ်း:သာပါတယ်။

Yes. *hou'ké* ဟုတ်ကဲ့။
No. *măhou'pabù* မဟုတ်ပါဘူး:။
come *lade* လာတယ်

go *thwàde* သွား:တယ်
Are you going there?
hoube'thwàmălà? ဟိုဘက်သွား:မလား။
How do I get to...?
...gou belou ...ကို ဘယ်လိုသွား:မလဲ
thwàmălè?
have *shíde* ရှိတယ်
Have you *...shídhălà?* ...ရှိသလား:။
(got)...?
I have... *...shíbade* ...ရှိပါတယ်
how *be lou* ဘယ်လို
How much is...?
...belau'lè? ...ဘယ်လောက်လဲ။
what *ba* ဘာ
What time is it?
be ăhceinshíbyilè? ဘယ်အချိန်ရှိပြီလဲ။
What did you say?
ba pyòdhălè? ဘာပြောသလဲ။
when *bedounká* ဘယ်တုန်:က
(in past)
When did you come to Myanmar?
Myămapyei bedoungálathălè?
မြန်မာပြည်ဘယ်တုန်:ကလာသလဲ။
when *bedó* ဘယ်တော့
(in future)
When is the next boat to...?
...gou nau'thinbò bedólè?
...ကို နောက်သင်္ဘော:ဘယ်တော့လဲ။
where *be hma* ဘယ်မှာ
Where is...? *...be hma lè?* ...ဘယ်မှာလဲ။
who *bădhu* ဘယ်သူ
Who do I ask?
bădhúgou mèiyádhălè?
ဘယ်သူ ကိုမေး:ရသလဲ။

Getting Around

I'm looking for...
...shaneibade ...ရှာနေပါတယ်။
Where is the...?
...be hma lè? ဘယ်မှာလဲ။
What...is this?
di...lè? ဒီ...လဲ။

airport	*leizei'*	လေဆိပ်
railway	*mìyăhtà*	မီး:ရထား:ရဲ့
station	*youn*	

bus station	*baskà gei'*	ဘတ်စ်ကား:ဂိတ်
riverboat jetty	*thìnbòzei'*	သင်္ဘောဆိတ်
town	*myóu bemyó*	မို့ဘယ်မို့
street	*làn belàn*	လမ်:ဘယ်လမ်:

When will the...leave?
  ...beăhcein htwe'mălè?
  ...ဘယ်အချိန်ထွက်မလဲ။

train	*mìyahtà*	မီး:ရထား:
bus	*băskà*	ဗတ်စ်ကား:
riverboat	*thìnbò*	သင်္ဘော
jeep	*ji'kà*	ဂျှစ်ကား:
taxi	*ăhngàkà*	အငှါး:ကား:

Where does this bus go?
  di baskà begou thwàdhălè?
  ဒီဘတ်စ်ကား:ဘယ်ကိုသွားသလဲ။
Where should I get off?
  behma hsìn'yámălè?
  ဘယ်မှာဆင်း:ရမလဲ။
How much is it to go to...?
  ...thwàyin belau'lè?
  ...သွား:ရင်ဘယ်လောက်လဲ။
Stop here.
  dihma ya'pa ဒီမှာရပ်ပါ။

Directions

left	*bebe'*	ဘယ်ဘက်
right	*nyabé*	ညာဘက်
straight	*tédé*	တည့်တည့်
north	*myau'hpe'*	မြောက်ဘက်
south	*taunbe'*	တောင်ဘက်
east	*ăshéibe'*	အရှေ့ဘက်
west	*ănau'hpe'*	အနောက်ဘက်

how far?
  belau'weidhălè? ဘယ်လောက်ဝေး:သလဲ။
very far away
  thei'wèbade သိပ်ဝေး:ပါတယ်။'
not so far away
  thei'măwèbabù သိပ်မဝေး:ပါဘူး။

Around Town

bank	*bandai'*	ဘဏ်တိုက်
market	*zèi*	ဈေး:
museum	*pyádai'*	ပြတိုက်
Myanmar Travels & Tours	*myăma htauri' yòun*	မြန်မာထွရှစ်ရိုး:

post office   *sadai*   စာတိုက်

I want to change...
  căno/cămá...lèjinbade
  ကျွန်တော်/ကျွန်မ...လဲချင်ပါတယ်။

money	*pai'hsan*	ပိုက်ဆံ
$	*dola*	ဒေါ်လာ
£	*paunhko*	ပေါင်ခေါ်
travellers' cheques	*(hkăyì)hce' le'hma'*	(ခရီး:)ချက်လက်မှတ်

Can you give me smaller bills?
  ngweise'ku ăthèiné pèi naindhălà?
  နိုင်သလား: ငွေစက္ကူ အသေး:နဲ့ ပေး:

Geographical Features

beach	*kànbyin*	ကမ်း:ပြင်
countryside	*tò*	တော
hill	*taun*	တောင်
island	*cùn*	ကျွန်း:
lake	*ain*	အိုင်
lake (small or artificial)	*kan*	ကန်
river	*myi'*	မြစ်
sand	*thè*	သဲ
sea	*pinle*	ပင်လယ်
town	*myóu*	မို့
village	*ywa*	ရွာ
waterfall	*yeidăgun*	ရည်တံခွန်

Accommodation

hotel	*hote*	ဟော်တယ်
guest house	*tè-ein*	တဲအိမ်

Can I stay here?
  dihma tènainbadhălà?
  ဒီမှာတဲင်ပါသလား:။
Can I see the room?
  ăhkàn cínainbadhălà?
  အခန်း:ကြည့်နိုင်ပါသလား:။
How much is the room?
  di ăhkàn belau'lè?
  ဒီအခန်း:ဘယ်လောက်လဲ။

Do you have...? *...shíbadhălà?* ...ရှိပါသလား:။

hot water	*yeinwèi*	ရည်နွေး:
a mosquito net	*hcindaun*	ခြင်ထောင်
a bed	*ei'ya*	အိပ်ရာ

How much is...?
...belau' lè?   ...ဘယ်လောက်လဲ။
  one night   *tăye'*   တရက်
  two nights   *hnăye'*   နှစ်ရက်

Shopping

How much is it?
  belau' balè   ဘယ်လောက်ပါလဲ။
How much is...?
  ...belau' lè?   ...ဘယ်လောက်လဲ။
It is very expensive.
  zèi thei' cìbade   ဈေးသိပ်ကြီးပါတယ်။

Do you have a
cheaper one?
  zèi póungèdé   ဈေးပိုငယ်တဲ့တခုရှိပါသလား။
  tăhkú shí badhălà?
OK (lit. 'good')
  kàunbabyi   ကောင်းပါပြီ။
Do you have a/any...?
  ...shíbadhălà?   ...ရှိပါသလား။
Where can I buy...?
  ...behma weyámălè?   ...ဘယ်မှာဝယ်ရမလဲ။
lacquerware *yùnde*   ယွန်းထည်
gems   *cau'mye'/*   ကျောက်မျက်ရတနာ
    yădăna
map   *myeiboun*   မြေပုံ
market   *zèi*   ဈေး
matches   *mìji'*   မီးခြစ်
shop   *hsain*   ဆိုင်
soap   *hsa'pya*   ဆပ်ပြာ

Time & Dates

What time is it?
  be ăhcein shíbyilè?   ဘယ်အချိန်ရှိပါပြီလဲ။
How long (time)?
  belau' caja lè?   ဘယ်လောက်ကြာကြာလဲ။

yesterday   *mănéigá*   မနေ့က
today   *gănéi*   ဂနေ့
tomorrow   *ne'hpyan*   နက်ဖြန်
year   *hni'*   နှစ်
month   *lá*   လ

week   *pa'*   ပတ်

Sunday   *tănìngănweinéi*   တနင်္ဂနွေနေ့
Monday   *tănìnlanéi*   တနင်္လာနေ့
Tuesday   *inganéi*   အင်္ဂါနေ့
Wednesday   *bou'dăhùnéi*   ဗုဒ္ဓဟူးနေ့
Thursday   *cadhăbădèinéi*   ကြာသပတေးနေ့
Friday   *thau'canéi*   သောကြာနေ့
Saturday   *săneinéi*   စနေနေ့

Numbers

zero   *thounyá*   သုည
1   ၁   *ti' / tă*   တစ်/တ
2   ၂   *hni'/hnă*   နှစ်/နှ
3   ၃   *thòun*   သုံး
4   ၄   *lèi*   လေး
5   ၅   *ngà*   ငါး
6   ၆   *hcau'*   ခြောက်
7   ၇   *hkúhni'/*   ခုနှစ်/ခုန
    hkúhnă
8   ၈   *shi'*   ရှစ်
9   ၉   *kòu*   ကိုး
10   ၁၀   *(tă)hse*   တဆယ်
11 (10 & 1)   ၁၁   *hséti'*   ဆယ့်တစ်
12 (10 & 2)   ၁၂   *hséhni'*   ဆယ့်နှစ်
20 (2 & 10)   ၂၀   *hnăhse*   နှဆယ်
100   ၁၀၀   *(tă)ya*   တရာ

1000   *(tă)htaun*   တထောင်
10,000   *(tă)thàun*   တသောင်း
100,000   *(tă)thèin*   တသိန်း
million   *(tă)thàn*   တသန်း

Health

Where is the...   *...behmalè*   ...ဘယ်မှာလဲ။
  doctor   *hsăyawun*   ဆရာဝန်
  hospital   *hsèiyoun*   ဆေးရုံ
  pharmacy   *hsèizain*   ဆေးဆိုင်

Please call a doctor.
  hsăyawun hkopèiba   ဆရာဝန်ကိုခေါ်ပေးပါ။

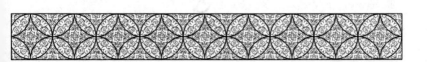

Facts for the Visitor

VISAS & EMBASSIES

The Myanmar government issues 12 types of visitor visas and border permits, including such quaint-sounding ones as 'caravan trader permit', 'seasonal mahjis permit' and 'frontier visa'. Leisure travellers are issued the tourist visa, which is now valid for four weeks (28 days) and is readily available through most Myanmar embassies or consulates abroad. At the embassy in Bangkok you can usually receive a visa the same day you apply for it. The simple application process requires three passport-size photos and around US$15 to US$20 for the visa fee.

For quite a period in the 1960s the doors into Myanmar were firmly shut, then they slowly reopened. First of all 24-hour stays were permitted, then along came the seven-day visa, until the 1988 civil disturbance when the door closed again for about six months. By the end of 1990, 14-day tourist visas were being issued with regularity, but only if you came as part of a package tour. Towards the end of 1992 Myanmar began to reintroduce 'foreign independent traveller' (FIT) visas which, although still limited to 14 days allowed much more freedom to plan things yourself. In March 1994 the tourist visa was lengthened to 28 days, making it now possible to see a good bit of the country at a comfortable pace.

The only fly in the ointment is that you have to exchange a non-refundable minimum of US$300 upon arrival into Foreign Exchange Certificates or FECs (this requirement is waived for package-tour visa holders). For most visitors this isn't much of a problem since the FECs may be used to pay for hotels as well as train and plane tickets; the average individual easily spends this much when staying three weeks or more. FECs may also be exchanged for kyat, the national currency, at the free-market rate – see the Money section further on for details.

Beware of travel agents in Bangkok (especially on Khao San Rd) who will try to sell you a 'special visa' (often said to be a business visa) or other type of visa that would exempt you from the US$300/300FEC exchange requirement. Only holders of tourist visas bearing the stamp 'package tour' are exempt from the FEC requirement.

Visa Extensions

Although some Myanmar embassies abroad will say tourist visa extensions aren't permitted, once in Myanmar you can usually extend your visa up to 30 days beyond the original 28-day validity – at the discretion of the Department of Immigration & Manpower. The usual procedure requires five photos plus payment of a US$36 fee, but this can vary from office to office. If you're refused at one office, try again at another location – in low-tech Myanmar there are no computer checks or other easily communicated record of visa extension applications. Some offices are slower than others; allow two or three days for the extension to go through. The type of permit issued for such extensions is called a 'stay permit'.

If you overstay your visa by a day or two due to unavoidable transport difficulties, there's usually little hassle at Yangon International Airport if immigration authorities can verify your story. If not, be prepared to part with some cash for a short-term extension.

Myanmar Embassies Abroad

Addresses of Myanmar's relevant embassies and consulates include:

Australia
22 Arkana St, Yarralumla, ACT 2600
(☎ 273 3811)
Bangladesh
89B Rd No 4, Banani, Dhaka (☎ 60 1915)
Canada
85 Range Rd, Apt 902-903, The Sandringham, Ottawa, Ont K1N 8J6 (☎ 232 6434/6446)
China
6 Dong Zhi Men Wai St, Chaoyang District, Beijing (☎ 532 1584/1425)

France
60 rue de Courcelles, 75008 Paris
(☎ 42.25.56.95)
Germany
Schumannstrasse 112, 5300 Bonn 1 (☎ 21 0091)
Hong Kong
Room 2424, Sun Hung Kai Centre, 30 Harbour
Rd, Wanchai (☎ 827 7929/9843)
India
No 3/50F Nyaya Marg, Chanakyapuri, New
Delhi 110021 (☎ 600 251/252)
Indonesia
109 Jalan Haji Agus Salim, Jakarta Pusat
(☎ 327 684, 314 040)
Israel
12 Zalman Schneor St, Ramat Hasharon 47239,
Tel Aviv (☎ 540 0948)
Italy
Via Vincenzo Bellini 20m Interno 1, 00198 Rome
(☎ 854 9374)
Japan
8-26, 4-chome, Kita-Shinagawa, Shinagawa-ku,
Tokyo 140 (☎ 3441 9291)
Laos
Wat Sokpaluang Rd, PO Box 11, Vientiane
(☎ 21 2789, 16 9114)
Malaysia
5 Taman U Thant Satu, 55000 Kuala Lumpur
(☎ 242 4085)
Nepal
Chakupat, Patan Gate, Lalitpur, Kathmandu
(☎ 521 788)
Singapore
133 Middle Rd, B & N Bldg No 05-04, Singapore
0718 (☎ 338 1073)
Switzerland
47 Ave Blanc, 1202 Geneva (☎ 731 7540)
Thailand
132 Sathon Neua Rd, Bangkok 10500
(☎ 233 2237, 234 0320)
UK
19A Charles St, London W1X 8ER
(☎ 629 6966, 499 8841)
USA
2300 'S' St NW, Washington, DC 20008
(☎ 332 9044/5/6)
Vietnam
Bldg No A-3, Ground Floor, Van Phuc Diplomatic Qrtrs, Hanoi (☎ 253 369)

TRAVEL PERMITS

Travel anywhere in the standard tourist
quadrangle – Yangon (Rangoon), Mandalay,
Bagan (Pagan), Inle Lake, Taunggyi and to
any points between or near these destinatons
– is freely allowed for anyone holding a valid
passport and tourist visa. This includes
places a little off the main linking routes such

as Bago (Pegu), Pyay (Prome), Shwebo,
Magwe, Monywa, Taungoo and Pyinmana –
basically any place in central Myanmar
between the Shan Yoma range to the east and
the Ayeyarwady (Irrawaddy) River to the
west – plus most places in the Ayeyarwady
Delta region (Pathein or Bassein, Twante,
Thanlyin and Letkhokkon).

Even for these places though, your passport is likely to be checked from time to time.
In fact every airport arrival, anywhere in
Myanmar, requires a passport and visa check
and the filling in of some papers with your
name and passport number. Hotel staff also
check passports and visas.

Travel to just about anywhere else in
Myanmar requires a permit – actually a typed
letter stamped with various government
seals – issued by the Ministry of Hotels &
Tourism and approved by the Ministry of
Defence. Such permits are available directly
from Myanmar Travels & Tours (MTT) in
Yangon or through many Yangon travel
agencies. MTT doesn't charge for a travel
permit but the catch-22 is they usually won't
issue a permit unless you arrange for the paid
services of a guide. We say 'usually' because
we've heard of cases – for example
Kyaiktiyo – where MTT simply handed over
a permit without requiring the services of a
guide. Travel agencies work similarly; you
must contract the services of a guide or driver
before they'll arrange for a permit.

As the time of this writing the government
hadn't published a list of places that officially require permits or a list of those which
don't. So it really becomes a sort of guessing
game as to which places you're allowed to
visit and which you aren't. We heard over
and over again in Yangon that one needed a
permit to go to Chaungtha Beach near
Pathein; we decided to chance it anyway and
found at least a half dozen foreigners there
who had also made it *sans* permit. At the
military checkpoint we passed on the road
from Pathein to Chaungtha, the soldiers just
glanced at our passports and waved us on.
Similarly many travellers go to Kyaiktiyo
and Lashio without a permit even though
permits are officially required.

Some places are more strict about permits, and some places are offically off limits, permit or no permit. In Myitkyina and Bhamo, for example, any foreigners who turn up will have their papers scrupulously checked and if you don't have the proper permit, you're sent back in the opposite direction immediately. Insurgent-controlled territory – for example, between Taunggyi and Kengtung in the Shan State or just about anywhere in the Kayin State – is absolutely not permitted. Military checkpoints placed at close intervals along every government-controlled road leading into these areas net anyone who tries to enter from Myanmar proper (these areas are in fact more accessible from Thailand – albeit very illegally).

Even *with* a permit, there's no guarantee the local authorities won't give you the boot – as happened to several visitors to Myitkyina in 1995. That year MTT was issuing permits to Myitkyina with the caveat that upon your arrival, the Myitkyina authorities could arbitrarily refuse entry. For other places – like Mawlamyine (Moulmein) – permits may be easy to get one week and impossible the next, depending on the level of rebel activity in the area.

Once you arrive, permit in hand, at your destination, there are other papers to be filled in. At the airport in Sittwe (Akyab) we had our passports checked by no less than five different persons, each of whom reviewed the permit letter and wrote our names, passport numbers and visa numbers in ledgers or on little scraps of paper! The scraps of paper were literally just the corners torn from a plain sheet of paper.

It's obvious that the most touchy destinations are in frontier areas where ethnic insurgencies are headquartered. Our experience has been that those places easily reached by road, river or rail can be visited either with or without a permit. Those places for which only air travel is allowed – for example, Myitkyina, and in the near future Loikaw, Dawei (Tavoy) and Myeik (Mergui) – require permits, and these permits will be thoroughly checked; even then, authorities may or may not recognise their validity. The

Chin State, on the other hand, has among the fewest checkpoints of any border state – even though MTT says it's off limits.

At some point in your Myanmar travels, you come to realise that the country is still run like a loose-knit collection of warlord states. Even when you're just moving from one Burman-majority division to another, your papers are checked. On top of this, every time you enter a small town or village by car, someone appears to exact tribute from the driver in the form of a 'road tax' (the same happens for Burmese road travellers).

All of this could change overnight, especially as Myanmar's frontier areas become more 'secure' following ceasefire agreements with insurgent groups and military victories over those groups which won't negotiate. By the time you read this, travel restrictions may have loosened considerably – or things could have gone the other way. Most likely the constant passport-checking will persist as long as the ruling junta maintains its warlord mentality – a centuries-old legacy in Myanmar.

To recap, for every destination in Myanmar, there exist these possible access scenarios:

- No permit is needed and you can travel to the destination freely – eg everywhere between Yangon and Mandalay, west to Pathein, Bagan and Salay, east to Taunggyi.
- A permit is officially required but not actually necessary in everyday practice – eg Chaungtha Beach, Lashio.
- A permit is required and you can travel there on your own once you have the permit – eg Thandwe (Sandoway), Kyaiktiyo, Bhamo.
- A permit is required but won't be issued unless you're accompanied by a licensed guide – eg Mawlamyine.
- A permit and guide are necessary but there are still no guarantees you won't be turned back – eg Myitkyina.
- An area is officially off limits but accessible by some routes – eg the Chin State, parts of the Shan State.
- An area is officially off limits and inaccessible due to the presence of military checkpoints – eg parts of the Shan, Kayah, Mon and Kayin states.

Confusing? Welcome to Myanmar!

Top: Tending the rice fields, Nyaungshwe
Bottom Left: Overloaded, Bagan
Bottom Right: Procession of monks, Pindaya

Top Left, Middle Right & Bottom: Market day at Shwenyaung
Top Right: Local toddy bar

New Areas

According to the best information we were able to obtain via strong rumour, innuendo and confidential sources, it looked like the following areas were going to open very soon to travel with or without permits:

- Hkamti, Kalewa and other destinations along the Chindwin River in the Sagaing Division
- Chin State (southern part) via the Kaladan River from Mrauk U (Myohaung), Rakhine (Arakan) State
- Pa-an in the Kayin State
- Dawei, Myeik, and Maungmagan Beach and Maungmagan Islands near Dawei, Taninthayi Division (all most likely by aeroplane only)
- Loikaw, Kayah State (by aeroplane or train only)

We haven't been to any of these places. Some may already be open when you read this and of course others not on this list may also have opened up.

Because what is 'officially' open seems to change week to week, sometimes it's better just to set off for your intended destination rather than ask MTT or wait around for permits. Your fellow travellers on their way out of the country will be the most up-to-date source of information on what's possible and what's not.

CUSTOMS

Besides personal effects, visitors are permitted to bring in the following items duty-free: 400 cigarettes (or 100 cigars, or 250 gm of unrolled tobacco), a quart of liquor and 500 ml of cologne or perfume. Cameras (including video cameras), radios, cassette players and calculators can be brought into the country, but they must be declared on arrival and taken out upon departure. Any foreign currency in excess of US$2000 must be declared upon entry.

See Export Restrictions in Things to Buy at the end of this chapter for a list of items that cannot be taken out of the country.

MONEY
Currency

Myanmar uses three currencies, two of which are legal tender for everyone, one of which Burmese citizens need a licence to use. All three currencies are strongly linked to the US dollar and the Japanese yen.

The first is the everyday national currency, called kyat (pronounced 'chat') and divided into 100 pyas with a confusing collection of coins that are rarely seen anymore since the kyat has decreased in value so much over the last few years.

At present the following kyat banknotes were in use: K1, 5, 10, 15, 20, 45, 50, 90, 100, 200 and K500. Make sure that any K50 or K100 bills you're offered are labelled 'Central Bank of Myanmar' rather than 'Union of Burma Bank'. To discourage the black market, K50 and K100 notes were demonetised in the 1960s, and K25, K35 and K75 notes underwent a similar fate in 1987; unscrupulous money-dealers occasionally try to foist these older bills on unsuspecting visitors. Just remember, any note reading 'Myanmar' rather than 'Burma' should be OK.

A sum of 100,000 is called *thein* in Burmese, so K100,000 is thein kyat; the Indian term *lakh* (100,000) is also common.

Foreign Exchange Certificates

As soon as you exit the immigration check at Yangon International Airport you're supposed to stop at a counter and exchange US$300 for 300 FECs – Myanmar's second legal currency. Printed in China, these Monopoly-like notes issued by the Central Bank of Myanmar 'for the convenience of tourists visiting Myanmar' come in denominations equivalent to US$1, 5, 10 and US$20.

Payment for FECs is accepted *only* in US dollars or British pound sterling, in the form of cash, traveller's cheques or credit card (at the time of writing, credit cards could not be used at the airport). Only travellers' cheques issued by the following banks are accepted: MasterCard, American Express, Bank of Tokyo. Citicorps, Visa, Bank of America, National Westminster Bank, First National CitiBank, Swiss Bankers and Commonwealth Bank of Australia.

One US dollar always equals one FEC; the pound equivalent fluctuates according to pound-dollar variance. Along with the FECs you'll also receive a 'Foreign Exchange Certificate Voucher' which you'll only need to save if you plan to convert more than US$300 at the official rate. Reconversion of kyat to dollars or pound sterling is possible only for conversions in excess of US$300 and only when accompanied by the FEC voucher.

FECs can be spent anywhere in Myanmar. No special licence or permit is necessary for a citizen of Myanmar to accept FECs; this is not the case for dollars. Officially approved hotel rooms, airlines, Myanma Railways (some stations) and larger souvenir shops require payment either in dollars or FECs. So the required US$300 purchase of FECs is not something necessarily to avoid since they can be used to pay your hotel costs.

FECs can also be exchanged for kyat – at the free-market rate – at shops or from moneychangers that accept FEC. If you run out of FECs while on the road, MTT is quite happy to sell you more. FECs may also be purchased at the Central Bank of Myanmar and the Foreign Trade Bank in Yangon and at state-owned hotels.

On the other hand, FECs aren't absolutely necessary for Myanmar travel, and if you can get away without having to purchase them you might as well. The staff at the FEC exchange booth at Yangon airport is sometimes lax about dragging each and every newly arrived visitor over to the booth and many travellers are able to simply walk past without buying FEC. Upon request, couples are usually permitted to exchange US$300 for both persons rather than US$300 each.

This entire complicated system revolves around the desire of virtually every Burmese – and of course the government – to get their hands on hard currency, commonly referred to as 'FE' (foreign exchange, pronounced like one word, 'effee').

Dollars
The 'effee' most desired is the US dollar, Myanmar's third currency – and the most basic to the country's overall economy. Cash dollars can legally be used only at establishments possessing a licence to accept dollars. In reality all merchants are happy to take them. They can also be used to exchange for kyat on the black market.

Where Does the 'FE' Go?
Perhaps the reason the airport customs staff don't expend too much effort in getting your dollars is that the government knows you'll have to spend dollars anyway to stay at approved hotels. Either way the government-owned banks – the only banks where dollar accounts are permitted – end up with a portion of the money you spend. For both dollars and FECs the government requires that 10% of every unit deposited be converted to kyat at the low official exchange rate. Any Burmese with a dollar account may exchange FECs for dollars at their bank (less the 10% official kyat government cut, of course).

For the Burmese, this means that a US$100 deposit in cash or FEC leaves them with US$90 in the account plus K55 (US$10 x the official rate of K5.5). Since the required conversions yield such a small amount of kyats, this is in essence a 9.45% tax. With these dollars or FECs the Burmese can then either buy goods priced in dollars (for example, by importing them from abroad or by buying at hard currency stores in Myanmar) or they can sell them to others who need dollars from an official source (namely, from a government bank). Depending on demand for official dollars, it's possible to get anything from K100 to K200 cash for each official (banked) dollar; when the government announced that extra telephone lines would be available to those Burmese who could pay in dollars, for example, the rate for official dollars in a bank account shot up to the K150 to K200 range. Otherwise it usually hovers at around the same rate you'd get for cash dollars or FECs on the street.

The government has taken to pricing scarce goods – eg certain pharmaceuticals, telephones – in dollars/FECs only so as to mop up the foreign exchange ('FE') in the private sector. It's one of the few economically sensible things they've done since it holds kyat inflation down, although Burmese without access to FE certainly wouldn't see it that way.

Burmese with official dollars engage in all sorts of speculation and arbitrage; for example, they may be able to get a better return by buying a TV with dollars and then selling it to someone for kyats than they could directly selling the dollars for kyat on the free market. ■

Exchange Rates

With the FEC system in place, it's quite rare – and plain stupid – for any foreign visitor to exchange money at the ridiculously low official exchange rate. Since it's legal for Burmese to possess FECs without any special permit (not so for US dollars, which require a licence issued by the government), the visitor no longer needs to consider the official exchange rate and can instead concentrate on getting the best free or 'black' market rate.

This means the old whisky-and-cigarette scheme – buying a bottle of Johnny Walker scotch and a carton of 555s at Bangkok airport's duty-free shop to sell for free-market kyat – is no longer necessary. In fact you'll lose money if you do it! These items are usually less expensive in Yangon than in Bangkok.

One can now choose to change either FECs (quasi-legally) or dollars (illegally) for currency at the free-market rate. Shops, hotels and even permanent moneychangers (so far only at Bogyoke Aung San Market in Yangon) make FEC exchanges quite openly. The government has never announced that this practice is legal but they haven't said it's illegal either. Since both FECs and kyats are legal tender for Burmese citizens as well as foreigners, it stands to reason that the currency-holder may trade back and forth.

Only foreign investors doing business in Myanmar need worry about the exchange rate – certain types of investment require a portion of the capital to be converted at official currency exchanges, though even for these the government usually compromises at a higher-than-official rate (usually somewhere between K30 and K85 to the dollar).

Where the official rate really comes into play is with regard to joint ventures between the government and foreign investors. For example Myanma Economic Holdings Ltd, an army-owned company, can contribute 'equal' capital to a joint venture and gain 50% voting rights while in reality investing only US$55,000 for every US$1 million contributed by the foreign investor (ie US$1 million figured at the official K5.5 rate is only worth US$55,000 in real-world, K100-to-US$1 purchasing ratios).

For the record, here are the official exchange rates – established by the Myanma Foreign Trade Bank:

Australia	A$1	=	K4.07
Canada	C$1	=	K4.09
Germany	DM1	=	K3.80
France	FF1	=	K1.09
Japan	¥100	=	K6.34
Malaysia	M$1	=	K2.21
New Zealand	NZ$1	=	K3.65
Singapore	S$1	=	K3.89
Thailand	1B	=	K0.23
UK	UK£1	=	K8.67
USA	US$1	=	K5.52

Again, the above rates are basically meaningless since no visitor with any sense changes foreign currency for 'official' kyat. In spite of the fact that no one changes at these rates, the government attempts to enforce their pipe dream exchange rate in two ways. First of all, it is illegal to bring kyat into the country. Second, it is illegal to exchange cash US dollars except at the official banking outlets. Neither of these makes much difference – if you want to smuggle money in, you will, and every second person on the street would love to buy cash dollars from you. The rate is usually best in Yangon – typically 10 to 15% higher than upcountry.

Free-Market Exchange The real exchange rate in 1995 was close to K100 per US dollar (for US$50 or larger-denomination US dollar bills), about 16 times better than the bank rate.

One can sidestep all illegality by changing FECs – legal tender for one and all – instead of cash dollars. Some people claim dollars get a slightly better free-market rate than FECs. Our experience was that both got a rate of around K100 per unit; any fluctuations between the two depended on which moneychanger we dealt with – and on which day we were changing since the rates bounce up and down from week to week. The lowest rate we've seen for either currency as we went to press was around 90, the highest 115. On any given day, if there seemed to be a difference between the two it was only a matter of K3 to K5, ie three to five cents per dollar.

To maximise your return, though, you can always reserve FECs for hotel, train and air payments, and use dollars to buy kyat. The rate seems to have stabilised due to the relaxation on foreign exchange holdings (caused by the introduction of FECs in early 1993) and the increase in national hard currency reserves, along with the greater influx of dollars brought by the increasing number of tourists and foreign businesses coming into Myanmar.

When to Change If you're newly arrived, always ask around for the going rate before changing large amounts. It's best to ignore money-changing touts at the airport – just use cash dollars for the taxi ride into Yangon. Some people bring a small amount of kyat purchased from travellers or moneychangers in Bangkok, and spend a few kyat on a bus into town if they're pinching pennies. There's a slight risk here, since it's illegal to bring kyat into Myanmar, but it's very seldom that anyone is searched on entry. Once in town you can check into any hotel or guest house using FECs or dollars, then ask other travellers what the current rate is.

Where to Change When you're ready to change dollars or FECs, it's safest to change in shops or hotels rather than on the street. Unscrupulous moneychangers are very good at short-changing new arrivals for several hundred or more kyat. Always count the kyat before releasing your dollars/FECs. And take your time counting: short-changing is all the easier with K15, K45 and K90 notes in the mix, as these are difficult for first-time visitors to add up quickly. Rumour says these odd-denominated notes may be discontinued in the near future to make currency calculations easier – and to make the government appear more 'normal' to the outside world.

Credit Cards
American Express, Diners Club, Visa and MasterCard are the only international credit cards accepted in Myanmar, albeit at few places so far. MTT accepts all four in payment for services purchased through their office. Air Mandalay and a handful of hotels in Mandalay and Yangon accept credit cards – and that's about it. The Foreign Trade Bank also accepts foreign credit cards for the purchase of FECs. Don't count on getting by with plastic money unless you plan to spend most of your time at hotels that do accept plastic.

So far Myanmar has no ATMs but there is an American Express agent (☎ 01-75361) at 148 Sule Pagoda Rd opposite the Yangon Duty Free Store. If the current trend toward banking modernisation continues, you can expect an increasing number of places to accept cards with every passing year. All transactions paid for with foreign credit cards in Myanmar are charged in US dollars, then converted to your home currency by the card's bank of origin.

In 1995 Myanmar Oriental Bank and Yoma Bank became the first private, Burmese-owned banks to issue credit cards. These cards charge in kyats only. Customers must deposit K50,000 to open a credit card account at either bank.

Banking
Myanmar now has 29 private banks in operation, including 17 foreign banks with representative offices. None of these so far are permitted to handle foreign currencies.

Of the two private Burmese banks, only Yoma Bank is authorised to arrange loans which can be repaid on instalment plans.

Only five banks – all government-owned, of course – are permitted to manage US dollar accounts: Myanma Foreign Trade Bank, Yangon City Bank, Yangon Cooperative Bank, Myawaddy Bank and Myanma Citizens Bank. There is a 10% 'tax' (actually a conversion to kyat at the piddling official rate) on such accounts.

Costs
Travel in Myanmar today is cheaper than it's

been at anytime since before the 1988-89 disturbances. Costs depend largely on where you decide to go and which hotels you choose to stay in. Generally speaking the farther off the beaten track you go, the cheaper (and let's face it, the more uncomfortable) travel becomes.

If you take a package tour or stay in any of the few remaining state-owned hotels, costs are certainly high by South-East Asian standards, especially considering the overall low quality of tourist facilities Myanmar has to offer.

Goods and services may be priced either in kyat or in US dollars/FECs. Hotel rooms, some train tickets, air tickets, car rental and guide services are generally priced in dollars/FECs – for some of these services dollars/FECs may be the only currencies accepted. Duty-free items at the airport and at the Yangon Duty Free Store are also priced in dollars/FECs. Food, taxis, buses and just about everything else in Myanmar are priced in kyat. In keeping with this two-currency system, prices in this guidebook are quoted in either US dollars or kyat; anytime dollars are quoted, FECs are equally acceptable.

Daily Expenses Over the last few years inflation in Myanmar, at least officially, has been high. Many costs – especially for state-owned tourist hotels – have shot up since the 1989 reopening. On the other hand, meals are very cheap if paid for with free-market kyats – US$4 or US$5 worth of free-market kyats per day will more than suffice for food.

Now that the hotel industry has privatised, it's possible to get rooms in well-touristed areas of Myanmar for as low as US$5 per person per night. For shoestring travellers this is high compared to Thailand and Indonesia, but about the same as in Laos and Vietnam. Virtually all hotels licensed to accept foreigners accept only US dollars or FECs for room payments. A few hotels here and there charge mixed rates for which you may pay a certain portion of the rate in US dollars/FECs and the remainder in free-market kyats. And in very out-of-the-way places you can even pay entirely in kyats,

which can bring room rates down to as low as K75 to K200 per person.

Most hotels and larger tourist restaurants add a 10% hotel and restaurant tax plus a 10% service charge to the bill. See the Acommodation section for details on potential ways to bring room costs down.

Except for those transport services monopolised by MTT (notably tickets for the Yangon-Mandalay express train and Mandalay-Bagan express boat), public ground transport is inexpensive and so slow that you're unlikely to be able to spend more than US$5 a day on long-distance movement. Using domestic air transportation speeds things up considerably but averages US$80 to US$120 per flight.

Although it's difficult to pin down a one-figure travel budget due to all the variables in the equation – particularly whether or not your desired itinerary requires travel permits – you can expect to spend a rock-bottom minimum of about US$10 a day. This assumes always taking the cheapest room available, using public ground transport (avoiding the Yangon-Mandalay express train and Mandalay-Bagan express boat) and eating in local restaurants and teashops rather than hotel restaurants or places geared to foreign tourists.

A comfortable budget for those seeking the extra convenience of a private rather than shared bathroom, as well as a broader range of restaurant choices, would be around US$25 to US$30 a day. Taking express ground transport and flying a couple of domestic air routes might add another US$5 or US$7 per person per day for anyone staying the full 28-day period permitted under the current tourist visa regulations.

Moving further upmarket you could easily spend US$25 to US$40 per day on the more well-appointed hotels and guest houses – and in Yangon there are an increasing number of US$75 to US$125 a night places. And for ultra-luxury, of course there's always The Strand, where rooms start at around US$300 a night and restaurant entrees cost US$8 to US$16.

Inflation It's important to remember that

Myanmar has an annual inflation rate of 25 to 30%, so any prices quoted in this book will probably need to be adjusted acordingly. One of the easiest and most accurate ways to calculate overall price increases is to check the price of a cup of tea in a typical Burmese teashop – such prices are more or less standard throughout urban Myanmar. In 1994, for example, you could sip a cup of tea for K6; a year later a sip at the same teashop cost K8. If this formula holds, a cup in mid-1996 would cost about K10. A trishaw ride cited in this guidebook as costing K200 would have increased to around K250 – and so on.

Corruption Minor bribes – called 'presents' in Burmese English (as in 'Do you have a present for me?') – are part of everyday life in Myanmar. Much as tips are expected for a taxi ride or a restaurant meal in the West, extra compensation is expected for the efficient completion of many standard bureaucratic services. A visa extension or customs inspection will move a little more quickly if a 'present' – a little cash, a package of cigarettes, a tube of lipstick, a ballpoint pen – is proffered along with whatever the regular fee is. T-shirts and up-to-date Western calendars – basically anything that can be re-sold for cash – will work minor miracles.

If a Myanma Airways flight is 'sold out', a whole carton of cigarettes or bottle of liquor – or the equivalent in cash (US$9 to US$11) – might buy a seat. Want to ride in the front seat of a passenger pickup truck instead of crammed in the back? Add 30 to 50% of the regular passenger fare.

In some cases a 'present' may be requested for no special service at all – just to get a government worker to do his or her job. Some visitors refuse to pay in such cases, though from the Burmese perspective you're liable for the unwritten 'leisure class tax' because of your relative wealth. You may have earned your meagre travel budget washing dishes at the dingiest dive in London, but to the Burmese your presence in Myanmar automatically means you're well off. The same happens to Burmese of obvious means, so it's not always a case of 'foreigners pay more'. The major exception is when it comes to hotels and plane or train transport, where foreigners really get soaked relative to what locals pay.

No matter how this system might bruise your sensibilities, you probably won't get through a Myanmar trip without paying at least a couple of minor bribes – even if you're not aware you've paid.

WHEN TO GO

Climate-wise, the best season for visiting most of Myanmar falls between November and February – during these months it rains least and is not so hot.

The cool hill stations of the Shan State or the wind-swept Rakhine State coast are best visited when the rest of Myanmar is miserably hot, March to May. Bagan, Mandalay and the rest of the 'dry zone' in central Upper Myanmar can be nearly intolerable during these months. During the height of the monsoon season, July to September, the dry zone gets less rain and humidity than the rest of the country, while roads along the Rakhine coast and delta region south-west of Yangon can become impassable.

The peak months for tourist arrivals are December, February, July and August. The least crowded months – though as yet Myanmar never actually seems to be overcrowded – are May, June and September.

WHAT TO BRING

Even at the height of the cool season you'll rarely need anything more than a sweater while on the plains – and that probably only for the nights in Bagan, where it can get a little chilly. It can get rather cold up in the hill country, so if you're going to Pyin U Lwin (Maymyo) or Inle Lake bring a warm sweater or light jacket. A sleeping bag might also be useful in the Inle Lake area, especially in Kalaw and Taunggyi where the one or two blankets per person supplied by guest houses is not always enough during the cool season.

Otherwise it's normal tropical gear – lightweight, but 'decent', clothes. Myanmar is a prim, conservative country; shorts (particularly when worn by women) or short skirts are inappropriate.

When travelling in Myanmar, we strongly advise that you wear sandals or thongs rather than shoes – simply because you take them off and put them on so often when visiting temples and *payas* (pagodas). Remember that the sunlight is intense in Myanmar – protect your head in open places like Bagan, or when out on Inle Lake. Mosquitoes can be a major irritant, so bring protection in the form of insect repellent, mosquito coils or even a mosquito net. Cheap hotels sometimes don't supply top sheets, so a sleeping bag or even just a sarong will provide some added protection against the little buggers.

Bring any items you feel may not be available in Myanmar – mosquito repellent or coils, film, batteries and medicines are obvious examples. Simple toiletries like soap, toothpaste or toilet paper are readily available; in fact toilet paper is much easier to find and is cheaper than in India. Remember that anything Western which is difficult to find in Myanmar will have an absurdly high value. Western clothes (interesting T-shirts), electronic gadgets, calendars, disposable lighters, ballpoint pens, lipstick and make-up are all items many Burmese would love to have. They have to be name brands though, something from the USA or Europe, not any old Asian product! You can always use them to barter for handicrafts, bribe sluggish bureaucrats or simply give away and make people happy.

A small but strong padlock is useful for locking your room door in small upcountry guest houses where locks aren't provided.

TOURIST OFFICES

Myanmar Travels & Tours (MTT), formerly known as Tourist Burma, is part of the Ministry of Hotels & Tourism (MHT) – the official government tourism organ in Myanmar. Their main office (☎ 01-78376, 75328, fax 89588) is at 77/91 Sule Pagoda Rd in Yangon, beside the Sule Paya.

MTT have little in the way of brochures or leaflets, unlike most other South-East Asian tourist offices. Their main function, in fact, is to sell tours and transport at premium rates, to channel as many visitors as possible into MTT-sanctioned hotels and to keep tabs on foreign visitors. They also sell reasonably good and inexpensive city maps for Yangon, Mandalay and Bagan.

Apart from the main Yangon office there are also MTT desks in Mandalay, Bagan, Nyaungshwe (Inle Lake) and Taunggyi. Until the early 1990s they were the only travel agency in the country; nowadays they compete with over a hundred private travel agencies.

With the privatisation of the tourist industry, it's no longer difficult to avoid MTT while travelling round Myanmar. Two of their remaining monopolies are express train tickets between Yangon and Mandalay and express boat tickets between Mandalay and Bagan, neither of which can be purchased by a foreigner except through MTT (or their representatives at the station/pier). But in both cases there are alternatives to using MTT transport, so even here you can bypass the bureaucrats.

In areas where until 1995 your only choice for a place to stay was a hotel owned by the Ministry of Hotels & Tourism (eg Mawlamyine), there are now alternative private hotels or guest houses. The only place we visited where it was impossible to avoid staying at an MHT-owned hotel was at Ngapali Beach in the Rakhine State; most likely even here private accommodation will soon be added. See the Accommodation section for more information on where to stay.

Just as the MHT is selling off all its hotel properties, there are rumours it may dissolve MTT in the face of competition from better-run travel agencies. In all honesty it must be mentioned that MTT actually has some very charming, very experienced guides, each of whom was trained at the long-running MHT school opposite the Baiyoke Kandawgyi Hotel. Many of the better private agencies in Yangon employ former MTT guides; some agencies are even owned by former MTT guides.

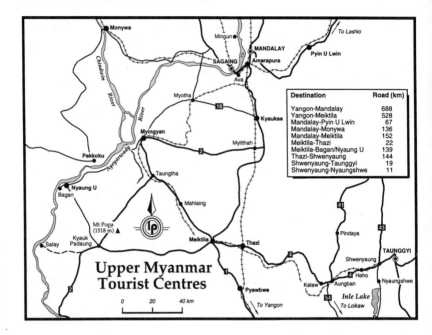

Destination	Road (km)
Yangon-Mandalay	688
Yangon-Meiktila	528
Mandalay-Pyin U Lwin	67
Mandalay-Monywa	136
Mandalay-Meiktila	152
Meiktila-Thazi	22
Meiktila-Bagan/Nyaung U	139
Thazi-Shwenyaung	144
Shwenyaung-Taunggyi	19
Shwenyaung-Nyaungshwe	11

Upper Myanmar Tourist Centres

0   20   40 km

BUSINESS HOURS

Most government offices are open Monday to Friday from 9.30 am to 4.30 pm (usually posted as 1630 in the military style). Don't arrive at a government office at 4 pm expecting to get anything done; most government workers start drifting away to the local teashops after 3.30 pm.

Banks are open from 10 am to 2 pm on weekdays only. Private shops are generally open from around 9.30 or 10 am till around 6 pm.

HOLIDAYS & CULTURAL EVENTS

Traditionally Myanmar follows a 12-month lunar calendar, so the old holidays and festivals will vary in date, by the Gregorian calendar, from year to year (see Time & Dates further on for a list of these months). Myanmar also has a number of more recently originated holidays whose dates are fixed by the Gregorian calendar.

Festivals are drawn-out, enjoyable affairs in Myanmar. They generally take place or culminate on full-moon days, but the build-up can continue for days. There's often a country-fair atmosphere about these festivals – at some convenient grounds there will be innumerable stalls and activities which go on all night. *Pwes* ('shows'), music and Burmese boxing bouts will all be part of the colourful scene. The normally calm Burmese can get really worked up during these festivals – at a full-moon festival on one of our visits to Yangon the supporters of the defeated favourite in a boxing bout were so enraged they wrecked the arena, and subsequent bouts had to be cancelled.

January/February
　Independence Day on 4 January is a major public holiday marked by a seven-day fair at Kandawgyi (Royal) Lake in Yangon. There are fairs all over the country at this time.
　Union Day on 12 February celebrates Bogyoke Aung San's short-lived achievement of unifying Myanmar's disparate racial groups. For two

weeks preceding Union Day, the national flag is paraded from town to town, and wherever the flag rests there must be a festival.

The month of Tabodwei culminates in a rice-harvesting festival on the new-moon day. *Htamane*, a special food-offering made and eaten at this time, consists of glutinous rice mixed with sesame, peanuts, shredded ginger and coconut. In villages large batches of htamane are cooked over open fires and stirred with big wooden paddles until they become a thick mass, after which the rice is wrapped in small banana-leaf parcels and distributed among all the members of the community.

February/March

The lunar month of Tabaung brings the annual Shwedagon Festival, the largest *paya pwe* or 'pagoda festival' in Myanmar. The full-moon day in Tabaung is also an auspicious occasion for the construction of new payas, and local paya festivals are held.

Two holidays fall during our month of March: 2 March is Peasants' Day, while 27 March is Resistance or Armed Forces Day, celebrated with parades and fireworks. Since 1989, the Tatmadaw has made it a tradition to pardon a number of prisoners on Armed Forces Day.

April/May

The full-moon day of Kason is celebrated as the Buddha's birthday, the day of his enlightenment and the day he entered *nibbana* (nirvana). Thus it is known as the 'thrice blessed day'. The holiday is celebrated by ceremonially watering *bo* trees, the sacred banyan tree under which Buddha attained enlightenment.

One of the best places to observe this ceremony is at Yangon's Shwegadon Paya, where a procession of girls carry earthen jars to water the three banyan trees on the western side of the compound. Although the government renounced socialism in 1989, the country still celebrates May Day – 1 May – as Workers' Day.

June/July

The full moon of Waso is the beginning of the three-month Buddhist 'Lent'. Laypeople present monasteries with stacks of new robes for resident monks since during the Lent period monks are restricted to their monasteries for a prolonged period of spiritual retreat. Ordinary people are also expected to be rather more religious during this time – marriages do not take place and it is inauspicious to move house. The most devout Burmese Buddhist will observe eight precepts – rather than the usual five – for the duration of the season. This is a good time for young men to temporarily enter the monasteries.

The 19th of July is Martyr's Day, commemorating the assassination of Bogyoke Aung San and his comrades on that day in 1947. Wreaths are laid at his mausoleum north of the Shwedagon Paya in Yangon. Government officials probably pray the Burmese people don't attempt to rein-

The Water Festival

Around the middle of April the three-day Thingyan or 'water festival' starts the Burmese new year. Thingyan, from the Sanskrit *samkranta* or 'fully passed over', celebrates the passage of the sun from the Sign of Pisces into the Sign of Aries in the zodiac. This is the height of the dry and hot season and, as in Thailand's Songkran, it is celebrated in a most raucous manner – by throwing buckets of cold water at anyone who dares to venture into the streets. Foreigners are not exempt!

In cities temporary stages called *pandal* (from the Tamil *pendel*) are erected along main thoroughfares. Each pandal is sponsored by civic groups, neighbourhood associations, student societies or government departments, the members of whom stand next to rows of water barrels and douse every person or vehicle that passes by.

On a spiritual level, the Burmese believe that during this three-day period the king of the *nats*, Thagyamin, visits the human world to tally his annual record of the good deeds and misdeeds humans have performed. Villagers place flowers and sacred leaves in front of their homes to welcome the god. Thagyamin's departure on the morning of the third day marks the beginning of the new year, when properly brought-up young people wash the hair of their elder kin, Buddha images are ceremonially washed and *hpongyis* (monks) are offered particularly appetising almsfood.

Although the true meaning of the festival is still kept alive by ceremonies such as these, nowadays it's mainly a festival of fun. In between getting soaked there will be dancing, singing and theatre. In the latter the emphasis is on satire – particularly making fun of the government, the latest female fashions and any other items of everyday interest. Cultural taboos against women acting in a boisterous manner are temporarily lifted, so women can 'kidnap' young men, blacken their faces with soot or oil, bind their hands and dunk their heads in buckets of water until the boys surrender and perform a hilarious monkey dance for the girls. ■

stall the planned civilian government aborted by Aung San's assassination.

July/August

At the festival in Wagaung lots are drawn to see who will have to provide monks with their alms. If you're in Mandalay, try to get to Taungbyone, about 30 km north, where there is a noisy, seven-day festival to keep the nats happy.

September/October

This is the height of the wet season, so what better time to hold boat races? They're held in rivers, lakes and even ponds all over Myanmar, but the best place to be is Inle Lake where the Buddha images at the Phaung Daw U Kyaung are ceremonially toured around the lake in the huge royal barge, the Karaweik. The latter comes just before the festival of Thadingyut and usually overlaps late September and early October.

In Thadingyut, the Buddhist Lent comes to an end and all those couples who had been putting off marriage now rush into each other's arms. Monks are free to travel from *kyaung* to *kyaung* (Buddhist monasteries) or to go on pilgrimmage to holy spots such as Kyaiktiyo or Mt Popa.

The Festival of Lights takes place during Thadingyut to celebrate Buddha's return from a period of preaching *dhamma* in Tavatimsa (the highest *deva* realm), his way lit by devas who lined the route of his descent. For the three days of the festival all Myanmar is lit by oil lamps, fire balloons, candles and even mundane electric lamps. Every house has a paper lantern hanging outside and it's a happy, joyful time all over Myanmar – particularly after the solemnity of the previous three months. Pwes may be performed on pandals erected along city streets, particularly in Mandalay.

October/November

The full-moon night of Tazaungmon is an occasion for another 'festival of lights', known properly as Tazaungdaing. It's particularly celebrated in the Shan State – in Taunggyi there are fire balloon competitions. In some areas there are also speed-weaving competitions during the night – young Burmese women show their prowess at weaving by attempting to produce robes for Buddha images between dusk and dawn. The results, finished or not, are donated to the monks. The biggest weaving competitions occur at Shwedagon Paya in Yangon.

Tazaungmon also brings *kathein* (Pali: *kathina*), a one-month period at the end of Buddhist Lent during which new monastic robes and requisites are offered to the monastic community. Many people simply donate cash; kyat notes are folded and stapled into floral patterns on wooden 'trees' called *padetha* and offered to the monasteries. This symbolises a much older tradition in which laypeople would leave kathina robes hanging from tree branches in the forest for monks to find. Myanmar's national day falls in late November or early December.

November/December

During Nadaw, many *nat pwes* or 'spirit festivals' are held; Nadaw is actually spelt with the characters for *nat* ('spirit') and *taw* (respectful honorific). Despite Myanmar's predominantly Buddhist background, Christmas Day is a public holiday in deference to the many Christian Karen.

December/January

Held on the first waxing moon of Pyatho, the Karen (Kayin) new year is considered a national holiday. Karen communities throughout Myanmar celebrate by wearing their traditional dress of woven tunics over red *longyis* (the sarong-style cloth covering the lower body) and by hosting folk dancing and singing performances. The largest celebrations are held in the Karen suburb of Insein, just north of Yangon, and in Pa-an, the capital of the Kayin State.

The Ananda Festival, held at the Ananda Paya in Bagan, also takes place during Pyatho.

Paya Festivals

In addition to the main pan-Myanmar festivals described above, nearly every active paya or kyaung community hosts occasional celebrations of its own, often called 'pagoda festivals' in Burmese English. The typical paya festival features the same kinds of activities as a major festival – craft and food vendors, music and dance – on a smaller scale. The biggest proliferation of paya fairs occur on full-moon days and nights during the January to March period following the main rice harvest, providing local paddy farmers and their families a good excuse to party. The festivals also offer added market venues for local basketweavers, potters, woodcarvers, blacksmiths, longyi-weavers and other artisans.

To the professional 'twelve-festival traders' or *say-hni-pwe-thi*, who travel from festival to festival following the lunar calendar, the smaller paya fairs serve as convenient filler between major gigs. Other assorted camp followers include fortune-tellers, movable teashops, tent barbers, homespun beauty consultants, pickpockets and professional beggars.

Particular paya festivals are described in the appropriate destination sections throughout this guidebook.

POST & TELECOMMUNICATIONS
Post
Surprisingly perhaps, mail out of Myanmar seems to get to its destination quite efficiently. Or at least we think so: a number of letter writers either agreed that everything they sent got through OK (even from Mandalay) or totally disagreed, saying that nothing at all ever arrived.

International postage rates are a bargain K5 per letter to the USA and Europe, K4 to Asia. For registered mail anywhere in the world add K14. Aerogramme and postcard postage cost just K3.5. Note also that there is no poste restante service in Myanmar.

Officially post offices all over Myanmar are supposed to be open Monday through Friday 9.30 am to 4 pm, but in reality the staff open and close when they feel like it. As a general rule of thumb, the smaller the town, the farther the post office deviates from the official schedule. Yangon's main post office keeps fairly rigorous hours; elsewhere it's often difficult to get any kind of service after 3.30 pm.

Embassies in Yangon recommend that if you are sending any important correspondence in or out of Myanmar you should send it by air freight rather than trust the mail. DHL Worldwide Express (☎ 01-71385, 85475) has an office at 524-B Merchant St. Other courier services include Mercury Air Cargo (☎ 01-76095) at 46 31st St and Overseas Courier Service (☎ 01-74045) at 147 40th St. For larger air or sea freight shipments, Myanmar International Moving Services (☎ 01-67057, fax 67058) at 14 A-1 Lane, A-1 Compound, Mile 9, Pyay Rd, is recommended.

A new domestic express service was recently introduced: for just K50, letters mailed to major cities before noon reportedly will arrive in one day.

Area Codes

The country code for Myanmar is 95; the area code for Yangon is 01, Mandalay 02. You need to dial the zero when calling from within Myanmar. Other cities with area codes include:

Bago	052
Chauk	061
Hinthada	044
Pa-an	035
Lashio	082
Loikaw	083
Kengtung	101
Magwe	063
Mawlamyine	032
Meiktila	064
Minbu	065
Monywa	071
Myingyan	066
Myitkyina	074
Pakokku	062
Pathein	042
Pyay	053
Pyinmana	067
Pyin U Lwin	085
Sagaing	072
Sittwe	043
Taunggyi	081
Taungoo	054
Thanlyin	065

Telephone
Domestic Calling other places in Myanmar is relatively simple and very inexpensive from the Central Telephone & Telegraph Office at the corner of Pansodan and Mahabandoola Sts in Yangon. Only larger cities with area codes can be direct-dialled. Smaller towns still use manual switchboards, so you must ask the national operator to connect you to a specific town operator, then request the local number. These numbers are usually listed with the name of the town. The telephone number for the Inle Inn in Nyaungshwe, for example, is 'Nyaungshwe 16' – which means you must first be connected with the operator in Nyaungshwe, then ask for the number 16.

International The only public place in the country where international telephone calls can be conveniently arranged is at the main telephone office described previously. International calls are charged by three-minute blocks; if you stay on the line for less than three minutes you still pay the full three-minute charge. If you want to talk longer than three minutes, you must start all over again for each additional three-minute block.

Destination	K per three-minute call
Africa	265
Australia	215
Europe	210
Hong Kong	105
Japan	160
UK	190
USA	265

You may have to wait for up to half an hour for a line. The phone office is open Monday to Friday 8 am to 4 pm, weekends and holidays 9 am to 2 pm.

So far few hotels in the country furnish international direct dial (IDD) room phones, but this will surely change as IDD phones become more common. The larger Yangon hotels – The Strand, Nawarat and Summit Parkview – feature in-room IDD phones as well as small business centres where guests may make international calls. All tack steep service charges onto the regular phone company rates. The Strand permits non-guests to use its business centre, which is open 24 hours, but calls are highly surcharged. Waiting is the norm even at the hotels, since not more than one IDD line is usually available.

You can also make surcharged phone and fax calls at the new International Business Centre (☎ 01-67133) at 88 Pyay Rd (Mile 6.5). Sponsored by the Ministry of Forestry, the International Business Centre offers a range of secretarial and business services in addition to basic telecommunications.

TIME & DATES
Hours
Myanmar Standard Time (MST) is 6½ hours ahead of Greenwich Mean Time (GMT/UTC). Coming from Thailand you turn your watch back half an hour, from India you turn it forward an hour. When it is noon in Yangon it's 9.30 pm the previous day in San Francisco, 12.30 am in New York, 5.30 am in London, 3.30 pm in Sydney or Melbourne.

When these cities are on daylight-saving time, these times are one hour off.

Days
Most Burmese Buddhists recognise an eight-day week in which Thursday to Tuesday conform with the Western calendar but Wednesday is divided into two 12-hour days. Midnight to 6 pm is 'Bohdahu' (the day Buddha was born), while 6 pm to midnight is 'Yahu' (Rahu, a Hindu god/planet). It's rare that the week's unique structure causes any communication problems, however, given that the Wednesday division mainly applies to religious rather than secular matters (for example, which planetary post a worshipper attends at a paya).

Months
The traditional Burmese calendar features 12 28-day lunar months which are out of sync with the months of the solar Gregorian calendar. To stay in sync with the solar year, the Burmese calendar inserts a second Waso month every few years – somewhat like the leap year day added to the Gregorian February. The Burmese months are:

Tagu	March/April
Kason	April/May
Nayon	May/June
Waso	June/July
Wagaung	July/August
Tawthalin	August/September
Thadingyut	September/October
Tazaungmon	October/November
Nadaw	November/December
Pyatho	December/January
Tabodwei	January/February
Tabaung	February/March

Most traditional festivals take place according to this scheme, making it difficult to calculate festival dates using a Gregorian calendar.

Each lunar month is divided into two 14-day halves; the two weeks during which the moon waxes (or appears to increase in size) are called la-zan, while the two weeks of the waning moon are la-gwe. These lunar phases determine the Burmese religious calendar. Four monthly 'holy days' – when it's most propitious to visit a paya or kyaung – occur on the 8th and 15th days of the waxing and waning moons.

Burmese months are cited more commonly than the Gregorian months in everyday speech. Ask villagers what the date is and they'll respond with something like 'It's Pyatho, eighth day of the waning moon'. Educated Burmese are familiar with the Gregorian calendar, which is used in most official capacities and in business situations.

Years

Over the centuries Burmese monarchs have established and counter-established several different year counts. The main one in current use, called *thekkayit*, is 638 years behind the Christian era. Since each new year begins in April (at the end of the Thingyan festival), this means the Christian year 1997 is equivalent of thekkayit 1359 until the month of April, after which it's 1360. Burmese archaeology is particularly challenging since historic chronicles and stone inscriptions use different year counts depending on who was king at the time.

Another calendar in use follows the Buddhist era as reckoned in Thailand counting from 543 BC; hence 1997 is 2540 BE. Private businesses typically cite years following the AD Christian calendar. Some official Burmese documents and many Burmese calendars state the year according to all three systems, ie thekkayit, BE and AD.

ELECTRICITY

Myanmar's national grid system covers only certain parts of central and southern Myanmar. Most of the power comes from a single hydroelectric plant at Lawpita in the Kayah State. Off the national grid, towns and cities may have their own diesel plants or small hydroelectric facilities. When it's working the current is supposed to run at 230v, 50 Hz AC. Most electrical wall outlets take British-style plugs with three flat lugs in a triangle; some older outlets accept round lugs and a few outlets feature combined round/flat holes for either type.

Even in the capital, however, there's never enough electric capacity to power the whole city, so Myanma Electric Power Enterprise (MPPE) rotates the supply from quarter to quarter and from day to day. The voltage often drops to levels that are barely enough for anything more than basic lighting. Brownouts and blackouts are common, except of course in the neighbourhoods where military officers or ministers live. In many towns and villages electric power is supplied only during the evening hours from around 6 to 11 pm.

Businesses and homes that can afford it maintain their own gas or diesel-powered generators. Often these are unable to supply enough voltage to power major appliances like air-conditioners; this is why many smaller hotels feature in-room air-con units which don't work. Transformers which 'step up' the voltage are becoming increasingly common but the cheaper models – those within economic reach of the Burmese middle class – don't seem to work very well.

In many villages lighting, heating and cooking sources are restricted to candles, paraffin and firewood.

WEIGHTS & MEASURES

For a country with such a professed anti-colonial stance, Myanmar is amazingly Anglo in the standard units of measures employed in everyday life.

Weight

The most common units of weight used in Myanmar are viss *(peiktha)*, pounds *(paun)* and ticals *(kyat tha)*. One viss equals 3.6 pounds (1.6 kg) or 100 ticals. One tical equals 16 gm.

Volume

At the retail level, rice and small fruits or nuts are sold in units of volume rather than weight; the most common measure is the standard condensed milk can or *bu*. Eight *bu* equals one small rice basket or *pyi* and 16 pyi make a jute sack or *tin*.

Petrol and most other liquids are sold by the imperial gallon (4.55 litres). One exception is milk, which is sold by the viss.

Length & Distance

Cloth and other items of moderate length are measured by the yard (91.5 cm), called *gaik* in Burmese. A half yard is a *taung* (45.7 cm), which is divided into two *htwa* (22.8 cm). Half a htwa is a *mait* (11.4 cm), roughly equivalent to an Anglo-American foot.

Road distances are measured in miles (one mile = 1.61 km). Shorter distances in town or in the countryside may be quoted in furlongs. There are eight furlongs in one mile; thus one furlong equals about two-tenths of a km.

BOOKS, PERIODICALS & MAPS
People, Culture & Society

Golden Earth by Norman Lewis (Eland Books, London), a re-issued edition of a book originally written in 1952, is a delightful tale of a ramble around Myanmar at a time when it was both more open and less open than it is today. At that time the varied rebellions were in full swing, but Myanmar had not yet entered its reclusive period. Much of the book sounds remarkably like Myanmar today, and the author's descriptions of Myanmar's antiquated trucks have the real ring of truth – no photograph could do a better job of summing up these miracles of mechanical endurance.

The Thirty-Seven Nats by Sir R C Temple, originally published in 1906 by Griggs in London, has just been redone in a beautiful colour edition by Kiscadale Publications. Though it costs an astounding US$180, it's still the most venerable description of the Burmese nat cult available and the colour plates provide artists' renderings of each of the 37 nats. If you read French, an even more informative book on the nat cult is *Rites et Possesions en Birmanie*, by Benedicte Brac de la Perriere (Edition Recherche sur les Civilisations). This one contains detailed descriptions of nat pwes and other spirit ceremonies. *Nat-Pwe: Burma's Supernatural Sub-Culture* by Yves Rodrigue (Kiscadale, 1992) sheds further light on this fascinating topic.

Other notable books from Kiscadale include a new edition of *The Burman: His Life and Notions*, a fascinating collection of essays by Shway Yoe, the pseudonym of Sir J G Scott, a colonial official and specialist in Burmese botany, linguistics and archaeology. In his many years in Myanmar, Scott acquired an extraordinary knowledge about every aspect of the country. Kiscadale has also re-published *The Silken East: A Record of Life and Travel in Burma*, a chronicle of turn-of-the-century travels along the Chindwin, Ayeyarwady and Thanlwin (Salween) rivers early this century by V C Scott O'Connor. Kiscadale, incidentally, devotes itself to Myanmar-related topics; for a catalogue write to Kiscadale Publications, Murray House, Gartmore, Stirling FK8 3RJ, UK.

Paul Theroux's amusing and cynical bestseller, *The Great Railway Bazaar* (Houghton Mifflin, 1975), includes chapters on the train trip from Yangon to Mandalay, and from Mandalay to Pyin U Lwin – with a perfect description of Candacraig, and his amusing visit to 'forbidden' Gokteik. Another witty account of pre-1988, seven-day-visa Myanmar is found in the essay 'The Raj is Dead! Long Live the Raj!' in Pico Ayer's book *Video Night in Kathmandu* (Vintage Departures, 1988).

The Soul of a People by H Fielding was an 1898 attempt to understand the Burmese. *Thibaw's Queen*, by the same author in 1899, is a romanticised story of the collapse of the final Burmese kingdom before British imperial might. It has been republished in Myanmar by the Buddha Sasana Council and is easily found. Maurice Collis *(Siamese White, Last & First in Burma)* also wrote about Myanmar.

Towards the end of WW II Longmans published a series of booklets about Myanmar known as *Burma Pamphlets*. You may see some of these long, long out-of-print books in Myanmar; they make interesting reading.

Mi Mi Khaing's *Burmese Family*, though first published in 1946 by Longmans, remains one of the best references on traditional Burmese customs and values. A blend of amateur sociology and personal memoirs, this book is available in reprinted form in Yangon.

Burman culture as it relates to religion is well covered in *Folk Elements in Burmese Buddhism* by Maung Htin Aung (Department of Religious Affairs, 1959), reprints of which are easy to find in Yangon since it's a standard exam text for Burmese students. The book most accurately describes what occurs in villages along the Yangon-Mandalay axis and as far north as Monywa and Shwebo only; customs in outer Myanmar – even in the predominantly Buddhist Shan, Rakhine, and Mon states – differ greatly.

Encounters on the Road to Mandalay, edited by Mya Than Tint and translated by Vicky Bowman (White Orchid, Bangkok, 1995), is a Studs Terkel-inspired collection of recent interviews with ordinary Burmese – an elephant oozie, a miner, a fortune-teller, a waitress etc – in which they describe their lives, loves, hopes and dreams.

For gourmets and cooking enthusiasts, *Cook & Entertain the Burmese Way* (Myawaddy Press) by Mi Mi Khaing makes interesting reading. This volume contains a wealth of information on preparing, serving and eating Burmese food in the correct style and includes instructions on how to mix Burmese salads by hand, recipes for 'salivators and tongue titillators', and a very useful appendix that lists fruits, vegetables, spices and fish with their Burmese and English names. It's available at bookstores in Yangon and at tourist hotels throughout the country. A slicker tome, *Under the Golden Pagoda: The Best of Burmese Cooking* by Aung Aung Taik (Chronicle Books, San Francisco), covers much of the same territory.

History & Politics

G E Harvey's *History of Burma* (Longmans, London, 1925) remains the classic work although parts are naturally out of date from today's historiographical perspective. *Burma* by F S V Donnison (Ernest Benn, London, 1970) gives a concise and very readable history of Myanmar from its earliest development through the British period and into the troubled 1960s. There are also chapters on the country's economy and culture. *The Union of Burma* by Hugh Tinker (Oxford University Press, London, 1961) is a scholarly study of the path to independence in Myanmar and the difficult U Nu period. Frank N Trager's *Burma: From Kingdom to Independence* (Praeger, New York, 1966) is an equally scholarly account of this same period and its particular ramifications for Asia.

Recommended French-written histories include *La Birmanie* by Guy Lubeigh (Presse Universitaire de France, 1973) and *Birmanie* by E Guillon and C Delachet (Seuil, 1975).

There are other more recent accounts of earlier Burmese history, such as *The Pagoda Wars* by A T Q Stewart (Faber, New York, 1972) which covers the British takeover of Myanmar. A number of books concern the dramatic events in Myanmar during WW II, particularly the behind-enemy-lines actions of Wingate's 'Chindit' forces. Find a complete description of their activities in *The Chindits* by Michael Calvert (Pan-Ballantine paperback), or read Bernard Fergusson's more personal accounts in *The Wild Green Earth* or *Beyond the Chindwin*. Fergusson's more recent *Return to Burma* provides an account of the author's postwar travels in Myanmar.

A French book, *Les Lautu-L'Organisation Sociale d'une Ethnie Chin de Haute-Birmanie* by André Bereigts (SELAF, 1981), contains an up-to-date description of Chin society and culture.

Essays on the History and Buddhism of Burma by Than Tun (Kiscadale, 1988) covers a range of social, religious, political and economic topics within the Burmese context. Anyone interested in colonial Myanmar's steamer era should read *Irrawaddy Flotilla* by Alister McCrae and Alan Prentice (James Paton, 1978), a history of the river fleet established by the British and still running today under the auspices of state-owned Inland Water Transport. Although the latter is out of print outside Myanmar, reprints are available in Yangon.

Two books by Myanmar expert David I Steinberg provide what is probably the most complete socio-political look at Myanmar between 1962 and 1988. *Burma: A Socialist*

Nation of Southeast Asia (Westview, Boulder, Colorado, 1982) contains an overview of Burmese history, geography, ethnicity, politics and economics, while *Burma's Road Toward Development: Growth & Ideology Under Military Rule* (Westview, Boulder, Colorado, 1981) is a history of the country since 1962, when Ne Win took power.

Burma – Insurgency & the Politics of Ethnicity by Martin Smith (Zed Press, London) contains a well-researched history and analysis of insurgent politics in Myanmar from the 1940s through to 1988. *Burma's Golden Triangle: On the Trail of the Opium Warlords* by André and Louis Boucaud (Asia Books, 1992; or in the French *Birmanie-Sur la piste des Seigneurs de la Guerre*, L'Harmattan, 1985) presents a collection of accounts detailing the Boucaud brothers' travels in insurgent Myanmar in the 1970s and '80s, along with some more recently updated material. Although it's sometimes difficult to tell which era is being covered, the book is an entertaining read.

Other French literature in this vein worth reading include two books by Martial Dasse – *La Face Politique Cachée de la Thailande* and *Montagnards, Revoltes et Guerres Revolutionaires en Asie du Sud-Est continentale*, both published by Duang Kamol, Bangkok. Another good one on insurgent Myanmar is *La Birmanie où la Quête de l'Unité* by Pierre Fistie (Ecole Francaise d'Extrême Orient, 1985).

Outrage: Burma's Struggle for Democracy by Bangkok journalist Bertil Lintner (White Lotus, London and Bangkok, 1990) chronicles the violent suppression of Myanmar's pro-democracy movement from 1987 to 1990, with particular focus on the events of 1988. It's a somewhat polemic, one-sided look at the student uprisings, but basically it's very informative. Lintner's *Land of Jade* by the same publisher describes a fascinating overland journey he and his Shan wife made through insurgent territories in northern Myanmar in 1985. The reporter's third book-length outing, *Burma In Revolt: Opium and Insurgency since 1948*

(Westview Press, 1994), discusses the relationship between opium production and insurgency among the Shan, Kayah, Pa-O, Mon, Lahu and Wa.

Edith Mirante's *Burmese Looking Glass* (Atlantic Monthly Press, 1993) follows similar political terrain in yet another mid-1980s first-person account featuring the ethnic rebel as noble savage. Among her many brief adventures, the author teaches Mon women to kill using ballpoints and flashlights as weapons.

True Love and Bartholomew: Rebels on the Burmese Border (Cambridge University Press, 1991) was written by Jonathan Falla, a nurse who worked in the KNU-controlled part of Karen State during the 1980s. His accounts of Karen society and the culture of insurgency form an important contribution to the literature on these topics.

Freedom from Fear & Other Writings by Aung San Suu Kyi (Viking, London and New York, 1991) presents a sometimes-brilliant collection of essays by and about the Nobel Peace Prize winner. She has also published an account of her father titled *Aung San of Burma* and the hard-to-find *Let's Visit Burma* (Burke Publishing, 1985), a thin children's guide to the country. A chapter in the latter, 'My Country and People', is an excellent encapsulation of Burmese culture.

Art & Archaeology
Several books offer histories and descriptions of the temple architecture at Bagan. The older *Pictorial Guide to Pagan* (Ministry of Culture, Yangon, 1979) contains illustrated descriptions of many of the important Bagan buildings plus a map inside the back cover. It's a useful book that you'll find fairly easily in Myanmar. The 1986 release, *Glimpses of Glorious Pagan* by the University of Yangon's history department, is basically an update of the earlier book. *Pagodas of Pagan* (Buddha Sasana Council Press) is also fairly readily available, but not so detailed or interesting. Top of the line is *Pagan: Art and Architecture of Old Burma*, by Paul Strachan (Kiscadale, 1988). This modern art history of Bagan monuments is available at larger

hotels in Yangon and costs around US$50 hardcover, US$25 soft.

Historical Sites in Burma by Aung Thaw (Ministry of Union Culture, 1972) is an excellent illustrated description of the major buildings at Bagan, Bago, Yangon, Amarapura, Ava, Sagaing, Mingun and Mandalay plus a number of other sites that are currently 'off limits'. It can be found at Yangon's Pagan Bookshop or in Bagan.

Mandalay & Environs, which is long out of print, can be very hard to find. It is very difficult to find any material on places other than the straightforward Yangon-Mandalay-Bagan triangle, however, *Historic Sites & Monuments of Mandalay & Environs* by U Lu Pe Win (Buddha Sasana Council Press) is fairly easy to come across and describes the ancient cities around Mandalay: Ava, Sagaing, Amarapura and Mingun.

One of the few books available with any information at all about archaeological sites other than Bagan or Mandalay is *A Guide to Mrauk U* by Tun Shwe Khine (Sittway Degree College, 1992). Available only in Yangon and Sittwe, it contains detailed descriptions and floor plans of the impressive Mrauk U monuments.

If you'd like to know a lot more about Shwedagon Paya then get a copy of *Shwedagon* by Win Pe (Printing & Publishing Corporation, Yangon, 1972). You might find it in street bookstalls in Yangon or at the Pagan Bookshop.

Burmese Art, written by John Lowry and published by the Victoria & Albert Museum in 1974, presents a detailed discussion of non-architectural art in central and Upper Myanmar from the early Bagan period through Mandalay. It's illustrated with 50 black-and-white photos of works in the museum's Burmese collection.

Aung San Suu Kyi's former secretary Ma Thanegi has published an informative volume on marionette theatre called *Burmese Puppets* (White Orchid, Bangkok, 1994). Around Yangon you may come across reprints of the drily written *Burmese Drama* by Maung Htin Aung, originally published by Oxford University Press India in 1937.

The slim *Kalagas: The Wall Hangings of Southeast Asia* (Ainslie's, Menlo Park, CA 1987) by Mary Anne Stanislaw contains photographs and descriptions of the Burmese tapestry *(kalaga)* craft. Sylvia Fraser-Lu's *Burmese Crafts, Past and Present* (Oxford University Press, 1994) is currently the most comprehensive volume covering handicrafts in Myanmar.

Novels, Short Stories, Poetry & Films

Quite a few writers set novels in Myanmar, the most famous being George Orwell's *Burmese Days* (Harcourt Brace, 1934), of course. It's available in a Penguin paperback and makes an engrossing, if slightly depressing, read on upcountry Myanmar in the British days. Orwell served with the British colonial police in Myanmar and his novel exhibits a strong grasp of the expat life.

Michio Takeyama's *Harp of Burma*, first published in Japanese in 1949, then in English in 1966 (Charles E Tuttle), novelises the desertion of a Japanese soldier in Myanmar during WW II. The story was made into a beautiful black-and-white Japanese film directed by Kon Ichikawa in 1956; it's now available on video with English subtitles under the title *The Burmese Harp*.

In 1983 Burmese author Wendy Law-Yone published *The Coffin Tree* (Alfred Knopf), a well-written, sensuous novel that follows the young female narrator on a cultural journey back and forth between the USA and Myanmar some time after the 1962 military coup. Law-Yone updated Burmese political themes and turned up the heat for her 1993 novel *Irrawaddy Tango*, in which the fictional country Daya stands in for Myanmar and a dictator's mistress turns rebel assassin. Set in colonial times, *John Dollar* (Harper & Row, 1989) is a riveting and haunting tale about another journey that a young woman makes to Myanmar. It recounts the English schoolteacher's experiences in the tightly-knit British community in Yangon as well as an exiting death-and-survival adventure on the high seas.

For a taste of Burmese verse, try *Modern*

Burmese Poetry (Thawda Press, Yangon, 1989), translated by Richard Win Pe and readily available in Yangon bookshops.

One chapter in *A Traveller's Literary Companion to South-East Asia* (In Print Publishing, Brighton, 1994) contains excerpted material from a number of works by foreign and Burmese writers on Myanmar, and includes an account of Orwell's sojourn in the country. The chapter editor, Anna Allott, also translated and edited *Inked Over, Ripped Out* (Pan American Center, New York, 1993 or Silkworm Press, Chiang Mai, 1994), which highlights the restrictions faced by Burmese writers in the 1990s and contains a number of censored and uncensored Burmese short stories from the SLORC period.

In 1995, the American director John Boorman's graphic *Beyond Rangoon*, a film dramatising the brutal suppression of the 1988 pro-democracy uprising, briefly focused international cinematic attention on Myanmar.

Travel Guides

We hope you'll find this the best guidebook available on Myanmar but there are, believe it or not, some other books to look for. Keep your eyes open for the Burmese-produced *Travellers' Guide to Burma* by Kanbawza Win, published by the YMCA in Yangon in 1977. It's quite a good little book but unfortunately it was banned; you'll be very lucky to find a copy anywhere in Myanmar.

In contrast, the readily available government productions are not worth looking at – just handfuls of statistics and drab pictures. Out of print, and unfortunately very difficult to find, is *Welcome to Burma*, published by the American Women's Association in Yangon – it has much rather out-of-the-way (and out-of-date) information about Yangon, Mandalay and around Mandalay.

Apa Productions of Singapore include *Insight Burma* in their collection of coffee-table guidebooks. Written by Wilhelm Klein with photographs by Gunter Pfannmuller, it has a superb selection of modern photographs complemented by some equally

> **Caring for your Elephant**
> One of my favourite Burmese books is *Burmese Timber Elephant* by U Toke Gale. It could be subtitled 'selection, care and use of your pet elephant' for it tells you everything you need to know and many things you don't need to know about timber elephants. Even what to do with your elephant when he's in *musth*. There's a chart showing the 90 nerve centres to which an *oozie* applies pressure to control his elephant or to get it to do things. But don't press 13, 25, 60, 61 or 63 for 'the animal will be infuriated'!
>
> **Tony Wheeler**

interesting old black-and-whites from the colonial era.

Anyone interested in quickly obtaining a broad understanding of Burmese customs and etiquette should pick up a copy of *Culture Shock! Burma* by Saw Myat Yin (Times Editions, Singapore, 1994). One of the few titles in the *Culture Shock* series to have been written by a local, this book simply and accurately explains male and female roles, business protocol, common Burmese ceremonies and festival, the naming system, how to extend and accept invitations, and even how Burmese perceive Westerners.

An arcane booklet of elephant lore you may come across moulding on a bookshelf somewhere in Myanmar is the 1922-vintage *A Short Treatise on the Management of Elephants* by A J W Milroy, deputy conservator of forests for the Raj.

Magazine Articles

National Geographic have done a number of features about Myanmar. The November 1940 issue carried an article called 'Burma Road, Back Door to China', which chronicled a trip through Hsipaw, Lashio and other places in northern Shan State to China. The February 1963 issue covered Myanmar as a whole, March 1971 was about Bagan, June 1974 had an article on the Inle Lake leg rowers, while in the June 1979 issue there was an article about the long-necked Padaung women – revealing that they're actually not long-necked at all; the heavy rings they wear around their necks actually push their shoulder blades and collar bones down, rather than extend their necks. Myanmar featured once again in July 1984, in a general article where it emerges that even *National Geographic* writers couldn't wangle more than a seven-day visa. Myanmar's latest *National Geographic* appearance occurred in the July 1995 issue, wherein the author excoriated the military regime in one of the most political articles the magazine has ever published.

Archaeology magazine ran an inspiring article on the archaeological significance of Bagan, 'The Power of Pagan', in its September/October 1992 issue.

Stan Sesser's detailed 22-page assessment of the country appeared in the 9 October 1989 issue of *New Yorker* and was reprinted in Sesser's book *Lands of Charm & Cruelty* (Vintage, 1994). Joe Cummings, co-author of this guidebook, published an article about black-market moneychanging in Myanmar called 'For a Few Kyats More' in *Outside* magazine, September 1994.

Hong Kong weeklies *Asiaweek* and *Far Eastern Economic Review* feature pieces on Myanmar at an average frequency of two or three times per month. With regard to Myanmar, *Asiaweek*'s reporting seems more factual and unbiased, though *FEER*'s coverage of guerrilla movements is more detailed.

Burmese Affairs Publications

Various groups outside the country produce newsletters and reports focusing on current political affairs and especially human rights in Myanmar. While all are very good sources of otherwise hard-to-find information, occasional articles seem designed more to inflame through anecdotal exaggeration rather than to inform through substantive reporting. Most groups will gladly send sample copies of their publications.

All Burma Students Democratic Front
  PO Box 1352, GPO Bangkok 10501, Thailand
  (☎ /fax 02-587 2400)

Amnesty International
  500 Sansome St, San Francisco, CA 94111, USA
  (☎ 415-291 9233)
Burma Action Group
  Collins Studios, Collins Yard, Islington Green, London N1 2XU, UK (☎ 0170-359 7679, fax 354 3987)
Burma Affairs Monitor
  3A Chatto Rd, London SW11 6LJ, UK
  (☎ /fax 0171-924 3146)
Burma Alert
  RR 4, Shawville, Quebec J0X 2Y0, Canada
  (☎ 819-647 5405, fax 647 5403)
Burma Debate
  PO Box 19126, Washington DC, 20036 USA (fax 301-983 5011)
The Burma Project
  45 Oak Rd, Larkspur, CA, 94939 USA
  (☎ 415-381 6905, fax 381 1326)
Burma Relief Centre
  PO Box 48, Chiang Mai University, Chiang Mai 50002, Thailand (☎ 053-21 6894)
Burma Review
  PO Box 7726, Rego Park, NY, 11374 USA
Coalition for Corporate Withdrawal from Burma
  Franklin Research & Development Corp
  711 Atlantic Ave, Boston, MA, 0211 USA
  (☎ 617-423 6655, fax 482 6179)
Human Rights Watch – Asia
  484 5th Ave, New York, NY, 10017 USA
  (☎ 212-972 8400, fax 972 0905)

Bookshops

Finding books in Myanmar is not that easy although there are a number of used-book vendors in Yangon. The best selection of English-language books, including many out-of-print editions, can be found at the Pagan Bookshop at 100 37th St, Yangon. Owner U Ba Kyi is a veritable national treasure for re-binding and reprinting rare, out-of-print literature on Myanmar. He has quite a large selection, although you may have to bargain a bit; the most expensive books are not, curiously, necessarily the rarest. Often the high prices are simply due to the books being currently out of favour – such as all books on Mahayana Buddhism! Joe found a first edition of Henry Miller's *City of Paris* here.

A little south from Pagan Bookshop along 37th St are a number of outdoor book vendors who stock English-language books on Buddhism, Burmese history, archaeology and other non-censored topics, including such oddities as the Raj-era *Civil List* (read *Burmese Days* to understand its all-consuming importance in the colonial era). Be sure to bargain – the street vendors tend to ask prices 100% or higher than bookshop prices for the same titles.

Inwa Book Store (☎ 01-71076) at 232 Sule Pagoda Rd and Sarpay Beikman Book Centre on Merchant St between 37th and 38th Sts are both government-owned bookstores with fair selections of new books as well as postcards.

Along Bogyoke Aung San St, across from the Bogyoke Aung San Market, are a number of other bookstalls, and there are some in the streets which run back from the main road. Several of these have quite a selection of Burmese books if you ask for them. You can also buy old issues of *Time, Newsweek* and foreign magazines here (and elsewhere in the street markets) for just K10 to K15 per copy.

The odd book can also be found in the bookstalls on the main approach to the Shwedagon Paya, which is a good place to look for books on Buddhism.

Away from Yangon you may spot some rare books in the pavement stalls at night or in the night market in Mandalay.

Maps

Good, up-to-date maps of Myanmar are virtually non-existent. For a country map, Nelles' *Myanmar* is sufficient for most purposes.

MTT publishes very useful and fairly detailed city maps of Yangon, Mandalay and Bagan. All are available from the main MTT office in Yangon on Sule Pagoda Rd, or from individual MTT offices in these respective cities.

MEDIA
Newspapers & Magazines
Before the 1962 Burmese military takeover, over 30 daily newspapers – including three in English, six in Chinese, five in Indian languages and 18 in Burmese – were published in the country. Today the only English-language daily newspaper readily available in the country is the *New Light of*

Myanmar – a thin, state-owned mouthpiece published by the Ministry of Information. Although much toned-down from its socialist predecessors, the *Working People's Daily* and the *Daily Guardian*, it still contains startling Orwellian propaganda of the 'War is Peace', 'Freedom is Slavery' nature, mixed in with a fair amount of non-controversial wire news.

There are now only four Burmese-language dailies, *Myanma Ahlin, Kyemon, Myodaw* and *Yadana Pon* (Mandalay only), none of which measures up to the *New Light* in total circulation numbers. According to the Ministry of Information, a second English-language daily called *The Yadanabon News* is available in Mandalay, though we've never actually seen a copy.

Fortunately the *New Light* isn't the only source of printed news in Myanmar. Recent issues of international magazines like *Time, Newsweek* and *The Economist* are often available at the Strand Hotel in Yangon. Whenever a feature about Myanmar appears in one of these magazines, however, that issue mysteriously fails to appear. Older issues are sold on the street by pavement vendors. Western newspapers are available at the British and American libraries.

Far Eastern Economic Review and *Asiaweek*, the Hong Kong-based weekly news magazines, regularly report on the latest major events within Myanmar and on the relatively calm acceptance of these events by Myanmar's neighbours.

A relatively new tourist-oriented publication called *Today*, available at the MTT office and at many hotels, contains short, noncontroversial articles on Myanmar's culture and the tourism industry, along with useful lists of embassies, current festivals, airlines and long-distance express bus services.

See the Bookshops & Libraries section in the Yangon chapter for information on where to find English and French-language publications.

Radio
All legal radio and television broadcasts are

state-controlled. Radio Myanmar (formerly Voice of Myanmar) broadcasts news in Burmese, English and eight other national languages three times a day. Only music with Burmese-language lyrics goes out on the airwaves.

Educated Burmese generally listen to shortwave BBC and VOA broadcasts for an earful of the outside world. Although these programmes appear nightly, the most popular time to listen is each Wednesday evening from 8.15 to 9 pm, when the BBC broadcasts Burmese-language special reports which contain translated Myanmar news stories extracted from the foreign press.

TV

TV Myanmar operates nightly from 6 to 10 pm via the NTSC system. Regular features include military songs and marching performances, locally produced news and weather reports and a sports presentation. Every evening a segment of 'national songs' is performed by women dressed in ethnic costumes; when the songs are over, the national flag is always tellingly hoisted by the singer wearing Bamar (Burman) dress.

National news in English is telecast on TV Myanmar nightly around 9.15 pm. Whenever a televised government speech or meeting is announced (which pre-empts all other programming for the evening), the local video rental shops are emptied as virtually no one watches these long, drawn-out events.

One of the most dramatic changes to occur in Myanmar's media since the advent of television is the recent arrival of satellite TV services. Over 4000 satellite dishes have appeared in Yangon alone over the last two years. The main signal received is the 'southern footprint' of AsiaSat 1 & 2, same as for Thailand and Indochina, which beam in STAR (Satellite Television Asia Region) channels such as BBC World Service, STAR Movies, the Chinese Channel, and Channel V (Asia's MTV clone). Myanmar also receives Doordarshan India (India Television), India's Hindi/Urdu Zee TV and Yunnan TV via satellite. Many of the newer hotels now provide satellite TV although for some reason it seems they're never able to provide a choice of more than two or three satellite channels at a time.

Every Friday at 12.20 and 4.30 pm, the American Center at 14 Tawwin St, behind the Ministry of Foreign Affairs in Yangon, packs them in for the satellite broadcast of the ABC World News Weekly Highlights. CBS News and the MacNeil/Lehrer Newshour are shown Monday throughout Friday at 10.30 and 11 am respectively. On occasions when the news is delayed (perhaps censored?), other programmes will be shown. This can be an interesting place to meet outward-looking Burmese, not all of whom are necessarily pro-American.

FILM & PHOTOGRAPHY

Myanmar is a very photogenic place so bring lots of film with you. Colour print films – mostly Kodak, Fuji and Konica brands – are readily and inexpensively available in shops in Yangon and Mandalay. Prices are around K200 for a 36-exposure roll of Fujicolor 100; Kodak costs a bit more.

Slide films are harder to find but some shops stock them. Generally the only types available are Kodak Ektachrome Elite 100 and Fujichrome Sensia 100, both of which sell for around K800 per roll. Pro grade films like Velvia and Provia are not distributed in Myanmar according to Fuji's head office, but they are occasionally available on the black market for K800 to K1000. Black-and-white print (or slide) films are very hard to come by. If you're shooting in this medium, be sure to bring your own supply.

Outside Yangon and Mandalay, film is scarce. Most film you might see on sale in the hinterlands will have come from visitors who sold it while in the country – with no guarantee on age or quality.

Photographic processing services are available but quality is erratic. You'll do best to wait until you've returned home – or have your film processed in Bangkok, where decent colour labs are plentiful.

The usual tropical rules apply to taking

photographs here. Allow for the intensity of the sun after the early morning and before the late evening. Try to keep your film as cool as possible, particularly after it has been exposed. Beware of dust, particularly at the height of the dry season when central Myanmar becomes very dusty indeed. And don't drop your camera in the Ayeyarwady!

A benefit of Myanmar's low tourist flow is that the Burmese are not over-exposed to camera-clicking visitors and are not at all unhappy about being photographed. Even monks like to be photographed although, of course, it's rude to ask them to pose for you and it's always polite to ask anybody's permission before taking photographs.

It is forbidden by law to photograph any military facility or any structure considered strategic – this includes bridges and railway stations – and any uniformed person.

If you happen to see a public demonstration taking place, be discreet about taking photographs as journalists are strictly unwelcome in Myanmar.

HEALTH

Travel health depends on your pre-departure preparations, your day-to-day health care while travelling and how you handle any medical problem or emergency that does develop. While the list of potential dangers can seem quite frightening, with a little luck, some basic precautions and adequate information few travellers experience more than upset stomachs.

Travel Health Guides

There are a number of books on travel health:

Staying Healthy in Asia, Africa & Latin America, Dr Dirk Schroeder, Moon Publications, 1994. Probably the best all-round guide to carry, as it's compact but very detailed and well organised.
Travellers' Health, Dr Richard Dawood, Oxford University Press, 1995. Comprehensive, easy to read, authoritative and also highly recommended, although it's rather large to lug around.
Where There is No Doctor, David Werner, Hesperian Foundation, 1994. A very detailed guide intended for someone, like a Peace Corps worker, going to work in an undeveloped country, rather than for the average traveller.

Travel with Children, Maureen Wheeler, Lonely Planet Publications, 1995. Includes basic advice on travel health for younger children.

Pre-Departure Preparations
Health Insurance A travel insurance policy to cover theft, loss and medical problems is a wise idea. There are a wide variety of policies and your travel agent will have recommendations. The international travel policies handled by STA Travel and student travel organisations are usually good value. Some policies offer lower and higher medical expenses options but the higher ones are chiefly for countries like the USA which have extremely high medical costs.

Medical Kit A small, straightforward medical kit is a wise thing to carry. A possible kit list includes:

* Aspirin or Panadol – for pain or fever.
* Antihistamine (such as Benadryl) – useful as a decongestant for colds, allergies, to ease the itch from insect bites or stings or to help prevent motion sickness. Antihistamines may cause sedation and interact with alchohol so care should be taken when using them.
* Antibiotics – useful if you're travelling well off the beaten track, but they must be prescribed and you should carry the prescription with you. Some individuals are allergic to commonly prescribed antibiotics such as penicillin or sulpha drugs.
* Bismuth preparation (Pepto-Bismol), Imodium or Lomotil – for stomach upsets and diarrhoea.
* Rehydration mixture – for treatment of severe diarrhoea; particularly important if travelling with children.
* Antiseptic such as Betadine, which comes as impregnated swabs or ointment, and an antibiotic powder or similar 'dry' spray – for cuts and grazes.
* Calamine lotion – to ease irritation from bites or stings.
* Bandages and Band-Aids – for minor injuries.
* Scissors, tweezers and a thermometer (note that mercury thermometers are prohibited by airlines).
* Insect repellent, sunscreen, suntan lotion, chap stick and water purification tablets.
* A couple of syringes, in case you need injections in destinations with medical hygiene problems. Ask you doctor for a note explaining why they have been prescribed.

Ideally antibiotics should be administered only under medical supervision and should never be taken indiscriminately. Overuse of antibiotics can weaken your body's ability to deal with infections naturally and can reduce the drug's efficacy on a future occasion. Take only the recommended dose at the prescribed intervals and continue using the antibiotic for the prescribed period, even if the illness seems to be cured earlier. Antibiotics are quite specific to the infections they can treat, so stop immediately if there are any serious reactions.

Health Preparations Make sure you're healthy before you start travelling.

If you require a particular medication take an adequate supply, as it may not be available locally. Take the prescription, or better still, part of the packaging showing the genuine rather than the brand name (which may not be locally available), as it will make getting replacements easier. Also visit your dentist, and if you wear glasses, take a spare pair and your prescription.

Immunisations There are currently no immunisation requirements for entry into Myanmar except for yellow fever if you come from an infected zone. The 'health check' at the airport means only a cursory look at your passport to see if you've come to Myanmar by way of Africa, in which case they may ask to see your immunisation certificate.

Plan ahead for getting your vaccinations; some of them require an initial shot followed by a booster, while some vaccinations should not be given together. Most travellers from Western countries will have been immunised against various diseases during childhood but your doctor may still recommend booster shots against tetanus, measles or polio. The period of protection offered by vaccinations differs widely and some are contraindicated if you are pregnant.

Basic Rules

Care in what you eat and drink is the most important health rule; stomach upsets are the most likely travel health problem but the majority of these upsets are minor. Don't

become paranoid, trying the local food is part of the experience of travel after all.

Water The number one rule is *don't drink the water* and that includes ice. If you don't know for certain that the water is safe always assume the worst.

Take care with fruit juice, particularly if water may have been added. Milk should be treated with suspicion, as it is often unpasterised. Boiled milk is fine if it is kept hygienically and yoghurt is always good. Tea or coffee should also be OK, since the water should have been boiled.

Water Purification The simplest way of purifying water is to boil it thoroughly. Technically this means boiling for 10 minutes, which rarely happens. Purified, bottled water is widely available from hotels, restaurants, markets and shops. Most restaurants provide weak Chinese tea in unlimited quantities, often as a matter of course.

Food Salads and fruit should be washed with purified water or peeled where possible. Thoroughly cooked food is safest but not if it has been left to cool or if it has been reheated. Take great care with shellfish or fish and avoid undercooked meat. If a place looks clean and well run and if the vendor also looks clean and healthy, then the food is probably safe. In general, places that are packed with travellers or locals will be fine, while empty restaurants are questionable.

Everyday Health A normal body temperature is 98.6°F or 37°C; more than 2°C higher is a 'high' fever. A normal adult pulse rate is 60 to 80 per minute (children 80 to 100, babies 100 to 140). You should know how to take a temperature and a pulse rate. As a general rule the pulse increases about 20 beats per minute for each °C rise in fever.

Many health problems can be avoided by taking care of yourself. Wash your hands frequently – it's quite easy to contaminate your own food. Clean your teeth with purified water rather than straight from the tap.

Avoid climatic extremes: keep out of the sun when it's hot, dress warmly when it's cold.

Climate & Geographical Considerations

Sunburn In the tropics, the desert or at high altitude you can get sunburnt surprisingly quickly, even through cloud. Use a sunscreen and take extra care to cover areas which don't normally see sun – eg your feet. A hat provides added protection, and you should also use zinc cream or some other barrier cream for your nose and lips. Calamine lotion is good for mild sunburn.

Prickly Heat Prickly heat is an itchy rash caused by excessive perspiration trapped under the skin. It usually strikes people who have just arrived in a hot climate and whose pores have not yet opened sufficiently to cope with greater sweating. Keeping cool but bathing often, using a mild talcum powder or even resorting to air-conditioning may help until you acclimatise.

Heat Exhaustion Dehydration or salt deficiency can cause heat exhaustion. Take time to acclimatise to high temperatures and make sure you get sufficient liquids. Wear loose clothing and a broad-brimmed hat. Do not do anything too physically demanding.

Salt deficiency is characterised by fatigue, lethargy, headaches, giddiness and muscle cramps and in this case salt tablets may help. Vomiting or diarrhoea can deplete your liquid and salt levels. Anhydrotic heat exhaustion, caused by an inability to sweat, is quite rare. Unlike the other forms of heat exhaustion it is likely to strike people who have been in a hot climate for some time, rather than newcomers.

Heat Stroke This serious, sometimes fatal, condition can occur if the body's heat-regulating mechanism breaks down and the body temperature rises to dangerous levels. Long, continuous periods of exposure to high temperatures can leave you vulnerable to heat stroke. You should avoid excessive alcohol or strenuous activity when you first arrive in a hot climate.

The symptoms are feeling unwell, not sweating very much or at all and a high body temperature (39°C to 41°C). Where sweating has ceased the skin becomes flushed and red. Severe, throbbing headaches and lack of coordination will also occur, and the sufferer may be confused or aggressive. Eventually the victim will become delirious or convulse. Hospitalisation is essential, but meanwhile get victims out of the sun, remove their clothing, cover them with a wet sheet or towel and then fan continually.

Fungal Infections Hot-weather fungal infections are most likely to occur on the scalp, between the toes or fingers (athlete's foot), in the groin (jock itch or crotch rot) and on the body (ringworm). You get ringworm (which is a fungal infection, not a worm) from infected animals or by walking on damp areas, like shower floors.

To prevent fungal infections wear loose, comfortable clothes, avoid artificial fibres, wash frequently and dry carefully. If you do get an infection, wash the infected area daily with a disinfectant or medicated soap and water, and rinse and dry well. Apply an antifungal powder like the widely available Tinaderm. Try to expose the infected area to air or sunlight as much as possible and wash all towels and underwear in hot water as well as changing them often.

Diseases of Poor Sanitation

Diarrhoea A change of water, food or climate can all cause the runs; diarrhoea caused by contaminated food or water is more serious. Despite all your precautions you may still have a bout of mild travellers' diarrhoea but a few rushed toilet trips with no other symptoms is not indicative of a serious problem. Moderate diarrhoea, involving half-a-dozen loose movements in a day, is more of a nuisance. Dehydration is the main danger with any diarrhoea, particularly for children, so fluid replenishment is the number one treatment. Weak black tea with a little sugar, soda water, or soft drinks allowed to go flat and diluted 50% with water are all good. With severe diarrhoea a rehydrating solution is necessary to replace minerals and salts. You should stick to a bland diet as you recover.

Lomotil or Imodium can be used to bring relief from the symptoms, although they do not actually cure the problem. Only use these drugs if absolutely necessary – that is, if you *must* travel. For children Imodium is preferable, but do not use these drugs if the patient has a high fever or is severely dehydrated.

Antibiotics can be very useful in treating severe diarrhoea especially if it is accompanied by nausea, vomiting, stomach cramps or mild fever. Ampicillin, a broad-spectrum penicillin, is usually recommended. Two capsules of 250 mg each taken four times a day is the recommended dose for an adult. Children aged between eight and 12 years should have half the adult dose; younger children should have half a capsule four times a day. Note that if the patient is allergic to penicillin, ampicillin should not be administered.

Giardiasis The *giardia* intestinal parasite is present in contaminated water. The symptoms are stomach cramps, nausea, a bloated stomach, watery, foul-smelling diarrhoea and frequent gas. Giardiasis can appear several weeks after you have been exposed to the parasite. The symptoms may disappear for a few days and then return; this can go on for several weeks. Metronidazole (known as Flagyl) is the recommended drug, but it should only be taken under medical supervision. Antibiotics are of no use.

Dysentery This serious illness is caused by contaminated food or water and is characterised by severe diarrhoea, often with blood or mucus in the stool. There are two kinds of dysentery. Bacillary dysentery is characterised by a high fever and rapid onset; headache, vomiting and stomach pains are also symptoms. It generally does not last longer than a week, but it is highly contagious.

Amoebic dysentery is often more gradual in the onset of symptoms, with cramping abdominal pain and vomiting less likely; fever may not be present. It is not a self-limiting disease: it will persist until treated and can recur and cause long-term health problems.

A stool test is necessary to diagnose which kind of dysentery you have, so you should seek medical help urgently. In case of an emergency the drugs norfloxacin or ciprofloxacin can be used as presumptive treatment for bacillary dysentery, and metronidazole (Flagyl) for amoebic dysentery.

For bacillary dysentery, norfloxacin 400 mg twice daily for seven days or ciprofloxacin 500 mg twice daily for seven days are the recommended dosages. If you're unable to find either of these drugs then a useful alternative is co-trimoxazole 160/800 mg (Bactrim, Septrin, Resprim) twice daily for seven days. This is a sulpha drug and must not be used by people with a known sulpha allergy. In the case of children the drug co-trimoxazole is a reasonable first-line treatment.

For amoebic dysentery, the recommended adult dosage of metronidazole (Flagyl) is one 750-mg to 800-mg capsule three times daily for five days. Children aged between eight and 12 years should have half the adult dose; the dosage for younger children is one-third the adult dose.

An alternative to Flagyl is Fasigyn, taken as a two gram daily dose for three days. Alcohol must be avoided during treatment and for 48 hours afterwards.

Hepatitis Hepatitis is a general term for inflammation of the liver. There are many causes of this condition: drugs, alcohol and infections are but a few.

The discovery of new strains has led to a virtual alphabet soup, with hepatitis A, B, C, D, E and a rumoured G. These letters identify specific agents that cause viral hepatitis. Viral hepatitis is an infection of the liver, which can lead to jaundice (yellow skin), fever, lethargy and digestive problems. It can have no symptoms at all, with the infected person not knowing that they have the disease. Travellers shouldn't be too paranoid about this apparent proliferation of hepatitis strains; hep C, D, E and G are fairly rare (so far) and following the same precautions as for A and B should be all that's necessary to avoid them.

Viral hepatitis can be divided into two groups on the basis of how it is spread. The first route of transmission is via contaminated food and water (leading to hepatitis A and E) and the second route is via blood and bodily fluids (resulting in hepatitis B, C and D).

Hepatitis A This is a very common disease in most countries, especially those with poor standards of sanitation. Most people in developing countries are infected as children; they often don't develop symptoms, but do develop life-long immunity. The disease poses a real threat to the traveller, as people are unlikely to have been exposed to hepatitis A in developed countries.

The symptoms are fever, chills, headache, fatigue, feelings of weakness and aches and pains, followed by loss of appetite, nausea, vomiting, abdominal pain, dark urine, light-coloured faeces, jaundiced skin and the whites of the eyes may turn yellow. In some cases you may feel unwell, tired, have no appetite, experience aches and pains and be jaundiced. You should seek medical advice, but in general there is not much you can do apart from resting, drinking lots of fluids, eating lightly and avoiding fatty foods. People who have had hepatitis must forego alcohol for six months after the illness, as hepatitis attacks the liver and it needs that amount of time to recover.

The routes of transmission are via contaminated water, shellfish contaminated by sewerage, or foodstuffs sold by food handlers with poor standards of hygiene.

Taking care with what you eat and drink can go a long way towards preventing this disease. But this is a very infectious virus, so if there is any risk of exposure, additional cover is highly recommended. This cover comes in two forms: Gammaglobulin and Havrix. Gammaglobulin is an injection where you are given the antibodies for hepatitis A, which provide immunity for a limited time. Havrix is a vaccine, where you develop your own antibodies, which gives lasting immunity.

Hepatitis E This is a very recently discovered virus, of which little is yet known. It appears to be rather common in developing countries, generally causing mild hepatitis, although it can be very serious in pregnant women.

Care with water supplies is the only current prevention, as there are no specific vaccines for this type of hepatitis. At present it doesn't appear to be too great a risk for travellers.

Hepatitis B This is also a very common disease, with almost 300 million chronic carriers in the world. Hepatitis B, which used to be called serum hepatitis, is spread through contact with infected blood, blood products or bodily fluids, for example through sexual contact, unsterilised needles and blood transfusions. Other risk situations include having a shave or tattoo in a local shop, or having your ears pierced. The symptoms of type B are much the same as type A except that they are more severe and may lead to irreparable liver damage or even liver cancer. Although there is no treatment for hepatitis B, a cheap and effective vaccine is available; the only problem is that for long-lasting cover you need a six-month course. The immunisation schedule requires two injections at least a month apart followed by a third dose five months after the second. Persons who should receive a hepatitis B vaccination include anyone who anticipates contact with blood or other bodily secretions, either as a health-care worker or through sexual contact with the local population, particularly those who intend to stay in the country for a long period of time.

Hepatitis C This is another recently defined virus. It is a concern because it seems to lead to liver disease more rapidly than hepatitis B.

The virus is spread by contact with blood – usually via contaminated transfusions or shared needles. Avoiding these is the only means of prevention, as there is no available vaccine.

Hepatitis D Often referred to as the 'Delta' virus, this infection only occurs in chronic carriers of hepatitis B. It is transmitted by blood and bodily fluids. Again there is no vaccine for this virus, so avoidance is the best prevention. The risk to travellers is certainly limited.

Typhoid Typhoid fever is another gut infection that travels the faecal-oral route – ie contaminated water and food are responsible. Vaccination against typhoid is not totally effective and it is one of the most dangerous infections, so medical help must be sought.

In its early stages typhoid resembles many other illnesses: sufferers may feel like they have a bad cold or flu on the way, as early symptoms are a headache, a sore throat, and a fever which rises a little each day until it is around 40°C or more. The victim's pulse is often slow relative to the degree of fever present and gets slower as the fever rises – unlike a normal fever where the pulse increases. There may also be vomiting, diarrhoea or constipation.

In the second week the high fever and slow pulse continue and a few pink spots may appear on the body; trembling, delirium, weakness, weight loss and dehydration are other symptoms. If there are no further complications, the fever and other symptoms will slowly diminish during the third week. However you must get medical help before this because pneumonia (acute infection of the lungs) or peritonitis (perforated bowel) are common complications, and because typhoid is very infectious.

The fever should be treated by keeping the victim cool and dehydration should also be watched for.

The drug of choice is ciprofloxacin at a dose of one gram daily for 14 days. It is quite expensive and may not be available. The alternative, chloramphenicol, has been the mainstay of treatment for many years. In many countries it is still the recommended antibiotic but there are fewer side affects with Ampicillin. The adult dosage is two 250-mg capsules, four times a day. Children aged between eight and 12 years should have half the adult dose; younger children should have one-third the adult dose. People who are allergic to penicillin should not be given Ampicillin.

Worms These parasites are most common in rural, tropical areas and a stool test when you return home is not a bad idea. They can be present on unwashed vegetables or in undercooked meat and you can pick them up through your skin by walking in bare feet. Infestations may not show up for some time, and although they are generally not serious, if left untreated they can cause severe health problems. A stool test is necessary to pinpoint the problem and medication is often available over the counter.

Diseases Spread by People & Animals

Tetanus This potentially fatal disease is found in undeveloped tropical areas. It is difficult to treat but is preventable with immunisation. Tetanus occurs when a wound becomes infected by a germ which lives in the faeces of animals or people, so clean all cuts, punctures or animal bites. Tetanus is also known as lockjaw, and the first symptom may be discomfort in swallowing, or stiffening of the jaw and neck; this is followed by painful convulsions of the jaw and whole body.

Rabies Rabies is found in many countries and is caused by a bite or scratch by an infected animal. Dogs are noted carriers as are monkeys and cats. Any bite, scratch or even lick from a warm-blooded, furry animal should be cleaned immediately and thoroughly. Scrub with soap and running water, and then clean with an alcohol solution. If there is any possibility that the animal is infected medical help should be sought immediately. Even if the animal is not rabid, all bites should be treated seriously as they can become infected or can result in tetanus. A rabies vaccination is now available and should be considered if you are in a high-risk category – eg if you intend to explore caves (bat bites can be dangerous) or work with animals.

Sexually Transmitted Diseases Sexual contact with an infected sexual partner spreads these diseases. While abstinence is the only 100% preventative, using condoms is also effective. Gonorrhoea and syphilis are the most common of these diseases; sores, blisters or rashes around the genitals, discharges or pain when urinating are common symptoms. Symptoms may be less marked or not observed at all in women. Syphilis symptoms eventually disappear completely but the disease continues and can cause severe problems in later years. The treatment of gonorrhoea and syphilis is by antibiotics.

There are numerous other sexually transmitted diseases, for most of which effective treatment is available. However, there is no cure for herpes and there is also currently no cure for AIDS.

HIV/AIDS HIV, the Human Immunodeficiency Virus, may develop into AIDS, Acquired Immune Deficiency Syndrome. HIV is a major problem in many countries. Any exposure to blood, blood products or bodily fluids may put the individual at risk. In many developing countries transmission is predominantly through heterosexual sexual activity. This is quite different from industrialised countries where transmission is mostly through contact between homosexual or bisexual males, or via contaminated needles shared by IV drug users. Apart from abstinence, the most effective preventative is always to practise safe sex using condoms. It is impossible to detect the HIV-positive status of an otherwise healthy-looking person without a blood test.

HIV/AIDS can also be spread through infected blood transfusions; most developing countries cannot afford to screen blood for transfusions. It can also be spread by dirty needles – vaccinations, acupuncture, tattooing and ear or nose piercing can potentially be as dangerous as intravenous drug use if the equipment is not clean. If you do need an injection, ask to see the syringe unwrapped in front of you, or better still, take a needle and syringe pack with you overseas – it is a cheap insurance package against infection with HIV.

Although by the end of 1993 only 189 cases were officially detected, estimates of HIV infections in Myanmar range from 200,000 to 300,000, which makes it the third-worst affected nation in Asia after India and Thailand. Rates among intravenous drug users are reportedly the highest in the world: for example, in Mandalay 84% of drug users tested were HIV-positive; in Yangon the rate for IV drug users was 74%; and in Myitkyina it measured over 90%. The closer you get to the Chinese border – where neighbouring districts record the highest HIV infection rates in Asia – the more prevalent the virus becomes.

HIV is also making the rounds in Myanmar's thriving prostitution underground. Prostitution exists in two parallel streams: the nearby invisible but larger Burmese trade in which Burman, Karen, Shan, Yunnanese and Kachin women service Burmese men on the 'guest house' circuit, and the more transparent but rather recent trade developed to service visiting Chinese businessmen from Hong Kong, Taiwan and Singapore through luxury hotels and karaoke lounges. So far no figures concerning the infection rates among Burmese prostitutes are available but it is likely to be quite high – probably higher than in Thailand where condom use is more prevalent.

Because of HIV's looming spectre over Myanmar, do not under any circumstances share needles or engage in unprotected sexual intercourse with Burmese nationals while in the country.

Insect-Borne Diseases
Malaria This serious disease is spread by mosquito bites. Myanmar is an endemic area and it is extremely important to take malarial prophylactics. Symptoms include headaches, fever, chills and sweating, which may subside and recur. Without treatment malaria can develop more serious, potentially fatal effects. Antimalarial drugs do not prevent

you from being infected but kill the parasites during a stage in their development.

There are a number of different types of malaria. The one of most concern is falciparum malaria. This is responsible for the very serious cerebral malaria. Falciparum is the predominant form in many malaria-prone areas of the world, including South-East Asia, Africa and Papua New Guinea. Contrary to popular belief cerebral malaria is not a new strain.

The problem in recent years has been the emergence of increasing resistance to commonly used antimalarials like chloroquine, maloprim and proguanil. Newer drugs such as mefloquine (Lariam) and doxycycline (Vibramycin, Doryx) are often recommended for countries like Myanmar and other chloroquine and multidrug-resistant destinations. Expert advice should be sought, as there are many factors to consider when deciding on the type of antimalarial medication, including the area to be visited, the risk of exposure to malaria-carrying mosquitoes, your current medical condition, and your age and pregnancy status. It is also important to discuss the side-effect profile of the medication, so you can work out some level of risk versus benefit ratio. It is also very important to be sure of the correct dosage of the medication prescribed to you. Some people have inadvertently taken weekly medication (chloroquine) on a daily basis, with disastrous effects. While discussing dosages for prevention of malaria, it is often advisable to include the dosages required for treatment, especially if your trip is through a high-risk area that would isolate you from medical care.

The main messages are:

1. Primary prevention must always be in the form of mosquito-avoidance measures. The mosquitoes that transmit malaria bite from dusk to dawn and during this period travellers are advised to:
   • wear light coloured clothing
   • wear long pants and long sleeved shirts
   • use mosquito repellents containing the compound DEET on exposed areas (overuse of DEET may be harmful, especially to children, but its use is considered preferable to being bitten by disease-transmitting mosquitoes)
   • avoid highly scented perfumes or aftershave
   • use a mosquito net – it may be worth taking your own
2. While no antimalarial is 100% effective, taking the most appropriate drug significantly reduces the risk of contracting the disease.
3. No one should ever die from malaria. It can be diagnosed by a simple blood test. Symptoms range from fever, chills and sweating, headache and abdominal pains to a vague feeling of ill-health, so seek examination immediately if there is any suggestion of malaria.

Contrary to popular belief, once a traveller contracts malaria he/she does not have it for life. One of the parasites may lie dormant in the liver but this can also be eradicated using a specific medication. Malaria is curable, as long as the traveller seeks medical help when symptoms occur.

Dengue Fever There is no prophylactic available for this mosquito-spread disease; the main preventative measure is to avoid mosquito bites. A sudden onset of fever, headaches and severe joint and muscle pains are the first signs before a rash starts on the trunk of the body and spreads to the limbs and face. After a further few days, the fever will subside and recovery will begin. Serious complications are not common but full recovery can take up to a month or more.

Cuts, Bites & Stings
Cuts & Scratches Skin punctures can easily become infected in hot climates and may be difficult to heal. Treat any cut with an antiseptic such as Betadine. Where possible avoid bandages and Band-aids, which can keep wounds wet.

Bedbugs & Lice Bedbugs live in various places, but particularly in dirty mattresses and bedding. Spots of blood on bedclothes or on the wall around the bed can be read as a suggestion to find another hotel. Bedbugs leave itchy bites in neat rows. Calamine lotion may help.

All lice cause itching and discomfort. They make themselves at home in your hair (head lice), your clothing (body lice) or in your pubic hair (crabs). You catch lice through direct contact with infected people or by sharing combs, clothing and the like. Powder or shampoo treatment will kill the lice, and infected clothing should then be washed in very hot water.

Snakes To minimise your chances of being bitten always wear boots, socks and long trousers when walking through undergrowth where snakes may be present. Don't put your hands into holes and crevices, and be careful when collecting firewood.

Snake bites do not cause instantaneous death and antivenenes are usually available. Keep the victim calm and still, wrap the bitten limb tightly, as you would for a sprained ankle, and then attach a splint to immobilise it. Then seek medical help, if possible with the dead snake for identification. Don't attempt to catch the snake if there is even a remote possibility of being bitten again. Tourniquets and sucking out the poison are now comprehensively discredited.

Women's Health
Gynaecological Problems Poor diet, lowered resistance due to the use of antibiotics for stomach upsets and even contraceptive pills can lead to vaginal infections when travelling in hot climates. Keeping the genital area clean, and wearing skirts or loose-fitting trousers and cotton underwear will help to prevent infections.

Yeast infections, characterised by a rash, itch and discharge, can be treated with a vinegar or lemon-juice douche, or with yoghurt. Nystatin suppositories are the usual medical prescription. Trichomoniasis is a more serious infection; symptoms are a discharge and a burning sensation when urinating. Male sexual partners must also be treated, and if a vinegar-water douche is not effective medical attention should be sought. Metronidazole (Flagyl) is the prescribed drug.

Pregnancy Most miscarriages occur during the first three months of pregnancy, so this is the most risky time to travel as far as your own health is concerned. Miscarriage is not uncommon, and can occasionally lead to severe bleeding. The last three months should also be spent within reasonable distance of good medical care. A baby born as early as 24 weeks stands a chance of survival, but only in a good modern hospital. Pregnant women should avoid all unnecessary medication, but vaccinations and malarial prophylactics should still be taken where possible. Additional care should be taken to prevent illness and particular attention should be paid to diet and nutrition. Alcohol and nicotine, for example, should be avoided.

Women travellers often find that their periods become irregular or even cease while they're on the road. Remember that a missed period in these circumstances doesn't necessarily indicate pregnancy. There are clinics in Myanmar where you can seek advice and have a urine test to determine whether or not you are pregnant.

Medical Facilities
It's very important that you watch out for your health and general physical condition as medical facilities in Myanmar are quite primitive by even other Asian standards. The country's best treatment facility is the Diplomatic Hospital (☎ 01-50149), also known as Kandawgyi Clinic, on Natmauk Rd near Kandawgyi Lake in Yangon.

Upcountry, foreigners are usually taken to military hospitals for medical emergencies that won't wait till Yangon. There are also a number of private clinics in Yangon, Mandalay and Pathein with passable standards. During the last Lonely Planet update Joe went to a private clinic in Mandalay for a tetanus injection after stepping on a rusty 20-cm nail and found the service quite satisfactory.

Even better for serious conditions – if you can afford the time and air fare – is to fly to Bangkok or Singapore, where excellent medical care is available.

WOMEN TRAVELLERS
In most respects Burmese women enjoy legal rights equal to those of Burmese men;

for example, they own property and aren't barred from any profession. Unlike in the West, females do not traditionally change any portion of their names upon marriage; in the event of divorce, they are legally due half of all property accumulated during the marriage. Inheritance rights are also equally shared. Female children are educated alongside male children and, by university age, women tend to outnumber men in university and college enrolment. Most professions grant women a maternity leave of six weeks before birth and one or two months afterwards.

Religion is one arena in which women perpetually take a back seat. A small number of Buddhist shrines, for example Mandalay's Mahamuni Paya, have small areas around the main holy image which are off limits to women. Many Burmese – women as well as men – believe a female birth indicates less religious merit than a male birth, and that it is easier for males to attain nibbana. A small but devoted minority of men and women refute this view, pointing out that the actual *suttas* or sayings of the Buddha do not support this assumption.

Just as boys between the ages of 5 and 15 usually undergo a pre-puberty initiation as temporary novice monks, girls around the

---

Burmese Beauty Secrets

Diet The typical Burmese dietary intake includes plenty of fibre via pulses, vegetables, fruit, and grains (rice and noodles). Fish and chicken are preferred to red meat, and vegetable oils (sesamum, sunflower and peanut) are used instead of animal fat. Few dairy products are eaten. Very weak green tea is drunk in large quantities and clear soups are taken with main meals.

Even in the cities, women rarely touch alcohol or cigarettes and the huge cheroots puffed by country women are very mild.

Climate Except for the central 'dry zone', the country's normally high humidity is kind to the skin. There are no frosts or drying winds and little pollution. Constant sweat keeps the pores active and flushed.

Personal Hygiene All-over washing with cold water two or three times a day – using unrefined, unscented soap – is a routine for all. It is believed that warm water is bad for the skin. Herbal shampoo is made by boiling the bark of a small shrub called *tayaw (Grewia)* with the pods of soap acacia *(Acacia concinna)*. The resultant brown liquid, which is widely sold in the markets, lathers quite well and leaves the hair soft and glossy. Hair is oiled with coconut oil and adorned with combs of woods, ivory and tortoiseshell.

Cosmetics The soft outer bark of the *thanakha* tree *(Linoria acidissima)*, which grows in central Burma, is ground on a whetstone with a little water and used as a paste on the face. Alternately, it can be bought prepared as a liquid cosmetic or in powder form. The paste is smeared on the face and body; some women cover their whole bodies with it at night. Thanakha is mildly astringent, and used as a combination skin conditioner, sunscreen, perfume and cosmetic. Older women put cold cream and light oil preparations on their faces before applying thanakha.

Traditionally, eyebrows and lashes were blackened with a mixture of oil and soot, but nowadays 'Western' cosmetics – some made domestically, some imported – are readily available. Burmese women are generally very brand-conscious and genuine Revlon lipsticks are a treasured gift.

Physique Most Burmese have small bones, high cheekbones in an oval face and slim bodies, although plumpness is frequently considered a sign of health and beauty. The expression *'Wa-laiq-ta'* ('How fat you're looking!') is considered a compliment. Although they are not tall, the *longyi* makes them appear so.

From early childhood, boys and girls carry water-pots or trays of food on their heads, which seems to result in fewer back problems and beautiful carriage. The longyi restricts the stride so the people move slowly and gracefully. Burmese women believe that squatting rather than standing helps prevent varicose veins.

Vicky Bowman

same age participate in an initiatory ear-piercing ceremony (often called 'ear-boring' in Burmese English). Some also become temporary nuns at this same age. For details on clerical differences between Buddhist monks and nuns, see the Religion section in the Facts about the Country chapter.

Saw Myat Yin, insightful author of *Culture Shock! Burma*, expresses a viewpoint common among the majority of Burmese women, who see their role as equal but 'supportive and complementary...rather than in competition' and that 'if they accept a role a step behind their menfolk they do so freely and willingly'. Though some Westerners may find this difficult to believe, this represents the most commonly expressed perception in Myanmar. Even Aung San Suu Kyi, Myanmar's torchbearer of democracy, has written:

Although theoretically men are considered nobler because only a man can become a Buddha, Burmese women have never really had an inferior status. They have always had equal rights of inheritance and led active, independent lives. Secure in the knowledge of her own worth, the Burmese woman does not mind giving men the kind of respectful treatment that makes them so happy!

As in most Buddhist countries, foreign women travelling in Myanmar are rarely hassled on the road as they might be in, for example, Malaysia or Indonesia.

DANGERS & ANNOYANCES

Tales of insurgents, terrorists, forbidden areas and so on make Myanmar sound as if it is a rather unsafe country to visit; the truth is actually very different. Myanmar's insurgency problem is a tricky one; the insurgents and guerrillas do not have enough support, equipment or energy to be more than a major irritation. They certainly have little hope of unseating the government. On the other hand the government is also sadly short of popular support and enthusiasm, so they have little hope of totally overcoming their armed opponents. The result is a long-running stalemate.

So long as you do not venture into those 'brown' or 'black' no-go areas (a possibility which the Burmese government is firmly determined not to let happen), you're very unlikely to run into any difficulty. Apart from occasionally blowing up the Yangon-Mandalay railway line, the insurgents seem happy enough to stick to their own territory and leave the government's territory to the government. See the Insurgency aside in the Population section of the previous chapter.

Added to this, one has the overwhelming impression that the Burmese would simply be too polite and well mannered to think of inconveniencing a foreigner! Of course in the government-controlled areas (the places where you are permitted to go), the possibility of being mugged, robbed, held up or otherwise enjoying any of those other unpleasant, everyday Western events is similarly remote, although there has been one isolated case of a woman getting robbed in Bagan. Basically Myanmar is a very friendly and safe country, though we do recommend that you keep a close eye on your valuables, particularly during overnight train trips. The shortage of luxury goods can make some of your possessions just a little bit too tempting at times.

You must also be cautious about talking Burmese politics with the locals, not for your safety but for theirs. The people who have the best chance of filling you in on the latest events are those Burmese who deal with foreign tourists on a regular basis – trishaw drivers, vendors, even the occasional candid MTT guide. Because of their occupations, these people can talk at length with foreigners without arousing suspicion; when not in the presence of other Burmese they can be surprisingly forthcoming with their views. The average Burmese on the street, however, would be very circumspect about conversing openly with a foreigner, especially about politics.

Night-time road travel is not recommended due to the frightful condition of most roads and public vehicles. In some

Top: The fabled *nats* of Mt Popa
Middle: Parasol-maker at work, Pathein
Bottom: A marionette performance, Mandalay

Traditional dancers and musicians performing a *pwe*

areas there are *dacoits* (highwaymen) who hold up vehicles at night; this is most common in the Kayin and Mon states.

See the previous Health section for cautions on personal health and conditioning.

HIGHLIGHTS

Now that visitors may stay nearly a full month (up to two months with extensions), and new areas have been opened up, closer to the full range of Myanmar's plentiful attractions are accessible. Still, because of the hassles with road travel and permits it usually pays to be under-ambitious with one's travel plans; don't try to see too much in too short an interval or your travels will quickly become a chore. Old Burma hands have found that more time to travel in Myanmar means more opportunity to become fed up and frustrated if you try to blaze through the country at the same pace as one used to during the one-week and two-week visa eras.

Virtually everyone begins their journey in Yangon. Under the old 'see-everything-in-two-weeks' system, travellers rushed immediately to Mandalay by night express train, leaving perhaps just a day at the end to see the capital. Nowadays there's less reason to rush, and Yangon is a good place to become accustomed to the climate, food and everyday customs before heading upcountry.

Your recreational and aesthetic inclinations will largely determine which direction you take upon leaving Yangon. The basic threads most visitors are interested in following include historic temple architecture, handicrafts, hiking, beaches and culture. These travel aspects are not necessarily mutually exclusive though it's hard to find one place that has them all!

Historic Temple Architecture

Myanmar's most magnificent temple ruins are of course those at Bagan, the country's number-one tourist attraction and for decades the most popular photo subject for tour brochures and posters. Nearby Salay boasts a little-known set of ruins from the same period, easily visited as a day trip from Bagan.

Nearly as impressive in form and style, if not in number of ruins, are the massive Mrauk U temples near Sittwe in the Rakhine State, which so far have seen few tourists.

Mandalay is surrounded by the ancient cities of Ava, Amarapura, Sagaing and Mingun, all easily visited on day trips. Though not as old or impressive in scale as those sites previously described, the atmosphere at the old Mandalay temples is energised by the continued worship of the local population.

Early stupas at the former Pyu capital of Thayekhittaya (Sri Ksetra) near Pyay rank third in architectural interest and are the most accessible of all the ancient capitals from Yangon. Additional Pyu ruins can be seen at the more obscure – and more off the beaten track – sites of Beikthano and Hanlin.

See the Architecture section in the Facts about the Country chapter for more information on art and archaeological styles.

Handicrafts

Myanmar's incredible ethnic diversity means a wide range of handicrafts are available for study or purchase throughout the country. As the culture and business capital of Upper Myanmar, Mandalay has been the main handicrafts centre for over a hundred years. Here you'll find virtually every type of craft produced in the immediate region, as well as materials from throughout the north. Mandalay specialities include silverwork, woodcarving, stone sculpture, embroidered tapestries *(kalagas)*, Burmese marionettes and jadework.

The Shan State is the country's centre for handrolled Burmese cigars *(cheroots)* and for the ubiquitous embroidered shoulder bags carried by practically every Burmese. Bagan is famed for its lacquerware and antiques.

Multi-coloured cotton longyis (a loom-woven length of cloth draped around the lower body and legs and tied at the waist) can be found in municipal markets throughout the country, but the most interesting Burman patterns seem to be those produced in small central Myanmar towns like Inma, Yezin,

'An' I seed her first a-smokin' of a whackin'
white cheroot' – Kipling

Pakkoku and Lindwin. The various frontier
states, ie the Kachin, Kayah, Mon, Kayin and
Rakhine states, produce patterns unique to
their regions.

Hiking

Northern Myanmar's potential as a serious
hiking venue remains virtually untapped due
to the sensitive political nature of the mountainous frontier states. Out-of-town hikes are
now permitted in the 'secure' area of the
Shan State stretching from Kalaw east to Inle
Lake. So far about the only place you'll find
hiking guides are in the small towns of
Kalaw and Nyaungshwe (Yaunghwe).

The area around Kalaw and Pindaya offers
a variety of possible mountain hikes to
minority villages. At present overnight hikes
don't seem to be officially permitted though
that hasn't stopped some visitors from

spending the night in the occasional village.
Guides in Nyaungshwe can lead hikes into
the hills east of Inle Lake – but not too far
east as Shan insurgent territory crops up
quickly in this direction.

Similar areas east of Taungoo seem like an
interesting possibility, though again this
takes one into insurgent areas (Kayin and
Kayah).

Kengtung, in the far eastern section of the
Shan State, would make an excellent base for
treks to nearby Wa, Shan, Kheun and Akha
villages. There are guides in Kengtung
gearing up for the day when the government
OKs such activities.

Mt Kyaikto, site of Kyaiktiyo Paya (see
Other Highlights below), offers an easily
navigated but physically challenging uphill
climb if you start from the bottom. Branch
trails around the mountain provide at least a
couple of days worth of side hikes that few
foreign visitors have so far experienced.

Mountaineers everywhere are awaiting
the day when snow-clad Hkakabo Razi
(5889 metres), on the border between
Myanmar and Tibet and the highest mountain in South-East Asia, and nearby Gamlang
Razi (5835 metres) are open to climbers. So
far there's been lots of talk about opening this
area up but little action. Those few foreigners
who have made it as far as Putao – a valley
town in the same general region – have been
disappointed; until the area north of Putao
opens there's little point in going to the
trouble of obtaining one of the rare permits
issued for Putao.

Beaches

Although Myanmar's coastline is the longest
in mainland South-East Asia, only the
Ayeyarwady Division and Rakhine State
sections stretching from the Ayeyarwady
River Delta north-west to Sittwe are generally accessible to foreigners. Because of the
lengthy travel times involved, stays of at
least one night are necessary at most seaside
areas. Most suitable for overnight visits are
Letkhokkon, Chaungtha, Kanthaya and
Ngapali. Between these points you'll find

plenty of other beaches, but few facilities and no 'licensed-for-foreigners' accommodation.

During the rainy season from June to November, many of the roads in these areas may be washed out and impassable. Only Ngapali is accessible by air. Ngapali is the most attractive beach of the four; the closer you get to the Delta the muddier the beaches become.

The beaches and islands south of Mawlamyine off peninsular Myanmar have incredible recreational potential, but all were off limits to foreigners at the time of writing. A resort hotel will soon be opening on Thahtay Island near Kawthoung, in the country's extreme south.

Culture

One of the main joys of travelling through Myanmar comes from just soaking up the general cultural ambience, which is plentiful throughout the country. You'll obtain less in terms of Burmese culture if you spend most of your time sitting around in foreigner-frequented guest houses and restaurants in Yangon and Mandalay, both of which are rapidly modernising. Try going to a small to medium-size town well off the main tourist circuit, staying at a local hotel and eating in Burmese curry shops and tea houses. It's not as easy as going with the crowd but you'll learn a lot more about the country.

Other Highlights

The Mon State's Kyaiktiyo Paya – the postcard-famous, stupa-topped gilded boulder perched on a mountain cliff – is fairly accessible these days and is a favourite among visitors interested in Myanmar's syncretic, animistic Buddhism. Mt Popa, the 'home of the nats' near Bagan, holds a similar lure although the overall atmosphere runs far behind that at Kyaiktiyo.

The old Mon capital of Bago – with the largest reclining Buddha in the country and a highly revered stupa – makes an easy day trip from Yangon or a convenient stopover on the way to Kyaiktiyo.

Inle Lake in the Shan State offers a nice variety of old Shan temples, boat tripping and relaxed evenings with nothing much to do except walking to the edge of town for a little stargazing before bed.

ACCOMMODATION

Following the privatisation of hotels that has occurred since the last edition of this guidebook, the accommodation scene in Myanmar has been turned upside down. In terms of new hotels under construction and on the drawing boards, Myanmar was in fact considered the hottest hotel market in the world in 1994 as dozens of large and small developers tried to meet the pent-up demand created by years of mismanagement by the Ministry of Hotels & Tourism. MHT is unloading its own properties as fast as it can sell them so by 1995 there were few government-owned places left in the country.

In Yangon alone over 70 new hotels and guest houses opened between February 1994 and February 1995; in Mandalay the number of hotels opened to foreigners reached 40, and in Bagan/Nyaung U about half that many new places opened. A mind-boggling 17 new foreign-owned hotels – with investments totalling US$600 million – were on the boards for Yangon in mid-1995. Such growth is all the more amazing given the overall political situation and the fact that foreign companies cannot buy land but must lease it instead.

Technically any hotel or guest house that accepts foreign guests must have a special lodging licence – this is usually displayed somewhere on the wall behind the reception desk. Such a licence requires these hotels and guest houses to charge dollars or FECs, and to have a minimum of five rooms (rumours say this may soon be raised to 10) and certain room standards that are substantially beyond the usual local inn. This seems partially designed to justify higher rates so that the government can collect more tax, partially to keep foreigners separate from Burmese and partially out of a concern that Myanmar will develop a poor image if foreigners see the inside of a typical Burmese guest house.

Traditionally, the Burmese don't stay in

hotels or guest houses when they travel but rather in the homes of family, friends or business associates, or at monasteries if none of the former are available. As in other countries in South-East Asia, until recently the hotel/guest house mainly functioned as a place where men enjoyed the company of prostitutes, gambled and drank – activities strongly discouraged by Burmese Buddhism – away from the disapproving eyes of their families.

While shopping for places to stay, keep in mind that the newer private hotels tend to represent better value than government-owned hotels or hotels that were previously government-owned. Many of the latter are now owned or managed by former MHT hotel managers who have long been accustomed to charging high rates for indifferent service and mediocre room quality. Of the countless new places to stay, among the best are the small, family-run places with fewer than 10 rooms.

Although the upcoming discussion of two-tiered rates, non-functioning amenities and tiresome breakfasts may sound intolerably discouraging, most people will find it's well worth putting up with these frustrations to be able to travel in Myanmar. The situation has actually improved a great deal over previous years when your only choices of places to stay were low-standard, high-priced MHT-owned hotels – of which there were relatively few. Rates and overall variety have improved tremendously over the last two or three years.

Rates, Services & Tax

Much of the whirlwind hotel development has arrived in over-anticipation of future tourism growth, so a lot of rooms will probably stay empty for the next few years. This means competition for your accommodation dollar will be keen and rates should settle out on the low side in the near future.

For the time being many of Myanmar's hotels can be a bit overpriced by most South-East Asian standards. In the first place almost all hotels follow a two-tiered pricing system

– charging one rate for locals in kyat and another for foreigners in US dollars/FECs. A typical middle-of-the-road, Burmese-owned hotel might charge K900 for Burmese and US$40 for foreigners – over four times the local price figured at the real exchange rate. A dingy guest house in the hinterlands might take K75 from locals and US$10 from foreigners – more than a ten-fold increase! If you complain the usual excuse is that hotels which accept payment in dollars must pay tax to the government in dollars – an irrational argument considering 10% of one currency's true value for any given amount is exactly the same as 10% of another.

Bargaining is the answer – for bottom and middle-range places you should expect to be able to talk the asking rate down. At the high end, rates aren't really much different from elsewhere in South-East Asia and you're not likely to get much of a discount – but it doesn't hurt to try.

Most places offer a 'free breakfast' as part of the room rate. This is where you should begin bargaining, as the breakfasts at most places (there are exceptions) are a uniformly boring plate of white toast and fried eggs with tea or instant coffee. Asking for a room without breakfast can net a savings of as much as US$2 to US$4 per night. You can usually buy a better and more filling breakfast at a local teashop for less than K50. If the hotel won't give you a discount for dropping breakfast, ask if you can at least get a changing variety of breakfasts, such as *mohinga*, *si htamin* or other Burmese specialities, from time to time to break the monotony.

Except for international-class places like The Strand, Traders Hotel and the Summit Parkview – where a uniform dollar pricing structure is used – and a few hotels way off the beaten track where everyone pays in kyat, virtually all hotels use the two-tiered pricing system. If you're travelling with a hired vehicle and driver, your driver can get a free room at most hotels – or at least he should get the much lower kyat rate reserved for Burmese.

Fortunately for travellers on a tight budget there are now a smattering of places in the

US$5 to US$10 per person range. Typically this gets a bare cubicle with two beds and a cold-water bathroom down the hall. Rooms with a private cold-water bath cost a few dollars more. A toast-and-egg breakfast is usually included.

Moving up from this category, room rates seem to make a big leap as hot water, air-con and TV suddenly become part of the picture. In fact, compared with the hotel scene in neighbouring countries, Myanmar seems to have way too many small hotels with air-con, hot water and TV in every room; somehow the Burmese are getting the message that all foreigners need every one of these amenities. Because of problems with inconsistent electric power supplies, the hot water and air-con units in these hotels frequently don't work properly, if at all – an especially frustrating situation when you're paying extra for these. For this type of room the minimum rate ranges around US$25 for a single and US$30 to US$35 for a double. Toast-and-egg breakfasts, of course, are included.

The next level of hotels offers larger rooms, usually a bit more atmosphere, perhaps a sitting garden, for US$40 to US$50 single/double. Toast and eggs again! Many of the places in this price range are older hotels that once belonged to the MHT but are now privately owned. The service in these hotels can be terrible at one place, great at another. Profit margins on foreigner rates are probably among the highest in the world since upkeep is obviously very low. Some hotels in this range are new, modern but characterless Chinese-owned buildings with tidy rooms and all the amenities. The same problems with non-functioning air-con and hot water tend to occur. In this category are a few rare exceptions where the hotel breakfasts include a variety of fresh fruits, eggs cooked in your choice of styles, or where Burmese breakfasts can be taken as an alternative.

Once you're in the US$60 and up range most of the amenities you pay for actually seem to function. At this level many of the hotels are owned by Singaporean, Taiwanese or Hong Kong companies, which usually don't insult you with 'free breakfasts'.

Depending on your luck and the current state of hotel development, you can usually find a few kyat-priced hotels to stay at in out-of-the-way areas, and even in fairly accessible but relatively untouristed Shwebo, Magwe, Myingyan and Pakkoku. We found other towns where guest houses cost no more than K200 a night, sometimes as low as K50. The rooms in such places are very basic – perhaps two hard beds in a room surrounded by wood partitions that stop 30 cm short of the ceiling. Once the local government begins enforcing the foreigner licence law this kind of place will become more difficult to find.

Most hotels and guest houses charge a 10% tax on top of room rates. Larger, more expensive hotels also add a 10% service charge.

Table Etiquette

At home most families take their meals sitting on reed mats around a low, round table about 30 cm in height. In restaurants chairs and tables are more common. The entire meal is served at once rather than in courses. In ordinary Burmese restaurants, each individual diner in a group eating together typically orders a small plate of curry for himself or herself while side dishes are shared amongst the whole party. This contrasts with China and Thailand, for example, where every dish is usually shared.

Traditionally, Burmese food is eaten with the fingers much like Indian food but nowadays it's also common for urban Burmese to eat with a fork *(hkayin)* and tablespoon *(zun)* in the Thai fashion. Such utensils are always available at Burmese restaurants and almost always given automatically to foreign diners. The fork is held in the left hand and used as a probe to push food onto the spoon; you eat from the spoon.

Except for *mohinga*, which is eaten with fork and spoon, noodle soups are eaten with a spoon and chopsticks *(tu)*. ■

FOOD

You can eat very well and very inexpensively in Myanmar. Until recently it could often be difficult to find Burmese food in local restaurants, but the economic development in urban areas has brought substantial improvements in the availability and quality of Burmese cuisine. Chinese and Indian food are also quite popular in the larger towns and cities. Street and market stalls tend to provide the regional dishes, but with these you must be a little wary of cleanliness. Like most South-East Asians, the Burmese are great snackers, and in the evening many street stalls sell tasty little snacks.

Myanmar has a wide variety of tropical fruits, and in season you can get delicious strawberries in Pyin U Lwin and Mandalay (even in Yangon). Don't miss the huge avocados if you're in the Inle Lake area. In Yangon and Mandalay snack bars have excellent, and seemingly healthy, ice cream but you should avoid the ice cream street vendors unless you have a very strong stomach.

Food can be incredibly cheap in Myanmar if you pay in free-market kyats – and this never seems to be a problem except at the Yangon International Airport snack bar and the biggest Yangon hotels.

Burmese & Regional Cuisines

Mainstream Burmese cuisine represents an intriguing blend of Burman, Mon, Indian and Chinese influences. Rice *(htamin)* is the core of any Burmese meal, to be eaten with a choice of curry dishes *(hin)*, most commonly fish, chicken, prawns or mutton. Very little beef or pork are eaten by the Burmese – beef because it's considered offensive to most Hindus and Buddhists, pork because the nats disapprove. Many Buddhists in fact abstain from eating the flesh of any four-legged animal, and, during the Buddhist Waso or rains retreat, may take up a 'fire-free' diet that includes only uncooked vegetables and fruit. Virtually all butchers in Myanmar are either Muslim or Chinese.

Burmese curries are the mildest in Asia in terms of chilli power – in fact most cooks don't use chillies at all in their recipes, just a simple *masala* of turmeric, ginger, garlic, salt and onions, plus plenty of peanut oil and shrimp paste. Heat can be added in the form of *balachaung*, a table condiment made from chillies, tamarind and dried shrimp pounded together, or from the very pungent, very hot *ngapi kyaw* – shrimp paste fried in peanut oil with chilli, garlic and onions. Curries are generally cooked until the oil separates from all other ingredients and floats on top. Some restaurants will add oil to maintain the correct top layer, as the oil preserves the underlying food from contamination by insects and airborne bacteria while the curries sit in open, unheated pots for hours at a time. When you're served a bowl of *hin*, you're not expected to consume all the oil; just spoon the ingredients from underneath.

Almost everything is flavoured with *ngapi*, which is a salty paste concocted from dried and fermented shrimp or fish, and can be very much an acquired taste. A thin sauce of pressed fish or shrimp called *nganpya-yay* may also be used to salt Burmese dishes. Mi Mi Khaing, author of one of the seminal works on Burmese cuisine, *Cook and Entertain the Burmese Way*, explains:

It is sometimes observed that cheeses, and the esoteric pleasures therefrom, are strangely absent in East Asian cuisines. Cheese needs milk, and so too herds lovingly bred; whereas our rivers, spreading into immense deltas and other waters, already abound with fish of kind upon kind there for the netting. Adjoining great fisheries are saltbeds of the long Burmese coastline. Deliciously odoriferous foods result from this conjoining.

One of the culinary highlights of Burmese cuisine is undoubtedly *thok* (also *lethok*) – light, spicy salads made with raw vegetables or fruit tossed with lime juice, onions, peanuts, chillies and other spices. Among the most exquisite are *magyi-ywe thok*, made with tender young tamarind leaves, and *shauk-thi thok*, mixed with pomelo, a large citrus similar to grapefruit. *Htamin lettap* are savoury salads made with cooked rice.

Another common side dish is Indian-influenced lentil soup or dal *(bei hin yei* in

Burmese); the better restaurants may serve dal fortified with chunks of boiled turnips, potatoes and okra. A mild soup *(hin-gyo)* of green squash may also be available. At an authentic *htamin zai* or 'rice shop', once you've ordered one or more curries then rice, dal, soup, side dishes and Chinese tea come automatically at no charge. Soft drinks, beer or Indian tea cost extra. Hotel restaurants will usually have a few Burmese dishes on their menus but these will be toned-down versions of the real thing with less chilli and seasonings, and they'll usually come with fewer accompanying dishes.

Noodle dishes are most often eaten for breakfast or as light meals between the main meals of the day. By far the most popular is mohinga (pronounced 'moun-hinga'), rice noodles served with a thick, yellow fish soup. Another popular noodle dish, especially at festivals, is *oh-no khauk-swe*, rice noodles with pieces of chicken in a spicy sauce made with coconut milk.

Shan khauk-swe or Shan-style noodle soup – thin wheat noodles in a light broth with chunks of chilli-marinated chicken – is a favourite all over Myanmar but is most common in Mandalay and the Shan State. A variation popular in Mandalay is made with rice noodles and called *myi shay*. Another Shan dish worth seeking out is *htamin chin*, literally 'sour rice', a turmeric-coloured rice salad.

A popular finish to Burmese meals is *lephet thok*, a salad-like concoction of pressed, moistened green tea leaves mixed with a combination of sesame seeds, fried peas, dried shrimp, fried garlic, peanuts, toasted coconut and ginger, and other crunchy flavourings. The 'slimy-looking' mass of leaves puts some foreigners off, but it's actually quite tasty once you get beyond the dish's exotic appearance.

In Mandalay and around Inle Lake (Kalaw, Pindaya, Nyaungshwe and Taunggyi) it is also fairly easy to find Shan food, which is very similar to northern Thai cuisine. Popular dishes are *khauk sen* – Shan-style wide rice noodles with curry – and various fish and meat salads. Large rice crisps or *maung jeut*, usually translated as 'rice cracker' (which in typical Burmese pronunciation comes out sounding like 'rice cricket'), are common throughout the Shan State.

Mon food, most readily available in towns stretching from Bago to Mawlamyine, is very similar to Burmese with a greater emphasis on curry selections. Where a Burmese restaurant might offer a choice of four or five curries, a Mon restaurant will have as many as a dozen, all lined up in curry pots for the prospective diner to see. Mon curries are also more likely to contain chillies. Otherwise the two cuisines are quite similar.

Rakhine cuisine most resembles those of Bangladesh and India's Bengal, featuring lots of bean and pulse dishes, very spicy curries and flatbreads. Because of the Rakhine State's long coastline, seafood is commonly eaten in the larger towns.

Chinese & Indian Food

Throughout Myanmar in towns large and small you'll find plenty of Chinese restaurants, including quite a few of the regional specialities which are a world (well, half of China anyway) distant from what we think of as Chinese food in the West. In a run-of-the-mill Chinese restaurant a meal will cost around K180, often less. In true Chinese fashion you almost invariably get soup with your meal and free Chinese tea.

Indian restaurants are also common although much more so in Yangon than in other towns. Most are run by Muslim Indians, a few by Hindus. Excellent chicken biryani *(dan bauk)* as well as all-you-can-eat, banana-leaf or thali vegetarian food is easy to find in the capital. The Burmese call Indian restaurants that serve all-you-can-eat thalis 'Chitty' or 'Chetty' restaurants. You can recognise Muslim Indian restaurants by the numeral '786' over the door, sometimes flanked by the star and crescent symbol. This number represents the Arabic phrase 'In the name of Allah the most beneficient and merciful'.

Some Useful Words & Phrases

(I am) hungry.

htămìn hsabade   ထမင်းဆာပါတယ။

(I) want to drink.

thau'hcinbade   သောက်ချင်ပါတယ။

(I) don't eat spicy food.

sa'té aĭsa măsàbù   စပ်တဲ့အစာ မစားဘူး။

I can't eat...

...măsànainbabù   မစားနိုင်ပါဘူး။

| meat | *ăthà* | အသား |
| chillies | *ngăyou'thì* | ငရုတ်သီး |

Do you have any drinking water?

thau'yei shíbadhălà? သောက်ရည်ရှိသလား။

I didn't order this.

èdiha măhmababù   အဲ့ဒီဟာမမှာပါဘူး။

This is delicious.

diha ăyádha shíbade ဒီဟာအရသာရှိပါတယ။

How much is it altogether?

àlòun belau'lè?   အားလုံးဘယ်လောက်လ။

breakfast	*măne'sa*	မနက်စာ
lunch	*néileza*	နေ့ လည်စာ
dinner	*nyáza*	ညစာ
snack/small meal	*móun/thăyeiza*	မုန့်သွေးစာ
food	*(ăsà)asa*	အစား;အစာ
eat	*sà(de)*	စား;တယ်
drink	*thau'(te)*	သောက်တယ်

Soups   *hìnjou*   ဟင်းချို

clear soup

hìnjouyòuyòu ဟင်းချိုရိုးရိုး

radish soup

mounla-ú hìnjou မုန်လာဥဟင်းချို

green soup

hìnnúnwé hìnjou ဟင်းနုနွေ ဟင်းချို

sizzling rice soup

hsanhlo hìnjou ဆန်လျော်ဟင်းချို

with prawn

băzunhsanhlo hìnjou ပုစွန်ဆန်လျော်ဟင်းချို

with fish

ngàhsanhlo hìnjou ငါးဆန်လျော်ဟင်းချို

duck soup

bèbaun hìnjou ဘဲပေါင်ဟင်းချို

'Thai soup' (sour; like Thai tom yam)

yòudăyà hìnjou   ယိုးဒယားဟင်းချို

Noodle Soups   *hìngà*   ဟင်းခါး

Mohinga: noodles, egg, fish

móunhìngà   မုန့်ဟင်းခါး

vermicelli with chicken

cazanhìngà   ကြာဆန်ဟင်းခါး

coconut & pea soup (Shan)

òunnóu hkau'hswè   အုံးနို့ ခေါက်ဆွဲ

large noodles (sweet)

móundi   မုန့်တီ

vermicelli & coconut (sweet)

móun cahsan   မုန့်ကြာဆန်

Rice

steamed rice	*htămìn*	ထမင်း'
fried rice	*htămìnjo*	ထမင်းကြော်
rice gruel	*hsanbyou'*	ဆန်ပြုတ်
sweet rice gruel	*htămănè*	ထမင်းနဲ
coconut rice	*òunhtămìn*	အုံးထမင်း
rice flour cake	*móunnye'*	မုန့်ညက်

Meat Dishes   *ăthà*   အသား

pork curry	*we'thà hìn*	၀က်သား;ဟင်း
chicken curry	*ce'thà hìn*	ကြက်သား;ဟင်း
beef curry	*ămèdhà hìn*	အမဲသား;ဟင်း
fried chicken	*ce'thà jo*	ကြက်သား;ကြော်
red pork	*we'thăni*	၀က်သား;နီ

pork curry in thick sauce

we'thà hsibyan hìn ၀က]သား;ဆီပြန်ဟင်း

beef in gravy

ămèhna'   အမဲနပ်

fried spicy chicken

ce'thà asa'hce' ကြက်သား;အစပ်ချက်

sweet chicken

ce'thà ăhcouje' ကြက်သား;အချိုချက်

grilled chicken (satay)

ce'thàgin   ကြက်သား;ကင်

Seafood

pinleza/yei tha'tawa   ပင်လယ်စာ/ ရည်သတ္တဝါ

shrimp/prawn curry

băzunhìn   ပုစွန်ဟင်း

eel

ngàhau'/ngàlinbàn   ငါး;ဟောက်/ငါး;လင်ပန်း

squid
ngàsălou' ငါးစာလုပ်

shellfish
hkăyú ခရု

fish
ngà ငါး

catfish
ngăhku ငါးခူ

steamed fried trout
ngàthăslau'pàun ငါးသလောက်ပေါင်း

steamed fish
ngàbàun ငါးပေါင်း

steamed fish in banana leaves
ngàbàundou' ငါးပေါင်းထုပ်

fish salad
ngàdhou' ငါးသုပ်

prawn salad
băzunthou' ပုစွန်သုပ်

Eggs   *ú*   ဥ

chicken egg   *ce'ú*   ကြက်ဥ
duck egg   *bè-ú*   ဘဲဥ
boiled (chicken)   *ce'ú byou'*   ကြက်ဥပြုတ်
egg
fried (chicken)   *ce'ú jo*   ကြက်ဥကြော်
egg

Vegetables
hìndhìhìnywe'   ဟင်းသီးဟင်းရွက်

vegetable curry
hìndhìhìnywe'hìn   နှင်းသီးဟင်းရွက်ဟင်း
fried vegetables
ìndhìhìnywe'jo   ဟင်းသီးဟင်းရွက်ကြော်
raw salad   *ăthou'*   အသုပ်
pickled salad   *thăna'*   သနပ်
beans   *pè.*   ပဲ
banana flower   *hngăpyòbù*   ငှက်ပျောဖူး
cabbage   *gohpihtou'*   ဂေါ်ဖီထုပ်
cauliflower   *pànmounla*   ပန်းမုန်လာ
carrot   *mounla-ú wa*   မုန်လာဥဝါ
corn (cob)   *pyàunbù*   ပြောင်းဖူး
cucumber   *thăhkwàdhì*   သခွါးသီး
eggplant/   *hkăyàndhì*   ခရမ်းသီး
aubergine
green beans   *pèdáunshei*   ပဲတောင့်ရှေ
green peppers   *ngăyou'thìzèin*   ငရုတ်သီးစိမ်း
lettuce   *hsăla'ywe'*   ဆလတ်ရွက်
mushrooms   *hmou*   မှို

sago/tapioca   *thagu*   ·သာဂု
semolina   *hsănwìnmăkìn*   ဆန်ပြင်းမကင်း
tomato   *hkăyànjindhì*   ခရမ်းချဉ်သီး
white radish   *mounla-úhpyu*   မုန်လာဥဖြူ
zucchini/   *bùdhì*   ဘူးသီး
courgettes

Snacks, Sauces & Condiments

betel   *kùndhì*   ကွမ်းသီး
lime (for betel)
htòun   ထုံး
fish sauce   *nganpyayei*   ငံပြာရည်
soy sauce   *pè nganpyayei*   ပဲငံပြာရည်
vinegar   *ăhcinyei*   အချဉ်ရည်
chilli sauce   *ngăyou'yei*   ငရုတ်ရည်
fish paste   *ngăpí*   ငါးပိ
whole salted fish
ngăpígaun   ငါးပိခေါင်
raw prawn fish paste
ngăpísèinzà   ငါးပိစိမ်းစား
pounded raw fish paste
dămìnngăpí   ဒမင်းငါးပိ
cooked fish paste
ngăpíyeijou   ငါးပိရေကျို
peanuts   *myei bè*   မြေပဲ
cashews
thihou thăye'séi   သီဟိုဠ်သရက်စေ
fried bananas
hngăpyòjo   ငှက်ပျောကြော်
raisins   *zăbyi'thìjau'*   စပျစ်သီးခြောက်
fried cicadas   *păyi'co*   ပုရစ်စကြော်
ginger salad   *jìndhou'*   ချင်းတုပ်
butter   *htòba*   ထောပတ်
ghee   *kălăhtòba'*   ကုလားထောပတ်
sugar   *dhăjà*   သကြား
salt   *hsà*   ဆား
honey   *pyàyei*   ပျားရည်
coconut cream   *òunnóu*   အုန်းနို့

Fruit   *thi'thì*   သစ်သီး

apple   *pàndhì*   ပန်းသီး
('flower fruit')
avocado   *htòba'thì*   ထောပတ်သီး
('butter fruit')
banana   *hngăpyòdhì*   ငှက်ပျောသီး
breadfruit   *paunmóundhì*   ပေါင်မုန့်သီး
coconut   *òundhì*   အုန်းသီး
custard apple   *òzadhì*   သြဇာသီး

durian	*dùyìndhì*	ဒူးရင်းသီး
lemon	*shau'thì*	ရှောက်သီး
lime	*thanbăyadhì*	သံပုရာသီး
lychee	*lainhcìdhì*	လိင်ချီးသီး
mandarin	*leinmodhì*	လိမ္မော်သီး
mango	*thăye'thì*	သရက်သီး
orange	*shau'hcoudhì*	ရှောက်ချိုသီး
papaya	*thìnbòdhi*	သင်္ဘောသီး

('steamboat fruit')

peach	*me'mundhì*	မက်မံသီး
pear	*hnìndhì*	နင်းသီး
pineapple	*nana'thì*	နာနတ်သီး
plum	*me'mandhì*	မက်မန်းသီး
jujube plum	*zìdhì*	ဆီးသီး
pomelo	*cwègòdhì*	ကျွဲကောသီး
rambutan	*ce'mau'thì*	ကြက်မောက်သီး

('cockscomb fruit')

tamarind	*măjìdhì*	မန်ကျည်းသီး
watermelon	*hpăyèdhì*	ဖရဲသီး

Foreign Foods

biryani (rice with spices and meat, an Indian dish)
  danbau'   ဒန်ပေါက်
dosa (potato-filled pancake; south Indian)
  toushei   တိုရှေ
Shan fried beancurd
  shàn touhùjo   ရှမ်းတိုဟူးကြော်
Shan rice, fish & potato
  shàn htămìnjin   ရှမ်းထမင်းချဉ်
bread
  paunmóun   ပေါင်မုန့်
toast
  paunmóungin   ပေါင်မုန့် ကင်
spring rolls/eggrolls
  koupyanjo   ကိုပြန်ကြော်

Herbs & Spices

cardamon	*hpalazéi*	ဖါလာစေ့
chilli	*ngăyou'thì*	ငရုတ်သီး
coriander	*nannanbin*	နံနံပင်
garlic	*ce'thunbyu*	ကြက်စွန်ဖြူ
ginger	*jìn*	ချင်း

galangal (white ginger-like root)
  mei'thălin/gán-ei'   မိတ်သလင်/ဂန့်အိတ်

lemongrass	*zăbălin*	စပါးလင်
rose syrup	*hnìn-yei*	နင်းရည်
sesame	*hnàn*	နှမ်း

turmeric	*hsănwìn*	ဆနွင်း

Sweets   *móun*   မုန့်

cake
  kei'móun   ကိတ်မုန့်
golden rice (sticky)
  shweihtămìn   ရွှေထမင်း
steamed sticky rice
  kau'hnyìnbàun   ကောက်ညှင်းပေါင်
palm sugar cake
  htàndhìmóun   ထန်းသီးမုန့်
steamed cake with shredded coconut
  móunsèinbàun   မုန့်စိမ်းပေါင်း
agar-agar
  cau'cò   ကျောက်ကျော
sago/tapioca in syrup
  thagumóun   သာဂူမုန့်
semolina pudding
  hsănwìnmăkìn   ဆနွင်းမကင်း
new-moon-festival sticky rice sweet
  htămănè   ထမနဲ
soft bread pudding ('brain sweet')
  móunòuhnau'   မုန့်ဦးနှောက်
fried cake
  móunjo   မုန့်ကြော်
rice/sticky rice wafer
  móunleibwei   မုန့်လေပွေ
hot circular rice sweet ('husband and wife sweet')
  móunlinma°yà   မုန့်လင်မယား
ice cream
  yeigèmóun   ရည်ခဲမုန့်
jaggery (toddy) candy
  htănye'   ထန်းလျက်
sugar candy
  dhăjàlòun   သကြားလုံး
jujube plums cooked in jaggery
  zìyou   ဆီးယို
sliced pickled green mango
  thăye'pyà   သရက်ပြား
durian cooked in jaggery
  dùyìnyou   ဒူးရင်းယို
rice cake soaked in jaggery ('egg sweet')
  móunce'ú   မုန့်ကြက်ဥ
fried rice jelly
  móunhsijo   မုန့်ဆီကြော်
flat sticky rice
  móunzàn   မုန့်ဆန်း
pancake
  móunpyi'săle'   မုန့်ပြစ်စလက်

DRINKS
Nonalcoholic Drinks
Only drink water when you know it has been purified – which in most restaurants it should be. One should be suspicious of ice although we've had lots of ice drinks in Myanmar without suffering any ill effects. Myanmar is a thirsty country and not a good one for slaking that thirst safely, pleasantly and at reasonable cost. Myanma Mineral Water is sold in bottles and is quite safe.

Burmese tea, brewed in the Indian style with lots of milk and sugar, is cheap. Many restaurants, the Chinese ones in particular, will provide as much weak Chinese tea as you can handle – for free. It's a good, safe thirst quencher and some people prefer it to regular Burmese tea. You can always buy some little snack if you'd like a drink but not a meal. Teashops are a good place to drink safely boiled tea and munch on inexpensive snacks like *nam-bya, palata* or Chinese pastries.

Soft drinks are more costly but reasonable by Asian standards. Made-in-Myanmar soft drinks are mostly terrible, but a few come in pleasant flavours – particularly if they're well diluted with ice. One of the better ones is Sparkling Lemon (called 'Lemon Sparkling' by most Burmese), but only the kind made in Yangon – its Mandalay counterpart is not so good. Half-and-half soft drink and soda water is another recommendation. Pepsi and other international brands are becoming increasingly common.

Sugar-cane juice is a very popular streetside drink – cheap, thirst quenching and relatively healthy.

Alcoholic Drinks
The Burmese are not big drinkers; according to the Food and Agriculture Organisation, Myanmar ranks 91st worldwide in the consumption of alcohol, consuming only about a quarter litre per annum. This is partially due to the general lack of disposable income and a socioeconomic context that classifies most alcoholic beverages as luxury items. Alcohol-drinking is also looked down upon by the many Burmese Buddhists who interpret the fifth lay precept against intoxication very strictly.

Beer Since foreign trade was freed up in the early 1990s, the beer brands most commonly seen in Myanmar are international: Tiger, Bintang, ABC Stout, Singha, San Miguel, Beck, Heineken and other beers brewed in Thailand, Singapore and Indonesia. At one time these brands were available only on the black market; they are now sold freely in shops and restaurants throughout the country and typically cost K65 to K90 per can or bottle.

Myanmar has its own brand, Mandalay Beer, which is very similar to Indian or Sri Lankan beer – rather watery but not bad on those hot and dusty occasions when only a beer will do. Most bottles contain a layer of sediment on the bottom resulting from inad-

---

Betel
Betel chews *(kunya* in Burmese) are often passed round at the end of a meal as a 'digestive'. These take a variety of forms, the most basic being small chunks of dried areca nut (or 'betelnut') wrapped in a betel leaf with lime paste. More elaborate kunya may contain flavoured tobacco (usually Indian snuff), peppermint and other spices. In villages in areas where areca palms are cultivated, people chew fresh areca nut as well as dried. Experienced chewers can hold betel cud in their mouths for hours without spitting.

The nut and leaf come from two separate plants, the areca or betel palm *(Areca catechu)* and the betel vine *(Piper betel)*. An alkaloid in the nut produces a mild stimulation and sense of well-being. It also kills certain worms that may take up residence in the digestive tract; modern veterinarians use an areca extract to de-worm pets. Though not habit-forming, the chewed nut stains the teeth dark red and is thought to be carcinogenic. ■

equate filtration. Unfortunately, considering its low quality, Mandalay Beer also happens to be the most expensive beer in Myanmar at K80 to K125 per bottle. Hence few Burmese or foreigners drink the national brew. Founded in 1886, Mandalay Brewery (129 Waden St, Yangon) also produces the New Mandalay Export label, which is better-tasting and doesn't bear sediment. 'Bucket beer' is also available here and there, served warm in a bowl and quite cheap.

Toddy Throughout central Myanmar and the delta, *hta yei* or 'toddy juice' is the farmer's choice of alcoholic beverage. Hta yei is tapped from the top of a toddy palm, the same tree – and the same sap – that produces jaggery or palm sugar. The juice is sweet and nonalcoholic in the morning, but by mid-afternoon naturally ferments to a weak beer-like strength. By the next day it will have turned. The milky, viscous liquid has a nutty aroma and a slightly sour flavour that fades quickly.

Villages in some areas have their own thatched-roof toddy bars where the locals meet and drink pots of fermented toddy. The toddy is sold in the same roughly engraved terracotta pots the juice is collected in for about K60 per pot (or K10 in a bottle to go), and drunk from coconut half-shells set on small bamboo pedestals. Favourite toddy accompaniments include prawn crackers and fried peas. Some toddy bars also sell *hta ayet* or 'toddy liquor' (also called 'jaggery liquor'), a much stronger, distilled form of toddy sap, for around K22 per bottle.

Burmese Drink Words

water	*yei*	ရည်
boiled cold water	*yeije'èi*	ရည်ချက်အေး
hot water	*yeinwèi*	ရည်နွေး
bottled water	*bíla'yei*	ဗီလတ်ရည်
cold water	*yei'èi*	ရည်အေး
soda water	*hsoudayei*	ဆိုဒါရည်
milk	*(nwà) nóu*	နွား နို့
tea	*lăhpe'yei (jàn)*	လက်ဖက်ရည်ကြမ်း

tea with milk	*lăhpe'yei nóuné*	လက်ဖက်ရည် နို့နဲ့
coffee	*kahpi*	ကာဖီ
beer	*biya*	ဘီယာ
toddy	*htăyei*	ထန်းရည်
rice whisky	*ăye'*	အရက်
wine	*zăbyi'yei*	စပျစ်ရည်
soft drink	*hpyoyei*	ဖျော်ရည်
coconut milk	*òunnóu*	အုန်းနို့
lime juice	*thanbăyayei*	သံပုရာရည်
orange juice	*leinmoyei*	လိမ္မော်ရည်
sugarcane juice	*canyei*	ကြံရည်
agar-agar	*cau'cò*	ကျောက်ကျော
moh letsaung	*móun le'hsàun*	မုန့် လက်ဆောင်း

The last two are sweets in liquid; they can also be eaten as sweets without the liquid.

one bottle	*tăbălìn*	တပုလင်း
one cup	*tăhkwe'*	တခွက်

Other Liquors & Wines Very popular in the Shan State is an orange brandy called *shwe le maw* which varies in price from K25 to K50 per bottle, depending on how close to the source you buy it – much of it is distilled in the mountains between Kalaw and Taunggyi. It's a pleasant-tasting liqueur, sort of a poor man's Grand Marnier, and packs quite a kick.

There is also a variety of stronger liquors, including *ayet piu* or 'white liquor', which varies in strength from brandy-like to almost pure ethyl; and *taw ayet* or 'jungle liquor', a cruder form of ayet pyu.

Foreign wines – especially those from Australia – are occasionally found in shops and restaurants frequented by foreigners.

THINGS TO BUY

Shopping in Myanmar is better than ever now that free-market kyat may be used openly for purchases. Bartering is also quite acceptable and many merchants would love to trade their wares for designer watches, handheld calculators, jeans, T-shirts with English writing on them, and so on.

In larger towns and cities the best bargains

are usually found in the public markets, called *zei* in Burmese. The main central market is often called *zei-gyo*; other markets will be named for the district or township where they're found.

The Bogyoke Aung San Market in Yangon and the Zegyo Market in Mandalay are good places to look for handicrafts; just about everything that can be bought around the country can be purchased just as cheaply right in these two markets. The big hotel shops, large air-con handicrafts emporiums and the shops in the departure lounge at Yangon airport are very expensive.

Note the warning below on precious stone rip-offs, but beware of other, more mundane rip-offs. A couple of travellers wrote of being persuaded to buy betel nut to resell in Bangladesh, which is something like taking coal to Newcastle!

Lacquerware

Probably the most popular purchase in Myanmar is lacquerware – you'll find it on sale in the main markets of Yangon and Mandalay, in the Mahamuni Paya entrance walks in Mandalay, and most particularly in Bagan – where most of the lacquerware is made. Burmese lacquerware is fairly similar to that made in the north of Thailand, and although connoisseurs of Japanese lacquerware say that in comparison the Burmese items are inferior, many people find it highly collectible.

Although the earliest lacquerware found in Myanmar today can be dated to the 11th century and was done in the Chinese style, the incised polychrome techniques known as *yun* in use today were imported from northern Thailand. 'Yun' is an old Burmese word for the inhabitants of Chiang Mai; in 1558 King Bayinnaung captured a number of Chiang Mai lacquer artisans and brought them to Bago to establish the Burmese incised lacquerware tradition.

At one time Mandalay artisans made relief lacquerware, a tradition that appears to have all but died out. The oldest bichromatic style applies gold or silver to a black background, a technique dating perhaps to the Pyay era

and kept alive by artisans in Kyaukka near Monywa, Mandalay Division. Lacquerware is also made in Kengtung.

Lacquer as used in Myanmar comes from the *Melanorrhea usitata* or *kusum* tree (not to be confused with 'lac', which comes from an insect), and in its most basic form is mixed with paddy-husk ash to form a light, flexible, waterproof coating over bamboo frames.

To make a lacquerware object, the craftsperson first weaves a frame. If the item is first-quality, only the frame is bamboo; horse or donkey hairs will be wound round the frame. In lower-quality lacquerware the whole object is made from bamboo. The lacquer is then coated over the framework and allowed to dry. After several days it is sanded down with ash from rice husks, and another coating of lacquer is applied. A high-quality item may have seven layers of lacquer altogether.

The lacquerware is engraved and painted, then polished to remove the paint from everywhere except in the engravings. Multi-coloured lacquerware is produced by repeated engraving, painting and polishing. From start to finish it can take five or six months to produce a high-quality piece of lacquerware which may have as many as five colours. Flexibility is one characteristic of good lacquerware. A top-quality bowl can have its rim squeezed together until the sides meet without suffering damage. The quality and precision of the engraving is another thing to look for.

Lacquerware is made into bowls, trays, plates, boxes, containers, cups, vases and many other everyday items. The octagonal-topped folding tables are another popular lacquerware item.

Clothes & Textiles

Myanmar is the only country in South-East Asia where the majority of the population wear non-Western clothes as part of their everyday dress. Native fabrics are for the most part limited to the longyi.

Men wear ankle-length patterns of checks, plaids or stripes. To tie them they gather the front of the longyi to create two short lengths of material, then twist them into a half-knot, tucking one end in at the waist while allowing the other to protrude from the knot; this protrusion of cloth can be allowed to hang freely or formed into a decorative bunch. It can even be used as a small pouch to hold money or keys. Any kind of shirt, from a T-shirt to the formal mandarin-collar *eingyi*, may be worn with a man's longyi. On very formal occasions such as weddings the Burman turban or *gaung-baung* is added to the outfit.

Burmese women favour calf-length longyis in solid colours, partial stripes or flower prints, topped off by a form-fitting, waist-length blouse. A black waistband is stitched along the waist end, which is folded in front to form a wide pleat, then tucked behind the waistband to one side. The most expensive designs feature wavy or zigzag *acheik* patterns, the most rare of which are woven using a hundred or more spools of thread and called *lun-taya* ('hundred spool') *acheik*. These are so thick and long-wearing

they may be handed down from generation to generation like Persian rugs.

Simple rubber or velvet thong slippers are the most common footwear for both men and women.

Tailoring in Myanmar is very inexpensive compared to just about anywhere else in the world. Many of the textiles seen in tailor shops are imported synthetics. If you want, say, a shirt made from pure cotton, consider buying a longyi in a market or longyi shop and having the tailor cut and sew from that.

Precious Stones & Jewellery

Myanmar generates a considerable income from the mining of precious stones, mostly in the north. Be very wary of people who come to you with stories of large profits from taking Burmese gemstones to sell in the West. There are a lot of red glass rubies waiting for the unwary.

Precious stones are supposed to be a gov-

Do Real Men Wear Longyis?

Men throughout South and South-East Asia commonly wore skirt-like waistclothes until the beginning of this century. European trouser-wearing gradually won over the rest of South-East Asia, and even in India the wearing of the *lungi* (the Indian equivalent to Myanmar's *longyi*) no longer predominates.

Myanmar's isolation since independence and general lack of income have thus far preserved the longyi-wearing tradition. Nowadays only around 10% of males in urban areas wear trousers; in rural parts of the country virtually no male (except for uniformed soldiers) is seen wearing anything other than a longyi. Jokes about what's found beneath a man's longyi parallel similar jokes about Scottish kilts.

The longyi is a very practical clothing choice for Myanmar. In the tropical heat, the billowing cotton keeps one's legs substantially cooler than even the thinnest trousers. The lower length can be pulled between the legs and tucked in at the back of the waist to create 'shorts' for swimming or running. In a country where people often bathe outdoors at riverbanks and streams, the longyi preserves the bather's modesty while he scoops water over his body, and dries quickly afterwards.

And one size fits all. They can easily be loosened at the end of a large meal, and as one's weight moves up or down, there's no need to buy a new set of longyis. More than just an article of clothing, a spare longyi can be used: as a shoulder sling to carry items while travelling; as a bedsheet, picnic blanket or towel; as a baby cradle; tied ankle-to-ankle for safely climbing coconut or toddy palms; and as an impromptu curtain when the hot sun pierces a train or bus window.

Different patterns hail from different parts of the country. In most of central Myanmar, small checks and plaids in relatively bright colours predominate. Solid reds bordered with horizontal stripes at the middle or bottom indicate a Karen-style longyi. Highly favoured – and somewhat expensive – Rakhine patterns feature a thick, high-relief weave in light, reflective greys and blues. Around Inle Lake weavers produce red, green and yellow *zin-me* and blue, brown and green *ban-gauk* ('Chiang Mai' and 'Bangkok') longyis modelled after Thai weaving styles introduced to the region in the early 20th century. You can also find *ikat* or tie-dyed longyis reminiscent of patterns used in north-eastern Thailand and Laos. Deep indigo, green and purple plaids are the hallmark of the Kachin style, which during the 1988-90 uprisings became a symbol of the pro-democracy movement – especially when worn with a white Mandarin-collar shirt and terracotta-coloured waistjacket. For a Burmese to wear the latter outfit today is to risk being branded as an undesirable dissenter by the authorities. ■

ernment monopoly and they are very unhappy about visitors buying stones anywhere except at licensed retail shops. If *any* stones are found when your baggage is checked on departure, they may be confiscated unless you can present a receipt showing they were purchased from a government-licensed dealer.

The finer imperial jade or pigeon-blood rubies can only be purchased at special dealer sessions during the government-sponsored Myanmar Gems, Jade & Pearl Emporium held each year in October, December and February at a special building next to Kaba Aye Paya in Yangon. Each is typically attended by only around 400 'key' buyers from around the world.

Still, many visitors manage to buy stones from unlicensed dealers, which far outnumber the licensed kind. The government turns a blind eye to most domestic trade; entire districts of southern Mandalay, for example, are engaged in the unlicensed buying, selling, cutting and polishing of jade.

Black-market prices are considerably lower than prices found in licensed retail shops, but of course the risk is far greater as well. The best place to buy unlicensed stones is at the source, where fakes are much less common; the reason being that anyone discovered selling fakes in a well-known gem town would be severely punished by dealers in legitimate minerals.

Dug from pit, strip and tunnel mines, Myanmar's finest rubies and sapphires hail from Mogok (Sagaing Division), Pyinlon (Shan State) and Maingshu (or Monshu, Shan State). The Kachin State is the sole domain of jadeite, or Burmese jade, which forms inside football-sized boulders in mountain streams. Emeralds are mined at Myadaung in the Kayah State. At the moment only Mogok is open to the average foreign visitor, but all of these precious minerals are traded heavily in Mandalay and Yangon.

In an effort to stem the unlicensed trade, the government is about to inaugurate a wholesale jade and gem market in a new building in Yangon's North Dagon district. Unlike the annual emporiums, the North Dagon wholesale market will be open to the public.

Tapestries

Along with lacquerware, tapestries are one of the better bargains in Myanmar. Called kalaga ('foreign curtain'), they consist of pieces of coloured cloth of various sizes heavily embroidered with silver- or gold-coloured thread, metal sequins and glass beads, and feature mythological Burmese figures in padded relief. The greatest variety is found in Mandalay, where most tapestries are produced, but mark-up can be high there because of a tout system (trishaw drivers or guides who hook customers typically receive high commissions). However, if you locate the shops on your own and bargain well, you can get very good prices. You can also purchase tapestries in Yangon at craft shops in the Bogyoke Aung San Market – prices are similar to those in northern Myanmar but the selection is not as great.

Good-quality kalagas are tightly woven and don't skimp on sequins, which may be sewn in overlapping lines rather than spaced side by side as a sign of embroidery skill. Metals used should shine, even in older pieces; tarnishing means lower-quality materials. Age is not necessarily a factor in value except when related to better-quality work. Prices vary according to size and quality, from smaller squares (say 30 cm by 30 cm) for US$5 to US$10, to the larger (say 1.5 by 1.2 metres) for US$65. You can usually get better deals by paying in cash dollars rather than the free-market kyat equivalent.

Antiques

They're not all as ancient as made out, but many people like to collect 'opium' weights *(a-le)*, the little animal shapes in descending sizes that are traditionally used for weighing out opium, gems and other precious goods (see Export Restrictions below, however).

The older scale system used a series of nine weights; the newer system uses six weights. Production of the traditional zoomorphic weights came to a halt once the British colonial administration standardised

Betel nut container in the shape of a *hintha*

the system of weights and measures in 1885. The pre-1885 weights were made of bronze; reproductions made for the tourist trade are usually brass. The most common animal figures are *to-aung* (a creature that looks like a cross between a bull and a lion), *hintha* (a swan-like bird) and *karaweik* (the Burmese crane). Folding scales in carved wooden boxes go with the weights. Check prices in shops in Bangkok before blithely looking for bargains in Myanmar.

Kammawa & Parabaik *Kammawa* (from the Pali *kammavacha* or 'karma-words') are narrow, rectangular slats painted with extracts from the Pali Vinaya – the *pitaka* concerned with monastic discipline, specifically extracts having to do with clerical affairs. The core of a kammawa page may be a thin slat of wood, lacquered cloth, thatched cane or thin brass, which is then layered with red, black and gold lacquer to form the script and decorations. The resulting 'pages' aren't bound but tied in stacks with similarly decorated wooden covers.

Traditionally a new monk may receive a kammawa from his sponsors (usually his family) upon ordination. They have become less common since the advent of the press-printed page in Myanmar and are now mostly seen in museums and antique stores.

The *parabaik* is a similarly horizontal 'book', this time folded accordion-style, like a road map. The pages are made of heavy paper covered with black ink on which the letters are engraved; some parabaiks may feature gouache illustrations, and some can be erased and written over again. Typical parabaiks contain *jatakas* (Buddha biographies) or royal chronicles, and less frequently, Buddhist scriptures.

Both kammawas and parabaiks are among the items prohibited for export. So unless you're setting up house in Myanmar you'd best leave them to the Burmese.

Woodcarving
You can still find some pleasantly carved new Buddha figures and other items from workshops in Mandalay or in the corridors leading to Shwedagon Paya in Yangon, but in general you will not see too much woodcarving on sale.

Older items from the Amarapura, Yadanapon and Mandalay periods are plentiful but you can't be sure Burmese customs will allow them out of the country.

Umbrellas
The graceful and beautifully painted little parasols you see around Myanmar are a product of the port of Pathein – in fact they're known in Myanmar as *pathein hti*. Everyday umbrellas have wooden handles, the more ceremonial ones have handles of silver. You can pick up a nice small umbrella for less than US$1. The Bogyoke Aung San Market is a good place to look in Yangon. See the Pathein section for details on where to observe them being made.

Shan Shoulder Bags

Brightly coloured, embroidered shoulder bags from the Shan State can be found all over Myanmar, but most particularly at Inle Lake. Fancy models have a zip pocket in the front. They are also now made by Chinese and Kachan weavers.

Export Restrictions

The following items cannot legally be taken out of the country: prehistoric implements and artefacts; fossils; old coins; bronze or brass weights (including opium weights); bronze or clay pipes; kammawas or parabaiks; inscribed stones; inscribed gold or silver; historical documents; religious images; sculptures or carvings in bronze, stone, stucco or wood; frescoes or fragments thereof; pottery; national regalia and paraphernalia.

Getting There & Away

AIR

Apart from day trips to Three Pagodas Pass from Thailand, five-day trips from Thailand's Mae Sai to the Burmese town of Kengtung, and group travel from China, people who arrive by land or sea are few and far between. That only leaves arriving by air, and even there the choice is fairly restricted since few airlines fly into Yangon (Rangoon).

KLM begin flying into Yangon in the 1930s and by the 1950s Yangon was an important air hub for a number of European airlines. Since the 1962 military takeover, increased restrictions and lack of traffic have led most carriers to delete Yangon from their schedules – not without a sigh of relief, one suspects. Yangon International Airport (located in the township of Mingaladon) is unable to take anything larger than an Airbus or 767, so large aircraft (747s and DC-10s) cannot fly there. A new, larger airport is under construction 50 km north-east of the capital on the highway to Bago (Pegu); when it opens in late 1996 it will have the capacity to field larger planes.

There are several major air route options. First, and most commonly, is to travel out-and-back from Bangkok in Thailand. The second possibility is to slot Myanmar in between Thailand and Bangladesh, India or Nepal – many people travelling from South-East Asia to the subcontinent manage a few weeks in Myanmar in between. The third alternative is to travel out-and-back from Calcutta. Kuala Lumpur, Singapore and Kunming round out the possibilities.

Bangkok is a good place to look for tickets to Myanmar. Some travel agents will not only sell you tickets at knock-down prices, but will fix up your visa too. It's usually cheaper to arrange visa and ticket separately, however. One discount ticket agency within walking distance of the Myanmar Embassy in Bangkok is Sun Far Travel (☎ 223 8179), at 48/5 Pan Rd. Typical costs for Bangkok-

Yangon-Bangkok tickets are around US$230 on Thai International Airways, US$220 on Myanma Airways International, and as low as US$144 on Biman Bangladesh. The latter flies Bangkok-Yangon-Calcutta for a similar figure and Bangkok-Yangon-Kathmandu for around US$200. Roundtrip flights to/from Kuala Lumpur, Singapore or Kunming cost around US$250.

Airlines

The airlines that currently fly into Yangon are:

Thai International Airways THAI currently fly Bangkok-Yangon-Bangkok daily Monday through Saturday; by the end of 1996, assuming passenger loads increase with 'Visit Myanmar Year', THAI may increase service to two flights daily, and may add Sundays to the schedule. THAI use Airbuses and the flight takes about 50 minutes. Although slightly more expensive than the equivalent Myanma Airways International flight, THAI's departure times are much more sane and the service more reliable.

Myanma Airways International MAI fly from Bangkok to Yangon and vice versa daily, from Hong Kong thrice weekly, Singapore four times weekly, Kuala Lumpur twice weekly and Dhaka once a week. They use Boeing 757-200ERs leased from Royal Brunei Airlines for all flights. Since 1993, MAI has been a joint venture between Myanma Airways (the government-owned domestic carrier) and a Singaporean company, with overseas offices in Singapore, Hong Kong and Bangkok. MAI's flights are first in line for daily flights to and from Bangkok, which means if they're running late then THAI goes late.

Biman Bangladesh Biman fly Bangkok-Yangon-Dhaka (via Chittagong) once a week. They are usually the cheapest operator although not always that reliable. In fact many people fly Biman simply because of their unreliability. There's always the chance of getting stuck in Myanmar for a bit longer than your 28-day visa would normally allow, due to the Biman flight not turning up!

If you're flying through to Calcutta with Biman you (sometimes) get a free night's stopover in Dhaka. Note that if you plan to stop in Bangladesh it's still worth getting a ticket to Calcutta since the price is the same and you may, therefore, start your Bangladesh travels with free airport transport and a free night's accommodation.

If you plan on a Dhaka overnight, be sure to get a hotel voucher from Biman before leaving Yangon; in fact it might be best to get it in Bangkok (or wherever you buy the ticket) first, just to be safe. A number of travellers have said they landed in Bangladesh and ended up sleeping in the airport because Biman wouldn't take them to a hotel without a hotel voucher.

Air China China's national carrier flies 737s between Kunming (Yunnan) and Yangon once a week. In the reverse direction this flight continues on to Beijing from Kunming every other week. If you are travelling around China and then continuing to South-East Asia this can be an economical choice, since from western China you would not have to backtrack all the way east to Hong Kong, then fly all the way west to Bangkok. Visas are obtainable from the Myanmar Consulate in Kunming.

Silk Air This subsidiary of Singapore Airlines flies to Yangon four times weekly from Singapore using Boeing 737s.

Other Airlines Several European airlines that used to fly into Yangon still maintain offices there for ticketing flights out of Bangkok and/or Singapore.

Aeroflot, the Russian airline, stopped flying into Yangon from Moscow and Vientiane in 1992 but may start operating again soon. Meanwhile you can book or confirm flights out of Bangkok from their Yangon office.

KLM has an office in Yangon to service its flights out of Bangkok and Singapore, as do Air France and Northwest for their Bangkok connections.

Bangkok Airways flew regularly scheduled flights between Chiang Mai and Mandalay for a short time in the early 1990s but are now only doing charters. Air Mandalay, Myanmar's new, privately owned domestic carrier, has its eye set on Chiang Mai and Chiang Rai flights for sometime in the future. For the moment Air Mandalay only runs charter flights to and from these destinations in Thailand.

Please see the Getting There & Away section in the Yangon chapter for a listing of airline offices in Yangon.

Arrival in Yangon

On arrival you will probably find there is a bit of a race on to get into the terminal building. Your first taste of Burmese bureaucracy is likely to be a lengthy one, and the early arrivals will save quite a bit of time. The process is first to squeeze past the health-control counter where your passport and/or vaccination certificate is checked to see if yellow fever immunisation is required. Then across to the immigration counter where your visa and immigration form is inspected.

Then it is on to the customs counter, where you will have to fill in a form if you have a camera, calculator, typewriter or any other marvel of Western technology. This form states number of items, brand name and value – undervalue them since if they are stolen or lost it's better to have a lower cost to argue about.

Arriving on a full Thai International flight, you may find that the immigration/customs procedures take a full hour to complete, which is all the more exasperating since it will be the only incoming flight at the time.

Once you've picked up your bags, you must pass the Foreign Exchange Certificate counter where you may or may not be stopped and asked to change dollars or pounds into FECs. (See the Money section in the previous chapter for details on this latest twist to the government's currency control system.)

Then it's through the arrival area exit, where you can book an official taxi into town or continue out the door to the street entrance, where you'll most likely meet your first 'black-market' dealer, eager to change money or buy anything you might have to sell. This brazen entry at the foot of Burmese officialdom doesn't seem to worry the Burmese entrepreneurs at all, nor the officials. But it's best to forego changing money till you get into town, where you can get a better rate than anywhere at the airport.

See the following Getting Around chapter for information on getting to and from the airport.

Flight Reconfirmation

If you are counting on flying out of Yangon on your scheduled date of departure, then you must reconfirm your outbound flight either at the appropriate airport ticket counter or at the relevant airline office in town. This applies regardless of whether your flight is officially confirmed ('OK' status) on the ticket or not. You may notice a sign in the airport waiting lounge which reminds you of this requirement.

For most flights, we have found the airline offices in town more reliable than the airport offices – mainly because you can't always find someone at the airport to fill out the proper forms. *None* of the airline offices in Yangon or at the airport are online with computer reservation systems yet, so a confirmation usually means filling in a form and calling back the next day (after the office has called abroad on your behalf) to see if you have 'OK' status.

If you do not reconfirm, the airlines (this goes for any of the airlines flying in and out of Yangon) cannot guarantee your outbound seat. Especially during the height of the tourist season (November-February), most flights out of Yangon seem to be intentionally overbooked. On the other hand, if you're looking for a few extra days in Myanmar, just

give it a miss and you're quite likely to get bumped – particularly if you neglect to arrive for check-in until an hour or less before departure.

If you do get bumped, make sure you visit immigration to extend your visa sometime before your rescheduled departure. Otherwise the airlines may refuse to give you a seat when you arrive for check-in and you will have to deal with the airport immigration office. This process has been known to delay check-in until the very last minute, in which case you may find yourself bumped a second time.

Departure Tax

Leaving Myanmar is much easier than in the recent past when you had to turn in a currency control form to prove you'd changed foreign currency for kyat. With the FEC system in place, no one checks to see what kind of currency you've spent or are leaving the country with.

A US$6 departure tax, payable in dollars or FECs, is collected at the airport from all ticket-holders before flight check-in.

In the departure lounge you can buy any handicrafts you forgot on your way round or purchase whisky and cigarettes at the duty-free counter – they're cheaper here than at Bangkok International Airport.

If you have time on your hands between check-in and boarding, there is a restaurant/bar/lounge on the 2nd floor of the departure lounge, where the food's not bad but rather expensive. Every item on the menu costs US$2, whether a sandwich, beer, soft drink or bag of potato chips.

LAND

'Overlanding' through Asia is nowhere near as popular an activity as it was some years back. Nevertheless, the idea of a route through Myanmar has long been a dream for overlanders. If you could only drive through Myanmar it would then be possible to travel by car all the way from London to Singapore, and Asia overland would be much more of a reality than it has been in the past.

Prior to WW II that route would not even

have been a dream – there simply were no roads through Myanmar. After the war there were three new roads and a railway across the Burmese borders, but these fascinating routes had a short civilian life. The railway was built by the Japanese, using the infamous 'Bridge on the River Kwai'. It went up to the Burmese border at the Three Pagodas Pass, from where it ran to Mawlamyine (Moulmein). After the war most of the railway was torn up, leaving only a stretch from Kanchanaburi in Thailand which runs into the jungle less than half way to the border. Forget that one.

From China

Originally built to supply the forces of Chiang Kai-shek in his struggle against the Japanese, the famous 'Burma Road' runs from Kunming in China's Yunnan province to the city of Lashio. Nowadays the road is open to travellers carrying permits for the region north of Lashio, although you can only legally cross the border in one direction – from the Chinese side (Ruili) into Myanmar via Mu-se in the Shan State. This appears to be possible only if you book a visa-and-transport package from Chinese travel agencies in Kunming. Once across the border at Mu-se you can continue on to Lashio and further south to Mandalay, Yangon and so on.

A second route a little further north-west from Lwaigyai to Bhamo is also open in the same direction. You cannot legally leave Myanmar by either route, however.

From India

During WW II the Indians and the British built a road from Imphal in India to Tamu on the Burmese border while further north the Americans, under General 'Vinegar Joe' Stillwell, built a 430-km road running from Ledo in the remote Indian North-East Frontier Province to Myitkyina in the north-east of Myanmar. At a cost in 1944 of US\$137 million it must rank as one of the most expensive roads in the world, because after a few months' use in 1944 it has hardly been used

since. Both these roads have now probably returned to the jungle.

You can read a quite fascinating description of driving through Myanmar, using the Stillwell road, in *First Overland* by Tim Slessor. It tells of a 1956 trip from London to Singapore by two Oxford and Cambridge University-crewed Land Rovers. They may well have been not only the first but also the last overland, for a 1962 edition of *The Motor Roads of Burma* (published by the Burma Oil Company) states that only the first 190 km from Myitkyina to Tanai is 'motorable during all weathers'. The rest of the way to Ledo required 4WD plus 'preparation, patience, perseverance and luck'. The road from Mandalay to Myitkyina via Pyin U Lwin (Maymyo), Lashio and Bhamo was 780 km long and generally motorable according to that same road guide. Turn-offs lead to the Chinese border from just beyond Mongyu and Bhamo.

The British-Indian road sounds equally forbidding. Mandalay-Tamu was 490 km via Amarapura, Sagaing, Shwebo, Yeu and Kalewa. After Shwebo, 93 km out, the road rapidly deteriorated (according to this 1962 report), with many unbridged *chaungs* (canals) to cross. In wet weather this would be an impossible proposition, although the booklet also noted that it was sometimes possible to ship vehicles from Monywa to Kalewa by riverboat – thus avoiding the worst part of the route. Once at Tamu the road on the Indian side of the border was quite good.

The latest word in Myanmar is that the Chin State is about to open to foreign travellers and that it will be possible to traverse the state via the Chindwin River all the way to the Indian border at Tamu. Whether foreigners will be permitted to cross into India or vice versa is a matter being discussed between the Indian and Burmese governments right now. Rumours suggest that Indian and Burmese traders may be allowed crossing privileges but that other nationalities will be denied such access.

From Thailand

Several border crossings between Thailand

and Myanmar are open to day-trippers or short excursions in the vicinity. As yet, none of these link up with routes to Yangon or Mandalay or any other cities of size.

Mae Sai-Tachilek The infamous bridge, Lo Hsing-han's former 'Golden Triangle' passageway for opium and heroin, spans the Sai River between Thailand's northernmost town and the border boomtown of Tachilek. Nowadays border permits for up to five days can be obtained from Burmese immigration officials at the border for excursions to Tachilek and beyond as far north as Kengtung. Travel west to Taunggyi is still off limits as well; you must leave the way you came, via Tachilek. During parts of 1994 and 1995 this border crossing closed for a few months due to fighting between Khun Sa's Shan armies and the Burmese.

Rumour has it that an overland route all the way to China via Kengtung will soon open here, but so far Kengtung's the end of the line. The road continuing west from Kengtung to Taunggyi is in useable condition, although this runs through the opium poppy harvesting area of the Golden Triangle, a common site for Shan army skirmishes with the Yangon military, and is most definitely off limits to non-Burmese. It is 163 km on from Tachilek to Kengtung, and another 450 km from Kengtung to Taunggyi.

Further to the south, in Thailand's Mae Chan district, it is possible to cross the border almost everywhere – with a local and reliable guide. This is opium country and Sunday strollers are not welcome.

Three Pagodas Pass A gateway for invading armies and a major smuggling route for many centuries, this is one of the most interesting and accessible of the border crossing points.

Now that the Burmese have wrested control from Mon and Karen armies, there is also much legal trade going on at Three Pagodas Pass. The settlement on the Burmese side, called Payathonzu ('Three Pagodas'), is open to foreign tourists for day trips. Travellers have been allowed to go as far as a dozen or so km inside Myanmar from this point, but the roads are so bad that almost no one makes it even that far.

From Kanchanaburi (the site of the 'Bridge on the River Kwai') you can get a minibus or rent a motorcycle and drive the 150 km along dusty, winding mountain roads to Sangkhlaburi. The trip takes about half a day. The road is OK as far as Thong Pha Phum, but deteriorates somewhat after that little town.

Pickup trucks make regular trips to Three Pagodas Pass from Sangkhlaburi. Along the way you must stop at a Thai military checkpoint and at the Burmese border you're required to sign your name and present your passport at the Burmese checkpoint. The pass itself is unreal – three little pagodas standing on a crest.

Payathonzu itself is not that interesting, just a collection of wooden teashops, a cinema, a couple of markets and several souvenir shops. The nearby Kloeng Thaw Falls take a couple of hours by motorcycle from Payathonzu. The road to the falls is only open in the dry season – reportedly the Karen control the waterfall area during the rainy season. No one actually stops you from going to the falls then, though many people will try to wave you back. Even in good weather, the two-rut track is very rugged; not recommended for motorcycle novices.

Mae Sot-Myawaddy This crossing begins a route from Myawaddy to Mawlamyine via Kawkareik along a rough road that has long been off limits to foreigners due to Mon and Karen insurgent activity in the area. There are regular buses from Tak to Mae Sot on the Thai side. In 1994 the Myanmar government signed an agreement with Thailand to build a bridge across the Moei River between Myawaddy and Mae Sot, so we can look for a possible opening up of this route sometime in the near future. It's possible to go right to the border on the Thai side of the Moei River, about six km beyond the town of Mae Sot.

On the Myawaddy side there's nothing very interesting, just a Buddhist temple, a village school and thatched-roof compounds. Here the government has kept the Myawaddy-Mawlamyine route open to black marketeers – in order to avoid civil unrest in Yangon due to consumer shortages and rising prices.

Just north of Myawaddy is Wangkha, and just to the south is Phalu (Waley on the Thai side), former Karen and Mon smuggling posts now controlled by Yangon. Between Mae Sot and Tha Song Yang, south of Mae Sariang on the Thai side, are several Karen refugee camps (at last report 12 camps with a total of about 100,000 refugees) populated by civilians who have fled Burmese-Karen armed conflicts, as well as political dissidents from Yangon. The fighting was particularly bad in 1995 when dissident Karen Buddhists – backed by Burmese troops – routed the leading Christian faction; this area continues to be a military hotspot.

Chiang Dao A dirt track turns left 10 km north of Chiang Dao and leads through the small town of Muang Ngai to Na Ok at the border. This was the most popular opium route from Myanmar 25 years ago, but the main trading items now are water buffalo and lacquer. It's wise to be very careful in this area though.

Prachuap Khiri Khan Not only is there a road over the Mawdaung Pass between Ban Huay Yang and Taninyarthi, there is a major business smuggling timber in from Myanmar. The 'toll gate', formerly controlled by Karen guerrillas from the Karen National Union/Karen National Liberation Army, is now once again controlled by Yangon forces. If you can find a local who knows the area well, it's possible to visit near the border crossing point of Dan Singkon.

WARNING
The information in this chapter is particularly vulnerable to change: prices for international travel are volatile, routes are introduced and cancelled, schedules change, special deals come and go, and rules and visa requirements are amended. Airlines and governments seem to take a perverse pleasure in making price structures and regulations as complicated as possible. You should check directly with the airline or a travel agent to make sure you understand how a fare (and any ticket you may buy) works. In addition, the travel industry is highly competitive and there are many lurks and perks.

The upshot of this is that you should get opinions, quotes and advice from as many airlines and travel agents as possible before you part with your hard-earned cash. The details given in this chapter should be regarded as pointers and are not a substitute for your own careful, up-to-date research.

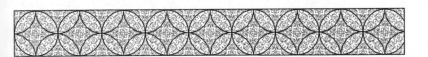

Getting Around

AIR

Myanmar has 66 airstrips around the country, 23 of which are served by regularly scheduled domestic flights. Most are short, one-strip fields that can land only one plane at a time. None have instrument landing capability, a situation which can be especially tricky during the May to November monsoon season even though all 23 are considered 'all-weather aerodromes'.

A new international airport is under construction outside Yangon (Rangoon) near Bago (Pegu), on a site used by B-29 bombers during WW II. Airports at Mandalay and Heho are soon to add sorely needed runways and expanded passenger facilities.

To/From the Airport

Since 1994 Burmese citizens without special permission or guide licences have been barred from the airport, hence nowadays you usually aren't approached by taxi drivers until you leave the airport. Hotel desks just outside the arrival area can arrange buses into Yangon for US$3 per person, or taxis for US$5 per cab (up to four passengers); most buses and taxis booked this way drop you off at a station on Bogyoke Aung San St. Some hotels will provide free transport if you book a room at their airport hotel desk. You can also book your own taxi from the motley collection of old, battered vehicles parked outside the airport for around US$4 to the destination of your choice.

Coming to the airport from Yangon you can pay in free-market kyats, though the fare works out to be about the same.

Departing from Myanmar is much simpler than arriving, unless you have an early-morning MAI (Myanmar Airways International) flight and have to crawl out of bed. MAI make it less pleasant by sending round their bus to collect you at an unnecessarily early hour. The bus starts from Strand Hotel and criss-crosses all over town on its way to Yangon's international airport in Mingaladon.

For MAI departures, taking a taxi gives you an extra hour (almost) in bed. From downtown Yangon to the airport the going rate for a tiny Mazda is K250 (about US$2.50 at free-market exchange rates) while the more comfortable 'saloon' sedans cost K300 to K350.

If you happen to be flying out of Yangon on Union Day, 12 February, you need to get out to the airport before noon because the road to the airport is closed to non-parade traffic after that time.

Myanma Airways

Until 1989 Myanma Airways (MA) was known as Burma Airways Corporation and, before that, Union of Burma Airways. MA's airline code remains UB.

MA's small fleet consists of two Fokker F-28 jets and four F-27 turboprops. Legroom and carry-on luggage space are minimal as the airlines have opted for the maximum number of seats the aircraft are designed to carry. All craft are in decidedly tatty condition and the whole operation seems to be a little on the haphazard side, which does not do wonders for one's nerves when flying with MA. The airlines employs safety procedures that haven't been updated since the 1950s, and between 1989 and 1991 MA logged four fatal crashes. In recent years, however, MA has beefed up its maintenance and crew; there have been no crashes since 1991. Even the often over-cautious US State Department has dropped its advisory against using Myanma Airways.

Why fly with MA at all when there is a better domestic airline available, not to mention buses and trains? Air Mandalay has a much smaller route net, flying only to the popular tourist destinations. Their fares are also significantly higher than MA's, though if you care about comfort, service, safety and punctuality the extra fare is definitely a worthwhile investment.

There are also places for which MA may be the only legal access; for example, MHT (Ministry of Hotels & Tourism) permits for Loikaw, Myitkyina and Myeik (Mergui) often require arrivals and departures by air. MA officials will usually also demand to see the MHT permit before selling a ticket.

Schedules Even with ticket in hand things may not go strictly to plan. Schedules don't mean all that much – if the passengers turn up early the flight may go early. If insufficient passengers show up the flight may not go at all. If too many passengers want to fly, another flight may be slotted in.

Even having a confirmed reservation and being first in line may not get you there because Burmese VIPs can jump the line with ease and package-tour people also get preference over independent travellers. Dates and departure times are rarely written on MA tickets so they don't have to honour these on the day and hour for which reservations were originally made.

Joe recently flew to Sittwe (Akyab) on MA and on the day he was to return to Yangon, General Than Shwe commandeered the entire craft to fly to Hanoi for a meeting with Vietnamese officials! All passengers were left stranded until the next day, when only those with bribe money or VIP connections emerged with seats as two plane-loads of passengers competed for that day's one and only departure.

Another annoying aspect of flying MA is that you inevitably waste a lot of time at the airports. Flights often go late, but given the difficulty of getting seats you daren't risk showing up late yourself. You'll be told to report at the airport at 8.30 am for a flight that isn't scheduled to leave until 12.45 pm.

At the airport you will find there is unlikely to be any announcement of impending departures. Simply keep an eye on everybody else, and when people start to move towards the plane, move too. It's wisest in Myanmar to travel as lightly as possible and carry your own baggage out to

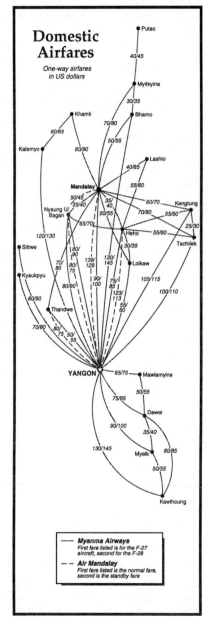

Domestic Airfares

One-way airfares in US dollars

Putao
40/45
Myitkyina
30/35
Khamti
Bhamo
70/80
60/65
Kalemyo
50/55
80/90
Lashio
40/65
Mandalay
55/60
50/45
35/40
35/40
60/70
Kengtung
Nyaung U/
Bagan
50/55
70/80
55/60
65/70
25/30
120/130
Heho
55/60
Tachilek
Sittwe
30/35
80/90
90
Loikaw
Kyaukpyu
139/129
130/145
105/115
70/80
75
90/100
75/85
100/110
80/90
123/113
113
Thandwe
55/60
70/80
80/75
50/55
YANGON
65/75
Mawlamyine
50/55
75/85
Dawei
90/100
35/40
130/145
80/85
Myeik
50/55
Kawthoung

Myanma Airways
First fare listed is for the F-27 aircraft, second for the F-28

Air Mandalay
First fare listed is the normal fare, second is the standby fare

the aircraft rather than trust that it will find its own way there. At many airfields, everyone except package-tour groups carry their own luggage on anyway, regardless of quantity. You will save time if you also carry it off at the other end. Except for international flights, you are unlikely to be served anything apart from a cup of Burmese tea or a glass of fruit juice on MA.

Fares & Payment Foreigners must purchase all tickets using Foreign Exchange Certificates (FECs) or US dollars cash. Burmese citizens pay much lower fares in kyat. If you cancel your booking within 24 hours of departure, MA collects a 25% cancellation charge; within six hours it jumps to 50%. Note also that you're not able to purchase tickets for MA outside the country – unlike Air Mandalay where you can.

Another wrinkle in booking procedures is that you can't take a MA flight that involves an intermediate connection straight through the connecting stop. For example, on Wednesdays MA flight UB 788 goes from Mandalay to Bhamo at 8.30 am and 20 minutes after arrival in Bhamo, the same plane continues northward to Myitkyina. But you can't book this flight straight through from Mandalay to Myitkyina; this is because the MA office in Mandalay apparently can't figure out how many people hold reservations on the Bhamo-Myitkyina leg. So you must stop over in Bhamo, and make a new reservation for a seat to Myitkyina. The same goes for flights to Mawlamyine via Dawei, flights from Kengtung to Yangon via Heho, and other such routings.

Though MA use both F-27 turboprops and F-28 jets, in everyday practice the more expensive F-28s are used only for long hauls, eg Yangon-Sittwe or Yangon-Myeik, so you'll usually end up paying the lower fare.

Air Mandalay

Flying with Air Mandalay (AM) saves visitors a whole list of headaches. In the first place they fly to places for which permits aren't necessary, so that's one layer of bureaucracy eliminated in their ticket lines.

Secondly, AM is usually punctual in arrivals and departures and for the most part schedules are arranged so that AM planes aren't waiting on line behind MA takeoffs. Finally, AM planes are substantially more comfortable and the attentive, professional service contrasts strongly with the cattle-car ambience at MA. AM also maintains its own separate departure lounge at each airport, where attendants make sure you know when your flight is leaving – unlike at MA where everyone seems to leap up in response to some secret signal!

Air Mandalay appears to have been created so that foreigners won't compete with Burmese citizens for perpetually tight seating space on MA aircraft. In other words the government would just as soon see you fly with upscale AM rather than with government-subsidised MA. A joint venture between MA and a private Singaporean company, AM currently operate two new French-built ATR-72s, comfortably configured to seat 66 passengers, allowing for ample legroom.

AM's Toulouse-trained pilots hail from Australia, France, Singapore and Myanmar; all flight attendants are trained in Singapore. The company has updated safety procedures for flying to each of the airports it serves in Myanmar – the first airline in Myanmar to undertake this task since the 1950s.

For the moment AM flies only to Mandalay, Bagan (Pagan), Thandwe (Sandoway) and Heho. Plans are under way to add more domestic routes as well as international flights to and from Chiang Mai and Chiang Rai in Thailand.

Ticketing & Reservations Unlike Myanma Airways, Air Mandalay has ticketing services overseas – but thus far only in Bangkok and Singapore: Mekong Land (☎ 66-2-712 5842, 381 0881, fax 391 7212), 399/6 Soi Thonglor 21, Bangkok, Thailand; MAS Travel Centre (☎ 65-235 4411, 737 8877, fax 235 3033), 19 Tanglin Rd, Tanglin Shopping Centre, Singapore.

Fares AM flights cost a bit more than MA

flights to the same destinations. They offer two categories of fare: normal and the slightly cheaper standby.

BUS & TRUCK

In general, buses in Myanmar operated by the state-owned Road Transport Enterprise tend to be crowded, ancient and unreliable. Within the last couple of years a fleet of new private, air-con express buses have caught on for services from Yangon to Meiktila, Pyay (Prome), Mandalay, and Taunggyi – with more sure to come with the ongoing privatisation of the transport industry. These new express buses beat Myanma Railway's express trains in both speed and ticket price; they also stop for meals along the way. Another major difference between bus and train is that all bus tickets may be purchased using kyat; if there's a dollar/FEC fare posted it's usually equivalent to the kyat fare figured at the free-market rate.

There are also many modern Japanese pickup trucks installed with bench seats (rather like an Indonesian *bemo* or Thai *songthaew)* coming into use in the country. In fact nowadays most intercity travel off the main routes is accomplished by Toyota pickups carrying 20 or more passengers plus cargo.

These days foreigners are permitted to buy bus tickets of any class, using kyat, to any destination within or near the main Yangon-Mandalay-Bagan-Taunggyi triangle. We also found buses were easily boarded in most other places, too, except for 'brown' areas toward the Thai border.

Trip durations for public road transport are very elastic. Burmese superstition says whenever you're on a journey, you shouldn't ask 'How much longer?' or 'When will it arrive?' as this is only tempting fate. Upcountry roads in central Myanmar are generally in reasonable condition on the main routes but they're always narrow. When oncoming vehicles meet or when one has to overtake another, both vehicles have to pull partly off the road. Breakdowns and tyre punctures are common.

TRAIN
Myanma Railways

Myanmar maintains 4684 km of metre-gauge railway line – much of which is now open to foreign tourists – and 550 railway stations. As of 1995 rolling stock consisted of 318 locomotives – 48 steam and the remainder diesel – plus 1130 passenger coaches.

The 716-km trip from Yangon to Mandalay is the only train trip most visitors consider – there are daily and nightly reserved cars on express trains on this route where you can be sure of getting a seat. One way to tell whether an approaching train is express or local is to check the engine colour; express engines are painted yellow, local ones blue.

Express trains hold the edge over buses for comfort, atmosphere and scenery. But if speed, punctuality or cost are important criteria, then the new private express buses are usually a better choice.

The express trains are far superior to the general run of Burmese trains. In fact we'd recommend avoiding most other trains for any long trip – one 12-hour train trip that ends up running 15 hours late is enough for most people. The Mandalay to Myitkyina route, though scheduled to take around 24 hours often takes 40 hours; in 1995 this train derailed, killing 120.

Apart from the straightforward Yangon-Bago-Thazi-Mandalay line, you can also take the branch line from Pyinmana to Kyauk Padaung (about 50 km from Bagan) or the branch from Thazi to Shwenyaung (about 11 km from Inle Lake). At Mandalay there are three branches: one running slightly north-west across the Ava Bridge and up to Yeu, one directly north to Myitkyina in the Kachin State, and one north-east through Pyin U Lwin (Maymyo) to Lashio in the northern part of the Shan State. From Yangon lines also run north-west to Pyay, with a branch off to Pathein (Bassein), while from Bago there is a branch off south-east to Kyaikto (jumping-off point for Mt Kyaik-tiyo) and Mawlamyine (Moulmein).

Note also that Burmese trains are classified by a number and either the suffix 'Up' for north-bound trains, or 'Down' for south-bound trains.

Private Railways

Although most trains are operated by state-owned Myanma Railways, a few private enterprises have come into existence as well. Between Yangon and Mandalay the private Dagon Mann line runs express trains that are a bit nicer than the state-run express trains. However the steep dollar fares are clearly designed to dissuade foreigners from taking the train, which caters to upper-crust Burmese rather than tourists. In fact the only reason the DM accepts foreigners is that the government requires the company to set aside a few seats to help fill the demand for space during the tourist season. For more detail on this train, see under Train in the Getting There & Away section of the Yangon chapter.

Two private companies operate trains along the Mandalay to Myitkyina line. In this case the only alternative is the very slow and uncomfortable ordinary government train. Ticket prices for foreigners, though many times higher those for locals, are reasonable compared to DM fares.

Classes

Express trains offer two classes of passage: upper class and ordinary class. The main differences between ordinary and upper are that the seats recline in the latter and can be reserved in advance, while ordinary features hard upright seats that can't be reserved.

The No 5 Up/No 6 Down train between Yangon and Mandalay is a 'special express' which utilises relatively new Chinese equipment. The upper-class Chinese cars contain 30 wide seats in rows of three; other express trains may use older South Korean cars, which also seat three across but contain a total of 40 seats so there's less room.

Myanma Railways and Myanmar Travels & Tours (MTT) no longer deny the existence of sleeping cars, but the one or two pulled by the No 5 Up/No 6 Down are usually occupied by Burmese VIPs or foreign tour groups. These sleeping cars contain five cabins, each with four berths, a fan, light and a small table with washbasin underneath. If demand is high enough the No 3 Up/No 4 Down may also pull a sleeper.

Private Cars Myanma Railways keeps a couple of private railcars at the Yangon station which are available for hire when not being used by government VIPs. Each comes with a kitchen, dining area, sitting area, double-berth cabin and six fold-down beds (in the dining and sitting cabins). The cars can be hooked on to any train along the Yangon-Mandalay and Thazi-Nyaungshwe (Yaunghwe) lines – and possibly other lines by special permit. The price is negotiable depending on how long the car is needed; a typical arrangement would be US$500 for up to nine days, including the services of an on-board cook. At night these private cars are usually parked on sidings within railway station limits along the way. For more information, see the stationmaster at Yangon Railway Station.

Bookings

For tickets along the Yangon-Mandalay trunk line, all foreigners are supposed to purchase train tickets from MTT or from the windows labelled 'Foreigner Ticket Centre' at the Yangon and Mandalay stations, open 8 am to 8 pm daily. Only Mandalay, Yangon and Thazi tickets are available from these sources. For Bago you must go to the Advance Booking Office (no English sign) on Bogyoke Aung San St adjacent to the station; the latter is only open 6 to 10 am and 1 to 4 pm.

There are two advantages to booking your express train tickets through MTT in Yangon: this office accepts Visa, MasterCard and American Express, and a seat quota set aside for foreigners means you might be able to get a seat even when the station window says the train is full. Contrary to rumour we found the fares to be exactly the same at both places (though fares differ according to which express train you take, even along the same line). A day's notice is usually enough for booking a seat.

If you want to try your luck at getting a coveted sleeper you'll need at least a couple of weeks notice. During the November to March tourist season berths are booked months in advance; assuming you hold a seat on a train pulling a sleeper car (No 5 Up/No 6 Down or No 3 Up/No 4 Down), your best bet is to try to upgrade to a berth after boarding. If any are available due to last-minute cancellations you should be able to move from seat to berth for a US$3 to US$5 additional fare paid directly to the conductor.

To buy tickets at other railway stations you can use the same ticket windows as the Burmese. For common tourist destinations – Bago, Pyin U Lwin, Kyaikto, for example – an inflated dollar/FEC fare is usually collected. To other points you may be able to pay in kyat. Some foreigners riding the scenic but slow train between Shwenyaung

and Thazi have been charged dollars/FECs while others have paid in kyat – even on the same day! Dollar/FEC fares run roughly ten times the local fare in real kyat; an upper class seat on an express train from Yangon to Mandalay costs foreigners US$30 to US$38 (depending on the train), while locals pay K350 for upper class, K140 for ordinary. Foreigners aren't permitted to ride in ordinary class on this line; on most other branch lines where foreigners are allowed to pay in kyat rather than dollars/FECs there's usually no problem buying an ordinary ticket if that's what you want – at least not yet.

If you're having trouble buying a ticket or making yourself understood at a station, try seeking out the stationmaster – the person at the station most likely to speak English and most inclined to help you out with getting a seat.

Train Schedules & Fares

Train	Departure	Arrival	Fare
Yangon to Mandalay			
11 Up	6.00 am	9.10 pm	US$30
17 Up	3.15 pm	5.40 am	US$18-50 (DM private express)
5 Up	5.00 pm	7.00 am	US$30
15 Up	6.30 pm	8.30 am	US$38 (special express)
3 Up	7.30 pm	10.35 am	US$30
7 Up	9.00 pm	11.30 am	US$30
Yangon to Thazi			
11 Up	6.00 am	5.52 pm	US$27
5 Up	5.00 pm	4.14 am	US$27
15 Up	6.30 pm	5.36 am	US$33 (special express)
3 Up	7.30 pm	7.17 am	US$27
Mandalay to Yangon			
12 Down	6.00 am	9.30 pm	US$30
6 Down	3.15 pm	5.20 am	US$30
18 Down	4.15 pm	6.20 am	US$18-50 (DM private express)
16 Down	5.30 pm	7.30 am	US$38 (special express)
4 Down	6.30 pm	10.00 am	US$30
8 Down	8.30 pm	12.50 pm	US$30
Thazi to Yangon			
12 Down	9.23 am	9.30 pm	US$27
6 Down	6.00 pm	5.20 am	US$27
16 Down	8.16 pm	7.30 am	US$33 (special express)
4 Down	9.43 pm	10.00 am	US$27

CAR

Prohibitions on car hire in Myanmar have lifted over the last few years and it's now very easy to hire a reasonably new, air-conditioned car with driver for around US$45 a day, less for older, non-air-con cars. The usual per-day asking price will be around US$50, including driver and all fuel. If you hire for five days or more and pay for fuel yourself the cost can drop to as low as US$30 a day. There are no car rental agencies per se, but most travel agencies in Yangon, Mandalay or Bagan – and some guest houses and hotels elsewhere – can arrange cars and drivers.

Foreigners with business or residence visas are permitted to drive themselves, although most still hire drivers. Driving conditions are poor and a driver adds little to the hire cost. Of the 24,000 km of roads in Myanmar, slightly less than half are bituminous or metalled; the remainder are graded gravel, unimproved dirt or simple vehicle tracks. To compound the difficulty, Myanmar traffic law requires vehicles be driven on the right-hand side of the road even though the vast majority of cars and trucks – because they are low-cost, basic Japanese models – have right-hand drive. Supposedly Ne Win changed driving customs from the left side of the road to the right in 1970 on the advice of a fortune-teller who vaguely suggested he move the country from left to right to improve his karma. This contradictory arrangement is brilliant for keeping an eye on pedestrians and oxcarts alongside the road, but terrible for observing oncoming traffic.

Among the most popular and reliable rental cars in the country are second-hand, reconditioned Toyota hatchbacks imported from Japan. Often called 'vans', one fresh off the boat costs US$5000. Myanmar assembles its own Mazda jeeps – or 'MJs' – using 85% local parts. Though mostly a monopoly of the government, these jeeps make decent off-road vehicles. The old US-made, WW II-era Willys jeeps that once characterised outback Myanmar travel are becoming few and far between.

Myanmar is no longer quite self-sufficient in oil, and petrol can usually only be purchased in the area where the vehicle is registered. Officially, petrol from a MPPE (Myanma Electric Power Enterprise) station costs just K25 a gallon but is rationed at four gallons a week (an increase from two gallons per week a year ago). At makeshift black-market pumps – often located just around the corner from an MPPE station – petrol costs up to K180 a gallon, over K200 in remote areas and small towns. When Burmese vehicle owners make an up-country 'road trip' (the Burmese English term for any ex-Yangon driving) they either have to buy fuel on the black market or carry numerous jerry cans of petrol along.

Another small cost to consider when travelling by car is the customary K5 'toll' collected upon entering many towns and villages throughout Myanmar – a legacy of the tributes paid to warlord states in centuries past. More a curiosity than a true financial burden, the road toll means you should carry lots of K5 bills along – Burmese drivers are adept at handing these to the toll collectors while barely slowing down.

MOTORCYCLE

Apparently there's no longer any restriction on hiring motorcycles in Myanmar – you may even drive them yourself if you possess a valid International Driving Permit. Almost any large motorcycle dealer will entertain a hire offer. In Yangon try Super Star Motorcycle Sale Centre (☎ 01-72290) at 222 Pansodan St or Mandalay Central Enterprise (☎ 01-73652) at 146 Pansodan St. Rates are high compared to Thailand, up to US$20 per day for nothing larger than a Japanese 125cc. A substantial deposit may be required. You might also consider buying a used bike and selling it back to the dealer at a slightly reduced price after a few weeks on the road.

Always check a machine over thoroughly before you take it out. Look at the tyres to see if they still have tread, look for oil leaks, test the brakes. You may be held liable for any problems that weren't duly noted before your departure. Newer bikes cost more than clunkers, but are generally safer and more reliable.

If you get a flat you can't deal with or just need air, you'll find plenty of tyre repair places along the road – look for oil drum tops painted with two Burmese characters spelling *lei* or 'air'.

Precautions

Wear protective clothing and a helmet (the dealer should be able to provide a helmet with the bike if asked). Without a helmet, a minor slide on gravel can leave you with concussion, cuts or bruises. Long pants, long-sleeved shirts and shoes are highly recommended as protection against sunburn and as a second skin if you fall. If your helmet doesn't have a visor, then wear goggles, glasses or sunglasses to keep bugs, dust and other debris out of your eyes. It is practically suicidal to ride on Myanmar's highways without taking these minimum precautions for protecting your body. Gloves are also a good idea – to prevent blisters from holding on to the twist-grips for long periods of time.

Distribute whatever weight you're carrying on the bike as evenly as possible across the frame. Too much weight at the back of the bike makes the front end less easy to control and prone to rising up suddenly on bumps and inclines.

For distances of over 100 km or so, take along an extra supply of motor oil and, if riding a two-stroke machine, carry two-stroke engine oil. On long trips, oil burns fast.

BICYCLE

Bikes can easily be hired in Mandalay, Bagan, Pyin U Lwin and around Inle Lake. Guest houses often have a few for rent at only K100 or K150 per day. Just about anywhere outside Yangon, bikes are the ideal form of local transport since they're cheap, non-polluting and keep you moving slowly enough to see everything. Outside Yangon and Mandalay vehicular traffic is generally very light. Carefully note the condition of the bike before hiring; if it breaks down you are responsible and parts can be expensive.

If renting doesn't appeal, you can buy a sturdy new made-in-India Hero for US$40, a slightly better Five Rams from China for US$50 or a 'top-of-the-line' Crocodile from Thailand for US$150. All are plain, utilitarian, all-black city bikes with moderately heavy frames.

A few visitors bring their own touring bikes into Myanmar; nowadays there doesn't seem to be any problem with customs as long as you make the proper declarations upon entering the country.

Grades in most parts of Myanmar open to tourism are moderate. Frontier regions, on the other hand – particularly the Shan, Kayin, Kayah and Chin states – tend to be mountainous. Everywhere you'll find plenty of opportunity for dirt-road and off-road pedalling – in fact you must come prepared for it! Especially in the north, a sturdy mountain bike would make a good alternative to a touring rig.

One of the most scenic routes is a loop that starts in Thazi (accessible by train), runs east through hilly Kalaw and Pindaya to Inle Lake, than north along the rugged road to Lashio via Loilem, back around to Mandalay and down the flat Ayeyarwady (Irrawaddy) River plains to Bagan. This itinerary can be accomplished in the 28 days allowed by the regular tourist visa. Shorter trips out of Mandalay to Monywa, Pyin U Lwin, Sagaing, Ava and Amarapura also make satisfying rides.

Anyone with previous Third World cycling experience will find Myanmar a fairly straightforward pedal, though an extra measure of resourcefulness and cycling savvy is called for due to the overall lack of accommodation and transport infrastructure. November through February are the best cycling months in terms of weather. Most larger towns have bike shops – there are several in Mandalay and Yangon – but they often stock only a few Indian, Chinese or locally made parts. All the usual bike trip precautions apply – bring a small repair kit with plenty of spare parts, a helmet, reflective clothing and plenty of insurance.

RIVER FERRY

A huge fleet of riverboats, heir to the old Irrawaddy Flotilla Company, still ply Myanmar's major rivers. Many of the boats date back 80 or 100 years to the British era. In Burmese English they're still called 'steamers' even though the original stern-wheelers have all been converted to diesel. River ferry is without doubt one of the most enjoyable ways to cover long distances in Myanmar. The main drawback is speed; where both modes of transport are available, a boat typically takes three to four times as long as road travel along the same route.

Today the Inland Water Transport Co (IWT) has over 500 boats totalling nearly 1½ million tons and they carry at least 14 million passengers annually. Another thousand or so private cargo and passenger boats ply the waterways. That is just a pale shadow of the former glory of the Glasgow-owned Irrawaddy Flotilla Company which ceased operations in 1948. Their Siam Class steamers carried 4200 deck passengers each plus 40 more in staterooms; they were 100 metres long and travelled faster upriver than the present-day boats can manage down! The captains of these mighty riverboats were so important that a Mandalay shop once had a sign announcing they were 'Silk Mercers to the Kings and Queens of Burma and the Captains of the Steamers'. The Flotilla Company was struck a disastrous blow by WW II, and the wrecks of 96 of their boats are still at Mandalay, scuttled in the river in 1942.

There are 8000 km of navigable river in Myanmar, with the most important river being the Ayeyarwady, of course. Even in the dry season boats can travel from the delta all the way north to Bhamo, and in the wet they can reach Myitkyina. Other important rivers include the Twante Canal, which links the Ayeyarwady to Yangon, and the Chindwin, which joins the Ayeyarwady a little above Bagan. The Thanlwin (Salween) River in the east is only navigable for about 200 km from its mouth at Mawlamyine.

Today the red-and-black boats of the nationalised water transport corporation are rather run-down and ramshackle, but it still takes great expertise to navigate Myanmar's waterways. Rapidly changing sandbanks and shallow water during the dry season mean the captains and pilots have to keep in constant touch with the changing pattern of the river flows. Seven pilots are used on the stretch from Mandalay to Pyay, for example. Each is an expert on his own particular segment of the river.

Many of the passengers on the long-distance ferries are traders who make stops along the way to pick up or deliver goods. Along the heavily travelled, 423-km Yangon-Pyay-Mandalay route, for example, there are 28 ferry landings where merchants can ply their trade.

Only a few riverboat routes are regularly used by visitors. Best known is the Mandalay-Bagan service which departs Mandalay early morning twice weekly and arrives at Nyaung U, just north of Bagan, 12 to 14 hours later – so long as you don't get stuck on a sandbank along the way, that is. There is a quite amazing amount of transport shuttling up and down this riverine 'road to Mandalay' and it's a trip which most people seem to enjoy. The new 'tourist boat', which carries foreigners on the upper deck, locals on the lower, isn't quite as adventurous an experience as taking the local ferries but it's faster. If you take local boats, this trip can be extended to Pyay or all the way to Yangon; it's two days travel downriver from Bagan to Pyay, where you change boats and have another couple of days travel before reaching Yangon.

There are other, less well-known, river trips the adventurous traveller can also consider. Twante, for example, is only a few hours from Yangon, and you can continue all the way to Pathein, 18 hours away. According to those who have managed to accomplish it (permits are necessary), the river journey between Bhamo and Mandalay is one of the most scenic. People in the Myanmar travel industry say Bhamo will be opening to tourism soon, which means this trip should become available to the average visitor in the near future.

Another shorter trip you can make quite

easily is the trip upriver from Mandalay to Mingun. You can also make short day-excursions by rented boat out of Yangon and Bagan.

Bookings

IWT fares, calculated by mileage, are inexpensive if you manage to pay in kyat. As with train travel, the collection of dollars/FECs versus kyat seems to be somewhat arbitrary. We easily managed to pay kyat for a cabin on the ferry from Pathein to Yangon, a fairly well-travelled route, but were charged dollars for the more remote Sittwe to Mrauk U (Myohaung) ferry. The dollar fare for the latter was quite reasonable considering the value received; the kyat fare for the Pathein trip was downright cheap.

The main IWT ticket office in Yangon sits one street back from Lan Thit St Jetty, in Bldg No 63. This is where all the locals purchase tickets. Foreigners are always referred to a small white building next to Transit Shed No 1, opposite nearby Kaingdan St Jetty. Here you can reserve tickets directly from IWT deputy division manager U Win Shwe, who has held the position for over a decade. To be safe, try to book a week in advance of travel, although a day's advance purchase may be sufficient in many cases.

Boats & Classes

The standard long-distance ferry features two large decks, a lower deck consisting of the bare steel hull and an upper deck finished in wood. These ferries typically hold 286 passengers altogether, 123 on the more costly upper deck and the remainder below. Only upper-deck passage can be reserved in advance; assigned numbers painted on the deck indicate the reserved spots. Some boats feature a dozen or so sling chairs toward the bow of the upper deck; these cost a bit more than regular upper-deck class. Boats running day routes usually feature a saloon compartment in the upper deck of the bow with a few wooden chairs and an attached toilet. Monks usually ride in a separate, wired-off section of the upper foredeck.

Those craft running overnight routes may contain a few beds in the saloon compartment. A few boats even have cabins with sleeping berths in the bow, usually no more than six cabins sleeping two each. (The Mandalay-Bagan tourist boat is an exception – it contains 10 cabins even though no overnight travel is involved!) On most routes, saloon- and cabin-class space is very difficult to come by, though foreigners have a better chance than the average Burmese. Military officers, of course, always have first choice.

A fleet of three new Chinese-built ferries featuring a triple-deck design will soon be put into service along the Yangon-Pathein route and along the Ayeyarwady River from Mandalay to Pyay via Nyuang U. These vessels feature 18 double cabins in 1st class, 10 double cabins in 2nd class, three 16-berth cabins in 3rd class and deck space for 270 passengers. First-class cabins on the triple-deckers have attached toilets and showers.

SHIP

Although the obstacles standing in your way are daunting, it's possible to travel along Myanmar's coastline via Myanma Five Star Line (MFSL), the country's state-owned ocean transport enterprise. MFSL maintains just 21 craft which sail north and south from Yangon about twice a month. Only eight vessels offer passenger service: *MV Taunggyi, MV Hakha, MV Myitkyina, MV Loikaw, MV Lashio, MV Bagan, MV Hpaan* and *MV Htonywa*. Shipping dates vary from month to month and are announced via a public chalkboard at the main MFSL office in Yangon.

Southbound ships sail regularly to Kawthoung, a two-night voyage from Yangon, to pick up goods shipped through Thailand's Ranong Province, with occasional scheduled calls at Dawei (Tavoy) and Myeik. Northbound ships call at Thandwe (a full day from Yangon) and Kyaukpyu (one night) before docking in Sittwe (five more hours) for cargo from India and Bangladesh.

Since to book passage on any MFSL ship you must show an MHT travel permit that specifies travel by ship, and since you must wait around for up to two weeks for a ship going your way, this is by far the most difficult public transport to arrange. Even if you have a date and permit at hand, as with Myanma Airways the government sometimes requisitions a whole ship at the last minute, thereby throwing all plans into disarray.

If you're bent on trying for a ticket, it would be best to have a Burmese citizen make inquiries on your behalf as the bureaucracy can be staggering. Tickets can only be purchased two days ahead; they are in such demand that locals are only able to buy them via a lottery system. The MFSL director told us the only foreign passenger he could remember having taken an MFSL voyage during the last five years was a German ambassador who sailed to Dawei.

Foreigners who have leapt all the hurdles will be issued one of the 20 coveted berths in saloon class. All ships leave from the MFSL Jetty (also known as the Chanmayeiseikan Jetty), just west of Pansodan St Jetty. Saloon fares: Kawthoung K1541; Dawei K858; Myeik K932; Thandwe K546; Kyaukpyu K793; Sittwe K978.

LOCAL TRANSPORT

Larger towns in Myanmar offer a variety of city buses *(kaa)*, bicycle rickshaws or trishaws *(sai-kaa)*, horsecarts *(myint hlei)*, vintage taxis *(taxi)*, more modern little three-wheelers somewhat akin to auto-rickshaws *(thoun bein* or 'three wheels'), tiny four-wheeled Mazdas *(lei bein* or 'four wheels') and modern Japanese pick-up trucks (also *kaa)* used like Indonesian bemos or Thai songthaews.

Small towns rely heavily on horsecarts and trishaws as the main mode of local transport. In the five largest cities (Yangon, Mandalay, Pathein, Mawlamyine and Taunggyi), public buses ply regular routes along the main avenues for a fixed per-person rate, usually no more than K2. Standard rates for taxis, trishaws and horsecarts are sometimes 'boosted' for foreigners. A little bargaining may be in order; ask around locally to find out what the going fares are. The supply of drivers and vehicles usually exceeds the demand, so it's usually not hard to move the fare down toward normal levels.

You can rent bicycles in Mandalay, Bagan, Pyin U Lwin and Nyaungshwe.

TOURS

Itineraries for Myanmar tours booked anywhere in the world look much the same. The cheapest (around US$400) is a four-day, three-night Yangon package that includes a visa, airport transfers in Yangon, guide service and accommodation only, booked through travel agencies in Bangkok. With a package of this sort, you must book your own roundtrip flight to Yangon, arrange for your own local transport outside Yangon and buy your own meals.

More expensive trips costing US$2000 and up run 14 or 15 days in Yangon, Mandalay, Pyin U Lwin, Bagan, Kalaw, Pindaya, Inle Lake, Taunggyi and Bago, including visa, roundtrip air from Bangkok, local transport, accommodation, all meals and guide service. Such tours can easily be booked in the USA, Europe, Japan, New Zealand and Australia, or from agencies in Bangkok.

It's also possible to arrange tours locally out of Yangon and Mandalay. There are well over a hundred travel agencies in Yangon, so it pays to shop around. Many will custom design a tour according to your requests for about the same price as a package tour booked abroad.

Yangon

Yangon (formerly Rangoon) lies in the fertile delta country of southern Myanmar, on the wide Yangon River about 30 km from the sea. Although the population hovers around four million, the city gives a very different impression from other Asian capitals of similar size. It seems full of trees and shade – even old growth teak here and there – and some neighbourhoods are practically jungle. Shimmering stupas float above the treetops. If you can close your eyes to the neglect, the lack of upkeep and the decay of the old colonial architecture downtown, you'll probably agree that this could be one of the most charming cities in the East. Downtown, the streets are wide and carefully laid out on a properly British colonial grid system.

The city appears to be on the threshold of major change following the 1989 banishment of socialism. Since April 1992, when the moderate, pro-capitalist General Than Shwe took power, many new cars and trucks have taken to city roads, cellular phones are commonly seen downtown and satellite dishes dot the horizon. Though the capital is still easygoing – the word 'rush' simply doesn't seem to be part of the Yangon vocabulary and there's little of the frenetic, neon-lit clamour of Bangkok to the east – one wonders for how much longer the city will escape the Asian megalopolis syndrome.

History

As Myanmar's capital city, Yangon is comparatively young – it only became capital in 1885 when the British completed the conquest of Upper Myanmar and Mandalay's brief period as the centre of the last Burmese kingdom ended.

Despite its short history as the seat of national government, Yangon has been in existence for a long time – although very much as a small town in comparison to places like Bago (Pegu), Pyay (Prome) or Thaton. In 1755 King Alaungpaya conquered Lower Myanmar and built a new city

Highlights
- Glittering Shwedagon Paya with its amazing mix of pavilions, stupas, images and bells
- Colonial architecture of old 'Rangoon' including the legendary Strand Hotel
- Colossal reclining Buddha in Chaukhtatgyi Paya
- Pro-democracy landmarks such as the Martyrs' Mausoleum and Aung San Suu Kyi's house
- Sprawling Bogyoke Aung San and Theingyi Zei markets
- Peaceful Kandawgyi and Inya lakes

on the site of Yangon, which at that time was known as 'Dagon'. Yangon means 'end of strife': the king rather vainly hoped that with the conquest of Lower Myanmar his struggles would be over.

In 1756, with the destruction of Thanlyin (Syriam) across the river, Yangon also became an important sea port. In 1841 the city was virtually destroyed by fire; the rebuilt town again suffered extensive damage during the Second Anglo-Burmese War in 1852. The British, its new masters,

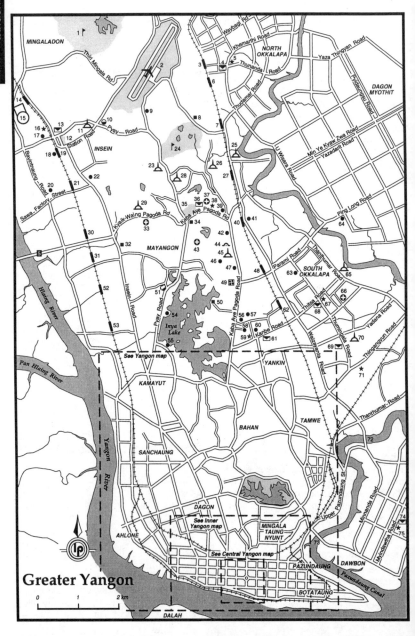

Greater Yangon

0   1   2 km

PLACES TO STAY	21	Gyogone Railway Station	48	Parami Railway Station
8 Airport Hotel (under construction)	22	Yangon Institute of Technology	49	Chanmyay Yeiktha Meditation Centre
32 Nawarat Hotel	23	Shan Kyaung	51	Philippines Embassy
34 Yangon City Hotel	24	Myanmar Golf Club	52	Thirimyaing Railway Station
50 Inya Lake Hotel	25	Mai La Mu Paya	53	Kamayut Railway Station
	26	Naga Cave Paya		
OTHER	27	Tadagale Railway Station	54	International Business Centre
1 City Golf Resort	28	Nagayon Paya	55	Boat Club
2 Yangon International Airport	29	Kyaikwaing Paya	56	Ministry of Forestry
3 Okkalapa Railway Station	30	Thamaing Railway Station	57	Ministry of Agriculture
4 Post Office	31	Okkyin Railway Station	58	Survey Department
5 Police Station			59	Police Station
6 Pweseikkon Railway Station	33	Hospital of the Disabled	60	Teacher Training College
7 Kyaukyedwin Railway Station	35	Myaing Haywun Park	61	Post Office
9 Department of Civil Aviation	36	Post Office	62	Kanbe Railway Station
10 Highway Bus Centre	37	Yangon Psychiatric Hospital	63	Nandawun Market
11 Ah Lain Nga Sint Paya	38	Police Station	64	Pinglong Market (new gem market)
12 Insein Park	39	Nawaday Cinema	65	South Okkalapa Paya
13 Post Office	40	Yegu Railway Station	66	Women and Children Hospital
14 Ywama Railway Station	41	Radio Transmitting Station	67	Police Station
15 Insein Prison	42	Department of Religious Affairs	68	Post Office
16 Police Station	43	Sangha Hospital	69	Post Office
17 Insein Market	44	Maha Pasan Guha	70	Kyaikkasan Paya
18 Railways Workshop	45	Kaba Aye Paya	71	Police Station
19 Insein Railway Station	46	State Pariyatti Sasana University	72	Thuwunna Bridge
20 Department of Health (Malaria Control)	47	Myanma Gems Enterprise	73	Thaketa Bridge
			74	Post Office
			75	Police Station

rebuilt the capital to its present plan and corrupted the city's name to 'Rangoon'.

Yangon's early history as Dagon is tied very closely to its grand Buddhist stupa, the Shwedagon Paya. It stands not in the downtown centre, but about three km to the north – yet totally dominates the Yangon skyline.

In 1988 around 15% of Yangon's downtown population – all squatters – were moved to seven new towns *(myo thit)* north-east of downtown. Many of the old colonial buildings once occupied by the squatters have now been refurbished for use as offices, businesses and apartments.

Starting in the early 1990s, the government began sprucing up the city's appearance by cleaning the streets and painting many public buildings. To try and keep blood-red spittle off the streets, the selling of betelnut was banned in 1995.

Orientation

The city is bounded to the south and west by the Yangon River (also known as the Hlaing River) and to the east by Pazundaung Canal, which flows into the Yangon River. The whole city is divided into townships, and street addresses are often suffixed with these (eg 126 52nd St, Botataung Township). North of downtown the city opens up like the top of a funnel and spreads along a network of long, curving avenues.

At the northern end of the city, most businesses and hotels are found along Pyay Rd, Kaba Aye Pagoda Rd or Insein Rd – long avenues running south from the airport area to the city centre. Addresses in this northern area often quote the number of miles from Sule Paya – the landmark *paya* (pagoda) in the city's centre. For example, 'Pyay Rd,

Mile 8' means the place is eight miles north of Sule Paya on Pyay Rd.

Two of the most important townships outside the downtown area are Dagon – where you'll find Shwedagon Paya, People's Park and several embassies – and Bahan, site of many of the city's medium and upper-range hotels and inns.

Downtown Yangon is a relatively simple area to find your way around and pleasant enough to explore on foot. The main downtown streets are laid out in a grid system, with the minor north-south streets numbered in the North American fashion. Many of the major roadways were renamed after independence, but some of the old names persist and this can be confusing. Mahabandoola Garden St, for example, is still often called Barr St and has both new and old street signs. Other old and new central city names include:

Old Name	New Name
Sparks St	Bo Aung Gyaw St
China St	Shwedagon Pagoda Rd
Latter St	Latha St
Phayre St	Pansodan St
Godwin Rd	Lanmadaw St
Dalhousie St	Mahabandoola St
Bigandet/Fraser St	Anawrahta St
Montgomery St	Bogyoke Aung San St

The English terms 'street' and 'road' are used interchangeably in Yangon for the single Burmese word *lan*. Hence some maps may read 'Shwegondine St' while others will say 'Shwegondine Rd'; in Burmese it's simply 'Shwegondine Lan'.

Maps The *Yangon Tourist Map,* put out by Myanmar Travels & Tours (MTT), is cheap and useful enough for most people. If you anticipate spending a lot of time in the capital, it's worth seeking out the harder-to-find *Yangon City Map* (Printing & Publishing Enterprise) or the more detailed and more up-to-date *Yangon Guide Map* (Ministry of Forestry, Survey Department). Both of the latter maps were first published in 1993; the Ministry of Forestry map can usually be purchased from the Indian vendor standing

just outside the MTT office on Sule Pagoda Rd; you might also find it at Sarpay Beikman Book Centre on Merchant St.

Information
Tourist Office The Myanmar Travels & Tours office (☎ 01-78376, fax 89588), right beside Sule Paya at the intersection of Sule Pagoda Rd and Mahabandoola St, is the main centre for tourist inquiries. Basically nothing more than a government-run travel agency, its main purpose seems to be to discourage visitors from going anywhere off the main tourist quadrangle. Decent city maps of Bagan (Pagan), Mandalay and Yangon are sold for K20 to K30 each; postcards are also cheap here.

The office is open 8 am to 8 pm daily.

Money With the new Foreign Exchange Certificate system in place, no one bothers to change money at the official rate any more. If you're foolish enough to want to, the MTT cashier will gladly take foreign currency.

Yangon is the best place in the country for changing money at the free-market rate. Ask around first to establish what the current rate is. If you've bought FECs at the airport, the best place to change them is at a hotel or shop licensed to accept FECs. In general, Bogyoke Aung San Market is a good place to shop for moneychangers; several here are licensed to exchange kyat for FECs. If you don't have FECs, cash dollars are the only alternative; free-market moneychangers usually aren't interested in other foreign currencies.

Post The GPO is a short stroll east of the Strand Hotel on Strand Rd. It's open Monday to Friday from 9.30 am to 4.30 pm.

Telecommunications The Central Telephone & Telegraph Office at the corner of Pansodan and Mahabandoola Sts is the only public place in the country where international telephone calls can be conveniently arranged. The office is open Monday to Friday 8 am to 4 pm, weekends and holidays 9 am to 2 pm.

See the Facts for the Visitor chapter for further details on making international calls.

Foreign Embassies Yangon can be a good place to get visas for other countries. You can usually pay for them with free (black-market) kyats so they're very cheap, and because Yangon isn't a big tourist stopover visas are usually issued quickly. Visas for Laos can be obtained directly from the Lao Embassy, for example; in Thailand you would have to go through a travel agency for the same visa.

Australia
88 Strand Rd (☎ 01-80711)
Bangladesh
56 Kaba Aye Pagoda Rd (☎ 01-51174)
Belgium
15 Myayagon St, Kandawgalay (☎ 01-76505)
Canada
c/o UK Embassy
China
1 Pyidaungsu Yeiktha Rd (☎ 01-21280)
Denmark
65-A Kaba Aye Pagoda Rd (☎ 01-60883)
France
102 Pyidaungsu Yeiktha Rd (☎ 01-82122)
Germany
32 Natmauk Rd (☎ 01-50477)
India
545-547 Merchant St (☎ 01-82550)
Indonesia
100 Pyidaungsu Yeiktha Rd (☎ 01-82550)
Israel
49 Pyay Rd (☎ 01-22290)
Italy
3 Inya Myaing Rd, Golden Valley (☎ 01-30966)
Japan
100 Natmauk Rd (☎ 01-52288)
Laos
A-1 Diplomatic Quarters, Taw Win Rd
(☎ 01-22482)
Malaysia
82 Pyidaungsu Yeiktha Rd (☎ 01-20248)
Nepal
16 Natmauk Rd (☎ 01-50633)
Netherlands
53-55 Mahabandoola Garden St (☎ 01-50633)
Norway
65-A Kaba Aye Pagoda Rd (☎ 01-60883)
Pakistan
A-4 Diplomatic Headquarter, Pyay Rd
(☎ 01-22881)
Philippines
56 Pyay Rd (☎ 01-64010)

Singapore
287 Pyay Rd (☎ 01-20854)
South Korea
97 University Ave (☎ 01-30497)
Spain
563 Merchant St (☎ 01-80608)
Sri Lanka
34 Taw Win Rd (☎ 01-22812)
Sweden
53-55 Mahabandoola Garden St (☎ 01-71495)
Thailand
91 Pyay Rd (☎ 01-21713)
UK
80 Strand Rd (☎ 01-81700)
USA
581 Merchant St (☎ 01-82055)
Vietnam
40 Komin Kochin (Thanlwin) Rd (☎ 01-50361)

Travel Agencies Because the number of airlines which fly in and out of Yangon are relatively few, most visitors to Myanmar never use domestic travel agencies except if they want to book a tour or hire a car. Of the more than 100 enterprises in Yangon calling themselves 'travel agencies', only a handful can be considered full-service, experienced tour agencies.

Among the more reliable agencies are:

Free Bird Tours
357 Bo Aung Gyaw St (☎ 01-94941, fax 89960)
Golden Express Tours
56 Wadan St (☎ 01-21479)
Journeys
Bldg 4/R-38, Mile 8, Pyay Rd (☎ 01-64275)
Myanmar Connection Travel
2 (B) Zizawa Lane (☎ 01-64169, fax 65230)
Tour Mandalay
194/196, 2nd Floor, Mahabandoola St
(☎ 01-90589, fax 62624)
White Horse Travel & Tours
218/5B Bo Aung Gyaw St (☎ 01-96837, fax 97946)

Bookshops & Libraries Inwa Book Store, at 232 Sule Pagoda Rd between Anawrahta and Bogyoke Aung San Sts, has a fair collection of new books in English. Sarpay Beikman Book Centre, on Merchant St between 37th and 38th Sts, carries most of the government-published books on Myanmar.

Pagan Bookshop on 37th St has the country's most complete selection of English-language books on Myanmar and South-East

Asia. The owner often has the front gate pulled across the entrance, but this doesn't mean the place is necessarily closed unless the door inside the gate is closed, too. Also check the many bookstalls around Bogyoke Aung San Market (sometimes known as Scott Market) or along 37th St. See the Books, Maps & Periodicals section in the Facts for the Visitor chapter for more details.

The UK Embassy has a small library of English-language magazines and books; it's open to the public Monday to Friday from 8.30 am to noon. The American Center at 14 Taw Win St also has a collection of books and magazines which can be perused Monday to Friday from 9 am to 4 pm.

For French-language material, check the Alliance Française (☎ 01-82122), attached to the French Embassy; it's open Tuesdays and Fridays only.

Religious Services For those seeking houses of worship in the Judaeo-Christian-Muslim tradition:

Anglican/Episcopal/Protestant
    Holy Trinity Cathedral, 446 Bogyoke Aung San St (☎ 01-72326)
    English Methodist Church, 63 Alaungpaya Rd (☎ 01-72808)
    Immanuel Baptist Church, Mahabandoola Garden St (☎ 01-85905)
    Kuo Yu Chinese Methodist Church, 47 Min Ye Kyaw Swa Rd, Ahlone (☎ 01-25141)
Catholic
    St Mary's Cathedral, 372 Bo Aung Gyaw St (☎ 01-72662)
    St Augustine's Church, 64 Inya Rd (☎ 01-30620)
Armenian Orthodox
    St John the Baptist Armenian Orthodox Church, 113 Bo Aung Gyaw St
Jewish
    Moseah Yeshua Synagogue, 85 26th St (☎ 01-75062), services on special occasions only
Muslim
    Surti Suni Jama Mosque, Shwebontha St
    Cholia Jama Mosque, Bo Soon Pat St
    Narsapuri (Moja) Mosque, 227 Shwebontha St

Laundry Professional laundry services usually do a better job of washing and ironing than Yangon's guest houses and small hotels. The latter tend to skimp on

detergent and clothes often come back looking almost as dirty as they were to begin with! Ava Laundry and Anglo Myanmar Laundry Service, two places on the southern side of Mahabandoola St between 41st and 42nd Sts, are fast, reliable and cheap.

Medical Services If you want medical attention in Yangon, your best bet is the Diplomatic Hospital (☎ 01-50149), also known as Kandawgyi Clinic, on Natmauk Rd at the north-eastern edge of Kandawgyi (Royal) Lake.

Emergency An ambulance can be summoned by dialling ☎ 192 or ☎ 01-71111. For police call ☎ 199 or ☎ 01-82511. At neither of these numbers can we guarantee an English-speaking operator; you may have to enlist the aid of a Burmese friend or acquaintance to make these calls.

Your embassy (see the Foreign Embassies list above) may also be able to assist with emergencies or serious problems. Many embassies and consulates maintain after-hours phone numbers which they'll disclose to passport-holders from the appropriate country. It's a good idea to register with your embassy upon arrival anyway so that the embassy staff will know where to reach you in case of an emergency at home.

Shwedagon Paya
The highlight of any visit to Yangon, and indeed Myanmar itself, Swedagon Paya is located just to the north of central Yangon, between the People's Park and Kandawagyi Lake. See the special section beginning on page 165 of this chapter for full details about Shwedagon, its design and historical significance.

Maha Wizaya (Vijaya) Paya
Almost opposite the southern gate to Shwedagon Paya, a pedestrian bridge links the Shwedagon complex with a well-proportioned zedi built in 1980 to commemorate the unification of Theravada Buddhism in Myanmar. The king of Nepal contributed

sacred relics for the zedi's relic chamber and Burmese strongman Ne Win had it topped with an 11-level hti – two more levels than the hti at Shwedagon.

Foreign media sometimes refer to the monument as 'Ne Win's pagoda' due to Ne Win's involvement in the project. Many Burmese citizens resent this phrase, pointing out that since the zedi was built by donations from the people it should rightfully be called the 'people's pagoda'. Furthermore, it is emphasised, any *kutho* or Buddhist merit created by its construction should accrue not to Ne Win but to the Burmese people who have enriched the man and his regime since 1962. Politics and religion aside, the Maha Wizaya stupa is one of the most attractive to have been built in Myanmar in decades.

Sule Paya

Situated in the centre of Yangon, beside the MTT office, the tall zedi at Sule Paya makes an excellent landmark; in fact it's used as a milestone from which all addresses to the north are measured. Legend says it's over 2000 years old but, as with many other ancient Burmese shrines, it has been rebuilt and repaired many times over the centuries so no one really knows when it was built. The central stupa is said to enshrine a hair of the Buddha; its Mon name, Kyaik Athok, translates as 'the stupa where a Sacred Hair Relic is enshrined'. Most likely, as with the zedi at Shwedagon, it was originally built by the Mon in the middle of this century.

The golden zedi is unusual in that its octagonal shape continues right up to the bell and inverted bowl. It stands 46 metres high and is surrounded by small shops and all the familiar non-religious activities which seem to be a part of every Burmese zedi.

Botataung Paya

Bo means 'leader' (usually in a military sense) and *tataung* is '1000' – the Botataung Paya was named after the 1000 military leaders who escorted relics of the Buddha brought from India over 2000 years ago. This ancient monument was completely des-troyed during WW II. It stood close to the Yangon wharves, and during an Allied air raid on 8 November 1943, a bomb scored a direct hit on the unfortunate paya.

After the war the Botataung was rebuilt in a very similar style to its predecessor, but with one important and unusual difference: unlike most zedis, which are solid, the Botataung is hollow and you can walk through it. There's a sort of mirrored maze inside the stupa, with glass showcases containing many of the ancient relics and artefacts, including small silver and gold Buddha images, which were sealed inside the earlier stupa. Above this interesting interior the golden stupa spire rises to 40 metres.

To the western side of the stupa is a hall containing a large gilded bronze Buddha cast during the reign of King Mindon Min. At the time of the British annexation it was kept in King Thibaw Min's glass palace, but after King Thibaw was exiled to India, the Brits shipped the image to London. In 1951 the image was returned to Myanmar and placed in the Botataung Paya.

Also on the grounds is a nat pavilion containing images of Thurathadi (the Hindu deity Saraswati, goddess of learning and music) and Thagyamin (Indra, king of the nats) flanking the thoroughly Burmese nat Bobogyi.

A short walk down from Botataung Paya at Botataung Jetty, you can watch ferryboats and oared water taxis cross the Yangon River.

Kaba Aye Paya

The 'world peace' zedi was built in 1952 for the 1954-56 Sixth Buddhist Synod. The 34-metre-high stupa also measures 34 metres around its base. It stands about 11 km north of downtown, a little beyond the Inya Lake Hotel. This attempt to construct a 'modern' paya was not terribly successful – it does not have much of the visual appeal of Myanmar's older, more graceful stupas. The interior of the monument, however, is hollow and inside are some nice Buddhist sculptures, including a *lei-myet-hna* or four-sided Buddha image sculpture.

YANGON

Maha Pasan Guha

The 'great cave' is a totally artificial one built close to the Kaba Aye Paya. It was here that the Sixth Buddhist Synod was held to coincide with the 2500th anniversary of the Buddha's enlightenment. The participants at the Synod were attempting to define a definitive text for the Buddhist scriptures known as the *Tripitaka*. The cavern measures 139 by 113 metres.

Chaukhtatgyi Paya

The reclining Buddha here is almost as large as the enormous figure in Bago. It's housed in a large metal-roofed shed on Shwegondine St, only a short distance east beyond the Shwedagon Paya. Surprisingly, this huge figure is little known and hardly publicised at all – if you can't get to Bago to see the Shwethalyaung, then don't miss this colossal image. Fortune-tellers on the surrounding platform offer astrological and palm readings.

Other Payas, Temples & Shrines

South of the Chaukhtatgyi Paya, there's a huge seated Buddha image at the **Ngahtatgyi Paya**. It's appropriately known as the

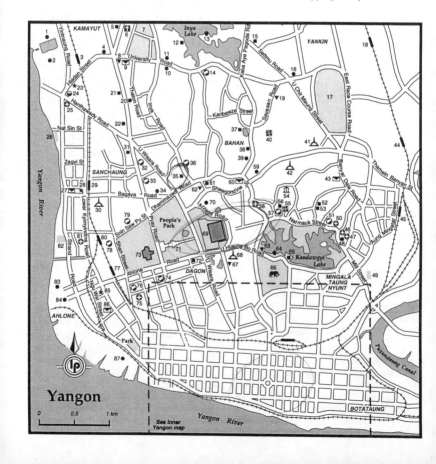

Yangon

'five-storey Buddha' and is located in the Ashay Tawya monastery. In Kemendine, in the west of the city, there's another huge seated Buddha in the **Kohtatgyi Paya** on Bagaya Rd; it stands (or sits) 20 metres high. There are many monasteries in the vicinity. Kemendine also has a busy night market.

Close to the airport, the **Mai La Mu Paya** has a series of images of the Buddha in his previous incarnations and also a reclining Buddha image. The paya is named after the mother of King Ukkalapa, the original founder of the city of Dagon. In Insein, west of the airport the **Ah Lain Nga Sint Paya** has

a five-storey tower and a particular connection with the nats and other spirit entities of Burmese Buddhism.

The **Yau Kyaw Paya** is a 30-minute drive from the city past the Kyaikkasan Paya. It's an interesting complex of buildings with tableaux depicting Buddhist legends, pet monkeys, deer and peacocks and an interesting museum crammed full of Burmese antiques. The paya is beside the Pazundaung Creek in a rural setting.

Kheng Hock Keong on Strand Rd is the largest Chinese temple in Yangon. Supported by a Hokkien association, the 100-year-old temple is most lively from around 6 to 9 am, when it's thronged with worshippers offering candles, flowers and incense to the Buddhist and Taoists altars within. Old men play Chinese checkers in the temple compound throughout the day. If you hang around long enough you may meet Mr Chan, an octogenarian *tai qi* and *qi gong* teacher who visits every morning after exercising at Mahabandoola Gardens. If you're interested in these ancient Chinese mental-physical disciplines, you can drop by Mr Chan's house at 322-B 25th St near Theingyi Zei.

The **Moseah Yeshua Synagogue**, at 85 26th St near Mahabandoola St, was founded over a hundred years ago by Sephardic Jews. In the classic Sephardic style, it contains a *bimah* in the centre of the main sanctuary and women's balcony upstairs. The wooden ceiling features the original blue-and-white Star of David motif. Myanmar counted around 2500 Jews – a combination of B'nai Israel, Cochin (Indian) and Iraqi heritages – up until nationalisation in the 1960s and '70s, when many began leaving the country. Today there are no more than 50 or so Burmese Jews left in the country, but surviving trustees maintain the synagogue for the occasional special service given by visiting rabbis from India. Caretaker Moses Samuels is happy to talk with visitors and show them the nearby Jewish cemetery with over 700 graves dating back to 1856.

Several Hindu temples can be found in the downtown section of the city, including **Sri Sri Siva Krishna** at 141 Pansodan St, **Sri Kali** on Anawrahta St between 26th and 27th Sts, and **Sri Devi** at Anawrahta and 51st Sts. These are the centres for the city's annual Murugu Festival, famous for colourful street processions featuring acts of ritual self-mutilation.

National Museum

Located on Pansodan St, close to the Strand Hotel, the building that houses the National Museum was originally the Bank of India. Inside, the pride of place is the eight-metre-high Lion Throne used by King Thibaw Min, the last Burmese king. The British took the throne from the Mandalay Supreme Court, outside the Mandalay Palace complex, and placed it in the Indian Museum in Calcutta following the annexation of Myanmar to the Raj. Thus it survived the destruction of the palace during WW II and after independence was returned to Yangon. The carving on the throne depicts the Lokanat or 'World Preserver' legend from Hindu-Burmese mythology, in which a battling lion and elephant cease fighting when a singing and dancing *deva* arrives on the scene.

Other exhibits include the Mandalay Regalia, a collection of gem-studded arms, swords, jewellery, bowls and other items. This too was taken by the British after the Third Anglo-Burmese War, and was returned to Myanmar in 1964 from the Victoria & Albert Museum in London. The museum also contains the royal couch that belonged to King Mindon's queen, a bronze cannon dating from 1757, the crocodile harp and other items – very few of which are labelled in English. The old photos of Mandalay Palace and Yangon are interesting, but everything else is second-best after the huge and intricately carved Lion Throne.

Note that the museum has a 2nd and a 3rd floor which are very easy to miss: access is from the ground floor, but you have to look for it as the only sign for the upstairs section is in Burmese – first of all you have to make your way through an empty room, then go round the lift shaft and climb some dingy stairs! Upstairs you'll find prehistoric and other early Burmese finds as well as traditional musical instruments. There are lots of English signs, though the excellent maps are mostly in Burmese. On the top floor are modern Burmese paintings by the talented U Ba Nyan and others.

Admission is US$5 and the museum is open from 10 am to 3 pm Monday to Friday. It is closed on weekends and on 'government-gazetted holidays'.

The government is building a new national museum on Pyay Rd, just around the corner from the Ministry of Foreign Affairs near the Indonesian and French embassies. No word yet as to when it will open but when it does the Pansodan St location will close and all exhibits will be moved to the new site.

Martyrs' Mausoleum

Close to the Shwedagon, on a hill offering a good view over the city, stands this memorial to Bogyoke Aung San and his fellow cabinet officers who were assassinated with him. It was here also that a bomb set off by North Koreans killed a number of South Korea's top government officials in late 1983.

Mahabandoola Garden

Just south-east of Sule Paya, this square urban park offers pleasant strolling in the downtown heart, especially early mornings when the Chinese come to practice tai qi and the air hasn't yet filled with fumes from the nearby traffic circle. Occupying the centre of the park's northern half, an **Independence Monument** is surrounded by two concentric circles of stylised lion sculptures or *chinthe*. A large fountain in the north-west corner sometimes functions; geese live in the somewhat stagnant pond at the park's southern end, where there is also a children's playground with a couple of mechanical rides.

For a year or two following the 1988-90 uprisings the park was occupied by Burmese soldiers; many of the more violent events of the time took place nearby.

Entry to the park costs K3 for locals and foreigners alike.

Yangon Zoological Gardens

These 70-acre gardens on Alaungpaya Pagoda Rd (formerly King Edward Ave) is a nice place for a stroll and encompasses a pretty decent zoo as well. Originally developed in 1906 by the British, the nicely landscaped grounds include a couple of artificial lakes, a playground and a miniature train circuit for kids, English and Latin labels (even on many of the trees) and maps of distribution. On weekends it's a favourite family picnic spot.

Tigers and lions pace about in the stately **King Edward VII Carnivora House**, built in 1915. Other open-air exhibits display an ele-phant house and a fair selection of both common and scarce Asian mammals (including sambar, leopard, serow, Eld's deer, Malayan sun bear, goral, Indian muntjac, great hornbill, pythons, cobras and huge marsh crocodiles).

A two-storey, school-like building on the grounds contains a **Natural History Museum**, free with zoo admission, with labelled static exhibits on rocks and minerals, mammals, birds, fishes, reptiles and amphibians – most of the specimens are stuffed or bottled. A separate room in the museum displays samples of tropical hardwoods and bamboos native to Myanmar.

A restaurant on one of the lakes offers cafeteria-style service. Zoo admission costs K20 for foreigners, plus K15 for every still camera, K150 for videocams. The zoo is open 6 am to 6 pm daily.

Across the street from the northern end of the zoo, on Kandawgyi Lake, stands the **National Aquarium**. When we visited the aquarium seemed only half in operation and none of the tanks were labelled – all in all, a disappointing contrast with the zoo. Admission to the aquarium is free.

Kandawgyi Lake

Since 'Kan' means 'lake' and 'Dawgyi' means 'royal', the common English name for this lake is actually a redundancy. Also known by its literal translation, 'Royal Lake', this natural body of water located close to the city centre is another good place for strolling or picnicking. The lake seems its most attractive at sunset, when the glittering Shwedagon is reflected in calm waters; you'll find the best sunset view from the lake's south-west edge.

Several of the city's embassies, clinics and smaller hotels are found in the lake's vicinity. Just east of the Baiyoke Kandawgyi Hotel (formerly the British Boating Club), on the southern side of the lake, floats a Shin Upagot shrine. Upagot is a bodhisattva or Buddhist saint who protects human beings in moments of mortal danger.

The **Karaweik**, a reinforced concrete reproduction of a royal barge, sits (it certainly doesn't float) at the eastern edge of the lake. Apart from being something of a local attraction in its own right, the Karaweik (Sanskrit: Garuda), the legendary bird-mount of the Hindu god Vishnu, is also a restaurant – see the Places to Eat section. Dance performances are held here in the evenings.

Inya Lake

Further north of the city, stretching between Pyay Rd to the west and Kaba Aye Pagoda Rd to the east, Inya Lake is roughly five times larger than Kandawgyi. Like the latter, it's a popular weekend relaxation spot for locals, although certain areas along the lakeshore – occupied by state guest houses and ministerial mansions – are off limits to the ordinary public.

Until mid-1995, two important figures in contemporary Burmese history resided on opposite sides of the lake, like powerful nats locked in a battle of wills. At the southern end at 54 University Rd sat Aung San Suu Kyi, under involuntary house arrest for six years with only her democratic ideals to keep her company; at the other end is willing recluse Ne Win, housed with his wizards and astrologers.

Other Attractions

Opposite Shwedagon Paya to the west, **People's Park** is a huge expanse of grass and trees bisected by **People's Square**, a wide, socialist-style pedestrian promenade. Near a set of fountains south of People's Square is a children's playground area and in the south-eastern corner of the park a couple of armoured tanks are on display. The park entrance faces the eastern side, opposite Shwedagon's western gate; admission costs a steep US$3 for foreigners, plus US$3 for still cameras, US$6 for video.

Swimming & Golf

Three public pools in Yangon charge small fees for daily use: Kandawgyi Swimming Pool (☎ 01-51327) on Kandawgyi Lake; Kokine Swimming Club (☎ 01-50034) at 23

Sayasan Rd; and National Swimming Pool (☎ 01-78550) on U Wisara Rd.

Yangon doesn't offer much in the way of golf, but at least greens fees are reasonable at the three public courses: City Golf Resort (☎ 01-40086), Thirimingala St, Mile 10, Insein; Myanmar Golf Club (☎ 01-61702), Pyay Rd, Mile 10; and Yangon Golf Club (☎ 01-45563), Danyingon Rd, Insein. All three have ties to the Burmese military. Players tend to be a cross-section of Tatmadaw officers and Singaporean and Japanese business execs. Greens fees average K150 to K200 for locals, US$15 to US$20 for foreigners.

Martial Arts & Weight Training

Burmese kickboxing instruction for beginners is offered on the ground floor of the YMCA on Mahabandoola St near Theinbyu St (☎ 01-94109), on Monday, Wednesday and Friday from 4 to 7 pm. The instructor is Ko Chit, a young but accomplished student of the renowned Nilar Win, who founded the YMCA programme and is now teaching Burmese kickboxing in Paris. Experienced students meet Tuesday, Thursday and Saturday from 3 to 5 pm. There's usually someone around who can translate the essentials, though you should mostly expect to learn and train by example. The techniques taught at the Y incorporate some moves borrowed from Thai and international boxing.

A bodybuilding/weight room next to the kickboxing room at the Y features a full range of cast-iron free weights. Visitors are welcome to participate in boxing or weight training upon becoming YMCA members. Inquire at the main office on the upper floor for more information.

Saya Pan Thu, founder of the Institute of Myanmar Traditional Advanced Boxing, 15 Aung Chan Tha St, Hledan St, Kamayut, teaches a more traditional Burmese kickboxing style most Saturdays at 4 pm at the Yangon University campus. Pan Thu doesn't speak English nor do any of his students seem to. If you're interested in learning Burmese kickboxing, watch a few training sessions at both the Y and Pan Thu's to see which style seems more suitable. Pan Thu and Ko Chit may also be able to refer athletes to other teachers and training situations in Yangon.

Places to Stay

Since the privatisation of the hotel industry in 1993, there has been an explosion of hotel and guest house development in Yangon. The number of places licensed to accept foreigners leapt from eight in 1992 – when you still had to book a package deal to receive a tourist visa – to 104 by the beginning of 1995, most of them entirely new places. The number of available rooms has skyrocketed from 78 to 1432! This number will undoubtedly have increased by the time you arrive in Yangon if current trends continue.

Places to Stay – bottom end

When Yangon's smaller hotels and guest houses began receiving licences allowing them to accept foreigners as guests in 1993, many proprietors reckoned they'd strike it rich by charging US$15 to US$20 per person per day for very basic rooms with shared bath. This was the going rate in 1993 and 1994; many bottom-end places have since dropped their rates a bit – some to as low as US$7 to US$10 per person. There still seems to be a general surplus of rooms, so more places may be lowering their rates over the next couple of years. Price quotes at the following places almost always include tax and service as well as a rudimentary eggs-and-toast breakfast. Payment is accepted in US dollars cash or FECs only.

The cheapest place to stay in Yangon so far is *Win Guest House* (no phone) at 10 Zay St in Kamayut township. It's near the three-way intersection of Strand Rd, Hanthawady Rd and Hledan St, a short walk from the Yangon River in the western part of the city. Plain rooms with two beds and little else cost US$7 single, US$12 double, with cold-water bath down the hall. Like many guest houses in this price category, the corridors between the rooms are air-conditioned; transoms over

the doors to each room allow some of the cool air to seep in.

Back downtown, the friendly and popular *White House Hotel* (☎ 01-71522) at 69/71 Konzaydan St, west of Sule Paya between Merchant and Mahabandoola Sts, offers similar room arrangements for US$10 per person. In addition each of the nine cubicles has an exhaust fan for aiding cross-ventilation. The guest house occupies two floors over a shop-house on a crowded street – a design pattern seen repeatedly in this price range.

The even more conveniently located *Zar Chi Win Guest House* (☎ 01-75407) sits on the western side of 37th St, just south of Merchant St and near the book vendors and Pagan Bookshop. The usual cubicles cost US$15 single, US$30 double with shared bath and toilet, or US$40 with private bath. Rates include breakfast and a left-luggage service is available. Some travellers have been able to bargain down to US$6 or US$8 per person without breakfast. The *Tea Camp* next door has decent Burmese breakfasts for less than K40.

Right around the corner on busy Mahabandoola St, between 37th and 38th Sts, the friendly *Myanmar Holiday Inn* (☎ 01-70016) charges US$12/22 single/double without breakfast or US$15/25 with breakfast. These rooms come with floor fans, exhaust fans and transoms admitting air-con from the corridors. Good-size double rooms with private bath and their own air-con duct are available for US$40.

Another downtown place, the *Grand Hotel* (☎ 01-97493, fax 83360) at 108 Bo Aung Gyaw St, near Merchant St, has a grand facade but little else that deserves the name. A tilting wooden stairway leads to narrow, cluttered rows of not-so-clean cubicles that cost US$10/20 single/double with shared bath. Much better, and cleaner, are the rooms with air-con and private bath for US$30/42 single/double. One redeeming feature is a terrace sitting area upstairs over the street.

Near the railway station at the corner of U Pho Kya Rd and Bo Min Yaung (U Ohn

YANGON

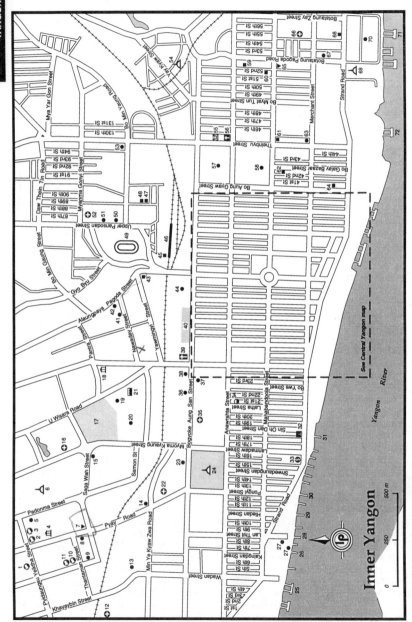

Inner Yangon

Yangon River

See Central Yangon map

PLACES TO STAY

43 Thamada Hotel
45 Sakhantha Hotel
47 Mann Shwe Gon Guest House
48 Sunflower Inn
59 Cozy Guest House
60 Three Seasons Hotel
61 YMCA
62 YWCA (under renovation)
64 Grand Hotel
68 Euro Asia Hotel

PLACES TO EAT

7 Sei Taing Kya Teashop
65 Home Sweet Home

OTHER

1 Egypt Embassy
2 Indonesia Embassy
3 France Embassy
4 National Museum (under construction)
5 National Archives
6 Ein Daw Yar Paya
8 Ministry of Foreign Affairs
9 American Center & USIS
10 Sri Lanka Embassy
11 Laos Embassy
12 Central Women's Hospital
13 Deaf & Dumb School
14 Than Zei (market)
15 School
16 No 2 Military Hospital
17 Myoma Ground
18 War Museum (under construction)
19 Tatmadaw Hall
20 National Theatre
21 National Swimming Pool
22 New General Hospital
23 Institute of Medicine
24 Thayettaw Kyaung
25 Wadan St Jetty
26 Kaingdan St Jetty
27 Inland Water Transport Ticket Offices
28 Lan Thit St Jetty
29 Hledan St Jetty
30 Pongyi St Jetty
31 Sin Oh Dan St Jetty (vehicle ferry to Dalah)
32 Kheng Hock Keong (Chinese temple)
33 Myanma Agricultural Bank
34 Pickups to Bago
35 Yangon General Hospital
36 School
37 Institute of Dental Medicine
38 School
39 St Mary's Cathedral
40 Bogyoke Aung San Market
41 Yuzana Pickle Tea
42 School
44 Myanma Railways Office
46 Yangon Railway Station
49 Aung San Stadium
50 School
51 School
52 Infectious Diseases Hospital
53 Theinbyu Zei (market)
54 Shwe Pon Pwint Paya
55 Sikh Temple
56 Salvation Army Church
57 School
58 Ministers' Offices
63 Myanma Five Star Line
66 General Hospital
67 University of Yangon (Botataung campus)
69 Botataung Paya
70 Saw Mill
71 Botataung Jetty
72 Myanma Five Star Line Cargo Jetty

Khine) Rd is the best of the budget places. From the street outside it doesn't look like much, but upstairs the *Sunflower Inn* (☎ 01-76503, 75628) offers very clean if small rooms with communal bath for US$15/20 single/double including breakfast. Or for US$25/30 single/double you can have a room with private hot-water bath, fridge and TV; there are only a couple of these rooms available and they're often booked. The Indian proprietors are friendly and helpful.

Next door, in the same row of buildings as the Sunflower Inn, the six-storey *Mann Shwe Gon* (☎ 01-72432) charges US$10 per person for plain rooms with shared cold-water shower and toilet. Most of the guests here seem to be Burmese, so it has more of a local feel than most of the other foreigner-licensed guest houses.

Close to the MTT office on Sule Pagoda Rd is the *Garden Hotel*, one of the original government-owned places which has now become private. Rooms cost from US$10/15 for a fan-cooled single/double with common bath to US$15/20 for a single/double with private bath. The rooms are just little cubicles with thin walls; they're small, spartan and not great value.

At 256-260 Sule Pagoda Rd toward Bogyoke Aung San St is another old standby, the newly privatised *Dagon Hotel* (☎ 01-89354, 78576). With a new paint job and better service than before, the fair-sized rooms aren't bad value at US$12 single, US$18 double with air-con, fridge, and shared bath and toilet. Rooms at the front near the street can be noisy. The tall, narrow hotel has a bit of character; there are nice city views from the balcony and a couple of good Chinese restaurants downstairs and nearby.

Pyin U Lwin Guest House (☎ 01-74005), up a rickety flight of stairs at 183 Mahabandoola Garden St, features small, cell-like rooms for US$15 per person on the main (1st) floor, US$10 per person on the 2nd floor, with shared cold-water bath and aircon in the corridors. The staff is friendly and there are usually Burmese as well as foreign guests.

For many years and through many visa changes budget travellers have stayed at Yangon's doddering *YMCA* (☎ 01-94109, fax 96848) on Mahabandoola St near Theinbyu St. The 18 rooms are large and in reasonable if somewhat tatty condition. Most cost US$8 per person with fan and common bath including breakfast. There are two rooms available for US$20 per person with air-con, private hot-water bath and fridge. The Y offers free transport to and from the airport and allows guests to store luggage while travelling upcountry. Another nice service is that there's no charge to hang out past checkout time if you have an afternoon flight. Both men and women are welcome at this Y, although couples are supposed to be married if they share double rooms.

The *YWCA* (☎ 01-97148) at 119 Bo Galay Bazaar St, a little closer toward the centre of downtown, is currently under renovation. When it reopens will have only two rooms sleeping four persons each; the management said the Y may add more rooms later but they were not sure whether these – or even the original two – will be open to foreigners. One thing's for sure, if it's open to foreigners it will remain open to women only.

Out past the YMCA in Pazundaung township, *Cozy Guest House* (☎ 01-91623, fax 92239) at 126 52nd St bridges the gap between budget and medium-priced inns. The Cozy's five small rooms offer air-con and carpeting, with a shared hot-water bath down the hall. Rates are US$20 single or US$30 double, including breakfast.

Places to Stay – middle

Yangon's accommodation in this category has expanded rapidly. Many of the newer medium-priced places consist of large converted residences in Bahan, Dagon and Mingala Taung Nyunt townships, just north of downtown in the vicinity of Kandawgyi Lake and Shwedagon Paya. Unless otherwise noted, rates do not include the 20% tax and service charges. Many hotels in this range will accept credit card payment.

Downtown *Best Inn* (☎ 01-72835, fax 86058) sits on busy Pansodan St at No 96/98, but is surprisingly cool and quiet inside. Clean, comfortable rooms with air-con, carpeting, TV and private hot-water baths cost US$42 single, US$54 double, US$66 triple; rates include breakfast, tax and service. Because of its location in the heart of downtown, the Best Inn is often full.

Further east near Botataung Paya, the modern, seven-storey *Euro Asia Hotel* (☎ 01-96731, fax 89960) at Strand Rd offers simple but clean air-con rooms with fridge, TV and attached hot-water showers. Budget singles cost US$20, while the more plentiful standard rooms are US$30 single, US$40 to US$45 double; suites are available for US$60. A rooftop terrace has sunset views of Strand Rd, Yangon River and the green cityscape stretching north. Rates include a choice of an Asian or European breakfast. Service is a cut above average since the manager came from the Inya Lake Hotel.

Not far from the YMCA, at 83/85 52nd St just north of Mahabandoola St, the two-storey *Three Seasons Hotel* (☎ 01-93304) offers seven large rooms for US$30 single, US$45 double, plus two large four-bed rooms for US$50 to US$60. All rooms come with hot-water showers, fridge, air-con, high ceilings and wooden floors. This is one of the quieter downtown neighbourhoods; other pluses include the tastefully decorated lobby and friendly, helpful staff. Rates include a full breakfast, served in an airy room overlooking the street; breakfasts of mohinga or htamin bei can be arranged with a day's notice.

Lai Lai Hotel (☎ 01-27878, fax 27342), on the edge of Chinatown at 783 Mahabandoola St, is a modern, eight-storey, thoroughly Chinese-style hotel with good city views from the upper floors. All rooms come with hot showers, satellite TV, phones, minibars and air-con for US$35/45/55 single/double/triple. A Chinese restaurant is downstairs.

The recently privatised, six-storey *Thamada Hotel* (☎ 01-71477), just across the railway line from the town centre at the northern end of Sule Pagoda Rd has been spruced up a bit and is a very popular venue for local wedding receptions. Done in the old socialist style, the hotel's 58 large rooms cost US$40 single, US$60 to US$65 double, or US$98 triple. All rooms feature high ceilings, air-con, TV and hot water; some have fridges. Roadside rooms offer bathtubs as well as showers but these get the most street noise. Rooms at the rear don't have tubs but they're quieter.

The woeful *Sakhantha Hotel* (☎ 01-82975), connected to the railway station with an entrance on the platform, has also recently been taken over by a private venture – although when we checked it out recently it looked just as dilapidated as it did under government auspices. With a seedy, postcolonial atmosphere reminiscent of the old Strand, this place might be considered by travellers who want to make the 6 am express to Bago, Thazi or Mandalay, although the Sunflower Inn on the other side of the station is a better deal. Big, dusty rooms with balconies, some of which overlook the train yard (well, train buffs would like it), go for US$36/42/54 single/double/triple with attached bath – and spotty plumbing. At these prices there are much better deals downtown. The bar, restaurant and platform coffeeshop downstairs, however, are quite pleasant and service is attentive.

Shwedagon & Kandawgyi Area This area of the city is generally quieter than downtown Yangon. It's also convenient for walking to Shwedagon Paya, the zoo and Kandawgyi Lake.

A residential compound-style inn typical of those found in Bahan township, *Beauty*

Land Hotel (☎ 01-51525) at 9 Bo Cho Rd offers a wide variety of rooms from US$10 to US$50, depending on whether you get hot water or cold water, shared bath or attached bath, air-con or fan. All rooms come with breakfast and the proprietors offer free airport transport.

A bit grander in style and more well kept, the mansion-like *Royal Hotel* (☎ 01-80339, fax 34158) offers spotless, large standard rooms with TV, fridge and phone for US$40/60 single/double, even larger superior rooms for US$50/70 single/double and huge suites with larger TVs and a bathroom with tub and bidet for US$80 single/double. Rates include breakfast. For foodies, one of the main advantages of staying at the Royal is that it's quite close to Aung Thuka, one of the best and most authentic Burmese restaurants in the capital.

The well-managed *Bagan Inn* (☎ 01-50489, fax 39660) sits in its own large, landscaped compound at 26 Natmauk Lane 2 (Po Sein Rd), a quiet street just north of Kandawgyi Lake. Owned by Hong Kong Chinese, the inn's 25 rooms, in three separate two-storey buildings, are large and nicely decorated with Burmese *kalagas* (tapestries). All rooms feature fridge, TV, air-con and phone; IDD phone and fax services are available. Standard singles cost US$40, doubles US$60 to US$70, superior doubles US$70 to US$80; there are also more expensive suites. Rates include full breakfast and laundry service. Next door and under the same ownership, the Silver Palace Restaurant offers a European, Thai, Chinese and Burmese menu.

Next to the Bagan Inn, the *Fame Hotel* (☎ 01-50179, fax 89960) at No 28 (A) offers slightly more basic but similar air-con rooms in its own compound for US$25 to US$45 a night. Four-bed rooms behind the main building are available for US$15 per person. Also on Po Sein Rd nearby are the *Green Hill Inn* (☎ 01-50330, fax 39388) and *Sharp Hotel* (☎ 01-51865), both with similar rates and facilities.

Situated right on the lake, the formerly state-owned *Baiyoke Kandawgyi Hotel*

(☎ 01-86523, fax 80412) on Kanyeiktha Rd was originally built as the British Boating Club. The Kandawgyi doubles as a training centre – begun by the United Nations Development Programme in 1982 – for all MHT (Ministry of Hotels & Tourism) staff. Now a joint venture between a Burmese and a Thai company (the Thai company is actually owned by a famous Burmese expat), the hotel is currently undergoing renovations. Refurbished standard rooms in the old wing, all with air-con, TV and fridge, cost US$55/65 single/double; those with lake views go for US$65 to US$70 single, US$75 to US$80 double. Frankly this is overpriced for rooms that are of about the same standard as the Thamada Hotel (though of course the latter doesn't boast a lakeside location) and of a lower standard than many of the newer hotels in the area. The Kandawgyi's famous lakeside chalets – for many years the best accommodation in the entire country – are being dismantled to make way for a swimming pool. An entire new guest wing is also under construction; once it's finished the old rooms may be converted to meeting facilities. The Baiyoke Kandawgyi's restaurant is one of the most tranquil dining/drinking spots in Yangon.

Two-storey *Comfort Inn* (☎ 01-33377, fax 34256) sits in a large compound at 4 Shwe Li Rd, between Inya Rd and U Wisara Rd and north of People's Park. Similar in standard to the Bagan Inn, the Comfort offers two standard rooms with air-con and TV for US$35 single, US$45 double, and 10 superior rooms with air-con, large bathrooms, TV, radio-cassette player and minibar for US$55/65 single/double. On the grounds is a putting green. Rates include free airport transfer and continental breakfast.

North The remainder of the hotels in this category are located well north of downtown; most are found along or just off Insein Rd or Pyay Rd, both long avenues running north to south.

A 15-minute bus ride north of Sule Paya is the French-owned *Aurora Hotel* (☎ 01-34080, fax 92239) at 477 Pyay Rd in Kam-

ayut township. Set well back from busy Pyay Rd, the inn encompasses two older buildings. The one at the back is decorated with antiques and contains a small French restaurant and bar, along with spacious guest rooms for US$20 to US$30 single, US$25 to US$40 double and US$30 to US$50 triple, depending on whether they come with fan or air-con. A second building located towards the front of the property (an English colonial brick bungalow) has budget rooms for US$15/20 single/double with shared bath, US$20/30/35 single/double/triple with attached bath. All rates include continental breakfast and laundry. IDD phone service is available.

Liberty Hotel (☎ 01-30050, fax 34144), at 343 Pyay Rd near the Hanthawady traffic circle in an elite residential neighbourhood, is a two-storey colonial mansion converted to a hotel. Large, high-ceilinged standard rooms cost US$30/40 single/double, while even larger superior rooms are US$40/50. Rates include breakfast but not tax and service.

Farther north at 69 Pyay Rd (Mile 6.5) is *Best Executive Suites* (☎ 01-35795, fax 64780), a branch of the downtown Best Inn. Its 12 well-kept rooms, each with air-con, TV and fridge, cost US$45/55 single/double.

Places to Stay – top end

Downtown & City Centre 'When in Singapore stay at the Raffles,' the saying used to go. (Actually it was 'feed at the Raffles' and stay somewhere else, but never mind.) Similarly, when you are in Yangon the place to stay if you can afford it is *The Strand* (☎ 01-81561, 81533), at 92 Strand Rd between 38th and Seikkantha Sts. Originally constructed by the Sarkies brothers of Raffles and Oriental fame in 1896, The Strand was one of those glorious outposts of the eastern British Empire early this century. During WW II it was forced to close, only to open again in 1948 under the auspices of London's Steel Brothers Co.

Ne Win nationalised the property in 1963 and in its latter-day socialist role The Strand became a run-down shadow of its former self

– certainly no competition for the well-kept likes of Raffles or the Oriental in Bangkok. Yet somehow the old colonial era lived on at The Strand. Many hardened travellers actually preferred staying here to staying at the heavily commercialised (and high-priced) Raffles and Oriental, insisting that The Strand had more character than either of these glossy stables.

All of this changed again in 1991 when Dutch-Indonesian resort impresario Adrian Zecha and company began spending US$36 million to renovate the grand dame. The original reopening was to take place at the end of 1992, but renovation on the front half of the hotel wasn't completed until 1994. By the beginning of 1995, 32 rooms had been totally redone and opened to the public.

Our verdict: of the three major Sarkies hotel renovations in South-East Asia, this one seems the most faithful to the original spirit. Though perhaps well beyond the budget of many visitors to Myanmar as a place to spend the night, The Strand is worth a visit for a drink in the bar, high tea in the lobby lounge or a splurge lunch at the cafe. Unlike the Oriental or Raffles, the hotel isn't appended to touristy shopping malls and souvenir shops. The decor doesn't bowl you over with a surplus of ornamentation, either, and the staff seem to be more laid-back and less snobbish to non-guest visitors – as long as you dress decently for your visit.

The renovated guest rooms are divided into eight superior suites for US$275 single/double a night, 23 deluxe suites at US$300 and one apartment-like Strand Suite for US$750. These rates do not include the mandatory 20% tax and service. Each suite is elegantly finished in the colonial style with plenty of brass and wood; IDD phones and all the other electronic gadgetry expected at hotels of this calibre are present. Among the public facilities are a dinner-only restaurant, an opulently finished bar decorated with local art, a cafe and a small business centre. Once the back half of the hotel has been redone, more facilities will undoubtedly be added. All guests are met at the airport.

For as long as they escape renovation,

there remain 39 rooms at the back of the building in much the same condition as they were before Mr Zecha came along. Rates here are US$42 single, US$54 double for standard rooms, US$48/60 single/double for superior rooms. The difference between standard and superior lies in the furnishings, not room size; the superior rooms seem slightly less musty! All rooms come with air-con and private baths – but don't expect luxury, as this is still the old Strand. Even the top-notch air-con rooms are a long way below the standards of other Asian 1st-class hotels. Downstairs you can bid farewell to what are surely the last of the hotel's old stylings: the sleepy, minimalist lobby; the remarkably economical restaurant; the casual but cheerful service; and the ancient but smoothly operating cage lift. The management says renovations on these remaining rooms will begin sometime in 1996; if the first phase can be used as a measure, it could be three years before they open again as an integral part of the luxurious new Strand.

A top choice among business travellers, the *Summit Parkview* (☎ 01-33862, fax 34071) stands at 350 Ahlone Rd within walking distance of Shwedagon Paya. The voluminous marble lobby is designed to impress; the US$30-million hotel is owned by a three-company consortium which includes Singapore's Tiger Balm Corp (owned by the Ow family, originally from Myanmar). All 252 rooms come with IDD phones, satellite TV, in-house movies and 24-hour room service for US$140 single, US$150 double. In addition to a useful hotel clinic and dispensary, the Summit offers a swimming pool, fitness centre, newsstand, bakery/cafe, restaurant, disco and the only full-service hotel business centre in Yangon. Airport transport is complimentary.

Bahan For those visitors who want luxury without the glitz, a number of converted mansions in Bahan township provide more intimate digs. Pick of the pack is *Mya Yeik Nyo Royal* (☎ 01-38310, fax 38318) at 20 Pale Rd, off Kaba Aye Pagoda Rd between Kandawgyi and Inya lakes. This stately, 50-

YANGON

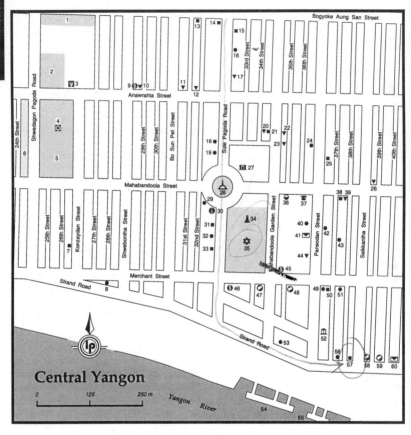

Central Yangon

0   125   250 m

Yangon River

year-old, two-storey edifice was built by the British as an office for the legendary Irrawaddy Flotilla Company and served later as a bank, kindergarten and state guest house. Large, high-ceilinged rooms contain IDD phones, adjustable air-con and minibars; rates start at US$90 for a single. The MYN Royal's perch on a nicely landscaped bluff affords clear views of the Shwedagon stupa. A Burmese music ensemble performs nightly in the spacious lobby/dining room, which is decorated with antiques and handicrafts. On the grounds are a pool and tennis court.

There are two other branches nearby, the

Mya Yeik Nyo Deluxe (☎ 01-56529, fax 65052) at 16B Thukhawaddy Rd, and the *Mya Yeik Nyo Supreme* (☎ 01-53818, fax 38318) at 23/25 Kaba Aye Pagoda Rd. Although architecturally not as interesting as the Royal, these hotels offer spacious and immaculate rooms with all the amenities inside quiet compounds for around US$70 a night including breakfast. The dining rooms at all three hotels enjoy reputations for good food. The Supreme has a woodcarving workshop on the premises.

Another converted colonial building, the *Shwe Hinthar Inn* (☎ 01-33295, fax 34170)

PLACES TO STAY

7	White House Hotel
13	Central Hotel (under construction)
14	Traders Hotel (under construction)
15	Dagon Hotel
21	Pyin U Lwin Guest House
25	Best Inn
31	Garden Hotel
33	Sofitel (under construction)
38	Myanmar Holiday Inn
50	Zar Chi Win Guest House
57	The Strand

PLACES TO EAT

10	New Delhi Restaurant
11	Simla Restaurant
12	Nila Briyane Shop
17	Golden Chetty Restaurant
20	999 Khauk Swai
22	Theingi Shwe Yee Tea House
23	Mr Guitar Cafe
26	Bharat Restaurant
39	Nilar Win's Cold Drink Shop
44	Nan Yu Restaurant

OTHER

1	New Bogyoke Market
2	Open-Air Market
3	Sri Kali Temple
4	Moseah Yeshua Synagogue
5	Theingyi Zei (market)
6	Theingyizei Plaza
8	Ministry of Trade
9	Myanma Oriental Bank
16	Inwa Book Store
18	Yangon Duty Free Store
19	Myanmar Airways International
24	Ava Tailoring
27	City Hall
28	Sule Paya
29	THAI Airways International
30	MTT
32	Air France
34	Independence Monument
35	Mahabandoola Garden
36	Buses to Thanlyin
37	Central Telephone & Telegraph Office
40	Supreme Court
41	Post Office
42	Biman Bangladesh
43	Pagan Bookshop
45	Myanma Foreign Trade Bank
46	Central Bank of Myanmar
47	US Embassy
48	India Embassy
49	Silk Air
51	Sarpay Beikman Book Centre
52	National Museum
53	Customs
54	Myanma Five Star Line Passenger Jetty
55	Pansodan St Jetty (passenger ferry to Dalah)
56	Myanma Airways
58	Australia Embassy
59	UK Embassy
60	GPO

at 51 Pyay Rd offers nine well-appointed rooms on spacious grounds for US$80 each, including continental breakfast.

North Another contender in Yangon's top hotel echelon is the *Nawarat Hotel* (☎ 01-67888, fax 67777), at 257 Insein Rd. Built originally as an office building and converted to a luxury hotel, the Nawarat is part of a huge Singapore hotel-conglomerate with properties throughout South-East Asia and Australia. The hotel's 170 rooms come with the coveted IDD phone and other similarly 'modern' amenities. Rates start at US$120/140 single/double. The business centre doesn't compare with the Summit's, but the hotel has plans to add convention facilities to the surrounding 10 acres, as well as executive service apartments, tennis courts, gym and pool. Other public facilities include a beauty salon, coffee shop, bar, two restaurants and a disco. Airport transport is provided by the hotel.

Renovations are underway – by the same company doing The Strand – at the 222-room *Inya Lake Hotel* (☎ 01-62866, fax 6519) on Kaba Aye Pagoda Rd, about six km north of the city centre on Inya Lake. Originally built with Russian aid and run, in its early days, by Israelis, the Inya Lake is big, imposing, dramatic and mostly empty except during the annual gem fairs. At the time of writing, only 94 deluxe rooms were open, with rates starting at US$110 a night. The hotel's biggest claim to fame was its swimming pool, until recently the only hotel pool in Yangon.

The Taiwanese-owned *Novel Garden* (☎ 01-34940, fax 33879) at 615 Marlar Lane, off Pyay Rd, is basically a two-storey, L-shaped, motel-like building around a pool. Its 22 immaculate rooms feature air-con, minibar, satellite TV and phone for US$60 single/double, including tax, service and breakfast. The architectural high points of the complex are the large coffee shop/dining room and reception area – both decorated with Burmese antiques and handicrafts – located in a separate building.

Farther north, the new Singaporean-owned *Yangon City Hotel* (☎ 01-67750, fax 67763) at the 'eight-mile junction' (the junction of Pyay Rd and Kaba Aye Pagoda Rd, Mile 8) features an interlocking complex of block-like buildings containing 80 modern rooms with air-con, satellite TV and IDD phones in the US$80 to US$95 range. Services include business centre, fitness room, restaurant and free airport shuttle. The airport is just a 10-minute drive away.

Hotels Under Construction As we went to press, 17 new luxury hotel projects worth a total of US$600 million were on the drawing boards for Yangon. Shangri-La Hotel Corporation, a Singaporean chain, is poised to invest US$12 million in two of these, *Traders Hotel* near the corner of Bogyoke Aung San St and Sule Pagoda Rd, and the *Shangri-La Rangoon* at a yet undisclosed location. The *Central Hotel,* a Macau enterprise, is going up next to Traders on Bogyoke Aung San St. The red brick Myanma Railways building opposite has supposedly been purchased for hotel conversion by a private company as well.

Farther south along Sule Pagoda Rd, a *Hotel Sofitel* is under construction just south of the Air France office. Traders, Central and Sofitel should all be open by 1997 and should cost from US$90 to US$150.

A Malaysian company will supposedly construct an *Airport Hotel* on Kaba Aye Pagoda Rd near the Department of Civil Aviation; should the international airport move north towards Bago, one wonders what will happen to this project.

Another 'pie-in-the-sky' project one frequently hears about is a luxury floating hotel to be moored somewhere along the Yangon River. Reportedly, Thailand's Central Plaza hotel group has plans to tow a Russian luxury cruise liner from the North Atlantic to the Mediterranean and through the Suez Canal to Yangon, where it will be refitted and ready for business by early 1997.

Places to Eat
Yangon has some interesting culinary possibilities for those willing to explore a bit. At the middle and top end of the scale are the ubiquitous Chinese restaurants, while the many Indian and Burmese places are cheap and basic. Eat early in the evening – by 9 pm virtually everything, except The Strand, will be closing up.

Burmese Two humble-looking restaurants in the Shwedagon Paya area enjoy reputations for serving the best traditional Burmese cuisine in the capital. *Aung Thuka* (no English sign) at 17(A) 1st St, between Shwegondine St and Dhammazedi Rd near Shwedagon Paya, People's Park and the Royal Hotel, features a clean, simple dining room decorated with Burmese calendars and movie posters, furnished with linoleum-top tables and wooden chairs. A long table along one side of the room displays dozens of cookpots containing the day's curries and special dishes, so all you need to do is point to what looks good. Curries made with prawn or venison are particularly good here, as are such side dishes as kazun ywet (stir-fried watercress and mushrooms) and shauk thi thok (citron salad). If you order one or more curries, you'll automatically receive soup, dal, rice and side dishes. Prices are very reasonable. Aung Thuka is sometimes known as 'Shwe Ba', because a famous Burmese actor of the same name once had his house nearby.

The nearby *Hla Myanma Htamin Zai* ('Beautiful Myanmar Rice Shop') at 27 5th St is also sometimes called 'Shwe Ba' for the same reason. Like Aung Thuka it's a very simple, plain restaurant where the food is served from rows of curry pots. They also have some Chinese and Indian dishes. It's a difficult place to find; it's best to go by taxi with a driver who knows the place. Both 'Shwe Ba' restaurants are open from around 10 am to 7 pm. Figure on spending no more than K200 per person for a full spread, not including beverages.

Daw Sawyi is a slightly more modern-looking Burmese restaurant with colourful tiled walls at the five-way intersection of Hledan St, University Rd, Pyay Rd and Insein Rd, quite near the main Yangon University campus, a little north of the Aurora Hotel. The food is traditional Burmese – a selection of curries, soups and vegetable side dishes. Daw Sawyi is also open for breakfast, when it serves fried vegetable rolls and noodles; like most Burmese rice shops it closes around 7 pm. A second branch called *Danubyu Daw Sawyi* can be found at 194 29th St, five blocks west of Sule Paya. *Khin Than Daw* at No 238 and *Nut Thoke Dar* at No 174 on the same street also serve inexpensive traditional Burmese cuisine.

Many of the Chinese and 'show' restaurants around town offer a few Burmese dishes, but nothing to compare with the places mentioned above. A few, such as the *Royal Rose Restaurant* (☎ 01-52707), 221 Shwegondine St, offer special 6 am to 10 am morning menus featuring traditional Burmese breakfast dishes such as nan gyi (rice noodle salad), nan pya (flat rice noodle salad), shwe taung (noodles in coconut milk gravy) and palata with chicken curry.

The Strand Cafe in the Strand Hotel serves some very good, 'updated' versions of classic Burmese cuisine at international prices. It's open 6.30 am to 11 pm.

Burmese foodstalls serving curries and rice – for experienced stomachs only – can be found along the eastern side of Bo Galay Bazaar St. The noodle stalls on 32nd St are very cheap and very good.

Shan & Thai *999 Khauk Swai*, at 130/B 34th St (behind City Hall, a short walk from Sule Paya) is a small shop serving the best Shan-style noodles in Yangon. The menu, printed in English and Burmese, includes delicious and filling shan khauk swe (thin rice noodles in a slightly spicy chicken broth), gyon khauk swe (same with wheat noodles), shan htamin chin ('sour' rice salad), myi shay (Mandalay-style noodles) and other delights. All noodle dishes cost K40 and are served with fried tofu triangles and jars of pickled cabbage. It's open 6.30 am to around 7 pm, though we'd recommend eating no later than

6 pm since the kitchen may sell out of some items.

Over on the next block at 203A 35th St, *Cherry* offers a similar Shan noodle setup. Yet another good spot for Shan noodles is *Thit Mwe* (no English sign) at 247 Mahabandoola St near 24th St. A broader representation of Shan cuisine, including the Shan State's famous salads and tofu, is available at the rustic *Shan Daung Tan* at 535C Pyay Rd in Kamayut township.

The Thai-owned *Sala Thai* (☎ 38661), at 56 Sayasan Rd in Bahan, is housed in a large Thai-style building made of teak with a full bar and both indoor and outdoor dining areas set around a small pond. The menu is extensive and authentic, featuring everything from tom yam kung (shrimp and lemongrass soup) to kai yang (Thai-style grilled chicken); seafood is the restaurant's strong suit. Prices are, for Yangon, medium high. There's an extra charge for dining in the indoor air-con rooms. Open 11 am to 9 pm daily.

Indian Along Anawrahta St, west of Sule Pagoda Rd toward the Shri Kali temple, are a number of shops serving Indian biryani (spiced rice with chicken, or kyettha dan bauk in Burmese), and at night the roti and dosa (North and South Indian pancakes) makers set up along the pavement on the side streets. Indian food is probably the cheapest way of eating in Yangon, particularly at places that serve thali – an all-you-can-eat meal of rice and various vegetable curries piled on a fresh banana leaf or stainless steel thali plate costs only around K45. Biryani costs a bit more, around K60 to K80.

The most popular biryani place downtown is still the *Nila Briyane Shop* on Anawrahta St between 31st and 32nd Sts. It's always crowded but the service is snappy. Nila Briyane may sell out by 7 pm, after which *Simla* (no English sign) next door at 222 Anawratha St takes over till closing around 9 pm. Some people prefer the Simla, others Nila; both offer vegetarian biryani as well as the usual chicken.

For more variety, try the *New Delhi Restaurant* on Anawrahta St between 29th and

Shwebontha Sts. This reasonably clean place serves a wide selection of North and South Indian dishes, including puris, idli and dosa (spelt 'toeshay' on the menu) with curry and coconut chutney in the morning, banana-leaf thalis and a variety of curries for lunch and dinner. Most Indian places serve tea; New Delhi serves only coffee, South Indian-style.

On Mahabandoola St, at the corner of Seikkantha St, is the dependable and cheap *Bharat*, which is similar to the New Delhi with more of a focus on South Indian. Bharat's a bit smaller – it's generally easier to get served – and the marble-topped tables make a nice change from the long cafeteria-style tables at the Indian places on Anawrahta Rd.

Golden City Chetty Restaurant at 170 Sule Pagoda Rd, just north of Sule Paya on the eastern side of the street, follows the usual pattern for Yangon's Indian restaurants – white-tile walls and bright fluorescent lights. The dosas, thalis, etc are nothing special. Like Simla, however, it's one of the few places open past 7 pm. Don't count on finding anything left worth eating past 9 pm, though.

Chinese You can sample the whole range of Chinese cuisine in Yangon – from the familiar Cantonese through the less well-known Shanghai, Sichuan, Beijing or Hokkien dishes. One of the more popular downtown spots these days is the recently remodelled *Nyein Chan Restaurant* at 234 Sule Pagoda Rd near the Dagon Hotel. It's packed nightly with Burmese and Chinese residents enjoying inexpensive but very acceptable southern Chinese food (duck dishes are especially good) and inexpensive, cold beer.

One of the oldest Chinese restaurants in the city is the *Palace* (☎ 01-77441) at 84 37th St, once widely considered by locals to be the best Chinese eatery in Yangon. Popular specialities include sour-hot fish, which makes heavy use of garlic. The menu here has no prices – most dishes are around K80; you might enquire when ordering, to avoid surprises. Servings are so generous that one dish here will be just as filling as two or three elsewhere. It's not the best Chinese

restaurant in Yangon by a long shot, but it's reliable.

The air-con *Nan Yu* (☎ 01-77796) has been in business at 81 Pansodan St since 1968 and has all the usual Cantonese specialities (including 'crabs thumbs') plus specials that require 24 hours' notice – soups are particularly good here. Another downtown spot, *Ruby* (☎ 01-95132), at 50 Bo Aung Gyaw St (round the corner from the GPO), is popular among foreign-embassy staff for dependable Chinese food and reasonable prices. The *Panda* (☎ 01-21152), at the corner of Bogyoke Aung San and Wadan (Keily) Sts, is popular among the same crowd.

For long, leisurely evening meals, a local favourite is the festive *Yan Kin* (☎ 01-58925), an indoor/outdoor place near Inya Lake at the corner of Kaba Aye Pagoda Rd and Kanbe Rd. The *Bamboo House* (☎ 01-20018), on Shin Saw Pu St to the west of Shwedagon Paya, has a reputable Chinese Muslim, Yunnanese-style menu and is also a popular evening spot. A similarly fancy place, *Yadana Garden Restaurant & Snack Centre* (☎ 01-77351), sits near the southern gate to Shwedagon Paya. In addition to an extensive offering of Chinese dishes, the menu features Burmese and international entrees.

For noodles, fried rice and other quick Chinese meals, try the night market on Lanmadaw St in Chinatown, around the corner from the Cantonese temple.

Good Chinese food is also available at the larger, banquet-style places described as 'dinner show' restaurants in the Entertainment section of this chapter.

Western Food & Hotel Restaurants At the northern end of the city, *Sylvan European Restaurant* (☎ 01-62603), 125 Pyay Rd (Mile 8.5), serves continental cuisine in an elegant public dining room and three smaller private rooms. Owned by a Scot and his Burmese wife, the restaurant features air-con, tablecloths and a high standard of service. Entrees are priced in the K550 to K1000 range; there are also special fixed-price buffets and set menus from K600 to K1500, and a rich dessert menu. Lunch is served from noon to 2 pm, high tea 2 am to 5 pm, dinner 6 to 9 pm and Sunday brunch 10 am to 2 pm.

French food is the emphasis at *Chez Sylvie*, a small dining room in the Aurora Hotel. Patrons may also choose to dine in an outdoor garden area. The fixed price menu changes daily and costs around K850. Live musical performances are provided most evenings; sometimes 'Joe Piano King', an elderly Burmese musician who played 55 years ago at The Strand, plays piano, guitar and sax for customers. It is open daily for lunch and dinner.

The Strand Hotel, quite predictably, has the best – and most expensive – hotel kitchen in town. At *The Strand Cafe*, off the southern end of the lobby facing Strand Rd, the menu offers well-prepared soups, salads and sandwiches as well as a number of Asian-inspired dishes. It's open from 6.30 am to 11 pm daily. Deeper into the hotel, *The Grill* features a changing continental menu and is open 6 pm to 11 pm only.

For as long as it lasts, the old Strand dining room in the 'annex' offers some of the best Western food in Yangon at very reasonable prices (downright cheap if paid in kyats). At lunch time they have a set lunch which usually features grilled fresh fish or chicken. Once The Strand is completely renovated, chances are the hotel will be adding at least one more restaurant to replace this old dining room.

Restaurants at the *Nawarat* and *Summit Parkview* hotels offer somewhat predictable but reliable menus featuring a variety of Chinese, European and pseudo-Burmese dishes. Both are open daily for breakfast, lunch and dinner.

Food at the *Inya Lake* is less palatable, but at the *Thamada* the Chinese food still has a good reputation. Of all the former MHT hotels, the *Baiyoke Kandawgyi Hotel* has perhaps the best (and most popular) restaurant overall, particularly since it's a government training centre and the kitchen staff seem to go out of their way to please

customers. The lake atmosphere is a major plus. The dessert menu features very good homemade ice cream and lemon meringue pie. Prices are listed in both kyat and US dollars; the hotel allows K30 to the dollar on US dollar prices (rather than the official K5.5) so that a US$3 burger can be paid for using K90.

The *Sakhantha Hotel* has Chinese, Burmese and European dishes on its menu. There are two dining rooms, one for hotel guests and one for nonresident diners and drinkers (usually people waiting for a train). They're both throwbacks to colonial days, with high ceilings and slow ceiling fans. If the nonresident room is crowded, they'll let you have a table in the room labelled 'House Guests Only'. The food isn't bad and portions are large. The 'bar' section of the restaurant serves hard liquor only – Mandalay Gin or Mandalay Rum – by the peg; if you want beer, you must be served in one of the dining rooms. Just outside the hotel on the railway platform is a table where you can sometimes get a very tasty boxed chicken biryani, prepared by the Sakhantha dining room, to take on the train.

Fast Food Modest Western-style restaurants catering to well-heeled Burmese clientele offering sandwiches, burgers, pizza, spaghetti and the like are multiplying quickly in the city. Typical of the genre is *Home Sweet Home* (☎ 01-93001), situated at the corner of Mahabandoola and 52nd Sts. When the voltage runs high enough, the place is air-conditioned. White-shirted waiters serve sandwiches and a variety of burgers made with a choice of chicken, beef, fish or pork for around K60 each. Other menu items include grilled lobster, pizza, omelets, spaghetti, macaroni and cheese, ice cream, milk shakes and imported beers; set menus are available for K550 to K650. Home Sweet Home is open 9 am to 10 pm daily.

An almost identical menu – in both selection and prices – is offered at *Excellent Burgers & Snacks*, on the northern side of Anawrahta St at 33rd St. The small downstairs dining area is open to the street, while the upstairs room is air-con. More popular – in fact it's packed with Burmese youth every evening – is *7 Store Snack* on the other side of Anawrahta St at No 165. It's a narrow room separated from the street by a beaded curtain. Along with the usual burgers-and-spaghetti menu, this one carries the odd Burmese and Chinese dish.

Behind Yuzana Supermarket on Bagaya Rd in Sanchaung, *Yuzana Burger Shop* has the usual menu of burgers, fish & chips, shakes and ice cream, but is a little less expensive than most of the aforementioned. Other spots with the same kind of menu include the modern-looking *Burgerbuster* (☎ 01-32890), at 114B Inya Rd, and *Woody House* (☎ 01-90836), 74 Bogyoke Aung San St.

At 377 Mahabandoola St, about midway between the YMCA and the Sule Paya (between 37th and 38th Sts), you'll find the long-running *Nilar Win's Cold Drink Shop* (☎ 01-78364). Founded by a famous Burmese boxer who now lives in Paris, it's a clean little cafe where you can get yoghurt, lassi (a delicious Indian yoghurt drink) and milk as well as fruit salad, avocado salad, toast and egg (just K30), French toast and other traveller faves. It's open 8 am to 11 pm daily.

Bakeries In Myanmar, bakeries where cakes and sweet pastries are produced are usually called 'confectioneries'. *Croissant Bakery House* (☎ 01-25414), at 779 Mahabandoola St between 13th and 14th Sts, sounds promising; in fact it has decent pastries and coffee but is not worth a special trip unless you're already in the area. Similarly there's a chain called *Paris Bakery House*, with shops on Insein Rd, Mahabandoola St and Sule Pagoda Rd, which is not all that great either.

The better places seem to be those which stick to the tried and true Burmese style of baking – itself a blend of local, Chinese, Indian and English styles. One find of this sort is *Shwe Pu Zun* at 246-248 Anawrahta St, west of Lanmadaw St. When it comes to the quality and variety of both Burmese and Western-style cakes and pastries, the Shwe Pu Zun has no peer.

The restaurant in the *Summit Parkview Hotel* stocks a small selection of European-style pastries in a bakery cabinet at the front for ordering in the dining room or for take-away.

Teashops Yangon abounds in teashops where cups of milk tea or coffee followed by endless tiny pots of Chinese tea and cheap Burmese, Chinese and Indian snacks are available. For breakfast, in fact, you're often better off spending a few kyat in a teashop than eating the boring toast, egg and instant coffee breakfasts provided by many hotels and guest houses.

The most famous tea-tippling spot in Yangon, perhaps all Myanmar, is *Sei Taing Kya*, which has three branches. The most happening branch is the one near the Lao and Sri Lankan embassies off Pyay Rd; there's another one 130 Anawrahta St. All three are open 7 am to 5 pm and specialise in first-quality tea, samosa, palata, mohinga and ei kyaw kwei.

Another famous one – and more conveniently located than Sei Taing Kya if you're staying downtown – is the smaller, more intimate *Theingi Shwe Yee*, three doors north of Mr Guitar Cafe on Mahabandoola Garden St. Quality tea is served here, along with sliced bei moke or 'opium cake', a moist, delicious brown cake made with poppyseeds and topped with slivered coconut. Other house specialities include seasoned sticky rice with pigeon peas, flaky coconut puffs, curry puffs and sanwin makein ('turmeric unavoidable'; sweetened sticky rice steamed in banana leaves). The teashop also makes hamburgers, which are popular throughout the day; Theingi Shwe Yee is open daily 7 am to 8 pm.

Down on Mahabandoola St are a couple of more modest establishments that typify the general division between Chinese-influenced and Indian-influenced teashops. *Yatha Tea Shop*, on the southern side of Mahabandoola St between Seikkantha and 39th Sts, represents the latter in providing fresh samosas and palatas. *Golden Crown Cafe*, on the other side of the street (diagonally opposite Myanmar Holiday Inn) offers Chinese pastries, steamed buns and eggrolls. Both places serve tea of average quality – nothing to compete with Sei Taing Kya or Theingi Shwe Yee.

The railway platform teashop attached to the *Sakhantha Hotel* features worn wooden booths under a corrugated metal shelter cooled by huge ceiling fans. Since it's rarely crowded it's a more relaxed spot to sip a slow tea or coffee than the average Yangon teashop (where the waiters are generally anxious for you to vacate your table as quickly as possible so other paying customers can sit down). Snacks are limited: in addition to tea and coffee there's a small selection of cakes and curry puffs, plus dan bauk (chicken biryani).

A certain crowd of Burmese writers congregate at *Lay Tan Kon* teashop on the upper block of 33rd St near Sape-Lawka Bookshop. *Ko Tin Hlaing* teashop on the upper block of Pansodan St is where movie extras and minor actors hang out waiting to be called for filming.

Entertainment

Yangon entertainment, never the highlight of any foreigner's Myanmar visit, was dealt a near death-blow by the 11 pm curfew imposed from 1988 to late 1992. The main form of local recreation is hanging out in the teashops or 'cold drink' shops.

On festival days local bands occasionally organise live outdoor concerts. During the water festival, sizeable rock-music shows are set up along Inya Rd and University Rd and feature local underground rockers such as The Wild Ones, Iron Cross, Aces and Aurora. Foreign observers who have seen the leather-clad performances said they are amazed the events are allowed by the SLORC (the State Law and Order Restoration Council).

National Theatre The Yangon goverment recently revived the performance of Burmese classical dance-drama at the National Theatre, a state-sponsored facility on Myoma Kyaung St, north-west of Bogyoke Aung San Market.

Scenes from *Ramayana* – called *yama thagyin* in Burmese – are only occasionally held. Finding out about them is the trick; check at the theatre itself or try asking staff at the larger hotels.

Dinner Shows In the last couple of years, a number of large, semi-outdoor, banquet-style restaurants with floor shows have opened in Yangon. Heavily used by the visiting business community, these dining spots are typically Chinese-owned and feature extensive Chinese menus plus a few Burmese dishes. Entertainment is provided by Burmese bands who perform a mixture of Burmese, Western, Chinese and Japanese pop songs – usually sung by a changing roster of female vocalists. Some places also feature Burmese classical dance and/or marionette theatre. There is no charge for entertainment, and no set charges for dinner – you simply order from a menu like at any other restaurant. Tax and service charges amounting to 20% of the bill are usually added.

Kandawgyi Lake seems almost ringed by such places, since a lake view is considered a prime asset for an evening out on the expense account. If this sounds like your cup of tea, among the best of the bunch is *Lone Ma Lay Restaurant* (☎ 01-50357) off Natmauk Rd on Kandawgyi Lake. Entertainment focuses on Burmese classical and folk dance early in the evening, pop later on. The Chinese food here is quite respectable, with huge portions and fresh ingredients at lunch and dinner. The Burmese dishes aren't too shabby, even if they show a little extra Chinese influence. The restaurant is also open in the morning for Burmese teashop snacks and noodles; breakfast is served 6 to 10 am, lunch and dinner 10 am to 11 pm.

Also on the lake, near the aquarium, is *Dolphin Seafood* (☎ 01-85084), which is a little less formal overall and is known for employing the best Burmese pop singers in town.

Another good choice for this sort of

evening out is *Golden View Restaurant* (☎ 01-80425), adjacent to the southern entrance to Maha Wizaya Paya, near Shwedagon. The restaurant's 'golden view' is of the Maha Wizaya stupa, which is illuminated at night. The restaurant is open 10 am to 11 pm daily.

Four similar restaurants share the rooftop of Theingyizei Plaza on Shwedagon Pagoda Rd in Chinatown. Access to all four is provided by a single lift open to the street. Directly opposite the lift exit on the roof is *Ayar Restaurant*, with the usual Chinese food and rotating pop singers. Turn left and you'll soon come to *Seafood*, which specialises in fresh seafood with no musical distractions. Turn right to reach *Ambassador*, which is similar to Ayar, followed by the popular *Smile World*, whose dynamic pop music show packs in lots of Burmese who let their *longyis* fly on the dance floor. The food isn't bad at Smile World either.

The first restaurant on the lake to offer musical entertainment was the state-owned *Karaweik* – you can't miss this huge replica of an old Burmese floating palace, which is made out of concrete and is most definitely not about to float anywhere. It is such a local attraction that all visitors and guests must pay the K1 admission – to keep gawkers out. Inside this superbly kitsch Yangon wonder you can get fairly ordinary Burmese, Indian or Chinese food, and prices are really not too outrageous. A traditional Burmese music ensemble sometimes plays the Burmese equivalent of 'music to dine by' in one of the several dining rooms, while a separate theatre-style room features a nightly performance of classical Burmese dance.

If you're waiting for a plane and haven't had enough fun yet, repair to *Penguin* (☎ 01-63751) or *Airport Oasis* (☎ 01-65865), two show-style restaurants near the airport with good Chinese and European food.

Cinema A half dozen or so cinemas along Bogyoke Aung San St, east of Sule Paya, show films for K10 or less per seat. The normal fare is pretty awful; a succession of syrupy Burmese dramas, kung-fu smash-ups and 'made for Third-World consumption' European or American action thrillers.

The American Center, behind the Ministry of Foreign Affairs at 14 Taw Win St, shows free American movies every Monday at noon; recent features have included *Back to the Future* and *In the Heat of the Night*. Music programmes such as *Austin City Limits* are also occasionally shown.

Bars, Cafes, Discos & Karaoke *The Strand Bar*, far more sophisticated than its funky predecessor, is open 11 am to 11 pm. Any foreign liquors you may be craving are bound to be among the huge selection of bottles behind the polished wooden bar. Modern watercolours of Burmese scenes decorate the walls and occasionally there's someone around to play the baby grand.

Founded by famous Burmese vocalist Nay Myo Say, *Mr Guitar Cafe* (☎ 01-85462) at 158-168 Mahabandoola Garden St is a small, two-storey cafe-bar decorated with old guitars. Live folk music is featured nightly from 7 to 10 pm. Most of the songs are sung in Burmese, with a few English chestnuts like 'Country Roads' thrown in from time to time. Well-known Burmese musicians drop by frequently, especially on weekends, to sit in with the regular house group. The clientele is a mix of Chinese, Burmese and European residents. Along with music, the cafe offers espresso drinks, imported beer and European food – expensive by Myanmar standards, moderate by international standards – from 6.30 to 11 pm. Mr Guitar has a second branch at the back of Bogyoke Aung San Market.

Although officially speaking discos are forbidden in Myanmar, the Singaporean company that owns the Yangon Duty Free Store at 143/149 Sule Pagoda Rd has managed to open *The Escapade* (☎ 01-77128) on top of the store. It's a full-on, high-tech disco with flashing lights and a chest-thumping sound system; at the back are a bank of posh, private, video karaoke rooms. Between DJ sets, a plastic Filipino band performs. High living doesn't come cheap; the cover charge is US$12 per person (includes two drinks), or you can purchase an annual membership for US$300. The Escapade is open nightly 8 pm to 12.30 am.

Take out the disco, add a large, Chinese banquet-style dining room, and you've got *Pegasus KTV Restaurant* (☎ 01-38058) at 5 Kaba Aye Pagoda Rd, Yankin township. In addition to a bar and lounge with a 100-inch TV, there are several private video karaoke rooms. The SLORC is contemplating a ban on all karaoke lounges, which are widely perceived by the Burmese to be fronts for prostitution.

The Nawarat Hotel's popular *Zawgyi Lounge* is a small but pleasant bar decorated with a series of original paintings by well-known Yangon muralist U Ba Kyi. The series depict various episodes in the life of a typical *zawgyi* or accomplished Burmese alchemist. A Filipino pop band performs Monday through Saturday nights, and on Sunday evening a local jazz band plays. There is no cover charge.

Things to Buy

Markets Shopping at the various markets *(zei)* in downtown Yangon can be fun and very educational. The sprawling, 70-year-old Bogyoke Aung San Market (sometimes called by its British name, Scott Market), appropriately located on Bogyoke Aung San St, has the largest selection of Burmese handicrafts you'll find under one roof (actually several roofs). Along the maze-like aisles you'll find a whole variety of interesting Burmese souvenirs, from lacquerware and Shan shoulder bags to T-shirts and cheroots. Gems and jewellery are also on hand, but be sure to read the relevant section on gems in the Facts for the Visitor chapter in this book before buying any.

Some of the more interesting shops in Bogyoke Aung San Market include: Depi Store, 39 West Block, for cheroots and cigars; Myanmar Lacquerware, 1/2 East Wing, for lacquerware; Eastern Queen, 18 Face Wing, 1st Floor, for rattan furniture; Maung Maw & Brothers, 115 Inner West Wing, for both modern and traditional musical instruments; Myat Sanda, 138 West

Wing and Sein Pan 69 West C, for *lephet* ('pickle tea'); and Mya Malar Longyi (Myanmar Traditional Nether Garments), West Wing. At least 20 other places in the market also specialise in longyis.

Another major market, especially for locals who find Bogyoke Aung San Market a little too pricey, is Theingyi Zei, the biggest market in Yangon. This rambling affair extends four blocks east to west from Konzaydan St to 24th St, and north to south from Anawrahta St to Mahabandoola St. Most of the merchandise for sale represents ordinary housewares and textiles, but the market is renowned for its large section purveying traditional Burmese herbs and medicines. A snake section features the fresh blood and organs of various snakes – including the deadly branded krait – eviscerated on the spot for medicinal consumption. Of more general interest is traditional Burmese herbal shampoo, made by boiling the bark of the *tayaw* shrub with big black acacia pods *(kin pun)* and sold in small plastic bags; this is the secret of how Burmese women maintain such smooth, glossy hair. A new mall-like section on Shwedagon Pagoda Rd, Theingyizei Plaza, contains less interesting modern shops.

Thirimingala Zei, on the Yangon River bank in Ahlone township off the northern end of Strand Rd (straight west about a km from People's Park), is a labyrinth of vendors selling fresh foodstuffs, vegetables, fruits and meat – it's worth a stroll for the amazing sights and smells, not all of them necessarily pleasant. Catch even more of an aroma further north along the riverfront at the San Pya Fish Market.

A little south-east of Kandawgyi Lake, Mingala Zei proffers textiles, clothes, electric appliances, plastic-ware, preserved and tinned foodstuffs, modern medicines, and cosmetics from Thailand, China and Singapore. This is the place to come if you're setting up house in Yangon on the cheap.

There are other markets around, such as the iron bazaar on the corner of Mahabandoola St and Lanmadaw St in Yangon's Chinatown – here you can find all the items that are used in Chinese cooking. Itinerant vendors set up along Anawrahta St east and west of Sule Pagoda Rd nightly from around 6 to 10 pm, selling everything from Chinese toothbrushes to fresh fruit and shishkebab. Chinatown itself extends east-west between Lanmadaw St and Shwedagon Pagoda Rd, and north-south between Mahabandoola St and Strand Rd.

Speciality Shops Myanmar Elephant House (☎ 01-32773), located at 24A Aung Min Khaung Rd, off Thanlyin Rd, produces a variety of high-quality, handmade wood, cane and rattan furniture plus design accessories.

Yuzana Pickle Tea (☎ 01-72456), at 22 Nawaday St, Dagon township, sells the city's best quality lephet in sweet, sour and chilli-laced varieties. You can buy an all-in-one kit containing prepared tea leaves, fried garlic, sesame, peanuts, fried peas, etc or buy each of the ingredients separately. The kit makes a unique souvenir. There is a second branch on the ground floor of Theingyi Zei, Shed D, E-60.

Myanmar Orchid and Flora Centre (☎ 01-72115), 119 Sule Pagoda Rd, offers fresh and artificial flowers, orchid plants and seeds; if you're moving to Yangon they can also provide landscape design.

For recommendations on where to buy books, see the Bookshops & Libraries section at the beginning of this chapter.

Tailors Yangon isn't a place you would usually think of for tailor-made clothes, but prices for tailoring are among the lowest in South-East Asia. The selection of fabrics at tailor shops, however, is mostly restricted to synthetics. Cotton lengths in prints, plaids, solids and batiks can easily be found in the larger markets, so you may do better to buy cloth at a market and bring it to a tailor shop for cutting and sewing.

If you want a traditional, Mandarin-collar Burmese shirt (for men), try Ava Tailoring (☎ 01-72973) on Pansodan St near the railway station at the Anawrahta St inter-

section. If you're measured the day you arrive, they can have it ready by the time you return from upcountry. Mohamed Esoof and Lain Lain Tailor at 142-143 Bo Galay Bazaar St are well regarded by local expats for women's as well as men's tailoring. Globe Tailoring (☎ 01-73416) at 367 Bogyoke Aung San St has also been recommended.

Film & Photo Supplies Along Anawrahta St between Sule Pagoda Rd and Maha-bandoola Garden St are at least a dozen shops that sell film and photo supplies. Several stock slide film – usually Kodak Ektachrome Elite 100 and Fujichrome Sensia 100 – for around K800 per roll. Colour print film is plentiful and cheap, black-and-white film very scarce.

Duty-Free Goods Most merchandise at the duty-free shop at Yangon International Airport is cheaper than in Bangkok, Hong Kong or Singapore. There's also a branch in town at the former location of the Tourist Department Store on Sule Pagoda Rd just north of Sule Paya. This time around it's called Yangon Duty Free Store. Both branches carry the usual airport stuff – perfume, cigarettes (US$9 a carton), booze (average US$10 per litre) and watches – plus a variety of other imported goods such as chocolate candies and breakfast cereal.

Getting There & Away
Air See the introductory Getting There & Away chapter for information on air travel in and out of Yangon.

Airline Offices Ten airlines have offices or agents in Yangon, though only Biman Bangladesh, Air China, Myanma Airways International, Thai International Airways and Silk Air actually have flights in and out of Yangon International Airport.

Aeroflot
  501-503 Pyay Rd (☎ 01-20295)
Air China
  15D Padonma St (☎ 01-73882, 87121)

BERNARD NAPTHINE

BERNARD NAPTHINE

BERNARD NAPTHINE

Yangon
Top: Yangon's legendary Strand
Middle: Yangon architecture from colonial times
Bottom: Downtown Yangon

RICHARD I'ANSON

BERNARD NAPTHINE

BERNARD NAPTHINE

BERNARD NAPTHINE

Yangon
Top Left: The great, gilded Shwedagon
Top Right: Robed devotee reflecting before the Shwedagon
Bottom Left: Monks beneath Botataung's golden stupa
Bottom Right: Glittering spires on the Shwedagon terrace

Air France
    69 Sule Pagoda Rd (☎ 01-77041)
Air Mandalay
    146 Dhammazedi Rd (☎ 01-82561)
Biman Bangladesh
    106-108 Pansodan St (☎ 01-75882)
KLM
    c/o Myanma Airways, 104 Strand Rd
    (☎ 01-74466)
Myanma Airways
    104 Strand Rd (☎ 01-82678)
Myanma Airways International
    123 Sule Pagoda Rd (☎ 01-89772)
Northwest
    36 Shwebontha St (☎ 01-81613)
Royal Nepal
    c/o Myanma Airways, 104 Strand Rd
    (☎ 01-77013)
Silk Air
    537 Merchant St (☎ 01-82653)
Thai Airways International
    441-445 Mahabandoola St (☎ 01-75936)

Buses North Most public and private buses
to destinations north of Yangon leave from
the Highway Bus Centre at the intersection
of Pyay Rd and Station Rd, just south-west
of Yangon's airport in Mingaladon. Each bus
line has its own little office at the station; for
the most part these offices are lined up
according to general route, eg one section for
Nyaung U/Bagan, another for the Mandalay
area, another for Taunggyi/Inle Lake and one
for Mawlamyine (Moulmein)/Dawei
(Tavoy). To buy a ticket to any destination
which requires a travel permit, you may be
asked to show your papers. There are a
number of snack shops with rice and noodle
plates in case you get hungry while waiting
for a departure.

Ordinary government buses are the cheapest and slowest: so slow that the Road
Transport Enterprise won't even give arrival
times. Virtually all trips listed below last at
least one day, some a day and a night. For
departure times and fares see the table opposite.

Private buses generally run better vehicles
on tighter schedules for up to twice the government fare. A company called Golden
Shuttle, for example, runs air-con buses to
Magwe which leave at 5 pm and arrive
around 3 am for K300 per person; the

company also has non-air-con buses to Pyay
for K100 which leave at 8 am and noon from
both ends of the route and take 6½ hours
to/from Yangon. Fares and departure times
change with regularity to account for passenger demand; the best way to get a ticket is to
show up around 5 am and start asking around
(or visit the station the afternoon of the day
before you want to go).

Most impressive of all are the new air-con
express buses which run to Pyay, Meiktila,
Mandalay and Taunggyi. These typically
feature large Japanese, Chinese or Korean
air-con buses with around 45 reclining seats,
and even onboard video. Typical fares are
K1000 to K1100 (or US$10/FEC) for Man-
dalay, Meiktila or Taunggyi, K400 (or
US$4/FEC) to Pyay. These lines also may
stop in Bago and Taungoo, where small
offices are maintained at roadside restaurants.

The major players on the popular Yangon
to Mandalay route are Rainbow Express,
Trade Express, Skyline Express and
Myanmar Arrow Express, all of whom maintain offices at the Highway Bus Centre as
well as in downtown Yangon. All depart the
terminal between 4.30 and 7 pm, arriving in
Mandalay 14 to 15 hours later. Meals en
route are usually provided. After inspecting
the equipment used for each of these, we
concluded that Skyline and Myanmar Arrow
ran the best buses, Trade Express the worst,

Yangon Government Bus Timetable

Destination	Departure times	Fare
Kyaikto	9.30 am, noon	K50
Kyauk Padaung	5 am	K215
Loikaw	5 am	K300
Magwe	5 am	K150
Mandalay	4 am, 5 pm	K300
	5 pm	K500
Meiktila	4 pm	K190
Mottama	5.30 am	K85
Pathein	5 am, 6 am	K60
Pyay	8 am, 9 am, 10.30 am	K80
Taunggyi	5.30 am	K350
Taungoo	8 am, 9 am	K100

but this could change. Enquire at the offices about hotel pickup; some companies transfer passengers from hotel to bus terminal in vans or pickups.

Express bus offices downtown include:

Myanmar Arrow Express
    19/25 Aung San Stadium, Southern Wing
    (☎ 01-74294, 41276)
Rainbow Express
    96/98 Pansodan St (☎ 01-72250, 83621)
Skyline Express
    284/286 Seikkantha St (☎ 01-71711)
Trade Express
    9 Yawmingyi St, Dagon (☎ 01-89291)

Buses to Bago, Pathein & Thanlyin Buses for Bago and Pathein (Bassein) leave from the Hsimmalaik Bus Centre near the intersection of Hanthawady Rd and Hledan St in the north-western part of Yangon. Pickups to Bago leave hourly from 6 am to 3 pm for K30 per person. There are two private buses to Pathein, both in the early morning around 5 am, for K80. Buses to Pathein are also available from the less convenient Highway Bus Centre.

Small pickups to Bago also leave from the eastern side of Latha St south of Anawrahta St. Buses to Thanlyin leave from the southern side of Mahabandoola St east of Sule Paya.

Train In addition to the many trains operated by state-owned Myanma Railways, one private company runs out of Yangon Railway Station along the Yangon to Mandalay line. Dagon Mann (☎ 01-71310) reserves just four berths and six upper-class seats for foreigners on its private express train (No 17 Up on the public schedule), which departs Yangon at 3.15 pm on Wednesday, Friday and Sunday, arriving in Mandalay at 5.40 am the next morning. Obviously this is no quicker than the Myanma Railways trains, simply because they use the same engines and tracks. In fact the train really caters to Burmese residents, who pay a good deal less – K200 – for a wooden seat in 64-seat ordinary class. The same seat costs foreigners US$18; in exchange for paying nine times the usual fare, the foreigner is rewarded with

a meal choice of hamburger, fried noodles or fried rice, plus one soft drink or beer.

Moving up a notch you'll pay US$45 for a 30-seat, air-con upper-class car, which features video programmes but is otherwise no better than the US$30 Myanma Railways express. At the top end, you can pay US$50 per person for a special upper-class sleeper, a four-person cabin with attached bath and fridge, video, air-con and audio; or US$48 for regular upper-class four-person sleeper with air-con and audio, no attached bath or video. A few two-person cabins are also available at the same price but it's rare that these become available for foreigners.

Dagon Mann upper-class tickets may be reserved up to a month in advance of departure. Ordinary-class travel can only be booked the day of departure. Reservations and tickets are available at the Dagon Mann ticket office on Bogyoke Aung San St alongside the railway station.

See the Getting Around chapter for information on rail travel between Yangon and Mandalay using Myanma Railways.

Boat Along the Yangon River waterfront, which wraps around southern Yangon, are a number of jetties with boats offering long-distance ferry services. Four main passenger jetties service long-distance ferries headed up the delta toward Pathein or north along the Ayeyarwady to Pyay, Bagan and Mandalay: Pongyi, Lan Thit, Kaingdan and Hledan. Named for the respective streets that extend north from each jetty, all four are clustered in an area just south of Lanmadaw township and south-west of Chinatown. When you purchase a ticket for a particular ferry from the IWT (Inland Water Transport Co) deputy division manager's office at the back of Lan Thit St Jetty, be sure to ask which jetty your boat will be leaving from.

Myanma Five Star Line ships leave from the MSFL jetty – also known as Chanmayeiseikan Jetty – next to Pansodan St Jetty.

Getting Around
To/From the Airport See under Air in the

introductory Getting Around chapter for details on getting to and from the airport.

Bus Over 40 numbered city bus routes connect the townships of Yangon. Many buses date back to the 1940s and carry heavy teak carriages. Often they're impossibly crowded; a Burmese bus is not full until every available handhold for those hanging off the sides and back has been taken. Other routes use newer Japanese and Korean buses that aren't too bad; some routes also use pickup trucks with benches in the back. If you can find a space you can get anywhere in downtown Yangon for K2 or less. Longer routes cost up to K5.

Useful bus routes include:

Bogyoke Aung San Market to Mingala Zei (southeast of Kandawgyi Lake) – Japanese pickup No 1 (၁)

Sule Paya to Thamaing Junction ('Eight-Mile Junction') along Insein Rd – Circular 1/2 (၁/၂) No 8 (၈)

Sule Paya to Hledan Junction, then Pyay Rd University of Yangon, along the west side of Inya Lake to Yangon City Hotel and the airport – blue bus No 9 (၉)

To Kaba Aye Paya and on to Mae La Mu Paya – bus No 5 (၅)

Similar route to No 8, starting from Insein, continuing on to Theinbyu St in the vicinity of the YMCA, Three Seasons Hotel, Cozy Guest House – green pickup No 48 (၄၈)

Mahabandoola Garden St to the Highway Bus Centre – yellow No 51 (၅၁)

To Shwedagon Paya – bus Nos 39 (၃၉), 31 (၃၁), 43 (၄၃) or 10 (၁၀) – the latter bus continues around Kandawgyi Lake and loops back into the city

To the Chaukhtatgyi Paya – bus to Shwedagon, then a No 16 (၁၆) east along Shwegondine Rd

Train A circular train route loops out north from Yangon to Insein, Mingaladon and North Okkalapa townships and then back into the city. There are actually two trains, one clockwise ('left-bound') and one counter-clockwise ('right-bound'), and it takes three hours to complete the loop in either direction. A run around this loop (trains leave hourly) will give you a cheap (about K7) but not particularly comfortable,

look around; trains depart seven times daily between 5 am and 5 pm.

This train isn't any good for getting around downtown Yangon – there's only one downtown station, the main one – but it can be useful for moving back and forth between the various townships north of the city centre. If you want to use the train to get around the city, the Ministry of Forestry's *Yangon Guide Map* shows the stations marked most clearly. The Kyaukyedwin station is not far from the airport, and there are also convenient stations for Hledan, Kamayut and Insein north-west of the city centre. Buses to these same areas are quicker, of course, unless you've just come from upcountry by train and are at Yangon Railway Station anyway. Yangon's main station is off Sule Pagoda Rd north of Bogyoke Aung San St; to buy tickets for the circular train, look for the ticket window next to an oval track map at the eastern end of the station.

Taxi Licensed taxis carry red licence plates, though there is often little else to distinguish a taxi from any other vehicle in Yangon. The most expensive are the car taxis – usually older, mid-sized Japanese cars. Fares are highly negotiable – most trips around the downtown area shouldn't cost more than K180 one way. You can hire a non-registered cab for the whole day for no more than K2500 or US$25.

Cheaper are the tiny three-wheeled and four-wheeled Mazda taxis, close relatives of the Indian *bajaj* or Thai *tuk-tuks*. A short trip of six to eight blocks or so should cost no more than K50, longer distances downtown K80 to 100 one way.

For all types of taxis the asking fares usually leap up 30% or so after sunset and on weekends, when rationed petrol isn't available. Late-night taxis – after 11 pm or so – often cost double the daytime rate, mainly because the supply of taxis on hand is considerably lower than in the daytime so the drivers are able to charge more.

Trishaw Every Asian country seems to have

YANGON

its own interpretation of the bicycle trishaw. In some countries the passengers sit beside the rider, side by side in a sort of sidecar; in others they sit in front or in the back. In Myanmar, trishaw passengers ride beside the driver, but back to back – one facing forward, one backward. These contraptions are called *sai-kaa* and to ride one costs roughly K10 per person every km or so.

Nowadays trishaws are not permitted on the main streets between midnight and 10 am. They're most useful for side streets and areas of town where traffic is light. As more cars and trucks deluge the roadways, it probably won't be too long before they're banned from the city centre altogether.

Boat Cross-river ferries to Dalah, on the southern bank of the Yangon River, leave from Pansodan St Jetty (for pedestrians), at the foot of Pansodan St, and Sin Oh Dan St Jetty (for vehicles) at the foot of Sin Oh Dan St. Dalah is the departure point for excursions to Twante and Letkhokkon. See the Twante section in the Around Yangon chapter for further details on cross-river transport.

You can hire sampans from the Pansodan or Botataung jetties for K100 per hour if you just want to have a look at river life. On a grander scale, for US$1000 you can charter a deluxe double-decker (normally reserved for VIP dinners and such) from the IWT office near Lan Thit St Jetty for a four-hour cruise between Thanlyin to the north-east and Bayinnaung Bridge to the north-west.

Since the completion of the Thanlyin Bridge, there are no more passenger ferries to Thanlyin across the Bago River from Yangon.

SHWEDAGON PAYA

THE GOLDEN DAGON

Kipling called it 'a golden mystery...a beautiful winking wonder'. As the setting sun casts its last rays on the soft orange dome of the great Shwedagon Paya you can feel the magic in the air. In the heat of the day the stupa glitters bright gold. It can be quiet and contemplative; colourful and raucous. The 'Golden Dagon' is the essence of Myanmar and a place that never fails to enchant.

For Burmese Buddhists, Shwedagon is the most sacred of all Buddhist sites in the country, one which all Burmese hope to visit at least once in their lifetime.

The great golden dome rises 98 metres above its base. According to legends this stupa – of the solid *zedi* type – is 2500 years old but archaeologists are nearly unanimous in suggesting the original stupa was built by the Mon sometime between the 6th and 10th centuries. In common with many other ancient zedis in earthquake-prone Myanmar, it has been rebuilt many times and its current form dates back only to 1769.

History

The legend of the Shwedagon tells of two merchant brothers meeting the Buddha, who gave them eight of his hairs to take back to be enshrined in Myanmar. With the help of a number of spirit *nats* the brothers and the king of this region of Myanmar discovered the hill where relics of the previous Buddhas had been enshrined. When the chamber to house the hairs was built and the hairs were taken from their golden casket, some quite amazing events took place:

...there was a tumult among men and spirits...rays emitted by the Hairs penetrated up to the heavens above and down to hell...the blind beheld objects...the deaf heard sounds...the dumb spoke distinctly...the earth quaked...the winds of the ocean blew...Mount Meru shook...lightning flashed...gems rained down until they were knee deep...all trees of the Himalayas, though not in season, bore blossoms and fruit.

Fortunately hairs of the Buddha are not unveiled every day.

Once the relics were safely enshrined, a golden slab was laid on their chamber and a golden stupa built on it. Over this a silver stupa was built, then a tin stupa, a copper stupa, a lead stupa, a marble stupa and finally an iron-brick stupa. Or so the legend goes. Later, the legend continues, the stupa at Dagon fell into disuse and it is said the great Indian Buddhist-emperor Asoka came to Myanmar and found the site only with great difficulty, but subsequently had the encroaching jungle cleared and the stupa repaired.

During the Bagan period the story of the stupa emerges from the mists of legend and becomes hard fact. Near the top of the eastern stairway you can see an inscription recording the history of the stupa up to 1485. King Anawrahta visited Dagon from his capital at Bagan in the 11th century, while King Bayinnaung, during his reign at Bago (1353-85), had the stupa rebuilt to a height of 18 metres. Succeeding kings alternately neglected, then improved, the stupa. During the 15th century it was rebuilt several times, eventually reaching 90 metres, not far short of its present height.

During this period the tradition of gilding the stupa also began – Queen Shinsawbu, who was responsible for many improvements to the stupa, provided her own weight (40 kg) in gold, which was beaten into goldleaf and used to gild the structure. Her son-in-law, Dhammazedi, went several better by offering four times his own weight and that of his wife's in gold. He also provided the 1485 historical inscription on the eastern stairway.

In 1586 the English visitor Ralph Fitch made probably the best early European description of the great stupa:

...it is called Dogonne, and is of a wonderful bignesse, and all gilded from the foot to the toppe...it is the fairest place, as I suppose, that is in the world; it standeth very high, and there are foure ways to it, which all along are set with trees of fruits, such wise that a man may goe in the shade above two miles in length...

The zedi suffered from a series of earthquakes that caused great damage during this time. In 1612 De Brito raided the stupa from his base in Thanlyin and carried away Dhammazedi's great bell, with the intention of melting it down for cannons. As the British were to do later, with another bell, he managed to drop it into the river. During the 17th century the monument suffered earthquake damage on eight occasions. Worse was to follow in 1768, when a quake brought down the whole top of the zedi. King Hsinbyushin had it rebuilt to virtually its present height, and its current configuration dates from that renovation.

British troops occupied the compound for two years after the First Anglo-Burmese War in 1824. In 1852, during the Second Anglo-Burmese War, the British again took the paya, the soldiers pillaged it once more and it remained under military control for 77 years until 1929. In 1871 a new *hti* (the decorative top of a paya), provided by King Mindon Min from Mandalay, caused considerable head-scratching for the British, who were not at all keen for such an association to be made with the still independent part of Myanmar.

During this century Shwedagon Paya was the scene for much political activity during the Burmese independence movement and also suffered from a serious fire in 1931. It started at the bottom of the western stairway, which had been reopened to the public for less than two years after the British military occupation had closed that entrance off. The fire rushed up the stairway and right round the northern side of the paya before being halted half way down the eastern stairway. The huge earthquake of 1930, which totally destroyed the Shwemawdaw in Bago, only caused minor damage to the Shwedagon. After another minor earthquake in 1970 the zedi was clad in bamboo scaffolding up beyond King Mindon's 100-year-old hti, and was refurbished.

Design

There are four covered walkways up Singuttara Hill to the platform on which the Shwedagon stands. The southern entrance, from Pagoda Rd, is the one which can most properly be called the 'main' entrance. Here and at the northern entrance there are lifts available should you not feel fit enough for the stroll up the stairs. The western entrance features a series of escalators in place of stairs and is the only entrance without vendors. The eastern stairway has the most traditional ambience, passing adjacent *kyaungs* (monasteries) and vendors selling monastic requisites. Foreigners are required to pay US$5 to enter the complex. A camera permit for the Shwedagon costs K5, but this fee is not always enforced.

Two nine-metre-high *chinthes*, the legendary half lion, half griffin 'leogryphs', guard the southern entrance. You must remove your shoes and socks as soon as you mount the first step. Like the other entranceways, the southern steps are lined with a whole series of shops. Here devotees can buy flowers, both real and beautifully made paper ones, for offerings. Paper ceremonial umbrellas, Buddha images, golden thrones, ivory combs, books, antiques and incense sticks are also on sale. However hot it may be outside, you'll find the walkway cool, shady and calm. It's this quiet, subdued atmosphere on the entrance steps which makes the impact so great as you arrive at the platform.

You emerge from semi-gloom into a visual cacophony of technicoloured glitter – for the Shwedagon is not just one huge, glowing zedi.

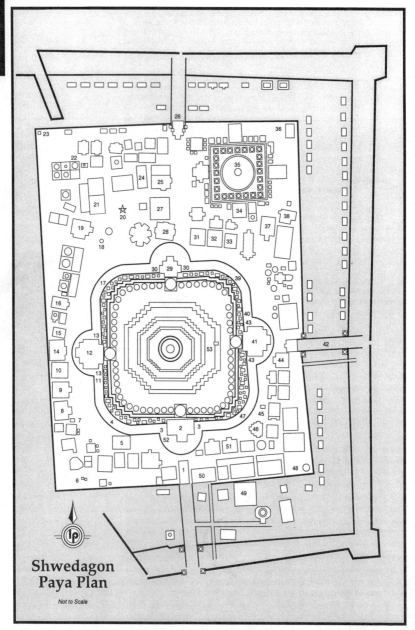

Shwedagon
Paya Plan

Not to Scale

1	Southern Stairway Landing	26	Northern Stairway Landing
2	Konagamana Shrine	27	Pavilion (where *hti* was placed)
3	Planetary Posts for Mercury	28	Hair Relics Well
4	Planetary Post for Saturn	29	Gautama Adoration Hall
5	Prayer Pavilion	30	Planetary Posts for Venus
6	Student Monument	31	Mahabodhi-Style Temple
7	Guardian Nat	32	Small Gilded Zedi
8	Rakhine Tazaung	33	Two-Pice Tazaung
9	Prayer Hall (with reclining Buddha)	34	Izza-Gawna Pavilion
10	Chinese Merchants' Tazaung	35	Golden Elder Stupa
		36	Dhammazedi Inscription
11	Mai Lamu & King of the Nats	37	King Tharawaddy's Bell
12	Western Adoration Hall	38	Pavilion (with wood carvings)
13	Planetary Posts for Jupiter	39	Planetary Post for the Sun
14	Two-Pice Tazaung	40	Shan Umbrellas
15	Low Pavilion	41	Kakusandha Shrine Hall
16	Pavilion (with tall columns)	42	Eastern Stairway Landing
17	Planetary Post for Rahu	43	Planetary Posts for the Moon
18	Eight Day Stupa	44	U Nyo Pavilion
19	Maha Gandha Bell	45	Hintha Prayer Post
20	Wish Fulfilling Place	46	Prayer Post Bell
21	Large Pavilion	47	Planetary Post for Mars
22	Wonder Working Image	48	Banyan Tree
23	North-Western Corner	49	Trustees' Office
24	Chinese Prayer Hall	50	Curio Museum
25	Pavilion (with Indian figures)	51	Pavilion (with wood carvings)
		52	Stairs to Zedi Plinth
		53	Tawa-gu Image

Around the mighty stupa cluster an incredible assortment of smaller zedis, statues, temples, shrines, images and *tazaungs* (pavilions). Somehow the bright gold of the main stupa makes everything else also seem brighter and larger than life.

Stupas, indeed all Buddhist structures, should properly be walked around clockwise, so at the top of the steps turn left, and like the crowds of Burmese, start strolling. During the heat of the day you'll probably have to confine yourself to the mat pathway laid around the platform – unless your bare feet can take the heat of the uncovered marble paving.

The hill on which the stupa stands is 58 metres above sea level and the platform covers 5.6 hectares. Prior to the British takeover of Lower Myanmar, there had been Burmese defensive earthworks around the paya, but these were considerably extended by the British and the emplacements for their cannons can still be seen outside the outer wall.

The main stupa, which is completely solid, rises from its platform in a fairly standard pattern. First there is the plinth which stands 6.4 metres above the clutter of the main platform and immediately sets the Shwedagon above the lesser structures. Smaller stupas sit on this raised platform level – four large ones mark the four cardinal directions, four medium-sized ones mark the four corners of the basically square platform and 60 small ones run around the perimeter.

From this base the zedi rises first in three terraces, then in the 'octagonal' terraces and then in five circular bands – together these elements add another 30 metres to the stupa's height. This is a normal solution to a standard architectural problem associated with stupas – how to change from the square base to the circular upper elements. Here,

YANGON

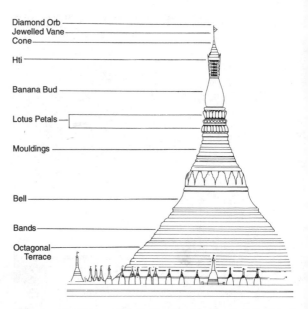

Diamond Orb
Jewelled Vane
Cone

Hti

Banana Bud

Lotus Petals

Mouldings

Bell

Bands

Octagonal Terrace

as in many other Burmese zedis, that transition is achieved with the help of the octagonal sections, which make a step between the square and the circle. Similarly, the circular bands make a transition from the horizontal design of these lower elements to the smooth vertical flow of the bell.

Earlier stupas were commonly hemispherical; a good example in Myanmar is the Kaunghmudaw at Sagaing near Mandalay. The more graceful bell design, as seen here, is a comparatively recent development. The shoulder of the bell is decorated with 16 'flowers'. The bell is topped by the 'inverted bowl', another traditional element of stupa architecture, and above this stand the mouldings and then the 'lotus petals'. These consist of a band of down-turned lotus petals followed by a band of up-turned petals.

The banana bud is the final element of the zedi before the hti that tops it. Like the lotus petals below, the banana bud is actually covered with no less than 13,153 plates of gold measuring 30 sq cm each – unlike the lower elements which are merely covered with gold leaf. The seven-tiered hti is made of iron and again plated with gold. Even without the various hanging bells it weighs well over a tonne. The seven tiers taper progressively and from the uppermost tier projects the shaft on which are hung gold bells, silver bells and various items of jewellery. The topmost vane with its flag turns with the wind. It is gold and silver plated and studded with 1100 diamonds totalling 278 carats – not to mention 1383 other stones. Finally, at the very top of the vane rests the diamond orb – a hollow golden sphere studded with no less than 4351 diamonds weighing 1800 carats in all. The very top of the orb is tipped with a single 76-carat diamond.

This central zedi is regilded every year; by 1995 it had reportedly accumulated 53 metric tonnes of goldleaf.

Around the Stupa

The mighty zedi is only one of many structures on the hilltop platform. Reaching the platform from the southern stairway (1), you encounter the first shrine (2), which is to Konagamana, the second Buddha. Almost beside the shrine stand the planetary posts for Mercury (3). If you were born on a Wednesday morning (as was the Buddha) then this is your post and the tusked elephant is your animal sign. Continuing around the plinth, you pass a double-bodied lion with a man's face, a laughing necromancer with his hands on his head and an earth goddess. At the south-west corner of the plinth you reach the planetary post for Saturn (4). Come here if you were born on a Saturday; your animal sign is the *naga* or dragon serpent. The pavilion (5) directly opposite has 28 images to represent the 28 'avatars' or previous incarnations of the Buddha.

Back towards the corner of the platform is a monument (6) with inscriptions in four languages, recounting a 1920 student revolt against British rule. Continuing around the platform, you come to a glass case with two figures of nats (7) – one is of the guardian nat of Shwedagon Paya. Close to these figures is a prayer pavilion (8), bare inside, but with fine woodcarving on the terraced roof. It is known as the Rakhine Tazaung since it was donated by brokers from the Rakine (Arakan) coast bordering Bangladesh. An eight-metre-long reclining Buddha can be seen in the next prayer hall (9). Next to this is the Chinese Merchants' Tazaung (10) with a variety of Buddha figures in different poses.

On the plinth opposite this prayer hall there are figures of Mai Lamu and the king of the nats (11), the legendary parents of King Ukkalapa who, according to the legend, originally enshrined the Buddha hairs here. The figures stand on top of each other. The western adoration hall (12) was built in 1841, but was destroyed in the fire which swept the zedi platform in 1931. The planetary posts for the Thursday-born (13) stand to the right and left of this pavilion – your planet is Jupiter, your animal sign the rat. A figure of King Ukkalapa can be seen further to the left, on the zedi plinth.

Directly opposite the west adoration hall is the Two Pice Tazaung (14) at the head of the western stairway. It was built with the proceeds of a daily collection of two *pice* (an extinct unit of Burmese currency) from the stalls in Yangon market. The western stairway, the steepest of the four entrances, was also built from this collection after the 1931 fire. The low pavilion (15) next to the entrance was built by manufacturers of monastery requirements – in contrast to the rather Chinese-looking roof. Next round is a pavilion (16) with tall columns and the *pyatthat* rising from the upper roof. Almost opposite this tazaung, at the north-western corner of the main zedi, is the planetary post (17) for those born on Wednesday afternoon, whose animal symbol is the tuskless elephant, planet Yahu (Rahu, a mythical planet in Hindu astrology which allegedly causes eclipses).

A small stupa with a golden spire (18) has eight niches around its base, each with a Buddha image. Between the niches are figures of animals and birds – they represent the eight directions of the compass and the associated sign, planet and day of the week. To get over the small complication of having an 'Eight Day Stupa' and a seven-day week, Wednesday is divided into Wednesday morning and Wednesday afternoon. The eight days, which can also be found with their corresponding planetary posts around the main stupa are (from the southern entrance):

Direction	Day	Planet	Sign
south	Wed am	Mercury	tusked elephant
south-west	Sat	Saturn	naga (dragon serpent)
west	Thu	Jupiter	rat
north-west	Wed pm	Rahu	tuskless elephant
north	Fri	Venus	guinea pig or mole
north-east	Sun	sun	garuda
east	Mon	moon	tiger
south-east	Tue	Mars	lion

Close to this small stupa stands the bell pavilion (19) housing the 23-tonne Maha Ganda Bell. Cast between 1775 and 1779, it was carted off by the British after the First Anglo-Burmese War in 1825. They managed to drop it into the Yangon River while trying to get it to the port for shipping to England; after repeatedly trying to raise it from the bottom of the river they gave up and told the Burmese they could have the bell back if they could get it out of the river. The Burmese placed logs and bamboo beneath the bell until it eventually floated up from the river-bottom. Venturing back into the open area of the platform, you come to the star-shaped 'wish-fulfilling place' (20). Here there will often be devotees, kneeling down and looking towards the great stupa, praying that their wishes will come true.

The large pavilion (21) across from the bell pavilion houses a nine-metre-high Buddha image and is often used for public meetings. Behind this pavilion stands a small shrine (22) with a highly revered 'wonder-working' Buddha image covered in goldleaf. From the north-western corner of the platform (23) you can look out over some of the British fortifications and the country to the north of the hill. There are also two banyan trees growing here, one of them grown from a cutting from the actual tree at Bodhgaya in India, under which the Buddha sat and was enlightened.

Amongst the cluster of buildings on this side of the platform is the Chinese prayer hall (24), with good woodcarvings and Chinese dragon figures on the sides of the zedi in front of it. The adjacent pavilion (25) has life-size figures of Indians guarding the side and front entrance doors. No one quite understands their relevance or that of the very British lions that guard the next pavilion.

In 1824 a force of Burmese 'Invulnerables' fought their way up the northern stairs to the entrance (26) of the platform before being repulsed by the better-armed British forces occupying the paya. The crocodile-like stair bannister dates from 1460. The Martyrs' Mausoleum of Bogyoke Aung San and his compatriots stands on the western side of the hill reached from this stairway; it doesn't open till 9 am and admission costs US$3.

Walking back towards the stupa, you pass the pavilion (27) built on the site where the great zedi's hti, provided by King Mindon Min, was placed before being raised to the zedi summit. The Hair Relics Well was located at the position of the Sandawdwin Tazaung (28) and is said to reach right down to the level of the Ayeyarwady (Irrawaddy) River and to be fed from it; the Buddha hairs were washed in this well before being enshrined in the zedi. In the northern adoration hall (29) the main image is of Gautama, the historical Buddha. On either side of the hall stand planetary posts for Friday (30), domain of the planet Venus and the guinea pig or mole.

Modelled after the Mahabodhi temple in Bodhgaya, India, the temple (31) a few steps away is distinctively different from the general style of buildings on the platform. A small gilded zedi (32) stands next to this temple, and next again is another 'two-pice' pavilion (33) enshrining a 200-year-old Buddha image. An opening behind this image is, according to legend, the entrance to a passage which leads to the chamber housing the Buddha hair relics. Although seen from the 'two-pice' pavilion, the image is actually in the adjacent stupa.

Izza-Gawna (the name means 'goat-bullock') was a legendary monk whose powers enabled him to replace his lost eyes with one from a goat and one from a bullock. In his pavilion (34) the figure off to the left of the main Buddha image has eyes of unequal size as a reminder of this unique feat. The golden Elder Stupa (35) is built on the spot where the hair relics were first placed before being enshrined in the great zedi. A straight line drawn from the centre of this stupa to the centre of the Shwedagon would pass through the small stupa reputed to be the entrance to the passage which leads to the relic chamber. Women are not allowed to ascend to the platform around the Elder Stupa, which is also known as the Naungdawgyi Stupa.

Back in the corner of the platform is the Dhammazedi inscription (36), which dates from 1485 and was originally installed on the eastern stairway. It tells in three languages – Pali, Mon and Burmese – the story of the Shwedagon.

Cast in 1841, King Tharawaddy Min's bell is housed in an elegant pavilion (37). The Maha Titthadaganda or 'three-toned bell' weighs 42 tons. Note the ceiling made of lacquer inlaid with glass. If you look closely, you can also discern red-billed green parrots nearly hidden in the scrolling among the devas. The adjacent small pavilion (38) has some good panels of woodcarvings. Back on the main platform the planetary post (39) for those born on Sunday (the sun) stands at the north-eastern corner of the stupa platform. The bird-like creature beneath the post is the garuda of Hindu-Buddhist mythology, called *galon* by the Burmese. Further round you will see golden Shan umbrellas (40) amongst the plinth shrines; there is also one over the Friday planetary post by the north pavilion.

Facing the eastern stairway, the eastern shrine hall (41) is said to be the most beautiful on the platform. It was renovated in 1869 but destroyed by the 1931 fire and subsequently rebuilt. The main image is that of Kakusandha, the first Buddha. The eastern stairway (42) is the longest and is lined with shops selling everyday articles as well as religious goods and antiques. On either side, the Monday-born worship at the planetary posts (43) ruled over by the moon and the tiger.

The graceful U Nyo pavilion (44) beside the eastern entrance has a series of interesting woodcarved panels illustrating events in the life of Gautama Buddha. The prayer post (45) close to the south-eastern corner of the zedi is topped by a mythological *hintha* bird. An interesting bell (46) hangs near this prayer post. Opposite these on the zedi plinth is the planetary post for Tuesday (47), presided over by the lion and the planet Mars.

In the corner of the platform stands another sacred banyan tree (48), also said to be grown from a branch of the original tree under which Gautama Buddha gained enlightenment in India. There is a good view from this corner of the platform over Yangon and across the Yangon River towards Thanlyin. You can, on a clear day, see the Kyaik-khauk Paya just beyond Thanlyin. The paya trustees have their office (49) on this side of the platform, and there's also a small curio museum (50). In front of the museum is a pavilion (51) with very fine woodcarvings. There is also a revolving hti and a telescope, possibly for looking at the real hti on top of the zedi.

Beside the southern shrine (2), the first stop on this circular tour, stairs (52) lead up onto the zedi plinth. With permission from the paya trustees, men only are allowed to climb up to the plinth terrace. Men come up here to meditate; the terrace is about six metres wide – a circular walkway between the great zedi and its 68 surrounding zedis. There's a K5 fee for entering the terrace. Behind the eastern shrine is a Buddha image (53) known as the Tawa-gu, which is reputed to work miracles.

Visiting the Shwedagon is far more than just wandering around and looking at the shrines, pavilions, images, bells and stupas. It's a place you feel as much as see. There's a quite amazing atmosphere here – sometimes serene, sometimes exciting, but always enjoyable. Sunrise and sunset are the best times for a visit.

Around Yangon

Several destinations in the Yangon, Bago and Ayeyarwady divisions surrounding the capital make good one to three-day excursions from Yangon. Thanlyin (Syriam) and Twante can be seen in out-and-back daytrips, while relaxing Letkhokkon begs an overnight stay. If your tastes are broad, the varied sights in Bago (Pegu) may be worth an overnight stay; Pathein (Bassein) and Chaungtha perhaps warrant several nights between them. Pyay (Prome), in the north-western corner of Bago Division on the Ayeyarwady (Irrawaddy) River, is a rewarding two-day detour for the modest ruins of Thayekhittaya (Sri Ksetra), a Pyu kingdom that existed around 1500 years ago.

Taungoo, a Bago Division town off the highway between Yangon and Mandalay, holds little of interest for the average visitor except as a resting place between Yangon and Mandalay.

Delta Region

A vast basin stretching from the Bay of Bengal coast across to the Bago Range receives year-round drainage from several major rivers, including the Ayeyarwady, Bago, Yangon (Hlaing) and Pathein (Ngawun). Intercut with canals, streams and tributaries, this riverine network irrigates millions of hectares of farmland, making the delta the central 'rice bowl' of Myanmar. Estuarine environments along the coast provide much of the country's saltwater and freshwater fish harvest as well. Because of such natural abundance, the delta has attracted Burmese from all around the country; hence it's one of Myanmar's most populated – and interesting – regions.

THANLYIN (SYRIAM) & KYAUKTAN
သံလျင် /ကျောက်တန်း
If you've got a morning or afternoon to spare

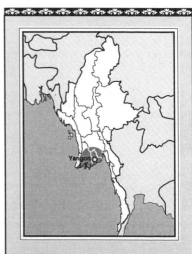

Highlights
- Rich delta life of the Pathein region
- Golden Buddha image at Shwemokhtaw Paya in Pathein
- Imposing paya of Shwemawdaw, an enormous reclining Buddha and the unusual Kyaik Pun Paya in Bago
- Ancient Pyu ruins of Thayekhitthaya near Pyay
- Day trips to Letkhokkon Beach and the pottery town of Twante

in Yangon, you can make an excursion across the river to Thanlyin and on to the 'mid-river' *paya* (pagoda) at Kyauktan. Thanlyin was the base during the late 1500s and early 1600s for the notorious Portuguese adventurer Philip De Brito. Officially a trade representative for the Rakhine, he actually ran his own little kingdom from Thanlyin, siding with the Mon (when it suited him) in their struggle against the Burmese. In 1599 his private army sacked Bago, but in 1613 the Burmese besieged Thanlyin and De Brito received the punishment reserved for those who defiled Buddhist shrines – death by impalement. It took him two days to die, due, it is said, to his failure to take the recommended posture where the stake would have penetrated vital organs. Thanlyin continued as a major port and trading centre until it was destroyed by Alaungpaya in 1756, after which Yangon took over this role.

Today there is nothing of this ancient city to be seen in Thanlyin, but a short bus ride out of town will take you to the large, golden **Kyaik-khauk Paya**, rising on a hillock to the north of the road. It's said to contain two Buddha hairs delivered to the site by the great sage himself, although it looks to be no more than a couple of hundred years old. Most likely the first stupa on this hillock was erected by the Mon sometime in the middle of this millennium. Just before this stupa are the tombs of two famous Burmese writers: Natshingaung and Padethayaza.

If you continue 12 km further until the road terminates at a wide river, you can visit the **Yele Paya**, or 'Mid-River' paya at Kyauktan. It's appropriately named since the complex is perched on a tiny island in the middle of the river. In the temple there are pictures of other famous payas all over Myanmar and even further afield. To reach the islet shrine, catch one of the many launch ferries from the river bank for a few kyat. Near the ferry landing are several food vendors.

Getting There & Away

With the opening of a Chinese-built bridge over the Bago River a few years ago, the journey from Yangon to Thanlyin no longer involves a ferry trip. Large pickups to Thanlyin leave frequently throughout the day from a spot on Sule Pagoda Rd opposite City Hall, a little east of Sule Paya. The fare costs K5 per person.

TWANTE တွံတေး:

It's an interesting day trip from Yangon to Twante, a small town noted for its pottery and cotton-weaving, and for an old Mon paya complex. One can travel there by public jeep from Dalah (on the opposite bank of the Yangon River) or by ferry along the Yangon

River and Twante Canal. The latter mode of transport is slower but provides a glimpse of life on and along the famous canal, which was dug during the colonial era as a short cut across the Ayeyarwady Delta.

A large market in the centre of town near the canal banks was destroyed by fire in January 1995 but has since been rebuilt.

Shwesandaw Paya

Standing 76 metres tall, this Mon-built *zedi* (bell-shaped paya) a km or two south of the canal is just a few years younger than the one at Yangon's Shwedagon Paya. Though the stupa itself fits the standard central Burmese mould, a walk around the compound will yield a few minor surprises. In a chicken-wire enclosure to one side is a casual display of ancient Twante pottery, plus religious and royal regalia from early Mon and Burman kingdoms. One corner of the compound, used by worshippers as a 'wish-fulfilling' station, commemorates King Bayinnaung's defeat of a local rebellion.

Along the western side of the stupa stand some old bronze Buddhas. Continuing counterclockwise, near the southern entrance you'll come to a 100-year-old sitting bronze Buddha in Mandalay style with unusual 'capped' shoulders in which the flowing monastic robes curl away from the shoulders. The left hand hovers above the crossed legs rather than resting on them – a difficult casting feat. Instead of focusing on the floor, the Buddha's eyes stare straight ahead. A low blue ledge in front of the image marks off 'footprints' allegedly left by an ogress who made a pilgrimage here.

The ruins of a smaller, older-looking zedi stand adjacent to the main compound, just off the road from the ferry landing.

Oh-Bo Pottery Sheds

Pottery is a major cottage industry in Twante, which supplies much of the delta region with well-designed, utilitarian containers of varying shapes and sizes. The pots are made in huge thatched-roof sheds in the Oh-Bo district south of the canal.

Near the entrance to the sheds are the

AROUND YANGON

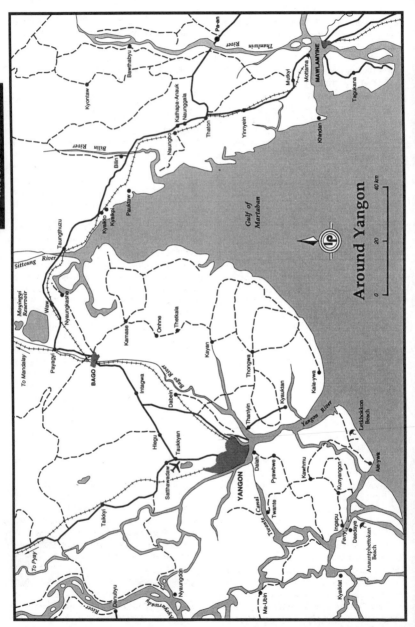

potters' wheels. Twante pots typically are half wheel-thrown, half coil-shaped, then air-dried on huge racks in the middle of the shed. After drying, the pots are fired in large wood-fired adobe kilns set towards the back of the sheds. To one side of the sheds stand stacks and stacks of cut wood – assorted jungle hardwoods, but especially rubber-wood, are the fuel of choice. The kilns are divided into two chambers, one for drying wood, one for firing the pots with a brown-black glaze. It takes around 15 days for the firing and cooling of one kiln-full. The typical shed turns out 70,000 pots a year, all of them handmade.

Twante pots can be purchased directly from the sheds or perhaps more conveniently at the central market near the Twante ferry landing.

Getting There & Away

The quickest way to get to Twante is via a short cross-river ferry and public jeep ride. Pedestrian ferries from Pansodan St Jetty, near the foot of Pansodan St, take passengers across the Yangon River to Dalah on the opposite bank in 20 minutes for K2 per person. In Dalah catch one of the dark green jeeps that leave for Twante every 45 minutes or so throughout the day. The jeep ride takes 30 to 45 minutes and the fare is K6 on weekdays, two or three times more on week-ends and holidays. Come prepared for a crush – these jeeps cram as many as 20 people into and onto the vehicle – or charter your own jeep for a few hundred kyat each way.

The seemingly slower but more scenic trip along the Yangon River and Twante Canal takes two hours – even though it's only 24 km from landing to landing. Although there are several boats that pass by Twante on their way across the western delta, including the Yangon-Pathein ferry (Lan Thit St Jetty), the most frequent departures are aboard Hpayapon-bound craft. These leave from the Hledan and Kaingdan St jetties in Yangon daily at noon, 1, 2, 3 and 4 pm, returning hourly till 7 pm. The fare is only K4.

When you add up the wait times for the cross-river ferry/jeep departure versus the canal ferry, both modes of transport end up taking about the same amount of time from start to finish. A good way to vary the trip would be to do the ferry-jeep combo out to Twante, then catch one of the canal ferries back to Yangon around sunset when the waterways look their best.

LETKHOKKON BEACH
လက်ခုပ်ပင်လယ်ကမ်း:

Letkhokkon, about three hours by road from Dalah, is the closest beach to the capital. Located in Kunyangon township near the mouth of the Bago River, it's a delta beach facing the Gulf of Martaban with fine powder-beige sand and a very wide tidal bore that tends toward mud flats at its lowest ebb. Copious coconut palms along the beach help make up for the less than crystalline waters. The lack of clarity is part of the estuarial milieu here and doesn't mean the water isn't clean. At low tide the local kids like to stage mudfights.

More than just a beach trip, a day or over-night excursion to Letkhokkon offers a glimpse of relaxed delta life. Along the way the road passes by rice fields, betel-leaf gardens and several mostly Karen villages. At Kunyangon a large stupa called **Payagyi** is a common stop for Burmese day-trippers. West of the road between Kawhmu and Ingapu is a hilly area studded with the por-celain remains of ceramics left behind by hundreds of years of sea trade.

Adjacent to the main beach area, the village of **Letkhokkon** itself is a fairly typical seaside village that prospers from coconuts and fishing. A little south-east in a neighbouring village is a monastery with a bizarre collection of mutant fruits, including a pineapple plant that bears a blossom not seen on other pineapples; coconuts whose outer husks bear likenesses of Kyaiktiyo Paya and the late *sayadaw* (chief abbot); and dead logs that bear fruit. Using a magnifying glass, the abbot likes to show visitors mark-ings in the fingerprint of his left index finger resembling a dancing peacock.

Myaseinthaun, a delta island offshore, is visited by many native and migratory waterfowl. **Daedaye**, on a delta peninsula north-west of Letkhokkon, is a small town that thrives on the production of processed seafood for export. Though the town itself isn't so interesting, there's a long beach nearby called **Anauntphettokan** ('West-ward-moving Beach', named for its heavy sand drift). The beach can be approached by boat from Ingapu or other spots along the coastline. You can rent a launch for visiting these areas from the Letkhokkon Beach Hotel. The asking price is K1200 per hour, but you should be able to arrange a better deal for multi-hour hires.

Places to Stay & Eat

As you approach Letkhokkon from the north, you'll see a two-lane, palm-flanked avenue leading off to the right to the *Letkhokkon Beach Hotel*, a tidy row of brightly painted wooden beach chalets. Under private ownership since mid-1994, the hotel charges US$36 single, US$42 double for spacious rooms with air-con, mosquito nets and attached cold-water showers. Rates include a choice of Western or Asian breakfast. Good seafood is available at the hotel restaurant. The hotel maintains a booking office in Yangon: Pyi Daw Mon International (☎ 01-23409), 76 Kaingdan St, Lanmadaw Township.

At the edge of Letkhokkon village is one other choice, a cluster of five simple thatched bungalows that rent for K150 per night. Although it's not an officially sanctioned place, several foreigners have stayed here, and the proprietors seem happy to have foreign guests. Sometimes the local authorities evict, sometimes not; you're less likely to be noticed if you enter from the beach rather than through the village. Adjacent to these bungalows is a rustic open-air restaurant with decent seafood.

There are a couple of other simple eateries in the village, as well as a thatched-roof bar where various palm distillates are available.

Getting There & Away

Vehicle ferries cross the Yangon River to Dalah from Sin Oh Dan St Jetty between 18th and 19th Sts in Yangon at 9 am, 1 and 4.30 pm, around the same time in reverse. The fare is K65 for autos and small trucks, K50 for larger trucks or buses plus a K20 tax to be paid on either side of the river. The crossing takes just 15 minutes.

The road between Dalah and Letkhokkon is in very poor condition in spots. Count on around three hours to complete the journey without stops, more by public conveyance. It's not easy getting to Letkhokkon by the latter. First you must cross to Dalah via the Pansodan St Jetty pedestrian ferry (K2) or charter a sampan for K30. Near the row of restaurants and teashops on the Dalah side you'll see a cluster of pickup trucks and jeeps; ask around to see if anyone's going to Letkhokkon. This isn't too common – usually only a couple of vehicles a day do this route direct.

There are more frequent departures to Kunyangon, but there's no guarantee you'll find a vehicle there to continue on to Letkhokkon. You might try chartering a jeep one way from either Dalah or Kunyangon; expect to pay at least K1000 or the dollar equivalent from the former, perhaps as little as K200 or K300 from the latter. Late morning is probably the best time to bargain – after the drivers have carried all their morning passengers to and fro and before the late afternoon driving circuit begins. Of course you could always hire a car and driver in Yangon; however, some drivers refuse to do the trip because the road is so hard on their vehicles.

Once in Letkhokkon it's usually not too difficult to find a vehicle heading back to Dalah.

PATHEIN (BASSEIN) ပုသိမ်

Situated on the eastern bank of the Pathein River (also known as the Ngawan River) in the Ayeyarwady Delta about 190 km west of Yangon, Pathein is the most important delta port outside the capital despite its distance from the sea. It is surrounded by a major rice-growing area which produces the best rice generally available in Myanmar, including a high-quality variety called *pawsanmwe htamin* or 'fragrant rice'.

Noted for its colourful hand-painted umbrellas, the town is of some historic interest and was the scene for major clashes during the struggle for supremacy between the Mon and the Burmans. Later it became an important trade relay point for goods moving between India and South-East Asia. The city's name may derive from the Burmese word for 'Muslim' – *pathi* – due to the heavy presence of Arab and Indian Muslim traders here centuries ago. The colonial Brits – or more probably their imported Indian civil servants – corrupted the name to 'Bassein'.

Today Pathein's population of 145,000 includes large contingents of Karen and Rakhine. Although once part of a Mon kingdom, Pathein is home to only a few Mon today. During the 1970s and '80s the Karen villages surrounding Pathein generated a bit of insurgent activity that has quelled to the point that Pathein is now open to foreign tourists. The recent growth of delta trade, particularly rice exports, has contributed to a general air of prosperity in Myanmar's fourth largest city.

The scenic waterfront area, markets, umbrella workshops and colourful payas make the city worth a stay of at least a night or two. It also serves as a jumping-off point for excursions to the small beach resort of Chaungtha and further north to Gwa and Thandwe (Sandoway) in the Rakhine (Arakan) State.

Post & Telecommunications

The main post office is located towards the western end of Mahabandoola Rd near the clock tower. Since there's no air service between Pathein and Yangon, mail is slow but the Pathein postal service is supposed to be reasonably reliable.

You can make domestic trunk calls, but not international calls, from the telephone office next door.

Shwemokhtaw Paya

In the centre of downtown Pathein near the riverfront looms the golden, bell-shaped stupa at Shwemokhtaw Paya. One legend says it was originally built by India's Buddhist King Asoka in 305 BC as a small stupa called Shwe Arna. Standing 2.3 metres tall, this original stupa supposedly enshrined Buddha relics and a six-inch gold bar. Another legend says a Muslim princess named Onmadandi requested each of her three Buddhist lovers to build a stupa in her honour. One of the lovers erected Shwemokhtaw, the others the less distinguished Tazaung and Thayaunggyaung payas.

Whichever story you believe, Bagan's King Alaungsithu is thought to have erected an 11-metre stupa called Htupayon over this site in 1115 AD. Then in 1263 King Samodagossa took power, raised the stupa to 40 metres and changed the name to Shwemokhtaw Paya, which means 'Stupa of the Half-Foot Gold Bar'. The stupa's main shape has remained the same since then, although the changing of the decorative *hti* top has increased the height to its present 46.6 metres. The current hti consists of a topmost layer made from 6.3 kg of solid gold, a middle tier of pure silver and a bottom tier of bronze; all three tiers are gilded and reportedly embedded with a total of 829 diamond fragments, 843 rubies and 1588 semi-precious stones.

The southern shrine of the compound houses the **Thiho-shin Phondaw-pyi** sitting Buddha image, which supposedly floated to the delta coast on a raft from Sri Lanka in ancient times. According to legend, an unknown Sinhalese sculptor fashioned four different Buddha images using pieces from the original bodhi tree mixed with a cement composite. He then placed them on four wooden rafts and set the rafts adrift on the ocean. One landed in Dawei (Tavoy), and is now housed at the Shin-Mokhti Paya; another landed at Kyaikkami (Amherst), and now is at Yele Paya; the third landed at Kyaikto and is now at Kyaikpawlaw; and the fourth landed near Phondawpyi, a fishing village about 97 km south of Pathein. In 1445 the Mon Queen Shinsawpu purportedly brought the latter image to Pathein, then known as Kuthima.

A marble standing Buddha positioned in a

AROUND YANGON

niche in the fence running along the western side of the stupa marks a spot where Mon warriors once prayed before battle. In the north-western corner of the compound is a shrine to Shin Upagot, the bodhisattva who floats on the ocean and appears to those in trouble. At this shrine his lotus raft is flanked by blue dragons representing the sea; live turtles swim in the water surrounding the small pavilion.

The people of Pathein celebrate 'thrice-blessed day' or Vesakha with a huge *paya pwe* ('pagoda festival') here during the full moon of Kason (April/May).

Settayaw Paya

Of the several lesser-known payas in Pathein, perhaps the most charming is this one dedicated to a mythical Buddha footprint left by the Enlightened One during his legendary perambulations through mainland South-East Asia.

The paya compound wraps over a couple of green hillocks dotted with well-constructed *tazaungs* – altogether a nice setting and a change from the flat paya compounds near the river. The footprint symbol itself is the usual oblong, metre-long impression and not very interesting. In the same pavilion,

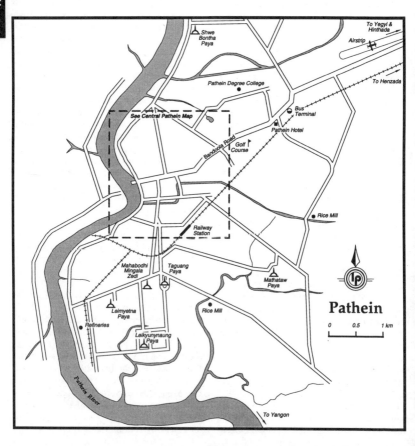

however, a well-done Mandalay-style bronze Buddha stands over the footprint. All too visible in the compound is a garishly painted 11-metre standing Buddha. The group of whitewashed stupas on the slight rise below were built by the famous Burmese musician Po Sein.

Other Religious Monuments

One of the standard sights in town is the so-called **Twenty-Eight Paya**, a rectangular shrine building containing 28 sitting and 28 standing images – none of them is particularly distinguished except that the latter appear in the open-robe Mandalay style rather than the closed-robe pose typical of Mandalay standing images. At one end of the hall stands a group of crude sculptures depicting a *jataka* scene in which Buddha teaches a disciple the relativity of physical beauty by comparing a monkey, the disciple's wife and a *deva*. Although it's not that interesting a sight, the shrine is a short walk from Pathein's main umbrella workshops. You may have to ask the caretaker to unlock the building.

More interesting from an artistic perspective is **Tagaung Mingala Zeditaw** (Tagaung Paya), centred around a graceful stupa that swoops inward from a wide, whitewashed base to a gleaming silver superstructure. Look for the small squirrel sculpture extending from the western side of the upper stupa and representing a previous incarnation of Buddha as a squirrel. One of the pavilions at the base of the stupa contains a very large sitting Buddha image. Local legend says the stupa is the same age as Shwemokhtaw but like most famous stupas in Myanmar the truth is buried beneath several layers of royal renovations. The latest refurbishing was carried out in 1979. Tagaung Paya is about three km south of Kaladan St, past the railway line.

West of Tagaung Paya a little way toward the river stands **Mahabodhi Mingala Zedi**, patterned after the world-famous Mahabodhi stupa in Bodhgaya, India. **Leikyunynaung Paya**, a couple of km directly south of Mahabodhi, was renovated by the SLORC using conscript labour in the early 1990s to create a facsimile of Ananda Paya in Bagan (Pagan). Its main distinguishing characteristic is that it can easily be seen at a distance, from boats passing along the river. Since the renovation few people outside the government worship here. A km or so north-east of Leikyunynaung is **Leimyetna Paya**, which features a large but particularly ugly sitting Buddha. Even worse is the gaudily painted sitting Buddha at **Shwezigon Paya** at the northern end of town.

Parasol Workshops

Most of the 'umbrellas' made in Pathein are actually parasols; that is they aren't waterproof but are used as a defence against the hot delta sun. Around 25 parasol workshops are scattered throughout the northern part of the city, particularly in the vicinity of the Twenty-Eight Paya shrine, off Mahabandoola Rd. The parasols come in a variety of colours; some are brightly painted with flowers, birds and other nature motifs. One type which can be used in the rain is the saffron-coloured monks' umbrella, which is waterproofed by applying various coats of tree resin over a two-day period. Parasols and umbrellas can be custom-ordered in any size directly from the workshops. Bargaining usually isn't too fierce as the parasols are quite reasonably priced, even cheap for basic ones.

Most workshops welcome visitors who want to observe this craft. One of the easiest to find – and one with high-quality work – is the workshop opposite the entrance to the Twenty-Eight Paya.

Other Attractions

At the **night bazaar** that is set up each evening in front of the Customs House along Strand Rd, vendors purvey food, clothing, textiles, tools, housewares and just about every other requisite for daily life at low prices. Just south of Shwemokhtaw Paya is the central market, and just south of that a newer market, with all manner of goods. Both of the latter markets are closed on Sunday.

The **golf course** next to the Pathein Hotel has 18 holes you can play for a reasonable K500 greens fee.

Places to Stay

At the time of writing the only place officially open to foreigners was the recently privatised *Pathein Hotel* (☎ 042-21162), an L-shaped, two-storey building on spacious grounds next to the golf course off Mahabandoola Rd. Large rooms on the upper floor come with air-con, fridge, TV and hot-water shower for US$44 single, US$56 double. Downstairs rooms are the same size but do not feature air-con, TV, fridge or hot water; these cost US$34 single, US$44 double. All rates include a mandatory US$4 charge for a cold toast-and-egg breakfast, possibly the biggest culinary ripoff in the country. By any standards elsewhere in South-East Asia, the rooms at this hotel are worth no more than a third the going rate. Besides price, another problem with the Pathein Hotel is its distance from downtown and all attractions.

Delta Guest House (☎ 042-22131), at 44 Mingyi Rd, is a good downtown choice. Although significantly smaller and simpler than the rooms at the Pathein Hotel, the Delta

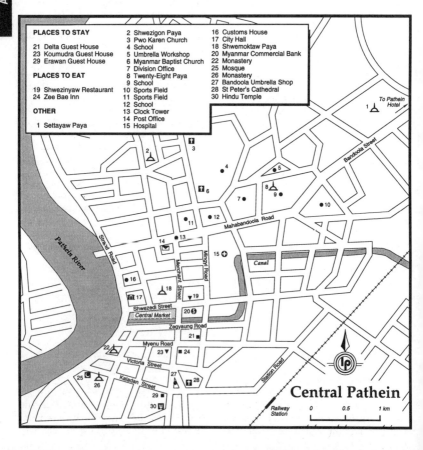

PLACES TO STAY

21 Delta Guest House
23 Koumudra Guest House
29 Erawan Guest House

PLACES TO EAT

19 Shwezinyaw Restaurant
24 Zee Bae Inn

OTHER

1 Settayaw Paya

2 Shwezigon Paya
3 Pwo Karen Church
4 School
5 Umbrella Workshop
6 Myanmar Baptist Church
7 Division Office
8 Twenty-Eight Paya
9 School
10 Sports Field
11 Sports Field
12 School
13 Clock Tower
14 Post Office
15 Hospital

16 Customs House
17 City Hall
18 Shwemoktaw Paya
20 Myanmar Commercial Bank
22 Monastery
25 Mosque
26 Monastery
27 Bandoola Umbrella Shop
28 St Peter's Cathedral
30 Hindu Temple

To Pathein Hotel

Pathein River

Strand Road

Mahabandoola Road

Bandoola Street

Mingyi Road

Merchant Street

Canal

Shwezedi Street

Central Market

Zegyaung Road

Myenu Road

Victoria Street

Kaladan Street

Station Road

Railway Station

Central Pathein

0   0.5   1 km

rooms are better kept and cost US$5 per person with common bath downstairs, US$15 for special single/double rooms upstairs with air-con and attached bath. Delta was on the verge of receiving its licence to accept foreign guests when we visited. A little west toward the river, at the corner of Merchant St and Myenu St, *Koumudra Guest House* offers similar facilities and will probably charge similar prices after it becomes 'licensed lodging' for foreigners.

South along Merchant St at Kaladan St, a colonial building that served as a Japanese hospital during WW II is now under renovation to become the *Erawan Guest House*. The proprietors say they plan to open to foreigners by late 1996.

Places to Eat

Pathein has several decent restaurants, most of them downtown. The Burmese restaurant revival sweeping Yangon and Mandalay hasn't yet reached this city, so most of the better places specialise in Chinese or Indian dishes. Among the more well-known and longest-running Chinese places is the *Zee Bae Inn* on Merchant St. This narrow, two-storey spot has been serving large bowls of noodles and other Chinese dishes since the 1950s. The downstairs area opens onto the street as usual, while upstairs there's an air-con dining room. The restaurant usually opens around 9 or 10 am and closes around 7 or 8 pm.

The *Morning Star Restaurant* on Mingyi Rd also has decent Chinese food – in fact better than its more famous rival, Zee Bae Inn. Several noodle shops occupy 1940s-vintage buildings along China St near the market.

Shwezinyaw Restaurant, at 24/25 Shwezedi St near Merchant St, is a Burmese/Indian Muslim hybrid with good curries and biryani. It's open 8 am to 9 pm daily. The biryani at nearby *Mopale* is even better, though the place closes down around 6 or 7 pm.

Opposite the golf course on Bandoola Rd, near the Pathein Hotel, is the *Shuginthat Tea Shop* (the English sign reads 'Golf Res-taurant'). This tranquil, indoor-outdoor spot is a good place to enjoy tea and Burmese snacks at a leisurely pace. At the other end of Bandoola Rd toward the river, turn right to reach the green and leafy, outdoor *Kanthaya Tea Garden*, another relaxing spot with Burmese snacks.

Yegyi If you're coming by car from Pyay, the town of Yegyi makes the best midpoint stop. *U Ba Gyi Rice Shop* (no sign), behind the railway station in the central market, is a dirty-looking place with decent Burmese food. A very good hot and sour vegetable soup comes as a side dish with all meals.

Getting There & Away

Air Pathein has an airstrip out at the northeast edge of the city, but at the moment it doesn't field any regularly scheduled flights. If it's ever expanded to handle Myanma Airways' Fokkers, it will only be a half-hour flight from Yangon.

Bus An ordinary bus to Pathein from Yangon's Highway Bus Centre costs just K60 but is crowded and slow – count on around eight hours to cover the distance. Better, if not faster, buses are available from Yangon's Hsimmalaik Bus Centre for K80; there are two departures daily, both at 5 am.

From Pathein's bus terminal on the southern side of Bandoola Rd, east of the Pathein Hotel, there are two or three buses per day to Pyay for K150. Yangon-bound buses depart from Pathein between 5 and 7 am.

Train Pathein is also accessible by rail, but since you have to travel some distance north towards Pyay and then turn south, making a ferry crossing along the way, the train trip takes a lengthy 14 hours or more.

Car Pathein can be reached by car from Yangon in five or six hours. The usual route is to drive 1½ hours (68 km) north-west to Nyaungdon (Yandoon or Yangdon on some maps) on the eastern bank of the Ayeyarwady River. Experienced drivers will know when it's best to leave to meet the vehicle ferry across the Ayeyarwady – it leaves every two hours between 6 am and 6 pm. From Nyaungdon to Pathein is another 122 km, about 2½ to three hours under normal driving conditions. Along the way you must cross several rivers and streams by bridge. There are a few military checkpoints along this route where foreigners are required to show their passports.

From Pyay you must first drive a little north to meet the ferry across the Ayeyarwady. Once across the river you continue west toward Taungup, turning south at the first major junction. From here a new road south to Myanaung runs smooth and wide for 60 km or so, then deteriorates considerably for the rest of the journey to Pathein. There are many checkpoints along this route; while foreigners supposedly do not need a travel permit to visit Pathein, some of the military at these checkpoints may ask for one. Yegyi is the most well-equipped stopoff point for trucks, buses and cars along the Pyay-Pathein road.

Boat German-built, double-decker 'express' boats leave Yangon's Lan Thit St Jetty around 3 and 5 pm daily and arrive at Pathein 16 to 18 hours later. In the reverse direction these boats leave Pathein at 4 and 5 pm daily. Passage costs K54 for upstairs-deck class (with assigned spaces), K48 downstairs and K161 per person for a comfortable two-bed cabin. The latter can be difficult to book since there are only eight cabins – you should reserve three days in advance. Along with the two beds, each cabin comes with a wash basin and mirror; a common toilet and shower are shared by all cabin passengers.

There is also one 'ordinary' boat that leaves Yangon at 6 pm, arriving at Pathein 20 hours later. This one costs K44 deck class, K88 per person in the 'saloon' – a single cabin in the upper bow which has four beds. For either type of boat, foreigners must buy tickets from the deputy division manager's office next to Bldg 63 at Lan Thit St Jetty.

AROUND PATHEIN
Horseshoe-shaped **Inye Lake**, 70 km north-

east of the city near the village of Kyonpyaw, is a favourite weekend picnic spot. Local fishermen sell fresh fish from the lake.

If you follow the Pathein River till it empties into the Andaman Sea you'll reach **Cape Mawdin** (Mawdinsoun), site of a famous festival during the lunar month of Tabodwe (February/March). On the sea side of the cape, at its point, is a sandy beach and the revered stupa of **Mawdin Paya**. Once a week or so a boat to Mawdin leaves the main Pathein jetty around 6 am and arrives at 2 pm, but since there's no lodging licensed for foreigners at Mawdin this is strictly a trip for risk-takers.

During the Cape Mawdin Festival there are special boats running daily – this would probably be the best time of year to attempt a trip since it would be easier to disappear into the crowds; also more guest houses open especially for the festival.

Huge **Diamond Island** lies in the midst of the mouth of the Pathein River (also known as the Ngawun River) and is an important sea turtle hatchery.

Other delta towns that might be interesting include **Labooda** and **Hpayapon**, both of which can be reached by long-distance ferry from Yangon.

Chaungtha Beach
West of Pathein on the Bay of Bengal coast, Chaungtha Beach has recently opened to foreign tourists. As western coast beaches go, this one fits somewhere between Let-khokkon farther south and Ngapali to the north in terms of quality. At low tide the very wide beach has a touch of the muddy delta look, but overall at medium and high tide it's attractive enough, with fine, beige sand backed by coconut palms and casuarina trees. **Kyaukpahto**, at one end of the beach near a cluster of boulders, is a large rock that's been carved into a *pahto* or 'cave' shrine. Offshore lies a modest coral reef with decent snorkelling except during the rainy season when water clarity is poor.

At the opposite end of the beach is the mouth of the U Do Canal, which wraps around the back of Chaungtha village to create a small peninsula. Because there's a military post at the southern end of the peninsula it's sort of a restricted zone – the Burmese don't usually walk in the area. Two islands can be seen offshore, **Theinbyu** and **Hpokkala**; although mainly inhabited by Burmese fisherfolk, the latter island is off limits to foreign visitors due to some kind of military presence as well.

The village has a network of sand roads lined with simple wood or thatch houses. Most Chaungtha residents fish or farm coconuts for a living; a couple of families also make furniture using rattan collected in nearby jungles. Many villagers speak the Rakhine dialect. The village market is most active from 6 to 9 am. Toward the beach is a string of restaurants and handicraft vendors.

If you follow a path east, past a solar-powered hospital, you'll pass through a mangrove swamp and end up at a canal beach with a wooden jetty. Also on the canal side of the peninsula are rickety stilted structures used by the villagers for drying fish. Ferry services to nearby villages along the canal are still available from the jetty.

Places to Stay & Eat Chaungtha receives heavy rainfall and high waves during the south-west monsoon. Few people from the interior visit then and all accommodation traditionally closes down from 15 May to 15 September.

At the overpriced *Chaungtha Beach Hotel* (☎ 042-22587; 01-87589 in Yangon) – also known as *New Paradise Hotel* – a bed in a rustic four-bed dorm room with attached cold-water shower costs US$24 per person. To add insult to high prices, these rooms stand next to an odiferous canal. The main section of the wooden hotel offers 'superior' rooms for US$54/72/96 single/double/triple. The rooms are large and feature air-con and fridges but are otherwise nothing special. Larger 'junior suites' cost US$60/US$84/US$108 single/double/triple. These rates include tax, service or breakfast, though it's still probably the most expensive hotel in Myanmar relative to what you get for your

money. Bargaining for lower rates may be possible.

Fortunately there's an alternative next door – an army-owned group of wooden bungalows that go for US$10 per person in four-bed rooms with mosquito nets, high ceilings and attached shower and toilet. Constructed to remain breezy and cool, these four-bed rooms beat the US$24 rooms at the Chaungtha Beach Hotel. Soap and towels are also available on request. During the week you may have a room to yourself; on weekends you may have to share, though the management is not likely to put foreigners in with Burmese.

In the restaurant area of the village are several very basic rooms for rent, but foreigners are unlikely to be admitted. Slightly better rooms are available at the *Diamond Guest House* in the village near the market; this place, too, is unlikely to accept foreigners but it might be worth a try. If the two licensed places are full, you may apply to the police for permission to stay at one of the unlicensed guest houses.

The main street into the village from the beach is lined with rustic seafood restaurants. The better ones include *Pearl, Golden Sea* and *May Khalar*, all of which serve fresh lobster, clams, scallops and fish. There are also a few teashops along this strip, one of which opens early in the morning and serves decent hsi htamin (turmeric-coloured sticky rice topped with sesame seeds and shredded coconut) and other Burmese tea snacks. The restaurant at the *Chaungtha Beach Hotel* isn't bad and does offer the advantage of a beach view.

Getting There & Away The rough 36-km road to Chaungtha from Pathein can be traversed in two hours by private car; public bus (actually a large pickup) takes three to four hours. Two passenger trucks leave the Pathein bus terminal daily at 7 and 11 am for Chaungtha for K45 per person. Pickups are also available from a road stop near the Shwemokhtaw Paya at 1 pm for the same fare.

Whether by public or private vehicle, from Pathein you first cross the Pathein

AROUND YANGON

River by ferry; the ferry runs roughly every hour 6 am to 6 pm daily. In the reverse direction if you get stuck waiting for a ferry back, there are five thatched-roof restaurants to hang out at.

Parts of the road to Chaungtha are sealed, some are unsealed. The road passes through nearly barren scrubland before crossing the U Do Canal by bridge, and after that climbs forested hills to an elevation of around 300 metres. This area is said to be inhabited by elephants, monkeys and leopards; at one point you'll pass through a lush forest reserve with an upper canopy of tall dipterocarps. From here the road descends into an area of coconut groves and rice fields. Over half the villages passed along the way are Karen.

Until the road was cut from Pathein, the only way to reach Chaungtha was by ferry along the U Do Canal. From the canal jetty in Chaungtha you may be able to book passage on a boat to Cape Mawdin, 12 hours south by schooner.

North of Yangon

TAUKKYAN ေထာက်ကြံ

On the road to Bago, beyond Yangon's airport at Mingaladon, you reach Taukkyan where the road to Pyay forks off to the north-west, while the Bago and Mandalay road continues on to the north-east. Shortly beyond the junction is the huge Taukkyan War Cemetery with the graves of 27,000 Allied soldiers who died in the Burma and Assam campaigns of WW II. Maintained by the Commonwealth War Graves Commission, the cemetery is beautifully landscaped.

You can get to Taukkyan on a No 9 bus from Yangon or aboard any Bago-bound bus.

BAGO (PEGU) ပဲခူး

Situated only about 80 km from Yangon, Bago is easily reached from the capital yet is just far enough off the beaten track to be very untouristed. There are now several hotels and guest houses where you can spend the night,

and if you're on your way to Mt Kyaiktiyo or Mawlamyine (Moulmein), an overnight stay here will break the journey up nicely.

Bago was reputedly founded in 573 AD by two Mon princes from Thaton who saw a female goose standing on the back of a male goose on an island in a huge lake. Taking this to be an auspicious omen of some kind, they founded a royal capital called Hanthawady (from the Pali-Sanskrit *Hamsavati* or 'Kingdom of the Goose') at the edge of the lake. During the later Mon dynastic periods (1287 to 1539) Hanthawady became the centre of the Mon kingdom of Ramanadesa, which consisted of all Lower Myanmar.

The Burmans took over in 1539 when King Tabinshwehti annexed Bago to his Taungoo kingdom. The city was frequently mentioned by early European visitors – who knew it as 'Pegu' – as an important sea port. In 1740 the Mon, after a period of submission to Taungoo, re-established Bago as their capital, but in 1757 King Alaungpaya sacked and utterly destroyed the city. King Bodawpaya, who ruled from 1782 to 1819, rebuilt it to some extent, but when the river changed its course the city was cut off from the sea and lost its importance as a sea port. It never again reached its previous grandeur.

In deference to legend, the symbol for Bago is a female *hamsa (hintha* or *hantha* in Burmese; a mythological bird) standing on the back of a male *hamsa*. At a deeper level, the symbol honours the compassion of the male hintha in providing a place for the female to stand in the middle of a lake with only one island. Hence the men of Bago are said to be more chivalrous than men from other Burmese realms. In popular Burmese culture, however, men say they dare not marry a woman from Bago for fear of being henpecked!

Kanbawzathadi Palace & Museum
Recently the original Hanthawady site surrounding a former Mon palace has been excavated just south of the huge Shwemawdaw Paya. Walled in the Mon style, the square city measured 1.8 km along each side and featured 20 gates in all. The palace

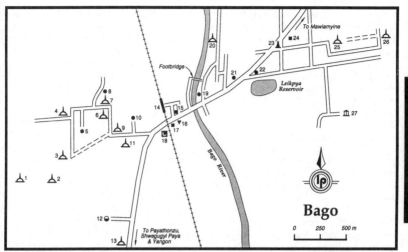

Bago

0   250   500 m

AROUND YANGON

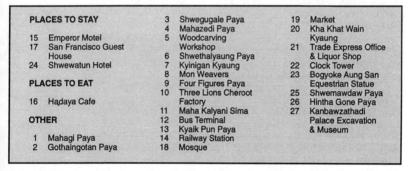

PLACES TO STAY	3	Shwegugale Paya	19	Market
	4	Mahazedi Paya	20	Kha Khat Wain
15 Emperor Motel	5	Woodcarving		Kyaung
17 San Francisco Guest		Workshop	21	Trade Express Office
House	6	Shwethalyaung Paya		& Liquor Shop
24 Shwewatun Hotel	7	Kyinigan Kyaung	22	Clock Tower
	8	Mon Weavers	23	Bogyoke Aung San
PLACES TO EAT	9	Four Figures Paya		Equestrian Statue
	10	Three Lions Cheroot	25	Shwemawdaw Paya
16 Hadaya Cafe		Factory	26	Hintha Gone Paya
	11	Maha Kalyani Sima	27	Kanbawzathadi
OTHER	12	Bus Terminal		Palace Excavation
	13	Kyaik Pun Paya		& Museum
1 Mahagi Paya	14	Railway Station		
2 Gothaingotan Paya	18	Mosque		

compound in the centre, known as Kanbaw-zathadi, housed King Bayinnaung (also spelt Bayint Nyaung) from 1553 (or 1566 according to some sources) to 1599 and covered 204 acres. About 64 acres of this area have been excavated. Bayinnaung, the brother-in-law of a Taungoo king, moved to Bago after conquering an older Mon principality called Oktha-myo, east of the Hanthawady site.

Only the palace's brick foundations are visible today. Everything else is being built anew as at the Mandalay Palace; the king's apartment and audience hall will open some-time in 1996. Among other marvels, the original audience hall featured a seven-level roof, two levels higher than Mandalay Palace, and was topped with solid gold tiles. The entire palace compound was originally surrounded by a teak stockade, a few stumps of which can be seen in the new museum. The government is keen to make the site into a showpiece of sorts since King Bayinnaung ruled during an era when Burmese domains reached their farthest in South-East Asia. The nearby Mon site of Oktha-myo, mean-while, is all but ignored.

The small but well-stocked, octagonal-shaped museum displays Mon, Siamese, and Bagan-style Buddhas; clay tobacco pipes; glazed tiles and pots; 'Martaban' jars (huge water jars from the delta area); bronze weights and scales; pieces of the original teak stockade; and weaponry. The museum is open Wednesday to Sunday from 9 am to 4 pm.

When we visited the Hanthawady site it wasn't officially open and the admission price hadn't been set. Unless the government has a change of heart about collecting fees for historical site visits, you can figure on spending US$4 or US$5 for the privilege of viewing what is essentially a facsimile palace.

Shwemawdaw Paya

The 'Great Golden God Paya' stands northeast of the railway station. You can't miss it since its height of 114 metres completely dominates the town. The Shwemawdaw is said to be over 1000 years old and was originally built by the Mon to a height of 23 metres to enshrine two hairs of the Buddha. In 825 AD it was raised to 25 metres and then to 27 metres in 840. In 982 a sacred tooth was added to the collection; in 1385 another tooth was added and the stupa was rebuilt to a towering 84 metres. In 1492, the year Columbus sailed the Atlantic, a wind blew down the hti and a new one was raised.

King Bodawpaya, in the reconstruction of Bago after the ravages of Alaungpaya, rebuilt the stupa to 91 metres in 1796, but from that point it has had a rather chequered career. A new hti was added in 1882, but a major earthquake in 1912 brought it down. The stupa was repaired, but in 1917 another major quake again brought the hti down and caused serious damage. Again it was repaired, but in 1930 the biggest quake of them all completely levelled the stupa and for the next 20 years only the huge earth mound of the base remained.

Reconstruction of the Shwemawdaw commenced in 1952 and was completed in 1954, when it reached its present height. The glittering golden top of the stupa reaches 14 metres higher than the Shwedagon in Yangon. Shady trees around the base make it a pleasant place to stroll or simply sit and watch the Burmese. At the north-eastern corner of the stupa a huge section of the hti toppled by the 1917 earthquake has been mounted into the structure of the stupa. It is a sobering reminder of the power of such geological disturbances.

Like the Shwedagon, the stupa is reached by a covered walkway lined with stalls – a number with interesting collections of antique bits and pieces. Along the sides of the walkway a collection of rather faded and dusty paintings illustrates the terrible effects of the 1930 earthquake and shows the subsequent rebuilding of this mighty stupa.

The mouths of the two *chinthe* or guardian lions at the western entrance contain two Mahayana bodhisattvas, Shin Upagot (Upagupta, on the left) and Shin Thiwali (Sivali, on the right).

On the full moon of the Burmese lunar month of Tagu (March/April) the Shwemawdaw Paya Festival attracts huge crowds of worshippers and merrymakers.

Admission to the paya, for foreigners, costs US$3.

Hintha Gon Paya

Located behind the Shwemawdaw, this shrine has good views over Bago from the roofed platform on the hilltop. According to legend this was the one point rising from the sea when the mythological bird (the hintha) landed here. A statue of the bird, looking rather like the figures on opium weights, tops the hill. The stupa was built by U Khanti, the hermit monk who was also the architect of Mandalay Hill. You can walk to it by taking the steps down the other side of the Shwemawdaw from the main entranceway.

Shwethalyaung Buddha

To the west of the Yangon-Bago road, only a little over a km on the Yangon side of the railway station, the Shwethalyaung is a huge reclining Buddha. Measuring 55 metres long and 16 metres high, it is a good nine metres longer than the reclining Buddha at Wat Pho in Bangkok. A sign on the platform in front of the image gives the measurements of each body part; the little finger alone extends 3.05 metres.

The Shwethalyaung is reputed to be one of the largest as well as the most lifelike of all reclining Buddhas. The Burmese say the image represents Buddha in a 'relaxing' mode – instead of death or *parinibbana* – since the eyes are wide open and the feet lie slightly splayed rather than parallel.

The sturdy iron shed which houses the image may look rough and ready, but it's spacious and airy and gives you a far better view than most reclining Buddhas in their cramped cells offer. The walkway up to the platform is crowded with souvenir and handicraft stalls.

Originally built of brick and stucco in 994 AD by the Mon King Migadepa II, the Shwethalyaung was allowed to deteriorate and was then restored several times during its existence before the destruction of Bago in 1757. The town was so completely ravaged that the huge Buddha was totally lost and overgrown by jungle. It was not found until the 1880s British era, when an Indian contractor, digging in a large earth mound for fill to be used in the construction of the railway line, rediscovered the image. Restoration began in 1881 and the present iron and steel tazaung, a product of a Calcutta engineering company, was completed in 1903. The 1930s saw another flurry of renovative activity, as mosaic was added to the great pillow on which the Buddha's head rests, and Italian marble was laid along the platform.

Near the huge head of the image stands a **statue of Lokanat** (Lokanatha or Avalokitesvara), a Mahayana Buddhist deity borrowed by Burmese Buddhism. Behind the reclining Buddha image is a set of huge painted reliefs depicting the legend of the founding of the image.

Foreigner admission is US$3 and worth it.

A Japanese war cemetery can be seen on the grounds of a monastery just north of Shwethalyaung, **Kyinigan Kyaung**. Northwest of this monastery, a settlement of **Mon weavers** use handlooms to produce cotton *longyis* and other textiles.

Lokanat (Lokanatha), a Mahayana deity better known as Avalokitesvara

Maha Kalyani Sima (Maha Kalyani Thein)

This 'Sacred Hall of Ordination' was originally constructed in 1476 by Dhammazedi, the famous alchemist king and son of Queen Shinsawpu. It stands beside the road en route from the railway station to the Shwethalyaung. It was the first of 397 similar *simas* or ordination halls he built around the country, copying plans brought back from Ceylon. De Brito, the Portuguese adventurer, burnt it down in 1599 during his period of plunder, and during the sack of Bago it was destroyed once again.

Subsequently it suffered from fires or quakes on a number of occasions before being levelled by the disastrous 1930 quake. As with the Shwemawdaw, reconstruction was completed in 1954. Next to the hall are 10 large tablets with inscriptions in Pali and

Mon. The hall itself features rows of tented arches around the outside, with an impressive separate cloister and marble floors inside. Niches along the inside upper walls contain 28 standing Buddha images.

Across the road from the Maha Kalyani Sima, by the corner, is a curious monument with four Buddha figures standing back to back, in somewhat similar fashion to the four seated Buddhas at the Kyaik Pun on the outskirts of town. An adjacent open hallway has a small reclining Buddha image, thronged by followers, and some macabre paintings of wrongdoers being tortured in the afterlife.

Mahazedi Paya

Continuing beyond the Shwethalyaung brings you to the Mahazedi or 'Great Stupa'. Originally constructed in 1560 by King Bayinnaung, it was destroyed during the 1757 sack of Bago. An attempt to rebuild it in 1860 was unsuccessful and the great earthquake of 1930 comprehensively levelled it, after which it remained a ruin. This current reconstruction was only completed in 1982. Stairways lead up the outside of the stupa, and from the top there are fine views over the surrounding area. Note the model stupa by the entrance.

The Mahazedi originally had a Buddha tooth, at one time thought to be the actual Buddha tooth of Kandy, Sri Lanka. After Bago was conquered in 1539 the tooth was later moved to Taungoo and then to Sagaing near Mandalay. Together with a begging bowl supposed to have been used by the Buddha, it remains in the Kaunghmudaw Paya near Sagaing to this day.

Shwegugale Paya

A little beyond the Mahazedi, this zedi has a dark 'tunnel' *(gu)* running around the circumference of the cylindrical superstructure. The monument dates to 1494 and the reign of King Byinnya Yan. Inside are 64 seated Buddha figures. From here you can take a short cut back to the corner in the road, just before the Shwethalyaung.

Kyaik Pun Paya

About three km out of Bago on the Yangon road, and then a couple of hundred metres to the west of the road, stands Kyaik Pun Paya. Built in 1476 by King Dhammazedi, it consists of four 30-metre-high sitting Buddhas placed back to back around a huge, square pillar. According to a legend, four Mon sisters were connected with the construction of the Buddhas; it was said that if any of them should marry, one of the Buddhas would collapse. One of the four disintegrated in the 1930 earthquake, leaving only a brick outline. It has since been fully restored.

En route to the Kyaik Pun you can detour to the prettily situated Gaung-Say-Kyan Paya, reached by crossing a wooden bridge over a small lake.

Other Attractions

North of the main town centre, near the eastern bank of the river, is one of the three largest monasteries in the country, **Kha Khat Wain Kyaung**. Watching the long line of monks and novices file out of the monastery in the early morning for their daily alms round is quite a sight.

Many Bago women work in local cheroot factories – there are around 15 large ones, many smaller ones. The **Three Lions factory** lies a little north of the road to Shwethalyaung from the main avenue through town; the proprietors don't mind receiving visitors. Further west toward Mahazedi Paya you can visit a **woodcarving workshop**.

Bago has a very interesting market just across the river from the railway station. Take some time to wander around the various market buildings. The market serves as a distribution point for cloth, household items and other imports from Thailand and beyond.

On the highway to Yangon south of town is **Hanthawady Golf Course**, a military-built course recently taken over by a Japanese company. Greens fees are around US$8 at the moment but will undoubtedly rise as the Japanese overhaul the course.

Places to Stay & Eat

Several places in the downtown area have recently received permission to accept foreign guests. The six-storey, modern-looking *Emperor Hotel* (☎ 052-21349) on the main avenue through town between the railway and the river has a friendly, English-speaking manager. Small but clean rooms cost US$10 single with fan and attached Asian-style toilet and bath, US$15 single with air-con and hot water. A rooftop terrace offers cityscape views. A new hotel under construction opposite the Emperor has no name yet but will post rates of US$6 with fan and shared bath, US$10 with fan and attached bath or US$15 double with air-con and attached bath.

The nearby *Htun Hotel* (☎ 052-21973) at 233 30th St costs US$10 for a single with shared bath, US$13 single with air-con and shared bath. Only doubles come with attached bath – US$20 double with fan or US$25 with air-con and hot water.

Further south-west near the railway crossing, the *San Francisco Guest House* has rooms with shared toilet and bath for US$6 per person, or US$12/15 single/double with attached bath. It's not particularly clean.

Out towards the Shwemawdaw Paya, on the road east to Mawlamyine, the government-owned *Shwewatun Hotel* (☎ 052-21263) offers clean singles/doubles for US$38/44 with ceiling fans, US$44/63 with air-con. Rooms have attached bathrooms with cold water only. This is clearly overpriced in comparison with the rates for downtown hotels. The hotel restaurant has decent food.

In the centre of town near the market are a number of foodstalls, including some good Indian biryani stalls. Indian breakfasts are good at a small, friendly place on a side street south of the main avenue. From the Emperor Hotel cross the road and go two short blocks, turn left, and look for a sign reading *Boss* on the counter inside; it's opposite a police post.

The *Hadaya Cafe*, opposite the Emperor, is a teashop with a nice selection of pastries, ice cream and good-quality tea.

One of the top places to eat in town is the *Three Five Restaurant* near the railway bridge. The extensive, mostly Chinese, menu includes 'goat fighting balls' (goat testicles) prepared a number of ways. Although expensive by local standards, meals here are cheap if paid for with kyats. In the same area, on the same side of the road, are several other Chinese places including the relatively expensive *Kyaw Swa* and the cheap and popular *Triple Diamond Ba Maung Restaurant*. The medium-priced *Panda Restaurant*, opposite the Three Five, is also good.

Getting There & Away

You can get to Bago by either rail or road; in either case the trip takes about two hours. It's very easy to day-trip to Bago from Yangon, but put aside the whole day. An early start is probably the best idea since Bago can get very hot around midday.

By road the route to Bago follows the Mandalay road to Taukkyan, about 30 km from the capital, where the Pyay road branches off. From here to Bago the country is much more open and the traffic somewhat lighter.

Air A new international airport is being built south-west of town on the way to Yangon. Intended to replace the current Yangon airport at Mingaladon, the new airport will make Bago an alternative to Yangon as a place to begin and end your trip.

Bus The buses from Yangon operate approximately hourly from 5 or 6 am and depart from Latha St. The fare is K30 and this can be a manageable bus trip. Avoid Sundays, however, when Bago is a very popular excursion from Yangon and the buses get very crowded. It can also be difficult to get back to Yangon because the buses will be booked out until late in the evening; you may want to catch a train back.

To/From Mandalay Some of the private bus companies running air-con express buses between Yangon and Mandalay stop in Bago. While they usually won't sell tickets for the short distance between Yangon and Bago, you can book tickets from Bago onward to Mandalay – for the full Yangon-Mandalay fare (around K1000).

Skyline Express departs for Mandalay from in front of the Hadaya Cafe around 7 pm. Trade Express leaves from a liquor shop near the Bogyoke Aung San equestrian statue at 7.30 pm.

Train It is possible to visit Bago by breaking the Yangon-Mandalay train journey here. It is wiser to do this coming down from Mandalay rather than going up from Yangon, because of the difficulties of getting a seat from Bago to Mandalay; from Bago to Yangon you could easily stand, wait for another train or change to the bus.

From Yangon there are about 10 trains a day from around 6 am to 9 pm. Although it's usually easy to buy Bago-Yangon tickets in Bago, Myanmar Travels & Tours (MTT) is reluctant to sell Yangon-Bago tickets even though Bago is definitely open! In that case you will have to go to the Advance Booking Office on Bogyoke Aung San St near the railway station in Yangon. The foreigner fare from Yangon is US$5 upper class, US$2 ordinary class on the express train. The local No 13 Up leaves Yangon at 5.20 pm and arrives in Bago at 8.50 pm for just K11; you should be able to buy the ticket on board after the train leaves the station. Obviously this would require an overnight stay in Bago.

If you miss the bus back to Yangon, try catching the train coming from Mawlamyine back to Yangon, which is supposed to arrive in Bago at 7.30 pm but is often one or two hours late. The fare is K11.

Taxi A third, more expensive, but also more convenient, alternative is to hire a taxi from Yangon. Start negotiating at around K2000, or the US dollar equivalent – no more than US$20. Taking a taxi or taxi-truck has the additional advantage of giving you transport from place to place once you get to Bago. Some drivers may feel that getting you to Bago and back, and to the two big attractions – the Shwemawdaw and the Shwethalyaung – is quite enough for one day. Don't accept

feeble excuses that other sites are 'too far off the road', are down tracks 'only fit for bullock carts' or are simply 'closed'. A good place to hire taxis for a Bago trip is near the Strand Hotel. Choose a driver with reasonable English-language skills.

To/From Kyaiktiyo A guide and driver to Mt Kyaiktiyo can be hired through any of the downtown hotels for around US$40. The same tour booked in Yangon costs US$80. See the Kyaiktiyo section in the South-Eastern Myanmar chapter for more information.

Getting Around
Trishaw is the main form of local transport in Bago. A one-way trip in the downtown area should cost no more that K20 to K25. If you're going further afield – say from Shwethalyaung Paya at one end of town to Shwemawdaw Paya at the other – you might as well hire one for the day, which should cost no more than K200.

TAUNGOO တောင်ငူ
Although Taungoo (often spelt Toungoo) was once the centre of one of the most powerful post-Bagan kingdoms, virtually nothing visibly historic remains to indicate its former 15th to 16th century glory. Today it's simply a typical central Myanmar town supported by the timber trade. It's situated toward the northern end of the Bago Division, within sight of mountain ranges to both the east and west, the source of teak and other hardwoods.

Among Burmese the town is most known for its bounteous areca palms, which yield the nut used in betel chews. In Myanmar when someone receives unexpected good fortune they are likened to a betel-lover receiving a paid trip to Taungoo.

Kayin State is less than 35 km east, and another 65 km or so further east is Kayah State. Karen and Kayah insurgents have been known to operate within these distances, and until very recently Taungoo was considered off limits for foreigners. A dry-weather road continues east all the way to Loikaw, but any

JOE CUMMINGS

JOE CUMMINGS

BERNARD NAPTHINE

Around Yangon
Top Left: The cylindrical Bawbawgyi Paya, near Pyay
Top Right: The graceful, silver-topped stupa of Pathein's Tagaung Paya
  Bottom: The inviting waters of Chaungtha Beach

JOE CUMMINGS

Around Yangon
The enormous reclining Shwethalyaung Buddha, Bago

travel beyond the Sittoung (Sittang) River a few km to the east of Taungoo still requires special permission. Such permission is nearly impossible to obtain unless you're a teak buyer or mineral engineer.

Shwesandaw Paya

Situated in the centre of town west of the main road, this is Taungoo's grandest pilgrimage spot. The central stupa, a standard-issue bell shape, is gilded and dates to 1597; local legend says an earlier stupa on the site was built centuries earlier and contains sacred hair relics. A pavilion on the western side of the stupa contains a large bronze Mandalay-style sitting Buddha, given to the paya in 1912 by a retired civil servant who donated his body weight in bronze and silver for the casting of the image. He died three years after the casting at age 72; his ashes are interred behind the image, which stands 3.6 metres high.

Another pavilion in the north-western corner of the compound houses a garish reclining Buddha surrounded by devas and monastic disciples. Glass cabinets along the wall display small religious objects and Buddhas donated by the faithful; only a few are old. Among the other tazaungs is one that displays sculptures of the seven Taungoo kings, a small Kuan Yin pavilion to placate the Chinese, a nat shrine with images of Saraswati and her attendants, and a Shin Upagot shrine.

Myasigon Paya

Though not as well known as Shwesandaw, this is the most interesting of the three famous zedis in towns. A brick *pahto* beneath the stupa features glass mosaic arches, paintings of Taungoo kings and a huge, bronze-and-silver-faced sitting Buddha in royal attire. The image is surrounded by planet Buddhas, an arrangement usually reserved for stupas. Smaller Buddhas, some of them old, are displayed in glass cases in the same building. Opposite the large sitting image, against a couple of pillars, are two Chinese bronze goddess statues, one sitting on an elephant, the other on a Fu dog. An inscription says the figures were donated to the paya in 1901 by a German Buddhist.

A small museum on the grounds contains bronze images of Erawan (the three-headed elephant who serves as Indra's mount), a standing Buddha captured from Thailand by King Bayinnaung and two British cannons dated 1897. Other items of lesser artistic or historic import include modern sculptures of famous disciples of the Buddha such as Mogalla and Sariputta, 100-year-old food-offering pedestals *(hsun ok)*, terracotta votive tablets, old coins and stamps.

Other Sights

In spite of the fact that seven kings reigned over Taungoo for a total of 155 years, all that's left of the secular kingdom known then as Kaytumadi are a few earthen ramparts and a moat on the western side of town. Nearby **Lay Kyaung Kandawgyi**, the town's 'royal lake', features a few small islands topped with pavilions.

Follow the road west of the lake to reach **Kawmudaw Paya**, said to be the oldest religious site in Taungoo. The central pink-and-white, bell-shaped stupa is not that impressive. A mirrored pillar marks the 'earth-conquering' spot from which Taungoo kings set off to conquer other armies. Worshippers walk clockwise around the pillar in the hope of conquering their personal problems.

Places to Stay

From the main road through town, turn west at the Taungoo Baptist Church onto Nansanda Rd to reach *Nansanda Guest House* (☎ 054-21089), opposite Myanma Economic Bank near a cinema and Sacred Heart Catholic Cathedral. Relatively clean rooms with air-con, ceiling fan, two beds, sink, mirror and shower (toilet outside) cost US$8/12 single/double. Similar triples with harder mattresses are available for US$12. The nearby *Soe Moe Guest House* looks more than adequate but has no licence to accept foreigners.

The *Myanma Thiri Hotel* (☎ 054-21764), well off the eastern side of the main road toward the southern end of town, is a two-storey, thick-walled, colonial-style building with colonnaded front. Large, well-maintained rooms with good beds, satellite TV, fridge, air-con, ceiling fans and private hot-water showers cost US$24/36/48/60 a single/double/triple/quadruple including breakfast. Although it once belonged to the state, Myanma Thiri is now privately owned. Very little English is spoken.

The owner of the *Sawasdee Restaurant* (see below) is building guest rooms above his restaurant. When finished, the rooms will probably rent for around US$8 to US$10 a night.

Places to Eat

Mandalay Htamin Zai (Mandalay Rice Shop) has been serving Burmese food since 1914 (at its current location since 1964) and thus claims the honour of being the oldest restaurant in Myanmar. It's on a side street off the western side of the main road near the main market – look for two peacock reliefs over the door. Burmese-style curries cost K60 and come with rice, soup and vegetables; it's not a very clean place but the food seems OK. It's open 6 am to 9 pm daily.

At the night market that convenes next to the central market, vendors specialise in chapatis and meat-stuffed palata. *Win Sanda* and *Sein Taik*, around the corner from Nansanda Guest House at the corner of the market, are two popular side-by-side teashops. One focuses on samosas, the other on bao-sii (Chinese buns); they're open 5.30 am to around 9 pm. The *Green Restaurant*, also near the market, is a small but very popular Chinese restaurant in a green building.

Several restaurants and teashops are found along the main north-south road through town. These are the only restaurants in Taungoo with English signs out the front, since they cater to teak buyers who come from all over Asia. *Kaytumadi Restaurant* and *Sakanthar Restaurant* serve good Chinese and Burmese food, while the *Min Min Cafe* is your basic teashop. *Tinechit Restaurant*, where several of the express

Yangon-Mandalay buses stop, also serves dependable Chinese and Burmese food.

South of the Myanma Thiri Hotel, *Sawasdee Restaurant* (☎ 054-21614) is owned by a local man who worked in Thailand for a couple of years. In addition to an indoor dining room there are a handful of little thatched-roof dining areas outdoors. The menu features a long list of Chinese dishes; Burmese and Thai food are available on request and prices are reasonable. Fresh prawns from the Sittoung River are a house speciality. It's open 7 am to 10 or 11 pm daily. The *Kayampya Restaurant* next door is similar.

The restaurant at the *Myanma Thiri Hotel* looks good but service is very slow and the food is bland.

Getting There & Away

Bus Taungoo is considered a midway point for road trips between Yangon and Mandalay. Trade Express, Asahi Express and Skyline Express all stop at the Tinechit Restaurant on the main road around 1 am. Myanmar Arrow Express stops on the opposite side of the road at Aungaba Teashop. Fares to either Yangon or Mandalay are K500 to K600 per person and the trip in either direction takes seven to eight hours.

Cheaper public buses are available to Yangon and Mandalay around 3 or 4 pm daily for just K100. These can be flagged down anywhere along the main road or at the central market. Count on around nine hours to either city.

See the Getting There & Away section in the Yangon chapter for bus departure times from Yangon.

Train The express train No 4 Down leaves for Yangon around 3 am and arrives around 11 am; express No 6 Down leaves at 11 pm and arrives in Yangon around 5.30 am; and express No 8 Down departs at 7 am and arrives at 1 pm.

In the northerly direction, the No 3 Up to Mandalay leaves around 2 am and arrives at 10 am; the No 5 Up departs at 11 pm and arrives at 5 am; and the No 7 Up leaves at 3 am and gets to Mandalay around 11 am. Step lively as the train only stops in Taungoo for 10 minutes. The fare is K69 ordinary, K140 upper class; for the moment no one at the station seems bent on collecting dollars though this could change.

See the Yangon Getting There & Away section for information on the Mandalay-bound express trains, which stop briefly in Taungoo. You can't buy Taungoo tickets at the MTT office or at the Foreigner Ticket Centre at the Yangon Railway Station; try the Advance Booking Office on Bogyoke Aung San St, where you'll probably be charged around US$15 for the trip. The same goes for Mandalay. If you're coming from Yangon or Mandalay, express bus would be a considerably cheaper option.

Car/Truck If you have your own vehicle and are feeling adventurous, the 100-km unpaved timber road from Oktwin (15 km south of Taungoo) to Pakkaung provides a unique shortcut to Pyay. From Pakkaung the road is sealed the remaining 39 km to Pyay. This is a lengthy and tiring all-day trip; start early and bring at least one spare tyre, plus food and plenty of water.

Forget about travelling east to Loikaw. Not only is the road beyond the Sittoung River in miserable condition, you may have to deal with both military checkpoints (at the river) and bandits (in the mountains).

PYAY (PROME) ဗြန်

Seven hours north of Yangon by road or an overnight riverboat trip south of Bagan, the town of Pyay lies on a sharp bend in the Ayeyarwady. Nearby are the ruins of the ancient Pyu capital of Thayekhittaya (Sri Ksetra). Very few visitors make their way to this remote site, although it has been the centre of the most intensive archaeological work in Myanmar almost all this century.

The current town site was established as a trade centre during the Bagan era, but Pyay didn't really hit its stride until the British developed the Irrawaddy Flotilla Company in the late 1800s. Today the town serves as an important transshipment point for cargo

moving between Upper and Lower Myanmar along the Ayeyarwady River, and between the Rakhine coast and the interior along the road from Taungup to Sinte (just across the river from Pyay). Sometimes the name of the city is spelt 'Pyi', although the everyday pronunciation is always 'Pyay'. The British called it 'Prome'.

Shwesandaw Paya

In the centre of the small town of Pyay itself, the Shwesandaw Paya is the main point of interest. A lift (K1) takes visitors from street level to the elevated main stupa platform, which, like the Shwedagon in Yangon, is perched on top of a hill.

As the name 'Golden Hair Relic' suggests, the zedi Shwesandaw purportedly contains a couple of Buddha hairs. Just over a metre taller than the main zedi at Shwedagon, the Shwesandaw stupa follows classic Burman Bagan lines similar to those seen at Bagan's oldest paya, Shwezigon. Along with Kyaiktiyo, Shwemawdaw, Mahamuni and Shwedagon, this is one of the most sacred Buddhist pilgrimage spots in Myanmar.

All in all, it's also one of the country's more impressive zedis, especially on its hillside setting. Looking east from the stupa you'll see an enormous seated Buddha figure rising up from the treeline. From the Shwesandaw terrace you look across to the image eye-to-eye; it's known as **Sehtatgyi Paya**, meaning 'Big Ten-Storey', for its height. Shwesandaw is at its most atmospheric at night, when the zedi is illuminated and the cityscape sparkles below. Daytime views are also good; so far the air over Pyay hasn't become too polluted.

Places to Stay

Only a few years ago if the authorities found foreigners without permits wandering around Pyay they were immediately sent back to Yangon. Today the city is officially open to foreign tourists – no permit is necessary – and there are now several accommodation choices.

Most comfortable is the recently privatised *Pyay Hotel* (☎ 053-21890) at the corner of Kan Rd and Strand Rd. The two-storey hotel stands well off the street on nicely landscaped grounds. The 10 spacious rooms on the upper floor come with fan, air-con and fridge, but since electricity is only supplied in the mornings and evenings these aren't terribly important. Toilets and showers (cold water only) are at the end of the hall. Rates are US$18 single, US$24 double and US$35 triple. Another 10 rooms on the ground floor appear to be reserved for Burmese only; these are slightly less well-furnished and don't contain air-con units or refrigerators. If you can talk your way into them, they should cost significantly less than the upper floor rooms. Rates include breakfast in the separate restaurant near the entrance gate.

Pan Ga Ba (Pangaba, Pangabar) Guest House (☎ 053-21277), nearby at 342 Merchant Rd, features basic rooms, with two beds and a mosquito net, in a big house-like building for just K300 per person. The manager speaks decent English and offers area maps and rental bikes. For the most part we've received nothing but raves about this place from travellers, though the latest report said a new wing was being added to the guest house and construction was noisy. In front of the guest house the proprietors run a restaurant popular with locals.

Near the Bogyoke Aung San statue in the middle of town, not far from the railway station, is *Aungapa (Aung Gabar) Guest House* (☎ 053-21332) at 1463 Bogyoke St. Although the rooms here are a bit small and dark, they're clean and the management is helpful. Bath and toilet are down the hall. Since it's an officially licensed place, only dollars or FECs are accepted; rates run from US$5 per person.

Up the road north a bit is the nicer *Shwemyodaw (Golden City) Guest House* (☎ 053-21990) at 353 High St. Rooms again are small but the place is bright, cozy and neat. Two-bed rooms with hard mattresses and fan cost US$15. For US$20 you get a

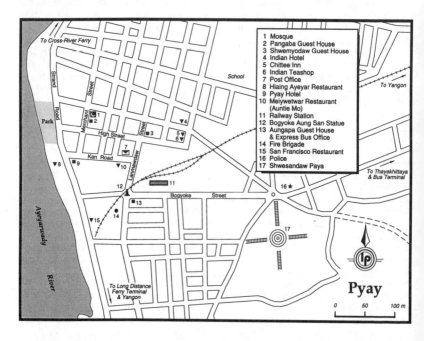

1 Mosque
2 Pangaba Guest House
3 Shwemyodaw Guest House
4 Indian Hotel
5 Chittee Inn
6 Indian Teashop
7 Post Office
8 Hlaing Ayeyar Restaurant
9 Pyay Hotel
10 Meiywetwar Restaurant (Auntie Mo)
11 Railway Station
12 Bogyoke Aung San Statue
13 Aungapa Guest House & Express Bus Office
14 Fire Brigade
15 San Francisco Restaurant
16 Police
17 Shwesandaw Paya

To Cross-River Ferry

Strand Street

School

To Yangon

Park

Merchant

High Street

Lanmadaw Street

Kan Road

To Thayekhittaya & Bus Terminal

Bogyoke Street

Ayeyarwady River

To Long Distance Ferry Terminal & Yangon

Pyay

0   50   100 m

similar room with softer mattresses and air-con, while US$25 rooms contain four beds and air-con. Showers and toilets are separate.

As Pyay becomes more tightly connected with the main tourist circuit over the next couple of years, more hotels and guest houses will probably open.

Places to Eat

The clean, friendly and inexpensive *Meiywetwar Restaurant* (no English sign), opposite the post office near Pyay Hotel, serves excellent traditional Burmese food. Also known as 'Auntie Mo', the restaurant offers curries made with chicken, shrimp, venison or steamed fish, plus fried chicken, roast duck, fried mackerel eggs and delicious Burmese salads made with your choice of tomato, fishball, pickled tea, horseshoe leaf or pomelo. There is no English menu as yet, so bring your best Burmese restaurant vocabulary or be prepared to point. It's open from 11 am until around 7 pm.

Around the corner from the Pyay Hotel on the river is *Hlaing Ayeyar*, an outdoor place that looks better from a distance than up close. You can dine at private chalet tables or in the large dining room. The menu consists mostly of Chinese dishes but the food isn't too special. Further south on the opposite side of Strand Rd, the *San Francisco Restaurant* offers slightly better Chinese fare.

The *Indian Hotel*, two streets north of the railway station, serves all-you-can-eat thalis (set meals) in a long, narrow, somewhat grubby dining room with tables along each wall. The only other Indian place we found, the *Chittee Inn* around the corner toward the railway station, was not as good and not as popular. Despite their names, neither of these places offers overnight accommodation.

The Indian teashop (no name) just south of the Chittee Inn offers decent potato curry and stuffed palatas for breakfast. There are also several Burmese teashops along Bogyoke St, east of the Bogyoke Aung San statue.

If your tastes run to palm toddy, there's a toddy bar behind the Ministry of Forestry's 'Static Workshop', just a bit west of Payagyi on the road to Hmawzaw. Take the narrow dirt road alongside the workshop till it ends next to a field of toddy palms. The rustic, thatched-roof bar is on the left; in addition to toddy sold by the pot or by the bottle, the bar sells prawn crackers and other snacks.

Getting There & Away

Bus Pyay lies 288 km north-west of Yangon via a decent sealed, two-lane road. From Yangon there are a couple of bus possibilities. A transport company at the corner of Shwebontha St and Bogyoke Aung San St operates one ordinary bus per day to Pyay that costs just K80 per person; it leaves at 9.30 am and arrives at 4.30 pm.

There are more choices from the Highway Bus Centre at the northern end of Yangon. A company called Golden Shuttle runs decent non-air-con buses between Yangon and Pyay for K100; they leave at 8 am and noon from both ends of the route and take about seven hours to/from Yangon. Aung Soe Moe Express operates a similar bus for the same fare. It leaves at 5.30 pm and arrives in Pyay around midnight.

Better yet is the Rainbow Express air-con, 45-seat bus to/from Yangon, which includes breakfast and door-to-door delivery for US$4 or K400. This leaves the company's Pansodan St office at 5 pm and arrives in Pyay around 10.30 pm. In the reverse direction the bus leaves Pyay at 5 am, arriving at the Pansodan St office at 10.30 am. In Pyay the office faces the traffic circle near the Bogyoke Aung San statue – the management told us they may move the office soon but will stay in this general vicinity.

Other companies at Yangon's Highway Bus Centre operate passenger transport to/from Pyay in the K100 to K200 range for ordinary pickups (seven to eight hours) or K400 for air-con express buses (five to six hours).

From the main bus terminal in Mandalay you can get an overnight express bus (three daily) for K300; these take a grinding 12 to 15 hours to reach Pyay, however. If you're coming from the north it would be better to break your journey in Nyaung U, Kyauk Padaung or Magwe. The road between

Magwe and Pyay is decent, but it's still a five-hour stretch.

Other bus routes to/from Pyay include: Kyauk Padaung (K200, three times daily, 10 hours), Taungup (K350, once daily, 13 hours), Taundwingyi (K80, three daily, four hours), Magwe (K100, three daily, five hours), Meiktila (K200, three daily, 12 hours) and Pathein (K150, once daily, 10 hours).

The Pyay bus terminal is about two km east of Shwesandaw Paya off the road to Paukkaung.

Train A branch railway line north from Yangon terminates at Pyay. There is only one express train per day, the No 71 Up, which leaves Yangon Railway Station at 1 pm sharp and is scheduled to arrive in Pyay at 8 pm. This train may arrive up to two hours late.

Probably neither the Foreigner Ticket Centre at the station nor the MTT office in Yangon will sell you a ticket. Your best bet is to try the Advance Booking Office on Bogyoke Aung San St one to three days before your intended departure; a ticket shouldn't cost more than US$10 one way in upper class, less in ordinary class, much less in either class if you manage to pay the regular kyat price of around K200. From the Pyay terminal back to Yangon, paying in kyat usually isn't a problem – so far.

Car A car and driver from Yangon to Pyay will cost less per day than hire to most other places outside the capital, since the road is decent and it's no more than a day's drive one way. Figure on paying around US$40 for an older, non-air-con car, up to US$50 for a newer model with air-con.

If you're coming to Pyay by private vehicle, you may want to break your journey in Paungde, a small town with a very trim, old colonial-style market building. It's only about 64 km short of Pyay, but is well-endowed as far as small Burmese towns go – since it was Ne Win's birthplace.

If you're continuing west to Thandwe and Ngapali Beach in Rakhine State (or south to Pathein), you'll have to drive a little north of Pyay on Strand Rd to meet the ferry which crosses the Ayeyarwady River to Sinte. From Sinte a road heads straight west to Taungup, then south to Thandwe. This same road crosses the road south to Pathein. The ferry leaves about every two hours from 6 am to 6 pm. For more information on these roads, see the Thandwe and Pathein sections.

Boat By riverboat from Bagan it's a two-day trip to Pyay with an overnight stop at Magwe. The boat leaves Nyaung U jetty (six km north-east of Old Bagan) every day, except Thursday and Sunday, around 5 am and arrives two evenings later in Pyay around 8 pm. Deck class costs K55, cabins K110. Bring your own food and water, as the food served at the deck canteen is of questionable quality and no bottled water is available.

You can continue on to Yangon for K68 deck, K136 cabin; this stretch takes 2½ days, with overnight stops in Myaungmya and Wakema. From Yangon, you could take the ferry upriver from Kaingdan St Jetty, but it's a slow, four-day journey.

The ferry pier in Pyay is a couple of hundred metres south of the San Francisco Restaurant. As the river level lowers during the dry season, the pier usually migrates downriver. You can book tickets at the IWT (Inland Water Transport Co) office on the opposite side of Strand Rd from the high-water pier or, for deck class only, on the boat itself.

From Pyay other ferry trip possibilities include Pakkoku (three full days; K60 deck, K120 cabin) and Mandalay (four nights upriver, three down; K86 lower deck, K135 upper deck, K272 cabin).

Getting Around

The main forms of local public transport are three-wheeled taxis and horsecarts, either of which should cost no more than K30 to K50 per trip anywhere in town.

AROUND PYAY
Thayekhittaya & Hmawza

The ancient site of Thayekhittaya – known to Pali-Sanskrit scholars as Sri Ksetra – lies eight km north-east of Pyay along a good road that leads to Paukkaung. Taking this road, you'll first come to the towering **Payagyi** ('Big Paya'), an early, almost cylindrical stupa, by the roadside about two km from the edge of the city.

Legend says Payagyi was erected by mythical King Duttabaung in 443 BC, but most likely it dates to the early Pyu kingdom which ruled the surrounding area from the 5th to 9th centuries AD – or from the 3rd to 10th centuries AD according to some sources. Nearby stand a couple of lofty teak trees, safe from the woodcutter's axe since they occupy sacred ground. Payagyi is thought to mark one of four corners which delineated Thayekhittaya; only two others are visible today, Bawbawgyi and Payama.

Very little is known about this kingdom or about the Pyus themselves. The earliest Pali inscriptions found here date to the 5th or 6th centuries AD and indicate the coexistence of Mahayana and Theravada Buddhism. A Chinese chronicle based on a Tang dynasty (618-905 AD) survey of the Pyu kingdom reads:

When the Pyu king goes out in his palanquin, he lies on a couch of golden cord. For long distances he rides on an elephant. He has several hundred women to wait on him...(The Pyus) are Buddhists and have a hundred monasteries, with bricks of glassware embellished with gold and silver...

A few km further brings you to the junction where you turn off the Bagan road towards Paukkaung. The road runs alongside the extensive city walls of Sri Ksetra, and ahead on the left you can see the decaying **Payama**, similar in form to the Payagyi, to the north of the road. Surrounded by rice fields, Payama is at its most picturesque in the rainy season. You must walk a half km or so from the highway along a trail which winds through these fields to reach it. On the grounds stands a stone plinth that once supported a *thein* or monastic ordination hall. A large brick-and-plaster pedestal near the stupa was a gift from the British to hold a large Buddha image (now in the Hmawza museum) excavated at the site. A bit of stucco relief still adheres to the pedestal. Two venerable banyan trees flank the stupa.

Just before crossing a stream, there's a turnoff south that leads into the village of Hmawza. This road terminates at a small railway station on the Yangon-Pyay line, which was built straight through the middle of Sri Ksetra. About a km and a half from the highway turnoff (six km total from Payagyi), by the old palace site, stands a small **museum** and a map of the area. Inside the museum is a collection of artefacts collected from Sri Ksetra excavations, including royal funerary urns, stone reliefs, a couple of bodhisattvas, a *dvarapala* (gate guardian), statues of the Hindu deities Tara Devi, Vishnu and Lakshmi, several 6th-century Buddha images, tile fragments, terracotta votive tablets and silver coins minted in the kingdom. There are no regular hours but the museum is usually unlocked for visitors.

Enquire at the museum for a guide to the outer ruins to the south, which can be hard to find. There's no charge for the service if someone's available, but a K100 tip is appreciated. At one time this area was considered dangerous due to the presence of 'insurgents' but it now appears secure. Archaeological enthusiasts could easily spend some time here, investigating these rarely visited ancient sites. The village itself holds some interest as an example of a typical farming settlement where rice, vegetables and flowers are brought to market or for shipment by train. Handmade basketry and pots are for sale in the village as well.

South of the museum, outside the city walls, are the cylindrical **Bawbawgyi Paya** and cube-shaped **Bebe Paya**. Standing over 45 metres high, the brick-and-plaster Bawbawgyi is the oldest stupa in the area. Bebe looks like a prototype pahto for some of the temples at Bagan; some sources say it was constructed in the 9th century but it may in fact have evolved during the Bagan era. The *sikhara*, a mound-like superstructure atop the cubic base, has been partially restored. Other cube-shaped pahtos in the area include one thought to have been used by a hermit, featuring eight Buddha reliefs along the lower half of the interior wall and a vaulted ceiling of brick. **East Zegu Paya** exhibits a similar vaulted brick ceiling, while **West Zegu Paya** lies in total ruins.

Leimyethna Paya is wider and squatter than the others; its doorways have been blocked off to prevent destruction by looters seeking valuable relics. The vaulted ceiling, no longer accessible for viewing, is reportedly supported by a pillar faced with original Buddha reliefs. The blocking of the doorways may be temporary until these valuable reliefs can be restored and moved to a museum.

The best English-language reference available on the Sri Ksetra monuments is an article entitled 'Excavations at Hmawzaw, Prome' which appeared in the 1911-12 annual report of the *Archaeological Survey of India*. The article contains detailed descriptions of objects and inscriptions found at each site, but almost no architectural information on the Pyu stupas.

Getting There & Away The most convenient way to reach Hmawza from Pyay is by three-wheeled taxi, which should cost around K100 one way and take no more than 15 or 20 minutes.

There are three local trains per day between Pyay and Hmawza at 7 am, 10 am and 5 pm. The fare is K2 and the journey takes about 15 minutes.

Hitching might also be possible as far as the turnoff to Hmawza, as the road out to Paukkaung is fairly well travelled.

Shwedaung

This small town about 14 km south of Pyay via the road to Yangon contains two famous payas. The more well-known is **Shwemyetman Paya**, 'Paya of the Golden Spectacles', a reference to a large, white-faced sitting Buddha inside the main shrine. The Buddha wears a gargantuan set of eyeglasses with gold-plated rims. Coming south from Pyay, the turnoff for Shwemyetman is located at the right-hand side of the road, opposite a small white-washed mosque bearing a 1962 imprimatur.

Spectacles were first added to the image during the Konbaung era, when a local nobleman offered them to the temple in an attempt to stimulate local faith through curiosity. Word soon spread that the bespectacled Buddha had the power to cure all kinds of ills, especially afflictions linked to the eyes. This pair was stolen early on, and a second pair was made and enshrined inside the image to protect them from thieves.

An English officer stationed in Pyay during the colonial era had a third pair fitted over the Buddha's eyes after his wife suffered from eye trouble and the abbot suggested such a donation. Naturally, as the story goes, she was cured. It requires nine monks to remove the glasses for their fortnightly cleaning.

The second major paya in Shwedaung, located to the north of the first, is **Shwenattaung Paya** (which means 'Golden Spirit Mountain'). As a stupa site, Shwenattaung reportedly dates back to the Sri Ksetra era, though the current 37-metre stupa features the post-Bagan style. Legend takes it back all the way to 283 BC, from which point it was supposedly reconstructed by a long line of Burman kings – hardly likely since there were no Burmans in the area before the 9th century AD – with the aid of local *nats* (or spirits). Although there is a nat shrine in the paya compound, there is little to suggest that nats play a more important role here than at any other central Burmese paya. A large paya pwe (pagoda festival) is held here each year on the full moon of Tabaung (February/March), the same time as Yangon's Shwedagon Festival.

The town of Shwedaung is also famous for *khauk swe* or rice noodles. Several noodle shops along the main road through town sell them from early morning till early evening.

Getting There & Away Large and small pickups leave for Shwedaung frequently throughout the day from the bus terminal east of Pyay for K5 per person. The last pickup back to Pyay passes the turnoff for Shwemyetman Paya around 5 pm.

Mandalay

Mandalay was the last capital of Myanmar before the British took over, and for this reason it still has great importance as a cultural centre. Historically it's the most Burmese of the country's large cities, a place where you'll come close to the 'heart' of Myanmar despite China-style modernisation. Mandalay still has considerable cultural and religious significance and its Buddhist monasteries are amongst the most important in the country – about 60% of all the monks in Myanmar reside in the Mandalay area. It's also said that Mandalay residents speak better Burmese than anyone else in the country.

The city takes its name from Mandalay Hill, the 236-metre-high bluff that rises just to the north-east of Mandalay Fort and its royal palace. Today the population ranges somewhere between 800,000 and a million; the largest in the country after that of the capital, Yangon (Rangoon), located 716 km to the south. It lies in the centre of Myanmar's 'dry zone' and is a surprisingly sprawling place – you'll find wandering around the city in the hot season a dry and dusty experience.

New townships are springing up along the edges of the township, many inhabited by former squatters who are being pushed out of the downtown area in the city's rush to modernise. The Chinese presence has become very large since the easing of foreign trade restrictions. Government truces with northern insurgents and trade with China have brought a boomtown atmosphere to Mandalay with a bevy of new hotels, high-rise office buildings and department stores.

The inhabitants of Kywezun and Ma Yan Chan, two districts on the river in the north-western part of the city, are scheduled to be moved out of the city to make way for parks and a new circular road around the city. These districts are considered 'black' by the authorities due to the flourishing presence of gambling, prostitution and heroin.

Highlights
- Shwenandaw Kyaung, the sole remaining building of the once extravagant moated palace
- Mandalay Hill with its spiralling stairways, temples and sweeping views
- Ancient Rakhine Buddha image at Mahamuni Paya
- Kuthodaw Paya, the world's 'biggest book'
- Bustling markets with produce and handicrafts from all over Upper Myanmar

Although it suffered considerable damage in the fierce fighting at the end of WW II – Mandalay Fort was completely burnt out – there is still much to be seen both in Mandalay and in the surrounding deserted cities of the old capitals.

History

Mandalay is a comparatively young city and its period as the capital of the last Burmese kingdom was a short one. Most of the monuments and buildings are therefore fairly recent, although some temples long pre-date the city. For centuries this area of Myanmar

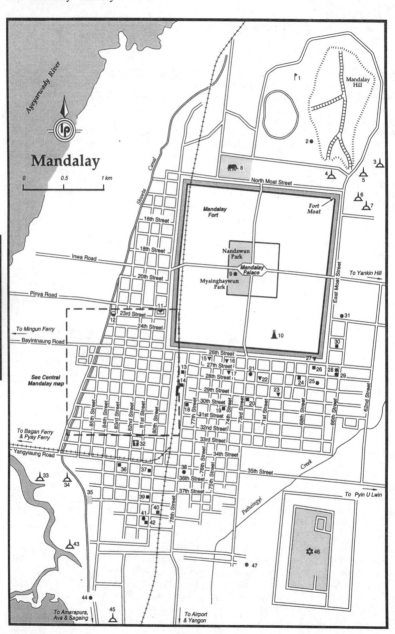

PLACES TO STAY		16	Marie-Min Vegetarian Restaurant	12	Buses to Lashio
13	Popa II Hotel	17	Too Too Restaurant	21	Mann Swe Gon Handicrafts
14	Popa I Hotel	22	Sakantha Restaurant	25	Police Academy
18	Pacific Hotel	23	Honey Garden Restaurant	29	Mandalay Marionettes
19	Boss Hotel	27	Pyigyimon Restaurant	31	School of Fine Arts, Music & Drama
20	Silver Cloud Hotel			32	Judson Baptist Church
24	Mya Mandalar Hotel	**OTHER**		33	Shwe In Bin Kyaung
26	Mandalay Swan Hotel & MTT			34	Thakawun Kyaung
28	Mandalay View Inn	1	Golf Course	35	Jade Market
30	Inwa Inn	2	Military Cemetary	38	Goldleaf Workshop
36	Shanghai Hotel	3	Kuthodaw Paya	41	Moustache Brothers Pwe Troupe
37	Sea Hotel	4	Kyauktawgyi Paya		
39	Tiger Hotel	5	Sandamani Paya	43	Kin Wun Kyaung
40	Great Guest House	6	Shwenandaw Kyaung	44	Buddha Image Makers
42	Power Hotel	7	Atumashi Kyaung		
		8	Yadanapon Zoo	45	Mahamuni Paya
PLACES TO EAT		9	Palace Watchtower	46	Royal Garden
		10	Independence Monument	47	Mandalay University
15	BBB Restaurant	11	GPO		

was the site of the capitals of the Burmese kingdoms; while in Mandalay you can easily visit three former royal cities – all now deserted.

King Mindon Min, penultimate ruler in the Konbaung dynasty, founded the city in 1857 and began construction of his new capital. The actual shift from nearby Amarapura to the new royal palace took place in 1861. In true Burmese tradition the new palace was constructed mainly from the dismantled wooden buildings of the previous palace at Amarapura. Mandalay's period of glory was short – Mindon was succeeded by the disastrous Thibaw Min and in 1885 Mandalay was taken by the British. Thibaw and his notorious queen were exiled and 'the centre of the universe' or 'the golden city' (as it was known) became just another outpost of the British Empire.

After independence Mandalay slumbered, like the rest of the country, through the socialist mismanagement of Ne Win and company. With the re-opening of the Burma Road through Lashio to China, however, the city is now undergoing an economic boom. The money fuelling this boom is generated by three trades, known locally as the 'red, green and white lines' – rubies, jade and heroin – and controlled by Kachin, Wa, Shan, Kokang and Chinese syndicates.

Orientation

The hill with the huge grounds of old Mandalay Fort at its base is the natural focus of Mandalay. The city sprawls away to the south and east of the fort, bounded on the west by the busy Ayeyarwady (Irrawaddy) River.

The city streets are laid out on a grid system with numbered streets running north-south and east-west. Some people may make a distinction between east-west 'roads' and north-south 'streets' but in everyday practice the Burmese use these terms interchangeably. The east-west streets run into the 40s only, while the north-south streets start in the 60s and run through the 80s. For moving across the city quickly, 35th St serves as the main east-west thoroughfare, while 80th St is the main north-south street.

Plans are underway to build a circular road around the city, which will speed travel to Sagaing and other outlying areas. All households now living along the river will have to move to a new town being established in Anisakan District, halfway between Mandalay and Pyin U Lwin (Maymyo).

MANDALAY

If you're thinking of making day trips to the 'ancient cities' outside Mandalay, it's best to do Sagaing one day and save Ava and Amarapura for another day,

Addresses In Mandalay a street address that reads '66th (26/27)' means the place is located on 66th St between 26th and 27th Sts. Some of the longer east-west streets take names once they cross the Shweta Canal (Shweta Chaung) heading west. Hence 18th St becomes Inwa Rd, 22nd St becomes Pinya Rd, 26th St changes to Bayintnaung Rd and 35th St is Yangyiaung Rd.

Information

Tourist Offices The Myanmar Travel & Tours office (☎ 02-22540) is in the Mandalay Swan Hotel, where you'll have to go if you need to buy train tickets (for Thazi or Yangon) or riverboat tickets (for Bagan). It's open from 7 am to 7 pm daily.

MTT also have a desk at the airport to meet flights, and at the railway station to meet tourist trains – in order to steer you towards their approved hotels.

MTT's *Mandalay Tourist Map* is useful for getting to the main tourist sites, though it only details four hotels.

Admission Fees The MTT office also collects fees for the various tourist attractions around the city – US$5 per person for Mandalay Palace, US$4 each for Mahamuni Paya and Mandalay Hill; US$3 for Kuthodaw Paya; and US$2 each for Sandamani Paya, Kyauktawgyi Paya and Sagaing Hill. If you visit all these sights, the fees will add up to a steep US$22. Admission fees can also be paid at each site; some people manage to avoid paying by visiting before 7 am or after 5 pm, or by claiming to be on Buddhist pilgrimage.

The Ministry of Hotels & Tourism (MHT) receives a steady trickle of complaints about these relatively high entrance fees and there is talk the fees may be reduced or abandoned in the future.

Guides Although most places in and around

Mandalay can easily be visited on your own, if you want someone to take care of all the travel details and provide a running commentary, there are several good guides in town. The going rate for a licensed guide is around US$20 a day, not including extras like car or driver.

Soft-spoken Richard at the Marie-Min Vegetarian Restaurant (☎ 02-24064), located on 27th St between 74th and 75th Sts, can arrange individual or small group tours in and around Mandalay and to Pyin U Lwin, Bagan (Pagan), Monywa and Inle Lake. An Indian Catholic, Richard is one of the few licensed non-MTT guides in Mandalay, and the only non-Burman one so far. Friendly English instructor U Nyunt, who lives at 122 74th St between 27th and 28th Sts is also recommended; he specialises in tours to Bagan and Mogok.

Experienced, French-speaking Than Tun ('Dominique') covers all of Upper Myanmar and can be contacted through the Royal Guest House. You'll find several tour agencies in town as well.

Some trishaw drivers act as guides for just a few dollars a day. Typically their foreign language skills aren't great and neither is their knowledge of Burmese history and architecture, but at least they know where everything is. Trishaw drivers accustomed to leading foreigners around usually park near the popular guest houses. But you don't have to worry about finding them – they'll find you. Keep in mind the typical trishaw driver will try to steer you into at least one or two handicrafts shop, where he'll earn commissions from anything you buy. Figure on paying K300 per day for all-day trishaw sightseeing in the central part of city, or K500 with jaunts to Mahamuni Paya to the south or Mandalay Hill to the north.

Post & Telecommunications The main post office was scheduled to move farther west along 22nd St to the corner of 22nd and 91st Sts by the end of 1995. It opens at 9.30 am and is supposed to close at 4 pm. In typical Burmese government fashion, the staff begin wandering off for tea at around 3

pm, and by 3.30 pm there's usually no one staffing the windows.

A block south of the main post office is the Central Telegraph Office, where both domestic and international calls can be made at low government rates. At least a few of the new luxury hotels on their way to Mandalay will offer IDD telephone service.

Mandalay Fort

King Mindon Min ordered the construction of his imposing walled palace compound in 1857. The immense walls measure eight metres high and three metres thick at the bottom, tapering to 1½ metres thick at the crenellated top, and are made of fired brick backed by earth ramparts. Each of the four sides extends two km; the surrounding moat is 70 metres wide and over three metres deep. A channel from the Mandalay irrigation canal fills the moat. After the British occupied the city in 1885, the compound was named Fort Dufferin and became the seat of the colony's government house and British Club.

On 20 March 1945, in fierce fighting between advancing British and Indian troops and the Japanese forces which had held Mandalay since 1942, the royal palace within the fort caught fire and was completely burnt out. The traditional wooden construction of Burmese palaces had often in the past led to severe damage by fire, and this – the last and most magnificent palace complex – was no exception. All that remains of the original palace today are the huge walls and moat, the base on which the wooden palace buildings and apartments stood, and a few masonry buildings or tombs. The Burmese army has re-occupied the fort; soldiers grow their own fruit and vegetables in the middle of the base to supplement meagre wages.

There were originally three gates to the fort on each of the walls. There were also five bridges leading into the fort, four running to the main gates. Each of the gates was topped by a *pyatthat*, or wooden pavilion. Smaller pyatthats stood at each corner and between the large ones – making 32 in all. Apart from some damage repaired after the war and

changes made when the railway was directed through the palace grounds, the wall and its pavilions are original.

Mandalay Palace was far more than just royal living quarters – it was really a walled city within the city. For the past few years the government has undertaken a massive reconstruction project and a new palace is taking shape for the benefit of tourists. Some visitors like the reconstruction while others abhor it. Instead of flammable wood, the new version – seven buildings so far – sports concrete construction topped by aluminium roofs.

The moat surrounding the fort is also under renovation. A 33-metre watchtower reached

Ornately carved teak watchtower,
Mandalay Fort

via a spiral staircase commands a view of the entire compound and cityscape. Nearby is the partially original 'tooth relic tower' and the tomb of King Mindon. The latter was once gilded and decorated with glass mosaics but an 1898 restoration obliterated all traces of the earlier craftsmanship. The large open sheds here contain over 600 inscribed stone slabs which were collected by King Bodawpaya (1782-1819) and were later moved to the palace from Amarapura just before WW II. Other reminders of the former glory of the old palace are the Royal Mint and the Sabbath Hall, which are also close by.

Much of the restoration of the palace and moat has been carried out using prison labour. For a while the municipal government required all young males in the city to contribute one day's worth of 'volunteer' labour per month to the project, but this practice was discontinued due to the negative publicity generated in the foreign press.

The palace museum has not yet reopened. It is planned to eventually combine this museum with the equally drab Mandalay Museum and library on 80th St, outside the fort walls.

Admission, for foreigners, to the palace compound costs US$5. The main entrance is the gate on the eastern wall. You can get a K5 glimpse of the compound by taking one of the public Mann Sit Thi buses, which run from Zegyo through the fort from east to west.

Mandalay Museum

Opposite the south-western corner of Mandalay Fort's wall, on the corner of 24th and 80th Sts, this mildly interesting museum contains a collection of Mandalay regalia, royally commissioned art and palm-leaf manuscripts that were formerly housed in the palace. Most of the articles date from the reigns of the last two Mandalay kings – Mindon and Thibaw. It's open Wednesday through Sunday 10 am to 4 pm and costs US$3 for foreigners. Eventually the holdings at this museum will be combined with those from the palace museum.

Kyauktawgyi Paya

Close to the southern entrance to Mandalay Hill stands the Kyauktawgyi Paya, the construction of which commenced in 1853 and was completed in 1878. It was originally intended that this paya, like its namesake a few km south in Amarapura, would be modelled after the Ananda Temple of Bagan, but due to a palace rebellion this grand plan was not carried through.

It is chiefly interesting for the huge seated image of the Buddha carved from a single block of marble. The marble block from the mines of nearby Sagyin was so colossal that it required 10,000 men labouring for 13 days to transport it from a canal to the current site. Ornamented with royal attire, the image was completed and dedicated in 1865. Around the shrine are figures of the Buddha's 80 *arahats* (disciples), arranged in groups of 20 on each of the four sides.

Mandalay's biggest festival is held here for seven days in early to mid-October to commemorate Thadingyut.

Admission for foreigners is US$2.

Sandamani Paya

To the south-east of Mandalay Hill, close by the bus stop, is the Sandamani Paya, a cluster of slender whitewashed stupas built on the site of King Mindon's temporary palace – used while the new Mandalay Palace was under construction. King Mindon had come to power after the successful overthrow of King Pagan Min, an operation in which he had been assisted by his younger brother Prince Kanaung.

Mindon tended to concentrate on religious matters and leave the niceties of secular rule to his brother, but in 1866 Prince Kanaung was assassinated in an unsuccessful revolt inspired by Prince Myingun. The Sandamani Paya was built as a memorial to Prince Kanaung on the spot where he was killed.

The Sandamani Paya enshrines an iron image of the Buddha cast in 1802 by Bodawpaya and transported here from Amarapura in 1874. Around the stupa lie a large collection of marble slabs inscribed with commentaries on the Buddhist canon.

A Stroll Up Mandalay Hill

Since it's such a natural focus for the city, and the only place with a good view over the pancake-flat central plain, the hill is where many people start their visit to Mandalay. The famous hermit monk, U Khanti, is credited with inspiring the construction of many of the buildings on and around the hill in the years after the founding of the city.

From the south, two covered stairways wind their way up the hill, meeting about half way up. Another path ascends more steeply from the west. It's a pleasant stroll, with plenty of places to stop for a rest. Shoes must be removed as you enter the walkways. For those who don't want to make the climb, a minibus to the top can be boarded for K3 per person. For most of the year, it makes most sense to climb before 10 am or after 4 pm to avoid the mid-day heat.

Close to the top of the hill you come to a huge standing Buddha image looking out towards the royal palace with an outstretched hand pointing in that direction. This image, known as the **Shweyattaw,** represents a rather interesting legend. The Buddha, accompanied by his disciple Ananda, was said to have climbed Mandalay Hill while on one of his visits to Myanmar. In the 2400th year of his faith, he prophesied, a great city would be founded below the hill. By our calendar that 2400th year was 1857 – the year King Mindon Min decreed the move from Amarapura to Mandalay. The statue represents the Buddha pointing to where the city would be built.

The first shrine you come to, half way up the hill, contains the so-called **'Peshawar Relics'**, three bones of the Buddha. The relics were originally sent to Peshawar, now in Pakistan, by the great Indian king Asoka himself. The stupa into which they were built was destroyed in the 11th century, but in 1908 the curator of the Peshawar Museum discovered the actual relic casket during excavations. Although Peshawar had once been a great Buddhist centre, it had by that time been Muslim for many centuries; so the British government presented these important relics to the Burmese Buddhist Society, and this relatively neglected temple was built to house them.

From the summit, 230 metres above the surrounding plain, there's a fine view back over the battlements of the palace to the city of Mandalay, while to the east you can see the hazy blue outline of the Shan hills. Those interested in military history can also find, in a small building attached to one of the shrines at the top of a wide, steep flight of steps, a monument to the British regiment which retook the hill from the Japanese in fierce fighting in 1945. The Mandalay Hill monasteries were renovated and enlarged in the early 1990s to accommodate Burmese army sentries.

Admission to the hill is US$4; there's an additional US$4 for the use of video cameras. Mandalay Hill can be reached via bus Nos 4 or 6, or via the red Mann Sit Thi bus. ■

They were another project of the venerable U Khanti. Do not confuse them with the 729 inscribed marble slabs of the Kuthodaw Paya which stands to the east of the Sandamani.

Admission to Sandamani, for foreigners, is US$2.

Kuthodaw Paya

Also known as the Maha Lawka Marazein Paya, the central stupa here was modelled after Shwezigon Paya at Nyaung U near Bagan. Building commenced in 1857, at the same time as the royal palace. The paya complex has been dubbed 'the world's biggest book', for standing around the central stupa are 729 marble slabs on which are inscribed the entire Buddhist canon, or *Tripitaka*. Each slab is housed in its own individual small stupa.

It took an editorial committee numbering over 200 to produce the original slabs. It has

been estimated that, reading for eight hours a day, one person would take 450 days to read the complete 'book'. King Mindon convened the Fifth Buddhist Synod and used a team of 2400 monks to read the whole book in a non-stop relay lasting nearly six months! In 1900 a paper edition of the stone original was printed in 38 volumes, each with about 400 pages. A 730th slab in the corner of the inner enclosure tells of the construction of this amazing book.

Foreigner admission is US$3.

Atumashi Kyaung

The ruins of the 'Incomparable Monastery', built by King Mindon in 1857, stand a little to the south of the Kuthodaw Paya. Built at the same time as the Kuthodaw Paya, this monastery was of traditional Burmese monastic construction – a masonry base topped by a wooden building – but instead of the usual multi-roofed design it consisted of graduated rectangular terraces. By all accounts it was one of the most magnificent temples in all of South-East Asia. Inside was a famous Buddha image, clothed in the king's silk clothing and with a huge diamond set on the forehead. The image was stolen in 1885, during the British takeover of the city.

In 1890 the monastery caught fire and, together with its contents which included four complete sets of the *Tripitaka* in teak boxes, was completely gutted. Today a huge quadrangle of colonnaded and arched walls, the main stairway and a few fine stucco reliefs survive. Although only a pale shadow of its original form, the ruined building is still impressive. Inside you can see the stumps of teak pillars that once supported the roof. Using convict labour, the government is currently renovating the site – one hopes the atmosphere won't be lost completely as at the Mandalay Fort. In the nearby Shwenandaw Kyaung you can see an early photograph of the Atumashi Kyaung prior to its destruction.

Admission to Atumashi Kyaung, for the time being, is free for all. Once the renovation is complete it's likely a fee will be collected from foreign visitors.

Shwenandaw Kyaung
Close to the Atumashi Kyaung stands the Shwenandaw Kyaung (or 'Golden Palace Monastery'). This monastery is of great interest not only as a fine example of a traditional Burmese wooden monastery, but as a fragile reminder of the old Mandalay Fort. At one time this building was part of the palace complex and was used as an apartment by King Mindon and his chief queen, and it was in this building that he died. After Mindon's death, King Thibaw Min had the building dismantled and reassembled on its present site in 1880 as a monastery. It is said that Thibaw used the building for meditation, and the couch on which he sat can still be seen.

The building is covered inside and out with carved panels; unfortunately, though, many of the exterior panels have weathered

badly and some have been prised off and removed. At one time the building was gilded and decorated with glass mosaics. The carved panels inside are still in excellent condition, particularly the 10 *jataka* scenes taken from the Buddha's life.

A couple of years ago an admission of US$3 was collected but this practice was recently discontinued. One rumour says the old *sayadaw* (chief abbot) in charge of the attached monastery thought it was disgraceful to charge admission to a religious building. Not even SLORC (the State Law and Order Restoration Council) goes against the most highly ranked sayadaws in matters of this kind.

Mahamuni Paya
South-west of the town, or about 1½ km north-west of Mandalay airport, stands the Mahamuni, or 'Great Sage', Paya. It is also sometimes called Payagyi, 'Big Paya', or the Rakhine (Arakan) Paya. It was originally built by King Bodawpaya in 1784, when a road paved with bricks was constructed from his palace to the paya's eastern gate. You can still find traces of this royal highway. In 1884 the shrine was destroyed by fire; the current one is comparatively recent.

The centrepiece of the this shrine is the highly venerated Mahamuni image which was transported to Myanmar from Mrauk U (Myohaung) in Rakhine in 1784. It was believed to be of great age even at that time – it may have been cast during the 1st century AD – and the surrounding complex was specially built for it. The four-metre-high seated image is cast in bronze, but over the years countless thousands of devout Buddhists have completely covered the figure in a 15-cm thick layer of goldleaf. Only men are permitted to walk up to the Mahamuni image and apply goldleaf. During the rainy season it is cloaked in monastic robes.

The image is thronged by so many worshippers that caretakers have installed video monitors in other parts of the complex so that the Burmese can pay their respects to the Mahamuni's video image; you'll actually see people bowing down before the TV screens.

Each morning at 4 am a team of monks washes the Mahamuni's face and even brushes its teeth – an event well worth getting up early to see. Photography of the image is forbidden.

In the courtyard a small building houses six bronze Khmer figures brought back from Rakhine along with the Mahamuni Buddha. Three are lions, two are male warriors and one is Erawan, the three-headed elephant. Originally these figures stood sentry at Angkor Wat in Cambodia, then were taken from Angkor by the Thais in 1431. King Bayinnaung subsequently looted them from Ayuthaya in 1564 and brought the figures to Bago (Pegu), where in 1663 they were nabbed by King Razagyi of Rakhine. According to legend, rubbing a part of the image will cure any affliction on the corresponding part of your own body – knee and stomach ailments seem to be the main preoccupation of the Burmese, who have polished these parts to a high gloss. Bars now protect the sculptures from further rubbing.

The temple courtyard contains more inscription stones collected by King Bodawpaya, who appears to have had quite a thing about this pursuit. Another small building, next to the one containing the bronze figures, has two large statues shouldering a pole between them, from which is slung a traditional Burmese gong said to weigh five tonnes. There are many interesting shop stalls at the entrance to the shrine; this was one of the few places in the country where photographs of Aung San Suu Kyi were openly sold during the period of her house arrest.

During the Mahamuni Paya Festival in early February, thousands of people from nearby districts make pilgrimages to the Mahamuni. The temple is always a centre of activity and during this festival it explodes with energy.

Admission to the Mahamuni Paya is US$4 for foreigners. The blue No 1 bus goes to Mahamuni from Zegyo Market and from Kuthodaw Paya.

Shwekyimyint Paya
Located on 24th St between 82nd and 83rd Sts, a little north-east of Zegyo Market or the clock tower, this paya's original construction considerably pre-dates Mandalay itself. It was founded in 1167 by Prince Minshinzaw during the Bagan period. He was the exiled son of King Alaungsithu and settled near the present site of Mandalay.

The shrine is notable because it contains the original Buddha image consecrated by the prince. It also contains many other images, made of gold, silver or crystal, which were collected by later Burmese kings and removed from Mandalay Fort after it was occupied by the British. These images are generally kept under lock and key and only shown to the general public on very important religious occasions. Here and at the Setkyathiha Paya you can find the ridiculous in close proximity to the sublime – glass cases with figures of the Buddha and disciples which, when you put a coin in the slot, parade around to noisy music.

Setkyathiha Paya
A short distance south-west of the Zegyo Market on 85th St, this stupa rises from an elevated masonry platform. It was badly damaged during WW II, but was subsequently repaired. Its main point of interest is the five-metre-high seated Buddha image cast in bronze by King Bagyidaw in Ava in 1823 just before the First Anglo-Burmese War broke out.

In 1849 King Pagan Min moved the image to Amarapura, just as the second war was about to begin. When the third and final conflict was about to commence, the image was brought to Mandalay in 1884. Reclining Buddha images can be seen in the paya courtyard along with a sacred bodhi tree planted by U Nu, a former prime minister of Myanmar.

Eindawya Paya
The beautifully proportioned stupa at Eindawya Paya stands west of Zegyo Market. It is covered in goldleaf and makes a fine, shimmering sight on a sunny day. The stupa was built by King Pagan Min in 1847, on the site of the palace where he lived before he ascended the throne – which at that time was still at Amarapura.

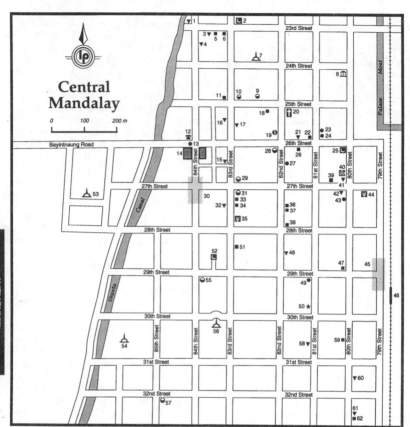

Central Mandalay

0   100   200 m

The shrine houses a Buddha image made of chalcedony – a quartz mineral with an admixture of opal – which was said to have come to Myanmar from Bodhgaya in India in 1839. Because the Eindawya Paya is a little more remote and less visited by the usual stream of tourists, you're likely to get an unusually open reception here.

Shwe In Bin Kyaung

This large and elegant wooden monastery was commissioned in 1895 by a pair of wealthy Chinese jade merchants. The wood-carved ornamentation along the balustrades

and roof cornices is of exquisite quality. You'll find it west of Shweta Canal and south of 35th St.

City Sights

Something is always happening on the streets of Mandalay, whether bustling street markets or neighbourhood *pwes* ('shows'). Mandalay's 'centre' is a short walk west from the south-western corner of the fort. Here you will find the clock tower, and nearby, the relocated **Zegyo Market**. The sprawling old market, designed in 1903 by Count Caldari (the Italian first secretary of the Mandalay

PLACES TO STAY		15	Man Thiri Restaurant	21	Sacred Heart
		16	Min Min Restaurant		Cathedral
5	Classic Hotel	17	Nylon Ice Cream Bar	24	Myanma Airways
6	Thailand Hotel	18	Mann Restaurant		Office
11	Garden Hotel	22	Shells Cafe	26	Central Mosque
19	Royal Guest House	33	Shwe Let Yar	28	Air Mandalay Office
23	Taung Za Lat Hotel		Myanmar Fast	29	Main Bus Centre
25	Sabai Phyu Guest		Food	30	Pickups to Monywa
	House	41	Punjab Food House	31	Night Market
27	Ayeyarwady Hotel	42	Everest Restaurant	32	Pickups to Pyin U
34	Modern Hotel &	48	Chin Shin Restaurant		Lwin
	Universe Hotel	58	Htaw Yin Restaurant	35	Hindu Temple
36	New York Hotel	60	Texas Cold Snack Bar	40	Sikh Temple
37	New Star Hotel	61	Shwe Wah Restaurant	43	Bamboo Fan Factory
38	Bonanza Hotel			44	Hindu Temple
39	Central Hotel &	**OTHER**		45	Night Market
	Dream Hotel			46	Railway Station
47	Man Ayeyarwady	2	Mosque	49	Fire Lookout Tower
	Hotel	7	Shwekyimyint Paya	50	Police
51	Hotel Sapphire	8	Mandalay Museum	52	Mosque
59	Kaung Myint Hotel	9	Buses to Taunggyi	53	Eindawya Paya
62	Palace Hotel	10	HMV Pyin U Lwin	54	Setkyathiha Paya
			Jeeps	55	Pickups to
PLACES TO EAT		12	Central Telephone		Amarapura, Ava &
			Office		Sagaing
1	Rainbow Restaurant	13	Clock Tower	56	Small Pagoda
3	Lashio Lay Restaurant	14	Zegyo Market	57	MMTA Pickups to
4	Thai Yai Restaurant	20	Bank		Pyin U Lwin

MANDALAY

Municipality) was dismantled – much to the dismay of the local folk – around 1990 and moved to two new three-storey buildings done in the People's Republic of China style on 84th St between 26th and 27th Sts. In spite of the less atmospheric location, the market still represents a fascinating collection of stalls selling every sort of Burmese ware you could imagine – and a fair assortment of smuggled goods from outside Myanmar. In the usual Asian manner there are sections for everything from jewellery or textiles to books or hardware. A lift and escalators were recently added – Burmese from the countryside often line up to take turn riding these marvels of modern technology.

In the evening, busy **night markets** spring up around the intersections of 84th and 27th Sts, and 79th and 29th Sts. A picturesque **open-air market** west of Zegyo specialises in onions, potatoes, and jaggery (the old English term for sugar produced by the sugar palm).

If you continue west along 26th St beyond the market you will eventually come to the **riverfront**, a scene of constant activity and interest; something is always happening down here. The boat landing at the end of 26th St (called Bayintnaung Rd at this point) is where you must come for the riverboats heading upriver to Mingun. You can see working water buffaloes at the western end of Pinya Rd (22nd St), the next landing north. A short distance north of the Mingun jetty is an area where people come to do their laundry; it can be a very colourful place. This may change if the government succeeds in its plan to move everyone out of the riverfront districts.

Yankin Paya, perched on Yankin Hill about three km east of Mandalay Fort, is a good spot for watching sunsets. If you go by rented bicycle you can park at the bottom and climb the hill on foot. Or you can take a white No 5 bus for K5 to the foot of the hill, then board one of the local pickups which climb the hill for K7 per person (K10 in a cab). Unlike at Mandalay Hill, there's no charge for climbing Yankin Hill.

Yadanapon Zoo, opposite the northern

side of the fort moat, has a small collection of animals but is a quiet place to wander around for a K3 entry fee.

Churches

Mandalay has some churches amongst the many temples. On the western side of 80th St between 34th and 35th Sts, **Father Lafon's Catholic Church** was built by the French in the gothic style in 1894, then rebuilt in 1919. Its gothic facade remains intact. **Sacred Heart Cathedral**, on the eastern side of 82nd St between 25th and 26th Sts, was constructed in 1873, bombed in WW II and rebuilt in 1951. Masses are held daily at both churches, twice on Sunday. The congregations are predominantly Indian and Chinese.

Tucked away at the junction of 23rd and 85th Sts, the **Church of the Province of Myanmar**, (formerly known as the Anglican Cathedral) was erected during the reign of King Mindon Min in 1873. The king's children were educated here in English. A baptismal font inside the cathedral was a gift from Queen Victoria.

The **Judson Baptist Church**, named for the American missionary who has virtually become a saint in Myanmar, stands on 82nd St between 33rd and 34th Sts. A sign posted on the church claims the church fathers oppose 'liberalism, modernism, ecumenism, formalism and worldliness'.

Places to Stay – bottom end

The budget end of the lodging circuit in Mandalay has substantially improved since the last edition of this guidebook, when nothing costing less than US$22 a night was approved for foreigners. Room rates at the bottom end now average US$5 to US$8 per person, high by Burmese standards but the lowest they've been in years. As more hotels and guest houses obtain licences to accept foreigners, rates may drop even further.

At all of these places, you can expect electric power and water pressure to be a little intermittent. Prostitution is common at most of the lower-end places; in fact in ordinary Burmese parlance, 'guest house' is

practically synonymous with 'whorehouse'. Often the cheap, multi-storey places will set aside certain floors for foreigners in an attempt to screen the flesh trade from view.

At the moment, two downtown guest houses stand out from the rest in terms of quality and variety of accommodation. The tidy *Sabai Phyu (Byu) Guest House* (☎ 02-25377), a multi-storey, modern building at 58 81st St between 25th and 26th Sts (near Zegyo Market), offers economy fan rooms with common bath for US$6 to US$10 single, US$10 to US$15 double. Standard rooms with air-con, carpet, good mattresses and attached hot-water showers cost US$12 to US$14 single, US$18 to US$20 double, US$28 triple; these rates include breakfast. The Sabai Phyu has one large superior air-con room with two double beds, bathtub and breakfast for US$45. Breakfasts are served on the rooftop, which affords views of Mandalay Hill.

Another popular place in the same general vicinity is the three-storey, 32-room *Royal Guest House* (☎ 02-22905) at 41 25th St between 82nd and 83rd Sts. Clean, if small, rooms here cost US$6 single, US$12 double with common toilet and shower facilities, or US$10 single, US$15 double with attached toilet and cold-water shower. The corridors adjacent to these rooms are air-conditioned, and open transoms allow some of the cool air to reach the rooms. For US$15 single, US$18 double you can get a room with an air-con unit inside and attached shower and toilet.

Over at 81st and 26th Sts, the 136-room *Taung Za Lat Hotel* (☎ 02-23210) offers rooms with common bath and toilet for US$6/10 single/double, with attached shower and common toilet for US$8/12, or with attached shower and toilet for US$10/15. There are also some newer rooms with air-con, hot-water showers and TV for US$15/25. Three of the five floors are reserved for Burmese only.

The *Garden Hotel* (☎ 02-25184) at 174 83rd St, between 24th and 25th Sts, is a typical Burmese-style hotel with decent economy rooms for US$6 to US$10 single,

US$15 to US$18 double and nicer standard rooms for US$10 to US$15 single, US$20 to US$35 double, US$40 triple. All rooms come with air-con, TV, fridge and breakfast; all except the more expensive standard rooms feature shared toilet and hot-water shower facilities.

The six-storey, 49-room *Modern Hotel* (☎ 02-28715), on the eastern side of 83rd St between 27th and 28th Sts, charges US$15 per person for air-con rooms with private cold-water shower, intercom phone and fridge. It's not very special – the lobby is especially dreary – but would do in a pinch. On the same block, the nine-storey *Universe Hotel* is under construction; when completed it will probably cost about twice as much per night as the Modern.

Still downtown, the three-storey *Ayeyarwady Hotel* (☎ 02-34332) on 26th St between 81st and 82nd Sts offers small but adequate rooms with ceiling fans, bath and toilet down the hall for US$5 per person, or 'special' rooms with air-con, TV, private hot-water bath and good mattresses for US$15/25 single/double. Watch out for the peepholes in the shared shower. The *Thailand Hotel* (☎ 02-21790) at 120 83rd St, between 23rd and 24th Sts, is similar but not as good value.

The friendly, quiet, Indian-run *Central Hotel* (☎ 02-25865), at 156 27th St between 80th and 81st Sts, has plain rooms with air-con for just US$5 per person with common bath or US$7 per person with shower.

Another good value hotel – seemingly undiscovered by foreigners though it has the proper licence – is the *Kaung Myint Hotel* (☎ 02-22790), between 30th and 31st Sts on the western side of 80th St. Air-con rooms with attached bath cost US$10 per person. The owner also speaks good English.

The nearby *Coral Rest House* (☎ 02-24407), on the eastern side of 80th St between 27th and 28th Sts, offers basic rooms with shared facilities for US$5 per person. It's a very local scene and not much English is spoken. The *Great Guest House* on the northern side of 39th St, between 80th St and the railway, is better; again, it sees few foreigners. This location is convenient to where the Moustache Brothers and other pwe troupes stage their performances.

Moving upmarket a bit, the modern, five-storey *Sea Hotel* (☎ 02-24142) on the western side of 80th St, between 35th and 36th Sts, charges US$15 single, US$20 double for rooms with air-con and private bath. The similar *Man Ayeyarwady* (☎ 02-27044), on the north-western corner of 29th and 80th Sts and near the Chinese market and railway station, looks more glittery from the outside – the attached karaoke lounge is larger than the lobby. Rooms with common bath and no breakfast cost US$7 per person, while 'special rooms' with hot-water shower and breakfast are good value at US$15/30 single/double. Ask for a room away from the street and karaoke lounge if you value quiet surrounds.

Catering mostly to budget tour groups, the *Natural Inn* (☎ 02-34336) at the end of 23rd St, between 80th and 81st Sts, has basic rooms with fan for US$5/10 single/double, nicer rooms with fan and attached hot-water shower for US$15/20 and junior suites with air-con for US$20/25. Although the compound outside is impressive, the rooms seem a bit overpriced and the service perfunctory.

Right next to the railway station, the *Popa I Hotel* (☎ 02-21988) has economy rooms for US$10 single, US$15 double, US$20 triple, plus better rooms with attached bath for US$20/25 and air-con rooms for US$30/35. The hotel was formerly known as the Manymo Hotel. A block north of the railway station, the *Popa Hotel II* (☎ 02-22555) has no economy rooms; standard and air-con rooms cost the same as at the Popa I.

The cheapest place to stay in Mandalay is also the quietest since it's quite removed from the central downtown area. *Si Thu Tourist Hotel* (☎ 02-26201), at 29 65th St, between 30th and 31st Sts, offers the usual cubicles-along-a-corridor setup with shared bath and toilet facilities for US$4 per person; it's not clear whether this is a licensed place or not.

The *YMCA* currently under construction at the corner of 25th and 81st Sts may rent rooms to foreigners once it opens.

MANDALAY

All of the foregoing hotels and guest houses offer a fair night's accommodation within this price range. Places which we think you should avoid, simply because of poor maintenance, overpricing and bad service, include *New Waves Hotel* at 27th and 80th Sts, the *Hotel Venus* on 28th St between 90th and 81st Sts and the government-run *Chanayethazan Hotel* in the bus station on 26th St.

Places to Stay – middle & top end

Mandalay has a fast-growing number of hotels with rooms in the US$30 to US$45 a night range. If you don't need to stay downtown, one of the nicer and quieter places is the Indian-operated *Mandalay View Inn* (☎ 02-22347), a two-storey residential compound on 66th St between 26th and 27th Sts, just north of the Mandalay Marionettes' theatre. Well-maintained standard rooms cost US$30/40 single/double, nicer rooms US$48 single/double. These rates include breakfast but not tax and service. Discounts are available for multi-day stays. All rooms come with air-con, TV, phone and hot-water showers; IDD phone service is available.

Another quiet spot in the same general neighbourhood is the less expensive *Peacock Lodge* (☎ 02-22092) at 5 Myaypadethar St, off 61st St near Mandalay Swan Hotel. Large, comfortable air-con rooms with attached hot showers cost US$24 single, US$35 double.

Downtown toward Chinatown on the north-eastern corner of 82nd and 28th Sts, the new Chinese-owned *Bonanza Hotel* (☎ 02-31032) offers good-sized rooms with air-con, TV and private hot-water showers for a reasonable US$15 per person. Better rooms with all of the foregoing plus fridge cost US$40 double.

In the same general area, the 103-room *Palace Hotel* (☎ 02-21422) on the eastern side of 80th St, between 32nd and 33rd Sts, caters to Wa, Kokang and Chinese business-people from the north and is the first hotel in Mandalay with a lift. All rooms come with TV, fridge, twin beds and hot water for US$25/35 single/double. Another Chinese-owned place, the smaller *Shanghai Hotel* (☎ 02-22490), at the corner of 35th and 83rd Sts, offers similar rooms in the US$30 to US$45 range. Seven blocks north on the same street, the six-storey *Hotel Sapphire* (☎ 02-24129, 27327), at 223 83rd St between 28th and 29th Sts, charges US$35 single/double for air-con, private bath and breakfast; a few economy rooms are also available for US$25.

South of the Air Mandalay office in two connected five-storey buildings on 82nd St, between 27th and 28th Sts, are the *New York* (☎ 02-28917) and *New Star* (☎ 02-27210). Air-con rooms with cold-water shower cost US$25 single/double at the New York, inexplicably US$5 more in the nearly identical New Star.

The *Dream Hotel* (☎ 02-26054), on 27th St between 80th and 81st Sts, presents a strong contrast between the busy outside world and a quiet interior. Run by an Indian family, the hotel offers a variety of lodgings, beginning with rooms with shared bath for US$12 single, US$20 double, superior rooms with attached bath for US$23/35 and larger suites for US$30 to US$35 single, US$41 to US$46 double, US$46 to US$69 triple. All rooms come with TV, air-con and fridge; both private and shared bath facilities feature hot water. The hotel has its own generator so the power supply is steady.

Several Chinese hotels convenient to both the train station and airport offer quality accommodation. Best of the bunch is the quiet and well-run *Tiger Hotel* (☎ 02-23234), a modern, five-storey inn well off the street at 628 80th St, between 37th and 38th Sts. All rooms feature air-con, minibar-fridge, satellite TV and private hot-water bath (yes, with bathtubs). Though it's the usual multi-storey box, the Tiger is a little classier than most and the rates are moderate at US$25/30 single/double for standard rooms, US$30/40 for larger rooms. Rates include breakfast but not tax and service. The hotel has its own generator.

The *Power Hotel* (☎ 02-52406), at 686 80th St between 39th and 40th Sts, tries to one-up the Tiger without success – it costs more and features a larger lobby but its service isn't as good. Two more hotels similar in facilities and rates are the *Boss Hotel* (☎ 02-22454) at 55 30th St between 74th and 75th Sts, and the *Silver Cloud Hotel* (☎ 02-27059) on the south-eastern corner of 29th and 73rd Sts.

Moving north to the Shan district around 23rd St, the new five-storey *Classic Hotel* (☎ 02-25635) at 59 23rd St, between 83rd and 84th Sts, offers comfortable air-con rooms with satellite TV and fridge for a very reasonable US$15 to US$20 single, US$25 to US$30 double including breakfast, tax and service.

Near the foot of Mandalay Hill, the modern, L-shaped *Yadanar Su Pon Hotel* (☎ 02-27054) features five large doubles with all the amenities for US$36. It's one of only three hotels in Mandalay so far with a swimming pool. Another new one with a pool and an out-of-the-way location is the two-storey, teak-panelled *Emerald Land Inn* (☎ 02-26990, 23578) on the southern side of 14th St, between 87th and 88th Sts. Eighteen well-kept air-con rooms in two buildings inside a walled, half-acre compound go for US$30/36 single/double. Along with a pool the Emerald Land features a pleasant outdoor dining area and offers free transport from the railway station and airport.

The sprawling, single-storey *Golden Express* (☎ 02-28767), at 43 9th St near the airport, was one of the first private hotels to open to foreigners in Mandalay. Large, tidy rooms with air-con and private hot-water showers cost US$25 single, US$32 double.

One of the last of the MHT-owned hotels, the *Mya Mandalar Hotel* (☎ 02-21283), sits a block east of Mandalay Fort on 27th St between 68th and 69th Sts. It may soon privatise, in which case facilities and rates will almost certainly change to compete with the local tourist market. For the moment, the hotel's spacious rooms cost a uniform US$36/42. All rooms have air-con and private hot-water showers; if you have a choice – which you should since the hotel is nearly always empty – ask for a downstairs room which tend to be nicer than those

upstairs. Behind the hotel are a swimming pool and dining room. In typical MHT fashion, the huge staff mostly lounge around the complex avoiding work.

The state-owned *Inwa (Ava) Inn* (☎ 02-27028) off 66th St near the eastern wall of Mandalay Fort has quiet but rather run-down bungalows for the same rates as the Mya Mandalar Hotel. Recent reports say the bar and restaurant are dismal.

The third in the remaining government trio, the Mandalay Hotel, has closed for renovations but will reopen as the *Mandalay Swan Hotel*, a joint venture between the Burmese government and a Singaporean company. The renovations have so far proceeded very slowly, so who knows when it will open.

At the time of writing, Mandalay boasts nothing that could truly be considered a 'top end' hotel but a few that would fit the category are under construction. Top of the list is a new *Sofitel* planned for the foot of Mandalay Hill, which when completed will be the most luxurious hotel in Upper Myanmar. At least 15 other hotels are planned or are under construction in the city, including the *Golden City Cooperative Hotel* near the edge of town on the way to the airport and the *Pacific Hotel* opposite the main railway station. We had a peek at the *Myit Phyar Ayer Hotel*, a new place one block south of Mandalay Fort on the western side of 80th St, while it was in the final construction phases. We only had a glimpse of the large lobby decorated with marionettes and classical musical instruments, but it looked promising. Rates are estimated to be in the US$40 to US$50 range.

Places to Eat

As in Yangon, the variety and quality of restaurants in Mandalay have multiplied with the recent economic development. Burmese, Shan and Chinese restaurants are particularly good, but the Indian food in Mandalay isn't quite up to Yangon's standards.

Burmese The long-running *Too Too*, on the

southern side of 27th St between 74th and 75th Sts, serves traditional Burmese food from pots lined up on a table, in typical Burmese fashion. It's a little more expensive than other restaurants of this type but the place is clean and the food is good. The similarly clean and reasonably priced *Shwe Let Yar Myanmar Fast Food* on 83rd St opposite the Modern Hotel serves traditional Burmese dishes and Burmese-style biryani.

Although it's oriented primarily towards visiting tourists, *Sakhantha* (☎ 02-21066) at 24 72nd St, between 27th and 28th Sts, offers a pleasant outdoor setting and consistently good if relatively pricey Burmese food. The long list of traditional Burmese thok, including the hard-to-find tamarind leaf salad, is particularly appetising. It's open 10 am to 9 pm daily. Another popular tourist venue is the *Pyigyimon Restaurant*, a replica of Yangon's Karaweik 'floating restaurant' at the south-eastern corner of the moat. There are as many Chinese as Burmese dishes on the menu. In the evening dinner is accompanied by a Burmese puppet show put on by Mandalay Marionettes.

Along the eastern side of 80th St between 28th and 30th Sts, many food stalls open up at night, selling everything from mohinga and chicken biryani to moonshine (ayet piu) and tea. Food is generally quite tasty here and you'll meet interesting people – it's less insular than most indoor restaurants in town.

Shan The best Shan restaurants are found in the vicinity of 23rd St west of the moat. The popular *Lashio Lay Restaurant*, next to the Classic Hotel on 23rd St between 83rd and 84th Sts, offers a large array of spicy Shan dishes which changes on a daily basis and usually includes four or five vegetarian dishes. The food is very good and it's easy enough to point out the dishes that look most appetising; virtually no English is spoken. There are at least four other Shan places in the immediate vicinity, including the *Lashio Gyi* opposite, and the *Bangkok* and *Taunggyi* on the same side of the street.

Thai Yai Restaurant, on the eastern side of 84th St south of 23rd St, serves Shan and

Thai dishes in a slightly nicer than average dining room. Among the house specialities are Thai-style roast chicken, papaya salad, noodles and chicken rice. It's open 6 am to 10 pm, later than most of the other Shan places.

Lashio Lay, Taunggyi and Thai Yai each serve delicious Shan khauk swe (spicy rice noodles) in the morning; this makes a nice change from teashop fare or the standard toast-and-egg breakfasts served at the guest houses and hotels. *Pan Cherry Restaurant*, on the north-eastern corner of 25th and 83rd Sts near the Royal Guest House, also makes decent Shan khauk swe.

Chinese There's quite a selection of Chinese eating places on 83rd St, between 26th and 25th Sts, not far from Zegyo Market. Here you'll find the popular *Mann Restaurant* – one of the city's better Chinese eateries. The nearby *Min Min*, on 83rd St between 26th and 27th Sts, has Chinese Muslim food – it's reasonably cheap, and the food is quite OK. A similar Chinese Muslim place, *Chin Shin*, on the eastern side of 82nd St between 28th and 29th Sts, serves curries, noodles, duck and Yunnan noodles.

Moving upmarket, the posh *Honey Garden Restaurant* (☎ 02-24098), at the corner of 70th and 29th Sts, offers superb service and a long list of well-prepared Chinese dishes (and a few Burmese ones) in outdoor dining areas. It's open 9 am to 10 pm.

Rainbow Restaurant, at the north-western corner of 23rd and 84th Sts, is a three-storey affair with a bakery on the bottom floor, an indoor dining room on the middle floor and an open-air dining area on the top floor. Although the setting is nice and it's clean enough, compared with the foregoing the Chinese food here is rather mediocre and the service is slow.

On the east rooftop of Zegyo Market, the *Ambassador Restaurant* features an extensive Chinese banquet-style menu with Burmese singing and dancing. The *Grand Restaurant* on the west rooftop is similar.

There are many small Chinese restaurants along 80th St in Chinatown, most open till 9 or 10 pm – late for Mandalay. *Shwe Wah*, a grubby-looking little restaurant on 80th St between 32nd and 33rd Sts, next door to the Palace Hotel, attracts many Wa and Kokang customers and serves a variety of southern Chinese and Shan dishes.

Not far away, the Chinese *Htaw Yin* restaurant at 396 81st St near 31st St is not only good but it also looks more hygienic. Another string of basic Chinese eateries is found along 29th St between 83rd and 84th Sts and along 30th St between 70th and 76th Sts.

Indian & Vegetarian Strictly vegetarian – though not strictly Indian – *Marie-Min Vegetarian Restaurant*, on 27th St between 74th and 75th Sts, is a godsend to many travellers. Owned and operated by an Indian Catholic family, Marie-Min serves delicious chapatis, papadums, curries, pumpkin soup and eggplant dip, plus such non-Indian delights as strawberry lassis (yoghurt shakes), muesli, guacamole, hash-brown potatoes, pancakes and various Western-style breakfasts (served all day). The menu, written in eight languages, is priced quite reasonably, with most dishes costing under K100; this place is less expensive than many Chinese restaurants in town. On Christmas Eve the devout family owners arrange special candlelight dinners accompanied by live Burmese music.

More traditional Indian places can be found near the Hindu and Sikh temples and the Central Mosque around the intersection of 81st and 26th Sts. A good find amongst these is the *Punjab Food House* on 80th St near 27th St. This friendly, Sikh-run curry shop serves very tasty chapatis, rice and vegetarian curries. Sometimes in the morning they also have aloo puri (fried flatbread with potato curry), though of late the price of potatoes in Upper Myanmar has kept this popular breakfast dish off most Indian menus in town. It's open from 8.30 am to 7.30 pm.

Across the street from Punjab House, next to the Nepali temple, is the slightly larger *Everest Restaurant*, with a tasty 'morning nasta' of chapati with vegetables, dosai and aloo puri on occasion. Rice and vegetable curry is served for lunch and dinner. It's open from 7 am to 7 pm. *Laksmi Restaurant* opposite the Hotel Venus on 28th St isn't bad for curries and rice.

The very basic *Devi Indian Restaurant* (no English sign), opposite the Arya Samaj temple on the eastern side of 82nd St between 25th and 26th Sts, does puri and dosai 6 to 8 am, rice and curries 10 am to 9 pm. Though it's basically just a grubby hole-in-the-wall place, this may be the only Indian eatery in town that serves beer (also tea and soft drinks).

Several shops around town serve biryani, a mixture of rice and spices usually served with roast chicken. *Thinn Biryani*, on the southern side of 28th St between 81st and 82nd Sts, serves both vegetarian and chicken biryani, plus rich ohn htamin (coconut rice). Look for the sign out front that says, 'Taste of Thinn will make you win; try Thinn's speciality, delicious Persian biryani in the heart of Mandalay City'. It's open 5 am to 10 pm.

Another reliable biryani shop, *May Myo Biryani*, has two branches, one on the northern side of 25th St between 83rd and 84th Sts, the other opposite Hotel Sapphire on 83rd St between 28th and 29th Sts; only the latter has an English sign. May Myo is open 10 am to 10 pm.

Teashops & Cafes Although Mandalay is absolutely jammed with teashops, two stand out from the pack. *Shwe Pyi Moe*, on 25th St between 80th and 81st (look for the thick phalange of bicycles parked out front), serves probably the best quality Burmese tea in town and is open 5 am to 5 pm. The selection of snacks leans toward Chinese, with ei kyar kway (Chinese you-tiao) a house speciality. *Minn Thi Ha*, at 72nd and 28th Sts, is of similar high quality and also very popular; it's open 5 am to 4 pm.

Shells Cafe, on the northern side of 26th St between 81st and 82nd Sts, serves the best selection of European, Chinese and Burmese pastries in town along with tea, coffee and soft drinks. It's open 6 am to 6 pm daily.

MANDALAY

MANDALAY

Burmese Teashops

At all times of day you'll see Burmese sitting in teashops where the tea flows freely and the assorted pastries are very inexpensive. Teashops are an important social institution in Myanmar, serving as meeting places for friends, family and business associates as well as a source of inexpensive nutrition and caffeine. The shops come in all shapes and sizes, indoor and outdoor, morning-oriented and evening-oriented. The morning teashops are typically open from 5 am to 5 pm and generally serve the best quality tea; many will also serve Burmese-style coffee. Evening teashops open around 4 or 5 pm and stay open till 11 pm or later – even all night in some places.

The relative tea quality can vary dramatically from one teashop to the next. The best use only fresh, first-quality Indian-style tea for every brewing cycle, while the worst recycle tea leaves until the flavour and colour are gone – to be replaced by ground tamarind and other natural flavour enhancers. The price differences between the good and the bad differ by only K1 or K2 per cup so it's usually worth seeking out the top-quality places – ask around, everyone knows the superior ones. In a city of 12 teashops, for example, two will stand out clearly as the best. If Burmese tea has received a bad international press in the past, it most likely comes from the low quality brews served in the lower class teashops. At a good place the tea can be very drinkable.

Most teashop servers know the English word 'tea' if nothing else, but if you want to order in Burmese ask for *laphet yei*, literally 'tea water'. Burmese tea is always served with milk and sugar. The shops will lighten up on the sugar if you say *cho bok* ('less sweet') or conversely add more if you say *kyauk padaung* (the name of a famous sugarpalm-growing region near Bagan).

Many tea-drinkers pour hot tea from the cup into the saucer and sip from the latter because it cools faster. Some Burmese add a dash of salt to their tea, a legacy perhaps of their Tibetan origins. A thermos of Chinese tea or *ahkayei* (also known as *laphet yei chan*) sits on every table and is drunk as a 'chaser' after finishing a cup or two of the Burmese-style milk tea. Don't remove the steel wool plug stuffed into the top of the thermos – it's meant to filter the tea leaves while pouring.

Tea Snacks

A good deal more than tea is available in a Burmese teashop. Cigarettes and cigars can be purchased singly, along with an array of snacks. Teashop menus fall into two main types, depending on whether they're mostly Chinese or Indian-influenced. A Chinese-style place typically offers *bao-sii* (steamed buns), *kaw pyant sein* (fried eggrolls) and *ei kyar kway* (long, deep-fried pastries known as *youtiao* in China).

An Indian-style teashop – slightly more common that the Chinese-style – typically serves *samosa* (fried triangular-shaped pastries stuffed with vegetables) and *palata* (Indian *paratha* or fried flatbread). The latter sounds like 'bladder' in Burmese pronunciation; a tasty variation is palata filled with mashed banana (ask for 'banana bladder'!). Another popular variation called *bei palata* is stuffed with pigeon peas. Some Indian-style teashops also offer *nam-bya*, a baked, unleavened bread similar to Indian *nan*, often served with a spicy split-pea dip.

Other more Burmese snacks that may be available at a teashop include *hsi htamin*, turmeric-coloured sticky rice topped with sesame seeds and shredded coconut; *kauk hnyin bauk*, sticky rice with salted and mildly spiced pigeon peas; *kua pyant leik*, deep-fried Burmese egg rolls stuffed with potatoes and vegetables; and *sanwin makein*, literally 'turmeric unavoidable', a packet of sweetened sticky rice and banana hunks steamed in banana leaves. Some urban teashops also sell hamburgers, which are gaining popularity as a breakfast food in Myanmar. ∎

European, Snacks, Ice Cream & Beer The *Barman Beer Bar* (☎ 02-25623), known as *BBB*, on the western side of 76th St between 26th and 27th Sts, offers an extensive menu of European, Burmese, Indian and Chinese dishes served in an air-con dining room furnished in rattan. Indian and European breakfasts cost K80, meat dishes K300, grilled lobster K600; plentiful set dinners cost K250. Other menu items include sandwiches, milk shakes and fruit juices. BBB is open 7 am to 11 pm daily.

Across the road from Mann Restaurant at 176 83rd St there's the very popular *Nylon Ice Cream Bar* – it's a strange name (actually Nai Lon), but the ice cream is excellent and seems to be safe. In the evening you can sit out at the pavement tables and try large servings of strawberry, pineapple or orange ice cream for just a few kyat. *Golden Land Cold Drink*, opposite the Shwe Wah Restaurant on 80th St, is owned by the same family as Nylon but some report the ice cream is better here. Golden Land also does delicious lassis. Friendly *Monterey Cold Drinks*, at 314 81st St between 26th and 27th Sts, is also quite popular.

Texas Cold Snack Bar, a block north of the Palace Hotel, is an 'old West' style place with swinging saloon doors. In addition to beer and soft drinks, this unlikely-looking spot serves burgers (K55) and steak (K200).

At Myainghaywun Park, inside Mandalay Fort, an informal outdoor cafe serves cheap draught beer from the Mandalay Brewery. Mandalay draught is also available at a bar on 26th St, between 83rd and 84th Sts, near Zegyo Market. At either place a bottle of fresh draught costs K45.

Towards the end of the dry season Mandalay becomes a very dusty, thirsty place. All over town there are sugar-cane vendors with their big, heavy crushing wheels ready to fix you a glass of iced sugar-cane juice (with a dash of lime). It's very refreshing and seems to be fairly safe. In season there are strawberry vendors around town; take a basket to one of the ice-cream bars and try strawberries and ice cream!

Entertainment

Marionette Theatre *Mandalay Marionettes and Culture Show* (☎ 02-24581), on 66th St between 26th and 27th Sts, is a small theatre where marionette shows, music and dancing are performed nightly at 8.30 pm. The same company puts on similar performances at the *Pyigyimon Restaurant* earlier in the evening at 7 pm. The show lasts around an hour and features selections from the *zat pwe* and *yama pwe* traditions. This includes colourful marionette dances that represent the zawgyi (immortal alchemist), naga (serpent), garuda and ogre figures from Burmese mythology. The puppetmasters are former students of the famous master Shewi-bo U Tin, who passed away some time ago. Preceding the marionette theatre are short performances of traditional music played on the Burmese harp and pattala (xylophone). The admission fee seems to fluctuate between K200 and K400 per person depending on the number of tourists in town. Trishaw drivers often bad-mouth the show or say it's closed because the theatre owners refuse to pay commissions. Handmade marionettes are available for sale.

An outdoor theatre in the compound of the *Natural Inn* on 23rd St, between 80th and 81st Sts, offers similar marionette, music and dance performances during the tourist season for an admission fee of US$5 per person.

Folk & Classical Pwe If you'd like to delve a little deeper into the art of the Burmese pwe, pay a visit to the *Moustache Brothers* on 39th St between 80th and 81st Sts. One of several pwe troupes headquartered in this district, brothers Par Par Lay and Lu Maw have opened their house to visitors interested in learning more about Burmese dance, comedy, music and puppetry. The Moustache Brothers' ensemble is somewhat unusual in that they use nothing but traditional instruments in their performances. Lu Maw, the comedian of the pair, speaks fair English and is very knowledgeable about the history of Burmese dance-drama and comedy. Par Par Lay is one of the few pwe performers who still does the full zawgyi dance, which he will gladly perform for visitors. If you give them advance notice, the brothers and their families will prepare a Burmese meal and perform for a small group in return for donations afterwards. The brothers also make and sell Burmese marionettes.

All of the pwe troupes in this area practice their craft during the months of June and July from 10 am to 4 pm daily. Visitors are welcome to wander from house to house and watch for free. During other times of year the troupes intermittently travel to perform at paya festivals, weddings, novitiations, housewarming rituals, monk's funerals and monastic robe-offering ceremonies.

Abbreviated examples of Burmese classical music and dance are performed at the *Grand* and *Ambassador* restaurants on the west and east rooftops of Zegyo Market.

Burmese Kickboxing You can watch Burmese kickboxing at a small training facility on 76th St between 27th and 28th Sts. If you're interested in attending a full-fledged match, this is the place to find out where and when the next one will be held in the Mandalay area. As in most places in Myanmar, matches most commonly take place at paya festivals.

Things to Buy
Markets Zegyo Market – a redundant term since 'Zegyo' *(zei gyo)* means 'Central Market' – encompasses two large buildings on 84th St; one between 26th and 27th Sts, the other between 27th and 28th Sts. You can find just about anything made in Myanmar here, from everyday consumer goods to jewellery and fine fabrics. Several markets have sprung in the surrounding area, including the large open-air Kaingdan Market a couple of streets west of Zegyo which specialises in fresh produce and jaggery. A night market which extends southwards from the intersection of 84th and 27th Sts offers all kinds foods, audio tapes and clothing.

In Mandalay's unofficial Chinatown, there's a daily market that sets up along each street between 29th and 33rd Sts, running east of 80th St and west of the railway. Produce and household goods are cheaper here than anywhere else in Mandalay.

Arts & Crafts Mandalay is a major crafts centre and you can get some really good bargains if you know what you're looking for. There are many little shops in the eastern part of the city near the Mya Mandalar and Mandalay Swan hotels selling a mixture of gems, carvings, silk, *kalaga* tapestries and other crafts. If you enter without a tout (most of the younger trishaw or horsecart drivers are into this), you'll get better deals than with a tout, as they are usually paid high commissions.

Among the better shops is Mann Swe Gon on 27th St between 72nd and 73rd Sts. The proprietors maintain a particularly good selection of kalaga tapestries as well as other handicrafts. Another decent one is Sein Win Myint, which claims to be the oldest crafts shop in town. It's a small place down an alley between 83rd and 84th Sts, and between 26th and 27th Sts. Handicrafts are also available at a few vendor stalls in Zegyo Market. Keep in mind that some of the items sold at these shops aren't legally supposed to be taken out of the country – older kalagas, *parabaiks* (folding manuscripts), *kamawas* (lacquered scriptures), gems, jade and any authentic antiques.

The very plush Yadanapura Art Centre, a government enterprise at the western end of 78th St toward the airport, purveys a high-quality selection of handicrafts and jewellery. As long as you keep the receipt, you'll be able to take any purchase from this shop out of the country.

If you have a dilapidated stupa in need of refurbishing, then head for the western exit of the Mahamuni – here you will find workshops manufacturing all sorts of temple paraphernalia. If the *hti* has toppled from the top of your stupa then this is the place to come for a new one.

Mandalay's goldleaf makers are concentrated in the south-east of the city, near the intersection of 35th and 78th Sts. Sheets of gold are beaten into gossamer-thin pieces which are cut into squares and sold in packets to devotees to use for gilding images or even complete stupas. The typical goldleaf square measures just .000127 cm, thinner than ink on the printed page. Gilding a Buddha image or a stupa with goldleaf brings great credit to the gilder, so there is a steady growth of goldleaf on many images in Myanmar. Gold-leaf stickers cost just a few kyat. Other crafts you may be able to see around Mandalay include silk weaving and silversmithing.

You can visit a bamboo paper factory on 80th St between 36th and 37th Sts. Here the artisans make fans of paper and bamboo for weddings and banquets.

Precious Stones & Sculpture Kyawzu and Minthazu, two villages attached to the urban sprawl of southern Mandalay, specialise in the cutting, polishing and carving of jade. Just north of there, outdoor jade markets meet daily in several spots along 86th St. The best quality jade is generally purveyed during the late morning (10 am to 1 pm) at the intersection of 38th and 86th Sts, where you'll see throngs of Burmese standing and squatting on the roadside or sitting in teashops, poring over red, white and green chunks laid out on empty rice sacks. Both rough and polished pieces, some carved, can be purchased here. None of the trade, of course is 'government approved'. While most of the jade seen here is genuine, not all is of high quality. Beware of vendors selling jade 'boulders' smuggled in from the Kachin State. Some are fakes with thin sheets of jade peering through the brown outer 'skin'; the inside may contain cement or worthless stone.

A street close by the Mahamuni Paya has a whole series of stone-carvers' workshops. Here Buddha images of all sizes are hewn from solid stone slabs. The best stone and marble cutters are found at the corner of 45th and 84th Sts. Bronze foundries and wood-carving workshops are clustered off Aung San St in the Tampawadi Quarter, south of Mahamuni. Bells and gongs are hand-beaten

at workshops near the Myohaung railway station (take pickup No 7).

Film & Photographic Supplies Winner Colour Lab, just north of the Air Mandalay office on 82nd St, has good prices on film and processing. The shop does a fair job on colour prints, and stocks some slide films. Similar photographic shops can be found nearby.

Getting There & Away
For information on travel between Mandalay and Bagan or Mandalay and Taunggyi, see the Bagan or Inle Lake sections in the relevant chapters. From Yangon you can fly, bus or rail 'up-country'.

Air Both Myanma Airways and Air Mandalay fly daily to Mandalay from Yangon. The former has the lowest fares, US$90 by F-27 turboprop, US$100 in an F-28 jet; the flights take about 1½ hours by F-27 and about an hour by F-28. Some of the F-27 flights stop in Bagan first, which adds another half hour to flying time. The Myanma Airways office (☎ 02-22590) is on 81st St between 25th and 26th Sts.

Flights aboard Air Mandalay's better-equipped, safer and more pleasant ATR-72s cost US$139 each way; standby fares cost US$10 less. Unlike Myanma Airways, which accepts only US dollars cash or Foreign Exchange Certificates in payment for tickets, Air Mandalay accepts major credit cards. Air Mandalay flights also tend to depart and arrive more punctually than those of Myanma Airways, so if your schedule is tight it might be worth paying the difference. The Air Mandalay office (☎ 02-27439) is on 82nd St, between 26th and 27th Sts.

A private taxi from Mandalay's airport to anywhere in the city costs K300. Bus Nos 10 and 12 also head downtown from the airport for K5 per person.

Bus Kipling never actually took the 'road to Mandalay', but now you can. Private buses from Yangon's Highway Bus Centre range in

MANDALAY

price from K500 to K1200 for a one-way fare.

The better air-con express bus services between Mandalay and Yangon are operated by Trade Express (☎ 02-27092) at 200 83rd, between 27th and 28th Sts, opposite the Modern Hotel; Myanmar Arrow Express (☎ 02-23404) at 32nd and 83rd Sts; and Rainbow Express (☎ 02-28809) at 262B 29th St between 82nd and 83rd Sts. Skyline and Trade also both have offices at Mandalay's main bus centre at the corner of 26th and 82nd Sts. For fares, departure times and trip durations, see the Getting There & Away section in the Yangon chapter.

For most other destinations outside Mandalay, the usual mode of transport is Japanese pickup truck. Several companies run pickups to Bagan, including Bagan Express at the corner of 82nd and 32nd Sts. This company usually charges foreigners K250, sometimes more, and has a reputation for rude service. A better-reputed company called Nyaung U Mann runs similar pickups from the main bus centre for K200. If you want to ride at the front of the cab, figure on paying double.

Pickups to Amarapura, Ava and Sagaing leave from a stand on 84th St near the corner of 29th St for K5 each. For Pyin U Lwin there are several places where you can hop a pickup, the first choice being the main bus centre, where the fare is K40 in the back, K100 in the front. Some companies also operate pickups to Pyin U Lwin from the southern side of 27th St near the corner of 83rd St and from the northern side of 25th St near the corner of 83rd St. In general it's less of a hassle just to show up at the main bus centre; the money collectors there seem less inclined to exact a 'foreigner tax', perhaps because there's more of a crowd watching.

For Monywa, private pickups leave from the northern side of 27th St near the corner of 83rd St, cost K45 and take three to four hours.

Private pickups offering reserved seats to Nyaungshwe (Yaunghwe) are available for US$10 from 23rd St near the Classic Hotel. If you feel like roughing it, you can catch a government bus to Taunggyi for K100 by large bus or for K300 by ordinary pickup from the bus centre. The trip takes at least seven hours.

From the main bus centre, buses to Lashio cost K100 for the full-day trip. For K400 you can get a nicer pickup from 23rd St, just north of Rainbow Restaurant. This is also the place to find transport to Mu-se on the Chinese border, although for the latter you'll probably need to show a permit.

Other departures from the main bus centre at the corner of 26th and 82nd Sts include Meiktila (K75, three times daily, 4½ hours), Monywa (K45, three times daily, 3½ hours), Kyauk Padaung (K150, twice daily, five hours), Shwebo (K45 to K60, three times daily, three hours) Pyinmana (K165, once daily, seven hours), Taungoo (K200, once daily, 11½ hours), Bago (K275, once daily, 14-15 hours).

Train The old British-designed Mandalay Railway Station is being razed and a new seven-storey complex, including two floors devoted to a hotel, will be built just south along the same stretch of track. While construction is going on, passengers will use the Mann Yadanabon Station (next to the present station) and Myohaung Station farther south.

Although there are a number of trains each day between Yangon and Mandalay, you should only consider the day or night expresses since the other trains represent everything that can be wrong with Burmese rail travel – slow, crowded, uncomfortable and so on. Additionally, it's possible to reserve a seat on the express services, and on these special 'impress the tourists services' you really do get a seat – not a half or a third of a seat. First class even has reclining seats and is quite comfortable. Sleepers are available but hard to reserve.

Trains leave both ends at the same time and should arrive at the same time. They are generally punctual, although you should reserve your seat as early as possible. Get an excellent chicken biryani wrapped in a banana leaf for lunch at one of the stations on the way or, if you take the night train, on the Yangon platform. Meals in the dining car, which is often packed, aren't bad; Mandalay Beer is available.

Upon arrival in Mandalay you may be given a ticket for 'free transport' to your hotel, endorsed by Myanma Railways. Although this does entitle you to a free ride to the hotel or guest house of your choice, it means Myanma Railways takes a K200 commission from the place you stay. As with any kind of tout/commission system, this means they may try to steer you away from places that don't pay commissions.

Myanma Railways operates daily trains from Mandalay to Myitkyina, Monywa and Lashio; see the Getting There & Away sections in the appropriate chapters for details. To purchase a ticket to Myitkyina you'll probably need to show a travel permit.

For schedule and fare information for the trains to and from Yangon, see the Getting Around chapter at the start of this book.

Car & Motorbike Cars can be rented through a number of sources, including most hotels and guest houses, and at Win Win Transport Services (☎ 02-21070) at 25 Bayintnaung Rd. Drivers are included in the deal.

Although motorcycle rental hasn't really caught on yet in Mandalay, you may be able to rent a bike at one of the following places: Astrea Grand (☎ 02-27679), on 35 St between 82nd and 83rd Sts; Honda Motorcycles (☎ 02-23491), 256 29th St between 82nd and 83rd Sts; or Yamaha (☎ 02-24243), 216 27th St between 82nd and 83rd Sts.

Boat The Inland Water Transport office (☎ 02-21144, 21467) is located at the Gawwein Jetty, at the western end of 35th St (Yangyiaung Rd). For information on ferries to Bagan or Pyay (Prome), see the appropriate Getting There & Away sections in the Bagan and Pyay sections.

Getting Around

Bus Mandalay's buses are virtually always crowded, particularly during the 7 to 9 am and 4 to 5 pm 'rush hours'. Somehow it feels rather strange to be talking about a rush hour

in Myanmar. The buses are also surprisingly friendly – so if that's more important to you than smooth comfort, you'll probably quite enjoy bussing around Mandalay. Some of the useful services include:

From Mahamuni Paya to Zegyo Market and Kuthodaw Paya – blue bus No 1 (つ)
To Gawwein Jetty, railway station and airport – blue bus No 2 ( ))
To Mandalay Hill from the clock tower and Zegyo Market – bus No 4 (၄)
Between Yankin Hill, Zegyo Market and the boat pier to Mingun – white bus No 5 (၅)
To the other side of Mandalay Hill, to the Institute of Indigenous Medicine – bus No 7 (?)
Via Setkyathiha Paya, Mahamuni Paya and Amarapura to Ava; starts from the corner of 27th St and 84th St – red or black bus No 8 (၈)
To U Bein's Bridge – yellow bus No 8 (၈)
Mandalay Hill to south of the city and airport – red bus No 12 (၁၂)
Mahamuni Paya to Mandalay Hill through Mandalay Fort – red and yellow 'Mann Sit Thi' bus

Taxi There are few car taxis in Mandalay; for the most part you take Japanese pickups or small three or four-wheeled Mazdas. Around Zegyo Market you'll find hordes of three and four-wheelers. They operate within the city for around K50 to K75 per trip. The level of English among most drivers is virtually nil; our experience is that it's easier for non-Burmese speakers to take a little time to make sense of the city bus system than it is to try and work out your destination with a Mazda taxi driver. It helps if you have the address of the place you're going written in Burmese.

There are usually a few car taxis waiting at the airport; these cost a standard K300 for the whole vehicle into town. Jeeps are also occasionally available, although there are fewer than in previous years.

It's possible to hire cars, jeeps or pickups by the day for tours around Mandalay. Count on around K1500 to K2000 for a trip to Amarapura and Sagaing that includes an English-speaking guide; the trucks will take up to eight people so it needn't be expensive.

Trishaw & Horsecart The familiar back-to-back trishaws are the usual round-the-town transport. Count on K25 for a short ride in a trishaw, K40 for a longer one – say, from the Mya Mandalar Hotel to Zegyo Market. Figure on K300 a day per trishaw for all-day sightseeing in the central part of the city, K500 if you include both Mahamuni Paya and Mandalay Hill toward the northern and southern ends of the city. You must bargain for your fare, whether by the trip, by the hour or by the day.

Trishaws can easily be flagged down on the street just about anywhere. Many drivers tend to hang out near the popular guest houses; at the time of writing this meant the Royal Guest House and Sabai Phyu Guest House but the trend could change tomorrow. Some of the trishaw drivers in these areas speak English or French. Those with language skills are usually keen to get you into souvenir or handicraft shops, since the shop owners will pay them a fee for every head they bring in the door. This goes for restaurants and other guest houses as well. If you're just trying to get from A to B it's better to flag down a trishaw driver on the street.

Horsecarts will take up to four passengers and cost double the fare of a trishaw, but you can hire one all day for sightseeing for K500. They only operate on the outskirts of town and along certain main thoroughfares in the city though – they're perhaps best for seeing the Mandalay Hill area.

Bicycle There are several places downtown where you can rent bicycles, including a couple of places near the Royal Guest House on 25th St and another place opposite the Mann Restaurant on 83rd St. The average cost is K25 to K35 per hour or K100 to K150 per day, depending on the bike's condition. If you're looking for cycle parts and accessories, try Ye Yint in Zegyo Market (No 1 Myout Bet Tait Tan).

Walking Mandalay is a surprisingly sprawling place. Think three times before setting out on a little stroll around the fort walls or out to Mandalay Hill. The downtown area is easily traversed on foot, however.

JOE CUMMINGS

JOE CUMMINGS

BERNARD NAPTHINE

JOE CUMMINGS

Around Mandalay

Top Left: The royal palace at Mandalay Fort
Top Right: Pyin U Lwin's delightfully coloured mosque
Bottom Left: Rickety U Bein's Bridge, near Amarapura
Bottom Right: Pyin U Lwin's pony wagons, reminiscent of bygone times

BERNARD NAPTHINE

BERNARD NAPTHINE

BERNARD NAPTHINE

Around Mandalay
Top: The massive Mingun Paya
Bottom Left: Marionette puppet crafted in Pyin U Lwin
Bottom Right: The impressive falls of Anisakan

Around Mandalay

The area around Mandalay has a number of attractions well worth visiting. The four 'deserted cities' (Amarapura, Ava, Sagaing and Mingun) are all within easy day-tripping distance, as is the atmospheric old 'hill station' of Pyin U Lwin (Maymyo). Though not as historic, Monywa to the north-west is one of Myanmar's most typically Burmese cities, though it receives few tourists.

Ancient Cities

After the fall of Bagan (Pagan), right up to when the third and last Anglo-Burmese war reached its final (and, for the Burmese, disastrous) conclusion in 1885, the capital of one of Myanmar's kingdoms stood in or close to Mandalay. Perhaps it's part of the Buddhist belief in the temporary nature of life, but many kings developed an overpowering urge to start their reign with a new capital and a new palace. Thus the capital seemed to play musical chairs around the countryside.

Additionally, masonry or brick construction was reserved almost solely for religious buildings. The palaces may have been magnificent and extensive, but they were made of wood. When the shift was made to a new capital the wooden palace buildings were often dismantled and taken along. When the royal entourage departed, the mighty cities soon reverted to farming villages – with neglected stupas picturesquely dotting the fields.

In the chaos after the fall of Bagan it was Sagaing that first rose to power in the early 14th century, but in 1364 it was succeeded by Ava. Not until 1760 was the capital shifted back across the river to Sagaing, where it remained for just four years. Ava regained its pre-eminent position only from 1764 to 1783, after which time Amarapura became the capital. In 1823 Ava was again the capital, but following the terrible earthquake of

Highlights
- Day trips to the ancient royal capitals of Ava, Amarapura and Sagaing
- Ferry rides along the Ayeyarwady to the massive Mingun Paya
- Scenic colonial hill-station of Pyin U Lwin
- Ruby capital of Myanmar at Mogok

1838, which caused great damage to all these cities, the capital was moved back to Amarapura in 1841. Amarapura was again capital for only a short period and in 1860 the seat of power was transferred to Mandalay, where it remained until the British finished their conquest of Myanmar 25 years later.

Three of the ancient cities are south of Mandalay. Amarapura and Ava are on the eastern (Mandalay) side of the Ayeyarwady (Irrawaddy), while Sagaing lies to the west of the river but is easily reached by the long Ava Bridge. Mingun, which was never a capital, is on the western bank of the Ayeyarwady to the north of Mandalay. It's easily reached by frequent riverboats from Mandalay.

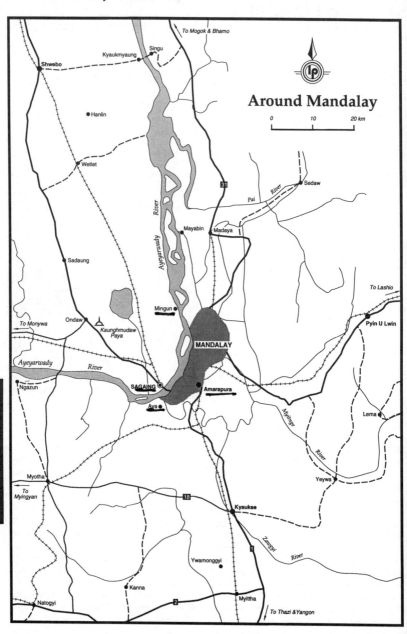

Don't try to do all the cities in one day. It's best to devote a half day each to Sagaing and Mingun; Amarapura and Ava can be seen together on a separate day.

The Last Kings

Alaungpaya founded the last dynasty (the Konbaung dynasty) of Burmese kings in 1752. It ended only 133 years later when King Thibaw Min was deposed by the British and exiled to India. Two of the kings, Hsinbyushin and Bodawpaya, were Alaungpaya's sons.

The kings were:

Alaungpaya	1752-1760
Naungdawgyi	1760-1763
Hsinbyushin	1763-1776
Singu Min	1776-1782
Bodawpaya	1782-1819
Bagyidaw	1819-1837
Tharawaddy Min	1837-1846
Pagan Min	1846-1853
Mindon Min	1853-1878
Thibaw Min	1878-1885

AMARAPURA အမရပုရ

Situated 11 km south of Mandalay, the modern town of Amarapura is often referred to as Taungmyo, 'the Southern City', to distinguish it from Mandalay, the northern city. The old name means 'City of Immortality', but Amarapura's period as capital was brief. Amarapura was founded by Bodawpaya as his new capital in 1783, soon after he ascended the throne, but in 1823 Bagyidaw moved his court back to Ava. In 1841 Amarapura again became the capital but in 1857 Mindon Min decided to make Mandalay the capital and the changeover was completed in 1860. Amarapura was also the site for the first British embassy in Myanmar in 1795.

Today little remains of the old Amarapura palace area, although there are several interesting sites to be seen. They are widely scattered, so if you don't have transport, allow enough time and energy for walking. The city walls were torn down to make quarry material for railway lines and roads,

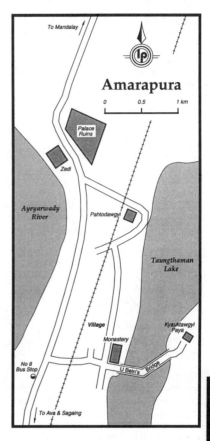

while most of the wooden palace buildings were dismantled and taken to the new palace in Mandalay.

Pahtodawgyi

Built by King Bagyidaw in 1820, this well-preserved paya stood outside the old city walls. The lower terraces have marble slabs illustrating *jataka* scenes from the Buddha's life. There's a fine view over the surrounding countryside from the upper terrace. An inscription stone within the temple precincts details the history of the monument's construction.

Palace Ruins

Little remains of the old Amarapura palace, but you can find two masonry buildings – the treasury building and the old watch tower in its old grounds. King Bagyidaw and King Bodawpaya were both buried here and their tombs also remain. The corner stupas still stand at the four corners of the once square city.

Bagaya Kyaung

Just out of town on the road to Sagaing stands one of Myanmar's largest and most active wooden monasteries, dating to the mid-19th century. King Mindon Min, Ava's penultimate king, was educated here and a full restoration of the older structures is currently underway. Over 400 Buddha statues, many rare works of art, are displayed on the ground floor of the monastery library. You'll find the monastery on the left side of the road as it forks right at Amarapura (the left fork goes to U Bein's Bridge); look for a Bagan-style *pahto* (a hollow, rectangular paya).

U Bein's Bridge

South of Pahtodawgyi, the shallow Taungthaman Lake is crossed by a long and rickety teak bridge. During the dry season the bridge crosses dry land. U Bein was the 'mayor' at the time of the shift from Ava, and he wisely salvaged material from the deserted Ava Palace to build this 1.2 km-long footbridge. It has stood the test of time for two centuries and remains the longest teak span in the world.

At the start of the bridge there's a monastery where the monks' quarters are designed to look like a row of paddle steamers. There is also a new, and rather ugly, temple with a gigantic seated Buddha. Near the bridge is a cluster of tables where you can take tea, beer and snacks. The best times to visit the bridge are just after sunrise or just before sunset, when hundreds of villagers commute by foot or bicycle back and forth across the bridge.

Kyauktawgyi Paya

If you stroll across the bridge (there are fine views across the lake to Pahtodawgyi and rest places where you can shelter from the sun) you'll come to Kyauktawgyi Paya. Constructed in 1847 by King Pagan Min, it is said to have been modelled on the larger Ananda Temple at Bagan, but it has the look of a Tibetan or Nepali temple, with its five-tiered roof.

While the paya does not have the perfectly vaulted roofs or the finer decorations of the original, it does have an excellent seated Buddha image and interesting and well-preserved frescoes in the four entrance porches. Religious buildings, zodiac charts and scenes from everyday life are all illustrated in the frescoes. You can even find some suspiciously English-looking figures in the crowds – they were beginning to make their presence felt at the time of the temple's construction. In 1979 the Kyauktawgyi was repainted in a most un-Burmese-looking shade of baby blue.

U Bein's Bridge in Amarapura, built of teak from Ava Palace

The atmosphere around Kyauktawgyi is very peaceful and shady, and this is a good place to be at sunset when people, bicycles and bullock carts pass on their way back from a day's work in the fields surrounding the shrine. There are several smaller overgrown stupas in the vicinity, including a unique 'honeycomb'-shaped stupa covered with Buddha niches. Lay people come here to practise meditation away from the worldly distractions of Mandalay. There are a couple of traditional outdoor teashops where those with time on their hands sit on woven mats around low tables, drinking small pots of Chinese tea and eating snacks such as fried gourd, soy cake and fried lentil balls dipped in a tasty tamarind sauce.

Other Attractions

On the bank of the Ayeyarwady, across from Amarapura, stand two 12th-century *zedis* (stupas) – the **Shwe Kyetyet** and the **Shwe Kyetkya** – which were built by a king of Bagan. Amarapura also has a **Chinese joss house**; when the decision was made to shift to Mandalay, the Chinese traders preferred to remain.

Amarapura is noted for silk and cotton weaving, and there are reportedly around 40,000 Siamese-style, four-heddle looms in the area. As you wander through the wooden buildings of the modern town you'll hear the looms' steady clackety-clack.

Bronze casting is also carried on in Amarapura.

Getting There & Away

A No 8 bus from 84th St near the corner of 29th St in Mandalay will take you to Amarapura and on to Ava if you wish. Get off the bus when you come to the palace wall on the left of the road and a temple guarded by elephants on the right, with the Ayeyarwady visible behind it. From here you can walk to Pahtodawgyi and through the village of Taungthaman to U Bein's Bridge.

You can also reach Amarapura from Mandalay by horsecart. This a good way to get from sight to sight once you reach Amarapura, although the trip to and from Mandalay

is an hour's ride each way. A one-way journey by horsecart costs K400; if you want to keep the horsecart all day, count on K500 to K600.

Touring by bicycle is a less expensive, and quicker, alternative. Bikes can be rented in Mandalay for K100 to K150 a day. Pedalling to Amarapura should take no longer than 40 minutes or so.

AVA အင်းဝ

A few km south of Amarapura, the Ava Bridge spans the Ayeyarwady River across to Sagaing. Just south of the bridge the Myitnge River flows into the Ayeyarwady, and south of this river stands the ancient city of Ava. A channel, known as the Myittha Chaung, was cut across from the Myitnge to the Ayeyarwady to make Ava into an island.

From 1364 Ava was the capital of a Burmese kingdom for nearly 400 years (apart from brief interludes) until the shift was made to Amarapura in 1841. No other capital has lasted as long. Although Myanmar was known to the outside world as Ava until comparatively recently, the classical Pali name of the city was Ratnapura ('City of Gems'), pronounced 'Yadanapon' in Burmese.

Prior to 1364 Sagaing had been the capital of the central Burman kingdom, but after Sagaing fell to the Shan the capital was moved across the river to Ava. The kings of Ava set about re-establishing Burman supremacy, which had been in decline since the fall of Bagan. Although the power of Ava soon extended as far as Pyay (Prome), the Mon rulers of Bago (Pegu) proved to be a strong match for the Burmans.

In 1555 Ava fell to another Burman kingdom, that of Taungoo, but in 1636 the capital of Taungoo was returned to Ava. This period as capital lasted only a century. The Mon again rose up and destroyed Ava in 1752. Only a few years later Alaungpaya vanquished the Mon forever, and after a period with Shwebo in the north as capital, Ava once again became the centre of the Burmese kingdom.

When the British occupied Lower Myanmar

AROUND MANDALAY

following the Second Anglo-Burmese War, much of Upper Myanmar was known as the Kingdom of Ava. An embassy report of a visit to Ava in 1795 enthused:

The Burmans are certainly rising fast in the scale of Oriental nations. They have an undeniable claim to the character of a civilised and well instructed people. Their laws are wise and pregnant with sound morality; their police is better regulated than in most European countries, their natural disposition is hospitable to strangers.

During his reign, Bodawpaya moved the capital to Amarapura, but his successor Bagyidaw shifted it back to Ava. When the disastrous earthquake of 1838 caused serious damage, the city was finally abandoned as a capital, in favour of Amarapura, in 1841.

Although there is not a great deal to be seen within the city, the massive old city walls are still easily traced. To the south of the city an ancient brick causeway leads from the city gate towards the town of Tada-u. A number of small villages have sprung up inside the city walls and peasants till the soil where once the palace used to stand.

Watch Tower
The 27-metre-high masonry watch tower, the Nanmyin, is all that remains of the palace built by Bagyidaw. The upper portion was shattered by the 1838 earthquake and the rest has taken on a precarious tilt – it's known as the 'leaning tower of Ava'.

Maha Aungmye Bonzan
Also known as the Ok Kyaung, this is a brick-and-stucco monastery built by the chief queen of Bagyidaw for her royal abbot (Nyaungganagan Sayadaw) in 1818. Monasteries were normally built of wood and were prone to deterioration from the elements or destruction by fire. Although this monastery was built in imitation of the traditional wooden style, its masonry construction has ensured its survival. The 1838 earthquake badly damaged it, but in 1873 it was restored.

Ava Bridge
This British-engineered, 16-span bridge

dates to 1934 and is the only structure that crosses the Ayeyarwady River, although a new bridge planned near Pyay may end that distinction. The bridge was put out of action by the British in 1942 when they demolished two spans in order to deny passage to the advancing Japanese. Not until 1954 was the bridge repaired and put back into operation. It carries two lanes of traffic plus a railway line.

Tolls are collected for every moving vehicle that crosses, from bullock carts and trishaws to cargo trucks. Due to the route's strategic importance, photography of the Ava Bridge – or from the bridge – is strictly forbidden.

Other Attractions
Farms, villages, monasteries and ruined zedis are scattered around the area within the old city walls. The walls are in particularly good condition near the northern gate, facing the Ayeyarwady. This was known as the **Gaung Say Daga**, or 'hair-washing' gate, since kings had their hair ceremonially washed at this gate. In places the moat outside the walls is also visible.

Located nearby, **Htilaingshin Paya** dates back to the Bagan period; in a shed in the compound an inscription records the construction of the wooden palace during the first Ava dynasty.

To the southern side of the city stand the remains of the huge four-storey **Leitutgyi Paya**. There is also the **Lawkatharaphu Paya**, while to the south of the city stands the **Ava Fort**.

The Ava Nat Festival celebrates the nat Thon Ban Hla from the 10th day of the waxing moon through to the full moon of Tabaung (February/March).

Getting There & Away
From Mandalay take a No 8 bus via Amarapura to Ava, or take a Zaya-Mann taxi-truck bound for Sagaing (K5) from the corner of 29th and 83rd Sts, and get off at the Ava Bridge. You can then follow the extremely dusty (in the dry season) track down to the ferry landing on the Myitnge River. You'll

be ferried across for K2. During the wet season you have to take a ferry from the Thabyedan Fort near the Ava Bridge. Ferries also shuttle across the Ayeyarwady between Ava and Sagaing for K2.

SAGAING စစ်ကိုင်း:
If you're unable to get to Bagan to poke around the ruins, Sagaing may provide you with an interesting substitute. There are certainly plenty of stupas here, and those scattered over the Sagaing hills – which rise on the western bank of the Ayeyarwady, just north of the modern town – provide a very picturesque spectacle from across the river. Flying in or out of Mandalay provides you with an even better view, but make sure you're sitting on the correct side of the plane – on the right when flying Mandalay-Bagan, on the left when flying Bagan-Mandalay.

Sagaing became capital of an independent Shan kingdom around 1315, after the fall of Bagan had thrown central Myanmar into chaos. Its period of importance was short, for in 1364 the founder's grandson, Thado Minbya, moved his capital across the river to Ava. For four brief years, from 1760 to 1764, Sagaing was once again the capital, but its historic importance is comparatively minor.

Today it's mostly known as a religious centre that supports dozens of Buddhist monasteries and nunneries as well as a major monastic hospital.

Thabyedan Fort
Just to the left of the Ava Bridge, on the Mandalay and Ava side, is the fort of Thabyedan which was built as a last-ditch defence by the Burmese before the Third Anglo-Burmese War. It was taken by the British with little effort.

Kaunghmudaw Paya
Best known of the Sagaing stupas, this huge whitewashed edifice is actually situated 10 km beyond the town of Sagaing. The enormous dome rises 46 metres in the shape of a perfect hemisphere and was modelled after the Mahaceti ('Great Stupa') in Sri Lanka – although legend also says that it represents

the perfectly shaped breast of a well-endowed Burmese queen. Also known as Rajamanicula, the zedi was built in 1636 to commemorate Ava's establishment as the royal capital of Myanmar.

Around the base of the zedi are 812 stone pillars, each 1½-metres high and with a small hollow for an oil lamp. Images of nats can be seen in the 120 niches which also circle the base. A nearly three-metre-high polished marble slab stands in a corner of the paya grounds – the 86 lines of Burmese inscriptions on the slab record details of the monument's construction.

Kaungmudaw Paya and guardian *chinthe*,
Sagaing, near Mandalay

Tupayon Paya

Constructed by King Narapati of Ava in 1444, Tupayon is of an unusual style for Myanmar: it consists of three circular storeys each encircled with arched niches. A temporary wooden bridge was constructed across the Ayeyarwady when the *hti* (the decorated top) was raised, and a huge festival was held. The 1838 earthquake toppled the superstructure, and although it was partially repaired in 1849 the reconstruction was never completed.

Aungmyelawka Paya

Situated on the riverfront, near Tupayon Paya, this zedi was built in 1783 by Bodawpaya on the site of his residence before he became king. It is built entirely of sandstone in imitation of the Shwezigon Paya at Nyaung U in Bagan. It is also known as the Eindawya Paya.

Other Payas

The **Datpaungzu Paya** is comparatively recent, but houses many relics from other, older temples which were demolished when the railway was built through Sagaing. **Ngadatkyi** to the west of Sagaing was built in 1657 and houses a fine and very large seated Buddha image.

Hsinmyashin Paya is on the way to the Kaunghmudaw Paya and is known as the 'Pagoda of Many Elephants' because of the elephant statues stationed at each entrance-way – a departure from the usual half-lion, half-dragon *chinthes*. Built in 1429, it was badly damaged in an earthquake in 1485. Although subsequently repaired, it suffered even worse damage in a 1955 earthquake.

Sagaing Hill

The hill itself has a number of zedis and monasteries, some of which are comparatively recent. **Padamyazedi** dates from 1300, while **Onhmin Thonze**, or '30-caves', contains many Buddha images in a crescent-shaped colonnade. The impressive **Soon U Ponya Shin Paya** nearby was constructed in 1312 and reaches 29.3 metres high with a 7.8-metre hti above that; in front of the principal altar, large bronze frogs on wheels serve as collection boxes. The view of Sagaing from Soon U Ponya Shin and its approach are outstanding. Mural paintings can be seen in the **Tilawkaguru** cave temple which was built around 1672. The **Pa Ba Kyaung** is typical of the many monasteries on the hillside.

Sagaing also has the remains of a fort by the riverbank. Silversmiths in the nearby village of **Ywataung** are renowned for their engraving skills.

The village of Sagaing at the foot of Sagaing Hill makes an interesting visit – it's chock-a-block with markets, shops and restaurants. Foreigners are charged an entry fee of US$3 to climb Sagaing Hill.

Places to Stay & Eat

Although a day trip to Sagaing seems sufficient to many visitors, an overnight stay will allow you to take in the sights at a more leisurely pace while absorbing the local ambience.

Near the central market in Sagaing, on a side street of the main road through town, the quiet *Happy Hotel* (☎ 072-21420) offers 21 basic but clean rooms for US$8/15 single/double including breakfast. Shower and toilet facilities are down the hall. Downstairs you'll find a very decent restaurant serving Chinese and Burmese food. Coming from Mandalay, turn right just past the cinema on the right side of the road, then make the first left and you'll see it on your left.

Some travellers have managed to stay at unlicensed guest houses in Sagaing for as little as K60 a night. There are plenty of teashops and restaurants in the vicinity of the Happy Hotel and central market.

Getting There & Away

Sagaing is about 20 km south-west of Mandalay and is easily reached by road. The Ayeyarwady flows south by Sagaing, then turns west and north, encircling the town in a loop. The road to Sagaing crosses the river on the 16-span Ava Bridge, which is well over a km long and also carries the railway line.

A Sagaing-bound taxi-truck (from the intersection of 83th and 29th Sts) will take you right to the middle of town for K5 from Mandalay. If you want to continue to the Kaunghmudaw Paya, it costs another K3 by taxi-truck.

MINGUN မင်းကွန်း

If we had to choose just one of the four ancient cities around Mandalay to visit, it would be Mingun. Not only are there some very interesting things to see within a comparatively compact area, but just getting there is half the fun.

Mingun, located about 11 km upriver from Mandalay on the opposite bank of the Ayeyarwady, is accessible only by river. It's just long enough to give you a pleasant feel for the river without being so long that you'll worry how much of your 28-day visa you're using up – as can happen on the Mandalay-Bagan riverboat (particularly if you get stuck).

The village itself is a very friendly place and worth exploring a bit. Several teashops and curry stalls in the vicinity of the huge Mingun Bell offer snacks, noodles and beverages. A footpath parallel to the river that runs the length of the ruins area and beyond makes an interesting walk and is less dusty than the main road in dry weather.

The **Mingun Sanitarium** (also called the Buddhist Infirmary), a nursing home for the elderly, is worth checking out. Visitors are welcome. The head nurse here is Than Than Sue – she speaks excellent English and is happy to impart info on the Mingun area. This is one of only two such facilities in all of Myanmar (the second is in Myeik). You might be able to stay here for the night if there's room.

The **Mingun Nat Festival** takes place between the 5th and 10th days of the waxing moon of Tabaung (February/March). This celebration pays homage to the brother and sister of the 'Teak Tree'.

Mingun Paya

If King Bodawpaya had succeeded in his grandiose scheme, Mingun might now boast

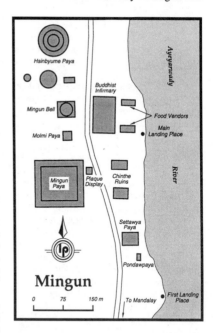

the world's largest zedi. Thousands of slaves laboured to build the massive stupa beginning in 1790. Work halted in 1819 when Bodawpaya died, leaving a brick base that stands about a third of its intended height.

An earthquake split the monument in 1838 and reduced it to partial rubble – possibly the world's largest pile of bricks. But what a pile of bricks! The base of his projected stupa, badly cracked by the earthquake of 1838, stands 50 metres high overlooking the river. Each side of the enormous base measures 72 metres, and the lowest terrace measures 140 metres. There are projecting four-layer lintels over the porticoes on each of the four sides. Beautiful glazed tiles in brown, pale brown, cream and green were intended to be set in panels around the terrace; some of these tiles can be seen in the small building in front of the enormous ruin. Had the stupa been completed it would have stood 150 metres high.

Despite its dilapidated state you must still

go barefoot if you intend to climb the base. You can climb the zedi on the crumbled corner, and from the top you have a fine view of the Hsinbyume Paya, Mingun village and the river.

A pair of commensurately large chinthes are crumbling away at their guard posts closer to the river. They, too, were badly damaged by the 1838 quake.

Pondawpaya Closer to the riverbank, a little downstream from the Mingun Paya, is this five-metre-high working model for the gigantic structure. It gives a clear picture of just what Bodawpaya intended to achieve. During the 15 years it took to build the base of his stupa he frequently set up residence on an island in the Ayeyarwady to supervise the construction.

Mingun Bell In 1808 Bodawpaya had a gigantic bell cast to go with his gigantic zedi. Weighing 55,555 viss (90 tonnes), it is claimed to be the largest hung, uncracked bell in the world. There is said to be a larger bell in Moscow, but it is cracked.

The same earthquake that shook the zedi base also destroyed the bell's supports, so it was hung in a new *tazaung* (shrine building) close to the riverboat landing. The bell is about four metres high and over five metres in diameter at the lip. You can scramble right inside it and some helpful bystander will give it a good thump so that you can hear the ring from the interior.

Between Mingun Paya and the bell stands a new pavilion sheltering a life-size standing bronze statue of Molmi Sayadaw, a famous Buddhist abbot from the nearby village of Molmi.

Hsinbyume (Myatheindan) Paya

Built by King Bagyidaw in 1816, three years before he succeeded Bodawpaya as king, this stupa was constructed in memory of his senior wife, the Hsinbyume princess. It is built as a representation of the Sulamani Paya which, according to the Buddhist plan of the cosmos, stands atop Mt Meru. The seven wavy terraces around the stupa repre-

sent the seven mountain ranges around Mt Meru, while the five kinds of mythical monsters can be found in niches on each terrace level. This zedi, too, was badly damaged in the 1838 quake, but King Mindon Min restored it in 1874.

Settawya Paya

Close to the riverbank, upstream from the Pondawpaya model, this hollow, vaulted shrine has a footprint of the Buddha which was brought to Mingun by King Bodawpaya when the relic chamber in the base of his huge pahto was sealed up. The temple was built in 1811.

Getting There & Away

Riverboats to Mingun depart Mandalay from the western end of Bayintnaung Rd (26th St) with reasonable frequency. The upriver journey usually takes about 45 minutes, though sometimes it can take as long as two hours. Depending on the currents, coming back may be rather quicker. It's best to get a boat out of Mandalay between 7 and 8 am; arrange transport to the jetty the night before. Boats leave every half hour or when full. The last boat back to Mandalay from Mingun usually leaves around 4 pm, so don't start this trip too late in the day. The cost is K10. For K800 you can hire an entire boat seating 20 or more people.

It's a pleasant, interesting trip with plenty to see along the way – fishing villages, bullock carts, corn fields, market boats, laundering. Joe sighted three Irrawaddy dolphins swimming near the boat during his last trip. The boat stops at a sandbank at the southern end of the Mingun area, then continues to the main landing place beyond the Mingun Paya base.

Pyin U Lwin ပြင်ဦးလွင်

During the British annexation of Myanmar, Pyin U Lwin was renamed Maymyo after a British Colonel May (Maymyo means 'Maytown'), and among many older locals (and tourist touts) the town is still known by its colonial name. Pyin U Lwin was long a British hill station where, during the hot season, the servants of the Raj went to escape the heat and dust of the plains. It is 67 km east of Mandalay and, at 1070 metres, considerably higher. The altitude makes all the difference. Even at the height of the hot season Pyin U Lwin is pleasantly cool and at certain times of the year it can get quite chilly. Best of all, the air is fresh.

As a legacy of the influx of South Asians during the British colonial era, Pyin U Lwin township is home to around 5000 Nepalis and 10,000 Indians. Sweater-knitting is the biggest occupation in town; most of this work is done by women, while the men roam the streets and hang out in teashops. A less publicised occupation is smuggling goods between Myanmar and China along the Burma Road to the north-east. Every day inbound pickups from the north drop off troops of men carrying backpacks stuffed with who knows what.

Getting to Pyin U Lwin is part of its attraction. From Mandalay you take a pickup or jeep which chugs its way across the plains, then up the winding road into the hills. There's no hurry about the trip, which is interspersed with stops to top up the vehicle's radiator. At the half-way mark you pass 'View Point', which has spectacular views.

Getting around Pyin U Lwin can be equally enjoyable; the standard transport around town is a miniature, enclosed wagon pulled by a pony. You're never sure if it's a half-scale replica from the Wells Fargo days of the American West or something from the British 'stand and deliver' era. The lodgings can be the most fun of all – see Candacraig in the following Places to Stay section, or read Paul Theroux's delightful account of Pyin U Lwin in his book *The Great Railway Bazaar*.

Around Town

Many of the colonial-era buildings along the town's main streets are being replaced by modern ones built by Chinese developers. You'll find the most intact colonial mansions along the circular road west and east of downtown. Chinese immigrants from Yunnan are buying up many of these old mansions using profits earned in the border trade.

Pyin U Lwin is a centre for growing many 'English' vegetables which do not flourish in the hotter conditions of the plains. Strawberries are one of the products of this higher altitude – in season (February-March) they're cheap and delicious. Mulberry trees, used to raise silk cocoons, are another important township product.

The town itself is easygoing and full of interest – a good place for an evening stroll or an interesting morning spent around the markets. There are still many English signs around.

Botanical Garden

Colonel May used Turkish POWs to develop this 237-acre botanical garden during WW I. The garden features wide expanses of manicured grass, large flower beds, 49 acres of natural forest with walking trails, a rose garden, an orchid house, a small stupa on an islet in a pond and several other ponds. It's very popular with picnicking families on weekends and holidays.

An open-air snack shop sits on a slope overlooking the park. It's open daily 7 am to 5.30 pm; admission is K3 per person.

Other Attractions

Purcell Tower, the clock tower near the town entrance coming from Mandalay, was a present from Queen Victoria, who offered an identical tower to Capetown in South Africa. Naturally, its chime copies Big Ben's.

There's a good view from **Naung Kan Gyi Paya** on a hilltop overlooking town, just north of the railway station. You can leave your bicycle at the shops at the bottom of the hill.

The hundred-year-old **Church of the Immaculate Conception**, south of the downtown area, features a large brick sanctuary with a belltower and cruciform floor plan. The vaulted wooden ceilings and well-appointed interior are more impressive than the outside. According to the Mother Superior here, Pyin U Lwin township counts

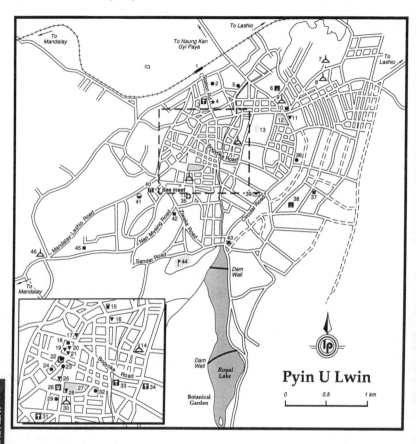

Pyin U Lwin

0   0.5   1 km

around 5000 Catholics; there are two other Catholic churches in town.

A few minutes walk from Candacraig is a colourful **Chinese temple** built by Yunnanese immigrants.

On the north-eastern outskirts of town is a small **Japanese war cemetery** containing around 50 graves. Each year during the months of December and January friends and families of the deceased come from Japan to pay their respects.

Maymyo Golf Club

This fairly well-tended 18-hole golf course near the Botanical Garden is one of the best in Myanmar. Greens fees are K500 per player; clubs (K300), shoes (K100) and caddies (K200 each) can be hired at the pro shop. With club rental you are provided 10 balls; you'll be fined K100 per each ball you lose. Men may be refused play if they're not wearing collared shirts ('polo' or tennis-style shirts are OK).

Places to Stay – bottom end

Although there are several local guest houses downtown in the vicinity of Purcell Tower, only a couple of places are licensed to accept

PLACES TO STAY		21	Myitta Thit Tea Shop	26	Hindu Temple
		25	Hlaing Tea Shop	27	Municipal Market
10	YMCA	28	Win Shwezin Cafe	29	Cinema
18	Ruby Guest House			30	Monastery
24	Golden Dream Hotel	**OTHER**		31	Church
37	Thiri Myaing Hotel			32	Fire Brigade
	(Candacraig)	1	Railway Station	33	St Matthew's Kachin
42	Grace Hotel	2	School		Baptist Church
43	Gandamar Myaing	3	Methodist Church	34	Church of the
	Hotel	4	Police Station		Immaculate
45	Nann Myaing Hotel	5	School		Conception
		6	Cantonese Temple	35	Hospital
PLACES TO EAT		7	Shwe Myan Tin Paya	36	School
		8	U Chanti Paya	38	YunnaneseTemple
11	Aung Padamya	9	Aung Chantha Paya	39	Post Office
	Restaurant	12	Shan Market	40	Town Hall
15	Tawthagi Cold Bar	13	Football Ground	41	Pickups to Mandalay
16	Lay Ngoon Restaurant	14	Shwezigone Paya		& Lashio
17	Shanghai Restaurant	22	Mosque	44	Maymyo Golf Club
19	Family Restaurant	23	Purcell Tower	46	Kyak Taung Paya
20	Maymyo Restaurant		(clock tower)		

foreign guests at this time. *Golden Dream Hotel* (☎ 085-22142), at 42/43 Mandalay-Lashio Rd close to the tower and the HMV pickup stop, is a rambling multi-storey place where rooms with shower and toilet down the hall cost US$5 per person. Rooms with private shower and toilet go for US$10 per person. The rooms are large but not very clean; rooms toward the back are quieter than those facing the street. Hot water is not available.

On a side street near a canal, east of Purcell Tower and north of Mandalay-Lashio Rd, *Ruby Guest House* (☎ 085-22494) charges US$5 for small singles or US$8/15 single/double for larger rooms with shared shower and toilet, US$10/20 for better rooms with private shower and toilet. Hot water is available 24 hours.

The *Grace Hotel* at 114A Nann Myaing Rd is a one-storey, 11-room inn, with small rooms with shared facilities, and larger rooms with private toilet and shower. Rates seem to fluctuate according to how many visitors are in town; on three different occasions we were quoted three different rates, from US$5 to US$7 per person for the smaller rooms, US$8 to US$10 per person in the larger. Mattresses are hard; hot water is available by advance arrangement only. Bargaining may be in order. The main advan-

tages to the Grace are its quiet location off the main streets and its garden sitting area out front.

The *YMCA* on Mandalay-Lashio Rd near the Shan Market has applied for permission to accept foreigners.

A local mafia of sorts tries to keep tabs on all foreigners coming into town from Mandalay. Their operation starts at the rest stop on the way up, where virtually every foreigner will be approached by a friendly chap asking where the foreigner plans to stay in Pyin U Lwin. Whatever your answer is – and regardless of whether you take the tout's recommendation or not – the representative will take note of your appearance, then later make a trip to Pyin U Lwin to collect a 'commission' from the hotel or guest house owner of the place you stay. There are two main gangs running this operation, both centred at Indian-owned crafts shops in Pyin U Lwin.

Places to Stay – middle & top end

For many visitors, half the reason for coming to Pyin U Lwin is to stay at *Candacraig* – even if it is now officially known as the *Thiri Myaing Hotel*. In the colonial era this was the 'chummery' or bachelor quarters for employees of the Bombay Burmah Trading Company. This trading firm was engaged in

AROUND MANDALAY

extracting teak in Upper Myanmar, and the chummery was built in 1906 in the form of an English country mansion – constructed, naturally, of the finest teak.

Today you can sweep up the imposing staircase to the upper landing where you will find huge, old-fashioned rooms, with high ceilings and wooden balconies overlooking the grounds. Three small single rooms with common shower and toilet cost US$12. Six huge standard rooms with fireplace (now blocked) and attached bathroom go for US$24/30 single/double. Rates include breakfast. Although fires are no longer permitted in the rooms, the hotel staff will light a fire in the large sitting room fireplace downstairs – guests must chip in 'to pay for firewood'. Hot water is available 6 to 8 am and 6 to 8 pm only.

Much of Candacraig's appeal was that Mr Bernard, the chummery cook back in the British era, ran the place exactly as if the British had never left. Unhappily Mr Bernard has now departed this world, but roast beef and roast chicken still appear on the set dinner menu (K300) every night and most travellers find it a great place to stay. You can sip a beer in front of the roaring log fire in the lounge, and at breakfast or lunch they may put a table out on the lawn so you can dine in open-air splendour. The hotel tends to be booked out in the December-January and July-August tourist seasons; at other times of the year you're liable to have the place to yourself. The hotel is still government-owned, although it's up for sale to any private interest that comes up with the cash.

The Ministry of Hotels & Tours (MHT) maintains two other large hotels in Pyin U Lwin. *Gandamar Myaing* is a brick, two-storey Tudor and Victorian mansion – similar in design to Candacraig – on the way to the Botanical Garden. Large rooms with attached bathrooms go for US$43/56 single/double; hot water is reportedly available 24 hours.

Off the Mandalay-Lashio Rd coming in from Mandalay is the *Nann Myaing* (☎ 085-22112, 23118), a large cluster of buildings vaguely designed in Tudor style. The separate reception building is the grandest; the guest rooms are rather more simple and modern. All rooms have wooden floors, high ceilings and blocked fireplaces. Standard rooms with cold-water shower and toilet cost US$43/56 single/double, larger 'superior' rooms are US$55/68 single/double and junior suites with sitting rooms and slightly nicer furnishings (fridge, TV, hot shower, portable radiators) cost US$91/104 single/double. These grossly overpriced rates include a mandatory breakfast charge of US$7.20; if you take lunch and dinner at the hotel (payable in kyat), you'll receive a discount of US$4 off room rates. This same 'discount', by the way, is available at the Thiri Myaing and Gandamar Myaing hotels.

All three MHT hotels accept Visa, MasterCard and American Express for room payments, but your card must be franked at the Nann Myaing location no matter where you stay. For reservations at any of the three MHT hotels, call the Nann Myaing number.

At least three upper-end hotels are planned for the near future. The first to be completed will most likely be the modern three-storey *Thiri Myanmar*, under construction along the eastern end of Circular Rd. A bungalow-style hotel is also under construction behind No 4 High School, and cottages along the golf course are also on the drawing board.

There are also three state-owned hotels that are for the most part reserved for VIPs, military officers and other state guests: *Thiri Myaing, Cherry Myaing* and *Yuzana Myaing*. All are on or just off the eastern end of Mandalay-Lashio Rd. On the rare occasion that the other hotels in town fill up, the military allows ordinary foreign visitors to stay at these places.

Places to Eat

Apart from Candacraig there are a number of assorted eating places in the town centre, including several Chinese and Indian places. The *Shanghai Restaurant*, a few blocks north-east of Purcell Tower on Mandalay-Lashio Rd, specialises in Shanghai-style and Sichuan food. Several blocks further east, the *Lay Ngoon Restaurant* specialises in Cantonese food and seems to enjoy more popularity.

Closer to the clock tower on the northern side of the street, the large *Myitta Thit Tea Shop* serves good quality tea, crispy biscuit-like *nam-bya* with dal dip and fresh butter from local Gurkha-run dairies, samosas (morning only) and mohinga (evening only). The *Maymyo Restaurant* next door serves decent Chinese at slightly lower prices than the Shanghai.

Just around the corner on a side street is the clean and popular *Family Restaurant* at 13 Block 4, 3rd St. The menu mixes Burmese and Indian dishes; order a chicken, vegetable or mutton curry and you'll also receive three or four side dishes, including vegetables and a delicious dal, plus rice.

Near the municipal market, *Hlaing Tea Shop* is a Nepali-style place serving good egg-fried rice, chapatis, aloo puri and samosas for breakfast, plus other snacks throughout the day. A little farther east along this same road is the large and very popular *Win Shwezin Cafe*, a standard Burmese-style teashop.

Further east near the Shan Market, the family-run *Aung Padamya Restaurant*, at Site 44, 28 Thu Min Galar, Zaythit Rd, serves very good home-cooked Indian food from 11 am to 6 pm daily. As at the Family Restaurant, a curry order (chicken, pork, fish or mutton) brings with it plenty of dal, vegetables and rice. The restaurant is owned by the golf pro from Maymyo Golf Club and his Catholic Indian family.

Indulge your sweet tooth at *Diamond Confectionery*, a small shop on the main street founded by an Italian who left Myanmar following nationalisation. Although it may not look like much from the street, the shop produces a nice variety of baked goods and Indian snacks, including shortbread, butter cookies, chocolate-cashew muffins, coconut puffs, vegetable puffs and various cakes.

The open-air *Tawthagyi Cold Bar*, off the road leading to the railway station, serves delicious yoghurt lassis made with strawberries, papaya, banana, avocado or coconut. Beer and soft drinks are also available.

Things to Buy

The main shed of the central municipal market near the clock tower contains vendor stalls selling textiles and household goods from India, China, Thailand and Myanmar. Behind this main shed is a large area where fresh produce and other goods brought in from the countryside are sold. Don't believe any touts in town who say there's nothing local for sale at this market; they're just trying to steer you away from the rival commission mafia and toward their own mafia at the smaller Shan market in the eastern part of town. Both markets are visited by tribespeople; the only real difference between the two markets is size, though it's true there are more Shan at the Shan market.

Two handicraft shops on the main street downtown vie for your dollars and kyat: Dream Merchant (opposite Maymyo Restaurant) and Zaw Crafts (next to the Golden Dream Hotel). Both carry similar collections of marionettes, *kalagas* (tapestries), shoulder bags, wood carving, lacquerware and other materials from around Upper Myanmar. Most of this stuff comes from Mandalay, though the store personnel may try to convince you it's Shan gear. Some Shan textiles and jewellery may be available but that's about it. Beware of offers of precious stones at these or any other shops; Pyin U Lwin has a very low reputation when it comes to dealing in gems. Many travellers have ended up with handfuls of worthless sapphires they thought represented a big score.

The 3D Art Gallery, at 10 Telegraph Rd near the municipal market, displays paintings and other art executed by local artists, some of it very good.

Getting There & Away

Pickups The famous WW II-era jeeps that once plied the route between Mandalay and Pyin U Lwin have been almost entirely replaced by Japanese pickups. Seven companies depart from several places around the centre of Mandalay from 5 am until about 3 pm. As soon as a full load of passengers has fitted itself on board, your truck will depart;

for comfort and view you are better off grabbing the front seats and letting the hardier Burmese cram themselves into the back. The cost is K40 in the back, K100 up the front and the trip takes three to 3½ hours up, two to 2½ hours down – barring breakdowns of course, which in Myanmar are always possible.

On the way up the trucks stop midway to allow the passengers to grab a snack, to give the driver a chance to top off the radiator and to give the touts time to try and steer you toward specific hotels and restaurants in Pyin U Lwin.

From Pyin U Lwin, pickups depart in the opposite direction from the Shan market, railway station, Cantonese temple, clock tower and municipal market. They're all pretty much the same – you might make your selection based on which staging point is most convenient for you. You can hire an entire pickup to Mandalay for K800 to K1000.

Pickups on to Lashio leave from near the clock tower and from in front of the Cantonese temple, for K300 in the back, K500 in the front. From the same areas more comfortable Toyota hatchback share-taxis take four passengers for K800 per person. It takes about six hours to cover the 209 km to Lashio.

Train There is a daily train up to Pyin U Lwin from Mandalay, but this is more a joy ride for railway enthusiasts than a sensible means of transport. The train (No 131 Up) departs Mandalay at 4.35 am and climbs the hills by a switchback system; the schedule says it takes 3½ hours to reach Pyin U Lwin but this is optimistic – count on four to five hours. The local fare is just K60 but we've heard of foreigners being charged about 10 times that in US dollars.

The same train continues on to Lashio. The stationmaster at the Pyin U Lwin station is adamant about charging foreigners US$11 for this leg of the journey.

Getting Around
Most of the town's famous horsecoaches are stationed near the mosque on the main street downtown. Fares are steep by Myanmar standards: figure on K50 to K60 to travel

from the mosque to the Shan market, K150 for the roundtrip to Candacraig or the Botanical Garden, K500 for all-day sightseeing.

You can hire bicycles to explore the town at the Grace Hotel or at either of the two crafts shops on Mandalay-Lashio Rd. The going rate is K10 per hour or K70 per day.

A fellow at the Hlaing Tea Shop asks K300 per hour to rent his motorcycle, but you can probably negotiate a lower daily fee.

AROUND PYIN U LWIN
Waterfalls & Caves
There are several natural attractions around Pyin U Lwin, including a number of caves, waterfalls and tribal villages. Most can be reached by a combination of public transport and hiking, though the Dream Merchant or Zaw Crafts in Pyin U Lwin can arrange a guided trip to any or all of them. Rates are negotiable depending on where you want to go.

Pwe Kauk Falls Called Hampshire Falls in British times, Pwe Kauk is about eight km from town off the Lashio road. Although the falls themselves aren't that spectacular, it's a pleasant picnic spot – popular on weekends and holidays with the locals. During or just after the rainy season, you can swim in the upper reaches, but not at the bottom where the undertow can be dangerous.

Three **Shan villages** – Mogyopyit, Yechando and Ye Ngeye – can be visited on the way to Pwe Kauk Falls. Or from Pwe Kauk you can take a one-hour hike to **U Naung Gu**, a natural cave containing several Buddhas and used by local meditators. Ask around at Pwe Kauk for a local guide to the cave.

You can charter a pickup out to the falls from any of the truck stands in Pyin U Lwin for a few hundred kyat. To visit the Shan villages you can sometimes hire a bullock cart at Pwe Kauk.

Anisakan Falls Although a fairly long walk is required to get to these falls, the hike is worth it. At the village of Anisakan, about eight km towards Mandalay, turn right at the railway station, continue about 600 metres to the railway crossing, then turn left on a dirt road for about 800 metres to a fork where you again take a left turn. After about half a km you reach a parking place from where you continue on foot. It's an hour climb down through a river gorge to reach the falls, which consist of five sections; the third is particularly impressive.

Jeep taxis go to Anisakan village from Pyin U Lwin for K15 per person – catch them in front of the cinema opposite the municipal market. You should allow at least a half day for the whole trip.

Peik Chin Myaung This large Hindu-Buddhist shrine cave, 27 km toward Lashio off main road, was developed by local Nepalis and later co-opted by the government as a tourist attraction in 1990. A 600-metre path leads through the cave, which is decorated with newish Buddha images and models of Myanmar's most famous stupas, eg the Shwedagon and Kyaiktiyo. Private HMV pickups make the one-hour trip direct to Peik Chin Myaung for K180 per person. You can also charter a pickup and driver for K2000; ask at the Dream Merchant, Zaw Crafts or at the Lashio truck stand.

Monywa, Shwebo & Mogok

These cities in Sagaing Division, to the north-west and north of Mandalay, are known as three of the most typically 'Burmese' towns in all of Myanmar. Although Monywa has been open to foreigners for some time, Shwebo only opened in 1994; neither place has so far received many tourists at all.

MONYWA မုံရွာ

Monywa is a worthwhile trip for Burmese temple enthusiasts or others who just want to go where few travellers go. It lies 136 km north-west of Mandalay along the Manda-

lay-Budalin branch railway line but is best reached by bus.

Situated on the eastern bank of the Chindwin River, Monywa serves as a major trade centre for agricultural produce from the surrounding Chindwin Valley, especially beans, pulses and jaggery (palm sugar). In addition to some 600 warehouses, Monywa supports mills for the production of cotton, flour, noodles and edible oils. Rough cotton blankets from Monywa are famous in Myanmar; some even end up sewn into knapsacks which are sold to tourists in Bangkok. Other regional crafts traded here include mats and baskets made of bamboo and reed, bullock carts and agricultural implements such as hoes and machetes.

Black-market goods from India, especially saris and bicycle parts, pass through Monywa on their way to other parts of Myanmar. A forest reserve west of the Chindwin River produces teak and other hardwoods.

The Monywa area – particularly the region west of the river – was for many years a centre for the Burmese Communist Party. Although the BCP is no longer active here or elsewhere in Myanmar, military intelligence in Monywa can be particularly watchful.

The old market near the river is still active despite the large new market sheds built by the government near the Monywa Hotel and Great Hotel. Most likely this is because the government ordered the relocation of a Muslim cemetery to make way for the new market; people fear the nats that may have been left behind.

There is talk of building a km-long bridge across the Chindwin at Monywa as part of the so-called 'Western Highway' that may some day link Pathein (Bassein) in the south-west delta with Ye U in the north-west. With the northern reaches of Sagaing Division opening up to foreigners, Monywa can serve as a stepping stone for Chindwin River trips north-west to Kalewa. From Kalewa it's just a short road trip to the Chin State.

Twinn Hill, in Budalin township about three km east of the river, stands only 200 metres above the surrounding plain but features a deep round lake. According to some sources the depression holding the lake was left behind by a volcanic eruption; others say a meteorite bounced off the earth's crust here.

Monywa is one of the hottest places in the entire country in April and May, when temperatures approaching or exceeding 40°C are not uncommon.

Festivals

Monywa sits at the north-western edge of what might be termed the 'nat belt', a region of Upper Myanmar where the nat cult is particularly strong. *Nat pwe* followers will find the Zeedaw Nat Festival at Zeedaw and Maungdon (cross the Chindwin River at Monywa and travel 22 km west along the Yinmabin road) between the 8th day of the waning moon and the new moon and between the first and seventh days of the waxing moon of Tabaung (February/March).

Coinciding with the festival at Zeedaw, the Ahlone Nat festival is celebrated at Ma Ngwe Daung (12 km north of Monywa on the Shwebo road).

Places to Stay & Eat

On the north-eastern side of the main road into town, the new *Great Hotel* (☎ 071-21930) has rooms with good mattresses and attached shower and toilet for US$10 per person. Although the rooms themselves aren't air-conditioned, the corridors are. Next door, in a similar style, is *Shweltaw Guest House* which didn't accept foreigners at the time of writing.

A bit further in towards the town centre on the same side of the road as the accommodation listed above is the recently privatised *Monywa Hotel* (☎ 071-21549). Wooden bungalows with corrugated metal roofs are divided into four rooms, each with attached hot-water bath, fridge and air-con for US$24/30 single/double, or US$30/36 for slightly better-furnished rooms with TV. All rates include breakfast. One of the Monywa Hotel's main advantages is its pleasant outdoor bar. This hotel is supposedly about to undergo renovation so prices may change.

The *Pann Cherry Restaurant* in the centre of town near the old market serves good Chinese food in both the open-sided dining room downstairs and the air-con room upstairs.

Getting There & Away

Bus From Mandalay you can catch a pickup to Monywa from 27th St near the corner of 83rd, or from the main bus centre at the corner of 26th and 82nd. Pickups leave about every 45 minutes between 4 am and 3 pm, cost K45 and take three to four hours. Larger government buses leave three times a day from the main bus centre for the same fare.

Train Myanma Railways operates trains from Mandalay to Monywa at 5.35 am (No 123 Up) and 1.45 pm (No 125 Up) daily, but the journey is a slow six hours compared to the 3½ hours by bus. The return journeys are scheduled for 1.20 pm (No 124 Down) and 6.50 am (No 126 Down). The fare is just K15.

As trade with India via Kalewa increases, it's only a matter of time before a faster express train is established along this line.

Car By car it's only a 2½-hour drive from Mandalay via a decent two-lane road. The going rate for car and driver between the two cities – as a day trip only – is US$35.

Boat Ferries upriver to Kalewa take around four days and cost K150 per person in two-bed cabins, about half that in deck class. Food can be arranged through the crew or at ferry stops along the way.

Getting Around

Horsecart and trishaw are the main forms of local transport. A trip between the Chindwin River and Monywa Hotel will cost around K25 by trishaw, K40 by horsecart.

AROUND MONYWA
Thanboddhay Paya

The big attraction in Monywa is this magnificent, Mt Meru-type structure. From the outside the central stupa is vaguely reminiscent of Borobudur in Indonesia, though considerably smaller. Small stupas numbering 845 surround the richly decorated central stupa.

First built in 1303 by Monywa Sayadaw, Thanboddhay assumed its present form during a major reconstruction in 1939. The solid section of the monument is said to enclose 7,350 relics and other holy materials. Inside the attached pahto, votive Buddhas of bone and other materials decorate every wall and archway halfway to the ceiling, and there are larger sitting and standing Buddhas in niches. Altogether these images reportedly number 582,363.

Ancillary buildings in the compound resemble palace architecture from the Konbaung era (18th and 19th centuries) and feature three-dimensional jataka reliefs on their exteriors.

The paya complex is open daily 6.30 am to 5 pm; admission is free. Thanboddhay is located 19 km south-east of Monywa on the north-eastern side of the main road from Mandalay, just past a small bridge.

Ledi Kyaung

This monastery at the north-eastern edge of the township, 21 km north-east of town on the road to Ye U, was constructed in 1886 by order of renowned Pali scholar Ledi Sayadaw. Similar in concept to Kuthodaw Paya in Mandalay, the *kyaung* features 806 stone slabs inscribed with Buddhist scriptures.

Shwe Gu Nyi Paya

About 20 km east of town via a scenic two-lane road is one of the most important pilgrimage spots in Upper Myanmar. Dating to the 14th century, the main zedi of Shwe Gu Nyi Paya rises to 33 metres (an auspicious height made even more so when measured in feet – 108) and is famous for its 'wish-fulling' powers. The main antechamber to the shrine hall contains exemplary jataka paintings and is well decorated with mosaics.

Kyaukka

This village just beyond Shwe Gu Nyi Paya has been a centre for the crafting of lacquerware since the Konbaung era. The pieces produced here are for the most part more basic and utilitarian than those made in Bagan. Consisting of simple bamboo frames finished in black, silver or gold (or some combination thereof), the lacquerware here shows more links to the pre-Chiang Mai styles which existed before the Bagan artisans began using a wider palette, finer materials, more layers of lacquer and incising techniques which allowed different colours to show through the outer layers. Because Kyaukka is less frequented by tourists, prices are particularly low though you won't find any pieces quite as striking as in Bagan. In output, however, the village is second only to Bagan and the pieces made here are very strong.

The road to Kyaukka is lined with picturesque tamarind trees and rice fields. Pickups to Kyaukka leave a couple of times in the morning from Monywa's central market; the last one back leaves around 4 pm.

Po Win Daung Caves

It's a short ferry ride across the Chindwin River to Nyaungbingyi, followed by a 25-km drive to this system of sandstone caves situated in a cleft in the Po Win Daung (Po Win Hills). The hills have probably been occupied since the dawn of human habitation in Myanmar; to the south-west lies the Pondaung-pon-nya mountain range, where the fossilised remains of 'Pondaung Man' – who may have lived 30 million years ago – were found.

The caves and surrounding hills are named after U Po Win, a famous *zawgyi* (alchemist) who once lived among them. The caves themselves contain Buddhist statues and murals dating to the 17th and 18th centuries. Most exhibit the Inwa style, though some may date as far back as the 14th to 16th centuries. A covered stairway climbs a hill to the main cave shrine, but there are dozens of large and small caves in the area filled with old Buddhas. There are said to be over

400,000 images in these and other nearby caves.

Shwe Ba Hill, just beyond Po Win Daung, features unique pavilions cut from the surrounding sandstone and filled with plain Buddha images.

The last ferry in either direction across the Chindwin River departs at 6 pm.

SHWEBO ရွှေဘို

The flat plain that lies between the Mu and Ayeyarwady rivers around Shwebo has been continuously inhabited since at least the 3rd century AD, when the Pyus founded a city-state at nearby Hanlin. With the coming of the Burmans from the north, Hanlin crumbled and the area became an agricultural supply satellite for the rotating Burman kingdoms of Upper Myanmar.

During the early 17th century, when the Portuguese adventurer Philip De Brito was defeated at Thanlyin (Syriam), all the Portuguese and Eurasians living at De Brito's 13-year-old colony were exiled to the villages of **Monhla** and **Chantha** near Shwebo. Called *bayingyis*, the rare fair-haired resident may occasionally be seen in these villages but no linguistic or cultural legacies remain.

Shwebo served as a royal capital from 1760 to 1764 under King Alaungpaya. A Shwebo native, Alaungpaya used the city as a base for the reconquest of Ava and Lower Myanmar, establishing what is known as the Third Burmese Empire. After defeating the Shan and the Mon, Alaungpaya destroyed several British trading posts, one of the first aggravated assaults against the Raj. His successor Hsinbyushin moved the capital to Amarapura in the 1780s.

Shwebo today has a Burman majority. As at Monywa the local economy depends on the trading of nuts, pulses, rice and sesame cultivated on the surrounding plains. During the months of April and May, Shwebo is extremely hot and dry.

Things to See & Do

You can get a good view of the city from **Maw Daw Myin Paya** on Eindathaya Hill at the north-eastern corner of town. Other famous religious monuments include the typical Burmese-style **Myo Daunt Zedi** nearby and **Shwe Daza Paya** in the southern part of town (said to be 508 years old).

Nay Rapan Paya, which is distinguished by the fact that the complex boasts five entrances instead of the usual four, is located south-west of downtown. **Aung Myae Su Taung**, the town's 'wishing ground', is said to be the spot used by King Alaungpaya as a staging point before going into battle. You'll find it just outside the city entrance toward Mandalay, within a larger paya compound.

The water-filled eastern moat, the most visible legacy of Alaungpaya's original city plan, stretches a couple of km and is about 10 metres deep. The British built a jail on the **Alaungpaya palace grounds**, next to the central market north of downtown. Burmese residents recently moved the jail to the outskirts of town and are now excavating the site. Alaungpaya's remains, entombed nearby, are marked with a headstone inscribed in English.

Places to Stay

Although Myanmar Travels & Tours (MTT) says Shwebo is officially open, when we visited there was no 'foreigner-licensed' accommodation. The five local guest houses in town all said they would accept foreigners, however – and at local rates.

Only two of those guest houses are particularly recommendable as places to stay. The relatively new *Zin Wai Lar Guest House* (☎ Shwebo 263) is located in the eastern part of town on Yangyi Aung Rd toward Kyauk Myaung. It's a modern, three-storey affair with 14 ordinary doubles for K300 a night, plus two 'special' rooms for K500. All rooms feature twin beds; the special rooms have attached shower and toilet. Rates include service and tax.

Tun Tauk Guest House, a converted private residence, stands opposite the central market downtown on Aungzeya (Lanmadaw) Rd. It costs K150 per person and is sometimes full with local clients. It's fairly clean and well run; shower and toilet facilities are shared throughout. Other guest houses in town include the less reputable *Myakantha Guest House, Khine Shwe Wa Guest House* and *Mya Theingi Guest House*.

Places to Eat

Eden Culinary Garden, located downtown on Aungzeya Rd, offers a mixed menu of European, Chinese and Burmese dishes in a relatively clean setting. *Shwe Taung*, north of the market and opposite the petrol station on the same road, is Shwebo's most popular Chinese restaurant. The Chinese food at the more modern-looking *Ngwe Zin Yaw*, at the

corner of Aungzeya Rd and Yangyi Aung Rd, is decent as well.

Quiet, well-decorated *Khine Thazin* serves Burmese and Chinese food on Min Nyo San St, near the cinema north of the town centre. There are several small no-name Burmese restaurants north of the central market along Aungzeya Rd. For good biryani and other Indian Muslim dishes, head for *Win Myint Gyi Muslim Restaurant* near the central market.

Getting There & Away

Pickup Several transport companies operate

PLACES TO STAY

6 Zin Wai Lar Guest House
17 Tun Tauk Guest House

PLACES TO EAT

7 Ngwe Zin Yaw Restaurant
10 Eden Culinary Garden
11 Shwe Taung Chinese
    Restaurant
12 Khine Thazin Restaurant

OTHER

1 Myo Daunt Zedi
2 Golf Course

3 Railway Station
4 Immigration Office
5 Yangyi Aung Park
8 Police Station
9 Shwekyettho Paya
13 Post Office
14 King Alaungpaya's Tomb
15 Alaungpaya Palace
    Grounds (under excavation)
16 Central Market
18 Chanthaya Paya
19 Shwe Daza Paya
20 Chanthaya-gyi Paya
21 Shwebo College
22 Highway Bus Terminal
23 Aung Myae Su Taung

AROUND MANDALAY

along the 113-km route between Shwebo and Mandalay. The busiest line, ie the one with the most departures, is Yangyiaung Mahn, which charges K40 for a back seat, K60 for a front seat for the three-hour trip. All lines leave from the main bus centre in Mandalay hourly between 6 am and 3 pm; there are some normal-sized buses available as well as the small and medium-sized Japanese pickups. Shwebo's Highway Bus Terminal stands opposite Alaungpaya's 'wishing ground' paya, just outside the city entrance toward Mandalay.

Pickups from Monywa use a new, more direct road at about the same cost, departure frequency and travel time as transport from Mandalay. There are only three lines to and from Mogok; pickups drive first to Singu and cross the Ayeyarwady River by ferry to Kyauk Myaung before continuing on to Shwebo. Total travel time is around six hours. Pickups leave at 5, 6 and 7 am only and cost K150 for a back seat, K300 for a front seat. This fare includes the cost of the vehicle ferry; if you arrive at the crossing by private vehicle a high ferry charge is collected – the transport companies collaborate with the ferry line to discourage travel by private car.

Train Shwebo is linked to Myitkyina in the north and to Mandalay in the south by rail. From Mandalay the No 55 Up leaves at 3 pm and normally arrives in Shwebo at 6 pm.

Fares must be paid in US dollars to continue on to Myitkyina – at whatever rate the Shwebo stationmaster decides to collect. The stationmaster has a very poor reputation; even the BBC reported on his arbitrary treatment of foreigners.

Getting Around
Trishaws and horsecarts are the main modes of public transport. Pickups can be chartered for K1500 a day (not including fuel) around town, K3000 for out-of-town excursions.

AROUND SHWEBO
Hanlin
The architectural remains of the Pyu kingdom (3rd to 9th centuries) at Hanlin consists of a few crumbling city walls, gates, pillars and melting zedis but little else. Pots and other artefacts excavated at the site are displayed in a small museum in the local monastery.

Hanlin is 11 km south-east of Shwebo; each morning a couple of pickups make the trip from Shwebo's central market. The last and only pickup returns around 4 pm.

Kyauk Myaung
This small town 27 km east of Shwebo is known for its glazed pottery, including the large 'Martaban jars' used to hold water throughout rural Myanmar. During the dry season local residents pan for gold along the riverbanks.

Although nothing in Kyauk Myaung justifies a special trip, if you're travelling by road between Shwebo and Mogok you'll have to stop here to wait for the ferry across the Ayeyarwady River to Singu.

Should you need to spend the night here, a small guest house in town offers basic but clean rooms for K300.

MOGOK မိုးကုတ်
Famed for the surrounding natural beauty and for the brilliant rubies and sapphires pulled from its red earth, the township of Mogok was until recently completely off limits to foreigners. Even now one is supposed to obtain a travel permit endorsed for Mogok before being permitted to stay overnight.

The municipality of Mogok, roughly 200 km north of Mandalay and 148 km north-east of Shwebo, belongs to Pyin U Lwin District of Mandalay Division. This district is open to foreigners in the main, thus the authorities in Mogok theoretically shouldn't be too zealous about enforcing the permit requirement. But the situation is fluid, so be sure to check in Yangon (Rangoon) and Mandalay about the town's current status with regard to permits and their enforcement. Your best bet is to go with someone from Mandalay who knows the town – a permit may not be necessary if you're in the right company.

At 1170 metres above sea level, the mountain basin surrounding 'Rubyland' enjoys a fairly temperate climate. Unlike much of Lower Myanmar, the rainy season here runs from January to May. Burmans are a majority in the township of 150,000 but there are also substantial numbers of Shan, Lisu, Palaung, Kachin, Nepali, Indians and Chinese, all vying for a piece of the gem action or its attendant industries.

Royalty throughout the world have sought Mogok rubies and sapphires for many centuries. Alluvial limestone gravels are the source, and deposits are exploited by means of tunnelling, pit-digging or panning – all performed by hand. Other precious and semi-precious stones found in Mogok District include peridot, lapis lazuli, moonstone, garnet and chrysoberyl.

Information
Mogok has no telephone office, no area code and no direct dialling capacity. Operator-assisted trunk calls to Yangon can be made from Mogok Motel and from private houses with telephones. The post office is considered unreliable.

Religious Monuments
The hilltops surrounding town are dotted with stupas and kyaungs. On a hillside north of downtown, **Min Paya Taun Chantha-gyi Paya**, said to have been built by King Min Gaun 456 years ago, offers the best panoramic view of Mogok.

Phaung Daw U Paya, on another hill south-west of Mogok Lake, was built by King Alaungsithu. A shrine in the complex contains two very old gilded Buddha images, one mounted on a ruby-studded pedestal, the other on a silver pedestal.

Lay Myet Hnar Paya, on Bidaung Hill to the south, and **Shwe Gu Gyi Paya**, on a hill to the north, are also highly revered though of less visual interest.

Gem Markets
Rubies and sapphires are Mogok's lifeblood, and several markets around dispense the red and blue crystals on a rotating basis depending on the time of day. Best for the casual visitor is the **Peik Swae Gem Market** toward the eastern end of Mandalay-Moe Meik Rd, where moderately priced gems are displayed on small metal trays daily from 9 am to noon.

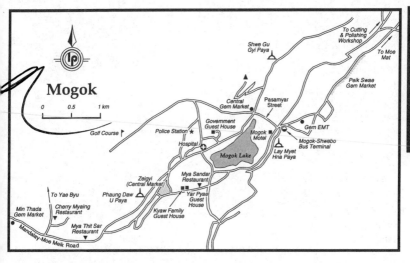

An unnamed downtown **gem market** near the cinema on Padamya St, west of the Mogok Motel, purveys high-priced stones to a nearly all-male crowd daily from noon to 2 pm only.

Finally the **Min Thada Gem Market**, on the westernmost edge of town on Mandalay-Moe Meik Rd near Min Thada Bridge, does business daily 3 pm to 6 pm.

Photography in the gem markets is frowned upon by both sellers and buyers.

Buying Gems In Mogok the main thing you must be concerned about isn't whether the stones are real but whether they're of good quality or whether the price is fair. Fake stones are rarely seen in town; this is because the supply of genuine rubies and sapphires is simply too great, and also because anyone caught selling fakes is run out of town immediately. One of the reasons Mogok has been a prohibited area for foreigners is that it's much harder for the government to control gem sales here, at the source, than in Mandalay or Yangon. In Mogok no one seems to care who's government-licensed and who's not. On the other hand, the customs officials at Yangon International Airport will definitely have something to say if they catch you with stones purchased from a non-government source. Be forewarned.

Other Markets
Every fifth day the **Zei Thit** ('New Market') or **Zeigyi** ('Big Market') is held at a site on the west side of Mogok Lake. It's most active in the morning, when it attracts several groups of tribespeople.

The **Aung Chantha Market** downtown is open daily and overall is busier than Zeigyi.

Places to Stay
The only officially licensed lodging in town is the three-story, 42-room *Mogok Motel*, south of downtown on Circular Rd. Still government-owned, the hotel has a tariff schedule which allows payment with a combination of kyat and dollars or FECs. Standard rooms with TV, fridge and attached toilet and hot-water shower cost US$9 plus K450 including breakfast, tax and service. Junior suites with sitting rooms and larger

The hill-side township of Mogok, Myanmar's 'Rubyland'

TVs are US$12.75 plus K720. Attached to the hotel are a restaurant and karaoke lounge. There is no electric power from midnight till 6 am.

Mogok Motel has been known to turn away foreigners who can't show a valid travel permit. When Mogok Motel is full, you're permitted to stay at either the *Yar Pyae Guest House* or *Kyaw Family Guest House*, which share a four-storey building near the Zeigyi in the southern part of town and are owned by the same family. Rooms at either place cost K200 per person with common bath, K220 per person with attached bath.

The *Golden Butterfly Park Bungalow*, in the western end of town off the main road, is a very nice guest house reserved for visiting gem buyers; however, the staff will not accept foreigners.

Places to Eat

There are plenty of Chinese, Shan and Burmese restaurants around town, though none of them are outstanding. *Cherry Myaing*, on the west side of town on Yae Byu Rd, near the town entrance from Mandalay, is good for both Chinese and Burmese cuisine. *May Thit Sar*, on Mandalay-Moe Meik Rd towards the same end of town, and *Mya Sandar* near the lake, east of Zeigyi on the same road as the Yar Pyae and Kyaw guest houses, are two of the better spots for Chinese food.

Getting There & Away

Several bus lines operate transport services to Mogok from Shwebo (Yan Aung Padamya and Kyandine Aung) and Mandalay (Mogok-Man, Golden Triangle, Padamyar-Man, Kanbawza and Nila-Man); most vehicles are Toyota Hilux pickups, with a few full-size buses mixed in.

From the main bus centre in Mandalay there are departures every half hour from 6 am to 9.30 am, all of which arrive between 3.30 and 4.30 pm. In the reverse direction buses leave Mogok every half hour from 5.30 am to 8 am. The fare is K350 (K600 for a front seat in the pickups).

From Shwebo the fare is K150 (K300 in the front seat) or in the reverse direction only K130/250. Pickups leave Shwebo at 5 am, 5.30 am, 6 am and 7 am and arrive in Mogok between 1.30 and 3 pm. In the reverse direction pickups leave Mogok at 5 am, 5.30 am and 6 am only. This route requires a ferry crossing from Singu to Kyauk Myaung across the Ayeyarwady River; it's important to get to Singu by 9 am in time to queue for the 11 am 'zed craft'. Since the ferry is owned by a consortium of bus companies, there's a heavy charge for private vehicles.

Getting Around

Mogok has no trishaws, taxis or horsecarts; local transport is limited to walking, renting a bicycle or hitching a ride on a private vehicle.

Because of the lack of local transport in Mogok, out-of-town buses and pickups customarily drop passengers anywhere they like in central Mogok.

AROUND MANDALAY

Bagan Region

Bagan (Pagan) is the most amazing sight in Myanmar, if not South-East Asia. Across 40 sq km of country, stretching back from the Ayeyarwady (Irrawaddy), stand literally thousands of stupas and temples. In every direction you look you'll see ruins of all sizes – huge and glorious temples like the Ananda soar towards the sky, small, graceful *zedis* stand alone in fields. Some come with all manner of historical tales, while others are identified only by a number.

One could easily spend a week or more exploring the Bagan area. In addition to the more well-known monuments found in the main archaeological zone of Old Bagan, there are sites worth visiting in several other nearby towns and villages.

What you will be able to see is very much limited by the amount of time at your disposal and how you intend to use it. If you can afford to hire a car (or horsecart) and a guide, you'll be able to visit more temples, particularly those further off the beaten track. The availability of bicycles to rent also makes the sites much more accessible than on foot.

If your time is very limited – just an afternoon or a day, for example – we suggest that you restrict yourself to the temples and stupas in the central Bagan Archaeological Zone, which is where most of them are concentrated.

Temples of Bagan

Detailed descriptions about the history and archaeological styles of Bagan's ancient temples and stupas have been combined in a special section at the end of this chapter, beginning on page 277. Practical information about transport, accommodation and restaurant options for all the major towns in the Bagan region is provided below.

HISTORY

The extraordinary religious fervour that resulted in this unique collection of buildings lasted two and a half centuries. Although

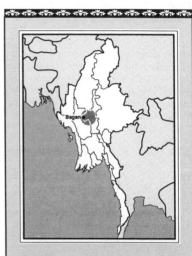

Highlights

• Spectacular plain of Bagan dotted with thousands of 800-year-old temple ruins
• Sunset over the Ayeyarwady River, viewed from the top of Mingalazedi or Shwesandaw Paya
• Mysterious Mt Popa, home to Myanmar's nats (guardian spirits)
• Little-known Bagan-era ruins of Salay

human habitation at Bagan dates back almost to the beginning of the Christian era, Bagan only entered its golden period with the conquest of Thaton in 1057 AD. Just over 200 years later, Bagan declined and in 1287 was overrun by the Mongols of Kublai Khan. But what fantastic effort went into those two and a half centuries – it's as if all the mediaeval cathedrals of Europe had been built in one small area, and then deserted, barely touched over the centuries.

Originally, this bend in the Ayeyarwady River was occupied by a stable and thriving Pyu city-state, perhaps allied with Beikthano and Thayekhittaya (Sri Ksetra) to the south as well as Hanlin to the north-east. Excavations along the ruined city walls indicate that by 850 AD the city had reached complex proportions. The name 'Bagan' may in fact derive from 'Pyugan', a name first written down by the Annamese of present-day Vietnam in the mid-11th century as 'Pukam'. In post-18th century Burmese parlance the name became 'Bagan', which was corrupted as 'Pagan' by the British.

Bagan's prime began with the Burman King Anawrahta's ascent to the throne in 1044. At this time, Myanmar was in a period of transition from Hindu and Mahayana Buddhist beliefs to the Theravada Buddhist beliefs that have since been characteristic of Myanmar. Manuha, the Mon king of Thaton, sent a monk to convert Anawrahta; the latter met with such success that Anawrahta asked Manuha to give him a number of sacred texts and important relics. Manuha, uncertain of the depths of Anawrahta's beliefs, refused the request. Anawrahta's reply to this snub was straightforward – he marched his army south, conquered Thaton and carted back to Bagan everything worth carrying, including 32 sets of the *Tripitaka* (the classic Buddhist scriptures), the city's monks and scholars and, for good measure, King Manuha himself. All in all some 30,000 Mon prisoners of war were brought to Bagan from Thaton.

Immediately Anawrahta set about a great programme of building, and some of the greatest Bagan edifices date from his reign. Amongst the better-known monuments he constructed are the beautiful Shwezigon Paya, considered a prototype for all later Burmese stupas; the Pitaka Taik, built to house the scriptures carried back from Thaton by 30 elephants; and the elegant and distinctive Shwesandaw Paya, built immediately after the conquest of Thaton. Thus began what the Burmese call the First Burmese Empire, which became a major centre for Theravada Buddhism and a pilgrimage point for Buddhists throughout South-East Asia.

Anawrahta's successors, particularly Kyanzittha, Alaungsithu and Narapatisithu,

continued this phenomenal building programme, although the construction work must have been virtually non-stop throughout the period of Bagan's glory. Pali inscriptions of the time called the city Arimaddanapura ('City of the Enemy Crusher') and Tambadipa ('Copper Land'). Marco Polo described the city-state in his famous 1298 chronicle:

The towers are built of fine stone; and then one of them has been covered with gold a good finger in thickness, so that the tower looks as if it were all of solid gold; and the other is covered with silver in like manner so that it seems to be all of solid silver...The King caused these towers to be erected to commemorate his magnificence and for the good of his soul; and really they do form one of the finest sights in the world, so exquisitely finished are they, so splendid and costly. And when they are lighted up by the sun they shine most brilliantly and are visible from a vast distance.

Historians disagree on what exactly happened to cause Bagan's apparent rapid decline at the end of the 13th century. The popular Burmese view is that millions of Mongols sent by Kublai Khan swept over the city, ransacking and looting. A more thoughtful view holds that the threat of invasion from China threw the last powerful ruler of Bagan into a panic; after a great number of temples were torn down to build fortifications, the city was abandoned, in which case the Mongols merely took over an already deserted city. This view finds support in Marco Polo's observation that the kingdom was taken by Kublai Khan's 'clowns and court jugglers'.

The Bagan scholar Paul Strachan argues that the city was never abandoned at all. For him the evidence suggests 'the physical arrival of the Mongols would seem to have affected Pagan little...Despite the political imbalances that the Mongols brought about Pagan remained a cultural centre, possibly even up to the present'. Evidence suggests Bagan may have continued as an important religious and cultural centre through to the 14th century, after which its decay can be blamed on the three-way struggle between the Shan, Mon and Burmans for supremacy over Upper Myanmar. Whatever happened, although some minor rebuilding and maintenance continued through the centuries the state's growth was effectively halted by 1300. Many of the religious monuments were later damaged by looters seeking precious metals and stones hidden in Buddha images and shrine walls.

From the 14th to 18th centuries, Bagan was considered a spooky region, ridden by bandits and *nats* (guardian spirits). The Burmese began moving back to Nyaung U and Bagan in some numbers only after the British established a presence in the area to provide protection from robbers and marauders.

It's hard to imagine Bagan as it once was because, like other Burmese royal cities, only the major religious buildings were made of permanent materials. The kings' palaces were all constructed of wood, and even most monasteries were partly or wholly wooden. So what remains today is just a frail shadow of Bagan at its peak. Today a few small farming villages are the only occupants of the great city. Grain fields stand where once there were palace grounds.

The kings who reigned over Bagan during its golden period were:

Anawrahta	1044-1077
Sawlu	1077-1084
Kyanzittha	1084-1113
Alaungsithu	1113-1167
Narathu	1167-1170
Naratheinkha	1170-1173
Narapatisithu	1174-1211
Nantaungmya	1211-1234
Kyaswa	1234-1250
Uzana	1250-1255
Narathihapati	1255-1287

1975 EARTHQUAKE & RESTORATION
In 1975 Bagan was shaken by a powerful earthquake. At first it was thought that this 1000-year-old wonder was totally ruined, but in actual fact events were not nearly so disastrous. Although many of the more important temples were badly damaged, major reconstruction started almost immediately.

Since renovation of these important religious monuments has been an ongoing project for many centuries, the old skills have not been lost and many monuments were rebuilt using traditional means. UNESCO's recent restoration projects now support dozens of local artisans, and although you certainly won't see any modern construction equipment in Bagan, modern techniques are being employed as well. UNESCO engineers, for example, are reinforcing some of the monuments by inserting iron beams in the masonry to preserve the structural integrity in case of earthquake.

As for the hundreds of lesser monuments, anything that was likely to fall off in an earthquake would have fallen off centuries ago. While it was quite evident which of the major temples were repaired, Bagan never looked like a huge building site. Some of the restoration, such as the repairs to the Gawdawpalin Pahto, took until the early 1980s to complete.

Bagan Archaeological Zone

Although Old Bagan is no longer inhabited except by hotel and government employees, it represents the core of the archaeological zone and contains several of the main temple sites, city walls and museum. It's right on a bend of the Ayeyarwady – sometime during your stay, wander down to the waterfront and watch the coming and going of the river trade. Boats will be passing by or pausing to unload goods, villagers will come down to the river with oxen carts to collect water. You can even take a boat across the river to the village on the other side. Note how Bagan's water supply is pumped up from a point just down below the Ayar Hotel.

ORIENTATION
Old Bagan sits on the eastern bank of a deep bend in the Ayeyarwady River. A paved road follows the river bend from Nyaung U, the

BAGAN REGION

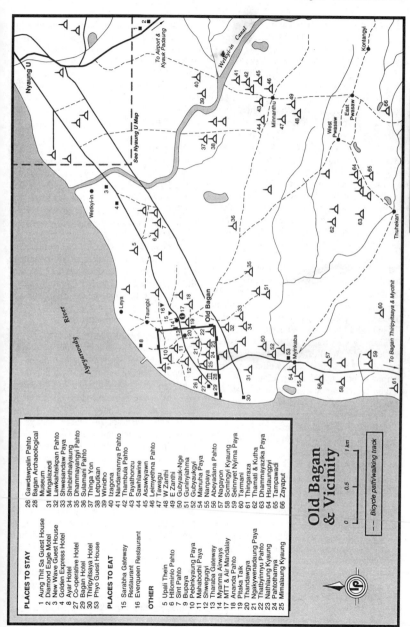

Old Bagan & Vicinity

0   0.5   1 km

-- - Bicycle path/walking track

PLACES TO STAY

1 Aung Thit Sa Guest House
2 Diamond Eagle Motel
3 New Wave Guest House
4 Golden Express Hotel
8 Ayar Hotel
27 Co-operative Hotel
29 Bagan Hotel
30 Thiripyitsaya Hotel
53 Phyo Guest House

PLACES TO EAT

15 Sarabha Gateway
    Restaurant
16 Everqueen Restaurant

OTHER

5 Upali Thein
6 Htilominlo Pahto
7 Sint Pahto
9 Bupaya
10 Pebinkyaung Paya
11 Mahabodhi Paya
12 Shwegugyi
13 Tharaba Gateway
14 Myanma Airways
17 MTT & Air Mandalay
19 Pitaka Taik
20 Thandawgya
21 Ngakywenadaung Paya
22 Thatbyinnyu Pahto
23 Nathlaung Kyaung
24 Pahtothamya
25 Mimalaung Kyaung
26 Gawdawpalin Pahto
28 Bagan Archaeological
    Museum
31 Mingalazedi
32 Lawkahteikpan Pahto
33 Shwesandaw Paya
34 Shinbinthalyaung
35 Dhammayangyi Pahto
36 Sulamani Pahto
37 Thinga Yon
38 Letputkan
39 Winidho
40 Izagona
41 Nandamannya Pahto
42 Thambula Pahto
43 Payathonzu
44 Sawhlawine
45 Asawkyawn
46 Leimyethna Pahto
47 Tawagu
48 W Zanthi
49 E Zanthi
50 Gubyauk-Nge
51 Guninyiahma
52 Gubyaukgyi
54 Manuha Paya
55 Nanpaya
56 Abeyadana Pahto
57 Nagayon
58 Somingyi Kyaung
59 Seinnyet Nyima Paya
60 Tarmani
61 Thingaraza
62 Thamati & Kutha
63 Dhammayazika Paya
64 Hsutaungpyi
65 Tampawadi
66 Zayaput

largest town in the area, and through the Bagan Archaeological Zone to the village of Myinkaba, and finally to Thiripyitsaya and Bagan Myothit (or New Bagan). Branching off this road is a vast network of tracks and trails between the various monuments.

Although the whole area is known to tourists as Bagan, only the archaeological zone is properly called Bagan nowadays. The village that grew up in the middle of the architectural area during the 1970s was moved to the middle of a peanut field several km away just before the May 1990 elections – much to the disgruntlement of Old Bagan residents. Back when tourist visits were limited to one week, this village was a place where some travellers spent nearly their entire seven days in Myanmar. Many residents depended on providing tourist services – lodging, food, souvenirs and moneychanging – for their livelihood. Now you can hardly tell that a village ever existed here, so thorough were the authorities in erasing all traces. At night a tomb-like silence has replaced the stimulating hum of international liaisons and black-market deals.

Clearing Old Bagan of guest houses has had one beneficial effect – it has dispersed visitors around the area and eliminated the tourist ghetto that had developed in Old Bagan. Accommodation is now scattered around Nyaung U, Wetkyi-in, Myinkaba, Bagan Myothit, Tetthe and Old Bagan.

The main town in the area, Nyaung U, is about five km upriver from Bagan. Nyaung U is also the terminus for buses and riverboats from Mandalay or further afield, and the airport is a couple of km south near the village of Tetthe.

Photography & Sunset-Viewing

For a panoramic view of as many ruined temples and stupas as possible, Mingalazedi is the best choice now that the upper terraces of the tallest monuments (Thatbyinnyu, Gawdawpalin, Dhammayangyi, Sulamani) are closed to visitors. The light for the eastward view from Mingalazedi is best in the late afternoon.

The westward view from Mingalazedi is of course also good for sunset, though some people prefer the sunset view from Shwesandaw Paya as it encompasses silhouettes of the monuments within Old Bagan to the north-west.

For Ayeyarwady River views at sunset the best choices are Bupaya in Old Bagan or Lawkananda Paya in Bagan Myothit; both stupas stand on the eastern bank of the river.

INFORMATION

Old Bagan itself contains just four hotels, the offices of Myanma Airways and Air Mandalay as well as Myanmar Travels & Tours. The latter is open from 8 am to 8 pm daily; it's main function is to administer the US$10 admission fee system for the Bagan Archaeological Zone.

You can also purchase two useful maps here, MTT's own *Bagan Tourist Map* and the independently produced *Tourguide Map of Bagan Nyaung U*. The MTT map is better-looking but the Tourguide map is more detailed.

Post & Telecommunications

There is a post office in Nyaung U; airmail letters are carried aboard daily flights to Yangon (Rangoon) so it's fairly reliable.

At the Thiripyitsaya Hotel in Old Bagan you can make international calls from an IDD phone for a steep US$9 a minute. Except for this hotel, the whole local phone system functions under a manual switchboard in Nyaung U. When telephoning to or from anywhere in the area you must therefore go through an operator.

Admission

MTT charges a US$10 entry fee for the first two nights spent in the archaeological zone, plus US$2 per night thereafter. For those arriving by air, the US$10 fee is collected at the airport on behalf of MTT, so it's difficult to get around it. Hotels collect the fee from those arriving overland. While wandering around the various sites we were never approached for the US$10 ticket inspection; the only place our ticket was checked was at the museum in Old Bagan. No one bothers to collect the US$2 for additional nights.

GETTING THERE & AWAY
Air
Both Myanma Airways (MA) and Air Mandalay (AM) fly to Nyaung U-Bagan Airport from Yangon, Mandalay and Heho.

From Yangon, AM flies daily; the flight takes an hour and 15 minutes and costs US$80 (US$75 standby). From Mandalay the AM flight costs US$50 (US$45 standby) each way and takes about half an hour. MA flies the same routes daily for US$80 and US$35 respectively. On either airline if you sit on the right-hand side of the aircraft flying Mandalay-Bagan or the left-hand side flying Bagan-Mandalay, you can keep the Ayeyarwady in sight most of the way and obtain a good view of Amarapura, Ava, the Ava Bridge and Sagaing while climbing out of or descending into Mandalay. You also get an excellent view of Bagan on the Bagan-Yangon flights.

From Heho both airlines fly daily to Bagan with a stopover in Mandalay. Aboard AM a ticket for this leg costs US$75; on MA it's US$65.

Air Mandalay flights can be booked or confirmed at the AM office next to the MTT office in Old Bagan. AM will soon be opening an office in Nyaung U as well. Ostensibly, MA flights can also be booked at the MA office on the opposite side of the road in Old Bagan, but repeated visits indicate that the staff are less than helpful. It's very difficult to find out whether you have a confirmed seat on the plane until it is too late to book the bus-train connection. Our recommendation – especially in light of MA's abysmal efficiency – is to forget about trying to fly in or out of Bagan on Myanma Airways. Stick to AM on this route – even though it costs a little more – or come via land or river.

Buses, Vans & Share Taxis
There are a number of options for travelling to the Bagan area by bus:

To/From Mandalay After flying, the fastest way to get to Bagan is on the regular bus from Mandalay to Nyaung U. Pickups operate daily from Mandalay's main bus centre on 26th St and cost K250 per person – the cramped vehicles are in poor condition so it's a rugged eight-hour trip. There are two departures from either end at 4 am and 9 am. Along the way you make a couple of tea stops – breakfast at Gume, lunch at Yewei.

There are also share taxis – Toyota hatchbacks – available to Bagan Myothit for K800 per person. Old cars or pickups can be chartered between Mandalay and Bagan for around US$60, new air-con vans for US$120. By share taxi or chartered private vehicle, the drive time for the 305 km between Mandalay and Bagan/Nyaung U drops to around six or seven hours.

To/From Taunggyi You can travel by bus, or rather pickup truck, directly between Nyaung U or Bagan Myothit and Taunggyi, for Inle Lake. From Bagan Myothit, Tiger Head Express operates Japanese pickups to Taunggyi for K500 per person. The pickup leaves the main north-south road in Bagan Myothit at 4 am and arrives in Thazi around 8.45 am, in time to catch the No 16 Down special express train south to Yangon. The pickup continues on to arrive in Taunggyi around 2 pm, stopping off for lunch along the way in Yemabay. Most travellers get off before Taunggyi at the junction town of Shwenyaung, from whence it's a short bus or taxi ride to Nyaungshwe (Yaunghwe) at the northern end of Inle Lake.

If you're really counting kyat you can hopscotch to Taunggyi/Inle Lake by taking a public pickup from Nyaung U to Kyauk Padaung (K25), changing to another pickup bound for Meiktila (K30), changing again to a Thazi-bound pickup (K10) and finally catching a pickup in Thazi all the way to Shwenyaung or Taunggyi (K60). The total fare for this trip may only be K125 but it's doubtful you'd make it all the way without having to spend the night somewhere. If you decide to overnight along the way, Thazi is your least expensive choice.

Those with a less limited budget can charter a pickup or old car all the way from the Bagan area to Taunggyi or Inle Lake for around US$50, or a new air-con van for up to US$100. Up over the hills east of Thazi the road is winding – beware if you suffer from motion sickness. Whether by public pickup or chartered van, this is a long and trying trip.

To/From Meiktila & Thazi When spare seats are available, Tiger Head Express will drop passengers off in Meiktila or Thazi on the way to Taunggyi for K250. If there's competition for the seats, Tiger Head sometimes charges the full Taunggyi fare, K500.

You can also take a regular pickup from Nyaung U to Kyauk Padaung at 5 am for just K25, than change to a Meiktila-bound pickup for K30. From Meiktila on to Thazi it's another K10.

To/From Yangon It is also possible to bus between Nyaung U and Yangon, although the trip is extremely long and wearing. Even by pick-up truck, with a few brief meals and rest stops, a look around Pyay (Prome) and much faster travel, Yangon-Bagan still entails a pre-dawn departure and an after-dark arrival.

Regular long-distance buses depart every other day or so from Nyaung U to Yangon for K300 to K500. You can also make the two-hour trip from Nyaung U to Kyauk Padaung, about 50 km south-east and costing K25. The Dagon-Popa bus line in Kyauk Padaung departs for Yangon twice daily at 4 am and 8 am. It should get to Yangon 12 to 14 hours later and costs about K250. Tickets can be booked a day ahead in Kyauk Padaung.

You could also bus to Meiktila and catch one of several Yangon-bound air-con express buses coming from Mandalay – see the Getting There & Away section in the Mandalay chapter for details. This is the most popular method among travellers these days.

A more interesting route to Yangon goes via the historic town of Pyay to the south. Myanmar Arrow Express runs an air-con bus

from the Nyaung U bus terminal to Yangon via Pyay at 5 pm every Monday, Wednesday and Saturday; the bus arrives in Yangon the next morning and costs K1500. Tickets may be purchased at the Pannu Book Store on the roundabout near Nyaung U's central market.

To/From Pyay You'll have to take a pickup to Kyauk Padaung first as described above. From Kyauk Padaung there are three daily buses to Pyay for K200 per person. The Kyauk Padaung to Pyay leg takes around eight hours. By private vehicle you can drive between Bagan and Pyay in as little as six or seven hours now that the road has been improved.

From Pyay you can continue on to Yangon by public bus (three departures daily) for just K100 and a ride of around seven hours. Air-con Rainbow Express buses from Pyay to Yangon are also available once a day around 5 pm for US$4 or K400 – see the Pyay section in the Around Yangon chapter for more details.

Train
There is no rail line all the way, so getting to or from Bagan by rail will also entail a sector by bus. It makes no sense at all to attempt to travel between Bagan and Mandalay by rail since you have to travel so far before getting a train – it's much easier to go by road all the way. Yangon-Bagan or Bagan-Yangon is a better possibility, although the first method is both very time-consuming and very uncomfortable.

Bus/Train via Kyauk Padaung To experience bus-train travel at its most miserable, try this option. Take a bus from Nyaung U to Kyauk Padaung, the nearest railhead to Bagan. At some time between 2 and 5 pm a train leaves for Yangon. Officially the train should arrive in Yangon around 8 am the following day, but in practice it can take closer to 24 hours. The fare is about the same as Thazi-Yangon if paid in kyat. The train is a dirty, uncomfortable, unlit, slow, crowded, tedious and unpleasant cattle train. It is best avoided. The hardy can also make this trip

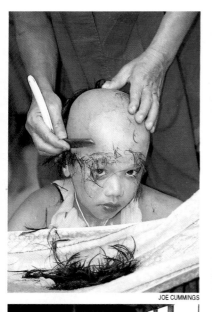
JOE CUMMINGS

BERNARD NAPTHINE

BERNARD NAPTHINE

JOE CUMMINGS

Bagan

Top Left: Buddhist head-shaving ritual, Bagan Myothit
Top Right: Sunset over the Ayeyarwady, Bagan
Bottom Left: On the deck, bound for Bagan
Bottom Right: Novitation ceremony, Bagan Myothit

BERNARD NAPTHINE

JOE CUMMINGS

Bagan
   Top: Mystical Mt Popa, rising over Bagan
Bottom: The elaborate Buddhist wood-carvings of Salay's Yoe Soe Kyaung

up from Yangon in a similar time, although you may have to change trains at Pyinmana, the junction on the Yangon-Mandalay line where the line branches off for Kyauk Padaung.

Bus/Train via Thazi This is a far better alternative. You first have to get to Thazi, which is about half way from Bagan to Inle Lake. A very efficient Tiger Head Express pickup goes straight through to Thazi from Bagan Myothit in plenty of time for the Mandalay-Yangon express. Departure time from Bagan Myothit is around 4 am.

The Bagan-Thazi road is very scenic, with a view of the Mt Popa volcanic dome in the distance near the start of the trip, as well as glimpses of villages, farms, bullock carts, pedestrians bearing cargo on their heads, etc. The ride is rather cramped with 18 official passengers in the back, two with the driver in front and three or four hangers-on. There are rest stops in Kyauk Padaung and Meiktila – the first a short intermission for fuel and the second a longer stop where you can refuel yourself with tea and *nam-bya* (Burmese roti). The fare is K250 per passenger.

The 6.30 pm express from Mandalay arrives in Thazi just after 9 pm and leaves a few minutes later. You can book your Thazi-Yangon tickets in Mandalay or Thazi, but if you wait till Thazi to buy your ticket there's no guarantee of a seat. A MTT official is sometimes at the station to meet foreigners coming in from Bagan. See the Thazi section for things to do while you're waiting for the train.

A more time-consuming option involves taking a truck to Kyauk Padaung from Nyaung U in the morning, changing to a Meiktila-bound truck in Kyauk Padaung and changing a second time in Meiktila to a Thazi-bound truck. There is really no reason to go this route but it is feasible so long as you get to Thazi in time for the Mandalay-Yangon express; otherwise you could end up on a slow train just as bad as the one from Kyauk Padaung. Anyone wishing to spend a night in Meiktila might also consider this option.

See the Getting Around chapter at the start of this book for the Thazi-Yangon train schedule.

Boat

It's possible to travel along the Ayeyarwady in both directions from Bagan, although the trip from Mandalay to Bagan is the one most commonly taken by travellers.

To/From Mandalay A passenger ferry departs Mandalay at 5.30 am every Thursday and Sunday on its downriver cruise to Bagan. The official foreigner fare is US$10 upper-deck class, US$30 for a cabin. Nowadays the entire upper deck is reserved for foreigners – sling chairs in deck class and 10 cabins with bunks and private toilets. If you were allowed to buy your ticket at the pier (slim chance) it would cost only K50 for lower-deck class.

You can get on board the boat the night before departure and grab a piece of deck space, thus saving the cost of a night's accommodation as well as staking your claim for deck space in the morning. The nights tend to be cold on the river so come prepared, and be ready to do battle with the mosquitoes too. The ferry arrives at Old Bagan around 5 pm when the water level is high, as late as 7.30 pm in the dry season when the pilots must sail more slowly to dodge sandbars. You must purchase tickets for the ferry at the Mandalay MTT office.

A slower, much cheaper ferry does the same route every day except Thursday and Sunday, taking roughly 26 to 29 hours and costing just K40. The slower boat stops one night on the western bank of the river at a town called Pakkoku, where there are several places to stay including the excellent Myayatanar Inn at 2288 Main Rd. It's about 250 metres down the main street from where you turn left out of the dock road. Rooms here are only K70 per person per night and they'll pick you up from the boat. They have good food too. Or you can also sleep on the boat if you want.

The next morning it's a further two hours downriver to Nyaung U, but don't worry if you over-sleep in Pakkoku and miss the boat as other boats pass by later in the morning. Only the faster 'tourist' ferry goes all the way to Old Bagan; all other boats land at the Nyaung U jetty, about six km north-east of Old Bagan. Pickups and horsecarts from the Nyaung U jetty to Old Bagan are plentiful.

Although it's quite an experience to travel by boat on the mighty Ayeyarwady, the river is wide and the banks flat with most of the villages set well back because of the risk of seasonal flooding, so you won't see too much off the river. There are plenty of stops, however, and people are always on hand to sell food and drinks.

Travelling upriver from Bagan to Mandalay involves another night stop on the way, so unless you can spare at least two full days, the upriver trip (on either ferry) is not worth considering unless you really have formed an attachment to Burmese river travel.

Think carefully before leaping on a Mandalay-Bagan ferry towards the end of the dry season (March or April). Getting stuck on sand bars can happen at any time of the year, but as the river level falls you're more likely to get stuck and it's liable to take longer to get unstuck. People have wasted a day or more sitting stationary in the middle of the Ayeyarwady.

To/From Pyay & Yangon From Nyaung U the slow ferries continue daily except Thursday and Sunday downriver to Pyay, where you could change boats and continue all the way to Yangon. The first day takes you from Bagan to Magwe, the second day from there to Pyay. From Pyay it's another two and a half day boat trip to Yangon. You'd use up a quarter of your four-week visa on this trip, but it would be quite a ride. See the Pyay section in the Around Yangon chapter for more details.

GETTING AROUND
To/From the Airport
The Nyaung U-Bagan airstrip is about five km south-east of Nyaung U, which is five km north-east of Old Bagan. Car taxis are available; figure on around K200 to Nyaung U or

Wetkyi-in, K500 to Old Bagan or Myinkaba, K600 to Bagan Myothit.

Bus
There is a bus service (pickup trucks once again) between Nyaung U and Bagan for K3; it departs about 200 metres from the bus terminal in Nyaung U.

Horsecart & Trishaw
You can hire horsecarts from place to place or by the hour; count on an hourly rate of around K50 to K60, K250 for the whole day, or K300 with two passengers. A horsecart from the Old Bagan jetty to Bagan Myothit costs around K75 with bargaining. Some of the horsecart drivers are pretty knowledgeable too, and some visitors reckon carts are preferable to bikes. Technically speaking, drivers are not supposed to act as guides – guides are required to have MTT licences and charge a separate guide fee – but with an informed driver, who needs a guide?

Trishaws are mostly confined to Nyaung U and Bagan Myothit, though they're occasionally seen elsewhere and always show up to meet the boat from Mandalay. A trishaw ride costs around K20 per km.

Bicycle
Although you can comfortably walk around the more central Bagan sites, if you want to travel further afield you'll need transport. Bicycles – available for hire at most hotels and guest houses – are a great way to get around. Traffic around Bagan is so light that bike riding is a delight, although you should steer well clear when the occasional motor vehicle does chance by. The usual cost is K80 per day or K50 for half a day. Riding can be hard going down the dustier tracks and punctures are inevitable, but they're fixed or the bike replaced with alacrity. An early-morning or late-afternoon ride along the sealed road between Wetkyi-in and Myinkaba is particularly pleasant.

When renting a bike, check it over thoroughly before accepting it – make sure it steers properly, that the brakes work and that the tyres hold air. One traveller told of seeing a rider discover his machine's total lack of braking just at the bottom of the long slope to the Thiripyitsaya Hotel. The staff picked him up, carried him inside and propped him up against the bar where a few beers restored his equilibrium. The same traveller was offered a bike with the suggestion that he pedal back every hour or so, 'to refill the tyres'. Riding out to some of the more remote temples can be hard going through the deep and dusty sand.

Boat

From the jetty near Bupaya in Old Bagan you can charter small boats for scenic trips along the river and to visit riverside shrines such as Lawkananda (near Bagan Myothit) and Kyauk Gu Ohnmin (east of Nyaung U). Hire rates are around K200 an hour.

OLD BAGAN ပုဂံဟောင်း:
Bagan Archaeological Museum

This small museum makes an interesting introduction before you start exploring the actual temples. It's housed in a cluster of modern buildings across from the Gaw-dawpalin Pahto. The central gallery contains a large number of religious images and other fine works found in temples around Bagan, including a bronze Buddha dating to the 16th century from Bago and many terracotta votive tablets from the 11th and 12th centuries. The stone images at the museum are crudely restored; better are the bronzes, many of which show Pallava influence. An 11th-century bronze lotus with Buddhas inside is particularly interesting.

Other museum pieces of note include fragments of painted cloth that were kept in the hollow forearms of large Buddha images, plus gems from the chests and heads of some images (many of the images in Bagan temple ruins have holes in the chest area where temple thieves made off with the cached gems). A lacquer Buddha in the museum's outside pavilion dates from the 13th century. Bagan-style Buddhas vary greatly in the proportion of head to body – some have huge heads and small bodies, some huge bodies and small heads – but all exhibit arched,

connected eyebrows and a knife-edged nose set in a squarish face.

There is also a small exhibit on the 1975 earthquake. The museum is open from 9 am to 4.30 pm Monday to Saturday; admission is US$4.

Tharaba (Sarabha) Gateway

The ruins of the main gate on the eastern wall are all that remain of the old 9th-century city wall. Traces of old stucco can still be seen on the gateway. The gate is guarded by highly revered brother and sister nats, the male ('Lord Handsome') on the right, the female ('Lady Golden Face') on the left. Since in their human histories the siblings died in a fire, worshippers offer the images flowers and water rather than candles or incense.

Anawrahta's original palace is thought to have been located near Tharaba.

Places to Stay

The accommodation situation in Old Bagan has changed radically since 1990. All of the cheap guest houses that used to line the main road through the archaeological zone were wiped out in one fell swoop before the May 1990 elections, when the entire village was moved to a new settlement called Bagan Myothit in 15 days. For several years afterwards, the only places open to foreigners were government-owned hotels in Old Bagan.

With the re-privatisation of hotels and guest houses, accommodation can now be found in Old Bagan, Nyaung U, Wetkyi-in, Myinkaba, Bagan Myothit and Tetthe (near the airport). Ironically the variety of places to stay has never been greater; around a dozen new places opened in 1994 and another 20 or so new hotels and guest houses are planned for the near future.

In or just outside Old Bagan proper there are four hotels, three of them now privately owned. Least expensive is the *Co-operative Hotel* (no phone) next to Gawdawpalin Pahto and opposite the museum. Basic rooms with mosquito nets, firm mattresses and shared shower and toilet cost US$8 single, US$15 double, US$20 triple. A six-bed 'dormitory' is also available for US$6 per person. A small new wing contains air-con rooms with fan and attached shower for US$10/18 single/double. Rates include breakfast, but the food at the Co-operative Restaurant is of very poor quality.

Though it costs more, currently the best all-around value in Old Bagan is the private Bagan (Thante/Thande) Hotel (☎ Nyaung U 12), continuing on the road that passes the museum. Fourteen large rooms in the two-storey 'guest house' building cost US$18/26 for a single/double with fan, US$20/28 with air-con. All rooms come with mosquito nets and good mattresses; some rooms have river views. The upstairs corner rooms are best since they get cross-ventilation and thus don't need air-con. Five 'chalet' bungalows with air-con, hot water and refrigerator cost a reasonable (for Myanmar) US$36/42. Verandah sitting areas are attached to each chalet. New chalets closer to the river, constructed of brick instead of wood, will cost US$50 when finished. On the grounds is a pleasant riverside garden.

Just north of the city wall near Bupaya is the privately owned Ayar Hotel (☎ Nyaung U 24; 01-95156 in Yangon), formerly the Irra Inn, which overlooks the Ayeyarwady and is close to the ferry landing. Economy rooms on the ground floor of the main U-shaped building cost US$18/24 single/double with fan and private cold-water shower. Standard rooms on the same floor add air-con and cost US$30/36. All ground floor rooms feature concrete floors. Upstairs are superior rooms of the same size, but with wood floors, TV, hot water, air-con and minibar, for US$36/42. Also on the upper floor, at the bottom of the 'U' facing the river, is the much larger Junior Suite with satellite TV, hot shower and minibar costing US$48/54, and the huge Ayar Suite with similar facilities for US$54/60. All rates include breakfast and free airport transfers but do not include the 20% service charge and tax. A new wing and bungalows under construction along the river will probably cost more.

About half a km south of the Old Bagan city walls – about a 20-minute walk from the centre – is the government-owned Thiri-pyitsaya Hotel, which does manage to take some advantage of its location and look like it belongs to an exotic place like Bagan – something which certainly cannot be said of most Bagan hotels. There are six separate bungalows, each with its own little verandah. Rooms have private bathrooms and fridges and are air-con. Recent visits have found it little run-down, with occasionally faulty plumbing. The nightly cost is US$45/55 for standard singles/doubles, US$56 for a deluxe one-bed bungalow or US$75 for a two-bed deluxe. The hotel also has a lounge area, pleasant restaurant and bar with a verandah, a good place for a beer around sunset. If after a hard day's temple-seeing you have not got the energy to drag yourself to a temple top to catch the sunset, this is a very acceptable substitute. Non-guests are permitted to swim at the hotel pool for K16. The hotel is now for sale; rumours say Ne Win's daughter may take the place over.

If all accommodation in Old Bagan is full (as it often is around New Year's) you can sleep on a platform at the old Bupaya stupa overlooking the river.

See the Nyaung U & Wetkyi-in, Myinkaba and Bagan Myothit sections for details on other accommodation in the area.

Places to Eat

Three of the four hotels in and around Old Bagan have decent restaurants; stay clear of the Co-operative dining room, which has made a number of travellers ill. The eating selections at each hotel are similar – the usual mixed Western and Burmese menu. The Thiripyitsaya usually has the best cooks, and it also has a bar.

Located just outside Tharaba Gateway, the friendly Sarabha Gateway Restaurant serves well-seasoned and reasonably priced Burmese, Chinese and Thai food in a simple, quiet, indoor-outdoor setting. Just a bit farther up the road toward Wetkyi-in, about 200 metres outside the city gate and north along a dirt road, is the inexpensive Ever-queen Restaurant, which has a similar menu and garden setting. The Burmese-style tomato and cucumber salad is particularly good at Everqueen.

Convenient to the Ayar Hotel, next to the boat landing below the hotel, is a cluster of local cafes and teashops. Although they're very rustic, the relaxed atmosphere makes for a pleasant evening. *Toe Toe*, on the left on a bluff as you walk toward the jetty, serves teashop snacks in the morning, decent curries in the afternoon.

There are many other places to eat in Wetkyi-in and Bagan Myothit – see the relevant sections for details.

Things to Buy
Like the guest houses and restaurants, the many craft shops that used to line the main road through the archaeological zone have been cleared out. A friendly Indian couple have managed to maintain a small lacquerware concession which they set up in front of Mahabodhi Paya on the road to the Ayar Hotel every morning. There is also a government-approved souvenir shop near the MTT office.

For a wider shopping selection, spend an afternoon wandering around Nyaung U or Bagan Myothit.

Getting There & Around
Nyaung U and Bagan Myothit are the main transportation centres for the area. See Getting There & Away and Getting Around earlier for details.

NYAUNG U & WETKYI-IN
ညောင်ဦး/ဝက်ကြီးအင်း
Nyaung U, about five km north-east of Old Bagan, is the major population centre in the Bagan area; you'll pass through Nyaung U if you arrive in Bagan by road or air, and by river if you take the slow boat from Pyay or Mandalay. It's an interesting little place for a wander around – it has lots of shops (look out for the cigar dealers), an excellent and colourful market and even a Burmese billiard hall. Recently several inexpensive guest houses have opened their doors to foreigners. Several small restaurants offer Indian, Chinese and Burmese food.

The small village of Wetkyi-in, roughly halfway between Nyaung U and Old Bagan, flanks the mouth of Wetkyi-in Canal. Along the two-km stretch between Wetkyi-in and Nyaung U are several guest houses and restaurants oriented toward travellers.

Although some of the monuments here are close to the Wetkyi-in and Bagan, or conveniently situated between both, others are rather inconveniently located far east of Nyaung U. You'll probably see some of them from the river or if you fly in or out of Bagan.

Aung Myi Bodhi Dhamma Yeiktha
Directly opposite Shwezigon Paya near Gubyaukgyi, this *kammathan kyaung* (meditation monastery) is home to the well-regarded 'Pakistan Sayadaw'. Also known by his Pali name U Ariyawananda, the *sayadaw* or abbot teaches a simple technique of breath-and-body awareness that attracts monks and lay practitioners from as far away as Yangon and even overseas. There's little to see among the simple collection of huts and buildings – no glittering stupas, just straight *dhamma* practice.

Places to Stay
Nyaung U and Wetkyi-in are fast adding places to stay, turning this side of the Bagan area into a modest accommodation centre. A number of guest houses and hotels are located near Shwezigon Paya, between Nyaung U and Wetkyi-in. The main advantage to these places are their proximity to the Nyaung U market and bus terminal.

The friendly *Aung Mingalar Hotel*, opposite Shwezigon, offers nine tidy rooms with small fridges, good mattresses, air-con and private cold-water showers and toilets for US$25/30/45 single/double/triple. It's next door to the well-run Aye Yei Thar Yar and Nation restaurants.

The less expensive, two-storey *Royal Guest House* (☎ Nyaung U 285), up the road a couple of hundred metres toward Nyaung U, has smaller economy rooms for US$7 per person with shared toilet and cold-water shower, and equally small standard rooms

BAGAN REGION

with attached facilities for US$10 per person. All rooms have ceiling fans.

Across the road toward Shwezigon is the *Pan Cherry Guest House* (☎ Nyaung U 74, 228), with 11 fan-cooled rooms for US$8/12 single/double with shared bath, and three rooms for US$12/20 with air-con and attached cold-water shower. The well-constructed, residential-style building stays fairly cool, even in hot weather.

Just south of this area off Thiripyitsaya Rd, the *New Heaven Hotel* (☎ Nyaung U 294) has quiet bungalow-style doubles with fan and attached toilet and cold-water shower for US$20.

About a km south-west of this area toward Old Bagan are two places located side-by-side. The residential-style *New Wave Guest House* features economy rooms with shared toilet and cold-water shower for US$8/15 single/double, and rooms with private facilities for US$12/18; rates include breakfast and all rooms have fans. Next door the much larger *Golden Express Hotel* (☎ Nyaung U 37) offers 15 cottage-style doubles on landscaped grounds for US$20/35/70 a single/double/triple including breakfast plus 24 economy rooms for US$10/15/20 not including breakfast. All rates are subject to

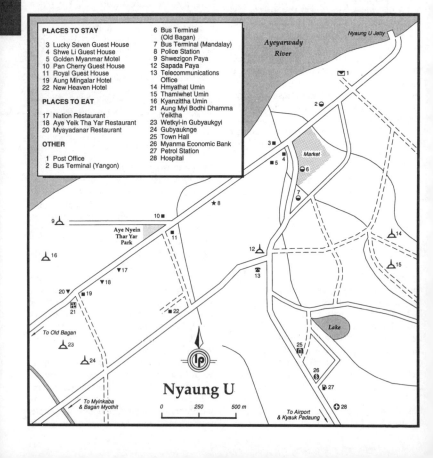

PLACES TO STAY
3 Lucky Seven Guest House
4 Shwe Li Guest House
5 Golden Myanmar Motel
10 Pan Cherry Guest House
11 Royal Guest House
19 Aung Mingalar Hotel
22 New Heaven Hotel

PLACES TO EAT
17 Nation Restaurant
18 Aye Yeik Tha Yar Restaurant
20 Myayadanar Restaurant

OTHER
1 Post Office
2 Bus Terminal (Yangon)
6 Bus Terminal (Old Bagan)
7 Bus Terminal (Mandalay)
8 Police Station
9 Shwezigon Paya
12 Sapada Paya
13 Telecommunications Office
14 Hmyathat Umin
15 Thamiwhet Umin
16 Kyanzittha Umin
21 Aung Myi Bodhi Dhamma Yeiktha
23 Wetkyi-in Gubyaukgyi
24 Gubyauknge
25 Town Hall
26 Myanma Economic Bank
27 Petrol Station
28 Hospital

Nyaung U

0   250   500 m

20% tax and service. These two hotels are 10 minutes walk to Shwezigon, five minutes to Htilominlo, 20 minutes to Nyaung U.

Two or three km north-east, at the western edge of Nyaung U on the main Nyaung U-Bagan road, are several other possibilities. Because of the general activity in the area, these places can be a little noisy during the day; nights are usually quiet though. The *Lucky Seven Guest House* (☎ Nyaung U 77), a large two-storey house on the northern side of the street, has rooms with ceiling fans for US$7 single, US$13 double. Rates include a substantial breakfast; toilet and cold-water shower facilities are shared. The local-style *Shwe Li Guest House* (☎ Nyaung U 291), on the southern side of the road a little west of the traffic circle and central market, features small rooms along a corridor for the same rates.

The larger *Golden Myanmar Motel* (☎ Nyaung U 98) stands off the main road a bit, opposite the Lucky Seven. The two-storey building features wooden walls, ceilings, floors and a sitting area on the upper floor overlooking the street. All rooms have fans and shared cold-water shower/toilet facilities; rates are US$8/15/20 a single/double/triple including breakfast. The management say they may add rooms with attached bath in the future. The hotel offers free transport to the bus terminal and jetty.

A couple of km south of Nyaung U are a couple of places near the airport and village of Tetthe. The residential-style, one-storey *Aung Thit Sa Guest House* (☎ Nyaung U 249) has two economy fan rooms, each with its own separate bathroom down the hall, for US$10/18/25 single/double/triple. There are also seven air-con rooms with attached bathrooms for US$20/28/40. All rooms have fans; showers are solar-heated.

Just up the road from the Aung Thit Sa, toward the airport, is the *Diamond Eagle Motel* (☎ Nyaung U 223, 138). Economy rooms with fan and attached bathrooms cost US$15/25 single/double, while larger air-con rooms with fridges go for US$25/35/45.

Places to Eat
Staying near Shwezigon puts you in the vicinity of three good places to eat, the *Nation, Aye Yeik Thar Yar* and *Myayadanar*. The menus at all three are similar, mostly Chinese with some Burmese dishes. The thatched-roof Nation, a leftover from the days when restaurants and guest houses were permitted in Old Bagan, has the best atmosphere and is the kind of place where travellers feel welcome to hang out a while. In addition to the usual fried rice, curries and noodles, the English-language menu includes several brands of beer, yoghurt, lassis and fruit juices.

In Nyaung U you'll find several less-than-clean rice and noodle shops, plus a couple of biryani places, but so far nothing special.

Things to Buy
Aside from the all-day central market, several small shops in town sell earthy, utilitarian ceramics, lacquerware and other crafts; what might be called 'folk utensils' elsewhere in Asia are everyday requisites here.

Getting There & Around
See the Getting There & Away and Getting Around sections at the start of this chapter for transport information about Nyaung U and Wetkyi-in.

MYINKABA မြင်းကပါ
Only a km or two south of Bagan, Myinkaba has a number of interesting temples and stupas from the Early Bagan period, and it is also worth visiting for its lacquerware workshops. Some of these accomplish the complete process of producing lacquerware in the one centre, while others specialise in a single phase of the production – such as making the bamboo frames on which the lacquer is coated.

Places to Stay & Eat
Next to Gubyaukgyi temple at the northern end of the village is the quiet and well-managed *Phyo Guest House*. Eight rooms along an air-con corridor share three bathrooms; the rates are US$8/15 single/double including breakfast.

Down the street, opposite Manuha Pahto, are a couple of decent teashops. One of them *Aung Mya Thi*, makes tasty samosas.

Things to Buy

A large lacquerware facility on the western side of the road is a good place to observe craft techniques or purchase a wide variety of well-priced lacquer items.

Getting There & Around

Old Bagan is a two-km walk north. Bicycles can be rented at Phyo Guest House for touring the ruins. Horsecarts are plentiful in Myinkaba. Bagan Myothit is about four km south, a K40 to K50 horsecart ride.

THIRIPYITSAYA & BAGAN MYOTHIT
သီရိပစ္စယာ/ပုဂံမြို့ သစ်

Thiripyitsaya is a small village that stands at the former site of a Bagan royal palace, about two km south of Myinkaba. The growth of Bagan Myothit (New Bagan) to its immediate south has for the most part swallowed up the village and the whole area is now more commonly known by the latter name. Lots of smaller ruins dot the area, including three very interesting monuments.

For the first couple of years after residents of Old Bagan were forced to move to the new town site, Bagan Myothit was a depressing place with little spirit. Today the residents have made the best of their unchosen new home and the place is abuzz with the construction of new hotels and guest houses, restaurants, souvenir shops and new homes. It now rivals Nyaung U as the main population centre, and is even beginning to draw migrants from Mandalay to serve the growing tourist industry.

Places to Stay

Bagan Myothit currently offers more choice of accommodation than any other town or village in the entire Bagan area. For several years there was a government monopoly on hotels; now that private hotels are again permitted to accept foreigners, many of the Burmese who had experience running guest houses in Old Bagan are participating in the development.

Just off the main road running between Old and New Bagan, near the police station, is the *Queen Hotel* a somewhat musty local-style place where 10 large rooms with ceiling fans and attached bathrooms (hot water on request) cost US$15/24 single/double for foreigners, much less for Burmese citizens.

South of here another main road heads east away from the river. On the northern side of this road is a short string of new places. First up on the left is the *Bagan Beauty Hotel*, a well-constructed, thick-walled two-storey house with three single rooms and nine double rooms for US$6 per person. All rooms have fans; toilet and shower facilities are shared.

On the opposite side of the street, the single-storey *Mya Thida Hotel* has just six rooms with attached hot-water shower and toilet, plus air-con in the corridor, for US$8 per person. This rate can sometimes be nego-

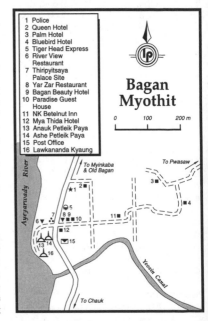

1   Police
2   Queen Hotel
3   Palm Hotel
4   Bluebird Hotel
5   Tiger Head Express
6   River View
    Restaurant
7   Thiripyitsaya
    Palace Site
8   Yar Zar Restaurant
9   Bagan Beauty Hotel
10 Paradise Guest
    House
11 NK Betelnut Inn
12 Mya Thida Hotel
13 Anauk Petleik Paya
14 Ashe Petleik Paya
15 Post Office
16 Lawkananda Kyaung

Bagan Myothit

0   100   200 m

To Myinkaba & Old Bagan
To Pwasaw
Ayeyarwady River
Yeosin Canal
To Chauk

tiated to as low as US$6/8 single/double, not bad value considering the facilities. Rates include breakfast.

Back on the northern side of the road, the two-storey *Paradise Guest House* offers 14 rooms with ceiling fans and hard beds in a modern house for US$8/15/21 a single/double/triple with breakfast.

Farther east on the same side of the street, the new *NK Betelnut Inn* (☎ Nyaung U 25) has eight separate but tiny cottages with air-con, hot water, fan and fridge for US$24/36 single/double including breakfast.

In a quiet north-eastern corner of Bagan Myothit, surrounded by an unnamed temple and stupa ruins, is the friendly and well-run *Palm Hotel* (☎ 01-90589 in Yangon, ☎ 02-21192 in Mandalay, ☎ 01-53297 radio phone), a one-storey building made almost entirely of local materials. Spacious rooms with ceiling fans and attached shower and toilet cost US$12 single, US$18 double, or with air-con US$18/24. A dining room in a separate building serves some of the best food in the Bagan area.

Several other small and medium-size hotels are under construction in Bagan Myothit, including the *Bluebird Hotel* south of the Palm Hotel. The Indian owners of Mandalay's popular Marie-Min Vegetarian Restaurant plan to build their own guest house on a piece of land opposite the Paradise Hotel.

Places to Eat

Along the main north-south road between Old Bagan and Bagan Myothit, near the Thiripyitsaya Palace site, three restaurants handle most of visitor dining trade. The *River View* stands on high ground above the river off the western side of the road. The menu features both Burmese and Chinese dishes, most of them well prepared. The indoor dining room is nothing special, but in good weather you can dine at breezy tables under shady trees out front. Prices are moderate to high. The nearby *Royal* and *Yar Zar* restaurants aren't quite as upscale but offer similar menus. The *Bwinmalar Burmese Restaurant* in the centre of town is very good – the

atmosphere is like eating in someone's home and a full Burmese meal costs only K100.

Of the three teashops in Bagan Myothit, the most traditional is *Yarkyaw (Yagyo)*, which attracts an older Burmese crowd with a taste for good tea. Younger folks hang out at *Moon* and *Bagan Cafe*, where the sound systems play rock'n'roll.

Things to Buy

One of the largest lacqerware shops in the area, U Ba Nyein, can be found on the main east-west road through town.

Getting There & Away

Tiger Head Express has its office on the eastern side of the main road, between the police station and the main east-west intersection. See Getting There & Away at the start of the chapter for details on Tiger Head's special pickups to Meiktila and Taunggyi.

Getting Around

Pickups to and from Nyaung U run roughly four times daily from the market for K10 per person. A horsecart to and from Old Bagan or the ferry jetty near Old Bagan costs K75.

Bicycles are a good way to get from place to place and they can be rented through any of the hotels or guest houses for K80 to K100 per day. The Palm Hotel can also arrange a car and driver for US$25 to US$30 per day.

MINNANTHU မင်းနန်သူ

Situated more or less directly south of Nyaung U, the monuments here are of a later period than those in the central Bagan area. Temples here are quite a way off the 'beaten track', and the track to the village can be very sandy, making bicycle riding difficult. These temples are generally locked up because of their valuable frescoes.

PWASAW ပွါးစော

Situated between Myinkaba and Minnanthu, Pwasaw was the site of the royal palace after it was transferred from Thiripyitsaya and before it was moved to Bagan in 874 AD. There are now two small villages, Anauk (West) Pwasaw and Ashe (East) Pwasaw.

Bagan Area

SALAY ဝင်္ဂဃ

During the Late Bagan era, specifically the late 12th and 13th centuries, Salay developed as the expanding spiral of Bagan's influence moved southward along the Ayeyarwady River.

Today's Salay is much more of a religious centre than Bagan, with many more working monasteries than found in Bagan today. Among the Burmese it's most famous as the historic home of Salay U Ponya, a Bagan-era writer/poet whose works are read by high school and college students all over the country.

The British established a presence here, as testified by the presence of several old two-storey colonial buildings in town, including one that still bears royal crown reliefs (typically removed in other parts of the country) on the facade. Following independence, the city was virtually abandoned until a Japanese firm built a huge fertiliser plant north of town around 20 years ago. The Japanese eventually turned the plant over to the Burmese, leaving behind the Salay Golf Club – a course built to serve the Japanese executives in charge of the project – near the town entrance.

Today the town, with its Burman majority, is bubbling with activity again. Aside from the atmospheric old colonial buildings and the ruins north of town, however, there's not a lot to see. A trip to Salay is warranted for anyone who develops a passion for Bagan-style architecture. For other visitors less consumed with Bagan, it's simply more of the same although the laidback town of Salay may be of interest for those who find Bagan and Nyaung U too touristed.

Bagan Era Monuments

Little of Salay's history is known outside a small circle of Burmese archaeologists working with limited funds. Western archaeologists too have yet to carry out a thorough study. Hence details on the 103 ruins – most of them known only by number rather than name – are sketchy. It is said that most of the

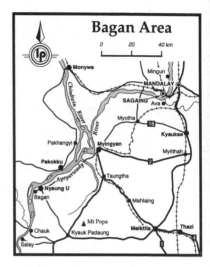

Bagan Area

monuments in Salay weren't royally sponsored but were instead built by the lower nobility or commoners. Hence there are no structures on the grand scale of Bagan's Ananda, Thatbyinnyu or Dhammayangyi.

Salay architects favoured designs similar to those found in the 'outer circle' Bagan monuments of Minnanthu and Pwasaw, particularly mid-sized *gu*-style sanctuaries (small, hollow temples) with prominent *sikharas* (corncob-like temple finials). The latter feature was often inspired by the Bagan namesake copy of the Mahabodhi stupa in Bodhgaya, India.

Among the named sites worth a look is **Payathonzu**, an interconnected complex of three brick shrines with corncob sikharas. All three shrines contain some form of mural painting but the most extensive graces the third one in the series, located to the south-west. This one also has a set of stairs that lead through a very narrow passage to reach the upper terrace. Legend says it was constructed by three sisters, but tripartite *pahtos* (temples) exist elsewhere in Salay and Bagan. If Payathonzu is locked you may have to ask a caretaker for keys.

In the same area, near the functioning

monastery of Thadanayaunggyi Kyaung and the meditation centre of Mogok Vipassana Yeiktha, a 19th-century shrine shelters a large lacquer Buddha known as **Nan Paya**. This image, said to date to the 13th century, may be the largest lacquer image in Myanmar; the fingertips alone measure about two metres high.

A short walk from Payathonzu stands what the locals call **Hkinkyiza Kyaung**, actually an old brick-and-stucco *pitaka taik* or library. Unlike similar libraries in Bagan, this one bears an intact superstructure. There is also some original stucco relief remaining on the lintels and pediments. Of the four entranceways, three are blocked off. The remaining unobstructed passage is bare except for an antique *pitaka* chest sitting at the back. The interior walls have been unfortunately whitewashed, probably covering murals underneath.

Yoe Soe (Youpson) Kyaung

On the other side of the main road from Kyauk Padaung is the oldest surviving wooden monastery hall in the Bagan area south of Pakkoku. The hall sports a new corrugated metal roof to protect the carved wooden structures below from rain or stray sparks from cooking fires. Only two sides of the 23-metre-long hall actually bear the original 120-year-old sculptures, which include nearly three-dimensional carvings of 19th-century court life, *jatakas* (stories from the Buddha's life) and *Ramayana* tales. Some panels are missing and there are some newer wood carvings mixed in with the old, but those that remain are lovingly cared for by the monks and caretakers, who apply oil regularly to prevent cracking.

Brick-and-stucco stairs featuring a *naga* (or serpent) design lead up to the hall, which is supported by 170 teak pillars two metres off the ground. The structure measures 23 metres long. Inside the hall is a collection of antique religious objects from the area including small wooden Buddha figures, heads, old pottery and votive tablets that may date from the 11th to 13th centuries, plus many wooden Konbaung or Mandalay-style

images. A wooden Bagan-style naga Buddha is particularly distinctive. A lacquer Konbaung-era Buddha image about a metre high sits in a separate section of the hall which features a painted carved-wood ceiling. In the same section is a graceful bronze and silver Mandalay-style sitting Buddha in the earth-touching pose; whether by design or not, the head is intriguingly tilted to the left very slightly.

Places to Stay & Eat

Salay has no hotels or guest houses – for foreigners or Burmese – but determined overnighters might be able to stay in one of the many monasteries. The central market has the usual noodle and sticky rice vendors, and there are a few teashops around town.

In Kyauk Padaung, on the way to Salay, you may be able to stay at the *Aung Chan Tar Guest House* for K300. It's unlicensed but usually accepts foreigners.

Getting There & Away

From Nyaung U/Bagan By public transport you can catch an early morning pickup from Nyaung U to Kyauk Padaung (48 km, K25) and change to a Salay-bound pickup (58 km, K30). Since the last pickup back to Nyaung U leaves around 4 pm, you'd hardly have any time to spend in Salay if you wanted to do it all in one day. Hence it's best to charter a vehicle or spend the night in Kyauk Padaung – or try your luck in Salay.

Salay can easily be visited as a day trip from Bagan if you have your own car or van. The 106-km trip via Kyauk Padaung takes around two and a half hours each way along a decent sealed road. There is also an unsealed secondary route that hugs the river south of Bagan Myothit and passes through Chauk. Although this road is considerably shorter, the bumpy drive can take up to four hours or more. Just south-west of Kyauk Padaung you leave Mandalay Division and enter Magwe Division.

You could also take a Pyay-bound ferry from Nyaung U, getting off in Salay around midday. The ferry leaves at 5 am every day except Thursday and Sunday and arrives in

Salay in the late afternoon; the deck class fare is around K20.

From Pyay The 380-km drive between Pyay and Salay takes six to seven hours by private vehicle along a paved road. By public transport you will have to change pickups in Magwe and Kyauk Padaung, making it a very long trip – plan to spend the night in Magwe to get an early start the next day for onward travel to Salay.

MAGWE မကွေး:

Capital of Magwe Division, this mid-size town on the eastern bank of the Ayeyarwady River is 531 miles north of Yangon and 152 km south-west of Nyaung U. The town has an estimated 99% Burman majority and, like the rest of the region surrounding Bagan, it's very hot and dry during the months of April and May.

There's very little of touristic interest in the town, although the locals will try to send you out to see the famous 1929-vintage **Mya Tha Lun Paya**, a typical Burmese stupa north-west of town on the river. Magwe's main value to the traveller is as a stopover on long road trips between Pyay and points north.

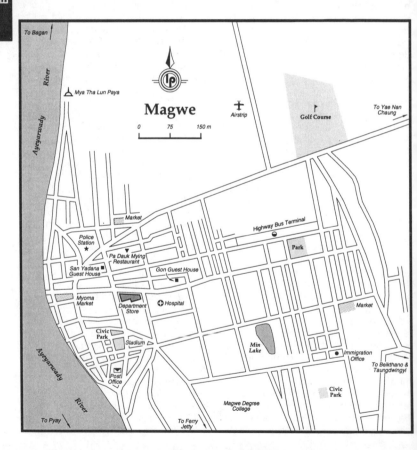

Places to Stay & Eat

A K25 trishaw ride from Magwe's bus terminal in the north-east part of town, *Gon Guest House* has very good rooms with aircon for K400. The more basic *San Yadana Guest House* near Myoma Market downtown offers passable rooms for K150. Other places in town where you may be able to stay include the *Sagawar, Ayeyar, Pyin U Lwin, Nyein Chan Phu* and *Thinn Cherry*, all basic guest houses with rooms in the K75 to K150 range. Of course none of the above are 'licensed lodgings' for foreigners, but that hasn't stopped most of them from taking in foreign guests.

Gon and San Yadana guest houses each have attached cafes that aren't too bad. In the vicinity of the market, *Sein Ya Tu* and *Nan Han* serve decent Chinese and Burmese food, while the *Chitty Htamin-zai (Chitty Rice Shop)* does very inexpensive Indian meals.

Getting There & Away

Bus & Pickup The main bus terminal is in the north-eastern part of town; from there you can catch pickups and buses to Pyay, Kyauk Padaung and Yangon.

Boat Ferries from Pyay arrive on Tuesday, Wednesday and Saturday for K29 deck class and K58 upper class, but it makes more sense to travel in the faster downriver direction on the intervening days (Sunday, Monday, Thursday and Friday). From Nyaung U expect to pay about the same as from Pyay. The office of the Inland Water Transport Co is near the Myoma Market; the ferry landing is south of town.

Getting Around

Trishaws and horsecarts are the main forms of local transport, but there are also a couple of regular pickup routes. A pickup from Myoma Market to the ferry landing costs K5 per person.

AROUND MAGWE
Beikthano

This ancient Pyu site is located near Taung-dwingyi, a small town 82 km south-east of Magwe. Don't even think of making a trip all the way out here unless you have a strong interest in ruins or Burmese history as there's little to see beyond piles of bricks, melting city walls and a few temple foundations.

Beikthano – a Burmese corruption of 'Vishnu' – was originally founded as Vishnu-loka under King Pyinbya, a Pyu monarch who may have been part Indian. Excavations among the ruins have uncovered beads, terracotta votives, stone and metal art objects, skeletal remains, stucco relief fragments, silver coins, potsherds and burial urns. The design of these items and their Pyu inscriptions indicate links with the Pyu principalities of Thayekhittaya and Hanlin, but little else is known about the city-state. A number of these artefacts are on display in a museum in Taungdwingyi.

With their wheel and swastika-shaped bases, the building plans of some of the structures bear a strong resemblance to Buddhist monuments found at Nagarjunakonda in South India. Since *dhammachakkas* (dharma wheels) and other Buddhist symbols – but no likenesses of the Buddha himself – were found here, one theory is that the settlement may have been started by Nagar-junakonda missionaries. If true, this would indicate a 3rd-century origin for Beikthano, representing a period when Buddhists didn't permit the sculpture or worship of Buddha images. Most scholars agree that Beikthano predates Thayekhittaya by about four centuries and that it was destroyed by fire in the 4th to 5th centuries.

Getting to Beikthano is difficult unless you have your own wheels. The road to Taungdwingyi is paved but not in very good condition. There may be one pickup per day between Magwe's Myoma Market and Taungdwingyi. The ruins lie just north of Kokkogwa, a village 19 km west of Taung-dwingyi; you should get off just before Kokkogwa when you see the city walls, which are bisected by the Magwe-Taung-dwingyi road.

Beikthano is contained within the old walls a short walk north-east of this point and

BAGAN REGION

BAGAN REGION

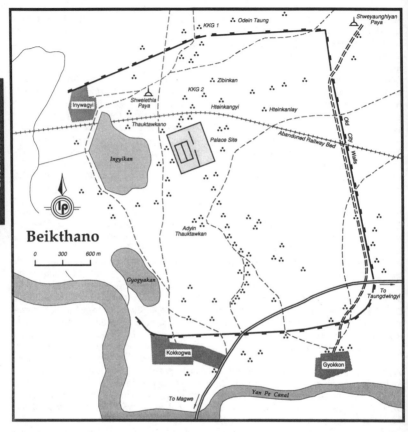

Beikthano

0   300   600 m

spreads over nine sq km. The old palace site sits a little north-west of the centre of the rectangle formed by the city walls. Just west of the old palace is a large pond called Ingyikan, an ancient reservoir still used by the villagers of Inywagyi to the immediate north-west. Less than a half km from the north-eastern corner of the old city is a famous stupa called Shweyaunghlyan Paya.

One of the only written English-language sources on the ruins is the 1969 archaeological survey *Report on the Excavations at Beikthano* by Aung Thaw, sometimes available in Yangon.

PAKKOKU ပခုက္ကူ

Now that the region is opening up and visa validities are longer, a trickle of travellers are stopping off in Pakkoku on the way to Bagan by river from Mandalay. A tobacco-trading centre, the town itself has little to see, but 20 km north-east of Pakkoku are the remains of **Pakhangyi**, a 19th-century town with old city walls, an archaeological museum and one of the oldest surviving wooden monasteries in Upper Myanmar. The latter is supported by 254 teak pillars. Further west is Myanmar's largest wooden monastery, a 19th-century structure with 332 teak pillars called **Pakhan-ngai Kyaung**.

Besides tobacco, which is cultivated in the surrounding Ayeyarwady floodplain, Pakkoku is famous for jaggery (palm sugar), *thanaka* logs, *longyis*, and checked blankets called *ok saung* made from cotton and wool. Vendors selling these items line up along the pontoon landing whenever a ferry calls at Pakkoku.

One of the town's biggest festivals, Thihoshin, is held from the 8th waxing day to the 8th waning day of Nayon (May/June). The festival is famous for its *pwe* performances, both human and marionette.

Places to Stay & Eat
The friendly *Myayatanar Inn* rents very simple rooms for K70 per person; someone from the inn usually meets arriving passengers at the pier. The inn can also arrange meals; the restaurants and cafes around town aren't much to crow about. A trishaw from the pier to the inn costs no more than K30. Less favourable accommodation is available at the *Tha Pye Nyo Guest House*, of which there are two (No 1 and No 2), for K75 per person.

Getting There & Away
The most convenient way to reach Pakkoku is by pickup from Mandalay. These cost K90 per person and leave the main bus centre at 7 am and 11 am, a schedule timed with the Chindwin River ferry crossings at 11 am and 3 pm.

Another way to reach Pakkoku is via the Mandalay-Bagan ferry – see the Getting There & Away section at the start of this chapter for details.

MYINGYAN ၿမင္းၿခံ
This Burman-majority township of 260,000 sits on a flat plain along the Ayeyarwady River about midway between Mandalay and Nyaung U. Roads to Mandalay, Nyaung U, Myittha and Meiktila all intersect here, and the long-distance ferries call here as well, so the township seat is a busy transport junction. A modern, two-storey central market

indicates trade is an important by-product of the town's transport function. **Yan Aung Daw Paya**, a standard bulb-tipped, bell-bottomed gilded stupa, is the town's only pride and joy after the market. The townspeople might also boast about the town's tidy green and white railway station, one of the better-kept stations in Upper Myanmar.

In the southern part of town at **Soon Lu Kyaung**, the remains of the well-known Soon Lu Sayadaw are draped in monastic robes and on display in an ornate gilded funerary dais. The sayadaw died 47 years ago; though desiccated, his body is remarkably well preserved.

Places to Stay
The Ministry of Hotels & Tourism's licencing division hasn't gotten around to Myingyan yet, but foreigners are occasionally accepted at *Aye Thukha, Yamon, Than Yadanar* and *Ngwe Phyo* guest houses. Each offers spartan rooms for K150 per person, plus a couple of air-con rooms for around K400. There are other less palatable places to stay as well.

Getting There & Away
Around a dozen intercity transport services run buses and pickups to Magwe (four hours, K120), Mandalay (three hours, K150), Nyaung U (three hours, K150), Meiktila (four hours, K200) and Yangon (15 hours, K450). The main bus station is in the centre of town near Aye Thukha Hotel.

Myingyan is linked by rail with Thazi, the junction for the Mandalay-Yangon express trains. The station is situated in the eastern downtown area. One train per day makes the six-hour journey to Thazi. Although the train fare is very cheap, buses do the same route (with a change in Meiktila) in around four hours.

Ferries between Mandalay and points south also stop off in Myingyan. The ferry landing is located west of town.

Getting Around
Trishaws, horsecarts and motorised three-wheelers ply the streets of Myingyan. At K15

BAGAN REGION

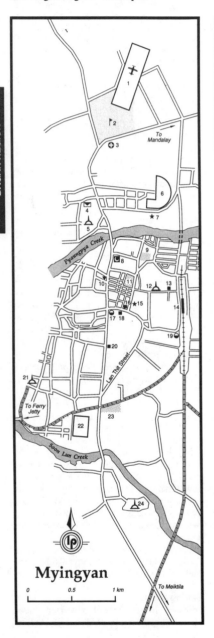

Myingyan

0   0.5   1 km

To Meiktila

PLACES TO STAY

13 Than Yadana Guest House
16 Yamon Guest House
18 Ayethukha Guest House
20 Ngwe Phyo Guest House

PLACES TO EAT

10 Sein Htay Restaurant

OTHER

1   Airstrip
2   Golf Course
3   Hospital
4   Post Office
5   Shwebontha Paya
6   Myingyan Jail
7   Police Station No 2
8   Mosque
9   Market
11 Central Market
12 Yan Aung Myin Paya
14 Railway Station
15 Police Station No 1
17 Bus Station
19 Aung Sit Thi Bus Terminal
21 Na Kyein Shae Hsu Paya
22 Stadium
23 San Pya Market
24 Soon Lun Kyaung

per km, trishaws are the cheapest options while three-wheelers and horsecarts cost about K25 to K30 per km.

MT POPA ပုပ္ပါးတောင်

If you look towards the range of hills that rise, shimmering in the heat, behind Bagan you'll see a solitary peak behind them. That is Mt Popa, which has been described as the 'Mt Olympus' of Myanmar. Rising to 1520 metres from the flat, surrounding Myingyan Plain, Mt Popa is said to be the core of an extinct volcano last active 250,000 years ago. The ground either side of the road is strewn with the remains of a petrified forest.

Volcanic ash makes the surrounding plains fertile and the heights capture the moisture of passing clouds, causing rain to drop on the plateau and produce a profusion of trees, flowering plants and herbs. 'Popa' in fact is derived from the Sanskrit word for flower. One of Mt Popa's presiding nats,

Mae Wanna, is considered the patron nat of medicinal and magico-religious herbs, many of which still grow in the area today. At one time the surrounding forests were home to elephants, rhinos, sambar and tigers; all had disappeared by the time a 1908 mammal survey was undertaken by the British Raj.

Mt Popa is considered the abode of Myanmar's most powerful nats and as such is the most important nat worship centre. The Mahagiri shrine, at the base of the rock out-cropping at the summit, contains a display of mannequin-like figures representing the 37 nats and is a major pilgrimage site. Burmese superstition says you shouldn't wear red or black on the mountain, nor should you curse, say bad things about other people or bring along any meat (especially pork) – any of these actions could offend the residing nats who might then retaliate with a spate of ill fortune.

Atop the impressive rocky crag clings a picturesque complex of monasteries, stupas and shrines which you can climb to via a winding, covered walkway. The 20-minute climb is steep and stiff, but it gets cooler as you get higher. When you reach the top the views are fantastic. You'll meet many other pilgrims along the way, including a class of non-ordained hermit monks called *yeti* (from the Pali-Sanskrit *rishi)* who wear tall peaked hats; part of their practice involves walking very slowly and mindfully while in the vicinity of Mt Popa.

Festivals
Mt Popa hosts two huge nat festivals yearly, one beginning on the full moon of Nayon (May/June) and another on the full moon of Nadaw (November/December). Before King Anawrahta's time thousands of animals were sacrificed to the nats during these festivals, but this practice has been prohibited since the Bagan era. Spirit possession and overall drunken ecstasy are still part of the celebration, however.

There are several other minor festivals, including ones on the full moons of Wagaung (July/August) and Tagu (March/April) which celebrate the departure and return of

the famous Taungbyon nats – Min Gyi and Min Lay – each year. The latter nats are brothers who were born to a marriage between Mae Wanna and an Indian Muslim in Anawratha's employ. The two sons were murdered at Taungbyon, where Anawratha built a shrine in their honour. Once a year the Taungbyon nats are believed to travel a spirit circuit that includes Mt Popa, Taungbyon (22 km north of Mandalay) and China.

Places to Stay & Eat
Most people visit Mt Popa as a day trip from Bagan or on their way east of Meiktila or Inle Lake. There's a rather utilitarian *Forestry Guest House* at the base of the mountain which may take visitors; or you could ask at the nearby monastery.

Near the Mahagiri shrine at the bottom of the rock outcropping are several small cafes with decent Burmese food. No beef or pork is served.

Getting There & Away
Mt Popa is about 50 km from Bagan or 10 km from the railhead at Kyauk Padaung. You can visit Mt Popa by day-tripping from Bagan or as a stop-off between Bagan and Thazi or Mandalay. Getting there by public transport would be a bit time-consuming, but with pickup truck charters becoming more readily available more travellers are managing to fit Mt Popa into their itinerary. A pickup, with enough room for 12 to 14 people at a squeeze, would cost about K2500 or US$25 for the round trip from Bagan.

MEIKTILA မိတ္ထီလာ
Only a short distance west of Thazi, Meiktila is the town where the Bagan-Taunggyi and Yangon-Mandalay roads intersect, just as Thazi is the place where the equivalent railway lines intersect. It's an important and prosperous trade centre which also draws revenue from a nearby air force base and training facility. Meiktila is officially open to foreigners and although there's nothing of particular historical interest here (a bad fire in 1991 almost wiped out the entire town), the town does offer the opportunity to savour

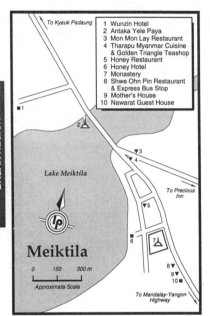

1	Wunzin Hotel
2	Antaka Yele Paya
3	Mon Mon Lay Restaurant
4	Tharapu Myanmar Cuisine & Golden Triangle Teashop
5	Honey Restaurant
6	Honey Hotel
7	Monastery
8	Shwe Ohn Pin Restaurant & Express Bus Stop
9	Mother's House
10	Nawarat Guest House

the atmosphere of a medium-size Burmese town that until recently has seen very few foreigners.

The town sits on the banks of huge Lake Meiktila, bridged by the road from Nyaung U. From one end of this bridge, a wooden pier extends out over the lake to small **Antaka Yele Paya**, a cool spot to rest on warm evenings. The municipality has plans to take further advantage of the town's lakeside location by adding a promenade around the lake, with restaurants to follow.

Shwebontha Kyaung is a monastery with huge lions out the front – you can't miss this main street landmark while passing through town. Just north of town, by the airfield, there's a WW II Spitfire on display in remarkably good condition.

Places to Stay & Eat

Honey Hotel (☎ 064-21847), a converted mansion on Pan Chan St next to the lake, offers large rooms with high ceilings, air-

con, private hot showers and good mattresses for US$20/33, or similar rooms with shared bath and air-con for US$10/17. Breakfast is available for US$1.

The *Nawarat Guest House* (no English sign), a two-storey green house next to a shop called Mother's House on the main street, rents simple but clean cubicles with shared facilities for K60 per day. The guest house has applied for a foreigner licence; expect rates to rise once the licence is posted.

Near the market in the bowels of the town, the *Precious Inn* (☎ 064-21818) at 131 Butar Houng (Air Force) St offers unimpressive rooms with shared facilities in a three-storey, concrete-and-wood box for US$8/14 single/double. A busy cafe downstairs serves Chinese and Burmese food.

The friendly *Wunzin Hotel* (☎ 064-21848), on the northern outskirts of town toward the air base, recently changed over to private ownership but standards are about the same as when the hotel was under MHT auspices. In the main building large, clean rooms have concrete floors, mosquito nets, air-con and attached hot-water bath for US$30/36 single/double a night; larger 'junior suites' cost US$36/42.

Out the back a separate two-storey wooden building contains a set of economy rooms. The rooms on the lower floor were undergoing renovation when we visited, but the upstairs section featured substantial, four-bed rooms with ceiling fans and attached large hot-water showers. For these the hotel charges US$18 single, plus US$6 for each additional person. The best thing about the economy section is that, unlike the main building, it faces the lake and thus catches the cool evening breezes. The dining room is quite decent if expensive by Burmese standards (breakfast US$3, lunch and dinner US$6 each), and the lakeside grounds are pleasant.

The *Meiktila Hotel* (☎ 064-21892) sits near the Yangon-Mandalay highway north of town and offers 24 clean rooms in chalet-style buildings. All rooms have air-con and attached toilet and hot shower; rates are US$36 single, US$42 double including breakfast.

Places to Eat

Meiktila has higher quality food than the typical Burmese town. Most famous of the local restaurants is *Shwe Ohn Pin* on the main street; a couple of the major express buses between Mandalay and Yangon stop here. One of the house specialities is a delicious 'curd curry', big hunks of Indian-style cheese (hlan no kei) mixed with cauliflower and okra in a thick and spicy sauce. You can order Chinese dishes from the English-language menu or look-and-point at the curry pots for Burmese food. All Burmese meals come with a complimentary dal stocked with lots of okra and turnips.

A block behind this restaurant, then two blocks north-west of the Honey Hotel, is the *Honey Restaurant* near the lake. Under the same ownership as the Honey Hotel, this small, humble wooden restaurant serves decent Chinese food.

Next door to Shwe Ohn Pin a snack shop called *Mother's House* stocks soft drinks, Mars bars, Pringles and cold beer along with traveller requisites such as mosquito repellent, shampoo and film. There are a few tables and chairs out front. The English-speaking father of the owner drops by occasionally and will share his English poems.

At the south-eastern end of the lake's bridge, where the road forks, are a couple of small places worth checking out. *Tharapu Myanmar Cuisine*, right at the point of the fork, offers a line-up of curry pots and a small beer garden in the front. Right around the corner, on the side of the fork which leads away from the main street and away from the bridge, is *Mon Mon Lay*, a small, reliable Burmese restaurant run by an Indian family.

For tea and snacks, the *Myayadanar Tea Shop* near the cinema downtown is a popular spot any time of the day. The *Golden Triangle Tea Shop* near Mon Mon Lay is favoured in the evening, while north-west of the bridge, past the turnoff for the Wunzin Hotel, the *Mya Hninsi (Emerald Rose)* is a good early morning and daytime teashop.

Getting There & Away

The public bus stop for Thazi (K10), Mandalay (K70), Pyinmana (K50) and Yangon (K500) is located at the northern side of the main bazaar downtown. You can also catch buses to Mandalay near the clock tower – this is the stop for buses and pickups west to Kyauk Padaung (K30) and Nyaung U (K50).

Trade Express and Skyline Express pick up passengers at the Shwe Ohn Pin restaurant on the way to Yangon. Myanmar Arrow stops at Shwe Kauko restaurant the next street over. See the Mandalay or Yangon section for details on these convenient express air-con bus services.

Getting Around

Horsecarts serve the western side of town; many of them park near the south-eastern end of the lake's bridge. Trishaws cruise the downtown streets. A trip from the Honey Restaurant to the Wunzin Hotel would cost, for example, around K40 by horsecart; Precious Inn to Shwe Ohn Pin restaurant by trishaw costs around K20.

PYINMANA ပျဉ်းမနား

One of the major towns along the Yangon-Mandalay rail and road routes, Pyinmana is a very leafy place with plenty of trees and many thatched roof homes at the edge of Shan Lake – a welcome change after visiting the 'dry zone' around Mandalay and Bagan. Overall it has a more colourful and interesting feel than Taungoo to the south, even though it's of less historic interest. Coconut palms are planted along the Ngalai River, which passes through town, and you can see the Shan Yoma and Lei Yoma mountain ranges to the east and west. The surrounding valley is carpeted with rice fields, many of which yield two crops a year.

The **Yezin Forest Research Institute**, located 15 km north of town, is an important facility for the study of Burmese hardwoods. Like Taungoo further south, a fair amount of Myanmar's teak trade is centred here. Korea, Japan, China, Taiwan and Singapore are the major players involved.

The town's diverse population supports three **mosques** downtown as well as **St Michael's Catholic Church**, a small brick

BAGAN REGION

edifice near the river. You may notice a higher than average number of propaganda signs in town, erected to scare visiting undercover rebels. Insurgent territory begins just 30 km east of town: the Kayin, Kayah and Shan states intersect around 80 km southeast of Pyinmana.

Places to Stay

Mingala Kanthaw (☎ 067-21226) is a government-owned guest house over a large auditorium on the eastern side of the main north-south stretch through town. Very basic rooms with thin mattresses, fan and mosquito nets cost K200 per person. Although the guest house has no licence to do so, the staff gladly welcome foreigners.

Much better is the *Shwe Tharapu (Golden Crown) Guest House* (☎ 067-21186), a two-storey house at 175 Bo Taya St downtown. Rooms with shared facilities cost K150 per person; there's air-con in the corridors. When we visited the management hadn't obtained 'licensed lodging' approval and they were reluctant to take foreign guests. It's worth checking here first before taking a room at the government place as it's much quieter and cleaner.

Other unlicensed but otherwise very suitable places to stay include the *Thukamyaing Motel* (☎ 067-21094) on the main street farther south and the *Pyinmana Guest House* (☎ 067-21283) downtown.

Places to Eat

One of the better places in town is the popular *Yan Naing Restaurant*, on the main drag south of the government guest house. The menu includes Burmese and Chinese food. There are several other small, rustic restaurants near here since this is where most buses stop on their way north or south. *Nankin Restaurant*, near the central market downtown, is also good for Chinese.

Getting There & Away

Pyinmana lies close to the southern end of Mandalay Division, just north of the Bago Division border, 303 km south of Mandalay and 393 km north of Yangon.

From near the central market buses leave frequently for Taungoo to the south for K100. Buses to Yangon (K185) and Mandalay (K165) cruise the main north-south strip for passengers a couple of times a day. The air-con express buses sometimes stop near the Yan Naing Restaurant for meals and to pick up passengers, but this is not as reliable a stop as Taungoo or Meiktila. Enquire at the Yan Naing for arrival and departure times.

The Yangon-Mandalay express trains stop briefly in Pyinmana. You may be allowed to pay in kyat if there are seats available; otherwise expect to pay around US$18 to reserve an express seat in advance to either terminal. Slower – much slower – trains also ply this route but you're much better off taking the bus.

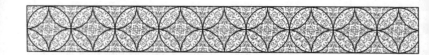

TEMPLES OF BAGAN

ARCHAEOLOGY OF BAGAN

Classification

Classifying the ancient monuments of Bagan by style and age is made difficult by the vast number of archaeological sites. The official count by the end of the 13th century is said to have been 4446. By 1901 surveys found 2157 monuments still standing and identifiable. According to resident Burmese archaeologist U Aung Kyaing, the last count was taken in 1978 when archaeologists found 2230 identifiable sites. Disregarding this living authority, most contemporary references on the subject quote a figure of 2217. These figures do not include brick mounds; if you include the latter there are still nearly 4000 separate visible sites.

The sheer variety of motifs and measurements to be studied also presents a challenge, though certain unifying factors can be found throughout. For the most part the proliferation of temples, stupas and monasteries are constructed of fired brick covered with plaster and decorated with stucco relief, polychromatic murals and glazed tiles. Sculpture materials included bronze, teak, brick-and-stucco, sandstone and lacquer. The most delicate of these media, the mural paintings, are endangered by the peeling of the plaster behind them, droppings left by resident bats and extensive soot from cooking fires lit during WW II when the Burmese sought shelter inside the monuments.

Temple paintings of such figures as Avalokitesvara, Manjusri and Shiva show an unmistakable Mahayana and possibly Tantric influence. Much of the mural work at Bagan is thought to be similar to how the interiors of Buddhist temples in north-eastern India may have appeared during the late Pala period before their destruction at the hands of Muslim invaders.

Looting & Restoration

Looters have made away with many of the sculptures and other religious objects once contained in the monuments. In the 1890s a German oilman removed glazed plaques from Mingalazedi, Dhammayazika and Somingyi, as well as Vishnu figures from Natlaung Kyaung, all of which ended up at the Berlin Völkerkunde Museum. Around the same time another German, Th Thomann, took some of the finest mural paintings known in Bagan from Wetkyi-in's Gubyaukgyi and Theinmazi Pahto. The latter were sold to the Hamburg Ethnographical Museum; the exquisite Wetkyi-in paintings never re-surfaced (fortunately Thomann left some murals behind, and they're still visible today).

Another complication comes in deciding what's original and what's been added or re-formed since the Bagan period. Restorations of several monuments, for example, were underway when British diplomat Michael Symes visited Bagan in 1795. Although writings from the colonial era for the most part show a great appreciation for Bagan art and architecture, the British did very little to further Bagan archaeology in terms of excavation or exploration.

Surveys

An example of the early carelessness with which research was carried out can be found in the early 1900s' *Archaeological Survey of India*. During the survey a representative from Yangon was accompanied by a local village headman who identified the monuments. When the headman didn't know a monument's name, he simply made one up to please the representative! Many of these names are still in use today.

It wasn't until a couple of decades later that inscriptions were seriously examined to learn Bagan's historical context. The eminent Cambridge scholar G H Luce published a pre-WW II three-volume study of the Early period monuments entitled *Old Burma-Early Pagan* that stands as the

Principal Bagan-Era Monuments

Monument	Estimated Date	Location
Ananda Pahto	early 12th C	Old Bagan
Ananda Ok Kyaung	11th C	Old Bagan
Shwegugyi	early 14th C	Old Bagan
Thatbyinnyu Pahto	mid-12th C	Old Bagan
Pitaka Taik	mid-11th C	Old Bagan
Nathlaung Kyaung	10th C	Old Bagan
Gawdawpalin Pahto	late 12th or early 13th C	Old Bagan
Pahtothamya	late 11th or early 12th C	Old Bagan
Bupaya	9th C	Old Bagan
Mahabodhi Paya	early 13th C	Old Bagan
Shwesandaw Paya	late 11th C	Old Bagan
Dhammayangyi Pahto	late 12th C	Old Bagan
Sulamani Pahto	late 12th C	Old Bagan
Mingalazedi	late 13th C	Old Bagan
Mimalaung Kyaung	late 12th C	Old Bagan
Shwezigon Paya	late 11th C	Wetkyi-in
Kyanzittha Umin	early 11th C	Wetkyi-in
Htilominlo Pahto	early 13th C	Wetkyi-in
Upali Thein	mid-13th C	Wetkyi-in
Wetkyi-in Gubyaukgyi	13th C	Wetkyi-in
Gubyauknge	12th C	Wetkyi-in
Sapada Paya	12th C	Nyaung U
Gubyaukgyi	early 12th C	Myinkaba
Myinkaba Paya	11th C	Myinkaba
Manuha Paya	11th C ?	Myinkaba
Nanpaya	late 11th C	Myinkaba
Nagayon	12th C	Myinkaba
Abeyadana Pahto	11th or 12th C	Myinkaba
Somingyi Kyaung	early 13th C	Myinkaba
Lawkananda Kyaung	mid-11th C	Thiripitsaya & Bagan Myothit
Leimyethna Pahto	early 13th C	Minnanthu
Payathonzu	late 13th C	Minnanthu
Thambula Pahto	mid-13th C	Minnanthu
Nandamannya Pahto	mid-13th C	Minnanthu
Dhammayazika Paya	late 12th C	Pwasaw

classic work. A well-researched art history of Bagan was finally carried out by Scotland's Paul Strachan in 1986 and 1987. Strachan published the results in his 1989 book *Pagan: Art and Architecture of Old Burma*, in which he divides everything from artefacts to buildings into three stylistic periods: Early (circa 850 to 1120), Middle (circa 1100 to 1170) and Late (circa 1170 to 1300).

The book has its flaws: the author questions why the reclining Buddha next to Shwesandaw Paya couldn't have been lying on its left side instead of its right, for example – an alternative that would have been a violation of classical Buddhist iconography never dared in Myanmar. Nonetheless, it is a very welcome addition to the literature on Bagan.

Strachan's book notwithstanding, no thorough archaeological study has been published since Myanmar's 1948 independence. UNESCO's work focuses on restoration rather than excavation or archaeology; this was perhaps mandated by government fears of any deep historical studies.

Pierre Pichard, an archaeologist from the École Francaise d'Extrême Orient (EFEO), the same faculty responsible for most of the authoritative work on Angkor and Champa in Indochina, has been working on a new treatise on the archaeology of Bagan for the last 15 years or so. If and when Pichard's work is published it may very well bring with it a whole new set of intriguing theories about the origins and demise of the kingdom of Bagan.

ARCHITECTURAL STYLES

Though there are a number of distinct architectural styles at Bagan, it is easy even for amateurs to trace the developments of temple design over the 240 years of construction. Buildings are primarily either solid *zedis* (stupas) or hollow *pahtos*. The latter – large, square buildings containing arched passageways – are sometimes referred to as 'temples' in their English names. A zedi customarily houses some relic from the Buddha – hair, tooth or bone – while the focal point of a pahto will be a number of Buddha images. The zedis can be seen in an earlier, more bulbous style and in a clearly Sinhalese design before they evolved into the more distinctively Burmese pattern.

Early pahtos were heavily influenced by late Pyu architecture as characterised by the monuments of Bebe and Leimyethna at Thaye-

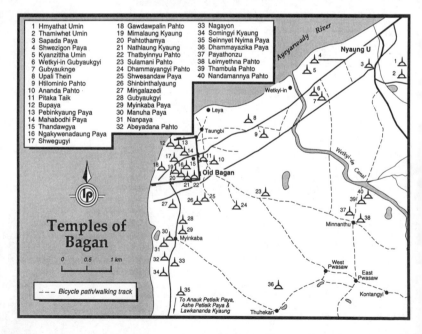

1 Hmyathat Umin	18 Gawdawpalin Pahto
2 Thamiwhet Umin	19 Mimalaung Kyaung
3 Sapada Paya	20 Pahtothamya
4 Shwezigon Paya	21 Nathlaung Kyaung
5 Kyanzittha Umin	22 Thatbyinnyu Pahto
6 Wetkyi-in Gubyaukgyi	23 Sulamani Pahto
7 Gubyauknge	24 Dhammayangyi Pahto
8 Upali Thein	25 Shwesandaw Paya
9 Htilominlo Pahto	26 Shinbinthalyaung
10 Ananda Pahto	27 Mingalazedi
11 Pitaka Taik	28 Gubyaukgyi
12 Bupaya	29 Myinkaba Paya
13 Pebinkyaung Paya	30 Manuha Paya
14 Mahabodhi Paya	31 Nanpaya
15 Thandawgya	32 Abeyadana Pahto
16 Ngakywenadaung Paya	
17 Shwegugyi	

33 Nagayon
34 Somingyi Kyaung
35 Seinnyet Nyima Paya
36 Dhammayazika Paya
37 Payathonzu
38 Leimyethna Pahto
39 Thambula Pahto
40 Nandamannya Pahto

Temples of Bagan

0   0.5   1 km

– – – Bicycle path/walking track

khittaya (Sri Ksetra) near Pyay (Prome). These early square temples are characterised by their perforated windows and dimly lit interiors. The common Burmese view holds that these early Bagan styles are 'Mon-style' buildings created by Mon architects imported from Thaton after its conquest, although no such architecture exists in the Mon lowlands. The latest theories suggest the Mon influence at Bagan was primarily confined to the religious and literary spheres rather than the artistic or architectural. Bagan's kings looked instead to the Pyu kingdoms and to India for architectural inspiration.

The pahtos can be primarily divided into two types: those having one entrance to a vaulted inner area and few windows and those having four entrances with images around a central cube. The smaller pahto characteristic of early Bagan is often called a *gu* or *ku*, a Pali-Burmese word for 'cave temple'; these monuments are particularly common around the town of Nyaung U. Seventeen pentagonal monuments – considered the earliest known five-sided buildings in the world – have also been found at Bagan.

Later pahtos added Indian design elements to the mix to produce a truly Burmese design in bright and well-lit pahtos like Gawdawpalin, Htilominlo and Thatbyinnyu. Ananda and Dhammayangyi are examples of an earlier transition phase; indeed, the Ananda is thought by some to have been built by imported Indian labour.

Other unique structures include the *pitaka taik* (Buddhist scripture library), *thein* (ordination hall) and *kyaung* (monastery). These are buildings that would normally have been constructed of wood and therefore would have disappeared; fortunately a few were constructed of brick and stone. Monastery buildings served as living quarters and meditation cells for resident monks. At one time much of the ground space between all the monuments visible today were filled with wooden monastery buildings, said to rival or even exceed the royal palace in design.

OLD BAGAN

Ananda Pahto

One of the finest, largest, best preserved and most revered of the Bagan temples, Ananda suffered considerable damage in the 1975 earthquake but has been totally restored. Thought to have been built around 1105 by King Kyanzittha, this perfectly proportioned temple heralds the stylistic end of the Early Bagan period and the beginning of the Middle period. In 1990, on the 900th anniversary of the temple's construction, the temple spires were gilded. The remainder of the temple exterior is whitewashed from time to time.

The central square measures 53 metres along each side while the superstructure rises in terraces to a decorative *hti* 51 metres above the ground. The entranceways make the structure into a perfect Greek cross; each entrance is crowned with a stupa finial. The base and the terraces are decorated with 554 glazed tiles showing *jataka* scenes (life stories of the Buddha) thought to be derived from Mon texts. Huge carved teak doors separate interior halls from cross passages on all four sides.

Facing outward from the centre of the cube, four 9.5-metre standing Buddhas represent the four Buddhas who have attained *nibbana* (nirvana). Only the Bagan-style images facing north and south are original; both display the *dhammachakka mudra*, a hand position symbolising the Buddha's first sermon. The other two images are replacements for figures destroyed by fires. All four have bodies of solid teak, though guides may claim the southern image is made of a bronze alloy. Guides like to point out that if you stand by the donation box in front of the original southern Buddha his face looks sad; while from a distance he tends to look mirthful. The eastern and western standing Buddha images are done in the later Konbaung or Mandalay style.

A small nutlike sphere held between thumb and middle finger of the east-facing image is said to resemble a herbal pill and may represent the Buddha offering *dhamma* (Buddhist philosophy) as a cure for suffering. Both arms hang at the image's sides with hands outstretched, a mudra unknown to traditional Buddhist sculpture outside this temple. The west-facing Buddha features the *abhaya mudra* with the hands outstretched in the gesture of 'no fear'.

At the feet of the standing Buddha, in the western sanctum, sit two life-size lacquer statues said to represent King Kyanzittha and Shin Arahan, the Mon monk who initiated the king into Theravada Buddhism. Inside the western portico are two Buddha footprint symbols on pedestals.

The British built a brick museum next to Ananda Pahto in 1904 in the provincial colonial style. It's now used as a storage facility and is closed to the public. Around the old museum stand a few ordination markers, inscribed stelae and Buddha images.

On the full moon of Pyatho (December/January), a huge paya festival attracts thousands to Ananda. Up to a thousand monks chant day and night during the three days of the festival.

Ananda Ok Kyaung

The name of the smaller *vihara* next door to Ananda means 'Ananda brick monastery' and this is one of the few surviving brick monastery buildings from the Early Bagan era. The interior of the building is lined with well-preserved murals whose colour palette stretches beyond the traditional brown, black and dull red to include a brighter red, plus a little green here and there. The paintings depict everyday scenes from the Bagan period, including Arab traders, market vignettes, bathing and

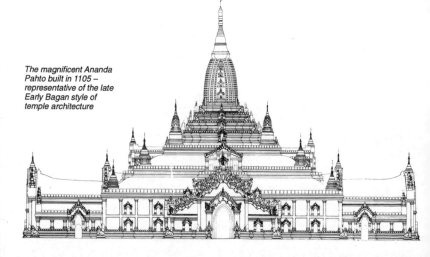

The magnificent Ananda Pahto built in 1105 – representative of the late Early Bagan style of temple architecture

cooking, and musicians playing *saing waing* (the Burmese drums) and Burmese harp.

Although the building is often locked, someone around the temple should have the keys and be able to let you in.

Shwegugyi

Built by Alaungsithu in 1311, this smaller but elegant pahto is an example of the Middle period, a transition in architectural style from the dark and cloistered to the airy and light. This brighter design was carried out through the use of more open doorways and windows. The basic profile of the temple, whose name means 'Great Golden Cave', presages the magnificent Gawdawpalin Pahto with its corncob *sikhara* (temple finial) – a scaled-down version of the one at Ananda Pahto – and the move toward verticality.

Shwegugyi is also notable for its fine stucco carvings and for the stone slabs in the inner wall which tell its history, including the fact that its construction took seven and a half months.

The elegant Shwegugyi Pahto, with distinctive corncob finial

BAGAN REGION

Thatbyinnyu Pahto

This 'Omniscient' temple, one of the highest in Bagan, rises to 61 metres and was built by Alaungsithu around the mid-12th century. The structure consists of two huge cubes; the lower one merges into the upper with three diminishing terraces from which a sikhara rises. Its monumental size and verticality make it a classic example of Bagan's Middle period. Indentations for 539 jataka plaques encircle the terraces; the plaques were never added, leading some scholars to surmise the monument was never consecrated.

In order to better preserve one of Bagan's greatest architectural achievements, since 1994 visitors have been barred from climbing through Thatbyinnyu's amazing inner passages to the top terrace. It was quite a maze climbing to the top – from the main eastern entrance you ascended a stairway flanked by two guardian figures. You then reached a corridor and climbed a narrow, steep flight of steps in the outer wall, and then some external steps to the huge Buddha image on the upper

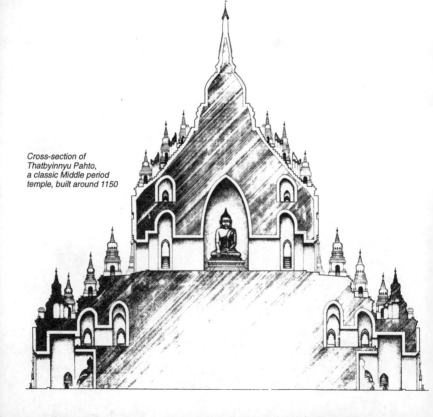

*Cross-section of
Thatbyinnyu Pahto,
a classic Middle period
temple, built around 1150*

floor. Another claustrophobic stairway within the wall took you to the upper terraces. Of course military officers and other VIPS are permitted to climb to the top whenever they visit Bagan.

In a monastery compound slightly to the south-west of the Thatbyinnyu you can see the stone supports which once held the temple's huge bronze bell. North-east of the temple stands a small 'tally zedi', which was built of one brick for every 10,000 bricks used in the main temple.

The elaborate front entrance detail of Alaungsithu's Thatbyinnyu Pahto

Ngakywenadaung Paya

Close to Thatbyinnyu Pahto, this ruined 9th-century stupa features the bulbous shape favoured by the Pyus. Many of the green-glazed tiles that covered it can still be seen.

Pitaka Taik

Following the sack of Thaton, King Anawrahta carted off 30 elephant-loads of Buddhist scriptures and built this library to house them in 1058. The design follows the basic Early Bagan gu or cave plan, perfect for the preservation of light-sensitive, palmleaf scriptures. It was repaired in 1738. The architecture of the square building is notable for the perforated stone windows – each carved from single stone slabs – and the plaster carvings on the roof in imitation of Burmese woodcarvings.

King Anawrahta's Pitaka Taik, an Early period Buddhist scripture library

Thandawgya

Slightly north of the Thatbyinnyu, this six-metre-high stone image of the Buddha was built in 1284, just before the Mongol invasion. It was in poor condition even before the earthquake.

Nathlaung Kyaung

Situated slightly to the west of the Thatbyinnyu, this is the only Hindu temple remaining in Bagan. It is said to have been built in 931 by King Taunghthugyi; if true, this was about a century before the southern school of Buddhism came to Bagan, following the conquest of Thaton. In design it resembles the Pyu Leimyethna or four-sided shrines of Thayekhittaya.

The temple is dedicated to the Hindu god Vishnu. Gupta-style reliefs of the '10 Avatars', of whom Gautama Buddha was said to be the ninth, were placed around the outside wall; seven of these survive. As a Vaishnava shrine, it's main function was to serve as a site for Brahmanic rituals deemed necessary adjuncts for royal ceremonies – an aspect of the Burmese monarchy that continued through the country's last kingship and one that still survives in neighbouring Thailand.

The central square of brick supports the dome and crumbled sikhara, and once contained free-standing figures of Vishnu as well as Vishnu reliefs on each of the four sides. The statues were stolen by a German oil engineer in the 1890s, but the badly damaged brick-and-stucco reliefs can still be seen. The temple may have been built by Indian settlers in Bagan – possibly the skilled workers brought to construct other temples. The Bagan scholar Paul Strachan, however, vigorously maintains the work was carried out by indigenous artisans.

This temple's name means 'Shrine Confining Nats', a reference to a purported time when King Anawrahta tried to banish nat worship in Bagan. He is said to have confiscated all non-Buddhist religious images – both indigenous Burmese nats and Hindu *devas* – and placed them in this shrine as part of an effort to establish 'pure' Theravada Buddhism. The king eventually gave in to the cult and standardised the current roster of principal Burmese nats by placing 37 chosen images at Shwezigon Paya. The veracity of this account has never been confirmed, but most Bagan residents – in fact virtually all Burmese – accept it as fact.

Gawdawpalin Pahto

One of the largest and most imposing of the Bagan temples, Gawdawpalin was begun during the reign of Narapatisithu and finished under Nadaungmya (1211-34) but was very badly damaged in the 1975 earthquake. Reconstruction of the Gawdawpalin probably represents the largest operation undertaken after the earthquake; it was not until the early 1980s that it was completed. The name literally means 'Platform to which Homage is Paid'.

In plan the temple is somewhat similar to the Thatbyinnyu – cube-shaped, with Buddha images on the four sides of the ground floor, with several refinements. It features the use of full pediments over the windows and stairways that ascend through the walls rather than from within the central cubes. The top of the restored sikhara, which toppled off in the earthquake, reaches 55 metres in height. Gawdapalin is considered the crowning achievement of the Late Bagan period.

Although the top terrace was once a popular place to catch the sunset over the Ayeyarwady, the passageways are now closed to visitors.

Pahtothamya

In the same temple-crowded central area, the Pahtothamya (or Thamya Pahto) was probably built during the reign of Kyanzittha (1084-1113), although it is popularly held to be one of five temples built by the non-historical king Taunghthugyi (931-964). The interior of this single-storey building is dimly lit, typical of the early type of Pyu-influenced temples with their small, perforated stone windows. In its vertical super-structure and lotus-bud sikhara, however, the monument is clearly beginning to move forward from the Early period.

Painting remnants along the interior passages may rate as the earliest surviving murals in Bagan.

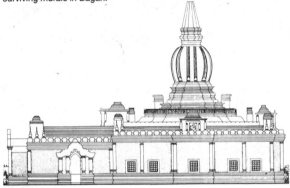

Pahtothamya, a Pyu-style temple with lotus-bud sikhara

Bupaya

Right on the bank of the Ayeyarwady, this cylindrical Pyu-style stupa is said to be the oldest in Bagan. Local residents claim it dates to the 3rd century AD, although there is little proof to support this belief. More likely it was erected about the same time as the city walls, that is around 850 AD – a dating which still distinguishes it as one of Bagan's earliest stupas.

Bupaya was completely destroyed when it tumbled into the river in the 1975 earthquake, but has since been totally rebuilt. The distinctively shaped bulbous stupa stands above rows of crenellated terraces.

Pebinkyaung Paya

If you have been to Sri Lanka you'll recognise the distinctly Sinhalese character of this small stupa. It was probably built in the 12th century and stands towards the river, near the Bupaya.

Mahabodhi Paya

Modelled after the famous Mahabodhi temple in Bodhgaya, India, which commemorates the spot where the Buddha attained enlightenment, this monument was built during the reign of Nantaungmya (1211-34). The pyramidal spire, covered in niches which enclose seated Buddha figures, rises from a square block. Stupas of this nature only appeared during the Late Bagan period; they were most common in the city of Salay further south.

Temples of Bagan
Top Left & Right: Shwesandaw Paya, Old Bagan
Bottom Left: Thatbyinnyu Pahto, Old Bagan
Bottom Right: Shwezigon Paya, Wetkyi-in

Temples of Bagan
Top: Touring the ruins by horsecart
Middle: Dhammayangyi Pahto, Old Bagan
Bottom: Mimalaung Kyaung, Old Bagan

BERNARD NAPTHINE

BERNARD NAPTHINE

JOE CUMMINGS

Temples of Bagan
   Top: Bagan's temples profiled at sunset
 Middle: Dusk on the Bagan plain
Bottom: Tharaba Gateway, Old Bagan

JOE CUMMINGS

BERNARD NAPTHINE

JOE CUMMINGS

JOE CUMMINGS

Temples of Bagan
Top Left: Manuha Paya's reclining Buddha, Myinkaba
Top Right: Gawdawpalin Pahto, Old Bagan
Bottom Left: Ananda Pahto, Old Bagan
Bottom Right: Mimalaung Kyaung's guardian *chinthe*, Old Bagan

Shwesandaw Paya

Following his conquest of Thaton in 1057, King Anawrahta built this graceful circular stupa at the centre of his newly empowered kingdom. The five terraces once bore terracotta plaques showing scenes from the jatakas, but traces of these, and of other sculptures, were covered by rather heavy-handed renovations. The zedi bell rises from two octagonal bases which top the five square terraces. This was the first monument at Bagan to feature stairways leading from the square bottom terraces to the round base of the stupa itself. This stupa supposedly enshrines a Buddha hair relic brought back from Thaton.

The hti, which was toppled by the earthquake, can still be seen lying on the far side of the paya compound. A new one was fitted soon after the quake.

Since the closing of the stairways to the upper terraces of Bagan's tallest monuments, the upper terrace of Shwesandaw Paya has become a popular sunset-viewing spot. This monument and Mingalazedi now offer the highest accessible points within the archaeological zone.

Close to Shwesandaw Paya stands **Lawkahteikpan Pahto** – a small but interesting Middle period gu containing excellent frescoes and inscriptions in both Burmese and Mon.

Shinbinthalyaung

Alongside a south-eastern portion of the wall around Shwesandaw, this long, vaulted-brick structure houses an 18-metre-long reclining Buddha from the 11th century.

Within the context of Burmese art history, the iconography of the image is a bit confusing. Although the head is oriented toward the south, which would indicate that the Buddha depicted is in a resting rather than dying or *parinibbana* state, the flat position of the right arm and the toes-together position of the feet suggests the opposite. A 'resting' Buddha is usually propped up on a crooked right arm, with his feet slightly splayed.

One view holds that the orientation and iconography clash because the architects didn't want the Buddha's back to face Shwesandaw. Naive critics might question why the builders couldn't simply have placed the figure on its left side so as to point the head north while still facing Shwesandaw. In Buddhist iconography throughout Asia, however, reclining Buddha figures always lie on their right side, a preferred sleeping and dying posture with antecedents in Indian yoga (to keep the left nostril clear, thus stimulating the *ida* nerve channel along the spine to induce a clear, restful state). The historical Buddha was thought to have passed into parinibbana while lying on his right side; even today Theravada Buddhist monks are often exhorted to sleep on their right rather than left sides.

The Shinbinthalyaung reclining Buddha, possibly dating to the Early period

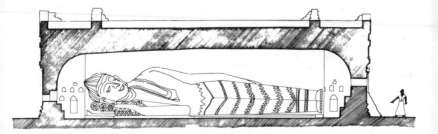

One explanation might be that, as the Cambridge scholar G H Luce suggested, this is an Early period image. Perhaps it shows relatively more Indian influence than later reclining images; in Tantric India the direction of the south *(dakshina)* is associated with death. At any rate, other parinibbana images with heads pointing south exist elsewhere in Myanmar. An appropriate conclusion may be that iconography overrides directional orientation.

Dhammayangyi Pahto

Similar in plan to Ananda Pahto, this later temple is much more massive-looking. It is usually ascribed to Narathu (1167-70), who was also known as Kalagya Min, the 'king killed by Indians', although other sources say it was the invaders from Sri Lanka who slew him. Other sources believe it was built a little earlier during the reign of Alaungsithu.

As at Ananda, the interior floor plan of the temple includes two ambulatories. Almost all the entire innermost passage, however, was intentionally filled with brick rubble centuries ago. No one knows for sure why the passage was blocked off; small open places near the top of the passage show intact stucco reliefs and paintings, suggesting that work on the structure had been completed. Local legend says that the work was so demanding – the king mandated the mortarless brickwork fit together so tightly so that even a pin couldn't pass between any two bricks – that when the king died the slave workers filled the inner ambulatory with rubble in revenge.

Three out of the four Buddha sanctums were also filled with bricks. The remaining western shrine features two original side-by-side images of Gautama and Maitreya, the historical and future Buddhas. Perhaps someday, when Myanmar's archaeological department, UNESCO or some other party clears out all the brick rubble, one of the great architectural mysteries of Bagan will be solved.

The interlocking, mortarless brickwork at Dhammayangyi, best appreciated on the upper terraces, is said to rank as the finest in Bagan. Unfortunately the highest terraces and hidden stairways leading to them are now off limits to visitors.

Sulamani Pahto

Like Htilominlo and Gawdawpalin, this is a prime example of later, more sophisticated temple styles, with better internal lighting. This temple, known as the 'Crowning Jewel', stands beyond Dhammayangyi Pahto and was built circa 1181 by Narapatisithu (1174-1211). Combining the horizontal planes of the Early period with the vertical lines of the Middle, the temple features two storeys standing on broad terraces assembled to create a pyramid effect. The brickwork throughout is considered some of the best in Bagan. The sikhara, badly damaged by the 1975 earthquake, remains unrestored. Stupas stand at the corners of each terrace, and a high wall, fitted with elaborate gateways at each cardinal point, encloses the entire complex. The interior face of the wall was once lined with a hundred monastic cells, a feature unique among Bagan's ancient monasteries.

Carved stucco on mouldings, pediments and pilasters represents some of Bagan's finest ornamental work and is in fairly good condition. Glazed plaques around the base and terraces are also still visible.

Buddha images face the four directions from the ground floor; the image at the main eastern entrance sits in a recess built into the wall. The interior passage around the base is painted with fine frescoes from the Konbaung period, and there are traces of earlier frescoes. Stairways lead very close to the top of this temple, from where the views are superb.

As at Thatbyinnyu and Gawdawpalin, however, ascents are now prohibited.

A walled enclosure in the north of the compound contains the remains of **Sulamani Kyaung**, a monastery building that housed Sulamani's senior monk and the *Tripitaka* (the Buddhist scriptures); it may also have served as an ordination hall. A water tank in the compound is thought to be the only original Bagan reservoir still in use by local residents.

Mingalazedi

Close to the riverbank, a little south of the Thiripyitsaya Hotel, Mingalazedi ('Blessing Stupa') was built in 1277 by Narathihapati. It was the very last of the large Late period monuments to be built before the kingdom's decline, thus representing the final flowering of Bagan's architectural skills.

Mingalazedi is noted for its fine proportions and for the many beautiful glazed jataka tiles around its three square terraces. Although many have been damaged or stolen, there are still a considerable number left. The smaller square building in the zedi grounds is one of the few *Tripitaka* libraries made of brick; most were constructed of wood, like monasteries, and were destroyed by fire long ago.

Mingalazedi's uppermost terrace is one of the highest points now accessible to visitors. Being the westernmost monument at Bagan, it's a particularly good spot for a panoramic afternoon view of all the monuments lying to the east.

Mimalaung Kyaung

A nice set of *chinthes* (half lion/half dragon mythical beasts) guard the stairway leading up this small, square monastery platform constructed in 1174 by King Narapatisithu. On top of the platform, a tiered-roof shrine contains a large Bagan-style sitting Buddha. Archaeologists discovered a remarkable six-cm dolomite votive tablet here so intricately carved that it depicted 78 fully sculptured figures.

In front of the monastery stands a brick-and-stucco *pitaka* library next to a large acacia tree. The juxtaposition of venerable tree, library and shrine makes for a special atmosphere, yet few tourists ever visit this easily accessible monument.

Delightful Mimalaung Kyaung, with guardian chinthes and pitaka library

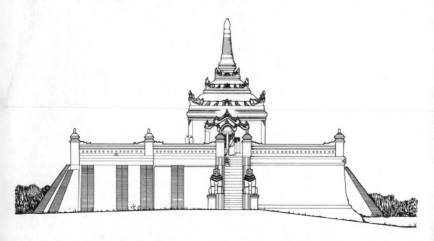

NYAUNG U & WETKYI-IN

Shwezigon Paya

Actually standing between the village of Wetkyi-in and Nyaung U, this beautiful zedi was commenced by Anawrahta but not completed until the reign of Kyanzittha (1084-1113). The latter is thought to have built his palace nearby. Supposedly the Shwezigon was built to enshrine one of the four replicas of the Buddha tooth in Kandy, Sri Lanka, and to mark the northern edge of the city; the other three tooth replicas went to Lawkananda, a smaller stupa to the south; to Tan Kyi, a stupa on the western bank of the Ayeyarwady; and to Tuyan Taung, a stupa on the summit of a hill 32 km to the east.

The stupa's graceful bell shape became a prototype for virtually all later stupas all over Myanmar. The gilded zedi sits on three rising terraces. Enamelled plaques in panels around the base of the zedi illustrate scenes from the previous lives of the Buddha. At the cardinal points, facing the terrace stairways, are four shrines, each of which houses a four-metre-high bronze standing Buddha. Gupta-inspired and cast in 1102, these figures are Bagan's largest surviving bronze Buddhas. Their left hands exhibit the *vitarka* or 'exposition' mudra while the right hands are held palm outward, fingers straight up, portraying the gesture of *abhaya* or 'no fear'.

A 10-cm circular indention in a stone slab near the eastern side of the stupa was filled with water to allow former Burmese monarchs to look at the reflection of the hti without tipping their heads backward (which might have caused them to lose their crowns). For a few kyat visitors can view the bejewelled hti through a telescope reserved for that purpose. Surrounding the zedi are clusters of *zayats* (rest houses) and shrines, some of them old, others more modern, though none of them are original.

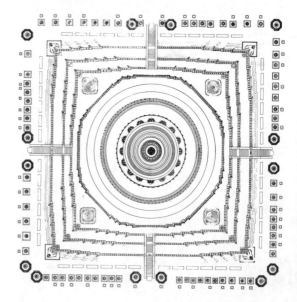

Aerial-view plan of Shwezigon Paya

In addition to ranking as one of the oldest stupas in Bagan, Shwezigon is known as the site where the 37 pre-Buddhist nats were first officially endorsed by the Burman monarchy. Figures of the 37 nats can be seen in a shed to the south-east of the platform. The 12th-century originals were spirited away by a collector and are now reportedly somewhere in Italy. At the eastern end of the shed stands an original stone figure of Thagyamin, king of the nats and a direct appropriation of the Hindu god Indra. This is the oldest known free-standing Thagyamin figure in Myanmar. Flanked by tigers representing her forest home, another small shrine in the south-eastern corner of the grounds is reserved for Mae Wanna, the guardian nat of medicinal roots and herbs.

Caretakers collect a fee of K10 for the use of still cameras, K25 for videocams.

The beautiful bell-shaped Shwezigon Paya – its design became a virtual prototype for all stupas in Myanmar

Kyanzittha Umin

Although officially credited to Kyanzittha, this cave temple may actually date back to Anawrahta. Built into a cliff face close to the Shwezigon, the long, dimly lit corridors are decorated with frescoes, some of which are thought to have been painted by Bagan's Tartar invaders during the period of the Mongol occupation after 1287.

Htilominlo Pahto

Situated close to the road between Nyaung U and Bagan, this large temple was built by King Nantaungmya in 1218. The name is a misreading of the Pali word for 'Blessings of the Three Worlds'. Nantaungmya erected the temple on this spot because it was here that he was chosen, from among five brothers, to be the crown prince.

Inside the 46-metre-high temple, which is similar in design to Sulamani Pahto, there are four Buddhas on the lower and upper floors. Traces of old murals are also still visible. Fragments of the original fine plaster

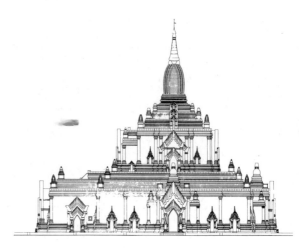

carvings and glazed sandstone decorations have survived on the outside. The doorways feature nice carved reliefs.

Upali Thein

Named after Upali, a well-known monk, this ordination hall was built in the mid-13th century and stands across the road from the Htilominlo Pahto. The rectangular building has roof battlements imitative of Burmese wooden architecture and a small central spire rising from the rooftop. Most buildings of this type were made of wood and have long since disappeared. Inside there are some brightly painted frescoes on the walls and ceilings from the late 17th or early 18th century. The building is usually kept locked in order to protect them.

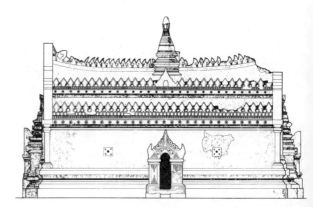

Top: Early 13th-century Htilominlo Pahto, similar in design to the earlier Sulamani Pahto

Bottom: Upali Thein, a mid-13th century ordination hall (thein)

Wetkyi-in Gubyaukgyi

Close to Wetkyi-in village, this 13th-century 'cave temple' has an Indian-style spire like the Mahabodhi Paya in Bagan. It is interesting for the fine frescoes of scenes from the jatakas, but unfortunately in 1899 a German collector came by and surreptitiously removed many of the panels on which the frescoes were painted.

To distinguish it from the temple of the same name in Myinkaba, this monument is sometimes called 'Wetkyi-in Gubyaukgyi'.

Gubyaukgyi in Wetkyi-in which has a Mahabodhi-style pyramidal spire

Gubyauknge

A little south-west of Gubyaukgyi near Wetkyi-in Canal, this Early period temple has some excellent stucco carvings on the outside walls.

Hmyathat & Thamiwhet Umin

These twin cave-temples are about a km from Nyaung U towards the airport – but off the main road. Dug into hillsides, the caves date from the 13th century.

Sapada Paya

Sited close to the road as you approach Nyaung U from Kyauk Padaung or the airport, this Late period zedi from the 12th century was built by Sapada, who originally came from Pathein (Bassein) but became a monk in Sri Lanka. His stupa is Sinhalese in style, with a square relic chamber above the bell.

Other Monuments

Closer to the river, about three km east of Nyaung U, you can find the 13th-century **Thetkyamuni** and **Kondawgyi** pahtos. The 11th and 12th-century **Kyauk Gu Ohnmin** cave temple, further from the river and built into the side of a ravine, is of the same period of Myinkaba's Nanpaya and contains some very impressive sandstone reliefs. It's best visited by boat.

MYINKABA

Gubyaukgyi

Situated just to the left of the road as you enter Myinkaba, this temple was built in 1113 by Kyanzittha's son Rajakumar, on his father's death. In Indian style, the monument consists of a large shrine room attached to a smaller antechamber. The fine stuccowork on its exterior walls is in particularly good condition.

The Early period temple is also of particular interest for the well-preserved paintings inside, which are thought to date from the original construction of the temple and to be the oldest remaining in Bagan. The temple is typical of the Pyu or Early Bagan style in that the interior is dimly lit by perforated rather than open windows; you need a powerful light to see the ceiling paintings clearly. It is generally kept locked – ask in the village for someone to open it. In high tourist season (December to February) it's open most of the day, however.

Right: Gubyaukgyi in Myinkaba, an Early period Pyu-style temple

Below: Wall painting, Gubyaukgyi, Myinkaba, Bagan

Next to the monument stands the gilded **Myazedi** or 'Emerald Stupa'. A four-sided pillar in a cage between the two monuments bears an inscription consecrating Gubyaukgyi and written in four languages – Pyu, Mon, Old Burmese and Pali. Its linguistic and historical significance is great since it establishes the Pyu as an important cultural influence in early Bagan and relates the chronology of the Bagan kings.

Myinkaba Paya

Situated in the village of Myinkaba, this 11th-century paya was built by Anawrahta to expiate the killing of his half-brother, the preceding king, Sokkade, in man-to-man combat. It stands at the Myinkaba stream, into which Sokkade's body and saddle were allegedly disposed. Since it was built before Anawrahta's conquest of Thaton, it is also an interesting example of the religious architecture existing before the influence of the southern school of Buddhism had made itself felt.

Manuha Paya

Manuha was named after the Mon king from Thaton who was held captive in Bagan by Anawrahta. Legend says that Manuha was allowed to build this temple in 1059, and that he constructed it to represent his displeasure at captivity. Stylistically the dating isn't consistent with the story, though intervening renovations may be responsible for any discrepancies.

The exterior and overall floor plan resemble the more remote Kyauk Gu Ohnmin, a rectangular box topped by a smaller rectangle. Inside three seated Buddhas face the front of the building, and in the back there's a huge reclining parinibbana Buddha. All seem too large for their enclosures, and their cramped, uncomfortable positions are said to represent the stress and lack of comfort the 'captive king' had to endure. However, these features are not unique in Bagan.

It is said that only the reclining Buddha, in the act of entering nibbana, has a smile on its face, showing that for Manuha only death was a release from his suffering. You can climb to the top of this paya via the stairs at

The unusual interior plan of Manuha Paya, allegedly illustrating King Manuha's discomfort in captivity

The mid-11th century Manuha Paya, supposedly built by the captured Manuha

the entrance to the reclining Buddha chamber, at the back of the temple. Through a window you can then see the face of the sitting Buddha, and from up at this level you'll realise that the gigantic face, so grim from below, has an equally gigantic smile! In the earthquake the central roof collapsed, badly damaging the largest, seated Buddha, which has since been repaired.

An outdoor corner of the temple compound is dedicated to Mt Popa's presiding nats, Mae Wanna and her sons Min Lay and Min Gyi. Devotees of Manuha Paya celebrate a large *paya pwe* (or pagoda festival) on the full moon of Tabaung (February/March).

Nanpaya

Close behind the Manuha Paya, this shrine is said to have been used as Manuha's prison although there is little evidence supporting the legend. In this story the shrine was originally Hindu. Supposedly his captors thought that using it as a prison would be easier than converting it to a Buddhist temple. Recent research now suggests that the temple was built by Manuha's grand-nephew in the late 11th century.

The masonry work – sandstone block facings integrated over a brick core – is particularly fine. Perforated stone windows are typical of earlier Bagan architecture – in fact it was probably Bagan's first gu-style shrine. It also features interesting arches over the windows.

In the central sanctuary the four stone pillars have finely carved sandstone bas-relief figures of four-faced Brahma. The creator deity is holding lotus flowers, thought to be offerings to a free-standing Buddha image once situated in the shrine's centre, a theory that dispels the idea that this was ever a Hindu shrine. The sides of the pillars bear ogre-like heads with open mouths streaming with flowers. The local Burmese say the face represents a Burmese legend in which an ogre eats (or, according to others, regurgitates) flowers. In fact the face is a typical representation of the Indian god of time and death, Kala, who devours all in his path.

This temple is generally kept locked up but someone at Manuha can usually arrange to have it opened.

Nagayon

Slightly south of Myinkaba, this elegant and well-preserved temple was built by Kyanzittha. It is generally kept locked to protect its interesting contents. The main Buddha image is twice life size and shelters under the hood of a huge naga, or serpent. This reflects the legend that Kyanzittha built the temple on the spot where he was sheltered while fleeing from his angry brother and predecessor Sawlu – an activity he had to indulge in on more than one occasion.

The outer, dark corridor has many niches with images of the earlier Buddhas. Paintings also decorate the corridor walls. The central shrine has two smaller standing Buddhas as well as the large one. Unfortunately the walls have been whitewashed, obscuring any traces of possible murals.

The small ruined stupa of **Pawdawmu Paya** is located nearby.

Abeyadana Pahto

While Kyanzittha sheltered at Nagayon during his flight from Sawlu, his wife Abeyadana waited for him a short distance away. At that site he subsequently built this temple, which is similar in plan to the Nagayon.

The inner shrine contains a large, brick-built seated Buddha (partly original, partly restored), but the fine frescoes are the main interest here. These paintings are now being cleaned by UNESCO staff. Of the many Buddha niches lining the walls, most are empty. Some contain bodhisattvas and Hindu deities – Avalokitesvara, Brahma, Vishnu, Shiva, Indra – showing a Mahayana influence accredited to the tastes of Kyanzittha's Bengali bride, who was said to have been a Mahayanist.

This temple is usually kept locked, though you can ask around in Myinkaba about getting someone to open it.

King Kyanzittha's Abeyadana Pahto, built in honour of his wife

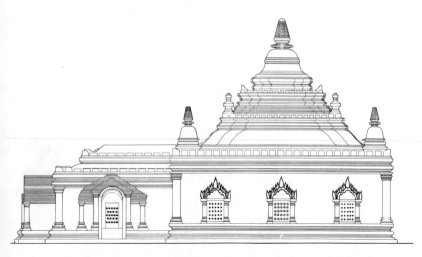

Seinnyet Nyima Paya & Seinnyet Ama Pahto

This shrine and stupa stand side by side and are traditionally assigned to Queen Seinnyet in the 11th century, although the architecture points to a period two centuries later. The zedi rests on three terraces and is topped by a stylised umbrella.

Somingyi Kyaung

Named after the lady who supposedly sponsored its construction, this typical Late Bagan brick monastery is thought to have been completed in 1204. A zedi to the north and gu to the south are also ascribed to Somingyi. Most brick monasteries in Bagan were single block structures; Somingyi is unique in that it features monastic cells clustered around a courtyard.

THIRIPYITSAYA & BAGAN MYOTHIT

Ashe (West) & Anauk (East) Petleik Payas

When the lower parts of these twin 11th-century payas were excavated in 1905 they revealed quite a surprise. The payas were built not on a solid base as expected, but on vaulted corridors, the walls of which were lined with hundreds of unglazed terracotta tiles illustrating scenes from the jatakas. New roofs were built over these twin tiers of tiles, many of which are still in excellent condition – particularly in the better preserved Anauk Petleik Paya. The buildings themselves are unimpressive.

Lawkananda Kyaung

At the height of Bagan's power, boats from the Mon region, Rakhine (Arakan) and even as far afield as Sri Lanka would anchor by this riverside monastery with its distinctive elongated cylindrical dome. It was built in 1059 by Anawrahta, who is also credited with the Petleik payas. It is still used as an everyday place of worship and is thought to house an important Buddha-tooth replica.

The riverside and sunset views from Lawkananda are very good. A couple of vendors on the riverbank provide snacks and soft drinks.

Sittana Paya

This large, bell-shaped stupa is set on four square terraces, each fronted by a standing Buddha image in brick-and-stucco. The stupa was built by Htilominlo and stands slightly south of Thiripyitsaya.

MINNANTHU

Leimyethna Pahto

Built in 1222, this east-facing temple standing on a raised platform has interior walls decorated with well-preserved frescoes. It is topped by an Indian-style spire rather like that on Ananda.

Payathonzu

This complex of three interconnected shrines (the name literally means 'Three Shrines') was abandoned shortly before its construction was complete – possibly due to the invasion of Kublai Khan. Dating to the late 13th century, each square cubicle is topped by a fat sikhara; a similar structure appears only at Salay, much farther south along the Ayeyarwady River. The design is remarkably similar to Khmer Buddhist ruins in Thailand.

Two of the shrines contain vaguely Chinese or Tibetan-looking mural paintings that contain bodhisattva figures. Whether these indicate possible Mahayana or Tantric influence is a hotly debated issue among art historians. Those who say the art is purely indigenous point to the lack of a scriptural context for the paintings; others argue from a purely aesthetic view that the overall iconography suggests Mahayana or Tantric content. The three-shrine design hints at links with the Hindu *trimurti* of Vishnu, Shiva and Brahma, a triumvirate also associated with Tantric Buddhism. Although one might just as easily say it represents the 'Triple Gems' of Buddhism (dhamma, Buddha, sangha), such a design is uncommon in Asian Buddhist archaeology although it does appear in the Hindu shrines of India and Nepal. At any rate Mahayana/Tantric versus indigenous was never a mutually exclusive polarity despite Anawrahta's efforts to the contrary.

The complex is usually locked. It's best to inquire at the museum in Old Bagan to make an appointment for an inspection; in high season, it will probably be open most of the day for group tours.

Thambula Pahto

This square temple is decorated with faded jataka frescoes and was built in 1255 by Thambula, the wife of King Uzana. On the eastern wall of the southern transept is an apparently secular painting of a boat race.

Nandamannya Pahto

Dating from the mid-13th century, this small, single-chambered temple has very fine frescoes and a ruined, seated Buddha image. The murals' similarity with those at Payathonzu has led some art historians to suggest they were painted by the same hand.

One of the murals represents the 'temptation of Mara' episode in which nubile young females attempt to distract the Buddha from the meditation session that led to his enlightenment. The undressed nature of the depicted females, actually quite tame by all but the most straight-laced standards, shocked French epigraphist Charles Duroiselle, who wrote in 1916 that they were '...so vulgarly erotic and revolting that they can neither be reproduced or described'.

PWASAW

Dhammayazika Paya

This circular zedi is similar to the Shwezigon or the Mingalazedi, but has an unusual and rather complex design. Built in 1196 by Narapatisithu, the stupa rises from three five-sided terraces. Five small temples, each containing a Buddha image, encircle the terraces; some of them bear interior murals added during the Konbaung era. An outer wall also has five gateways.

Departing from the usual Leimyethna or four-faced type, the plan adds a fifth aspect in tribute to Mettaya or Maitreya, the Buddha to come. This Buddha plays a major role in historical Mahayana Buddhism. In the context of all the other Mahanayist art seen in Late Bagan temples, one cannot help but wonder if during the Late period the kings weren't drifting towards Mahayana Buddhism.

The three terrace levels still bear intact jataka plaques in places, and on the pediments some fine stucco reliefs have survived very well.

North-Eastern Myanmar

Shan State

Nearly a quarter of Myanmar's geographic area is occupied by the Shan State. Before 1989 the area was broken into several administrative divisions collectively known as the 'Shan States'. It's the most mountainous state in the country, divided down the middle by the huge north-south Thanlwin (Salween) River. To the west of the river lies the 1000-metre-high Shan Plateau, to the east a jumble of north-south mountain ranges and international borders with China, Laos and Thailand.

About half the people living in the Shan State are ethnic Shan, who for the most part live in valleys formed by the Thanlwin River and its tributaries. The traditional Shan ruling system revolves around the *sao pha loang* (*sawbwagyi* in Burmese) or 'great sky lord', an hereditary, feudal leadership-position installed in each of the original nine Shan states. Under the British, a system of indirect rule created 37 administrative divisions, with a sao pha in charge of the largest ones. After independence the Shan leadership signed away their hereditary rights in the 1947 Panglong Agreement, which guaranteed a cooperative, semi-autonomous administration of the Shan States. Much of the current conflict in the state dates from this time: Shan commoners were appointed to government positions after the formation of the Union of Burma, much to the dismay of the sao pha who expected the appointments; and from the perspective of most Shan, the degree of expected autonomy never materialised.

In addition to the Shan, the state's major ethnic groups include the Palaung in the mountainous north-western corner, the Kachin in the far north, the Kaw (Akha) and Lahu (Musoe) in the far east and north-east, the Kokang and Wa in the north-eastern

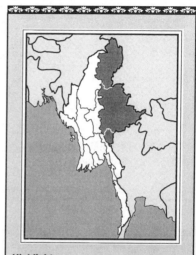

Highlights
- Hiking to hill-tribe villages in the Shan State
- Intriguing Buddhist shrine-caves of Pindaya
- Serene waters of Inle Lake and its famous leg rowers
- Holy temple of Phaung Daw U, site of a distinctive Shan festival
- Golden Triangle centre of Kengtung with its diverse hill tribes and colourful markets
- Newly opened regional capital of Myitkyina, home of the Kachin people

mountains and the Padaung and Taungthu in the south-west. Dozens of smaller groups also inhabit various parts of the state, particularly the mountainous areas.

Because of its elevation, most of the Shan State – even the river valleys – is ill-suited for the cultivation of lowland crops like rice. One crop that flourishes even at high elevations is *papaver somniferum,* the opium poppy, from which flows the state's main source of income. Although the opium trade extends to most parts of the state, poppy cultivation and processing is concentrated in the far north and south-east. Not coinciden-

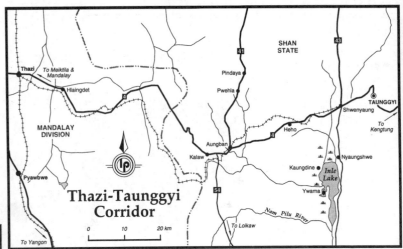

SHAN STATE

MANDALAY DIVISION

Thazi-Taunggyi Corridor

0   10   20 km

To Yangon

Thazi   To Meiktila & Mandalay

Hlaingdet

Pyawbwe

Pindaya
Pwehla

Aungban
Kalaw

To Loikaw

Nam Pilu River

Heho

Kaungdine

Ywama

Inle Lake

Nyaungshwe

Shwenyaung

TAUNGGYI

To Kengtung

---

tally, these are the areas where Shan rebel armies and opium warlords operate, hence travel to these areas is restricted by the government. The areas most accessible now include the highway/railway corridor between Kalaw and Taunggyi and the Inle Lake area which extends east from Thazi in the Mandalay Division, a similar corridor between Pyin U Lwin (Maymyo) and Lashio north-east of Mandalay, and the isolated township of Kengtung in the far east of the state.

THAZI သာစည်

Although Thazi is located about 65 km west of the Shan State border in the Mandalay Division, most visitors begin or end their journey into Shan territory in this rail-junction town. It's little more than a place where people embark or disembark from the train when travelling to or from Bagan (Pagan) or Inle Lake.

Places to Stay & Eat

At the time of writing the only licensed lodging is the spartan *Moon-Light Rest House* (☎ Thazi 56) on the top floor of the *Red Star Restaurant*. Simple rooms with two beds, mosquito nets and shared shower and toilet cost US$5 per person. The busy dining room downstairs serves very good Indian Muslim food, including fresh yoghurt. The proprietors will also allow you to bathe and rest upstairs while waiting for a train.

Around the corner is the larger *Thazi Htun Rest House* (☎ Thazi 16), a nice two-storey guest house with no foreigner licence as yet. The management said they might be getting a licence soon; room rates for foreigners should run around US$6 to US$10 if they follow the same pattern seen elsewhere in Myanmar, or as little as K300 if local rates are charged.

Near the Red Star Restaurant, the *Wonderful* has Chinese food and an English menu. Around the bus stop there are several teashops with endless free tea and cheap pastries.

There is a decent snackbar on the railway platform with good food and service.

Getting There & Away

Bus The Thazi bus stop is a couple of hundred metres from the railway station – just an empty building and a patch of dirt. Buses (Japanese pickups) to Kalaw and Taunggyi will only leave when they get 20 passengers or when some impatient traveller pays the fare differential for any number less. Thazi to Kalaw costs K200 for a seat in the back, K300 up the front; there's usually only one departure a day at around 7 am.

If you want to travel between Mandalay and Thazi by bus, you must change buses in Meiktila; this will no longer be the case after the new highway between Mandalay and Thazi is finished. A passenger pickup between Meiktila and Thazi costs K10 to K15.

Train See the Getting Around chapter at the start of this book for details on train travel to and from Thazi. Travellers from Thazi have managed to get ordinary class seats to Yangon (Rangoon) for US$9, or as far as Bago (Pegu) for US$7.

For information on the train to Shwenyaung, for Inle Lake, see the Inle Lake section.

Car Ask at the bus stop or at the Red Star about car, jeep or pickup rental. The going rate is K3000 to 5000 per day, depending on the condition of the vehicle. It's hard to get the lower rental rates available around Mandalay or Bagan simply because the steep winding roads of the Shan State require more vehicle upkeep.

KALAW ကလော

Situated 70 km west of Taunggyi, about half way along the Thazi-Taunggyi road, Kalaw sits high on the western edge of the Shan Plateau. This was a popular hill station in the British days and it's still a peaceful and quiet place with an atmosphere reminiscent of the colonial era. At an altitude of 1320 metres it's also pleasantly cool and a good place for hiking amid gnarled pines, bamboo groves and rugged mountain scenery. There's good accommodation, and you can make interesting excursions around Kalaw.

The small population is a peculiar mix of Shan, Indian Muslims, Burmans and Nepalis (Gurkhas retired from British military service), many of whom are missionary-educated. As recently as the 1970s there were still American missionaries teaching in the local schools. Because of the colonial and

missionary heritage, many people speak English.

Things to See & Do
There are three mildly interesting temples to see in town. Perched on the hill overlooking the Thazi-Taunggyi road is the **Thein Taung Paya**. In the 'downtown' area is a glittering stupa, covered in gold-coloured mosaics, called **Aung Chan Tha Zedi**. Just across the street is the dilapidated **Dama Yon**, a two-storey temple; it's not particularly interesting in itself, but upstairs you get fair views of the town, Dama Yan Thi Paya and the ruins of

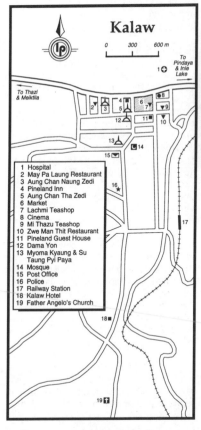

Kalaw

0   300   600 m

To Thazi & Meiktila

To Pindaya & Inle Lake

1 Hospital
2 May Pa Laung Restaurant
3 Aung Chan Naung Zedi
4 Pineland Inn
5 Aung Chan Tha Zedi
6 Market
7 Lachmi Teashop
8 Cinema
9 Mi Thazu Teashop
10 Zwe Man Thit Restaurant
11 Pineland Guest House
12 Dama Yon
13 Myoma Kyaung & Su Taung Pyi Paya
14 Mosque
15 Post Office
16 Police
17 Railway Station
18 Kalaw Hotel
19 Father Angelo's Church

NORTH-EASTERN MYANMAR

the **Su Taung Pyi Paya**, now a field of crumbling stupas behind the Dama Yon towards the Kalaw Hotel.

Near the Kalaw Hotel is **Christ the King Church**, a brick Catholic church under the supervision of the Italian Father Angelo Di Meo, who has been in Myanmar since 1931 – despite Japanese suspicion of his possible British sympathies during WW II, British suspicion after the war and the SLORC suspicion today. The Christ figure over the altar inside came from Italy, and Father Angelo himself painted the mural background. A stone grotto built behind the church is believed to have curative powers. Mass is held daily at 6.30 am; and at 8 am and 4 pm on Sunday.

Places to Stay

The historic *Kalaw Hotel* (☎ Kalaw 47, 081-21425 in Taunggyi), which looks like a cross between a Tudor mansion and a hunting lodge, was built between 1903 and 1906 as resort quarters for British officers. The Japanese used it as a hospital during WW II, after which it became a private hotel until 1984, when the government took it over. Privatised once again in late 1994, the Kalaw Hotel offers licensed accommodation in the bare economy wing for US$15/24 a single/double with shared facilities. In the middle wing attached to the lobby and reception area, large rooms with high ceilings and private bathrooms go for US$30/36 a single/double, while in the new wing there are superior rooms with carpet and a fridge for US$36/42. Hot water is available from 6 am to 10 pm. Set back well behind the town, it's a very quiet and peaceful place to stay. The hotel is famous for its restaurant service.

The *Pineland Inn* (☎ Kalaw 99) is a new two-storey guest house right on the highway through Kalaw. Basic but clean two-bed rooms with shared cold-water shower and toilet cost US$5 per person.

We've heard rumours that one of the old British manor houses at the edge of town is being converted into a hotel by a French enterprise.

Places to Eat

The *Pineland Inn* serves basic Chinese and Burmese fare, nothing great but quite edible. For a splurge the famous *Kalaw Hotel* dining room is highly recommended for well-prepared Burmese or European set meals. Palatable Australian wine is also available by the bottle at reasonable prices.

The clean, Shan-owned *May Pa Laung Restaurant* (☎ Kalaw 132) near Aung Chan Naung Zedi (three blocks west of the market) offers a good menu of Chinese, Burmese and Shan dishes; the cooks can also prepare delicious Indian food with advance notice.

There are quite a few teashops in Kalaw but nothing fancy. The *Royal Tea Garden* near the cinema is large and popular. Across the street the tiny Nepali-operated *Lachmi Tea House* serves very good tea, chapatis and curry, and is open from 5 am till around 9 pm, longer than any of the other places. Around the corner is a larger Nepali teashop, *Mi Thazu*, where chapatis, tea and *raksi* (local moonshine) are available.

The *Zwe Man Thit Restaurant* opposite Mi Thazu is basic-looking but serves the best Chinese food in town.

Getting There & Away

From Thazi, buses leave for Kalaw in the morning, for K40 per person. Travel time is about three hours. From Taunggyi to Kalaw it's about two to three hours for the same fare. To charter a vehicle to either destination will cost around US$30. For Aungban and Pindaya, see the following Pindaya section.

It's possible to take the train from Thazi or Shwenyaung; it takes around 4½ hours from either end and is a scenic, if slow, trip. If you can pay in kyat, the fare for either ordinary or upper class is less than K30. In dollars the fare will run as high as US$4.

To get back to Yangon, it's possible to book a seat on one of the Taunggyi-Yangon air-con express buses for US$10 to US$15 through the Kalaw Hotel. In Yangon check with Skyline Express. There's also the usual Mandalay-Yangon train connection via Thazi.

AROUND KALAW
Visiting Nearby Villages

The plateau near Kalaw is inhabited by people of the Palaung and Pa-O tribes. Palaung women wear colourful blue and red costumes and families tend to live in 'long houses'. One of their main livelihoods is the cultivation of *tanapet*, a large leaf used to wrap Burmese cigars. The Pa-O wear more somber dark blue or indigo costumes and are known as shrewd businesspeople. Tribespeople often come into town to do business, especially on Kalaw market day, which comes around every five days.

Several nearby villages can be visited in half-day or whole-day hikes. Some guides are beginning to lead multi-day trips, although it's not clear if this is officially permitted. Guides in Kalaw typically charge K300 to K500 per day.

If you want to trek to nearby villages, ask at the Kalaw Hotel, Pineland Inn or May Pa Laung Restaurant for directions or guide assistance. Father Paul at Christ the King Church is also quite helpful. When visiting the villages, it's better to contribute cash to the village health fund rather than hand out medicines, toys or food. Pencils and ball-point pens are also welcome. Usually the abbot of the village monastery or the village headman handles such donations; it's always better to offer gifts intended for children

---

Five Day Market

In the Shan State, community markets are held on a traditional rotating basis in which each town or village within a given area hosts a market every five days. Hence a five-day market held on Saturday in Pindaya will come around again five days later, not every Saturday.

The schedule in the Kalaw-Inle Lake corridor is as follows:

Day 1   Phaung Daw U Monastery (Inle Lake), Kalaw, Shwenyaung
Day 2   Pindaya, Nyaungshwe
Day 3   Heho, Kyoung (on the way to Pindaya)
Day 4   Ywama, Taunggyi, Aungban
Day 5   Pwehla (on the way to Pindaya)

---

through an adult rather than directly to the children.

AUNGBAN အောင်ဘန်း

This small highway town is an important transport junction for cargo and passengers moving west or east between Thazi and Taunggyi, north to Pindaya or south to Loikaw, the capital of Kayah State. As such Aungban's main function is to feed and fuel; among Shan State truck drivers it's also infamous for its brothels.

There is little of substance to the town itself except when the five-day market is held. For seekers of Buddhist wisdom, the **Taungpulu Meditation Monastery**, a little east of town off the highway, has been an important waystation for many years. Founded by the late Taungpulu Sayadaw, the meditation system used here is said to be particularly effective in countering lust.

Places to Stay & Eat

The new *Myatmanaw Guest House* just east of the junction offers plain but comfortable rooms in a two-storey building for US$5 per person. There are other guest houses around, but most are devoted to the brothel trade.

Padonmar Restaurant, on the same stretch of road just outside town, is a big, clean place with Chinese and Burmese food, plus snacks (including chocolate and cheese) to take on the road. Myatmanaw Guest House has an attached cafe with inexpensive Burmese meals.

Getting There & Away

See following Pindaya Getting There & Away section for information on transport from Pindaya and Kalaw to Aungban.

Loikaw, the capital of Kayah State, is 155 km south of Aungban – four to five hours by car, longer by public transport. Officially this road was closed to foreigners when we visited; there are four military checkpoints between Aungban and Loikaw so the chances of getting through undetected are virtually nil.

Trains along a new rail line from Aungban to Kalaw – reported to have been at least

NORTH-EASTERN MYANMAR

partially built using prison and conscript labour – take about 10 hours to cover the distance. The fare is K50. For more information, see the Loikaw section at the end of this chapter.

PINDAYA ပင်းတယ

About 40 km north of Aungban is the town of Pindaya, noted for its extensive limestone caves and picturesque lake. The highly scenic Aungban-Pindaya road passes through the Pa-O and Danu villages of Pwehla and Ji-Chanzi. There are fields of dry-cultivated mountain rice along the way and potato fields where the tuber is grown in red mud mounds.

Pindaya itself is a centre for the Burmese-speaking Taungyo people. Local handicrafts include Shan paper made from mulberry bark and parasols made from the same paper.

Pindaya Caves

The famous Pindaya Caves are ensconced in a limestone ridge overlooking the lake. It's a long walk from the lake to the foot of the cliff containing the caves; if you've chartered a jeep from Kalaw or Taunggyi, make sure that you're driven all the way up to the cliff. Travel from town to the foot of the cliffs costs K30 by horsecart. A 200-step stairway leads to the cave entrance – leave your shoes at the bottom or carry them with you. Foreigners are charged a US$3 admission fee.

Inside the cavern are 8,094 Buddha images – made from alabaster, teak, marble, brick, lacquer and cement – which have been put there over the centuries and arranged in such a way as to form a labyrinth throughout the various cave chambers. Some of the smaller side chambers are only accessible on hands and knees, and in these you may come across lay people practising meditation.

Among the more unusual features in the cave is a set of stalagmites that can be struck with large wooden mallets to produce 'gong' tones. In one corner of the cave stand three 'perspiring Buddhas', sitting images that stay wet because of a condensing reaction between the lacquer sculptural medium and the surrounding air. Burmese worshippers

believe they will gain good fortune and beauty by rubbing the drops of 'sweat' on their faces.

Although many areas within the caves are illuminated by electric lights, a torch (flashlight) would help make out the darker corners. Take care on the slippery paths.

From a temple complex built along the front of the ridge you can view the nearby lake and the ruins of **Shwe Ohn Hmin Paya**, a cluster of low stupas just below the ridge. Beginning on the full moon of Tabaung (February/March), Pindaya hosts a colourful *paya pwe* at Shwe Ohn Hmin.

Padah-Lin Caves

North-west of Pindaya, and near the village of Ye-ngan, is the most important prehistoric site in Myanmar, the Padah-Lin Caves. The interior of one of the caves is decorated with the remains of very old paintings of animal and human subjects, not unlike Neolithic cave paintings in Europe. To get here you will have to charter a jeep – this can be added on to a Pindaya jeep trip from either Kalaw or Taunggyi for an extra K400 to K500 per vehicle.

Places to Stay & Eat

The *Pindaya Hotel* is a clean and comfortable two-storey place about half way between the town and the caves, just off the road to the caves and facing the lake. Standard singles/doubles with fan and attached shower and toilet cost US$24/30, superior rooms with fridge are US$31/38. A cheaper alternative, the unlicensed *Diamond Eagle Guest House*, is next to the lake and if you can manage to get a room there you'll pay less than K200 a night.

The owners of the Pindaya Hotel are building bamboo bungalows with kitchenettes near the town entrance which should open soon. The rates are projected to be US$24 to US$40 a night.

The Pindaya Hotel has a restaurant that is usually empty unless a tour group is passing through for lunch. Good food can be found in the market area in town – the best is at *U Aseik*, where you can get a delicious full

Burmese meal for around K60. The *Kyanlite Restaurant* has an English menu and is recommended for Chinese food. At the cave temple as well as in the market you can buy delicious local avocados (called dopa-thi in Burmese).

Getting There & Away

From Kalaw it costs K10 to Aungban and another K25 to Pindaya by public transport. It can be difficult to find buses, especially between Aungban and Pindaya, so leave early in the morning and allow a whole day for the trip. From Taunggyi there's one bus per day at 2 pm for K40; the same bus travels in the opposite direction at 6 am the next day.

You can also charter a jeep and driver in Kalaw. If you don't want to stay in Pindaya, you could hire a jeep to take you from Kalaw to Pindaya, get it to wait for a couple of hours while you take in the caves and have lunch in town, and then take you on to Nyaung-shwe (for Inle Lake). This should cost about US$30 or the kyat equivalent for the whole day – it's better to pay in dollars than kyats. One jeep can take four or five passengers with baggage. Actual road time is about two hours for the 50 km from Kalaw to Pindaya and three hours or more for the 93 km from Pindaya to Nyaungshwe (Yaunghwe). Add waiting time (which can be considerable) in Aungban and Shwenyaung if you go by public transport.

HEHO ဟဲဟိုး

Another highway town, Heho is about halfway between Aungban and Shwe-nyaung, which is the junction for the road south to Nyaungshwe and Inle Lake. North of town is an airstrip that fields Air Mandalay (AM) and Myanma Airways (MA) flights from Yangon and Mandalay (see the Inle Lake Getting There & Away section for details).

Heho has a dusty market area just off the highway that hosts the largest of the five-day markets in the southern area of the Shan State. The several guest houses in town admit locals only. On the highway near the market area are a couple of decent places to eat, including the *Oasis Cafe* (tea snacks),

San San Restaurant (Chinese food) and *Island Restaurant* (Chinese and Burmese meals).

SHWENYAUNG ရွှေညောင်

Few people stop off in Shwenyaung, except to change from a Thazi-Taunggyi pickup to one going to Nyaungshwe. Should you find yourself needing overnight accommodation here, there is one good choice; in fact it may be good enough to warrant an intentional stopover for those seeking something away from the lake scene.

The two-storey, L-shaped *Remember Inn* near the crossroads has budget singles with shared facilities for US$6, standard single/double rooms with air-con, fridge and attached toilet and bath for US$25, or superior rooms for US$30 a single/double with the same plus TV. All rooms are spacious and there's a rooftop terrace with umbrellas and chairs. The proprietors lead treks to local Shan and Pa-O villages.

Getting There & Away

You can get all the way to Shwenyaung, the railhead, by train, but it's time-consuming. From Yangon or Mandalay the programme would be to take one of the Yangon-Manda-lay expresses and disembark at Thazi – the place where visitors to Bagan usually catch the train. See the Getting Around chapter at the start of this book for timetable details.

The train from Thazi to Shwenyaung is rather slow – the average speed must be around 10 km/h with occasional sprints of 15 km/h – but the route is very picturesque and having the run of a carriage can be more comfortable than sitting in the back of a cramped pickup. It's a spectacular eight to nine-hour journey through the Shan mountains and local villages, partially on a zig-zag railway. Stations en route have masses of fruit, snacks and flowers for sale. From Thazi the No 143 Up leaves at 5 am and arrives in Shwenyaung around noon. From Shwen-yaung back to Thazi there are two trains: one that leaves at 8.30 am and arrives around 5 pm, and a second train around 10 am (No 144 Down) which arrives in Thazi at 7 pm.

Coming from Shwenyaung both trains arrive in plenty of time to connect with the No 10 Down from Mandalay to Yangon, which is scheduled to depart Thazi around 8.30 pm but usually doesn't actually leave till around 9 pm. If you take the earlier Shwenyaung-Thazi train you'll leave yourself more connecting time in case it's late arriving in Thazi. On occasion, there's even a through carriage, so enquire at the Shwenyaung station if it's your intention to continue on directly to Yangon.

If you can manage to pay in kyat, the fare between Thazi and Shwenyaung is K15 in ordinary class, K40 in upper class (available only on the 8.30 am train). Of late the ticketsellers in Shwenyaung have been charging foreigners US$3 in ordinary class, US$7 in upper class (8.30 am train only).

INLE LAKE အင်းလေးအိုင်

Inle Lake is 22 km long, 11 km wide, 1328 metres above sea level and outrageously picturesque – it has dead calm waters dotted with patches of floating vegetation and busy fishing canoes. High hills rim the lake on both sides; the lakeshore and lake islands bear 17 villages on stilts, mostly inhabited by the Intha people. Culturally and linguistically separate from their Shan neighbours, the Inthas are thought to have migrated to this area from Dawei (Tavoy) on the Taninthayi peninsula (Tenasserim) in southern Myanmar. The Intha dialect is related to standard Burmese but also shows similarities with the Mon-influenced Dawei dialect. The Burmese 'th' sound becomes an 's' in Intha, so that the Burmese 'beh-thwa-ma-lay' ('Where are you going?') becomes 'beh-swa-ma' among the Intha.

According to one story, two brothers from Dawei came to Nyaungshwe in 1359 to serve a Nyaungshwe *sawbwa* (Shan chief). The latter was so pleased with the hard-working demeanour of the Dawei brothers that he asked them to invite 36 more families from Dawei; purportedly all the Intha around Inle Lake are descended from these migrant families. Another theory says they migrated from the Mon region in the 18th century to avoid

wars between the Thais and Burmans. Like the Shan, Mon and Burmans, the Intha are Buddhist; there are around 100 Buddhist *kyaung* (monasteries) around the lake and perhaps a thousand stupas. The Inle style of religious architecture and Buddhist sculpture is strongly Shan-influenced.

The hard-working Intha are famous for propelling their flat-bottomed boats by standing at the stern on one leg and wrapping the other leg around the oar. This strange leg-rowing technique offers relief to the arms – which are also used for rowing – during the long paddles from one end of the lake to

Inle Lake

another. It also enables the rower to better see floating water hyacinth (*kyunpaw*) – it's sometimes necessary to stand up to plot a path around the obstacles – and to spot fish. Although outboard motors are used for cross-lake ferries and for carrying tourists to the islands and lakeshore villages, most people still use oars and paddles to avoid petrol shortages, to save money and to preclude the hassle of hyacinth-tangled propellers.

The entire lake area is contained in the township of Nyaungshwe and supports a population of 126,000 that consists of Intha, Shan, Taungthu, Taungyo, Pa-O, Danu, Kayah, Danaw and Burman people. The township seat of the same name sits north of the lake and is approached by road from Shwenyaung or from the lake to the south via a long, narrow channel. Around 70,000 people live on the shores and islands of the lake. In the hills east of town, the Pa-O Liberation Army was active until the recent signing of a truce with the Yangon government.

The industrious villagers inhabiting the lake region support themselves by growing a wide variety of flowers, vegetables and fruits all year round, including tomatoes, beans, cauliflower, cabbage, eggplant, garlic, onions, betel vine, melon, papaya and banana. They also grow rice, especially at the northern end of the lake around Nyaungshwe. Many of these crops are cultivated on floating islands, where marsh, soil and water hyacinth have combined to form incredibly fertile solid masses which are staked to the lake bottom with bamboo poles. Between the islands and peninsulas thus formed is a network of canals that are the main avenues of transportation for the Intha. Tall lattices of betel vine line the canals in some of the villages, providing a curtain of privacy and another source of income. Ywama is known as the floating village since it has *chaungs* (canals) for streets, and much of the day-to-day village activity, including marketing, is carried on from canoes.

Using cone-shaped nets stretched tautly over wood and bamboo frames, Intha fishermen harvest *nga-pein* (a type of carp) and other kinds of freshwater fish. Women in the villages (especially Ywama and Heya at the southern end of Inle Lake) weave Shan-style shoulder bags and silk *zin-me* (Chiang Mai-style) *longyis* on wooden handlooms. Using raw silk brought from China, these weavers in fact produce more silk garments than anywhere in the country after Amarapura.

When they aren't busy with fishing or farming, the men of Inle produce silver and brassware as well as pottery and lacquerware. The area around Kaungdine on the western shore is famous for the production of noodles, tofu and other soybean products which end up in kitchens all over Myanmar.

The lake itself is very shallow and clear – a swim looks inviting and the **Inlai Bo Te** is a good place to have one. Inlai means 'middle of', Bo is 'officer' or 'official' and Te is 'house', so the Inlai Bo Te is literally an official's house in the middle of the lake. It's no longer used as such, but makes a good place to stop for a mid-lake picnic or swim.

One of the best times of the year to be here is during September and October. The ceremonial Phaung Daw U festival, which lasts for almost three weeks, is closely followed by the Thadingyut festival, when the Inthas and Shan dress in new clothes and celebrate with fervour the end of Waso, or Buddhist Lent. They are so religious that it's not unusual for families to spend all of their meagre savings during this one annual event.

During January and February, the nights and mornings around the lake area are cold, so you should bring socks and sweaters, and a warm sleeping bag would also be handy.

Around the Lake

To really experience Inle Lake culture you need to get out onto the lake itself. Myanmar Travels & Tours (MTT) no longer has a monopoly on lake tours and you can hire watercraft from just about anyone who has a boat. MTT does, however, collect a US$3 entry fee from anyone entering the lake area.

The exact price per person or per boat depends on the kind of boat and number of people. For longboats with outboard motors

NORTH–EASTERN MYANMAR

– the type preferred by many visitors with limited time since they travel the fastest – 12 passengers is usually the maximum, although anything over eight people is a bit cramped. A typical motorboat of this sort goes for K800 to K1200 per day; MTT charges K1500 for its boats. The typical motorboat trip is not bad – you will see the floating gardens, leg-rowers, fishermen, Phaung Daw U Kyaung and whatever lake commerce is going on. Ywama market day is best, when there is a sizable floating market with both shoppers and merchants in canoes. Guides may tell you that there is a floating market every day, but except on Ywama market day, the only 'floating market' is a small fleet of souvenir boats.

The lake itself is rich in wildlife, especially various waterfowl. All avifauna on the lake and adjoining wetlands are reportedly protected by law, as Inle Lake has been an official bird sanctuary since 1985. Egrets fly in formation over the lake every day about an hour before sunset. The boat trips usually include stops at souvenir shops near Phaung Daw U. The selection isn't bad at these shops, but prices are lower at the five-day floating market or at the paya – at all these places you'll see Shan shoulder bags, Burmese clothing, tapestries, pottery, jewellery and all the other usual Myanmar souvenirs.

Canoe Trips With all the package tours heading to the southern end of the lake by noisy powerboat nowadays, a quiet canoe paddle through the villages at the northern end of the lake and along the lake channel has become an attractive alternative. Several people in town do shorter canoe trips on the canals branching off the lake and along the Nyaungshwe shores of the lake for rates of about K150 per two or three-hour paddle. Although you won't get to see the more famous lake sights, like the floating gardens, Ywama or Phaung Daw U, life along the canals is itself pretty fascinating and the villagers are very friendly. Canoes are also better for photography since they move more slowly.

One place that can only be visited by

canoe is the large **nat shrine** in the middle of a swampy banyan tree jungle near Nanthe village, west of the main channel. No one dares cut the trees for fear of the nats' wrath, so it's a good place to see unfettered nature, including plenty of waterfowl. The house-sized, wooden nat shrine sits on stilts and contains a rustic altar.

If you become especially enamoured with Inle canoes and want to paddle yourself you could buy your own vessel. The better craft are made of teak; a good quality teak canoe costs US$50 to US$90 depending on the size. Some teak canoes have served the same Intha families for over a hundred years.

Hiking Extended walks to the north or south of Nyaungshwe pass among extensive rice fields dotted with Shan stupa ruins. Trails into the hills east of town lead to Pa-O villages and aerial views of the lake area. Guided day hikes can be arranged through any guest house or hotel in town; guides typically charge US$2 to US$3 a day.

Nyaungshwe (Yaunghwe)
Nyaungshwe ('Golden Banana Tree', also called Yaunghwe) is the small town at the northern end of the lake. Here there are a number of places to stay and eat, and boats run out onto the lake from the wide channel that runs along the western side of town. At first it appears there's not a lot to do around town, but between the lake itself, the nearby villages, countryside walks and historic ruins there's actually enough to occupy an active visitor for a week or more.

Shan Palace Museum (Yaunghwe Haw Museum)
Housed in a large teak and brick mansion in the north-eastern part of town, this was the palace (*haw*) of the 33rd and last Shan sawbwa, Sao Shwe Thaike. Thaike, who became the first president of Myanmar in 1948, was imprisoned when Ne Win came to power and died in jail. Overall the collection of Shan regalia and photos is not that interesting but the building itself is worth a visit as it's the best surviving example of a

Shan haw since the demolition of the *haw sao pha* in Kengtung in 1991.

Most of the two-storey building, laid out in a double cruciform floor plan, is in disrepair. An upstairs room displays original wood carvings that once decorated the exterior of the palace. A small room off to the side contains a royal bed and throne. When we last visited, the bottom floor of the main building was under renovation. Most impressive is the huge teak-floored throne and audience hall in the north wing, behind the front building.

Shrines, Monasteries & Stupas The oldest temple in town, **Yadana Man Aung Paya**, is worth a look around for its unique step-spired stupa. Look for the 'you will be old' and 'you will be sick' figures in glass cases in one of the shrine buildings.

There are several good-sized monasteries in the centre and south-eastern parts of town, including **Kan Gyi**, **Shwe Gu** and **Yangon**. On the south-eastern outskirts of town the ruins of an old Shan monastery called **Nigyon Taungyon** – originally built by the Nyaungshwe sawbwa – features a set of slender whitewashed Shan stupas and some very old plinths with surviving stucco relief. The monastery is now being restored under the supervision of an old monk who is trying to breathe life back into the complex as a *kammathan kyaung* (meditation monastery). A new shrine hall on the grounds contains five alabaster sitting Buddhas in the Mandalay style, and there are a few thatched huts for meditators.

Less than a km north of the town entrance, an old 18th or 19th-century monastery called **Shwe Yaunghwe Kyaung** features a venerable wooden *thein* (consecrated hall) with unique oval windows. A long, low, rectangular brick and stucco *pahto* (shrine) on the premises bears slender Shan *zedis* (bell-shaped payas) on top and Buddha images of various ages inside.

A short walk south of town along the eastern side of the main channel leads to the small but atmospheric ruins of **Kyauk-pyugyi (Big White Stone) Paya** next to the

Intha village of Nanthe. Surrounded by brick and stucco devas, lions and stupas is a huge sitting Buddha, said to be 700 years old. The cloister around the image is lined with intact stucco reliefs, while the stupas behind the main shrine are topped with surrealistically bent and twisted *htis* (decorative metal umbrellas).

Mingala Market The main municipal market near the town's northern entrance is busiest in the morning when vendors congregate to ply their wares. In addition to mountains of fresh produce, Shan noodles and other local products, there are a few stalls selling pottery and textiles.

Ywama

Regular boats run from Nyaungshwe to the village of Ywama – if you want to see the famed floating market, you must calculate the day according to the local five-day market scheme. Any guest house or hotel in Nyaungshwe will have the current schedule. If the timing isn't right for the Ywama market day, ask about the secondary five-day circuit that rotates among the lake villages of Kaungdine, Mainthauk, Nanpan, Intein and Thandaung.

As you approach Ywama, you pass through floating fields where the Inthas grow everything from vegetables to flowers. The fields make an unusual and picturesque sight.

On the way to Ywama you can stop at **Nga Phe Kyaung**, a wooden monastery built on stilts over the lake four years before the construction of Mandalay Palace. It's known among the package-tour crowd as the 'Jumping Cat Monastery' because the monks there have trained a few cats to leap through small hoops. But a better reason to visit is to see the modest collection of Buddha images in Shan, Tibetan, Bagan and Inwa styles. Just as impressive as the Buddhas themselves are the tall, highly ornate, wood-and-mosaic pedestals and cases built for the images. Such pedestals are a speciality of Shan and Northern Thai Buddhist art and those at the monastery are over a hundred years old. Many of the original Shan images they once

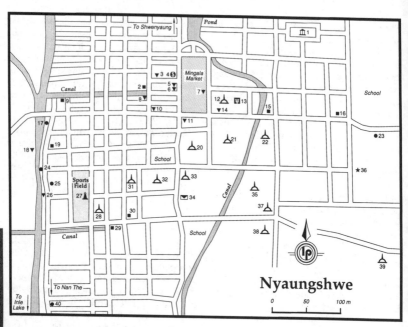

Nyaungshwe

PLACES TO STAY

2   Hu Pin Hotel
9   Joy Hotel
15 Evergreen Hotel
16 Inle Inn
19 Shwe Hintha Guest
    House
29 Pyi Guest House
30 Golden Express Hotel

PLACES TO EAT

3   Hu Pin Restaurant
5   Shwe Inlay Bakery
6   Kong Kong
    Restaurant
7   Teashop
8   Love Village Cafe &
    Sunflower
    Restaurant
10 Golden Crown
    Restaurant
11 Thuka Cafe
14 Teashop
18 Big Drum Restaurant
26 Nyaungshwe
    Restaurant & MTT

OTHER

1   Shan Palace Museum
4   Bank
12 Stupa
13 Sri Jagdish Hindu
    Temple
17 Boat Landing
20 Monastery
21 Yangon Kyaung
22 Hlain Kyu Kyaung
23 Township Office
24 Boat Landing
25 Moe Ma Kha Boat
    Hire
27 Independence
    Monument
28 Shwe Zali Paya
31 Stupas
32 Yadana Man Aung
    Paya
33 Stupas
34 Post & Telegraph
    Office
35 Shwe Gu Kyaung
36 Police
37 Kan Gyi Kyaung
38 Monastery
39 Nigyon Taungyon
    Kyaung
40 Four Sisters

contained have been sold or stolen, so the cases mostly contain newer images. A few 150-year-old Shan images are unceremoniously kept off to the side on a smaller altar;

crafted by Intha artisans, the gilded wood images feature crowns and royal attire decorated with mosaic.

If your tolerance for souvenir hawkers is

low, you may find Ywama over-touristy; if so, make it clear to your boat pilot or guide that you'd prefer to spend more time at other lake sights. Another way to beat the crowds is to go early in the morning; peak visitation times tend to occur around 10 am and again around 4 pm. The typical motorboat charter to Ywama costs K800 to K1200 for a half-day trip – the route takes at least two hours each way from Nyaungshwe. Public ferries make the trip a couple of times in the early morning from the public boat landing in Nyaungshwe for K30 per person.

Phaung Daw U Kyaung The main landing at Ywama stands in front of Phaung Daw U Kyaung, the holiest religious site in the southern area of the Shan State.

Stalls on the ground floor of the shrine and nearby sell brightly coloured cotton Shan shoulder bags, other local crafts and 'antiques'. Silk and cotton fabrics are a local speciality; there are over 200 handlooms in Ywama. A shady *khamauk* (conical straw hat) is another popular purchase here.

Kaungdine

Also spelt Kaungdaing, this Intha village on the north-western shore of the lake is known for the production of soybean cakes and noodles. It's easy to wander around the village and observe the methods used, since just about every other household is involved in these cottage industries. Potting and weaving can also be seen. Just outside the village are some interesting Shan temple ruins featuring brick-and-stucco zedis, pahtos and *chinthes*; the villagers use some of the pahtos for storing straw or hay.

A little north of Kaungdine is a hot springs spa which is open 8 am to 5 pm daily. You can bathe in unisex communal baths for a few kyat or take a private room for K150 per day. The water is very hot but the overall cleanliness could see some improvement.

Kaungdine and the hot springs are a 15-to 20-minute drive from Nyaungshwe around the top of the lake or two hours across the lake by boat. A boat charter costs K700 to K800 to Kaungdine, K800 to K1000 to the hot springs. There are a couple of hotels near Kaungdine; see the Places to Stay section below.

Places to Stay – bottom end & middle

A number of new places have opened in

Phaung Daw U Festival

The biggest event in the southern area of Shan State takes place at Phaung Daw U Kyaung, one of the state's holiest sites, from the first day of the waxing moon to the third day after the full moon of Thadingyut (September/October). The focus of the large two-storey sanctuary is five gold-leaf-covered statues, of which three are said to be Buddha images, while the remaining two are reportedly Arahats or historical disciples of the Buddha. The goldleaf on the figures has become so thick that it's hard to tell what the figures represent; they look a bit like short, squat bowling pins or lop-sided dumbbells.

The statues were reportedly fashioned during the reign of King Alaungsithu (1112-67). The gold lumps are so holy that pilgrims rub red strips of cloth against them, then tie the cloth strips to their bikes, cars and trucks to create protective spiritual force-fields around themselves and their vehicles.

During the 20 days of the festival, a ceremonial barge carries four of the five Phaung Daw U images from village to village around the lake to bless the village monasteries. The smallest of the five figures stays at Phaung Daw U to act as 'guardian' of the temple, following an incident that happened many years ago when the procession used to carry all five images around the lake. About eight km from Phaung Daw U, in the middle of the lake, you can see a pillar mounted by a *shwe hintha* or golden swan figure (actually a *hamsa*, a swan-like creature from Indian mythology). This monument marks the spot where the ceremonial barge once capsized. Only four of the five figures were immediately recovered but when the stunned crew returned to Phaung Daw U they found the fifth sitting on its pedestal, covered with lake weeds. Ever since the legendary incident that image has never left the monastery.

Hundreds of other vessels travel in the entourage in a general celebratory atmosphere. Thousands of people from around the Shan State attend this most holy of Shan celebrations. ∎

Nyaungshwe since the privatisation of the hotel industry. Facing the lake access canal on the western edge of town, the friendly *Shwe Hintha Guest House* (☎ Nyaungshwe 62) offers a variety of rooms in a rambling converted house. Economy rooms with common hot-water shower and toilet cost US$5/10 a single/double, while standard rooms with attached cold-water shower and toilet are US$12 a single/double. All rates include breakfast. Some of the economy rooms upstairs have balconies overlooking the canal; there is also a small canal-view terrace where anyone can sit.

Further north on a narrower, more quiet canal that heads east into town, *Joy Hotel* (☎ Nyaungshwe 83) has 12 basic but clean rooms in a two-storey house for US$7/12 a single/double with shared hot-water shower and toilet, or US$13/16 with hot-water shower and toilet attached. Breakfast comes with the rooms. A small sitting area overlooks the canal.

East of Mingala Market on a stream that runs through town is the long, two-storey *Evergreen Hotel* (☎ Nyaungshwe 79, 24). Basic economy rooms here with common toilet and hot-water shower cost US$5 per person. Slightly larger standard rooms with softer mattresses and attached hot-water shower and toilet cost US$12/20 a single/double.

Further east along the same road, the well-run and quiet *Inle Inn* (☎ Nyaungshwe 16, 21, or 081-21347 in Taunggyi) is one of the oldest privately owned inns in the country. In the back of the main building a thatched wing signed 'Inle Bamboo Lodge' has simple economy rooms with shared toilet and cold-water shower cost US$5/8 a single/double. Better rooms in the main building and in a new wing off to the side come with attached toilet and hot-water shower and are US$15/22/33 a single/double/triple. There is a pleasant garden sitting area out the back. Good food is available; a Shan dinner and puppet show is offered nightly for K350 per person.

Pyi Guest House, in the southern part of town, three blocks east of the main canal, is a big thatched-roof building with very spartan cubicles for US$5 per person, toilet and shower outside. There is also one nicer room with attached shower for US$18 a single/double. As at the Inle Inn, the proprietors sometimes arrange dinner shows with Shan food, music and dancing.

At all these places there seems to be a shortage of blankets during the cool season, which happens to coincide with high tourist season – you may have to beg for even a second blanket for your bed. Power blackouts are common, but since none of the rooms contain electric appliances beyond simple lightbulbs, it's not that noticeable.

As the Nyaungshwe guest houses seem to be running at near full capacity during the high tourist season, we can expect some new places to appear over the next couple of years. A new spot called *Queen Guest House* is planned for the western bank of the main canal next to the Big Drum Cafe; reportedly it will be built of bamboo and palm thatch and will feature rates similar to those at Shwe Hintha.

Places to Stay – top end
Nyaungshwe The top end in Nyaungshwe isn't luxurious but is comfortable enough for people who desire softer beds, hot water and screened windows. Of the two places that fit this category, the best value is the modernised Shan-style, two-storey *Golden Express Hotel* (☎ Nyaungshwe 37) on Phaungdawpyan St, a long block and a half south-east of Yadana Man Aung Paya and a block east of Pyi Guest House. The hotel has 11 well-furnished, spacious rooms, each with hot-water shower, toilet, fridge, fan and carpet, for US$24/30/42/54 a single/double/triple/quadruple. A discount may be possible during the low season or any time the place has several vacancies. Generator power is steady.

Located a block west of Mingala Market, the modern four-storey *Hu Pin Hotel* (☎ Nyaungshwe 23) is owned by the famed restaurant of the same name nearby. Plain rooms with attached hot-water shower cost US$20/24 a single/double, add TV and fridge for US$30/36 or pay US$48 for a larger single/double with bathtub, fridge and TV. All rates include breakfast at the rooftop restaurant or around the corner at the Hu Pin Restaurant. Although Hu Pin has its own generator, electric power is nonetheless spotty.

Kaungdine Near Kaungdine the quiet and relaxing *Inle Hotel* overlooks the lake and offers 26 spacious rooms with private facilities in two wooden buildings for US$24 to US$36. Near the hotel pier, eight thatched bungalows belonging to the Inle Hotel sit on stilts over the lake's edge; these cost US$24 a single/double. The village is a short walk away. Closer to the hot springs, the two-storey *Innlay (Kaungdaing) Hotel* is similar.

South of Kaungdine in the middle of the lake – 13 km south of Nyaungshwe – *Dak Bungalows* is a small wooden resort on stilts. It's reserved for government VIPs, so you're not likely to be allowed to stay there.

Places to Eat

Vegetarians will find Inle Lake a fine place to eat because of the year-round variety of vegetables, fruits and soy products. Mingala Market is a good place to shop for local produce; there are also plenty of Shan *khauk swe* (noodle soup) vendors at the market every morning. Another local delicacy is *maung jeut*, round, flat rice crisps usually translated 'rice cracker', which in typical Burmese pronunciation comes out sounding like 'rice cricket'.

A teashop on the outside, north-eastern corner of the market sells good *nam-bya* (flat bread similar to naan) with bean dip. Another nam-bya shop can be found next to the ruined stupa near the Evergreen Hotel.

In the centre of town near the market, the popular *Thuka Cafe* serves a variety of Burmese teashop snacks. On the opposite side of the street a bit north, *Shwe Inlay* bakes tasty Chinese and European-inspired pastries daily; it opens early but closes by late afternoon. On the next street west is the *Love Village Cafe*, which in spite of its imaginative name is just an ordinary youth-oriented Burmese teashop. Next door, the *Sunflower*

Restaurant serves noodles and tea snacks but closes around 5 pm.

Three local restaurants serve mostly Chinese food. The *Hu Pin* is known to be Nyaungshwe's best Chinese restaurant and is also easily the cleanest place in town. The English menu is divided into three sections: chicken, fish and pork. The Hu Pin closes around 8 pm – late for a town that is almost completely shut down by 7 pm. Three blocks south the *Golden Crown Restaurant* has a very similar Chinese menu that's about 15% cheaper. On the same block as the Shwe Inlay pastry shop, *Kong Kong* is a distant third choice for Chinese.

The only place that serves Shan food outside the market and hotels is the friendly *Big Drum Restaurant*, a set of thatched A-frame shelters on the western bank of the canal opposite Shwe Hintha Guest House. A Shan dinner of fish curry, bean soup, fried peanuts, rice and maung jeut costs K150 here. Chinese food is also on the menu. Shan food can also be arranged at the *Inle Inn* and *Pyi Guest House* in conjunction with Shan cultural shows.

Another place for local food is a house at the south-western edge of town known as *Four Sisters*. The Intha family that live here serve dinner to guests by advance arrangement; there's no set charge for the meal but donations are gladly collected. Some nights the sisters dance and sing as well as cook. One of the four sisters is a student in Mandalay now, but the remaining three, plus their brother, carry on the tradition. They also arrange canoe and motorboat trips, again by donation only.

The Chinese places are the only restaurants in town that serve beer (and Mandalay Rum), although some smaller shops sell *ayet piu* (white liquor) by the shot, which mixes well with lemon-lime soda. A government liquor shop in town sells beer and ayet piu at special government rates – K80 for a large bottle of beer, K35 for a bottle of 'white lightning'.

Getting There & Away

Apart from flying, all the routes to the Inle

Lake area are time-consuming. There are several things to consider which can save you much time and trouble getting to the lake. First of all there is no need to go to Taunggyi, the main town in the area and the location of the main MTT office. If you want to simply go to the lake you'll save a couple of hours by skipping Taunggyi.

Air Both Air Mandalay and Myanma Airways fly to Heho, which is 30 km from Shwenyaung, from where it is a further 11 km to Nyaungshwe or 20 km to Taunggyi. The airstrip at Heho is only 12.5 meters wide; according to AM this is the smallest ATR landing in the world. There are a couple of small restaurants behind the terminal.

AM, which provides the most comfortable and most punctual service, has direct flights from Yangon to Heho three times weekly and flights via Mandalay on the same day (Monday, Wednesday and Saturday). The Yangon-Heho fare is the same on both flights, US$113 standby or US$123 with a confirmed seat; from Mandalay the fare is US$45/50. MA flies from Yangon to Heho daily except Thursday for US$75 by F-27, US$85 by F-28, and from Mandalay four times weekly for US$35/40.

From Heho both airlines fly daily to Bagan with a stopover in Mandalay. Aboard AM a ticket for this leg costs US$75; on MA it's US$65.

Car taxis from Heho to Nyaungshwe cost US$13 to US$15. If you wait for a collective pickup, you can get a ride as far as the Shwenyaung junction for K30; from Shwenyaung another pickup goes to Nyaungshwe for K20. If you're continuing on to Taunggyi it's K40 straight through.

Bus & Pickup By road, most people travel to Inle Lake from Bagan, Thazi or Mandalay. In January the trip up over the mountains from the plains to Inle Lake can be very cold in an open truck – make sure you have some warm clothes.

To/From Thazi & Meiktila The road between Thazi and Taunggyi has improved considerably over the last few years but it's still a stiff ride of around six hours by public transport, around five hours if you have your own vehicle.

The fare for the better Thazi-Taunggyi trucks varies from K80 to K250 depending on the type of vehicle and number of passengers. The less expensive trucks don't leave till there are passengers hanging off every protrusion on the truck; the better ones have more leg room and fewer passengers. Most trucks depart from either town at 9 and 11 am. If you're heading for Inle Lake, get off at the Shwenyaung junction and catch one of the frequent pickups (6 am to 6 pm only) to Nyaungshwe, 11 km south, for K20. Share taxis do the same trip for K50 per person.

There are also a couple of trucks a day between Shwenyaung and Meiktila for K90.

The staging area for most public transport in and out of Nyaungshwe is the street that runs south of the Hu Pin Hotel, one block west of Mingala Market.

To/From Mandalay Pickups and regular buses between Mandalay and the lake area cost K250 to K400 per person depending on the company; all leave between 4 and 6 am and arrive at the other end in 10 to 12 hours. One of the more reliable companies, Naung Inle, has an office in Mandalay on 23rd St between 82nd and 83rd Sts. From Nyaungshwe their vehicles leave from in front of the Sunflower Restaurant. Inle Inn in Nyaungshwe operates a daily private bus to Mandalay for US$10, leaving at 5 am and arriving at 5 pm. It's main advantage is door-to-door pickup and dropoff at either end.

At the moment all road transport goes through Meiktila, west of Thazi; once the new highway between Mandalay and Thazi is completed, the trip will probably become half to one hour shorter.

There are also several bus lines that go between Mandalay and Taunggyi for roughly the same fares. They leave from the market in Taunggyi or from 25th Rd in Mandalay; reserve your seat the day before. Bus lines on this route include Thanlwin-Mann, Cherry-Mann and Taunggyi-Mann. The old buses are cheaper, but also much more crowded, slower and far less reliable than the modern pickups.

To/From Bagan For the most part an overland trip from Bagan entails getting to Meiktila or Thazi, then changing to a Nyaungshwe, Shwenyaung or Taunggyi-bound bus or pickup. See the Bagan section for more information.

Tiger Head Express operates a bus from Bagan Myothit (New Bagan) to Taunggyi for K500 which leaves at 4 am; as usual, get off at Shwenyaung and continue on to Nyaung-shwe by public pickup for K20. Inle Inn runs a private pickup with door-to-door pickup and dropoff to/from Bagan Myothit for US$10. For both of these you should reserve a seat the day before you would like to make the journey.

To/From Taunggyi See the following Taunggyi Getting There & Away section for details.

To/From Yangon Several companies run buses between Yangon and Taunggyi; see the following Taunggyi Getting There & Away section for details. Inle Inn in Nyaungshwe sometimes organises a bus straight through to Yangon for US$17 per person.

TAUNGGYI တောင်ကြီး:
Situated at 1430 metres, the pine-clad hill station of Taunggyi provides a cool break from the heat of the plains. There are some pleasant walks if you are in the mood, but basically it's a just a growing trade centre for the south-western area of Shan State.

Taunggyi is the official end of the line for eastern-bound foreigners in Myanmar. Beyond lies a world of black marketeers, insurgent armies and opium warlords. The town was once a place of respite for perspiring Brits, although all that remains of the colonial era are an overgrown graveyard, a stone church, a line of cherry trees and a handful of timbered cottages, all on the fringes of town. The main street is strictly socialist realism, with signs done in raised

concrete letters just like in Myanmar's current mentor China.

But because of its function as a conduit for smuggled goods from Thailand, China and India, this is one of Myanmar's most prosperous and enterprising towns. Long-haired smugglers in army fatigues saunter down the street alongside turbaned hill people and sleek-suited Chinese businesspeople. An abundance of black-market consumer goods are displayed in the Taunggyi market, which is located at the edge of a Chinese enclave whose residents include many illegal immigrants. The remainder of the population of 100,000 includes tribespeople, Shan, Burmans, Sikhs, Punjabis and retired Gurkhas who once fought for the British. Along Taunggyi's main streets you'll see Buddhist, Sikh and Hindu temples, mosques and churches.

The temple on the hill overlooking the plains and Inle Lake is nothing special, but the views of Taunggyi are good and the walk is nice.

Information
Find information on the street and at the MTT office (☎ 081-21601, 21227) located in the Taunggyi Hotel. At the post office near the hotel you can make long-distance calls to Yangon and other parts of Myanmar, but not abroad. The mail is said to be reliable.

Things to See & Do
Taunggyi has an interesting **municipal market** area in the centre of town where you're likely to see colourful hill tribespeople – there's a daily market plus one that comes to town every five days. From Taunggyi, the market moves to Pwehla (on the way to Pindaya), then the third day to Kalaw, and from there in turn to Pindaya, Heho and back to Taunggyi. One of the local handicrafts most in evidence is basketry.

There is also a **gem market** in the north-eastern part of town where jade, rubies and sapphires are bought and sold daily from noon to 4 pm. While it doesn't compare with the gem markets of Mogok, the well-

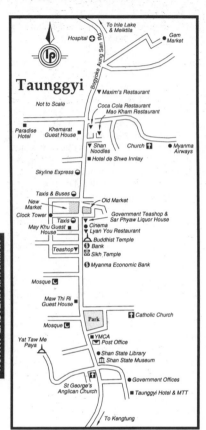

Taunggyi

Not to Scale

To Inle Lake & Meiktila
Hospital
Gem Market
Maxim's Restaurant
Coca Cola Restaurant
Mao Kham Restaurant
Paradise Hotel
Khemarat Guest House
Shan Noodles
Church
Myanma Airways
Hotel de Shwe Innlay
Skyline Express
Taxis & Buses
Old Market
New Market
Clock Tower
Taxis
Government Teashop & Sar Phyaw Liquor House
May Khu Guest House
Cinema
Lyan You Restaurant
Buddhist Temple
Teashop
Bank
Sikh Temple
Myanma Economic Bank
Mosque
Maw Thi Ri Guest House
Mosque
Park
Catholic Church
Yat Taw Me Paya
YMCA
Post Office
Shan State Library
Shan State Museum
St George's Anglican Church
Government Offices
Taunggyi Hotel & MTT
To Kengtung

different ethnic groups officially recognised in the state. There's also a display of royal Shan regalia and an exhibit of religious art that includes Buddhist sculpture in mixed Shan and Mandalay styles, Shan *jataka* (life stories of the Budha) paintings, *pitaka* chests, *kammawas* (Buddhist lacquered scriptures), *parabaik* (folding manuscripts) and ornate votive tablets.

One room upstairs is devoted to the Panglong Agreement of 1947 in which Shan, Kachin and Chin leaders signed a document promising cooperation in the proposed Union of Burma. Admission to the museum is free and English-speaking lecturers are available to lead visitors around.

There's a cheroot factory called **Flying Tiger Mashua** on a side street south of the Myodaw Cinema. The handrolling technique is impressive, and cigar bundlers are able to bunch 50 cigars in bundles without counting the individual cigars – they judge simply by feel.

Places to Stay

An old standby in Taunggyi, the *May Khu Guest House*, is a rambling wooden structure not far from the market and off Bogyoke Aung San Rd, the north-south avenue through town. Although it's run-down and a bit noisy, it does have some atmosphere. Foreigner rates are US$10 per person in simple two-bed rooms with common bath.

The new *Khemarat Guest House* at 4B Bogyoke Aung San Rd, at the northern end of town in a quieter semi-residential quarter, has economy rooms with shared bath for US$9/12 a single/double plus rooms with bath attached for US$15/18. The friendly manager speaks fair English. Overall this is the best value in town.

Paradise (Paradiz) Hotel (☎ 081-22009) at 157 Khwa Nyo Rd, west a few blocks from the Khemarat, is a new four-storey (no lift) modern Chinese-style place. Well-appointed rooms with good mattresses, hot-water showers, polished wood floors and TV cost US$24 single, US$30 double. Slightly nicer rooms with fridge cost US$36/42. There are plush sitting rooms at the end of each floor.

informed may be able to ferret out a deal or two.

For those interested in the Shan State's cultures, the modest **Shan State Museum** and **Shan State Library** near the Taunggyi Hotel are worth a visit. Although only a relatively small number of items are labelled in English, you can look at items including local native costume, musical instruments, ceramics and weapons. If nothing else, you may begin sorting out hill tribe names: Kaw for Akha, Tai for Shan, Jin-Phaw for Kachin, Lahta and Yanglai different Karen groups; and identifying kinds of dress for the 35

JOE CUMMINGS

BERNARD NAPTHINE

JOE CUMMINGS

North-Eastern Myanmar
   Top: The amazing jumping cats at Nga Phe Kyaung, Ywama
Middle: Coming in for market, Nyaungshwe
Bottom: An illuminated cave-chamber, Pindaya

JOE CUMMINGS

JOE CUMMINGS

JOE CUMMINGS

North-Eastern Myanmar
Top: Sailing the calm waters of the Sittoung River
Bottom Left: Moared, Inle Lake
Bottom Right: Checking the nets, Intha fisherman, Inle Lake

Also near the Khemarat, on the opposite side of Bogyoke Aung San Rd, is the *Hotel de Shwe Innlay*, which despite its French-inspired name doesn't yet accept foreign guests. It's a fairly well-maintained two-storey place that would probably cost around US$10 per person if/when it obtains a foreigner licence.

The recently privatised and relatively efficient, 56-room *Taunggyi Hotel* (☎ 081-21127, 21302) sprawls over landscaped grounds near the southern end of town. Spacious rooms with attached hot-water bathrooms cost US$30/36/54 a single/double/triple, superior rooms with TV and fridge are US$36/42/63 and a bigger junior suite costs US$42/48 a single/double. The old MHT-style bar and restaurant attract a mix of well-heeled businesspeople and military types. The hotel is a short stroll from the town centre and is one of the more comfortable older hotels in Myanmar.

The other places in Taunggyi are all quite central and pretty much alike – small and basic – but since 1989 they're all off limits to foreigners. If you want to visit the old standbys, check out the *San Pya Guest House*, on the main street toward the Taunggyi Hotel end of town, near the post office and the museum. Also on the main drag lie the *Maw Thi Ri* and *Myodaw* guest houses and the *Lyan You Hotel*, none of which currently admit foreigners.

Places to Eat

A row of small food stalls in the market serve decent Chinese and Shan dishes. Very little English is spoken here, however, so brush up on your Burmese and/or point-to-order technique. The unassuming *Maokham* serves basic Shan and Chinese fare from 10 am to 8 pm; walk east off the main street down the road near the Hotel Shwe de Innlay, make an immediate left and it's the unmarked wooden place on the right.

On the main street in the same area, the *Coca Cola Restaurant* has an all-Chinese menu; it's nothing great, but it's popular.

The *Lyan You Hotel* prepares good noodle dishes; sometimes Australian wine is available here for just K200 per bottle. Next door the *Taunggyi Cafe & Confectionery* and *City Tea Shop* serve decent tea and snacks.

Another favourite, with a more pleasant decor, is *Shwe Le Maw*, across from the Sikh temple. They specialise in an extensive variety of pastries and tea snacks and also have a take-away window – Burmese fast food. *Sambya*, a small shop near Myodaw Cinema, serves basic *dan bauk* (biryani).

Getting There & Away

Trucks to Taunggyi from Inle Lake charge K30 and leave frequently from the Nyaungshwe market area between 7 am and 5 pm for the 45-minute trip; in the downhill direction the fare is only K15. A taxi along the same route costs US$15 or K1500.

There's one pickup per day from Taunggyi to Pindaya at 2 pm which arrives at 5.30 pm and costs K40; it starts back the next day at 6 am. The pickup fare to Heho is also K40, taxi US$13 to US$15.

From Bagan Myothit and Mandalay, pickups cost K250 to K300 per person and take seven or eight hours.

Express air-con buses to/from Yangon are available for K1000 to K1200 and take around 16 hours. Skyline Express (☎ 081-21670) has an office at 40 Bogyoke Aung San Rd north of the market area.

HOPONG ဟိုပုံး:

Although few foreigners have seen it, the valley around Hopong, just 20 km east of Taunggyi, begins a beautiful stretch of forested hills that continue more or less all the way to Kengtung in the extreme eastern end of Shan State.

From Hopong a decent sealed road leads 155 km south to Loikaw, the capital of Kayah State. Wanyin, 40 miles south of Hopong and surrounded by 2400-metre peaks, is a centre for the Taungthu and Padaung people, who outnumber the Shan five to three in this area.

Although not officially open, foreigners making day trips to Hopong from Taunggyi aren't usually stopped by the authorities. Along the way the hills are dotted with Shan-style stupas, and in Hopong itself there's an interesting paya trimmed with hundreds of bells and chimes.

Around 16 km east of Taunggyi, off the highway, a spring-fed pool is a popular spot for picnicking and swimming.

KENGTUNG (KYAINGTONG) ကျိုင်းတုံ

Tucked away in a far eastern corner of the Shan State, 456 km north-east of Taunggyi and 163 km north of the border town of Tachilek (opposite Mae Sai, Thailand), is the sleepy but historic centre for the state's Khün culture, Kengtung, surrounded by Wa, Shan, Akha and Lahu villages. Built around a small lake, and dotted with aging Buddhist temples and crumbling British colonial architecture, Kengtung is probably the most scenic town in the Shan State.

Its opening to foreign visitors in January 1993 came as a complete surprise considering this was – and still is – one the most remote inhabited mountain valleys in Myanmar. Access is difficult and restricted to MA flights from Myanmar's interior or a rough overland road trip from Tachilek/Mae Sai. It is also a strategic Burmese government stronghold in the middle of the shifting seas of Shan insurgency and the opium trade. Its position is doubly strategic considering the area is a crossroads with outlets in four different countries – Myanmar, China, Thailand and Laos. As such it is a critical linchpin in the country's defence. During WW II the town was occupied by Japanese and Thai soldiers because it is 160 km equidistant from three international borders.

Although Kengtung lies about midway between the Thanlwin River and Mekong River valleys, it is more or less cut off from the former by a series of north-south mountain ranges. Hence, culturally, the area has more of an affinity for the nearby cultures of the Mekong – Laos, Xishuangbanna (southeastern Yunnan) and Thailand – than for the Shan and Burmese cultures west of the Thanlwin.

The Khün speak a Northern Thai language related to Shan and Thai Lü and use a writing script similar to the ancient Lanna script of Chiang Mai in northern Thailand. The orig-

inal Khün are in fact said to have been 13th-century migrants from Chiang Mai, and their rulers claim to be descendants of the Lanna (or Lan Na Thai, 'Million Thai Rice-Fields') dynasty.

Before the Khün began paying tribute to the Burmans under King Anawrahta, they had their own independent kingdom variously called Muang Tamilap, Muang Ong Puu, Muang Sanlawachilakam, Muang Khemmaratungkburi and Tungkalasi before settling on Kengtung, which means 'Walled City of Tung'. 'Tung' is a reference to the kingdom's mythical founder, a hermit named Tungkalasi who used his magic staff to drain a lake of near-sea proportions, leaving behind the current town lake. Remains of the original city walls and gates can still be seen. Today the Thais know the city as 'Chiang Tung' while the Burmese call it 'Kyaingtong'.

Traditional Khün dress consists of a horizontally striped longyi and Shan-style jacket with a crossover front that ties on the side. Nowadays most Khüns dress similarly to their counterparts in neighbouring countries. About 80% of the township population of 180,000 are Khün; roughly 15% are Shan-Chinese, the remainder a mix of other ethnicities from around the Shan State and beyond. About half the population is Buddhist, another 17% Christian and the rest belong to various spirit cults.

About 70% of all foreign visitors to Kengtung are Thais seeking a glimpse of ancient Lanna. Few Westerners are seen around town save for contract employees working for the UNDCP (United Nations Drug Control Project), whose sizable expenditures lead many of the locals to believe all Western arrivals are similarly flush.

Crossing the Border from Mae Sai

Since 1993 foreigners have been intermittently permitted to cross the bridge over the Sai River from Mae Sai, Thailand, to Tachilek and from there to continue by air or road the 163 km to Kengtung. Three to seven-day tours to Kengtung may be arranged through any Mae Sai guest house or travel agency at rates starting at US$200 per person. Or you can do it on your own. You must leave your passport and three photos at the border, fill out some papers and pay the US$18 fee for a four-day border pass. You must also pay a mandatory exchange of US$100 for Foreign Exchange Certificates (FECs), which, as elsewhere in Myanmar, can be spent on hotel rooms or exchanged on the black market for kyat. The permit can be extended for up to three months at a cost of US$36 at the immigration office in Kengtung.

In May 1994 Khun Sa's Mong Tai Army (MTA) bombed the Tachilek dyke, draining the reservoir that supplied the town with water. The border was closed to foreigners for several weeks, then opened again but other incidents in April 1995 closed the border once again. This same pattern will probably be repeated again and again until the Shan and Burmese come to an agreement – an unlikely event in the near future.

Hence if you're contemplating an overland trip to Kengtung from Thailand, you'll simply have to take your chances on finding the border crossing open or closed – more often than not it has been open.

Foreigners are not at direct risk from the fighting between the MTA and Burmese troops although the possibility of getting caught in the crossfire somewhere along the road between Tachilek and Kengtung cannot be ruled out. Kengtung itself seems relatively safe; the MTA hasn't attacked the town since the 1980s. Foreigners are rarely given permission to travel north of Kengtung; the border area between Kengtung and China is controlled by the Eastern Shan State National Democratic Army (ESSNDA), a rebel Shan splinter group. Neither the MTA nor the ESSNDA have ever been known to threaten or harm tourists.

See the following Tachilek section for more information on border crossings.

Things to See & Do

When the British settled into Kengtung, they centered the town around a large, natural lake. Decaying colonial-style buildings, taken over by the Burmese government or by squatters, are reminiscent of British colonial provincial architecture found elsewhere in Myanmar and India. The faded colonial air, along with the pagoda spires of over 30 local temples, the surrounding green hills and narrow, winding streets combine to create something of a Burmese counterpart to Luang Phabang (Laos).

Kengtung's many well-kept monasteries – called *wats* rather than kyaungs by the Khün – reflect Shan, Siamese, Burmese and Chinese influences. The most impressive is **Wat Jom Kham (Zom Kham)**, which features a tall gilded zedi topped by a gold hti inlaid with silver, rubies, diamonds, sapphires and jade, and hung with tiny gold bells. The interior walls bear older goldleaf-on-lacquer jatakas as well as modern painted ones, sparkling mirrored pillars and a dozen or so Buddha images on an altar draped with gilded cloth. Much intricate tinwork outlines the gables and plinthes of the temple. Legend says Jom Kham dates to a visit by Gautama Buddha and that the zedi contains six strands of his hair. Most likely the site dates to the 13th century Chiang Mai migration. The temple was substantially renovated in 1906 and 1936, when the height of the stupa rose to 38 metres. The zedi was regilded in 1988 and 1989. Wat Jong Kham is located north of the town centre.

Right in the centre of town are a couple of busy and visually striking 19th-century temples, **Wat Pha Jao Lung** (Burmese name 'Maha Myat Muni') and **Wat Ho Kong**.

On a hill to the south-west of town, **Wat Pha That Jom Mon** features an older wood-and-plaster sanctuary with good tinwork. Further up the hill behind the monastery are some very tall dipterocarp trees and two picturesque white stupas. The surrounding hillside provides good views of the town below. In the same area is the modest **Wat Mahabodhi Vipassana**, a forest-style monastery where the monks practice intensive meditation.

On the road leading west out of town toward Taunggyi, the British-era **Roman Catholic Mission (RCM)** and the 12-year-old **Immaculate Heart Cathedral** are still

NORTH-EASTERN MYANMAR

thriving on a hillside where the original town was founded a thousand years ago. Visitors are welcome. The mission cares for nearly one hundred orphaned boys, many from Shan State hill tribes.

One of the great sights in Kengtung was the large **Haw Sao Pha Kengtung**, considered the most outstanding example of Shan-style palace architecture in Myanmar. The stucco-and-teak structure combined Buddhist temple-style pavilions with Islamic-looking domes, said to have been inspired by the suggestions of a visiting Muslim Indian prince. Despite a protest mounted by a group of monks and Khün residents who appealed to the local army commander to preserve the building, the Burmese government demolished the palace in 1991 to make way for a hotel that remains unbuilt. Reportedly there are two other smaller royal residences surviving in town – **Haw Sao Pha Yong Huay** and **Haw Sai Paa Si Paw Lae**.

The **central market** draws people from all over Kengtung District, including a variety of hill tribe people. Fresh produce and household goods are the market's main emphases, but some handicrafts are also available. Look

Kengtung

0   250   500 m

To Mong Yang
To Mong Ma
To Airport
To Taunggyi
To Loi Mwe & Tachilek
To Pha Yang Gate
To Tachilek

Nawng Tung Lake

Naung Yarng Lake

PLACES TO STAY		6	Wat Kae Min	38	Yang Kham Gate
		7	Wat Yang Kon	39	Water Buffalo Market
1	Harry's Trekking	8	Pottery Works	40	Roman Catholic
	House	10	Wat Naung Kham		Mission &
9	Win Guest House	11	Mangala Kyaung		Immaculate Heart
17	Noi Yee Hotel		(Wat Tamawtaya)		Cathedral
20	Kyaing Tonge Hotel	12	Wat Jong Kham	41	Fax & Telegram Office
28	Kyi Lin Star Guest		(Zom Kham)	42	Myanma Airways
	House	13	Wat Noi Naw	43	Wat Asok
48	Barami Motel	14	Wat Chiang Ing	44	Police
56	Hsam Yawt Guest		(Keng Ing)	45	Independence
	House	15	Jail		Monument
		18	Immigration Office	46	Sports Field
PLACES TO EAT		19	Wat Chiang Ying	47	Maung Ming Kyaung
			(Keng Yun)	49	Maung Mai Kyaung
16	Keng House	21	Wat Pha Kaew	51	Khemarat Cinema
	Restaurant	22	Wat Pha Jao Lung	52	Thai Flying Service
25	Tai Khun Restaurant		(Maha Myat Muni)	54	Regional Offices
31	Golden Banyan	23	Wat Ho Kong	55	Chinese Clan House
	Restaurant	24	Kengtung Cinema	57	Town Hall
50	Honey Teashop	26	Tai Khun Silverworks	58	Central Market
53	Lauo Tien Lu	27	Wat Chiang Jan	59	Wat Chiang Khom
	Restaurant		(Keng San)		(Keng Khom)
		29	Wat Ho Kat	60	Wat Si Naw
OTHER		30	Buses to Tachilek	61	Wat Mahabodhi
		32	Paleng Gate		Vipassana
2	Chinese School	33	Hospital		(Kamathan
3	Naung Pha Gate	34	Mosque		Kyaung)
4	UNDCP Office	35	Wat Jom Mai	62	Wat Tuya
5	American Baptist	36	St Mary's Convent	63	Wat Pha That Jom
	Church	37	Buses to Taunggyi		Mon

NORTH-EASTERN MYANMAR

for Kengtung-style lacquerware, which, like that found in Kyaukka in the Mandalay Division, doesn't employ the polychromatic incising techniques found in Bagan but rather two-colour lacquer-moulding reliefs.

A **water buffalo market** convenes daily on the southern side of the road to Taunggyi on the western outskirts of town; visitors are welcome to wander around and observe the negotiations. It's like touring a used-car lot, with pedlars extolling the virtues of their animals while buyers point out their flaws until finally a price is agreed upon, money changes hands and the new owners walk off leading their buffaloes by the nose.

The lake in the centre of town, **Nawng Tung** (Nawng is the Shan word for 'small lake'), is a popular spot for morning and evening strolls.

Places to Stay

Blackouts are common in Kengtung, so be sure to bring along a torch (flashlight). *Harry's Guest House & Trekking* (☎ 101-21418), at 132 Mai Yang Rd, Kanaburoy Village, 500 metres north of the Naung Pha gate at the northern edge of town, has basic rooms in a large house for US$5 per person. Harry is an English-speaking Kengtung native who spent many years as a trekking guide in Chiang Mai.

The *Noi Yee Hotel* near the centre of town costs US$10 per person per night in large multi-bed rooms with mosquito nets, high ceilings, and attached cold-water bathrooms (some rooms share bathrooms).

MTT tries to steer tourists toward the more expensive, government-run *Kyainge Tong Hotel*, where rooms with air-con and hot water cost US$36/42 a single/double in the 'A' and 'B' sections, similar rooms without air-con or hot water are US$30/36 in the 'C' and 'D' sections, and cheaper rooms in the 'E' section cost US$15. The management has been known to deny the existence of the latter. At night the hotel dining room is converted into a taxi dancing parlour; a Shan ensemble plays live music while male patrons dance with women dressed in traditional garb, each dance timed by a matron armed with a whistle.

Win Guest House, on the road to the airport north-east of town, offers decent rooms in a modern-looking house for US$25 a single, US$30 a double, each with private toilet and cold-water shower. Although it's a bit removed from the town centre, it's quiet.

Other places in town which are poised to accept foreigners if and when they receive licences include the *Barami Motel* (☎ 101-21089) at 3 Loi Mwe Rd, *Hsam Ywat* (☎ 101-21235) at 21 Conner Jenglan Rd and *Kyi Lin Star* near Paleng gate. The Barami and Hsam Yawt plan to ask US$10 to US$15 per person.

Places to Eat

Two Chinese restaurants a few blocks south-east of the central market get more than their share of regular clientele. The longest-

Opium, Khun Sa & the Golden Triangle

The opium poppy, *papaver somniferum*, has been cultivated and its resins extracted for use as a narcotic at least since the time of the early Greek Empire. The Chinese were introduced to the drug by Arab traders during the time of Kublai Khan (1279-94). It was so highly valued for its medicinal properties that hill-tribe minorities in southern China began cultivating the opium poppy in order to raise money to pay taxes to their Han Chinese rulers. Easy to grow, opium became a way for the nomadic hill tribes to raise what cash they needed in transactions – willing and unwilling – with the lowland world.

Many of the hill tribes that migrated to Myanmar in the post-WW II era in order to avoid persecution in China took with them their one cash crop, the poppy. The poppy is well suited to hillside cultivation as it flourishes on steep slopes and in nutrient-poor soils. Large tracts of land are needed for the crop, however; it takes the sap of 3000 poppies to produce one *joi* (1.6 kg), the standard unit of weight in the opium trade.

For many hill tribes opium plays an important role in traditional medicine. Among some ethnic groups, such as the Lolo, raw opium sap (which in small amounts is non-intoxicating) is also a significant element of their daily food intake. In the lowlands, opium poppyseeds are the main flavouring in *bei mok* – opium cake.

Because of all the money earned via opium trafficking in the region where Myanmar, Laos and Thailand meet, the area has been dubbed the 'Golden Triangle'. The term might more accurately be expanded to 'Golden Quadrangle' in order to include south-western China, a major location for the refining and smuggling of illicit opiates.

One of the region's most colourful figures is Khun Sa (also known as Chang Chi-Fu, or Sao Mong Khawn) a half-Chinese, half-Shan opium warlord. Born in Lashio District in 1934, Khun Sa started out in the 1950s and '60s working for the Kuomintang (KMT) – Chiang Kai Shek's Nationalist Chinese troops who had fled to Myanmar. The KMT were continuing military operations against the Chinese communists along the Myanmar-China border, financed by the smuggling of opium (with CIA protection). They employed Khun Sa as one of their prime local supporters/advisors. Khun Sa broke with the KMT in the early 1960s after establishing his own opium-smuggling business, with heroin refineries in northern Thailand.

From that time on, the history of heroin smuggling in the Golden Triangle has been intertwined with the exploits of Khun Sa. In 1966, the Burmese government deputised Khun Sa as head of 'village defence forces' against the Burmese Communist Party (BCP), which was at maximum strength at this time and fully involved in opium trade. Khun Sa cleverly used his government backing to consolidate power and build up his own militia by developing the Shan United Army (SUA), an anti-government insurgent group heavily involved in opium throughout the Golden Triangle in competition with the BCP and KMT.

When the KMT attempted an 'embargo' on SUA opium trade by blocking caravan routes into Thailand and Laos, Khun Sa initiated what has come to be known as the Opium War of 1967 and thwarted the embargo. However, the KMT managed to chase Khun Sa, along with a contingent of SUA troops running an opium caravan routed for Thailand, into Laos, where Burmese officials arrested Khun Sa and the Laotian government seized the opium. Khun Sa escaped Burmese custody by means of a carefully planned combination of extortion and bribery in 1975 and returned to take command of the SUA. About the same time, the Burmese government broke KMT control of opium trafficking and Khun Sa stepped in to become the prime opium warlord in the Triangle, working from his headquarters in Ban Hin Taek, Chiang Rai Province, Thailand. Coincidentally, US forces pulled out of Indo-China at this time so there was no longer any competition from CIA conduits in Laos.

running and most reliable is *Lauo Tien Lu* (also known as Lawt Tin Lu), a branch of a restaurant owned by the same family in Thailand's Chiang Khong. It's a simple open-sided restaurant with good southern-Chinese food. The second is *Golden Banyan* (also called Shwe Nyaung Bin or Ton Pho), near Wat Chiang Jan (Keng San) and opposite Kyi Lin Star Guest House. The main feature of the latter is outdoor tables beneath a huge banyan tree.

On the eastern shore of Nawng Tung is *Keng House Restaurant* a pleasant, open-air spot with an extensive Chinese menu; hotpot is a house speciality. *Tai Khun Restaurant*, east of Kengtung Cinema, serves authentic Shan/Khün food.

The *Honey Teashop* next to the central market is one of the best places in town for morning samosas and palata.

Getting There & Away
From Elsewhere in Myanmar If current

Since the late 1970s, Khun Sa's armies have continued to buy opium from the Shan, Kokang, Wa and hill-tribe cultivators in Myanmar, Laos and Thailand, transporting and selling the product to Yunnanese-operated heroin refineries in China, Laos and Thailand, who in turn sell to ethnic Chinese syndicates who control access to world markets via Thailand and Yunnan.

A turning point in Khun Sa's fortunes occurred in 1982 and 1983 when the Thais launched a full-scale attack on his Ban Hin Taek stronghold, forcing him to flee to the mountains of the Kok River valley across the border in Ho Mong, Myanmar, where he now directs his independent empire from a fortified network of underground tunnels. This move led to the breaking up of opium and heroin production in much of north-western Thailand.

The SUA has since merged with several other Shan armies to form the Mong Tai Army (MTA), led by the Shan State Restoration Council; in 1992 Khun Sa declared the Shan State an independent nation. Recent MTA strength has been estimated at 25,000, the largest and best-equipped ethnic army in Myanmar – well beyond that of the Karen National Union, the country's second-largest insurgent group (among the 30-odd different groups operating since the 1940s). From time to time Khun Sa announces his 'retirement' but like his Yangon nemesis Ne Win, Khun Sa has outwitted many international players before and will probably maintain de facto control until his death or capture. Khun Sa is now a 'marked' man (with a price of US$200,000 on his head, roughly the wholesale value of one hundred kilos of pure heroin) who may soon be sacrificed by corrupt Burmese and Thai generals in order to appease the US government. Recently there have been rumours that the MTA leadership would like Khun Sa to step down as commander-in-chief in order to disassociate the independence movement from Khun Sa's notorious past.

By all estimates there has been a steady increase in Triangle production for the last ten years; only 1.9 to 2.5% of the opium crop is intercepted by national or international authorities each year. The yearly output of the Shan State alone now reaches over 500 tonnes. Khun Sa likes to boast that although his armies have been attacked by US-backed Thai troops on over 40 occasions, no opium or heroin has ever been seized as a result of the assaults. To the USA, Khun Sa has proposed a seven-year poppy eradication programme which he says can be accomplished with US$210 million in aid.

Meanwhile power shifts from warlord to warlord while the hill-tribe and Shan cultivators continue as unwilling pawns in the opium-heroin cycle. The planting of the poppy and the sale of its collected resins has never been a simple moral issue. Cultivators who have been farming poppies for centuries and heroin addicts who consume the end product have both been exploited by governments and crime syndicates who trade in opium for the advancement of their own interests. Because of the complexities involved, opium production in the Golden Triangle must be dealt with as a political, social, cultural and economic problem and not simply as a conventional law-enforcement matter.

> There is an end of joy and sorrow
> Peace all day long, all night, all morrow
> But never a time to laugh or weep.
> Their end is more than joy or anguish,
> Than lives that laugh or lives that languish,
> The end of all the poppied sleep.

Charles Swinburne (1837-1909)

economic and political conditions in Myanmar prevail, the road between Kengtung and Taunggyi should open to foreign travel at some point in the future. At the moment only Myanmar citizens are permitted to use this road. Fighting between Myanmar's Yangon government and the Shan insurgents (the only ethnic rebel group besides the Karen that haven't yet signed a ceasefire with Rangoon) makes the Kengtung-Taunggyi journey potentially hazardous.

The drive from Taunggyi takes two long days (sometimes four or five days in wet weather) over a narrow and winding road. The main overnight stops are **Loilem, Kunhing** and **Mong Ping**, each of which has rustic guest houses and rudimentary cafes.

You can fly MA to Kengtung from Yangon (US$105 by F-27, US$115 by F-28), from Mandalay (US$60/70), from Heho (US$50/50) and from Tachilek (US$25/30). Most of these flights run three times a week; during periods of heavy fighting between the Burmese and Shan armies (typically in the December to May dry season), half the seats in the return direction may be taken up by wounded Burmese soldiers. It's not unusual to see the cargo-hold on a Tachilek or Kengtung-bound MA flight filled with Chinese rocket launchers or other military equipment.

From Mae Sai/Tachilek The cheapest form of transport to Kengtung is the pickup truck for K200 (50B in Thai currency) that leaves each morning from Tachilek. You can rent jeeps on either side of the border, but Thai vehicles with a capacity of five or fewer passengers are charged a flat US$50 customs fee; it's US$100 for vehicles with a capacity of over five. The nearest car hire agencies on the Thai side are in Chiang Rai; some agencies won't allow their cars to be taken into Myanmar while others require a substantial deposit.

Burmese vehicle hire is more expensive (about 2000B or US$80) and requires the use of a driver although of course you save on the customs fee. Whatever form of transport you use, count on at least six to 10 gruelling

hours to cover the twisting, pot-holed and rutted stretch of road between the border and Kengtung. Until this road is sealed it should be avoided during the monsoon season (July to September).

The unsealed road passes through steep narrow river valleys and past numerous Akha, Wa and Shan villages. Along the way the main rest stops are **Talay**, a small town with interesting Shan temples and an army post, and **Mong Phyak**, the most popular food stop.

The road is currently being improved and reportedly will eventually be sealed all the way to the Chinese border, 100 km beyond Kengtung. If the Chinese border opens – and a truce agreement is reached with the ESSNDA – perhaps Thai immigration authorities in Mae Sai may allow visitors to travel with their passports, which would make an overland trip into China possible.

From Chiang Rai Small planes operated by Thai Flying Service (☎ 053-779 020 in Thailand) fly from Chiang Rai to Kengtung once a week for US$150 return. Obviously this is no bargain when you can cross the border and hop a MA flight from Tachilek for US$25. Then again, there are no guarantees the MA flight will leave remotely close to its scheduled departure time – or that there will be seats available when it does.

AROUND KENGTUNG

Foreigners are restricted to travel within a 25-km radius around town except for the road to Tachilek. Just south of town on the road to Tachilek is a large public **hot springs spa**. Entry to one of the gender-segregated bathhouses costs K25 per person. Shampoo and soap are available for sale, so this is a great spot to clean up if you're staying at one of the cold-water guest houses in town during the cool season. Vendors on the grounds sell noodles and other snacks, so you could easily spend an entire afternoon here. The spa is busiest on weekends.

On the northern outskirts of town in the village of **Yang Kong**, on the road to Mong Ma, you can visit pottery works where roof tiles, utilitarian bowls and other ceramic items are made.

Hiking to nearby Lahu (Musoe), Akha (Kaw), Shan and Wa villages is permitted in the company of a licensed guide, available at the Kyainge Tong Hotel or Harry's Guest House for around US$5 a day per person. The private Khemarat Tour Guide Centre at 14 Zaydangyi Rd, just south of the traffic circle and Wat Pha Jao Long, can also provide guides. Overnighting in the villages is not officially permitted.

Although it lies a little outside the permitted radius, no one seems to care if you visit **Loi-mwe**, 33 km south-east of Kengtung. Located at over 1600 metres, this 'hill station' features a number of old colonial buildings and a century-old Catholic church. The main attraction, though, is the scenery on the ascent to Loi-mwe, which passes through forests, terraced rice fields and a lake. You'll have to hire a car or motorcycle as there doesn't seem to be any regular public transport between Kengtung and Loi-mwe.

TACHILEK တာချီလိတ်

Burmese authorities have spruced up Tachilek ('Thakhilek' in the Thai-Shan-Khün spelling), the town opposite Mae Sai, Thailand, and now allow foreigners to cross the Sai River bridge, for the day, upon payment of a US$5 fee (formerly US$10) and deposit of passport at the Thai immigration post. The economies of the twin border towns are tightly bound; many Burmese cross from Tachilek to Mae Sai during the day to work or do business, hurrying back by sunset. Burmese lacquerware, gems, jade and other goods from Laos and Myanmar are sold in shops but prices are about the same as on the Thai side; many big-time dealers from around Thailand come here to buy gems and crafts wholesale.

You can spend more time in Tachilek if you obtain one of the seven-day permits available for US$18, but most travellers head straight for Kengtung to the north rather than linger at the border. Whichever type of pass you hold, you're restricted to a radius of five km (Tachilek-Kengtung road excepted). See the Kengtung section above for information on permits.

In January 1995 the oddly named 'Wa and Burma VIP Casino' – reportedly a joint venture between the Thais and the Wa, established with Yangon's approval – opened in a four-storey shop-house in Tachilek. Admission is 50B – neither kyat nor dollars are accepted. Inside are the usual Chinese and Western games of chance with the setup typically seen in Macau, the Genting Highlands (Malaysia) and on cruise ships in the South China Sea.

Fighting is common in the vicinity of Tachilek, as the MTA controls the large area to the immediate west.

Border Crossings

The Mae Sai-Tachilek border is usually open 6 am to 6 pm weekdays, 6 am to 9 pm weekends and holidays. This early closing time on weekdays can be a problem if you're driving back from Kengtung, given the unpredictability of road conditions between Kengtung and Tachilek.

Should you find yourself stranded in Tachilek after the border has closed you have two choices. One option is to check in at the A-frame bungalows strung with coloured lights on the Tachilek riverbank west of the town centre, where adequate rooms facing the river cost US$8 to US$14 a night. This is the only foreigner-licensed lodging in town as of this writing.

Alternatively you can check in with the immigration office near the western side of the bridge on the Myanmar side, where an immigration officer will undoubtedly escort you to the bridge and show you how to climb over the border gate at the Thai end. If you have a Thai vehicle along, you can leave it parked at the immigration office and pick it up the next morning; ask for a note from Myanmar immigration that will allow you back into Tachilek without obtaining a new permit.

PYIN U LWIN TO LASHIO
Gokteik

The unusual Gokteik railway viaduct is 55

km out of Pyin U Lwin en route to Lashio. When, on behalf of the British, the Pennsylvania Steel Co built the Gokteik Bridge over the deep gorge a hundred years ago, it was the second-highest railway bridge in the world. A British insurance policy expired just 15 years ago and until then the Burmese government didn't service it much – they finally renovated it recently. But its age shows; even today Burmese trains slow to a crawl when crossing the viaduct to lessen undue stress on the structure.

If you go by train, get off at the station before the bridge to get the best view. You're not permitted to go under the bridge since there's a military camp there. In fact you should be careful wandering around the bridge as land mines are reputed to be planted in some areas – to fend off insurgents who might want to destroy the span. You'll only have a few minutes before you must get back on the train – if you're continuing on to Hsipaw or Lashio.

Getting There & Away From Pyin U Lwin catch the Mandalay-Lashio train between 7 and 8 am for the two-hour journey to Gokteik; the fare is US$4 (or a lot less if you can manage to get a kyat ticket). Or start at Mandalay aboard the 5 am train.

You can also go by car or bus to Gokteik via the Mandalay-Lashio road – see the Lashio and Mandalay sections for details.

Kyaukme & Hsipaw

These market towns between Gokteik and Lashio are in many ways more interesting and atmospheric than Lashio. Unlike Lashio, which has a large Chinese and Burman population, Kyaukme and Hsipaw are Shan-majority towns with small numbers of Chinese and Indian traders.

Both towns are located on the road and rail routes between Mandalay and Lashio, the main China-Myanmar trade route. Kyaukme is also joined by road with Mogok to the north-west, so it sees a steady stream of gem traders on their way to plug into this route. Hsipaw was once the centre of a small Shan state of its own and is joined by road with the

surrounding Shan towns of Namhsan, Nam Pe, Kyethi and Mon Hsu – the latter is a 'new' gem-mining area.

A haw sao pha (sawbwa haw in Burmese) or **Shan Palace** still stands at the northern end of Hsipaw – see it quick before it disappears. The last sao pha was arrested in 1962 and hasn't been heard from since. His nephew is taking care of the palace and will admit foreign visitors. It's a K100 trishaw ride from the clock tower in the centre of town.

Hsipaw's large **market** is best in the morning when Shan and other tribal people

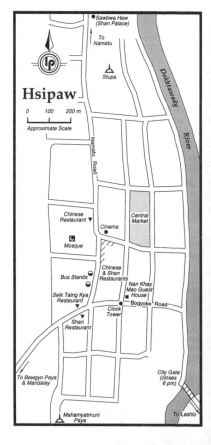

from nearby villages come to trade. The Dokhtawady River just east of the market is cool and clear.

One of the busiest religious sites in Hsipaw is **Mahamyatmuni Paya** at the southern outskirts of town. A shrine in the compound contains a large Buddha image inspired by its Mandalay namesake.

More interesting architecturally is the Shan-style **Bawgyo Paya** south-west of town off the Mandalay-Lashio road. This is the most revered paya in northern Shan State – equivalent to Inle Lake's Phaung Daw U Kyaung in the southern half of the state. One of the oldest and largest Shan festivals, the Bawgyo Paya Pwe, is held here from the 10th waxing day to the first day after the full moon of Tabaung (February/March). Shan pwes traditionally served as important economic and administrative, as well as social, events since this was when the sawbwa collected taxes and reviewed the accounts of his lieutenants and subjects. The Bawgyo pwe still draws a large encampment of traders and festival-goers who pay tribute, in spirit if not in pocketbook, to the old Shan ways. *Zat pwe* (costumed dance-drama based on jataka stories) is performed nightly.

Places to Stay & Eat *Nan Khay Mao Guest House* (☎ Hsipaw 88), near the clock tower at 134 Bogyoke Rd, is the guest house most likely to take foreigners. It's convenient to both the market and bus terminal and costs K90 per person for clean, spacious rooms with shared facilities.

Seik Taing Kya Restaurant, also on Bogyoke Rd, has good Burmese food, and there's a decent Shan restaurant on the opposite side of the road, east towards the clock tower. A cluster of smaller, simpler Chinese and Shan cafes on Namtu Rd, north of the Bogyoke Rd intersection near the cinema and market, serve OK food.

Getting There & Away The city gate to Hsipaw from the Lashio side closes at 6 pm – a custom representing both the warlord legacy, and possible threat from Shan rebels to the north and east.

Buses and pickups come and go from stands along Namtu Rd in the centre of town near the market. Pickups cost K100 to Lashio (72 km north-east) or K300 to Mandalay (209 km south-west) and leave once or twice a day in the early morning. See the Mandalay section for information on other public vehicles to Lashio, all of which make stops in Hsipaw.

The only public transport around town are trishaws, which cost around K10 to K15 per person per km.

LASHIO လားရှိုး:

This township of 103,000 mostly Shan-Chinese and Chinese inhabitants is located at the southern end of the infamous 'Burma Road'. Until recently Lashio was off limits to foreigners because of its proximity to China – and the hated Chinese communists – and to ethnic insurgent territory. Since the 1950s the town has been flanked by the Shan State Army to the west and south, the Kachin Independence Army to the north and the United Wa State Army to the east. Recent truces with two out of three of these armies, along with the tremendous boost in trade with China, led to an announcement in 1992 that the town of Lashio – and the town only – would be open to foreign visitors.

Even now MTT usually say a guide must be hired before they'll issue a permit. Many travellers make it to Lashio without anyone asking for either a guide or a permit – in fact we've never heard of anyone being turned back in the last two years.

Shan insurgents are still around, and you're not likely to be allowed beyond the military checkpoints at the north-eastern edge of town without special permission from the regional army command. Although the Myanmar government allows foreigners to travel from China to Lashio with permits obtained at the consulate in Kunming, it doesn't sanction travel in the opposite direction (see the Getting There & Away chapter and Mu-se in the Around Lashio section).

Lashio is in a mountain basin at 855 metres – clouds may form and deliver rain just about any time of the year. It is divided into two main districts, Lashio Lay (Little Lashio) and Lashio Gyi (Big Lashio), connected by Theinni Rd. Lashio Lay is the newer and bigger of the two districts.

Information

Post, telephone and telegraph services are available at the main post office, opposite the Lashio Motel on Mandalay-Lashio Rd at the corner of Station Rd. Although direct dialling is only possible within the city (you can direct dial *to* Lashio from other places), overseas and trunk calls may be made through the operator.

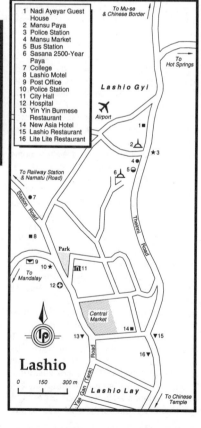

1 Nadi Ayeyar Guest House
2 Mansu Paya
3 Police Station
4 Mansu Market
5 Bus Station
6 Sasana 2500-Year Paya
7 College
8 Lashio Motel
9 Post Office
10 Police Station
11 City Hall
12 Hospital
13 Yin Yin Burmese Restaurant
14 New Asia Hotel
15 Lashio Restaurant
16 Lite Lite Restaurant

To Mu-se & Chinese Border

To Hot Springs

Lashio Gyi

Airport

To Railway Station & Namatu (Road)

Station Road

Theinni Road

Park

To Mandalay

Central Market

Lashio

0   150   300 m

Yee Gan (Track)

Lashio Lay

To Chinese Temple

Things to See & Do

Mansu Paya stands between Lashio Lay and Lashio Gyi on a hill to the western side of Theinni Rd, and is said to be over 250 years old. It is unremarkable except for the fact that it has no planetary post for Monday; the Monday-born pay homage to the main Buddha image instead. More impressive is the **Sasana 2500-Year (Pyi Lon Chantha) Paya**, reportedly built by the last Shan *sawbwa* in the area, Sao Hon Phan. One of the shrines in the paya complex contains a Bagan-era Buddha image. A second stupa of similar name, **New Pyi Lon Chantha Paya**, sits on Mya Kantha Hill in the northern part of town and offers good views of the city. The latter is also known as 'Kyaw Hein's Pagoda' because the famous Burmese film actor of the same name paid for its construction.

More interesting than any of the Buddhist shrines in town is the large and busy **Quan Yin San Temple** in Lashio Lay. Built around 40 years ago, it's the main Chinese temple in Lashio and possibly the largest in Myanmar; the steady traffic here bears testimony to Lashio's heavily Chinese population.

Markets include the larger main one in downtown Lashio-Lay and a smaller one called Mansu Market on Theinni Rd closer to Lashio Gyi. The central market has just about everything while the other one focuses on produce and foodstuffs. Some visitors to Lashio expect its markets to be very exotic and colourful – if you want to see people from various ethnic groups participating, you're better off in Hsipaw, Kyaukme or Kengtung.

Places to Stay

Just about any hotel or guest house in Lashio seems prepared to accept foreign guests. Rates quoted bounce back and forth between kyat and dollars, or are sometimes quoted in both. *Nadi Ayeyar Guest House* (☎ 082-21725), on Theinni Rd in Lashio Gyi, one km from the town centre, has clean but small rooms with carpet and good mattresses for US$6/10 a single/double. Toilet and bath facilities are shared; hot water is available on request. The friendly owner, Moira Yang, speaks English.

Mo Shwe Li Guest House, near the bus terminal and Mansu Market, charges K200 for a simple single with shared facilities, K300 to K400 for a double, or K700 with attached hot-water shower. Some visitors have been charged US$10 for the latter room. Other places in the vicinity, eg *Aung Dagon* and *Lwin*, charge K150 per person for simple cubicles.

New Asia Hotel (☎ 082-21622), on San Gaung St at the northern end of Lashio Lay, is a modern four-storey place which has simple rooms with attached bath for US$8 a single, US$15 a double. The *Yedana Theingi* at 1 Yakan Rd nearby costs K600 for rooms with a common bath.

The three-storey *Lashio Motel* (☎ 081-21702, 21738), at the intersection of Mandalay-Lashio Rd and Station Rd, charges a hybrid rate of US$9 plus K540 for good rooms with air-con, TV, fridge, toilet and hot-water shower. The price includes breakfast. Larger suites with sitting rooms cost US$12 plus K900. Favoured by visiting Chinese businesspeople, the motel features an attached karaoke lounge and an expensive restaurant.

Places to Eat

Chinese and Shan eateries are abundant in Lashio Lay. The famous *Lashio Restaurant*, on Theinni Rd just east of New Asia Hotel, is one of the most reliable for both kinds of cuisine. Another good restaurant serving both Chinese and Shan meals is *Lite Lite Restaurant*, near the New Asia Hotel on Chinese Temple St. The *Ngwe Sanda Shan Restaurant* (☎ 082-21297), at 206 Thukha Rd, Block 3 in the centre of town, receives high marks for authentic Shan food. There are also many Shan restaurants, large and small, near the central market on Yae Gan (Tank) Rd.

For Yunnanese cuisine, the *Winlight Chinese Muslim Restaurant*, downtown near the Aung Dagon Hotel, is inexpensive and good. The recently opened *Yin Yin Burmese Restaurant*, near the central market, is the best place for Burmese food – there are also a few Shan and Chinese dishes available.

In the same area, the very modest *786 Restaurant* serves Indian Muslim food at a small shop on Yae Gan Rd west of the market.

Getting There & Away

Air There are three MA flights weekly from Yangon (US$110 by F-27, US$120 by F-28), Mandalay (US$40/65), and Heho (US$55/65). To purchase an air ticket for Lashio you must present a travel permit valid for that destination.

The airport is north of Lashio Gyi. A taxi pickup from the airport into town costs K300.

Bus, Van & Pickup Many visitors choose to travel to Lashio by bus or train simply because no permit is (usually) required. From Mandalay there's a ramshackle RTA bus once daily at 5 am for K200. Better buses are available from several private companies including Shan Taungtan, Pinlon, Shwe Family, Yoma and Golden Border Express. Some operate from the main bus centre in Mandalay, others from the Shan neighbourhood around 23rd St, but this seems to change depending on the season (or perhaps on bribes paid, since the 23rd St departures are illegal). To be safe, check both places and reserve a seat a day in advance.

Tickets ranges in price from K250 to K400 depending on whether the vehicles are pickups or full-size buses; the average fare is K350 for a newer pickup, the most abundant type of vehicle. Small air-con vans are also available for K1000 in the rear seats, K1500 up the front; these deliver their passengers door-to-door but they fill up fast.

Most vehicles leave Mandalay around 5 am, although you must be at the vehicle by 4.30 am to be assured of a seat – even if you have a reservation. In the reverse direction, pickups depart Lashio for Mandalay around 6 am and seats cost K50 more, on average, as passengers must compete for space with cargo imported from China and the 'Golden Triangle'.

In either direction the 220-km ride takes a slow nine to 11 hours on a rough, dusty road. To break the trip up, it's a good idea to schedule at least a day's stopover in Pyin U Lwin along the way. From Pyin U Lwin it's only six or seven hours by road to Lashio. See the earlier Pyin U Lwin section for details.

The main bus terminal in Lashio stands on Theinni Rd south of Mansu Paya and near the Mansu Market.

The road entrances to Lashio from Mandalay and from Mu-se close at 6 pm, so don't count on any night-time travel into or out of town.

Train Although it sometimes takes longer, travel to Lashio by train is definitely more comfortable than by pickup. Another important point in favour of the train is we've heard of travel permits occasionally being requested for the Mandalay-Lashio bus trip. We have never heard of anyone being asked for one on the train.

The No 131 Up leaves Mandalay at 4.35 am and arrives in Lashio around 6 pm – when it's not delayed by track conditions (9 pm arrivals aren't unusual). Along the way you'll cross the famous Gokteik Bridge and wind around four monumental switchbacks. This route is known as the 'black-market train' among the Burmese because of all the goods smuggled on board in both directions.

In Pyin U Lwin the same train picks up passengers around 7.30 am. The Mandalay to Lashio fare costs US$13 in the only upper-class coach on the train. In this car only five seats are under Myanma Railways control; the remainder are controlled by the military. Tickets for this route can be bought 11 days ahead of time, and they sell out fast. From Pyin U Lwin the fare drops to US$11. Apparently, ordinary class isn't available to foreigners, but it might be worth asking.

In Lashio the railway station lies three km north-west of the centre of Lashio Lay.

Car If you hire your own vehicle and driver

in Mandalay you can make it to Lashio in six or seven hours. Permits don't seem to be necessary. The going rate for car hire in either direction is K4500 or US$45 one way, or the same amount per day for a multi-day hire. The tough road conditions between the two cities boosts the rate higher than rates for rentals around Mandalay or Bagan.

Getting Around
Pickups circulate between the railway station, Lashio Lay and Lashio Gyi for K5 to K10 per person.

Small vans and taxi pickups with black numbered plates park at the Lashio Motel and central market in Lashio Lay, as well as at the railway station and airfield. The drivers charge K350 per hour for vans, K300 per hour for pickups, with a one-hour minimum rental.

AROUND LASHIO
If you want to leave town via the northern entrance (toward Mu-se), you must have a permit from the regional military headquarters. Taxi drivers or staff at the Nadi Ayeyar, New Asia, and Lashio Motel can sometimes help arrange these.

Hot Springs & Caves
The **Lashio Hot Spa** is a hot springs about 10 km north-east of Lashio Gyi via Theinni Rd. If you've come by road from Mandalay or Pyin U Lwin you might want to head straight there to wash all the dust off! It's open till 8 pm and there's a K5 entry fee, on top of which you pay K45 for up to 30 minutes in a small bathhouse, K130 to K200 for one of the larger, nicer ones. Vendors on the premises sell Chinese and Shan snacks.

Although you're not officially allowed to visit them, **Paitchinhmyaing Caves**, 72 km north-east of Lashio, features Buddha-filled caverns up to 793 meters deep.

Mu-se
The Shweli River forms the border between Myanmar's Shan State and China's Yunnan

Province at Mu-se. Although it extends all the way to Lashio (and to some degree beyond), the Chinese influence is of course stronger here than elsewhere in the Shan State. You're not likely to be allowed to visit Mu-se from the south. If you managed to enter Myanmar with a permit from Kunming, Yunnan, on the other hand, you can't avoid it.

Such permission is best obtained through private travel agencies in Kunming. You will need three photos, your passport and US$18 for the permits. It should be noted that we haven't yet met or heard from anyone who has actually done this trip, although according to the Yangon government this is the procedure.

Most people will find little of interest in Mu-se, although fans of border towns worldwide will recognise the charged atmosphere generated by the friction of two cultures resting side by side. A disco just across the river in Ruili draws the country boys from the Burmese side, who manage to scrape together the K50 cover charge, as well as urban traders and moneyed smugglers who are just passing through. Discos are still illegal in Myanmar. The area around Mu-se is one of the primary pipelines for opium and heroin smuggling from the Shan State to Yunnan, and from Yunnan to Hong Kong. East of Mu-se along the border there are reportedly several major heroin refineries. This area to the east is strictly off limits to foreigners.

The area around Mu-se is thought to have been the centre of one of the first consolidated Shan kingdoms – called Kawsumpi or Mong Mao – as early as the 7th century. From this point the Shan dispersed to other river valleys to the west, east and south.

Cut by the Shweli River, the verdant **Namkham Valley** south-west of Mu-se is a beautiful patchwork of bamboo and rice fields. Most of the people living off the land in this area are Shan and other Tai ethnic groups. **Namkham** itself is renowned as the WW II-era location of Dr Gordon Seagrave's American Medical Center. Seagrave renounced his associations with the American Baptist Mission in order to offer medical service free of Christian proselytisation; people from all over the northern frontier states emerged from his medical centre trained as doctors and nurses. He and his staff tended to wounded soliders around the clock during the Allies' siege of Myitkyina in 1944. In 1951 Seagrave was briefly imprisoned by the post-independence Burmese government for his alleged associations with Kachin rebels. After his release he remained in Namkham till his death in 1965.

Places to Stay & Eat If you cross from China in the late afternoon, you'll have no choice but to put up at the government-owned *Muse Hotel*, a 40-room place with rooms for US$25/30 a single/double. There are better – and cheaper – places to stay on the Chinese side, including the *Ruili Guest House* and *Mingrui Hotel* on the bottom end, *Yongchang Hotel* and *Nanyang Hotel* at the upper end.

Getting There & Away From Mu-se it's six or seven hours by pickup or car along the famed Burma Road to Lashio, a distance of 187 km. There's usually only one pickup a day, leaving around 6 am and costing K300 per person. Air-con shared taxis – Toyota hatchbacks – are sometimes available for K800 to K1000 per person. Hitching is possible but any driver who picks you up will probably want some money for fuel plus a little extra for stopping.

Since 1992 there has been a bridge over the Shweli River (called Ruili River on the Chinese side), which you'll be permitted to cross from China if you've brought the proper paperwork from Kunming. There are also one-day border passes available to foreigners for US$10, but you'd have to be pretty twisted to go all the way to China to spend one day in Mu-se.

From Kunming, Ruili can be reached by air (50 minutes, Y350) or by bus (24 hours, Y155 for a sleeper).

NORTH-EASTERN MYANMAR

Kachin State

Myanmar's northernmost state borders India and China to the north and east, the Sagaing Division to the west and the Shan State to the south. Major rivers flowing north to south – the Malika, Mekha, Tanaingka and Ayeyarwady (Irrawaddy) – form fertile upland valleys where most of the state's meagre population live. Above these valleys stand the nation's highest mountain peaks, part of the southern tip of the Himalayas.

Most people living in the Kachin State are of Tibeto-Burman origin, representing four main language groups: the Jingpaw, Maru, Yaywin and Lisu. The Jingpaw, who are known to the Burmese as 'Kachin', are the majority, and since their language can be written (using a Roman alphabet system devised by 19th-century Christian missionaries), Jingpaw has become a lingua franca for the state.

Although many Kachin people nowadays are nominally Christian or Buddhist, certain of the old beliefs are practised syncretically. Under the British and today to a much lesser degree under the SLORC, the Kachin tribes have continued to practice their own form of semi-democratic civil administration, *gumlao-gumsa*. One of the distinctions of this system is that the youngest in the family – rather than the eldest – is the legal heir when a parent dies.

Until the early 1990s the Kachin Independence Organisation (KIO) and its tactical arm, the Kachin Independence Army (KIA), operated with near impunity throughout the state. Following the 1993 signing of a truce with the Yangon government, the KIA have ceased active insurgency. The Burmese government, however, still considers the state a 'sensitive' area and the movements of both foreigners and Burmese are strictly curtailed.

The jade trade may also have something to do with travel restrictions in the state. During the Konbaung era, roughly 75% of all Kachin jade ended up in China. The Chinese are still the biggest market for Burmese jadeite, which is preferred over China's nephrite although both minerals can be called 'jade'.

The Manao

Traditionally, the Jingpaw are animists who recognise a spirit world presided over by Karai Kasang, a supreme deity who requires animal sacrifice. Hereditary chieftains called *duwa* maintain ceremonial and cultural leadership, especially with regard to the *manao* (also spelt manau or manaw), important festivals held periodically to placate or pay homage to the Jingpaw nats. There are several types of manao depending on the region and time of year. One of the most common types, the *sup manao*, looks toward the future, insuring good weather for farming and serving to ward off danger and general ill fortune; a *padang manao*, on the other hand, celebrates a past victory or success.

A typical manao involves the sacrifice of 29 cows and/or buffaloes, one for each of the 28 Jingpaw nats plus one dedicated to all of them. Participants dance to music played on a large doubled-headed drum, brass gong,

Gauri Kachin girls, from the far north of Myanmar

cymbals and buffalo-horn oboe. These festivities are centred around *manao-taing*, brightly painted totems strung with banners of red, black and white – the colours considered most attractive to the nats. Dancers often carry fans in imitation of bird feathers; the lead dancer wears a headdress designed to resemble the head and beak of a great hornbill. Other dances mimic the movements of horse-riding, fishing and cattle herding. There is much drinking of local rice beer (*churu*) and feasting on special meal packets called *shat kada*.

On 10 January – Kachin State Day – a major manao in Myitkyina draws Kachin groups from all over the state and beyond.

MYITKYINA မြစ်ကြီးနား

At the moment this is the only place in the Kachin State open to foreign visitors – and by permit only. The waiting time for a Myitkyina permit can extend up to two weeks since authorities in Yangon must check with the regional military command to ensure all is still calm in the state. Even with your permit in hand, there is no guarantee you won't be turned back by the local authorities once you arrive in Myitkyina – a situation that proves yet again how the country is run like a loose conglomeration of warlord states.

Set in a flat valley that becomes extremely hot in the hot season and very rainy during the monsoon, the town itself is not that interesting. The pride of Myitkyina, indeed the entire state, is the abundance of fruits available in the local markets, especially in the cooler months. In addition to the large variety of fruit, many local hill tribe people can be seen haggling over produce and consumer goods in the **central market**. The most popular souvenir among visitors is, of course, the dark indigo and green Kachin longyi, which has become something of a pro-democracy symbol among many Burmese.

Hsu Taung Pyi Zeditaw is a pretty, gilded, 'wish-fulfilling' stupa on the banks of the Ayeyarwady River. The larger **Andawshin Paya** boasts a silver-plated zedi said to contain tooth relics and a Buddha footprint; there are a couple of adjacent monasteries. Other religious structures of interest in town include the **Sri Saraswati Gurkha Hindu Temple, Ja-me Mosque** and a Taoist-Buddhist **Chinese Temple**.

If permitted to stay in Myitkyina you'll be restricted to a 25-km radius around the city, in basically a flat river valley surrounded by hills. Rice produced in this valley, known as *khat cho*, is considered the best in Myanmar; highly valued for its delicate texture and fine fragrance, khat cho is scarce and expensive outside the Kachin State.

There are plenty of Kachin villages in the area, and with a guide you may visit those that lie within the 25-km limit. Kachin men living in the lowlands wear dark blue and green longyis, while those from the mountains wear trousers. The most colourful dress is reserved for weddings and festivals, events that would make any village visit much more compelling. In a Kachin wedding the groom presents his bride with a silver sword and a shoulder bag to symbolise the offering of protection and material support.

Myit-son, the confluence of the Mekha and Malika Rivers, 45 km north of town, forms the beginning of the great Ayeyarwady River. Although it lies outside the restricted area, foreigners are sometimes permitted to travel this far since it's one of the few 'sightseeing' attractions in the Myitkyina area. A government rest house overlooking the water was burned to the ground by Kachin insurgents in the 1960s; there is talk of a new hotel replacing it one day.

Another spot you might be able to visit is the jade mining centre of **Pakkhan**, 148 km west, and outside the limit, of Myitkyina. The first 80 km to Kamaing is via a sealed road, the rest is an unsealed dry-weather road. You'd need to charter a vehicle from Myitkyina or Kamaing to complete the whole route. If you're only interested in buying jade, however, there's plenty in Myitkyina. South-west of Kamaing is the huge **Indawgyi Lake**, said to be beautiful but currently off limits to foreigners.

Most of the Kachin people living in and around Myitkyina have been missionised

NORTH-EASTERN MYANMAR

and there are now around 15 churches in town – mostly Baptist with a few Methodist and Catholic churches sprinkled in. About 14 km north is **Praying Mountain**, a sacred site for Kachin Baptists and location of a bible school and seminary.

Many older Kachin people speak English since they were educated in mission schools. There are also a few elderly WW II veterans around who like to talk about Merrill's Marauders and the various campaigns fought in the region.

Places to Stay & Eat

Hotel and restaurant infrastructure in Myit-kyina is well behind that found in more touristed regions of the country, and rates are high. The friendly *YMCA* downtown has rooms with common bath for US$15/20 a single/double. It's nothing special but is the best value if you're avoiding government hotels.

The *Popa Hotel* (☎ 074-21746) at the railway station charges US$20 to US$30 for simple rooms with a fan and a common bath. Somewhat better is the government-owned but well-maintained *Nan Thiri Hotel*, which costs US$15 per person in very large rooms with attached toilet and cold-water shower. Once open only to VIPs, the Nan Thiri will take foreign tourists until more hotels open.

Most of the restaurants in town serve Chinese food. One of the better ones is *Shwe*

Ledo-Bhamo-Burma Road

The so-called Burma Road – actually a network of three major routes – came about during WW II when Japanese invasion forces closed in on Myanmar from the north via China and from the south via Thailand. In what was known as the China-Burma-India (CBI) Theatre, Allied supplies for the ground war fought in Lower Myanmar were easily flown or shipped in from India. Supplying the China front, however, required dangerous flights over 'The Hump', a series of high Himalayan peaks that separate Myanmar and China.

Over a thousand airmen died flying this route, prompting the Allies to look for a new way to supply Chiang Kai-shek's nationalist Kuomintang (KMT) army, who were fighting the Japanese in western China. The Yunnanese themselves built the original Burma Road from Kunming to Wanting, China, between 1937 and 1939. They then laid an extension into Myanmar from Wanting to Lashio in 1940 for a total length of 1200 km. Early in the war this Lashio-Kunming route served as the main supply line for the KMT, but as Japanese pressure from the south increased, the Allies looked for an alternate route from India.

American General Joseph ('Vinegar Joe') Stillwell proposed the construction of an all-weather two-lane road from India to China via northern Myanmar. The plan was to link up not with the original Lashio-Kunming route, but with a rough dry-weather track developed by the Chinese between Bhamo in southern Chin State and Yunchang, Yunnan. British army engineers, using a trail created by war refugees fleeing to India from Upper Myanmar, began building the 800-km Ledo Road from Ledo, Assam, to the Bhamo terminus of the Bhamo Road in 1942. Although the engineers originally had 5000 laborers at their disposal, progress was slow and work on the Ledo Road was abandoned in May 1942.

A huge contingent of American engineers took over in November 1942 and assembled 35,000 Burmese, Indian, British and Chinese troops to tackle the enormous task of cutting through thick jungle, upgrading the Bhamo track, and spanning 10 major rivers and 155 secondary streams between Ledo and Wanting. So many men were lost along the way that the builders sardonically dubbed the route the 'man-a-mile road'.

Completed in May 1945, the Ledo Road – also known as the Stillwell Road – was maintained until a year later when all Allied units were withdrawn from the CBI Theatre. The Myitkyina Bridge, which spanned the Ayeryarwady River south of Myitkyina and was the longest pontoon bridge in the world, was deemed an obstacle to river traffic and was dismantled in 1947. One of the chief postwar effects of the Bhamo-Myanmar road network was the opening up of the Kachin State to some measure of development. Little remains of the Ledo Road, which quickly fell into disuse.

The main Lashio-Kunming route, though in poor condition nowadays, sees much traffic as a major smuggling route to China for opium, heroin, gems, jade and teak. In the reverse direction, traders bring finished goods such as auto parts, pharmaceuticals, processed foods, clothing and housewares. The Yangon government has made such trade – legal and illegal – much easier than in the past by making the border crossing at Mu-se a legal overland port of entry from China. ■

Ainsi (Ein Zay), which doesn't look like much but serves quite reasonable food. Its owned by the proprieter of a Pakkhan jade mine and is favoured by gem dealers.

Getting There & Away

There are two easy ways to reach Myitkyina from other parts of the country: air and rail. However, if you're determined to arrive by surface, you can travel by road or complete part of the journey by boat.

Air MA flies to Myitkyina from Mandalay on Sunday, Monday and Friday; the flight takes 50 minutes and costs US$70 by F-27, US$80 by F-28. MA has one 25-minute flight on Wednesday to/from Bhamo for US$30/35. On Friday there is also a flight between Myitkyina and Putao that lasts 35 minutes and costs US$40/45. A taxi into town from the airport costs K150.

Train Anyone who can afford to fly from Mandalay rather than take the train usually does – the fare differential is not that great considering the time factor.

The No 55 Up train from Mandalay leaves daily at 3 pm and is supposed to take 22 hours

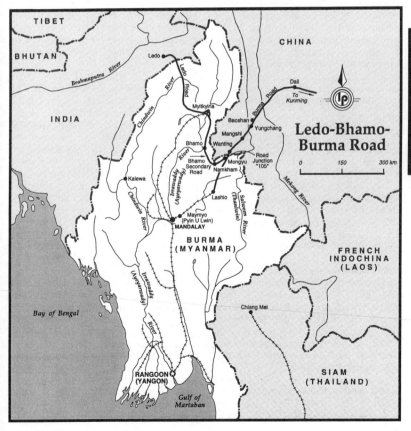

to reach Myitkyina. In everyday practice it often takes longer – up to 40 hours due to the poor condition of the railbed. In early 1995 a derailment at the railway bridge near Mohnyin killed over 100 passengers.

Two private companies run better trains to Myitkyina certain days of the week. Malika Railways departs Monday to Friday at 7 pm, arriving around 5.30 pm the next day. A seat costs US$15 for foreigners, or you can get a sleeper for US$20. The Malika ticket office is at the southern end of the railway station in Mandalay. Across the street, a slightly more upmarket company, STT, charges US$30 for a seat and US$60 for a sleeper with dining car. This one runs Wednesday and Sunday at 7.30 pm and arrives at 6 pm; it returns on Friday and Tuesday. STT is more likely to have berths available as they have three sleeper carriages with a total of 60 berths; Malika has two carriages totalling 40 berths. In the seat-cars, both lines feature 40 seats per coach. Should you be accompanied by a guide, STT will allow the guide to take a berth for US$20.

Road There are no regular public transport services along the road between Mogok and Myitkyina as road conditions are quite bad between Mogok and Bhamo.

The 188-km road between Bhamo and Myitkyina, which runs parallel to the China-Myanmar border, is passable in all weather. Strictly speaking you're not supposed to arrive in Myitkyina by road, however. This may change as 'security' improves.

Boat & Road You can ride a ferry north from Mandalay as far as Bhamo, then continue on to Myitkyina by road. The ferry trip is fairly straightforward (see the following Bhamo section for details), and the Bhamo-Myitkyina road was recently improved. Before the 1993 KIA ceasefire went into effect, this road closed whenever the KIA took control of the area.

Boat & Rail Another alternative is to travel by ferry as far as Katha (about two-thirds of the way between Mandalay and Myitkyina),

and continue by train from there. Of course you would still have the shaky Mohnyin Bridge to contend with, as it's north of this junction.

PUTAO ပူတာအို

It's very difficult to obtain permits for Putao in the far north of the Kachin State. So far, the only foreigners who have received permission to travel there have been missionaries and tour operators scouting new territory. Word from the latter is that there's virtually nothing of general interest to see or do in Putao. Although tantalisingly close to Hkakabo Razi, whose name is derived from the Tibetan for 'Snow-White Ridge Mountain', Putao itself is not that high up and since travel infrastructure is practically non-existent you can't really travel into the high country without mounting an expedition.

Putao and the surrounding area lie above the Tropic of Cancer, in a zone characterised by subtropical, broadleaf, evergreen forest up to 2000 metres; temperate, semi-deciduous, broadleaf rainforest from 2000 to 3000 metres; and evergreen, coniferous and sub-alpine snow forest passing into alpine scrub above 3000 metres. The highlands north of Putao are considered one of the most pristine Himalayan environments in Asia and could become a major ecotourism destination if made accessible to foreigners. Plans are afoot to bring tourism here; the runway at Putao is being extended so that large jets can land safely.

Hkakabo Razi stands 5889 metres high and is, as its name suggests, snowcapped year round. Satellite peaks in adjoining massifs include **Namni-Lka** (4664 metres) in the Adung Valley and **Diphuk-Ha** (4360 metres) in the Seingku Valley. A protected 'trans-frontier reserve' has been proposed by neighbouring countries.

During the late British colonial era, a military post called Fort Hertz was based in Putao. By the end of WW II most westerners used this name instead of Putao – it still appears on some older maps. Most of the population of around 10,000 are Kachin and

Lisu, followed by Burman, Shan and various other smaller tribal groups.

Places to Stay & Eat

Until recently, most foreigners who travelled to Putao ended up staying and dining at the *Government Guest House* at a cost of US$25 per night per room. The alternative now is the *Tokyo Guest House*, a thatched-palm house operated by a Lisu family, not far from the airport. Simple rooms cost US$50 per person; a pit toilet and well out the back are the only facilities.

The town has one Chinese 'restaurant', as usual called *Sein*, which serves more as a local bar than anything else. The *Yadanapon Tea Shop* serves a few tea snacks, at prices significantly higher than elsewhere in Myanmar.

Getting There & Away

Foreigners are not allowed to travel to Putao by road. Even with permission the narrow, unsurfaced 356-km road is passable only in dry weather. See the Myitkyina section for information on MA flights.

BHAMO ဗန်းေမာ်

Those who have been there say Bhamo, 186 km south of Myitkyina, is more interesting than the latter. The **daily market** draws Lisu, Kachin and Shan participants from the surrounding countryside. The overgrown city walls of **Sampanago**, an old Shan kingdom, can be seen around five km east of town. **Theindawdye Paya** downtown features an older stupa.

Places to Stay

The *Golden Dragon Hotel* has been known to accept foreigners for K100 a head. The hotel – really more of a guest house – can provide a guide to nearby Kachin villages such as Aungtha. Adequate Chinese food is available from *Sein Sein Restaurant*.

Getting There & Away

Air MA flies to Bhamo from Mandalay on Wednesday; the flight costs US$50 in an F-27, US$55 by F-28 and lasts one hour. This flight originates in Yangon – the fare all the way from Yangon to Bhamo via Mandalay is US$130/145. It then continues on to Myitkyina (US$30/35 from Bhamo). Due to the infrequency of this flight, it's often full.

Boat A double-decker ferry plies the Ayeyarwady River between Mandalay and Bhamo twice weekly. When the water level is optimum, the upriver journey takes one and a half days, but when the river's low it can take as long as two and a half days. The overcrowded boat stops along the way in Kyauk Myaung and Katha. Lower-deck class costs K45, upper-deck class K96 and cabins K290. Some foreigners have reported having to pay in dollars to board this boat in Mandalay; you might have better luck paying in kyat from Kyauk Myaung, which is a short road hop east of Shwebo.

The scenery along the upper reaches of the Ayeyarwady is supposed to be very fine, especially north of Kyauk Myaung where the riverbanks are lush with bamboo and other flora and the boat passes through steep rock gorges.

Kayah State

This small state is wedged between the Shan State to the north and west, the Karen State to the west and south, and Thailand to the east. Eight ethnic groups reside in this mountainous state, including the Taungthu, Padaung, Yinbaw, Bre, and Kayah who form the majority.

The culture of the Kayah people, also known as Karenni or Red Karen, appears to the outsider to be a blend of Karen and Shan influences. Hereditary chieftains called *saopya* have obvious similarities with the *sao pha* of the Shan, while bronze frog drums are used ceremonially as in the Karen culture. Most of the Kayah are animist, although there are significant numbers of Christians and Buddhists as well. Animists, Buddhists and Christians alike participate in the annual Kuhtobo Festival in May, which pays homage to the rain spirits.

Most known to the outside world are the minority Padaung, whose women traditionally stack up to 22 kg of brass rings around their necks. The rings depress the collarbone, making it look as if their necks have been unnaturally stretched. No one knows for sure how the ring custom got started; one theory says it was to make the women's appearance strange enough that men from other tribes wouldn't pursue them. The Padaung also wear thin hoops, made of cane or lacquered cord, in bunches around their knees and calves.

Until the early 1990s, Kayah rebel groups controlled much of the eastern half of the state. The Yangon government has concentrated on securing the capital, Loikaw, and the very important hydroelectric plant at nearby Lawpita. The recent ceasefire has allowed the government to build a railway between Aungban and Loikaw.

LOIKAW လွိုင်ကော်

The Kayah State is open by permit only, and so far permits are only valid for the state capital, Loikaw – located near the state's northern tip at an elevation of just over 1200 metres.

Loikaw's colourful **Thirimingala Market** sees participants from several tribal groups, including the Padaung. Naungyar, situated towards the northern quarter of town, is inhabited by mostly Kayah people; now that a ceasefire with the insurgency is in effect, it's not unusual to see Kayah rebel soldiers in this area. Two small lakes and a chaung (stream) add visual interest to the town. Visit the **Taungkwe Zedi** on Taungkwe, a twin-peaked mountain on the edge of town, for Loikaw vistas.

Twenty km south-east of Loikaw is a huge

hydroelectric facility built by the Japanese as war reparation. A dam impounds the Balu River, which flows from Inle Lake 120 km to the north. The facility supplies most of the power in the national grid system and so is highly strategic. Nearby **Lawpita Falls** is said to be beautiful; it's in insurgent territory so you're unlikely to be permitted to visit, despite the ceasefire.

Pinlaung, roughly halfway between Aungban and Loikaw, is the highest point on the road/railway route at over 1500 metres. It's inhabited mainly by Pa-O and it can be quite cold in the winter.

Places to Stay
The *Garden Hotel* provides economy rooms for US$12/18 a single/double, standard rooms for US$18/24 and superior rooms for US$24/30; there are some smaller superior singles for US$18. This is where visiting government officials and VIPs stay; rumour says the hotel may be leased by a Thai enterprise in the near future.

Getting There & Away
At the time of writing, travel to Loikaw for foreigners was only permitted by air. MA flies to Loikaw from Yangon on Sunday, Tuesday and Friday. The flight takes 70 minutes and costs US$55 in an F-27, US$60 in an F-28. There's also one flight on Thursday from Heho (55 minutes, US$30/35).

The new railway open between Aungban and Loikaw takes six to 10 hours but it isn't open to foreigners as yet. Locals pay K50 for the ride.

The road trip from Aungban takes four to five hours by car, longer by public transport. Officially this road is closed to foreigners; there are four military checkpoints between Aungban and Loikaw so you probably won't get through undetected.

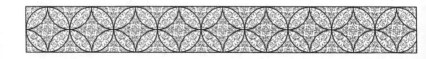

South-Eastern Myanmar

Mon State

The homeland of the Mon wraps around the eastern coast of the Gulf of Martaban from the mouth of the Sittoung (Sittang) River to the northern end of Taninthayi Yoma (Taninthayi Range). Once native to a broad region stretching from Lower Myanmar to Cambodia, the Mon have been absorbed – sometimes willingly, sometimes unwillingly – by the more powerful Burman and Thai cultures in Myanmar and Thailand over the last thousand years or so. The absorption has been so effective that their own history and culture have received little attention by scholars, even though vestiges of the Mon culture and language clearly survive in both countries.

Though no one knows for sure, the Mon may be descended from a group of Indian immigrants from Kalinga, an ancient kingdom overlapping the boundaries of the modern Indian states of Orissa and Andhra Pradesh. They are responsible for much of the early maintenance and transmission of Theravada Buddhism in mainland South-East Asia even though Sri Lankan monks may have initially introduced the *Tripitaka* and ordination lineage. In the case of Myanmar, the Bagan kingdom forcefully captured these elements, while in Thailand it was the peaceful interest of King Rama IV that amplified Mon Buddhism.

Since 1949 the eastern hills of the state (as well as mountains further south in Taninthayi Division) have been a refuge for the New Mon State Party (NMSP) and its tactical arm, the Mon National Liberation Front, whose objective has been self-rule for the Mon State. In addition to harassing the Burmese government, the Mon have occasionally fought the Karen over control of the remote border crossings along the Thai border. With growing government influence along this

section of border – and following a string of Karen defeats – the situation has cooled. In 1995 the NMSP signed a ceasefire with the Burmese government.

Despite these events the lower half of the state south of Mudon is still a 'brown area' where road travel is considered unsafe. Highway robberies are common, even in broad daylight. Regardless of claims on either side, it's very unclear whether these assaults are politically motivated or whether the robbers are simple *dacoits*. For political reasons the government tends to lump both kinds of attacks together as 'insurgent act-

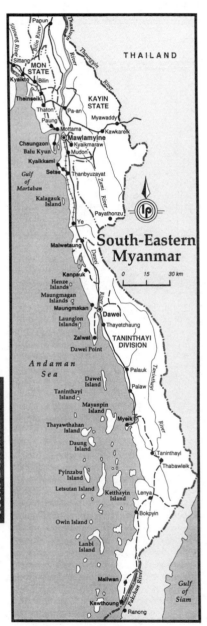

South-Eastern Myanmar

0   15   30 km

ivity'. For the traveller, the upshot is that it can be difficult to get permission for travel south of Mawlamyine (Moulmein).

KYAIKTIYO ကျိုက်ထီးရိုး

One of the most interesting formerly 'off-limits' trips is to the incredible balancing boulder stupa at Kyaiktiyo. It's about 20 km from the town of Kyaikto, which in turn is about midway between Bago (Pegu) and Thaton. The small stupa, just 7.3 metres high, sits atop the 'Gold Rock', a massive, goldleafed boulder delicately balanced on the very edge of a cliff at the top of Mt Kyaikto. Like Shwedagon Paya in Yangon (Rangoon) or Mahamuni Paya in Mandalay, Kyaiktiyo is one of the most sacred Buddhist sites in Myanmar.

Legend relates that the boulder maintains its precarious balance due to a precisely placed Buddha hair in the stupa. The legend goes on to say that King Tissa received the Buddha hair in the 11th century from a hermit who had secreted the hair in his own topknotted hair. The hermit instructed the king to search for a boulder whose shape resembled the hermit's head, then enshrine the hair in a stupa on top. The king, who inherited supernatural powers as a result of his birth to a *zawgyi* (an accomplished alchemist) father and *naga* princess, found the rock at the bottom of the sea. The boat used to transport the rock turned to stone upon its miraculous arrival on the mountaintop and can be seen about 300 metres from the main boulder – it's known as the Kyaukthanban, or 'stone boat stupa'.

The atmosphere surrounding Kyaiktiyo during the height of the pilgrimage season, November to March, is charged with magic and devotion, especially when the glinting boulder is bathed in the purple, sometimes misty light of dawn. Pilgrims chant, light candles and meditate all through the night. Men are permitted to walk along a short causeway and over a bridge spanning a chasm to the boulder and affix goldleaf squares on the rock's surface. It's said that if you wedge a short piece of wood or bamboo into the space between the bottom of the boulder and the cliff on which it rests, you can watch it flex as the boulder gently rocks back and forth.

A new terrace allows devotees to view the boulder from below. There are several other stupas and shrines scattered along the ridge at the top of Mt Kyaikto; though none are as impressive as Kyaiktiyo, the interconnecting trails sometimes lead to unexpected viewpoints of the valleys below.

Permits for Kyaiktiyo

The permit policy for Kyaiktiyo is vague, though it's clear you're supposed to have a permit to make the trip. If you enquire at Myanmar Travels & Tours (MTT) or most travel agencies, you'll most likely be told that you need not only a permit but a guide as well. There are three or four checkpoints between Bago and the town of Kyaikto on the main Yangon-Mawlamyine road – the most stringent being the military and cus-

toms checkpoints at the bridge over the Sittoung River. When tour buses make the trip they're often required to carry an armed guard.

For individual travellers, Bago makes a better starting point for road trips to Kyaiktiyo than Yangon since the hotel staff there are adept at arranging inexpensive alternatives. A guide and driver to Mt Kyaiktiyo can be hired through any of the downtown Bago hotels for around US$40. The same tour booked in Yangon costs US$80.

On the other hand there are no checkpoints along the rail route, so many foreigners travel to Kyaikto by rail without permits. See the Getting There & Away section below for details on road and rail transport.

Once you've reached Kinpun at the base of the mountain, you're supposed to show your permit at a checkpoint placed near the trailhead. In everyday practice the police

---

Visiting the Boulder Stupa of Kyaiktiyo

Mt Kyaikto's 'base camp', Kinpun, is 12 km from the town of Kyaikto. At Kinpun you'll find several decent foodstalls, souvenir shops and a tourist office with restrooms and a washbasin.

From the camp there are two ways to reach the summit. The most time-consuming, but most meritorious for Burmese Buddhists, is a strenuous 13-km climb along a winding footpath. This hike takes around four hours to reach the boulder shrine itself; it's a pretty hike once you get into the wooded uplands, and there are around 30 rest stops along the way. Foodstalls serve Burmese and Chinese food, water, tea and fruit. As the mountain is flush with bamboo, many souvenir vendors along the path hawk items made from the sturdy grass, including huge, toy machine guns labelled 'Rambo'!

You certainly won't be alone on the hike; a trip to the top accumulates considerable merit and there are steady streams of pilgrims making the ascent during the dry months, November to April. On full moon days the number swells to the thousands.

The path ascends about 1000 metres from base to summit and it's impossible to miss – just follow the crowds. In addition to the various rest halts at the side of the path, there are shrines which relate the legend of the temple's creation.

The quicker, less meritorious way to reach the summit is to catch one of the large trucks that carries pilgrims most of the way up. After a 20-minute, white-knuckle ride around precipitous hairpin curves, the trucks stop at a point that's within a 45-minute hike of the top along a winding footpath. Like the main trail, this one's lined with snack and souvenir stalls; eventually it joins the main trail. The ride costs K90 up, K60 down. From the upper terminal, if you can't physically make the 45-minute hike, you can hire a sedan chair and four bearers to carry you to the top for US$4 or K400; it takes about an hour for a sedan chair to make this final ascent. When descending this trail back to the truck stop, be sure to bear right at the first fork; the left fork leads to the long way down – four hours instead of 45 minutes.

Note that it is only really possible to get to the top when the pilgrimage season commences, at the end of the rainy season in late October. Few pilgrims come in April or May since the weather is so hot then that the climb becomes very trying, and the haze from local slash-and-burn agriculture obscures views from the summit. Once the rainy season starts in June, the whole mountain more or less closes down for four or five months; both the original footpath and the truck road become virtually impassable. There is some discussion about sealing the truck road and cementing the steps in the final 45-minute climb to allow all-weather travel. ■

usually accept a US$10 entry fee if you don't possess a permit, US$4 if you do.

Places to Stay & Eat

Although Kyaiktiyo can be visited as a day trip from Bago, the advantage of staying at the top is that you can catch sunset and sunrise – the most magical times for viewing the boulder shrine.

Along the ridge at the top of Mt Kyaikto, the well-situated *Kyaikto Hotel* features a couple of long wooden buildings overlooking the valley below. It's a friendly and reasonably clean place, though the hotel's monopoly on accommodation keeps rates rather high in view of what you get. Standard rooms with attached toilet and shower cost US$33 single, US$44 double or US$108 for five beds. The 'shower' doesn't actually have on-demand running water, though it's plumbed for it; instead a couple of large plastic buckets are filled daily for use as scoop showers. We heard that a Yangon businessman had offered to donate a couple of water pumps to bring water up the mountain, so this may change. 'Economy' rooms with two beds and two buckets of water cost US$24/36 single/double, while simple bamboo huts with mattresses on the floor cost US$10 single, US$15 double. For the latter you bathe outside with bucket and bowl. All rates include the standard toast-and-egg breakfast.

Foreigners aren't permitted to stay in the *zayat* or rest shelters for pilgrims, nor are they permitted to camp in wooded areas on the mountain. When Kyaikto Hotel is full, people have been permitted to sleep on the reception floor for US$5 a head. The hotel has a booking office at 69 Theingyi St (☎ 01-31563) in Yangon if you want to try booking a room in advance.

Located in the town of Kyaikto at the foot of the mountain is another *Kyaikto Hotel*. Noisy and not very clean, it charges US$12 per room.

In addition to the foodstalls at the Kinpun base camp and along the footpaths, there's a decent teashop opposite the front entrance of the Kyaikto Hotel at the summit. As well as

serving the usual teashop snacks, the tiny kitchen can make fried noodles and fried rice.

If you're coming by road from Bago, *Yadana Oo Restaurant* just north-west of the town of Waw (35 km from Bago) serves good Burmese food in clean surroundings.

Getting There & Away

Bus Buses straight from Yangon to Kyaikto cost K150 from the Highway Bus Centre, but as the trip takes all day (because the road is so bad) it means you'll end up staying at the miserable Kyaikto Hotel at the bottom of the mountain. Buses from Bago to Kyaikto cost K60, leave early in the morning from the bus terminal at the south-western end of town and take around five hours.

There are several checkpoints along the road where the military may board the bus to check permits.

For travellers wanting to visit Kyaiktiyo, pickups bound for Kinpun (12 km from Kyaikto at the base of Mt Kyaikto) leave from a spot near the Kyaikto railway station every half hour or so between 6 am and 4 pm, depending on the number of passengers. The fare for the half-hour ride is K20 per person.

Train A direct train from Bago to Kyaikto leaves daily at 4.30 am, arriving two and a half to three hours later, substantially quicker than the equivalent bus trip. In the reverse direction the train from Mottama (Martaban) arrives around 5 pm, sometimes later if the train is delayed. The foreigner fare is US$3 per seat.

We've never heard of travel permits being checked on the Bago-Kyaikto train.

Car If you're coming to Kyaikto by car keep in mind there are checkpoints along the way and that the Sittoung Bridge closes at 6 pm.

AROUND KYAIKTO TO MAWLAMYINE

South-east of Kyaikto is **Bilin**, a dusty town of wooden buildings and a favoured stop for truckers making the Yangon-Mawlamyine haul. Among the mechanic shops that line the main road through town are a couple of cheap but quite decent Burmese restaurants. A few km south-east of town there's a toll bridge over the Bilin River.

Thaton

Long before the rise of Bagan (Pagan), Thaton was an important centre for a Mon kingdom that stretched from the Ayeyarwady River Delta to similar river deltas in Thailand and possibly as far east as Cambodia. Early on it may have been known as Suvannabhumi, the 'Golden Land' – legend says Asoka, the great Indian Buddhist emperor, sent a mission here in the 3rd century BC – and later as Dvaravati when it reached it's dynastic peak between the 6th and 10th centuries AD. The thriving port carried on trade with the south of India and Sri Lanka. Shin Aran, a monk from Thaton, carried Theravada Buddhism north to the Burmese kingdom of Bagan, and in 1057 Thaton was conquered by King Anawrahta of Bagan.

Today Thaton sits on the main road and rail line that stretches from Bago to Mottama. Little of ancient Thaton is visible, as the modern town has been built over the old sites; piles of brick here and there are all that remain of the massive city walls. The town's core is a leafy place lined up on either side of the highway with colonial mansions dotted among thatched-roof homes, and a few older stupas on hillsides surrounding town. A picturesque canal network irrigates rice fields and fruit orchards.

Shwe Zayan Paya, on the northern side of the road just beyond the clock tower, features a nice set of monastery buildings and a large stupa supposedly built during the early Mon era. A famous 10th-century standing Buddha stele found at this paya was sculpted in the classic Mon style and shows strong similarities with Dvaravati-period Buddhas from central Thailand.

Taunzaung Paya, another large and interesting old *zedi*, can be found at Zokthok village, slightly south-east of town. The most famous of the many hillside stupas is **Myathapeik Paya** or 'Emerald Alms-Bowl Stupa', which can be reached by road and offers good overhead views of town.

Places to Stay & Eat An overnight rest stop in Thaton might be worthwhile if you're travelling between Yangon and Mawlamyine without any other stops. A large, two-storey, no-name guest house (☎ Thaton 186) off the northern side of the main street through town has clean and comfortable rooms with shared facilities for K300 per double. The friendly staff report that although the guest house isn't yet officially licensed to accept foreigners, they can arrange permission for overnight stays through local immigration authorities on a case by case basis.

There are several teashops and basic Burmese-style restaurants along the busy main street.

Mottama (Martaban)

The narrow, patched and potholed road from Bago terminates at Mottama, where the wide Thanlwin (Salween) River empties into the Gulf of Martaban. The railway from Yangon also terminates here, although an extension picks up on the other side in Mawlamyine and continues 145 km to Ye, where a new line leads further south to Dawei (Tavoy). If you're continuing to Mawlamyine on the other side of the river you must present a travel permit valid for Mawlamyine to immigration authorities at the ferry station.

Double-decker passenger ferries depart for Mawlamyine from the Mottama landing every half hour from 7.15 am to 6.45 pm. The fare is K1 and the trip takes 20 to 30 minutes depending on tides.

Less frequent vehicle ferries from Mottama to Mawlamyine cost K30 per passenger plus K30 per car or van, more for trucks and buses. Departures depend on the tides; the last boat leaves just before sunset, and the crossing lasts about half an hour.

If you don't feel like waiting for a ferry, you can charter a passenger boat across the river for around K300.

See the Mawlamyine Getting There & Away section for details on bus and rail transport to Mottama.

MAWLAMYINE (MOULMEIN) မော်လမြိုင်

If you're wondering what Yangon and Mandalay looked and felt like six or seven years ago before they hit the development fast track, come to Mawlamyine. The atmosphere of post-colonial decay is still palpable here; it's also an attractive, leafy, tropical town with a ridge of stupa-capped hills on ɔ side and the sea on the other.

Mawlamyine served as capital of British Burma from 1827 to 1852, during which time it developed as a major teak port. Much coastal shipping still goes on, although Pathein (Bassein) and Yangon have superseded it as Myanmar's most important ports. Today it's Myanmar's fourth largest city with a population of around 300,000, composed roughly of 75% Mon or some mixture of Mon, plus Karen, Burman, Indian, Chinese and other ethnicities.

Orientation

The city's main north-south thoroughfares begin with North Bogyoke Rd, which runs south from the vehicle ferry landing at the northern end of Mawlamyine and links with Upper Main Rd in the centre of town. Upper Main Rd continues south past several government buildings to the main bus terminal at the southern end of town, then connects with the highway southward to Ye. Along the western side of town, South Bogyoke Rd links with Lower Main Rd through the market and commercial districts. Another block west, Strand Rd hugs the waterfront and offers access to various local and long-distance passenger ferry jetties.

The main west-east avenue is Dawei Jetty Rd, which leads from the Dawei Jetty on the coast across town to the southern end of the ridge where most of the city's famous temples and shrines are located. On the eastern side of the ridge stand several grand colonial-era mansions that have been converted to government offices.

Taungwaing Rd cuts diagonally from the centre of town south-east to the airstrip and Mawlamyine University, terminating near Taungwaing Paya.

Mon Cultural Museum

This two-storey building at the north-eastern corner of Boho St (formerly Dalhousie St) and Dawei Jetty Rd is dedicated to the Mon history of the region. Exhibits are displayed downstairs, while upstairs are reading rooms and toilets.

The museum's modest collection includes: stelae with Mon inscriptions; hundred-year-old wooden sculptures depicting old age and sickness (used as *dhamma*-teaching devices in monasteries); ceramics, *thanaka* grinding stones; silver betel boxes; an English-language letter dated 22 December 1945 from Bogyoke Aung San to Mo Chit Hlaing, a famous Mon leader; lacquerware; *parabaik* (folding manuscripts); royal funerary urns; Mon musical instruments; and wooden Buddha altars.

In front of the museum is a British cannon dated 1826, plus a huge Burmese gong. Some labels are printed in English though most are in Burmese only.

The museum is open Wednesday to Sunday 9.30 am to 4 pm. Admission is free.

Religious Monuments

In the city's east, a hilly north-south ridge is topped with five separate monasteries and shrines. At the northern end is **Mahamuni Paya**, the largest temple complex in Mawlamyine. It's built in the typical Mon style with covered brick walkways linking various square shrine buildings. The main image resembles its namesake in Mandalay – without the thick goldleaf. Another difference is that women may enter the main Buddha chamber here. Tilework on the chamber walls includes colourful peacock representations. In the outer cloister several well-executed paintings depict local scenes from the 1920s and '30s.

Further south along the ridge stands **Kyaikthanlan Paya**, the city's tallest and most visible stupa. It was probably here that Rudyard Kipling's poetic 'Burma girl' was 'a-setting' in the opening lines of *Mandalay:* 'By the old Moulmein Pagoda, lookin' lazy at the sea'.

For K2 you can take a lift to the main

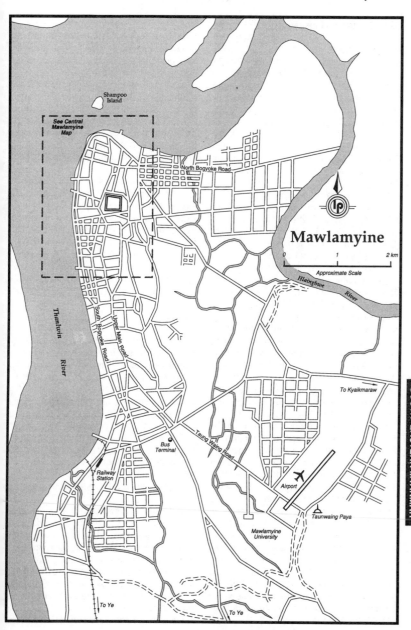

platform surrounding the 40-metre stupa, which offers fine views over the city and harbour. You can also see the plains to the east toward Kyaikmaraw and the coconut tree-shrouded islands in the mouth of the Sittoung River. The zedi's name comes from the Mon word for stupa, *kyaik*, while *than-lan* is thought to mean 'Siamese-defeating' *(than = shan = siam)*. The defeat refers to the Mon effort in building the highest stupa in the region, rather than a military manoeuvre. A large bell at the shrine's western entry dates to 1855 and weights 600 viss (960 kg).

Below Kyaikthanlan is the hundred-year-old **Seindon Mibaya Kyaung**, a monastery where King Mindon Min's queen, Seindon, sought refuge after Myanmar's last monarch, King Thibaw Min, took power. On the next rise south stands the isolated silver- and gold-plated **Aung Theikdi Zedi**.

A viewpoint on the western side of the ridge a bit further south looks out over the city and is a favoured spot for catching sunsets and evening sea breezes. Just beyond the viewpoint stands **U Khanti Paya**, built to commemorate the hermit of Mandalay Hill fame; supposedly U Khanti spent some time on this hill as well. It's a rustic, airy sort of place centred around a large Buddha image. Various bells and gongs are suspended by ropes from the sanctuary's steel ceiling supports.

U Zina Paya, on the southern spur of the ridge, was named after a former monk who dreamt of finding gems at this spot, then dug them up and used the proceeds to build a temple on the site. One of the shrine buildings contains a very curvy, sensual-looking reclining Buddha topped with a blinking electric halo; a second recliner in the same room has blinking lights all over its body.

In the centre of town toward the waterfront, on Lower Main Rd, are three mosques built during the colonial era when many Indians arrived to work for the British. Since the Indian exodus of the 1970s, Muslim congregations have declined substantially but the survival of these grand old buildings makes a walk along Lower Main Rd and its extension South Bogyoke Rd a fleeting exercise in nostalgia. The most impressive, **Kaladan Mosque**, is a grey and white structure designed by Sunni Muslims in the elaborate 'wedding-cake style' similar to that seen in Penang or Kuala Lumpur. Further south, on the same side of the street, is the smaller **Moghul Shah Mosque**, a white Shia place of worship with austere Moorish arches. A couple of blocks further on, the Sunni **Sulati Mosque** fills a similar space but presents a more brilliant turquoise and white facade.

Just up from Dawei Jetty, on the eastern side of Strand Rd, the small but colourful **Htyan Haw** Chinese temple serves the local Chinese community. Of historic interest is the sturdy brick **First Baptist Church**, also known as the Judson Church, located at the corner of Upper Main Rd and Dawei Jetty Rd. Founded by the American missionary Adoniram Judson, this literally was Myanmar's first Baptist church.

Markets

Mawlamyine's central market, **Zeigyi**, is a rambling area on the western side of Lower Main Rd just north of the main pedestrian jetty for Mottama. This market specialises in dry goods, from inexpensive 'bale' clothes to housewares. Much of the merchandise includes items which have 'fallen off the boat' on the way from Singapore to Yangon, such as untaxed cigarettes and liquor.

On the same side of the street a block north is the **New Market**, a large shed built as 'People's Market No 2' during Myanmar's recently ended socialist era. Fresh fruits, vegetables and meats are the main attraction here.

A variety of street vendors set up shop all along both sides of Lower Main Rd, in the area of these two markets. Fresh areca nut, pomelo and durian are among the specialities Mawlamyine is renowned for. The entire district is busiest in the early morning from 7 to 8 am; by 9 am business is considerably slower.

A newer bazaar next to the football field on Upper Main Rd, several blocks east of the old market area, was recently opened but so

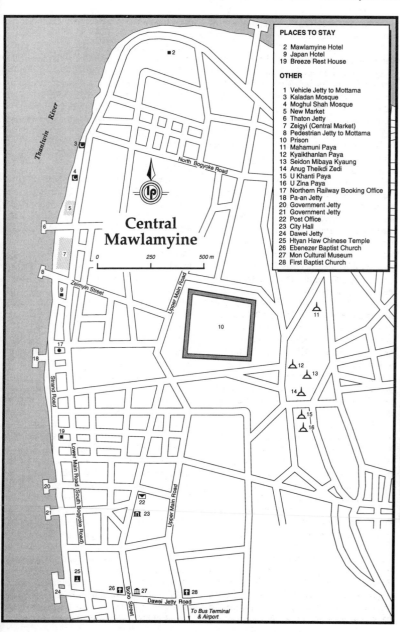

PLACES TO STAY

2 Mawlamyine Hotel
9 Japan Hotel
19 Breeze Rest House

OTHER

1 Vehicle Jetty to Mottama
3 Kaladan Mosque
4 Moghul Shah Mosque
5 New Market
6 Thaton Jetty
7 Zeigyi (Central Market)
8 Pedestrian Jetty to Mottama
10 Prison
11 Mahamuni Paya
12 Kyaikthanlan Paya
13 Seidon Mibaya Kyaung
14 Anug Theikdi Zedi
15 U Khanti Paya
16 U Zina Paya
17 Northern Railway Booking Office
18 Pa-an Jetty
20 Government Jetty
21 Government Jetty
22 Post Office
23 City Hall
24 Dawei Jetty
25 Htyan Haw Chinese Temple
26 Ebenezer Baptist Church
27 Mon Cultural Museum
28 First Baptist Church

Central Mawlamyine

0   250   500 m

Thanlwin River

North Bogyoke Road

Zeimyin Street

Upper Main Road

Strand Road

Lower Main Road (South Bogyoke Road)

Upper Main Road

Bogyo Street

Dawei Jetty Road

To Bus Terminal
& Airport

SOUTH-EASTERN MYANMAR

far it hasn't attracted a large number of vendors or shoppers.

Gaungse ('Head-Wash') Kyun

Commonly known in English as 'Shampoo Island', this picturesque little isle off Mawlamyine's north-western end is so named because during the Ava period the yearly royal hairwashing ceremony customarily used water taken from a spring on the island.

You can hire a boat out to the island for K150. Other than just walking around and soaking up the island ambience, you can visit **Sanhawshin Paya**, a whitewash-and-silver zedi said to contain hair relics, and a nearby Buddhist meditation centre. Among other islands in the river, you can find the largest one – **Balu Kyun** or 'Ogre Island'.

Places to Stay

In the north-western corner of the city, not far from the Mottama vehicle ferry landing, the recently privatised *Mawlamyine Hotel* (☎ 032-22560) offers a well-spaced selection of bungalows with three large guest rooms in each. Rooms come with two beds, an assemblage of cane and rattan chairs, desk, coffee table, mini-fridge, TV (with TV Myanmar only) and private toilet and hot-water shower. The uniform foreigner rate of US$48 single, US$60 double includes breakfast, service and tax; Burmese citizens pay one-sixth these rates. Slightly faulty plumbing seems to be the norm; on the plus side, it's a quiet location and service is good. An elaborate Shin Upagot shrine sits at the water's edge next to the hotel, within sight of Shampoo Island.

When we visited, the pricey Mawlamyine Hotel was the only foreigner-licensed lodging available. The *Thanlwin Hotel* (☎ 032-21518) on Lower Main Rd, currently under renovation, will probably run in the US$15 to US$25 range when it reopens – and if the requested licence is granted.

The funky but quite adequate *Breeze Rest House* at 6 Strand Rd was on the verge of receiving its foreigner licence. This two-storey wood building has a typical arrangement of high-ceilinged cubicles with open transoms off a central hallway. At the moment all rooms come with two beds, fan and shared facilities for K120. The English-speaking owner claims he will be adding air-con to at least some of the rooms, for which the rate will be approximately US$10.

The *Japan Hotel* on Strand Rd just south of the Mottama pedestrian jetty looks slightly nicer than the Breeze Rest House, but at the moment it doesn't accept foreign guests.

Getting There & Away

Air Myanma Airways flies direct from Yangon to Mawlamyine on Wednesday, and via Dawei on Saturday. For the latter flight, an overnight in Dawei is necessary since seats from Dawei to Mawlamyine can only be reserved in Dawei, not in Yangon. From Yangon to Mawlamyine the fare for the 35-minute flight is US$65 by F-27, US$75 by F-28. From Dawei, an hour away by plane, the fare is US$50/55. There is an additional flight from Dawei to Yangon on Wednesday.

There are also flights to Mawlamyine from Mandalay on MA for US$75/85.

Bus Private buses to Mawlamyine are available from the Highway Bus Centre in Yangon for just K250 but these are very slow and involve overnighting by the side of the road just west of Sittoung Bridge – passengers pass the night in their seats, beneath the bus or in nearby monasteries. You'd be much better off breaking your journey in Bago or Kyaikto, and starting fresh from either town. Most buses terminate in Mottama on the northern bank of the Thanlwin River, where you can catch one of the frequent pedestrian ferries to Mawlamyine on the southern bank; a few through buses to Dawei and beyond actually board the less frequent vehicle ferries across the river from Mottama to Mawlamyine. At either ferry landing immigration authorities check passports and travel permits.

Mawlamyine's main terminal for southbound buses or pickups is near the southern end of town off the road to Ye. Here you can board public vehicles to Thanbyuzayat (six

South-Eastern Myanmar
The remarkable balancing boulder-temple of Kyaiktiyo

Western Myanmar
Top: Mrauk U's fort-like Shittaung
Bottom Left: Carrying water home, Mrauk U
Bottom Right: Silent observers, Mrauk U

times daily, K50), Kyaikkami (previously Amherst; six times daily, K50), Dawei (once daily, K324) or Payathonzu on the Thai border (once daily, K1500). Two small indoor restaurants at the terminal serve decent Burmese and Chinese fare.

Train Two express trains run from Yangon to Mottama daily, the No 81 Up at 3 am and the No 83 Up at 8 am. When the trains are running on time the trip takes seven and a half hours – beating even the fastest bus lines by several hours. The local price for an upper-class seat is K200, while the foreigner price is US$8. Ordinary-class seats cost K75, although they aren't officially available to foreigners. To arrange a train ticket in Yangon you'll have to go to the Advance Booking Office as the Foreigner Ticket Centre refuses to sell tickets to Mottama. You may find it easier to purchase train tickets to Mottama in Bago or Kyaikto.

In the reverse direction, the No 84 Down leaves Mottama at 8 am and is scheduled to arrive in Yangon at 4.10 pm; the No 82 Down leaves at 11.45 am and arrives in Yangon at 7 pm. In Mawlamyine tickets may be purchased one day in advance at the Northern Railway Booking Office, which stands between Strand Rd and Lower Main Rd just north of the Pa-an Jetty.

A separate southern railway line begins at the southern end of the city and terminates in Dawei. At the time of writing, foreigners weren't allowed to travel on this railway due to a lack of security further south.

Boat See the Mottama section for details on the Thanlwin River ferry crossings to Mawlamyine. There are two main jetties on the Mawlamyine side for ferries to and from Mottama: the vehicle jetty at the northern end of town and the pedestrian jetty just south of the central market off Strand Rd.

The next jetty south of the Mottama pedestrian jetty handles boats to Pa-an in the Kayin State. Next south are two jetties reserved for government boats only, followed by the larger Dawei Jetty for boats to Dawei and Myeik (Mergui). It's quite difficult for foreigners to arrange passage on any of these boats, though it's rumoured that the Pa-an ferry will likely open to non-Burmese in the near future.

Getting Around

Motorised *thoun bein* or 'three-wheelers' are the main form of public transport around the city. The highest concentration of three-wheelers is found on Lower Main Rd in front of the Zeigyi market. The going rate is K20 for a short hop within the centre of town, and as much as K50 or K60 for a ride up the ridge to Kyaikthanlan.

AROUND MAWLAMYINE

The authorities frown upon foreigners travelling south of Mawlamyine, even though the local tourist brochures are flush with photos of Thanbyuzayat, Kyaikkami and Setse. However **Mudon**, 29 km south of the city, is considered a 'white area' and there are no checkpoints on the way. Verdant mountains to the east are a source of 'jungle food' – deer, snake and other wild forest species – for restaurants in Mudon itself. The town is known for cotton weaving as well.

Just north of Mudon is a turn-off east to **Azin Dam**, a water storage and flood control facility that's also used to irrigate local rubber plantations. A tidy recreation area at **Kandawgyi** – a lake formed by the dam – is a favourite picnic spot; bring your own snacks or rely on the vendors that gather here on weekends and holidays. At the northern end of the lake stands the gilded stupa of **Kandawgyi Paya**.

Just off the road between Mawlamyine and Mudon there are two interesting hilltop shrines at **Kyauktalone Daung** and **Yadana Daung**. The former is a flat-topped limestone crag crowned with stupas. On the opposite side of the road is a similar but smaller outcropping surmounted by a Hindu temple. On Yadana Daung, local Buddhists are constructing a huge reclining Buddha which when completed will reportedly measure around 160 metres long, making it the largest such image in the world. Many

SOUTH-EASTERN MYANMAR

other stupas and standing Buddhas dot the countryside around the reclining image.

South of Mudon begins a 'brown area'. Most locals will warn against travelling along the roads here after 3 pm. The government attributes road attacks in this area to Mon or Karen insurgents, but since the attacks don't discriminate between government and private vehicles, and since the motive always seems to be robbery, it's hard to conceive that the perpetrators are anything other than common highway bandits. One of the methods used – to which we can testify since it happened to us – is to roll a log across the road to force vehicles to stop, at which time armed men appear and demand money from driver and passengers. We were fortunate to be able to remove the log from the road before any robbery attempt occurred. Incidents between 8 am and 2 pm are apparently quite rare because that's when most people travel – increased traffic means increased safety. Public transport – buses or pickups – are comparatively safer from attack than private vehicles.

Kyaikmaraw

This small but charming town 24 km southeast of Mawlamyine is accessible via a good sealed road. For the most part Kyaikmaraw is considered a 'white area' although insurgents or bandits have been known to rob the rubber plantations along the road to Mawlamyine.

Hugging the banks of the Ataran River, a branch of the Thanlwin River, the town consists of mostly wooden homes with thatched palm or corrugated metal roofs.

Kyaikmaraw Paya The pride of the town is this temple built by Queen Sinsawbu in 1455 in the late Mon regional style. Among the temple's many outstanding features are multi-coloured glass windows set in the outside walls of the main sanctuary, an inner colonnade decorated in mirrored tiles and beautiful ceramic tile floors. Painted reliefs appear on the exterior of several auxiliary buildings; one wall of the *thein* bears a large relief of Myei Sountmatham, the Hindu-

Buddhist earth goddess (Ma Dharani in Pali), twisting her wet hair to create a flood to wash away Mara the tempter.

Covered brick walkways lead to and around the main square sanctuary in typical 15th-century Mon style. The huge main Buddha image sits in a 'European pose', with the legs hanging down as if sitting on a chair rather than in the much more common cross-legged manner. The Burmese call this the 'going-to-leave' pose, a transition between the canonical sitting and standing/walking postures. A number of smaller cross-legged Buddhas surround the main image, and behind it are two reclining Buddhas, one with eyes open, one with eyes closed. The robes of all the Buddha figures in the main sanctuary are gilded; some are encrusted with semi-precious stones. Another impressive feature is the carved and painted wooden ceiling.

A side room to the inner sanctuary contains sculptures depicting the Buddha in various stages of illness and death – other than the traditional *parinibbana* reclining posture, these are unusual motifs for Buddhist temples. Two images show the Buddha lying on his back with hands folded on his abdomen; another depicts an ill Buddha stooping over slightly with one hand clasped to his chest, the other hand against the wall as his disciples reach out to assist him. Another elaborate sculpture display features *devas* dividing the Buddha's remains to serve as relics while his monastic disciples watch.

Next to the main sanctuary is a small museum with Buddha images donated by the faithful on the upper floor; other artefacts from the area are on the lower floor. Some of these objects are over 500 years old.

Getting There & Away Two kinds of trucks ply the Kyaikmaraw road frequently from Mawlamyine; green Chevy trucks with wooden passenger compartments cost K10 per person and take about 45 minutes, while smaller white Japanese pickups cost K15 per person and take 30 minutes. Lined with toddy palms and rubber plantations, the road passes through eight villages before ending at the riverbank in Kyaikmaraw.

Thanbyuzayat

South of Mudon little traffic is seen and the hills to the east grow more densely forested. Thanbyuzayat ('Tin Shelter'), situated 64 km south of Mawlamyine, was the western terminus of the infamous Burma-Siam Railway, dubbed the 'Death Railway' by the thousands of Allied POWs and Asian coolies who were forced by the Japanese military to build it. It was here that the Japanese broke into Myanmar after marching over the rugged mountain range separating Myanmar from Tak in Thailand via Three Pagodas Pass.

The strategic objective of the railway was to secure an alternative supply route for the Japanese conquest of Myanmar and other Asian countries to the west. Construction on the railway began on 16 September 1942 at existing terminals in Thanbyuzayat and Nong Pladuk, Thailand. Japanese engineers at the time estimated that it would take five years to link Thailand and Burma by rail, but the Japanese army forced the POWs to complete the 415-km, one-metre-gauge railway, of which roughly two-thirds ran through Thailand, in 16 months. Much of the railway was built in difficult terrain that required high bridges and deep mountain cuttings. The rails were finally joined 37 km south of the town of Payathonzu ('Three Pagodas'); a Japanese brothel train inaugurated the line. The railway was in use for 20 months before the Allies bombed it in 1945.

An estimated 16,000 POWs died as a result of brutal treatment by their captors, a story chronicled by Boulle's book *The Bridge Over the River Kwai* and popularised by a movie based on the same. The notorious bridge itself still stands in Kanchanaburi, Thailand. Only one POW is known to have escaped, a Briton who took refuge among pro-British Karen guerrillas.

Although the statistics of the number of POWs who died during the Japanese occupation are horrifying, the figures for the labourers, many from Myanmar, Thailand, Malaysia and Indonesia, are even worse. It is thought that in total 90,000 to 100,000 coolies died in the area.

A clock tower in the centre of Thanbyuzayat stands at a road junction; the road south leads to Ye while the road west goes to Kyaikkami and Setse. About a km and a half south of the clock tower, a locomotive and piece of track commemorating the Burma-Siam Railway are on display. A km west of the clock tower in the direction of Kyaikkami, on the south side of the road, lies the **Thanbyuzayat War Cemetery**, which contains 3771 graves of Allied POWs who died building the railway. Maintained by the Commonwealth War Graves Commission, the landscaped cemetery is reminiscent of, but much smaller than, the Taukkyan War Cemetery near Yangon. Most of those interred were British, but there are also markers for American, Dutch and Australian soldiers.

Thanbyuzayat is easily reached by public pickup from the Mawlamyine bus terminal; there are six departures, all before noon, for K50 per person. As there is no legal lodging in Thanbyuzayat, start early so that you can catch the last pickup back to Mawlamyine around 2 pm.

Kyaikkami

Located 24 km north-east of Thanbyuzayat, Kyaikkami was a small coastal resort and missionary centre known as Amherst during the British era. Adoniram Judson (1788-1850), an American missionary and linguist who has practically attained sainthood among Burmese Baptists, was sailing to India with his wife when their ship was blown off course, forcing them to land at Kyaikkami. Judson stayed on and established his first mission here; the original site is now a Catholic school on a small lane off the main road.

Among other accomplishments, Judson developed the first Burmese-English dictionary in 1849 and was the first to translate the Bible into Burmese. He was buried at sea, but the grave of his wife, Anne Judson, can still be see in Kyaikkami a couple of hundred metres off the main road near the school.

But the main focus of Kyaikkami is **Yele Paya**, a metal-roofed Buddhist shrine complex perched over the sea and reached via a long two-level causeway; the lower level is submerged during high tide. Along with 11 Buddha hair relics, the shrine chamber beneath Yele Paya reportedly contains a Buddha image which supposedly floated here on a raft from Sri Lanka in ancient times. According to legend, a gifted Sinhalese sculptor fashioned four different Buddha images using pieces from the original bodhi tree mixed with a cement composite. He then placed them on four wooden rafts and set the rafts adrift on the ocean; the other three landed near Pathein, Kyaikto and Dawei. A display of 21 Mandalay-style Buddha statues sit over the spot where the Sinhalese image is supposedly buried. Some of the seashells for sale on the premises have been fashioned into religious charms.

During the early half of the day there are occasional pickups to Kyaikkami from Thanbyuzayat for K20 per person. You can also charter a car or truck taxi for K400 or K500.

Setse

This low-key Gulf of Martaban beach lies 24 km south of Kyaikkami, or 16 km south-west of Thanbyuzayat. It's a very wide, brown-sand beach that tends toward tidal flats when the shallow surf-line recedes at low tide. The water doesn't look particularly clean but it may just be the colour of the sand; the beach is lined by waving casuarina trees.

As yet there are no foreigner-approved hotels at Setse, though 10 private unlicensed bungalows are available for Burmese citizens. Vendors sell fresh young coconuts full of juice, and a few modest restaurants offer fresh seafood. The biggest, *Mya Annwa* or 'Emerald Sea', serves delicious lobster and prawns.

There is no public transport to Setse; from Thanbyuzayat you can charter a taxi for K400.

Kayin State

Most districts in Kayin State and Taninthayi Division (which both share borders with Thailand) are very much off limits to foreign visitors travelling from Yangon. The Kayin State, homeland to around a million Karen (Kayin is the Burmese pronunciation), has probably received more foreign visitors who have crossed over – unofficially – from Thailand than from any other direction. Many international volunteers have ventured into the frontier area to assist with refugee concerns.

Ever since Myanmar attained independence from the British in 1948, the Karen have been embroiled in a fight for autonomy. The main insurgent body, the Karen National Union (KNU), controls much of the northern and eastern parts of the state although recent Yangon military victories have left the KNU and its military component, the Karen National Liberation Army (KNLA), without a permanent headquarters. A split between Christian and Buddhist factions has also weakened the KNU, which had become the de facto centre of the Democratic Alliance of Burma (DAB), an alliance of a dozen rebel groups fighting for regional autonomy. KNU headquarters was also the seat of the National Coalition Government of the Union of Burma, a 'parallel government' established by a group of disaffected National League for Democracy members who won parliamentary seats in the ill-fated May 1990 national elections. Much of the state remains a potential battleground as fighting between Burmese troops and the KNLA continues.

PA-AN ဘားအံ

A new road from Mawlamyine to the Kayin State capital of Pa-an will span the Gyaing River north-east of the city, thus linking Mawlamyine with a Thanlwin River crossing east of Thaton. Tourism authorities in Yangon say Pa-an will soon be added to the list of places foreigners may visit with a permit.

Double-decker ferries from the Pa-an Jetty in Mawlamyine leave daily at 6 am and noon for the four-hour trip up the Thanlwin River to Pa-an on the river's eastern bank. The fare is K10 and every conceivable inch of deck space is used for cargo and passengers.

We have no information on what to expect upon arrival in Pa-an, though the town itself is probably little different from Thaton or other small to medium-sized towns in the region.

From Pa-an a rutted, unsurfaced road heads 143 km south-east to **Myawaddy**, a town controlled by the Tatmadaw ('armed forces') on the western bank of the Thaungyin River (known as Moei River to the Thais) opposite the northern Thai town of Mae Sot. As many as 100,000 Karen refugees fleeing KNLA-Tatmadaw battles are encamped on the Thai side of the border in this area. In late 1994 the Burmese and Thai governments agreed to span the river with a vehicle bridge but construction was halted in mid-1995 because of disputes over the repatriation of refugees. Yangon is demanding that the Thais send the refugees back; so far the Thai government has refused on humanitarian grounds.

Although it's possible to drive from Pa-an (or Mawlamyine) to Myawaddy in six or seven hours, the final 64 km between Kawkareik and Myawaddy is considered unsafe due to fighting in the area. There are several military checkpoints along the way and it's highly unlikely any foreigner would be permitted to make this trip.

Tourist brochures printed in Yangon sometimes mention that Myawaddy is open to day visits from the Thai side but in practice the border situation is now so tense that this is rarely allowed.

PAYATHONZU ဘုရားသုံးဆူ

Another Yangon-controlled town on the Thai-Burmese border, Payathonzu ('Three Pagodas') is around 110 km south-east of Thanbyuzayat via an unsurfaced road. Three small zedis mark a mountain pass used for many centuries as a route for overland trade as well as military invasion. The zedis today

stand on Thai turf, a dozen metres from the Burmese border crossing. Control of the Burmese side of the border once vacillated between the Karen National Union and the Mon National Liberation Front, since Payathonzu was one of several 'toll gates' along the Thai-Burmese border where insurgent armies collected a 5% tax on all merchandise passing through.

The Karen also conduct a huge multi-million dollar business in illegal mining and logging, the products of which are smuggled into Thailand by the truckload under cover of the night – not without the 'palms-up' co-operation of the Thai police, of course. Pressure for control of these border points has increased since the Thai government enacted a ban on all logging in Thailand in 1989, which has as a consequence led to an increase in teak smuggling.

In late 1988, heavy fighting broke out between the Karen and the Mon for control of the 'toll gate' here. Since this is the only place for hundreds of km in either direction where a border crossing is geographically convenient, this is where the Mon army (who traditionally have controlled this area) have customarily collected the 5% tax on smuggling. The Karen insurgents do the same at other points north along the Thai-Burmese border. Burmese government pressure on the Karen further north led to a conflict between the Karen and the Mon over Three Pagodas trade and the village on the Burmese side was virtually burnt to the ground in the 1988 skirmishes.

In 1989 the Yangon government wrested control of the town from both the Karen and Mon, and the Burmese seem firmly established at the border for the time being. The town has been entirely rebuilt and filled with shops catering to an odd mix of occupation troops and Thai tourists.

Foreigners are allowed to cross the border here for day trips upon payment of 130B in Thai currency or US$5 cash. Payathonzu lies 470 km by road from Yangon but is considered '75% safe' by the Burmese military. Insurgent Karen forces are still in the area and there are occasional firefights.

Payathonzu has three Burmese tea houses, one cinema, several mercantile shops with Burmese *longyis*, cheroots, jade, clothes, and a few souvenir shops with Mon-Karen-Burmese handicrafts. Bargaining is necessary but in general goods are well priced. About 20 Thai merchants operate in town – the Burmese government offers them free rent to open shops. A new temple, given the Thai name **Wat Suwankhiri**, has been constructed on a bluff near town.

Kloeng Thaw Falls, located 12 km from the border, takes a couple of hours by motorcycle to reach from Payathonzu. The road to the falls is only open in the dry season – reportedly the Karen control the waterfall area during the rainy season. Even in good weather, the two-rut track is very rugged – not recommended for motorcycle novices. Lately the falls area has been closed more often than it has been open.

The border is open from 7 am to 6 pm daily.

Getting There & Away
Only military vehicles or commercial vehicles under armed guard use the road from Thanbyuzayat. For the time being foreigners are only permitted to visit Payathonzu from the Thai side; the nearest Thai town of any size is Sangkhlaburi, where lodging and food are readily available.

On the Thai side, a 19-km paved road to Three Pagodas Pass begins four km before

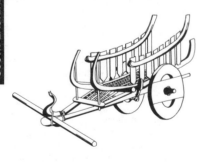

Burmese bullock cart made of *padauk* wood and bamboo

you reach Sangkhlaburi off Thailand's Highway 323. At this intersection a Thai police checkpoint may stop you for minor interrogation, depending on recent events in the Three Pagodas Pass area. Along the way you'll pass a couple of villages inhabited entirely by Mon or Karen; at one time there was a branch of the All Burma Students Democratic Front here, where self-exiled Yangon students had set up an opposition movement with the intention of ousting the Ne Win government from Myanmar. The students have since moved north to Thailand's Tak Province.

Pickups to Three Pagodas Pass leave about every 50 minutes between 6 am and 5 pm from Sangkhlaburi's central market area. The fare is 30B; the last pickup back to Sangkhlaburi leaves Three Pagodas Pass at around 4.30 pm.

Taninthayi Division

Taninthayi Division, known to the outside world as Tenasserim until 1989, is relatively more accessible than the Kayin State. However, the KNLA (and its Mon equivalent, the Mon National Liberation Front) have been pushed into the northern reaches by the Tatmadaw and much of the Thai border area is considered 'black territory'. Permits are occasionally available for Dawei and Myeik, and Kawthoung is easily accessible from Ranong, Thailand.

DAWEI (TAVOY) ထားဝယ်
The area round the mouth of the Dawei River has been inhabited for five centuries or more, mostly by Mon and Thai mariners. The present town dates to 1751 when it was a minor 'back-door' port for the Ayuthaya empire in Thailand (then Siam). From this point it bounced back and forth between Burman and Thai rule until British annexation in 1826.

Still a port of medium importance, Dawei today is a sleepy, tropical seaside town only recently connected to the rest of Myanmar by road and rail. In spite of its remote location – or perhaps because of it – Dawei has become a significant Burmese Buddhist centre.

Among local religious monuments, **Shinmokhti Paya** is the most sacred. Reportedly constructed in 1438, this is one of the four shrines in the country that house a Sinhalese Buddha image supposedly made with a composite of cement and pieces of the original bodhi tree – see the Pathein or Kyaikkami sections for an account of the legend. **Gathita Yama Kyaung**, one of the largest monasteries in south-eastern Myanmar, is headed by a highly respected octogenarian *sayadaw* (chief abbot) who has turned down invitations by the Burmese government to become the *sangharaja* or Supreme Patriarch of the Burmese monkhood.

Completed in 1931, the largest reclining Buddha in the country – 74 metres long, 21 metres high – can be seen at **Lyaung Daw Mu** at the edge of town. Further out of town on a hillside, **Su Taungpyi** features two revered stupas (one plated with silver, the other with goldleaf), and an attached *kammathan yeiktha* (meditation centre) under the direction of Sayadaw U Eida Wuntha.

Dawei's sleepy, laid-back demeanour is threatened by the development of a new Ye-Dawei railway, which was largely built using locally conscripted labour. Hundreds of Taninthayi Division residents fled to Thailand rather than work on the railway under conditions – if refugee reports are to be believed – that almost rival those described in chronicles of the Japanese army's 'Death Railway'. According to Amnesty International, one of the camps of refugee labourers at the Thai border was attacked by a battalion of Myanmar's 62nd Infantry and some of the refugees were forcefully repatriated.

Dawei is also near the starting point for a massive gas pipeline project sponsored by the French company Total. If completed as planned, the pipeline will carry natural gas from the Gulf of Martaban to Thailand. Reportedly the government is relocating villages that fall in the pipeline's proposed path with little or no compensation for the villagers.

Beaches & Islands

Few foreigners have been permitted to visit coastal areas around Dawei so details are still sketchy. The best local beach area reportedly lies on the coast around 18 km west of Dawei in Maungmakan township. Here a sand beach stretches eight km, and has some government bungalows usually reserved for VIPs.

Opposite Maungmakan is a collection of three pretty island groups which were named the Middle Moscos Islands by the British – they are now known as Maungmakan, Henze and Launglon (or collectively as the Maungmakan Islands). Due to a natural profusion of wild boar, barking deer, sambar and swiftlets, these islands belong to Myanmar's only marine sanctuary – established by the British in 1927 and still officially protected.

A long peninsula ending in Dawei Point (Dawei Angu), about 60 km south of Dawei, creates a vast estuarine bay dotted with islands. Because the waters of the lengthy bay are to some degree protected from strong ocean currents, these islands may be more easily accessible by boat than the Maungmakan Islands.

Places to Stay & Eat

Sibin Guest House lodges government officials in six-bed rooms with shared facilities for just K15 per person. This is where you'll most likely stay if you are able to obtain a permit for Dawei, though you'll undoubtedly be charged more.

Myanma San and *Daw Khin San,* in the centre of town, serve decent Burmese food. For breakfast your best bet is the *Beik Tea & Coffee Shop*.

Getting There & Away

Air Myanma Airways fields daily flights from Yangon to Dawei for US$75 on an F-27, US$85 by F-28. The flight takes an hour and 20 minutes. There are also flights from Mawlamyine (Wednesday and Satur-

SOUTH-EASTERN MYANMAR

day, US$50/55, one hour), Myeik (Monday and Saturday, US$35/40, 30 minutes) and Kawthoung (Thursday, US$80/85, one hour). You will have to show a travel permit valid for Dawei in order to purchase tickets for Dawei-bound flights.

Bus A company called Snowflake operates buses from Yangon's Highway Bus Centre all the way to Dawei beginning at 7 pm for K500 per person. Along the way passengers spend a night each at the Sittoung Bridge and at Thanbyuzayat, usually sleeping in nearby monasteries.

A more reasonable overland approach would be to start out fresh from Maw-lamyine. The 317-km trip may require an overnight at Ye since drivers are loathe to drive in late afternoons or evenings. Even during supposed 'safe hours', dacoits and KNLA/MNLF regulars sometimes collect a 'road tax' from the drivers along the way. The tropical scenery between Ye and Dawei is superb.

Boat Myanma Five Star Line occasionally sails between Yangon, Dawei, Myeik and Kawthoung but travel is very slow and permits endorsed for ship are difficult to obtain.

MYEIK (MERGUI) ဗိုက်

The Taninthayi coast, in the extreme south of Myanmar where Myanmar and Thailand share the narrow peninsula, is bounded by the beautiful islands of the Mergui Archipel-ago. Myeik – known to the colonials as Mergui and locally as Beik or Myeit – sits on a peninsula that juts out into the Andaman Sea.

The area inland from Myeik is a major smuggling route into Thailand as well as a 'brown area' from the military perspective, so Myeik is very much off limits to those without permits. Permits are hard to come by unless you work for an international oil company or have government connections. Whether for anticipated tourism or for oil exploration, the Myeik airport is being expanded to field bigger aircraft. So far one

sees very few Westerners wandering around town.

In the 18th century Myeik served as a port for Thailand's Ayuthaya empire. Ocean-going visitors from the West would land here and continue up the Taninthayi River on smaller boats to Taninthayi, then finish the trip by road to Ayuthaya via Dan Singkon (in present-day Prachuap Khiri Khan Province, Thailand). As Myeik became an important trade entrepôt, many European traders and envoys in the employ of the Ayuthaya court settled in the area. The British occupied the region following the First Anglo-Burmese War in 1826.

Along with rubber and coconuts, marine products are a major source of livelihood for Myeik residents, and the *ngapi* (fermented fish or shrimp paste) made here is renown throughout Myanmar. Another local product is the sea swallow's nest, collected and exported as the main ingredient in the 'bird's nest soup' favoured by Chinese throughout Asia. The nests are made of saliva which the birds secrete – the saliva hardens when exposed to the air. Cooked in chicken broth, the nests soften and separate and look like bean thread noodles. The Chinese value the expensive bird secretions highly, believing them to be a medicinal food that imparts vigour.

The sea swallows (*Collocalia esculenta*), also known as 'edible-nest swiftlets') like to build their nests high up in limestone caves, in rocky hollows which can be very difficult to reach. Many such caves are found on islands in the Mergui Archipelago. Agile col-lectors build vine-and-bamboo scaffolding to get at the nests but are occasionally injured or killed in falls. Before ascending the scaf-folds, the collectors pray and make offerings of tobacco, incense and liquor to the cavern *nats* (spirits). The collectors sell the nests to intermediaries who then sell them to Chinese restaurants abroad. Known as 'white gold', premium teacup-sized birdnests sell for US$2000 per kilo – Hong Kong alone imports US$25 million worth every year.

Perhaps far beyond the value of these nests is the archipelago's huge, untapped potential in the beach-going and eco-tourist market. The Burmese say there are over 4000 islands in the archipelago, though British surveyors recognised only 804. Many are inhabited by 'sea gypsies' (called 'Moken' by anthropologists, 'Salon' by the Burmese), a nomadic seafaring people who sail from island to island, stopping off to repair their boats or fishing nets. With stones tied to their waists as ballast, a Moken diver can reportedly descend to a depth of 60 metres while breathing through an air hose held above the water surface.

Things to See & Do

The city's most venerated Buddhist temple, **Theindawgyi Paya**, contains a European-pose Buddha and a reclining Buddha, both similar to those at Kyaikmaraw Paya near Mawlamyine; a tall gilded stupa overlooks the harbour.

At the edge of town, the three gilded stupas of **Pawdaw Mu Aung Theikdigon** are mounted on shrine cubicles picturesquely close to the seashore and a rubber plantation.

Pataw Patit Island, a five-minute boat ride from the harbour, is devoted to several religious buildings, stupas and sculptures. A large, hollow reclining Buddha lies at the island's south end. A nearby monastery, **Kokthein-nayon Kyaung**, has square shrine buildings in the regional Mon style. One of the shrines contains scenes of the sick-and-dying Buddha, reminiscent once again of Kyaikmaraw Paya. The name of the monastery, in fact, is the Burmese pronunciation of Kusinara, the place in India where the historical Buddha is supposed to have died. Also displayed at the monastery are a few Buddha images made in Thailand, possibly dating to the era when Myeik was a Siamese territory. There are several other shrines on the island.

Mayanpin Kyun, known to the British as King Island, is a huge island a good distance offshore. In spite of its size and geographic variation, reports say there are no good beaches on the island. A government guest house accommodates visitors to a hydroelec-tric power station – reportedly built with forced labour – on the island.

Boats to nearby islands can be chartered for US$60 per day from Myeik's harbour.

Places to Stay & Eat

Myeik has no commercial lodging licensed to accept foreigners. Those with permits may be allowed to stay either at the *Eindaw Pyu Guest House* (K100 per person in tiny bare rooms with shared facilities) at 57 Main Rd or at the much better government-owned *Annawa*, next to Theindawgyi Paya overlooking the harbour. At the latter, large rooms with mosquito net, fan and shared bath cost K500; there's a pleasant sitting terrace out front.

Decent restaurants in town include the *Bamboo House* (Chinese and Burmese) and *Welcome* (Chinese). There's also a better-than-average selection of teashops around town.

Getting There & Away

Air Travel permits valid for Myeik usually stipulate that the bearer arrive by air. Myanma Airways drops in daily from Yangon for US$90 aboard F-27s, US$100 on F-28s. The flight takes an hour and five minutes. There are also flights from Mawlamyine (Wednesday, US$75/85, one hour and 50 minutes), Dawei (Monday and Saturday, US$35/40, 50 minutes) and Kawthoung (Monday, Tuesday, Thursday and Friday, US$50/55). MA also runs a Mandalay-Myeik service.

Bus There are daily buses and pickups from Dawei, 249 km north, but it's highly unlikely any foreigner will be permitted to travel by bus to Myeik. The road is so bad – and so plagued by bandit attacks – that the trip sometimes requires an overnight at Palaw, 73 km north of Myeik. On top of this there are four ferry crossings, one each at Palauk Chaung, Pyicha Chaung, Pawal River and Tomok River.

Boat Myanma Five Star Line occasionally sails between Yangon, Dawei, Myeik and

SOUTH-EASTERN MYANMAR

Kawthoung but travel is very slow and permits endorsed for ship are difficult to obtain.

KAWTHOUNG ကောသောင်

This small port at the southernmost tip of Taninthayi Division – and the southernmost point of mainland Myanmar – is only separated from Thailand by a broad estuary in the Pakchan River. To the British it was known as Victoria Point and to the Thais it's known as Ko Sawng, which means 'Second Island' in Thai. The Burmese name, Kawthoung, is probably a corruption of the latter.

The main business here is trade with Thailand, followed by fishing. Among the Burmese, Kawthoung is perhaps best known for producing some of the country's best kickboxers.

Most Kawthoung residents are bilingual in Thai and Burmese. Many of the residents who were born and raised in Kawthoung, especially Muslims, also speak Pashu, a dialect that mixes the Thai, Malay and Burmese languages. Nearby islands are inhabited by bands of nomadic Moken or sea gypsies.

At the moment Kawthoung is only accessible to foreigners by boat from Ranong, Thailand. It's probably not worth making a special trip to Ranong just to visit Kawthoung, but if you're in the area and decide to cross over, you'll find it's similar to the rest of Myanmar except there are many more motorcycles!

Visiting Kawthoung

Boats to Kawthoung leave the pier in Ranong regularly from around 7 am till 3 pm for 30B per person. Immediately as you exit the Kawthoung jetty there's a small immigration office on the right, where you must pay US$5 for a day permit. For the same rate you can stay up to three nights but then you're required to buy US$50 worth of Foreign Exchange Certificates. If you want to stay longer, you can extend your permit up to 29 days upon payment of US$36 and the exchange of US$200 into FECs. Whether this will allow you to travel further north is another matter – road travel is impossible

and boat travel beyond the immediate Kawthoung area is forbidden. You may be permitted to fly to Yangon with the stipulation that you return to Kawthoung when exiting the country. Then again, once you're in Yangon you could probably apply through the immigration office for a permit to exit by air via Yangon.

Our experience indicates it's better to deal with the small immigration office at the pier rather than with the larger immigration on the road leading to the motel. The staff at the larger office may claim only day visits are allowed.

Islands

The Mergui Archipelago continues south to Kawthoung and many islands lie tantalisingly offshore in this area. Unfortunately there is no regular transport to any of these islands and boat charters are expensive.

Thahtay Kyun or Thahtay Island (also known as Pulau Ru), one of the closest isles, sports a large new resort owned by Thailand's Dusit chain. Known variously as *Andaman Club* and *Thahtay Island Resort* (☎ 01-956 4354, radio phone in Ranong), the resort's main features will include a casino, duty-free goods and a golf course – an arrangement obviously designed to appeal to well-heeled Thais and Singaporeans. There are no beaches to speak of on the island, but the resort will offer trips to a beach on St Luke's Island (Adetgyi Kyun), about 45 minutes away by speedboat.

A more interesting nearby island known as **Salon Island** (Sea Gypsy Island) or Pulau Besin is heavily wooded and boasts a lagoon in its centre and sand beaches on its shores. A Malaysian company started the construction of a few bungalows here but quit after a year. A Yangon company currently has tentative plans for two developments here, *Yadana Beach Resort* and *Suwanna Bhumi Resort*.

Tours

Jansom Thara Hotel (in Thailand: ☎ 077-821511, fax 821821) in Ranong offers Kawthoung and island tours aboard four boats with capacities ranging from 15 persons to 200 persons. A 'half-day tour' costing 600B per person sails from Ranong, visits a couple of payas in Kawthoung and returns to Ranong around 11 am. The 'full day tour' costing 850B goes to Pulau Besin for beach swimming and lunch and returns at 2 pm. Rates include immigrations procedures on both sides, guide and boat transport; lunch costs an extra 120B per person.

Places to Stay

There's only one place approved for foreigners, the simple *Kawthoung Motel* not far from the waterfront. For simple double rooms with private cold-water bath, Thais pay 350B, foreigners US$25.

Getting There & Away

Air Myanma Airways flies between Yangon and Kawthoung on Monday, Tuesday and Friday; the flight costs US$130 by F-27, US$145 by F-28, and takes an hour and 10 minutes. There are also flights from Kawthoung to Myeik (Monday, Tuesday, Thursday and Friday, US$50/55) and Dawei (Thursday, US$80/85, one hour).

Boat Myanma Five Star Line occasionally sails between Yangon, Dawei, Myeik and Kawthoung but travel is very slow and permits endorsed for ship are difficult to obtain, even in Yangon.

See Visiting Kawthoung above for details on boats from Ranong.

SOUTH-EASTERN MYANMAR

Western Myanmar

The Rakhine Yoma (Arakan Range) separates the Rakhine and Chin states from the central Ayeyarwady River plains. Isolated from the Burman heartland, in many ways the inhabitants of both states have more in common with the peoples of eastern India and Bangladesh.

The Rakhine

Rakhine ethnicity is a controversial topic – are the Rakhine actually Burmans with Indian blood, Indians with Burman characteristics or a separate race (as is claimed by the Rohingya insurgents)? Although the first inhabitants of the region were a dark-skinned Negrito tribe known as the Bilu, later migrants from the eastern Indian subcontinent developed the first Hindu-Buddhist kingdoms in Myanmar before the first Christian millennium. These kingdoms flourished before the invasion of the Tibeto-Burmans from the north and east in the 9th and 18th centuries. The current inhabitants of the state may thus be mixed descendants of all three groups, Bilu, Bengali and Burman.

Much of the English-speaking world knows the region as 'Arakan', a Bengali/Arab/Portuguese version of the local term 'Rakhine', which in turn becomes 'Yakhine' in standard Burmese. The main language spoken in the state is a dialect of Burmese; some groups in the state also speak Bengali-related dialects. The term 'Rakhine/Arakan' probably comes from the Pali name 'Rakkhapura' (in Sanskrit 'Raksapura'), which means 'Land of Ogres', and was a name given to the region by Buddhist missionaries. The obviously pejorative connotation may be a racist reference to the aboriginal Bilu inhabitants (Bilu means 'ogre' in Burmese) whose dark skin, frizzy hair and neolithic lifestyle may have invoked the comparison, or it could have referred to the ruthless exploits of pirates and slave traders who operated along the coast.

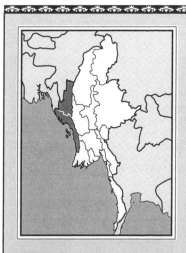

The earliest Rakhine kingdom, Dhanyawady, arose around the first century AD, possibly even earlier. The famous Mahamuni Buddha image today kept at Mahamuni Paya in Mandalay may have been cast here during the reign of King Chandra Suriya (Sandrasuriya in Rakhine) around 150 AD; the locals claim the statue was cast during the 6th century BC, using the living Gautama Buddha as a model! (Art historians agree that no images representing the Buddha were created until several centuries later.)

Dhanyawady was followed by a kingdom known as 'Wethali' ('Vesali' in Pali, 'Waithali' in the Rakhine dialect) in the third century AD. Wethali suffered from invasions by the Mongols in 957 AD, and by Bagan Burmans in the late 11th century. The Burman dominance remained strong until the 15th century when Rakhine came under the influence of the Bengali Islamic kingdom of Gaur. Although the Islamic faith didn't take hold in the area, Islamic ideas regarding maths and science were incorporated into the *zeitgeist* of the increasingly powerful Mrauk U dynasty.

In the 16th and 17th centuries, ports along the coast began receiving Arab, Central Asian, Danish, Dutch and Portuguese traders. Growing international trade enabled Mrauk U (Myohaung) to break free of Burman suzerainty once again and the Mrauk U dynasty came to rule the entire coastline from Chittagong to Yangon (Rangoon), and as far north as Bago (Pegu). The latter was conquered by the Rakhine King Razagyi in 1663. During this period the area's unsavoury reputation as a home for slave traders, pirates and petty tyrants grew. Rakhine rulers combined Brahman astrology, Buddhist cosmology and Islamic mathematics in a series of bell-ringing and chanting rituals called *yadaya* which they believed made them and their kingdom invincible.

Rakhine was re-taken by the Burmans in 1784 under King Bodawpaya, who sent the crown prince and a force of 30,000 to conquer the region and capture the talismanic Mahamuni image. The British annexed the Rakhine region in 1824 after Rakhine refugees in adjacent Raj territories were attacked by the Burman military.

Today the Rakhine harvest marine products from the third-largest fishery site in Myanmar (after the Ayeyarwady Division and Taninthayi Division coasts). Fed by western Myanmar's copious rainfall, four major rivers – the Kaladan, Lemyo, Mayu and Naff – irrigate large and productive rice fields in the lowland areas. The 348-km Kaladan River and its tributaries also serve as the major transport routes to the inland areas of the entire state. Opium is produced at higher elevations in the interior.

The Burmese government denies the existence of a Rohingya minority, a group of around three million people who distinguish themselves from the Rakhine majority by their Islamic faith. Many Rakhine Muslims – or Rohingyas as they prefer to be called – have fled to neighbouring Bangladesh and India to escape Burman persecution.

The Chin

The Chin State, to the immediate north, is hilly and sparsely populated. The people and culture exhibit an admixture of native, Bengali and Indian influences similar to that found among the Rakhine, with a much lower Burman presence. As in the Rakhine State, there have been clear governmental efforts in recent years to promote Burmese culture at the expense of Chin culture, and many Chin have fled west to Bangladesh and India.

Of Tibeto-Burman ancestry, the Chin call themselves Zo-mi or Lai-mi (both terms mean 'mountain people') and share a culture, food and language with the Zo of the adjacent state of Mizoram in India. Outsiders name the different subgroups around the state according to the district in which they live: eg Tidam Chins, Falam Chins, Hakha Chins, etc.

Traditionally the Chin practice swidden (slash-and-burn) agriculture. They are also skilled hunters, and animal sacrifice plays a role in important animistic ceremonies. Currently Chin State has the largest proportion of animists of any state in Myanmar, but the Zo culture is fast disappearing in the face of Christian and Buddhist missionary influences. Some Chin follow the Pau Chin Hau religion, which is based on the worship of a deity called Pasian and named after Pau China Hau, a spiritual leader from the Tidam District who lived from 1859 to 1948. Hau also devised the written Chin language and is at least partially responsible for growing Chin nationalism.

The more traditional Zo or Chin groups live in the south near the Rakhine State border. Chin Christians from the north have bombarded the area with a project called Chin Christianity in One Century (CCOC),

BANGLADESH

Hakha
Tabayin
Shwebo

SAGAING
DIVISION

Budalin
Ayadaw

Chindwin River

Monywa

Lotaw

Gangaw

CHIN STATE

Tilin

Myaing
Yesagyo

Matupi

Pauk
Pakokku

Myingyan

Aungthabye

Paletwa
Sami
Pindawa

Mindat

Nyaung U
Bagan

MANDALAY
DIVISION

Taungbyo

Lemyo River

Buhitaung

Mahamuni

Kyuaktaw

Teinnyo

Chauk
Salay

Kyauk Padaung

Meiktila

Maungtaw

Kaladan River
Magu River

Mrauk U
Myaungbwe

Salin

Koetankauk

Ponnagyun

Minbya

Sidoktaya

Yenangyaung

Donpauk

Pauktaw

RAKHINE
STATE

Dalet
Chaung

Ngape

Minbu

Magwe

Boister
Island

Sittwe

Thoebagwin

Ann
Chaung

Padan

Taungdwingyi

Hanka
Bay

Dalet
Kandauntgyi

Ann

MAGWE
DIVISION

Baronga
Islands

Sakhanmaw

Yebok

Ma-ei
Chaung

Mindon
Thayet
Myayde

Kyaukpyu

Sane

Lamu
Chaung

Yinnbye
Island

Ramree

Isarbyin

Bay of Bengal

Manaung Channel

Taungup
Chaung

Paukkaung

Manaung

Taungup

Padaung

Sinde
Pyay

BAGO DIVISION

Manaung
Island

Ayeyarwady River

Ngapali
Lontha

Thandwe

Gulf of Indu
Thabyugyine

Kyaukki

Thandwe
Chaung

Western
Myanmar

Kyeintali

AYEYARWADY
DIVISION

Minhla
Sitdwin

Kyeintali
Chaung

Letpandon

0   10   20 km

Gwa

Hinthada

Ngathaingchaung

the goal of which is to convert all Chin to the 'one true faith'. The Yangon government, on the other hand, has its own Buddhist missions in the area and are pushing against both the animists and Christians in a battle for the Chin soul.

The Chin National Front, a non-violent nationalist movement active on both sides of the India-Myanmar border, would like to create a sovereign 'Chinland' divided into the states of East Zoram (the current Chin State, Myanmar), West Zoram (part of southeastern Bangladesh plus Tripura, India), Central Zoram (the state of Mizoram, India), and North Zoram (Manipur, India) – a unified area before the British came along.

SITTWE (AKYAB) ဝင်္သင္း

Known to the Bengalis as 'Akyab' and to the Rakhine as 'Saitway', this port city of the Rakhine State sits at the mouth of the Kaladan River where it empties into the Bay of Bengal. Offshore delta islands form a wide protected channel that has served as an important harbour for many centuries. Sittwe has at least a 2000-year history of habitation, though in its modern form the city started as a trading port around 200 years ago and further developed after the British occupation of 1826.

During the British era, international trade along the coast bloomed. Two huge cargo steamers a day plied back and forth between Calcutta and Sittwe; old timers in Sittwe and Mrauk U still wistfully recall the huge Indian mangoes and creamy Bengali halvah that arrived on the ships. Among British colonials, Sittwe had a reputation for malaria and cholera epidemics, although historical records don't seem to support that image – nor is Sittwe a particularly swampy place compared to places further south in the Delta. A historical footnote: Scottish short-story writer and novelist Hector Hugh Munro, known by his pen name 'Saki', was born here in 1870.

For both Buddhists and Muslims in Sittwe, there is a distinctive Rakhine twist on standard Burmese culture that includes the enjoyment of much spicier foods and brighter-coloured clothing. Rakhine women, for example, tend to wear blouses and *longyis* that are pink, orange or red, colours that are somewhat uncommon elsewhere in Myanmar except in conjunction with Buddhist monastic robes.

Information

The main post office sits on the riverfront toward the southern end of town. There is a branch post office one block west of the Prince Guest House on the same side of the street. Mail is said to be fairly reliable here and phone calls to Yangon and abroad may be arranged.

During the monsoon season, July to October, it can rain often and heavily in Sittwe. As in other larger cities in Myanmar, electric power rotates from quarter to quarter, but even when up and running it's generally available from 6 to 11 pm only.

Payagyi

This temple (full name: Atulamarazei Pyilonchantha Payagyi) is located in the centre of town and features a large plain shed supported by pillars decorated with glass mosaic. A large sitting image beneath the shelter was cast in 1900 in the Rakhine style – minus the 'royal attire' (crown and jewelled chestpiece) common to many Rakhine images. The face of the figure shines with gold, while the rest of the body is bronze. It weighs a reported 5425 viss (8680 kg). Next door the **Kyayok Kyaung** features both a Sinhalese and a Burmese-style stupa.

Buddhistic Museum

Housed in a colonial-style building on the grounds of Mahakuthala Kyaungtawgyi ('Large Monastery of Great Merit'), about three blocks east of the canal that runs through town, this modest two-storey museum is the best place in Myanmar to view Rakhine-style Buddha images. Maintained by resident monks, the collection here represents a rare instance of historical preservation in a country where older Buddhas are stolen, bought and sold with frequency – partially due to the dire need for foreign exchange, partially because the Burmese in general associate older Buddhas with karmic accumulations they would rather not contend with.

Most of the images are under a metre in height and feature the royal attire common to Rakhine Buddhas. The majority date to the Mrauk U period, although a few date as far back as the Wethali era, and are made of bronze, silver, nickel, quartz or alabaster. Unique motifs include Buddhas seated on pedestals which are in turn supported on the backs of elephants standing in a circle. In glass cases are numerous small saucers filled with white pebble deemed to be bone relics of the Buddha.

There are also some Indian Buddhas and Hindu deities on display, a few Thai and Japanese Buddhas, plus silver coins from the Mrauk U era, clay pipes, terracotta votive tablets and engraved astrological charts. Entry is free, though donations are gratefully accepted. The sayadaw in charge somewhat narrow-mindedly insists his is the only museum of its kind in the world, even when told that similar Buddhist museums exist in neighbouring countries. He claims the museum will be moving to a new building near the airport, which would be much less convenient, appropriate and atmospheric than its current monastery location.

Around Town

An old steel **clock tower** topped with a weathervane in the centre of town was erected by the Dutch in the 18th century. As a counter-symbol of Burmese nationalism, SLORC (the State Law & Order Restoration Council) built the more ornate white clock tower on Main Rd in 1991.

The tomb of **Babagyi**, a local Muslim saint who lived 200 years ago in Sittwe, can be seen in the town's heavily Bengali Bodawma Quarter – this quarter is also where Sittwe's oldest mosque and oldest Hindu temple are found.

The state government is building a large **cultural museum** next to the mosque on the main road through town, about four blocks south of the Prince Guest House. It will

probably contain exhibits pertaining to the cultural history of the Rakhine State, with a Burman bias naturally.

Waterfront

As a seaside town, Sittwe has plenty of waterfront action. As in many other British-influenced towns in Myanmar, the road along the river is called **The Strand**; a new promenade is being built along the river toward the southern end of town, which when finished will provide a nice walking route between the centre of town and The Point.

The Point is a land projection at the confluence of the Kaladan River and Bay of Bengal. A large terrace constructed over the flat, shale-and-sandstone point is a good spot to catch the breeze and to cool off on hot afternoons. A former lighthouse tower now serves as a viewing platform. There are picnic tables available for public use, and a snack bar at one end is open sunrise to sunset. Fresh coconut juice is available from vendors. Admission to The Point costs K5 per pedestrian, K15 for trishaws, K30 for cars.

South-west of The Point is a beach area with grey-brown sand. Trucks drive onto the beach to collect sand for construction use, but overall it's okay for swimming especially if you move farther west away from The Point toward the new Sittwe Hotel.

About halfway up the shore side of town heading north is an inlet where fishing boats moor. During low tide the boats rest on mudflats, and the fishermen retire to a group of huts on shore. Just north of here is the harbour proper, where ocean-going vessels dock – including oil tankers operated by Myanma Electric Power Enterprise and cargo and passenger ships run by Myanma Five Star Line.

Places to Stay

At the time of writing, the best choice in Sittwe is the *Prince Guest House* (☎ 043-21395) at 27 Main Rd in the centre of town, next door to a small, century-old mosque. This simple three-storey building features basic but clean rooms with ceiling fans and bathroom down the hall at a cost of K500. One huge room with air-con, fridge, private bath and beds with decent mattresses and mosquito nets is available for K2500. Since electric power is only available 6 to 11 pm, the air-con and fridge don't mean much; even when the power is on there's rarely enough voltage to run an air-con unit! As it's at the back of the building, however, this room is quieter than those at the front. There is a small sitting terrace off the third floor.

Gisspa Guest House, just west of the branch post office on a side street, is a three-storey modern building with plain rooms for K75 per person. The mattresses here are exceptionally thin.

In the vicinity of the central market, main post office and Sittway Degree College, *Mya Guest House* (☎ 043-21888) is housed in a massive colonial building with a colonnaded carriageway. The interior is disappointing, however, with unkempt rooms created from wooden partitions that stop well short of the ceiling and mosquito nets for K75 per person. Toilet facilities are down the hall. A couple of rooms with attached bath are also available for K400.

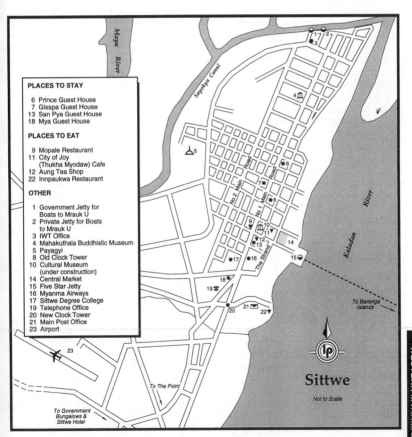

PLACES TO STAY

6 Prince Guest House
7 Gisspa Guest House
13 San Pya Guest House
18 Mya Guest House

PLACES TO EAT

9 Mopale Restaurant
11 City of Joy
   (Thukha Myodaw) Cafe
12 Aung Tea Shop
22 Innpaukwa Restaurant

OTHER

1 Government Jetty for
   Boats to Mrauk U
2 Private Jetty for Boats
   to Mrauk U
3 IWT Office
4 Mahakuthala Buddhistic Museum
5 Payagyi
8 Old Clock Tower
10 Cultural Museum
   (under construction)
14 Central Market
15 Five Star Jetty
16 Myanmar Airways
17 Sittwe Degree College
19 Telephone Office
20 New Clock Tower
21 Main Post Office
23 Airport

Sittwe

Not to Scale

Farther east and closer to the market, the large *San Pya Guest House* offers plenty of the usual cubicles with chicken-wire transoms, plus a couple of rooms with attached bath. The staff don't accept foreigners yet; an ice factory behind the San Pya operates at night and could be noisy.

About a km west of The Point is a government beach hotel open to government officials and state guests only. Supposedly it's being expanded to accommodate foreign tourists and is tentatively named the *Sittwe Hotel*. There are several other very nice-looking government guest houses in the area.

Places to Eat

Seafood and spicy Rakhine curries are what Sittwe kitchens do best. If you can find it, order *kakidit*, a delicious white-fleshed fish caught off the coast of Sittwe, best lightly fried whole and served with a tasty lime-garlic-chilli sauce.

The top place in town is the all-wood, brightly painted *Innpaukwa Restaurant*, directly opposite the main post office on the waterfront. Service is slow and perhaps only two of three dishes served will actually correlate with your order, but it still has good food. The menu is mostly Chinese and seafood; a multi-course meal for three costs around K1000. You can dine indoors or on the terrace which juts out over the adjacent mangrove swamp.

Mopale Restaurant, diagonally opposite the new cultural museum, serves Rakhine and Burmese food. It's the only proper restaurant in town that serves Rakhine dishes and it's open 9 am to 10 pm. Recommended dishes include the roast chicken in curry sauce, the fish curry and dal soup.

Hotter Rakhine curries can also be obtained from various street vendors and *htamin zai* ('rice shops') around town, especially on the street behind the new culture museum. One of Sittwe's specialities is moundi, a Rakhine version of mohinga usually served dry but it may also be served in a light broth instead of the thicker fish stew native to central Myanmar. It usually comes with grilled onions and garlic, chilli sauce and crumbled dried fish. At night vendors light candles along No 1 Main Rd to sell sticky rice and coconut steamed in bamboo joints.

Aung Tea Shop near the market opens early and by 7 am is full of locals savouring the shop's delicious chapati, nam-bya, palata and potato curry. The *City of Joy (Thukha Myodaw) Cafe* in the same general vicinity serves decent si htamin and bei palata, and what looks like slabs of thick French toast – bread fried in egg batter with banana essence. *Two Stars Tea Garden*, opposite Sittway Degree College, is popular with students.

Things to Buy

At the central market, or at one of the few longyi shops in town, you can purchase the famous Rakhine-style longyis. These feature a supplementary-weft weaving technique that creates dense, geometric patterns with a sometimes shimmering patina.

Getting There & Away

Air Myanma Airways fields direct flights from Yangon daily except Tuesday, when flights go via Thandwe (Sandoway). The fare is US$80 on F-27s, US$90 on F-28s. Because of the long distances involved, this is one sector where Myanma Airways tends to use its F-28 jets more frequently.

Sittwe's tiny airport is only 10 minutes from town. It costs K250 to charter a pickup for this short ride, or K50 in a shared pickup. Three small shops next to the airport serve fried rice, moundi, tea, coffee, soft drinks, and beer. Check-in is chaotic; don't forget to clear immigration and customs, for which there are no English signs.

Boat The Inland Water Transport office is near the government Mrauk U Jetty, which sits on Sayokya Canal, a tributary of the Mayu River, which in turn runs north-west off Kaladan River. See the Mrauk U section for details on ferries to Mrauk U.

Myanma Five Star Line ships take two days to reach Sittwe from Yangon, with an overnight at Kyaukpyu. Fares to Yangon are K200 deck class, K400 for a cabin. Check the MFSL office in Yangon or the MFSL office near the Five Star Jetty in Sittwe for shipping dates. See the Getting Around chapter at the beginning of this book for a description of MFSL booking procedures.

Getting Around
Trishaw is the main form of public transport around Sittwe. A ride from Mrauk U Jetty to the Prince Guest House costs K20 per person one way.

AROUND SITTWE
Baronga Islands
Also spelt 'Phaynoka', 'Bayonga' and 'Bayonka', these three islands just offshore, near the mouth of the Kaladan River, could make an interesting day excursion. Hand-dug, privately owned oil wells are a major source of livelihood on the island of East Baronga. The hereditary owners of the wells, called *twin-zar* (literally 'well-eater'), typically employ five worker-partners to operate the well, each of whom receives an equal share of the daily production. Simple tripod pumps extract the crude product, which is sold to local agents who refine the petroleum into diesel, kerosene and wax for local distribution. Although the island oil deposits tapped by the twin-zars are generally too small for industrial purposes, foreign oil companies have recently begun offshore explorations in the area.

Fishermen and coconut farmers live on Middle and West Baronga. The fishing is said to be especially good in the channel between Middle and East Baronga and there are some decent beaches on the western side of West Baronga and along the south-western shore of East Baronga. Regular boats to East Baronga leave from the Mrauk U Jetty (also called Sayokya Jetty) twice a week, but foreigners are supposed to have permission from the regional army command to make this trip. One boat stops at a jetty on the eastern side of the island while a larger one operated by Myanma Oil & Gas Enterprises stops on the western side before continuing on to Yangon. You can also charter a boat to the islands for a round trip

costing US$100 to US$200, depending on the boat.

MRAUK U မြောက်ဦး:
Once a centre for one of Myanmar's most powerful kingdoms, Mrauk U straddles the banks of Aungdat Chaung, a tributary of the Kaladan River, 72 km from the coast. The surrounding rice fields are well watered by the annual monsoon, which brings up to 508 cm of rain per annum. Also cultivated in the region are coconut, banana, jackfruit, mango, areca nut, citrus, lychee and a variety of vegetables.

The Rakhine King Minzawmun founded Mrauk U ('Myauk U' in the Burmese pronunciation) in 1433, though in the common practice of the times, dynastic legends endowed the kingdom with a make-believe 3000-year history. A network of canals allowed access by large boats, even ocean-going vessels.

In the next century the city became a free port that traded with the Middle East, Asia, Holland, Portugal and Spain; elephants were one of the main commodities supplied from the Rakhine region. A Dutchman who visited Mrauk U in the 16th century described it as one of the richest cities in Asia, and compared it with Amsterdam and London in size and prosperity. The remains of a European quarter called Daingri Kan can still be seen south-west of town.

The Mrauk U dynasty, which lasted 352 years, was much feared by the peoples of the Indian subcontinent and central Myanmar, who called the Rakhine warlords 'Magh' (the origins of this name are lost). Mrauk U kings even hired Japanese samurai as bodyguards against assassination. At Mrauk U's peak, King Minbin (1531-53) created a naval fleet of 10,000 warboats that dominated the Bay of Bengal and Gulf of Martaban.

Mrauk U was a successor to two earlier kingdoms in the area: Dhanyawady (circa 1st to 6th centuries) and Wethali (3rd to 10th centuries), the remains of which are still visible to the north. All three kingdoms blended elements of Theravada and Mahayana Buddhism with Hinduism and Islam. In the late 18th century, the Konbaung dynasty asserted its power over the region and Mrauk U was integrated into the Burman kingdoms centred around Mandalay.

After the First Anglo-Burmese War (1824-26), the British Raj annexed Rakhine and set up its administrative headquarters in Sittwe, thus turning Mrauk U into a political backwater virtually overnight. The Burmese name gradually changed to Myohaung, 'Old City', though the Rakhine continued to call the town Mrauk U. According to Maurice Collis, author of *Into Hidden Burma*, the name Mrauk U means 'Monkey Egg' though he never ascertained the origin of this meaning.

Today the original city lies in ruins and a small, poor town with simple buildings of brick, wood and thatch has grown up adjacent to the old city site. It's the kind of town where every man, woman and child seems to chew betel and smoke cheroots. The town is intersected by several canals, the main source of transport and water. Much of the daily activity seems to be taken up in water trips to and from the canals. Instead of the usual clay pots or rectangular oil cans employed in most of the rest of Myanmar, Mrauk U residents carry shiny aluminium waterpots imported from India on their hips with one arm crooked around the pot's neck.

One of the best times – or worst depending on your tastes – to visit Mrauk U is during the huge *paya pwe* ('pagoda festival') held in mid-May. Centred on the large grassy open area to the southern side of Dukkanthein, the festival lasts around a week and features the usual menu of fortune-tellers, craft vendors, seriocomic theatre, music and food.

Temples of Mrauk U

For a full description of the history and architectural styles of the temples of old Mrauk U, turn to the special section at the back of this chapter, beginning on page 379. This section also incorporates the map of the general Mrauk U area.

Places to Stay & Eat

The only place to consider staying in town

so far is the very basic *Myanantheingi Guest House*, which costs K50 for locals, K200 for foreigners. It has a thatched roof and walls with wooden partitions and floors. There are only six small rooms; the corner rooms have the best ventilation and are a bit larger. Toilet and shower facilities are located in the rear of the house. There are a couple of other places closed to foreigners that cost around K50 per person – the *Dhanyawady* and the *Co-operative* – but the quality is far below that of the Myanantheingi.

The *Mrauk U Hotel*, a joint government and private venture, will supposedly be built near the ruins area. Only a sign announcing it would open in October 1996 had been erected when we visited. If the project is completed, rates will probably run from US$30 for an economy single to US$45 or US$50 for a standard double.

Decent food is hard to come by in Mrauk U. An unnamed restaurant opposite Khite San Tailor on the main street serves fried rice, noodles, soup, fried vegetables and noodle soup. The *Dhanyawady Tea & Cold Drink Shop* (no English sign) opposite the market isn't bad. It has the usual teashop snacks and is especially good for breakfast, when kyet-u palata (egg palatas) with onions and chillies are served.

U Kyaw Taw, the English-speaking owner of *U Yebaw Rice Mill*, may be able to provide lodging and very good Rakhine food if you give him a day's notice.

Getting There & Away

Both government and private ferries make the river trip between Sittwe and Mrauk U. The government boats are old double-decker Irrawaddy Flotilla craft that carry at least twice the number of passengers they were designed to carry. The lower steel deck is chaos, while the upper deck is also quite crowded but has a limited number of sling chairs, plus a salon cabin. Foreigners are supposed to pay US$4 to IWT for a round-trip ticket in 'sling-chair class' but if you manage to get the local price you'll pay K11 for the basic passage plus K15 for a sling chair.

The salon cabin has 10 or so wooden chairs and a table and seems to be reserved for VIPs or those who can afford the expected bribe of K100 to move from the sling chair area into the salon. It's the coolest part of boat since it gets direct breezes through windows, and it has an attached toilet room.

Before you're allowed on the boat in Sittwe you'll probably be sent to fill out some papers at the IWT office, where most of the 20-odd staff sit around gossiping and drinking tea amid thick stacks of tattered, yellowing forms wrapped in brown paper. It can take around 30 minutes to complete these formalities, though we would expect this procedure to streamline in the future as more foreigners make their way to Mrauk U.

The ferries leave from the Mrauk U Jetty on Sayokya Chaung at the northern end of Sittwe on Monday, Tuesday, Thursday, Friday and Saturday. Departure times depend on the tide, but boats usually leave in the early morning on the way upriver, early afternoon on the way down.

On the way the boat stops at the town of Ponnagyun ('Brahman Island') on the 26-km-long island of the same name. On a hill nearby you can see the stupa of U Yit Taung Paya, supposedly erected in 993 AD and renovated in 1521, 1641 and 1688. The lower half of the large bell shape is whitewashed, the upper half gilded. Vendors standing on the pier extend bamboo poles holding plastic bags of curry and rice to passengers on the boat. It takes about four hours to reach Mrauk U.

Private ferries to Mrauk U cost K50 per person and go on Wednesday and Sunday, the two 'off' days for the government boats. These are single-deck boats that are usually every bit as crowded as the government boats and overall less comfortable. For K15,000 you can charter a private boat to Mrauk U and back, half that in one direction. Most types of boats take about 4½ hours to Mrauk U, five hours back. For part of the way the boats move against the current on the Kaladan River, then they turn east onto the Theinganadi River and go with the current before turning upriver again on the Henyakaw River. The government boat terminates in Kyauktaw, another four hours north of Mrauk U on the Kaladan River, connected to Mrauk U by the Theinganadi River.

Coming back, the government boat arrives from Kyauktaw on the way to Sittwe around 11.30 am, depending on tide and season. This is usually the most crowded direction because people from the villages upcountry are carrying goods to sell in Sittwe.

Getting Around

Mrauk U is small enough that you can get around most of the town easily on foot. A trishaw costs K10 to K15 anywhere in town, about double that if you want to be taken out to the major ruins or to the ferry jetty. Few trishaw drivers seem to be able to change a K100 note.

AROUND MRAUK U
Wethali

Just under 10 km north of Mrauk U are the remains of the Wethali or Vesali ('Waithali' in the local parlance) kingdom. According to Rakhine chronicles, Wethali was founded in 327 AD by King Mahataing Chandra. Archaeologists believe that this kingdom lasted until the 8th century. Of the oval-shaped city boundaries that remain, only parts of the moat and walls are still visible amid the rice fields. Many of the hillocks around this area are actually overgrown stupas. A central palace site – whose walls are relatively well preserved – measures about 500 by 300 metres. The palace prayer hall is now used as an irrigation tank during the rainy season.

Other than these meagre, unexcavated ruins, there is but one other sight worth seeing in Wethali. The **Great Image of Su Taung Prai** sits in the base of a large pahto that is missing all of its superstructure. Now covered with a corrugated metal roof, the five-metre, Rakhine-style sitting Buddha and its pedestal are said to be made from one piece of solid stone and date to 327 AD. The highly revered image is swathed in embroidered red holy cloth and attended by monks and nuns; an umbrella painted with runes stands over the figure. Pilgrims are starting to gild the image from the top down by handing goldleaf squares to an attendant, who climbs a bamboo scaffold to affix the gold to the head of the image.

Regular public transport to Wethali from Mrauk U is scarce, but you can arrange to charter a jeep or pickup through the Myanantheingi Guest House from between US$8 to US$10 for a roundtrip. The once or twice-daily pickup north to Mahamuni and Kyauktaw passes Wethali. Hitching might be possible though traffic on this road is light.

Mahamuni

The **Mahamuni Paya**, located 40 km north of Mrauk U and about 10 km east of the farm town of Kyauktaw, sits at the north-eastern corner of the old Dhanyawady city site. This was the original site for Mandalay's famous Mahamuni Buddha, a huge and very old bronze image which Rakhine kings believed provided supernatural protection for their successive kingdoms. When the Burmans under King Bodawpaya invaded Rakhine in 1784, they dismantled the image into three pieces and hauled it over the Rakhine Yoma to Amarapura to further legitimise the Konbaung dynasty.

Some Rakhine say the Burmans unknowingly took a counterfeit figure and that the true Mahamuni image lies hidden somewhere in the jungle. Nowadays three smaller stone images sit on the pedestal where the Mahamuni image once sat. A famous sandstone stele found here depicts a Gupta-style Buddha dating from 400 to 500 AD.

The current Konbaung-style shrine buildings date to the 18th or 19th centuries, as the earlier ones were destroyed by fire. One of the infamous yadaya bells used by Rakhine rulers to keep invaders at bay was once displayed here but has disappeared in recent years.

You can reach the town of Mahamuni by taking a boat to Kyauktaw (four hours from Mrauk U) and from there catching a pickup east to Mahamuni. It's quicker to go to

Kyauktaw by road from Mrauk U (50 km, about three hours) but this would involve a vehicle charter.

NGAPALI BEACH ငပလီပင်လယ်ကမ်း

Of the four beach resorts most accessible to Myanmar visitors, Ngapali is the prettiest. The origins of the name is something of a mystery, though the most popular story says a homesick Italian who lived here for awhile told everyone the beach reminded him of beaches near Naples. The Burmese name does have a meaning of its own – roughly 'Inveigling Fish'. It's the kind of name that should come with a story but no one in the area seems to know one, so perhaps the meaning has been grafted to the Burmese pronunciation.

Backed by swaying palms and casuarinas, the Ngapali area is a good place to relax and take a break from the rigours of Myanmar road travel. The very broad, pristine stretch of sand known as Ngapali Beach reaches over three km, and is separated from several more beaches by small, easily negotiated rocky headlands. Surfing is possible during the monsoon season (mid-May through to mid-September), but unfortunately the beach hotels tend to close down then because of the heavy rains. If you're determined to visit during this time of year you may still be able to find a place in the nearby township seat of Thandwe.

There's more to do around Ngapali than just sit on the white sand and splash around in the sea, though for many people that's motivation enough. Even the beach in front of the main hotel is a centre of activity. Fishermen begin setting and drawing drift nets before dawn and continue into the late morning, when they load their catches in baskets. Women carry the baskets of fish on foot to nearby villages, then return with lunch for the men; everyone breaks to eat at midday, then some pack up while others continue fishing till early evening.

If you manage to rent a bicycle (at the Ngapali Beach Hotel, or at one of the restaurants near the hotel or in Thandwe), you can tour several of the villages. Just north of

Ngapali Beach are the small villages of **Ngapali** and **Lintha**, both supported by the area's bounteous harvest of fish, coconuts and rice. **Kyiktaw** to the immediate south of Ngapali Beach is similar, followed by **Myabyin**, a larger and more interesting village with a market, a couple of teashops, monasteries and a government rice-storage facility.

If you choose to walk along the beach to these villages, rather than cycle along the paved road opposite the beach, you'll pass large areas of the beach where the villagers sun-dry fish, shrimp and coconut on cane mats spread over the sand. Just offshore near these villages are several small, rocky islets reachable during low tide, and a bit farther south there's a mangrove marsh. Further offshore are the larger islands of **Balet** and **Kayi**; a two-hour boat trip to these islands can be arranged at Zaw Restaurant, opposite Ngapali Beach Hotel, for K1500.

Further south still is the village of **Lontha** and an inlet of the same name backed by a sweeping curve of mangrove and sand. It's prettiest at high tide; during ebb tide the bay becomes muddy and rocky. There's a pier here, and the inlet is heavily used by smaller fishing boats since it's the most protected harbour in this area. The inlet is connected to a larger bay called the **Gulf of Indu** on recent government maps, 'Andrew Bay' on older colonial maps. All of these villages are connected by a sealed, two-lane road that ends at the Lontha jetty.

On the other side of the bay (accessible only by boat from this point – or by taking another road further inland) is the village of **Thabyugyine**. This village has a MFSL jetty used by the big fishing trawlers and MFSL ships as well as a large seafood processing plant near this jetty.

Places to Stay
You don't have much choice when it comes to accommodation at Ngapali. The mainstay is the *Ngapali Beach Hotel* (☎ Thandwe 28), positioned right on the beach, where two-room wooden bungalows with louvred walls and shaded verandahs cost US$25/30 single/double for a 'standard' room, US$40/45 for a 'superior' room. Both types of rooms are large and feature mosquito nets and attached cold-water baths. The only difference between the two we could readily discern was that the superior rooms feature a partition on the verandah for more privacy, along with a slightly newer paint job. Electric power is provided at night only. Trees and palm-thatch umbrellas on the beach provide shade. Treehouse-like platforms built into the banyan trees on the beach are a nice place to read or nap while catching a breeze.

Immediately south, the *New Ngapali Beach Hotel* (☎ Thandwe 27) is a new section under the same management but with a different name. These two-storey modern bungalows lack any sort of treeline in front, so are unshaded and exposed to full sun; unlike the old section there are no louvred walls to admit sea breezes. Air-con is provided but you're at the mercy of a generator that may or not be able to provide enough voltage to operate more than one or two air-con units at a time. Rooms here cost US$70 single, US$80 double and feature carpets and private baths with hot water.

North of the old section stands the *Shwer War Kyaing Hotel*, a two-storey wooden affair with several large, decaying buildings. It was closed and locked when we visited, even though it was Ngapali's high season; rumours say it's up for sale.

Ngapali Beach is most popular during the months of March and April, when rooms at the Ngapali Beach Hotel and New Ngapali Beach Hotel may be full. You'll have a better chance mid-week than on weekends.

Places to Eat
The Ngapali Beach Hotel has an open-air beachside restaurant with decent and reasonably priced food (kyats acceptable). Sunset views are a bonus.

Almost opposite the New Ngapali Beach Hotel section is *Kyi Nue Yake (Reik) Restaurant*, a small, friendly family-run place with fresh seafood plus Burmese and Chinese dishes – and an English-language menu. *Zaw Restaurant*, opposite the hotel, is very similar. Prices at both are low to moderate.

Getting There & Away

See the Thandwe section for details on air and road travel to Thandwe, the transport hub for the region.

Getting Around

A jeep taxi from Thandwe or Thandwe Airport to the Ngapali Beach Hotel costs K800. Thandwe, Kyiktaw, Myabyin, Lintha and Lontha are all linked by narrow sealed roads and can be visited by bicycle. Though there are no regular bike rental places, you should be able to make arrangements through the staff at the hotel or through one of the restaurants across the road.

THANDWE (SANDOWAY) သံတွဲ

Located around 9.5 km north-east of Ngapali Beach, Thandwe (also spelt Thantwe) is the seat of a township by the same name with a population of approximately 80,000. Around 25% of the township population is Muslim, most of whom live in the small township and attend the five mosques located there. For the most part the surrounding villages are Buddhist.

Thandwe has been a key Rakhine centre for many centuries and may originally have been an independent principality with the Sanskrit name of Dvaravati (roughly translated as 'Gated Kingdom', a name borrowed from India's *Ramayana* epic). Thandwe ('Iron-Fastened') may in fact be a Burmese corruption of this name. When the British stationed a garrison here at the turn of the century, they twisted the name into 'Sandoway'.

The town boasts a network of sealed and unsealed streets lined with two-storey buildings around 50 to 100 years old, constructed of masonry on the ground floors and wood on the upper floors. Away from the centre of town, virtually all houses are made of thatch. A former British jail in the centre of town is now used as a market where vendors sell medicinal herbs, clothes, textiles, hardware and free-market consumer goods. Among the many small shops surrounding the market are a number of gold shops, which

suggests that the area is marked by some wealth.

Along the road between Thandwe and Ngapali you'll see a number of rubber plantations, including terraced ones – a deviation from the usual flat groves seen in most parts of the world. Rice and coconuts are also heavily farmed in the area. A battalion from the Tatmadaw's 55th Regiment has replaced the old British garrison outside town – so it's not unusual to see trucks overflowing with men in green on the roads.

Three stupas perched on hillsides at the edge of town are of mild interest. **Sandaw Paya**, reportedly built in 784 AD by the Rakhine King Minyokin to house a Buddha hair relic and rebuilt by the Burmese in 1876, is a fairly ordinary stupa that affords good views of the town, river and surrounding hill. **Nandaw Paya**, on a higher hill opposite, was supposedly erected in 761 by King Minbra to enshrine a rib or piece of a rib of the Buddha. **Andaw Paya**, on a lower hill, claims a molar relic and a dating of 763. Outside one of the shrine buildings at Nandaw stands an old sculpture of a Rakhine king that reportedly dates to the 6th century. A stone niche, inscribed in the Pali language using Rakhine script, says the king reigned from 525 to 575 AD.

Places to Stay & Eat

The *San Yeik Nyein Guest House*, a set of bare but adequate wooden rooms with shared facilities set over a video house a block south of the market, charges K60 per person. This guest house was not accepting foreigners when we came along but it may be worth a try. At the eastern edge of town near a mosque is the less preferable *Mla Guest House*, similarly priced and unlicensed – this one doubles as a brothel.

Thandwe has little in the way of restaurants despite its apparent relative prosperity. Next to the market, almost opposite a large mosque, is a very good teashop called *Point*, which offers whitewashed chairs instead of the usual tiny stools. Sticky rice and palatas are usually available here. There are several other tea and cold drink shops in this area, and in the market itself there are a few questionable-looking noodle vendors.

On the next street south, a few blocks west of the San Yeik Nyein Guest House, *Jupiter Food & Drink* serves a mix of Chinese and Indian pastries, including baosi, ei kyar kway and samosas.

Getting There & Away

Air Air Mandalay (AM) flies from Yangon to Thandwe and back on Monday, Wednesday and Saturday. The flight takes 50 minutes and costs US$80 confirmed, US$75 standby.

Myanma Airways (MA) also flies to Thandwe from Yangon on Tuesday, Thursday and Saturday. For this route MA usually employs an F-28, which takes only 40 minutes to reach Thandwe; by F-27 the flights take a little longer. The fare from Yangon is US$55 by F-28, US$50 by F-27. On Tuesday MA also fields planes from Sittwe for US$50/55 and on Saturday there's a flight via Kyaukpyu for US$30/35.

MA doesn't fly to Thandwe during the rainy season (mid-May through to mid-September). AM is asking for permission to fly year round, though it may turn out there aren't enough passengers during the rainy season to make a year-round schedule worthwhile.

MA maintains a ticket office in the centre of Thandwe. AM has no office in Thandwe yet; eventually they may establish a local office, most likely at the Ngapali Beach Hotel. Until then the only time you can speak with a representative is when there's an AM plane on the runway at Thandwe Airport – the rep accompanies each flight from Yangon, spends about an hour taking care of business at the airport, then boards the return flight to Yangon. If you want to buy or confirm a ticket out of Thandwe, be sure to turn up at the airport around 3 pm on Monday, Wednesday or Saturday, when the AM flights are scheduled to arrive.

Bus & Taxi A variety of buses, pickups and taxis operate regionally out of Thandwe. A government bus between Thandwe and Yangon costs only K400, with an overnight in Pyay (Prome) when heading north or Sinde (opposite Pyay) when heading south, but anyone who would endure this 24-hour trip without planning a more appealing stopover must be either crazy or in a very big hurry (and too impecunious to fly).

If you decide to break the trip up into sections there are two different routes to choose from. The longer and more trying, but more scenic route from the south starts in Pathein (Bassein). A bus from Pathein north-west to Ngathaingchaung costs K50 and takes around four or five hours. Buses continue along a new road from Ngathaingchaung to Gwa (mornings only) on the coast for K100; this leg takes six hours or more. From Gwa one bus per day heads straight north to Thandwe on a dusty, unsealed road, a nine-hour trip that costs K50. Much of the trade on this route is cargo rather than passengers.

If you're coming from the north there's no need to go all the way south to Pathein as there are direct buses from Hinthada on the Ayeyarwady River – or better yet use the shorter route from Pyay. Direct buses from Pyay to Thandwe cost K200 – there are only one or two per day, starting early in the morning. It takes around five hours to cover the 167 km from Pyay to Taungup on the coast (including a ferry trip across the Ayeyarwady River at Pyay), then another three hours to finish the 86 km from Taungup to Thandwe. The Taungup Pass in the Rakhine Yoma was only breached in 1960.

Thandwe's bus terminal sits at the side of the road that leads to Andaw Paya on the edge of town.

Car If you can find a car and driver willing to endure the wear and tear, you can accomplish the same routes described above by private vehicle. A set of new roads under construction will allow continued road travel north of Taungup as far as Sittwe and beyond to Taungbyo on the Bangladesh border. By the time you read this the entire route from Ngathaingchaung to Sittwe – about 840 km – should be driveable.

Boat MFSL sends ships from Yangon to Thabyugyine Jetty south of Thandwe every 15 days or so. If you can manage a permit, the journey will take you around 12 hours at the cost of K200 for deck class or K546 for a berth in saloon class. MFSL maintains an office in Thandwe right around the corner from the Myanma Airways office. Dates for voyages to Yangon are posted on a chalkboard.

You can charter a boat from the Thabyugyine Jetty to the Lontha Jetty for K400. From Lontha there are regular buses to Thandwe for K5.

Getting Around
Most of Thandwe is easily seen on foot. Trishaws are available for short trips around town for K15 or K20 per person per km.

A taxi-jeep ride from Thandwe to Thandwe Airport, a distance of 6.5 km, will cost around K800. Valiant trishaw drivers will pedal the latter distance for K450.

Local buses – real buses as well as pickups – cruise several times a day from Thandwe to Lontha for K5; you can get off at Ngapali Beach along the way.

THAYA BEACH သာယာပင် လယ်ကမ်း
The Rakhine coast's latest beach resort is 26 km north of Gwa, a small town on the coast just north of the Ayeyarwady Division border, and 130 km south of Thandwe. Thaya Beach extends a sandy five km, but few people know about the place yet.

The bungalow-style *Kanthaya Beach Resort* should be open by the time you read this. Accommodation will cost about the same as at the Ngapali Beach Hotel, starting at US$25. As elsewhere in Myanmar, cheaper accommodation may come along as demand grows.

It's about six to seven hours by car from Yangon via Ngathaingchaung, about four to five hours from Pathein or five hours from Ngapali. See the Getting There & Away section under Thandwe for details on public transport to Gwa from Ngathaingchaung and Thandwe.

An old airfield outside Gwa may eventually be renovated for use by Air Mandalay and/or Myanmar Airways flights.

EXCURSIONS INTO SOUTHERN CHIN STATE
Although it's possible to visit the northern part of the Chin State by road from Kalewa in the Sagaing Division, the true heart of traditional Chin culture is found in the south. **Paletwa**, just over the state line from the Rakhine State, can be reached via boat along the Kaladan River from Sittwe or Kyauktaw. A new road under construction between Mahamuni and Paletwa will also allow vehicle travel direct from Mrauk U when completed.

In the Chin Hills some women still tattoo their faces, though it's a custom that's fading fast. At higher elevations they wear thick, striped cotton blankets draped over the body and ornaments of copper and bronze. Among the Khamui, a sub-tribe that inhabits the lower elevations of southern Chin State, unmarried women wear short skirts and little else. Chin men tend to wear simple Western-style dress such as shirts and trousers.

While the Chin State is currently off limits to foreigners, a source at the Ministry of Hotels & Tourism told us it would soon be open to visitors with travel permits and guides. At the moment there is no licensed lodging in the state.

WESTERN MYANMAR

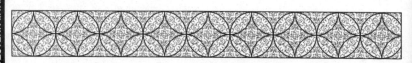

TEMPLES OF MRAUK U

TEMPLES OF MRAUK U

Unlike Bagan (Pagan), where temple ruins are strewn over a vast plain, the ruins of Mrauk U sit on or against bluffs in hilly terrain interlaced with streams and leafy trees. Overall this lends a more intimate, friendly feeling to the place. In addition to the major sites located a km or two north-east of town, there are lots of crumbling stupas next to the town itself, especially on hillocks along the stream at the southern end of town – a nice area for sunrise or sunset strolls.

Altogether there are around 70 named temple, stupa or city wall sites around Mrauk U, plus dozens of other unnamed sites. Only the more significant temple and stupa sites are described below. Most of the city walls are found to the eastern side of town, since the west, north and south provided natural defences in the form of hills and streams. The walls were built to fill in the gaps in these natural barriers, so they appear intermittently.

Palace Ruins & Museum

Walls and gateways of sandstone blocks and earth are all that's left of the Mrauk U royal palace, built in 1430 according to some sources, as late as 1553 according to others. A Portuguese monk and envoy to Mrauk U described the palace as it appeared during his visit in the 1630s:

The royal palaces...have massive wooden columns of such extraordinary lengthy and straightness that one wonders there are trees so tall and so straight. The inside columns are entirely gilt, without any admixture of other materials. In the same palace there is a hall gilt from top to bottom which they call the 'Golden House' because it has a vine of the purest gold which occupies the whole roof of the hall, with a hundred and odd gourds of the same pure gold. There are also in that very rich house seven idols of gold, each of the size and proportions of an average man. These idols are adorned on the forehead, breast, arms and waist with many fine precious stones, rubies, emeralds and sapphires, and also with some brilliant old rock diamonds of more than ordinary size.

Unfortunately the palace buildings were lost to fire long ago. A museum within the old palace walls contains a good collection of religious sculpture and other artefacts unearthed around Mrauk U. In the yard out front there are several sandstone figures, including a Hindu *yoni* (a vagina-shaped pedestal designed to support a Shiva *lingam* or phallus), headless Buddhas, Vishnu figures and various inscribed stelae.

Inside is a collection of Wethali, Mrauk U and Konbaung period Buddhas and bodhisattvas, votive tablets, small bronze stupas, Krishna statuettes, Buddha heads, musical instruments, sandstone lintels from 15th-century monuments, some broken pieces of painted frescoes from the Shittaung temple, painted ceramics, one large 4th-century relief from Kyauktaw depicting the Buddha teaching one of his disciples, *dvarapalas* (gate guardians) from the 14th-century Mrauk U palace and ornate 16th-century Portuguese headstone slabs bearing astrological runes. Among the more historically interesting artefacts are a set of stelae dating between the 8th and 16th centuries and inscribed with several different scripts, including Arabic. Some of the Mrauk U Buddhas on display are exquisite in design.

Hours for the museum don't seem to be regular – in fact it's often locked. However, it's well worth seeking out the caretaker to get in. Some items are English-labelled, though most labels appear in Burmese only. Admission is free.

Shittaung

The most complex and well-preserved of the surviving Mrauk U temples,

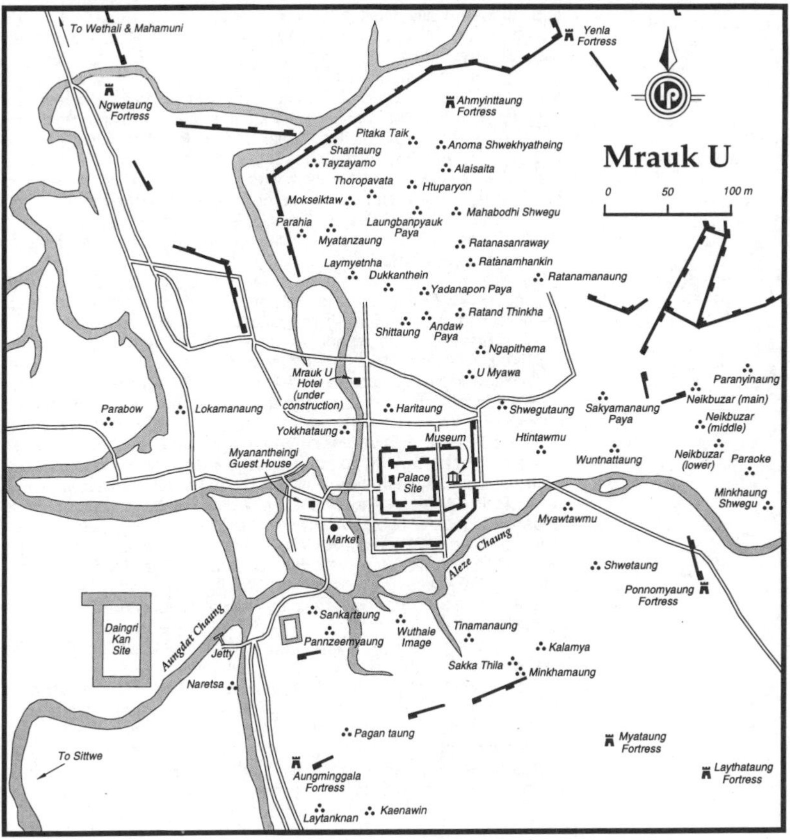

Mrauk U

Map labels (clockwise/by region):

To Wethali & Mahamuni · Yenla Fortress · Ngwetaung Fortress · Ahmyinttaung Fortress · Pitaka Taik · Shantaung · Anoma Shwekhyatheing · Tayzayamo · Thoropavata · Alaisaita · Htuparyon · Mokseiktaw · Laungbanpyauk Paya · Mahabodhi Shwegu · Parahia · Myatanzaung · Ratanasanraway · Laymyetnha · Ratanamhankin · Dukkanthein · Yadanapon Paya · Ratanamanaung · Shittaung · Ratand Thinkha · Andaw Paya · Ngapithema · Mrauk U Hotel (under construction) · U Myawa · Lokamanaung · Haritaung · Shwegutaung · Sakyamanaung Paya · Paranyinaung · Neikbuzar (main) · Parabow · Yokkhataung · Museum · Htintawmu · Wuntnattaung · Neikbuzar (middle) · Neikbuzar (lower) · Paraoke · Myanantheingi Guest House · Palace Site · Minkhaung Shwegu · Market · Myawtawmu · Alezz Chaung · Myawtawmu · Shwetaung · Daingri Kan Site · Jetty · Aungdat Chaung · Sankartaung · Pannzeemyaung · Wuthaie Image · Tinamanaung · Ponnomyaung Fortress · Kalamya · Naretsa · Sakka Thila · Minkhamaung · Pagan taung · Myataung Fortress · To Sittwe · Aungminggala Fortress · Laytanknan · Kaenawin · Laythataung Fortress

0   50   100 m

Shittaung (Sittaung to the Burmese) was built in 1535 by King Minbin, the most powerful of the Rakhine kings. The name means 'Shrine of the 80,000 Images', a reference to the number of holy images found inside. A maze-like floor plan – which vaguely resembles a square-cornered pinwheel – suggests the shrine was originally used for Tantric-like initiation rituals. A walk through each of the interior passages exposed the initiate to different set of formulaic Buddhist messages carved in sandstone on the walls. With its thick walls, tiny windows and commanding views of the surrounding area, the temple may have also served as a royal fortress during times of attack.

Shittaung sits on a bluff known as Phokhaung Taung and presents a layered quadrangle studded with straight-sided stupas that curve gently at the top where they are joined to their *sikharas* (temple finial). Though much fewer in number, the stupas are very reminiscent of Indonesia's Borobudur in shape, general absence of ornamentation and in the way they rise platform to platform. The large central and topmost stupa is flanked by 33 smaller stupas lined up in flaring angles to the northern and southern walls, while two significant sandstone stupas sit on the lowest platform – the circular Nay Win Paya ('Sunset Paya') and octagonal Nay Htwet Paya ('Sunrise Stupa').

The entire monument features a mortarless assembly of laterite and sandstone blocks carried to Mrauk U by boat along local rivers and streams. At the northern entrance to the complex stands the Shittaung Pillar, a three-metre, four-sided obelisk brought from Wethali to Mrauk U by King Minbin in 1535. Three sides of the pillar are inscribed in Sanskrit; the earliest inscription, facing east, is for the most part illegible but has been dated to between the 3rd and 6th centuries, ie the middle of the Dhanyawady era. The western face dates to the early 8th century and displays a list of Rakhine kings, while the northern face is ascribed to King Minrazagyi in 1593.

A walking tour of the monument takes one through four separate passages, five if you include the reliefs on the exterior walls. The latter are difficult to see unless you climb out onto the crumbling ledges in front of the reliefs. The reliefs appear to represent figures from Hindu-Buddhist mythologies – considered nats by the Burmese today – who are both protecting and paying homage to the temple interior. Many of these reliefs have decayed into an unrecognisable state and some are missing altogether.

The first outer chamber inside Shittaung features arched passages along the outside wall with pairs of Buddha images sitting back to back. The inner wall of the 94-metre passage bears sandstone slabs with high relief cut into six tiers. The lowest tier depicts people in Rakhine dress engaged in festival-oriented activities – boxing, dancing, drama, wrestling – plus work-related activities using elephants, water buffaloes and oxen. On the middle four tiers over a thousand separate sculptures chronicle 550 *jatakas* (scenes from the Buddha's life). Along the top layer of reliefs male and female figures participate in devotional activities. The teaching impetus of the reliefs perhaps implies that festival-going and making a living are lower sorts of human activities; learning about the history of the Buddha represents a step up, and then actually taking an active role in the religion is the highest custom. Some of the reliefs bear paint remnants. Small depressions along lower ledges were designed to hold oil for illumination. Nowadays the temple caretakers request a small donation to turn on electric lights in the concentric passageways.

The two inner galleries display hundreds of Buddha images in niches, while a Buddha footprint is the terminal point of the innermost passage,

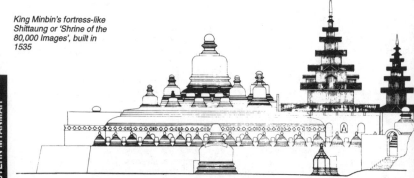

King Minbin's fortress-like Shittaung or 'Shrine of the 80,000 Images', built in 1535

taking the visitor from an appreciation for the serenity and wisdom of the Buddha to the knowledge that he actually walked on this spot – or so it is said – during his post-enlightenment travels. The route set by the first three passages moves in the traditional clockwise direction but when you come to the Buddha footprint, you're forced to double back counterclockwise through the smallest and darkest chamber – a twist perhaps further indicative of Tantric influence. Due to the insulating quality of the surrounding laterite substructure, each passageway feels cooler than the last – a perfect sensual metaphor for the psychologically 'cooling' effect of the Buddhist teachings.

The best of the Buddha sculptures are reserved for the innermost sanctuary and for the large prayer hall added to the eastern side of the temple where there was once a courtyard. Throughout the monument the images represent typical Rakhine style, though most have been restored and many are badly painted. Several images were gathered from other monuments in the region, including the Wethali and Dhanyawady sites. One Wethali image we couldn't identify looked like it had worms crawling out of its ears.

The prayer hall itself features an impressively carved and painted wooden ceiling. A lintel around the large portico into the main chamber has been restored in the original style. A Kala head over this entry is surrounded by devas, and a Brahma sits above Kala – a Hindu schema adopted by the Buddhists to show the devotion practised by Hindu deities in the presence of the Buddha.

Andaw Paya

Less than a dozen metres to the north-east of Shittaung stands a smaller, eight-sided monument with a similar linear layout – rectangular prayer hall to the east, multi-spired sanctuary to the west. Sixteen *zedis* are aligned in a square-cornered U-shape around the southern, northern and western platforms. As at Shittaung, small windows admit light and ventilation. In this case there are only two concentric passageways lined with Buddha niches; at the innermost core of the shrine an eight-sided pillar supports the roof.

The original construction of the shrine is ascribed to King Minhlaraza in 1521. King Minrazagyi then rebuilt Andaw in 1596 to enshrine a piece of the tooth relic supposedly brought from Sri Lanka by King Minbin in the early 16th century. Most likely the roof-line sikharas date to his later reconstruction, as their slender, terraced style is very different to that found at Shittaung.

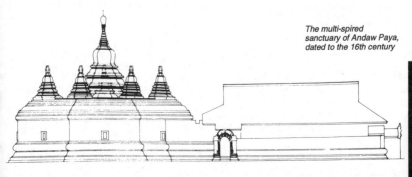

The multi-spired sanctuary of Andaw Paya, dated to the 16th century

WESTERN MYANMAR

Yadanapon Paya

The largest stupa in the area stands just north of Andaw Paya. Damaged by WW II bombing, only the bottom 'bell' portion and base remain standing. Even minus the original sikhara – now a pile of brick rubble lying to the sides – the brick structure reaches 60 metres in height. According to local chronicles, the mammoth stupa was sponsored by Mrauk U's Queen Shin Htway in 1612.

Sandstone *chinthes* at each of the four corners of the surrounding wall remain semi-intact. Along one side of the monument bricks have either fallen or been removed to form a rudimentary stairway to the top – a good spot for a sunset view of the surrounding ruins.

Dukkanthein

Said to have been constructed by order of King Minphalaung in 1571, Dukkanthein stands on a bluff a hundred metres opposite and to the north-west of Shittaung. A loose translation of the name is 'ordination hall that spiritually reinforces the town', and it certainly looks like a huge bunker from the outside. Although the overall structure is intact, a closer inspection shows it to be in a state of disrepair, with weeds and plants sprouting from cracks between the laterite and sandstone bricks.

Wide stone stairways lead up the eastern and southern sides of the tall base. Simple dome-shaped stupas similar to those at Shittaung stand atop receding terraces over a large, slope-sided sanctuary. Two inner cloisters form a U shape around the central rectangular sanctum in which a series of steps ascend to an egg-shaped Buddha chamber. The cloisters are lined with 146 Buddha niches along with sandstone reliefs depicting 64 different types of hairstyles for the wives of Mrauk U nobility. A tall entranceway on the east side admits light into this interior chamber.

Pitaka Taik

This compact, highly ornate building is now surrounded by rice fields in a secluded site accessible by a narrow path around 300 metres north-east of Dukkanthein. It was built in 1591 under King Minphalaung as a repository for the *Tripitaka* or Buddhist canon and is one of the few 48 such Mrauk U-period libraries that have survived. Originally it is said to have contained 30 *pitaka* sets brought from Sri Lanka in the mid-17th century, though at the moment it contains nothing but a pile of brick rubble.

The rectangular structure stands only 2.75 metres high, with a floor plan that measures four metres by three metres. The monument's most distinguishing features are its five-tiered roofline and beautifully decorated east-facing entranceway.

Laungbanpyauk Paya

Built in 1525 by order of King Minkhaungraza, this zedi stands roughly midway between Yadanapon Paya and Pitaka Taik. Locally it's known as the 'Plate Pagoda' because a wall in front of the structure is embedded with plate-like tiles in bright yellow, red, white, celadon and blue. Not all the tiles are intact; many broken pieces lie strewn on the ground.

Stylistically, the octagonal stupa itself somewhat resembles the sikharas atop Andaw Paya, with a receding terrace effect from the base to halfway up each side, followed by a smoothly rising bell shape topped by a lotus-bud sikhara that's only half intact. Before the latter toppled, the zedi is said to have reached 37 metres in height; it now measures only 23 metres. Sixteen Buddha niches surround the base; unfortunately

The intricately carved facade of Laungbanpyauk Paya

art thieves have emptied some entirely and taken the heads of the remaining figures. However, the carved lintels over the niches are still impressive.

Sakyamanaung Paya

Situated about a km north-east of the old palace walls, this graceful zedi was erected in 1629 under King Thirithudhammaraza. At this point in the development of Mrauk U architecture, the stupa had been modified into a more vertical and highly ornate form, an obvious absorption of Burman and especially Shan styles by way of Bagan and Ava.

The lower half of the well-preserved, 85-metre zedi features a multi-tiered octagonal profile as at Laungbanpyauk Paya, but beyond this the bell reverts to a layered circular shape mounted by a decorative *hti*. The western gate into the surrounding compound is guarded by a pair of half-kneeling, half-squatting *yakka* or giants.

Glossary

Acheik longyi – *longyi* woven with intricate patterns and worn on ceremonial occasions
Apyodaw – dancer responsible for placating the appropriate deities at the start of a *pwe*
Ayet piu – 'white liquor', a strong alcoholic beverage distilled from rice or palm sap

Bamar – Burman ethnic group
Bedin-sayas – astrologers; very important people in Myanmar, where everything must be done on an auspicious day
Beimok – Burmese 'opium' cake, made with poppyseeds
Betel – the nut of the areca palm which is chewed as a mild intoxicant throughout Asia
Bodhi tree – the sacred banyan tree under which the Buddha gained enlightenment; also 'bo tree'
Bo gyi – literally 'big leader'
Brahman – Vedic priest
Buddha footprints – large, flat, stylised sculptures that represent the Buddha's feet, distinguished by 108 identifying marks; footprint shrines mark places where the Buddha himself is reputed to have walked

Cantonment – the part of a colonial town occupied by the military, a carry-over from the British days
Chaung – stream or canal; often only seasonal
Cheroots – Burmese cigars; in Myanmar they range from slim to massive, but are actually very mild since they contain only a small amount of tobacco mixed with other leaves, roots and herbs
Chindits – the 'behind enemy lines' Allied forces who harried the Japanese during WW II
Chinlon – an extremely popular Burmese sport in which a circle of up to six players attempts to keep a rattan ball in the air with any part of the body except the arms and hands
Chinthe – half lion/half dragon mythical beast that guards *paya* entrances

Dacoit – a Hindi-Urdu term for robbers who specialise in roadside assaults
Dah – long-bladed knife, part of the traditional costume for the Shan and several hill tribes
Deva – Pali-Sanskrit word for spirit beings
Dhamma – Pali word for the Buddhist teachings; called *dhamma* in Sanskrit
Dobat – rural musical instrument; a small, two-faced drum worn around the neck

Eingyi – traditional long-sleeved jacket

Flat – covered pontoon used to carry cargo on the river, often up to 30 metres long
Furlong – obsolete British unit of distance still used in Myanmar; one-eighth of a mile

Gaung baung – formal male hat made of silk over a wicker framework

Haw – Shan word for 'palace', a reference to the large mansions used by the hereditary Shan sawbwas
Highway trip – journey up-country (away from Yangon) by road
Hintha – mythical, swan-like bird; *hamsa* in Pali-Sanskrit
Hne – a wind instrument like an oboe; part of the Burmese orchestra
Hti – umbrella-like decorated top of a stupa
Htwa – half a *taung*

Jataka – life stories of the Buddha; a common theme for temple paintings and reliefs

Kalaga – embroidered tapestries
Kamma – Pali word for the law of cause and effect; called *karma* in Sanskrit
Kammathan – meditation; *kammathan kyaung* is a meditation monastery
Kammawa – lacquered scriptures
Karaweik – the royal bird-mount of Vishnu (Garuda in Sanskrit); also the royal barge on Inle Lake

Khauk swe – noodles with vegetables and meat

Kutho – merit, what you acquire through doing good

Kyaung – Burmese Buddhist monastery; pronounced 'chong'

Kye waing – circle of gongs used in a Burmese orchestra

Lawkanats – guardian spirits of the world

Lin gwin – cymbals in a Burmese orchestra

Longyi – the Burmese unisex sarong-style lower garment, sensible wear in a tropical climate; unlike men in most other South-East Asian countries, few Burmese men have taken to Western trousers

Manuthiha – half-lion/half-human mythical creature; visible around the Shwedagon Paya

Ma ya nga – 'lesser wife', a man's second wife

Mohinga – traditional and very popular Burmese dish found at many street stalls (pronounced 'moun-hinga'); it consists of noodles, fish and eggs

Myanma let-hwei – Burmese kickboxing

Myit – river

Myo – city; hence Maymyo (after Colonel May), Allanmyo (Major Allen) or even Bernardmyo

Myothit – 'New City'

Naga – snake, often seen sheltering or protecting the Buddha

Nam-bya – flat bread cooked in a clay oven, similar to *nan* in South Asia

Nat – guardian spirit being; Myanmar's Buddhist beliefs also embrace a wide variety of good and bad nats

Nat pwe – spirit festival; see also *pwe*

Ngapi – fermented fish or shrimp paste, an all-purpose Burmese flavouring

Oozie – elephant rider

Ozi – a big, goblet-shaped, one-faced drum used for accompanying folk music in the country

Pagoda – generic English term for zedis or stupas as well as temples; see also *paya*

Pahto – Burmese word for temple or shrine

Pali – language in which original Buddhist texts were written; the 'Latin' of Theravada Buddhism

Parabaik – folding manuscripts

Patma – Burmese bass drum

Pattala – bamboo xylophone used in the Burmese orchestra

Paya – a generic Burmese term meaning 'holy one'; often applied to Buddha figures, zedis and other religious monuments

Phongyi – Buddhist monk

Phongyiban – important cremation ceremony for a *sayadaw*

Phongyikyaung – monastery; see also *kyaung*

Pi say – traditional tattooing, believed to make the wearer invulnerable to sword or gun

Pwe – generic Burmese word for festival, feast, celebration, ceremony or gathering; also refers to public performances of Burmese song and dance, often all-night (and all-day) affairs

Pyatthat – wooden, multi-roofed pavilion, usually turret-like on palace walls, as at Mandalay Palace

Pyithu Hlutaw – Peoples' Congress

Ro-Ro – 'roll on, roll off', a ferryboat that carries vehicles; see also 'zed craft'

Saing waing – circle of drums used in a Burmese orchestra

Sanei gyo-daing – 'planetary post', a small shrine near the base of a zedi containing a Buddha image to which worshippers make offerings according to the day of the week they were born; there are usually eight posts, one for each day of the Burmese week (Wednesday is divided into two days)

Sanskrit – very ancient Indian language and source of many words in the Burmese vocabulary, particularly those having to do with religion, art and government

Saung gauk – musical instrument; 13-stringed, boat-shaped harp

Sawbwa – Burmese corruption of the Shan word *sao pha* or 'sky lord', the hereditary chieftains of the Shan

Sayadaw – the usually venerable chief abbot of a monastery

Shawtaing – popular event at country fairs in which participants attempt to climb a greased bamboo pole to collect prize money from the top

Shinpyu – ceremonies when young boys from seven years old upwards enter a monastery for the period required of every young Buddhist male; girls have their ears pierced in a similar ceremony

Shwe le maw – orange brandy distilled in the Shan State

Sikhara – Indian-style, corncob-like temple finial, found on many temples in Bagan

Sima – see *thein*

Sinbyudaw – royal white elephant

Singoung – head elephant man, above an *oozie*

Soon – alms offered to monks

Stupa – see *zedi*

Tatmadaw – the armed forces

Taung – traditional Burmese measure, 46 cm or 18 inches

Tazaung – shrine building, usually found around *zedis*

Thabeik – monk's food bowl; also a traditional element of stupa architecture

Thanaka – yellow sandalwood-like paste, worn by many Burmese women on their faces as a combination of skin conditioner, sunblock and makeup

Thein – ordination hall; called *sima* in Pali

The Thirty – the '30 comrades' of Bogyoke Aung San who joined the Japanese during WW II and eventually led Burma to independence

Tripitaka – the 'three baskets'; the classic Buddhist scriptures consisting of the Vinaya (monastic discipline), the Sutta (discourses of the Buddha) and Abhidhamma (Buddhist philosophy)

Up-country – out of Yangon

Vihara – Pali-Sanskrit word for sanctuary or chapel for Buddha images

Viss – traditional Burmese weight, 1.6 kg

Votive tablet – inscribed offering tablet, usually with images of the Buddha

Wah let-khoke – bamboo clapper, part of the Burmese orchestra

Yagwin – Burmese cymbals

Yama pwe – Burmese classical dancing based on the Indian epic *Ramayana*

Yok-thei pwe – Burmese marionette theatre

Yoma – mountain range

Zat pwe – Burmese classical dancing based on *jataka* stories

Zawgyi – an alchemist who has successfully achieved immortality through the ingestion of special compounds made from base metals

Zayats – rest houses around a *zedi*

Zed craft – large vehicle ferry

Zedi – stupa, a traditional Buddhist religious monument consisting of a solid hemispherical or gently tapering cylindrical cone, and topped with a variety of metal and jewel finials; zedis are often said to contain Buddha relics

ACRONYMS

AM – Air Mandalay

FEC – Foreign Exchange Certificate

IWT – Inland Water Transport Co

MA – Myanma Airways

MFSL – Myanma Five Star Line

MHT – Ministry of Hotels & Tourism

MTT – Myanmar Travels & Tours

SLORC – State Law and Order Restoration Council

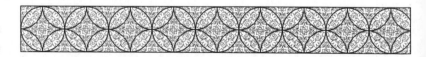

Index

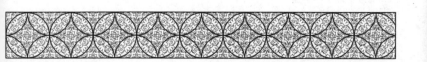

LONELY PLANET TV SERIES & VIDEOS

Lonely Planet travel guides have been brought to life on television screens around the world. Like our guides, the programmes are based on the joy of independent travel, and look honestly at some of the most exciting, picturesque and frustrating places in the world. Each show is presented by one of three travellers from Australia, England or the USA and combines an innovative mixture of video, Super-8 film, atmospheric soundscapes and original music.

Videos of each episode – containing additional footage not shown on television – are available from good book and video shops, but the availability of individual videos varies with regional screening schedules.

Video destinations include:
Alaska; Australia (Southeast); Brazil; Ecuador & the Galapagos Islands; Indonesia; Israel & the Sinai Desert; Japan; La Ruta Maya (Yucatan, Guatemala & Belize); Morocco; North India (Varanasi to the Himalaya); Pacific Islands; Vietnam; Zimbabwe, Botswana & Namibia.

Coming in 1996:
The Arctic (Norway & Finland); Baja California; Chile & Easter Island; China (Southeast); Costa Rica; East Africa (Tanzania & Zanzibar); Great Barrier Reef (Australia); Jamaica; Papua New Guinea; the Rockies (USA); Syria & Jordan; Turkey.

The Lonely Planet television series is produced by:
Pilot Productions
Duke of Sussex Studios
44 Uxbridge St
London W8 7TG
United Kingdom

Lonely Planet videos are distributed by:
IVN Communications Inc
2246 Camino Ramon, San Ramon
California 94583, USA

107 Power Road, Chiswick
London W4 5PL, UK

For further information on both the television series and the availability of individual videos please contact Lonely Planet.

PLANET TALK
Lonely Planet's FREE quarterly newsletter

We love hearing from you and think you'd like to hear from us.

When...is the right time to see reindeer in Finland?
Where...can you hear the best palm-wine music in Ghana?
How...do you get from Asunción to Areguá by steam train?
What...is the best way to see India?

For the answer to these and many other questions read PLANET TALK.

Every issue is packed with up-to-date travel news and advice including:

- *a letter from Lonely Planet founders Tony and Maureen Wheeler*
- *travel diary from a Lonely Planet author - find out what it's really like out on the road*
- *feature article on an important and topical travel issue*
- *a selection of recent letters from our readers*
- *the latest travel news from all over the world*
- *details on Lonely Planet's new and forthcoming releases*

To join our mailing list contact any Lonely Planet office.

Also available: Lonely Planet T-shirts. 100% heavyweight cotton (S, M, L, XL)

LONELY PLANET PUBLICATIONS
Australia: PO Box 617, Hawthorn 3122, Victoria
tel: (03) 9819 1877 fax: (03) 9819 6459 e-mail: talk2us@lonelyplanet.com.au

USA: Embarcadero West, 155 Filbert St, Suite 251, Oakland, CA 94607
tel: (510) 893 8555 TOLL FREE: 800 275-8555 fax: (510) 893 8563
e-mail: info@lonelyplanet.com

UK: 10 Barley Mow Passage, Chiswick, London W4 4PH
tel: (0181) 742 3161 fax: (0181) 742 2772 e-mail: 100413.3551@compuserve.com

France: 71 bis rue du Cardinal Lemoine – 75005 Paris
tel: 1 46 34 00 58 fax: 1 46 34 72 55 e-mail: 100560.415@compuserve.com

World Wide Web: http://www.lonelyplanet.com/

THE LONELY PLANET TRAVEL ATLAS

Tired of maps that lead you astray?
Sick of maps that fall apart after a few days' travel?
Had enough of maps that get creased and torn in all the wrong places?

**Lonely Planet is proud to announce the solution to all these problems –
the Lonely Planet travel atlas!**

Produced in conjunction with Steinhart Katzir Publishers, a range of atlases designed to complement our guidebooks is now available to travellers worldwide.

Unlike other maps and road atlases, which look good on paper but often lack accuracy, LP's travel atlases have been thoroughly checked on the road by Lonely Planet's experienced team of authors. All details are carefully checked to ensure that the atlas conforms with the equivalent Lonely Planet guidebook.

The handy book format means that the atlas can withstand months of rigorous travelling adventures. So whether you're struggling through an Icelandic gale or packed like a sardine on a backcountry bus in Asia, you'll find it easier to get where you're going with a Lonely Planet travel atlas. (Ideal for armchair travellers too!)

- full colour
- travel information in English, French, German, Spanish and Japanese
- place names keyed to LP guidebooks; no confusing spelling differences
- one country - one atlas. No need to buy five maps to cover large countries
- multilingual atlas legend
- comprehensive index

Available now:
Thailand; India; Zimbabwe, Botswana & Namibia and Vietnam

Coming soon:
Israel; Turkey; Laos and Chile

Guides to South-East Asia

Bali & Lombok – a travel survival kit
This guide will help travellers to experience the real magic of Bali's tropical paradise. Neighbouring Lombok is largely untouched by outside influences and has a special atmosphere of its own.

Bangkok – city guide
Bangkok has something for everyone: temples, museums and historic sites; an endless variety of good restaurants, clubs, international culture and social events; a modern art institute; and great shopping opportunities. This pocket guide offers you the assurance that you will never be lost...or lost for things to do in this fascinating city!

Cambodia – a travel survival kit
As one of the last nations in the region opens its doors to travellers, visitors will again make their way to the magnificent ruins of Angkor. Another first for Lonely Planet!

Indonesia – a travel survival kit
Some of the most remarkable sights and sounds in South-East Asia can be found amongst the 13,000 islands of Indonesia – this book covers the entire archipelago in detail.

Jakarta – city guide
Jakarta offers a myriad of opportunities for visitors, from the business person to the backpacker. This indispensable guide is packed with practical tips and suggestions to ensure you get the most of your visit.

Java – a travel survival kit
Explore Java, the heartland of Indonesia, with this comprehensive guide. It's packed with all the down-to-earth information and insider tips you need to enjoy this fascinating and diverse island.

Laos – a travel survival kit
From the fertile lowlands of the Mekong River Valley to the rugged Annamite highlands, Lao hospitality, natural scenery and the attractive capital of Vientiane have survived decades of war and now offer travellers an unparalled glimpse of old Indochina.

Malaysia, Singapore & Brunei – a travel survival kit
Three independent nations of amazing geographic and cultural variety – from the national parks, beaches, jungles and rivers of Malaysia, to the tiny oil-rich Brunei and the urban prosperity and diversity of Singapore.

Philippines – a travel survival kit
The friendly Filipinos, colourful festivals and superb natural scenery make the Philippines one of the most interesting countries in South-East Asia for adventurous travellers and sun-seekers alike.

South-East Asia on a shoestring
The well-known 'yellow bible' for travellers in South-East Asia covers Brunei, Myanmar (Burma), Cambodia, Hong Kong, Indonesia, Laos, Macau, Malaysia, the Philippines, Singapore, Thailand and Vietnam.

Thailand – a travel survival kit
This authoritative guide includes Thai script for all place names and the latest travel details for all regions, including tips on trekking in the remote hills of the Golden Triangle.

Vietnam – a travel survival kit
From the wide avenues and pavement restaurants of Hanoi and Saigon to the spectacular verdant countryside, travelling in Vietnam is packed with challenges and surprises. A comprehensive and informative guide to one of the region's most popular destinations.

Also available:
Lao phrasebook**, Thai** phrasebook, **Thai Hill Tribes** phrasebook, **Burmese** phrasebook, **Pilipino** phrasebook, **Indonesian** phrasebook, **Papua New Guinea Pidgin** phrasebook, **Mandarin Chinese** phrasebook and **Vietnamese** phrasebook.

Lonely Planet Guidebooks

Lonely Planet guidebooks cover every accessible part of Asia as well as Australia, the Pacific, South America, Africa, the Middle East, Europe and parts of North America. There are six series: *travel survival kits*, covering a country for a range of budgets; *shoestring guides* with compact information for low-budget travel in a major region; *walking guides*; *city guides, travel atlases* and *phrasebooks*.

Australia & the Pacific
Australia
Australian phrasebook
Bushwalking in Australia
Islands of Australia's Great Barrier Reef
Outback Australia
Fiji
Fijian phrasebook
Melbourne city guide
Micronesia
New Caledonia
New South Wales & the ACT
New Zealand
Tramping in New Zealand
Papua New Guinea
Bushwalking in Papua New Guinea
Papua New Guinea phrasebook
Queensland
Rarotonga & the Cook Islands
Samoa
Solomon Islands
Sydney city guide
Tahiti & French Polynesia
Tonga
Vanuatu
Victoria
Western Australia

North-East Asia
Beijing city guide
China
Cantonese phrasebook
Mandarin Chinese phrasebook
Hong Kong, Macau & Canton
Japan
Japanese phrasebook
Korea
Korean phrasebook
Mongolia
Mongolian phrasebook
North-East Asia on a shoestring
Seoul city guide
Taiwan
Tibet
Tibet phrasebook
Tokyo city guide

South-East Asia
Bali & Lombok
Bangkok city guide
Cambodia
Indonesia
Indonesian phrasebook
Ho Chi Minh City city guide
Jakarta city guide
Java
Laos
Lao phrasebook
Malaysia, Singapore & Brunei
Myanmar (Burma)
Burmese phrasebook
Philippines
Pilipino phrasebook
Singapore city guide
South-East Asia on a shoestring
Thailand
Thailand travel atlas
Thai phrasebook
Thai Hill Tribes phrasebook
Vietnam
Vietnam travel atlas
Vietnamese phrasebook

Middle East
Arab Gulf States
Egypt & the Sudan
Arabic (Egyptian) phrasebook
Iran
Israel
Jordan & Syria
Middle East
Turkey
Turkish phrasebook
Trekking in Turkey
Yemen

Africa
Africa on a shoestring
Central Africa
East Africa
Trekking in East Africa
Kenya
Swahili phrasebook
Morocco
Arabic (Moroccan) phrasebook
North Africa
South Africa, Lesotho & Swaziland
West Africa
Zimbabwe, Botswana & Namibia
Zimbabwe, Botswana & Namibia travel atlas

Mail Order

Lonely Planet guidebooks are distributed worldwide. They are also available by mail order from Lonely Planet, so if you have difficulty finding a title please write to us. US and Canadian residents should write to Embarcadero West, 155 Filbert St, Suite 251, Oakland CA 94607, USA ; European residents should write to 10 Barley Mow Passage, Chiswick, London W4 4PH; and residents of other countries to PO Box 617, Hawthorn, Victoria 3122, Australia.

The Lonely Planet Story

Lonely Planet published its first book in 1973 in response to the numerous 'How did you do it?' questions Maureen and Tony Wheeler were asked after driving, bussing, hitching, sailing and railing their way from England to Australia.

Written at a kitchen table and hand collated, trimmed and stapled, *Across Asia on the Cheap* became an instant local bestseller, inspiring thoughts of another book.

Eighteen months in South-East Asia resulted in their second guide, *South-East Asia on a shoestring*, which they put together in a backstreet Chinese hotel in Singapore in 1975. The 'yellow bible' as it quickly became known to backpackers around the world, soon became *the* guide to the region. It has sold well over half a million copies and is now in its 8th edition, still retaining its familiar yellow cover.

Today there are over 140 Lonely Planet titles in print – books that have that same adventurous approach to travel as those early guides; books that 'assume you know how to get your luggage off the carousel' as one reviewer put it.

Although Lonely Planet initially specialised in guides to Asia, they now cover most regions of the world, including the Pacific, South America, Africa, the Middle East and Europe. The list of *walking guides* and *phrasebooks* (for 'unusual' languages such as Quechua, Swahili, Nepali and Egyptian Arabic) is also growing rapidly.

The emphasis continues to be on travel for independent travellers. Tony and Maureen still travel for several months of each year and play an active part in the writing, updating and quality control of Lonely Planet's guides.

They have been joined by over 50 authors, 110 staff – mainly editors, cartographers & designers – at our office in Melbourne, Australia, at our US office in Oakland, California and at our European office in Paris; another five at our office in London handle sales for Britain, Europe and Africa. Travellers themselves also make a valuable contribution to the guides through the feedback we receive in thousands of letters each year.

The people at Lonely Planet strongly believe that travellers can make a positive contribution to the countries they visit, both through their appreciation of the countries' culture, wildlife and natural features, and through the money they spend. In addition, the company makes a direct contribution to the countries and regions it covers. Since 1986 a percentage of the income from each book has been donated to ventures such as famine relief in Africa; aid projects in India; agricultural projects in Central America; Greenpeace's efforts to halt French nuclear testing in the Pacific; and Amnesty International.

Lonely Planet's basic travel philosophy is summed up in Tony Wheeler's comment, 'Don't worry about whether your trip will work out. Just go!'